David Hume

MORAL PHILOSOPHY

David Hume

MORAL PHILOSOPHY

Edited, with Introduction, by
Geoffrey Sayre-McCord

Hackett Publishing Company, Inc.
Indianapolis/Cambridge

23 22 21 20   5 6 7 8 9

For further information, please address:
  Hackett Publishing Company, Inc.
  P.O. Box 44937
  Indianapolis, IN 46244-0937

  www.hackettpublishing.com

Cover design by Listenberger & Associates
Text design by Abigail Coyle
Composition by Westchester Book Group

Library of Congress Cataloging-in-Publication Data

Hume, David, 1711–1776.
  Moral philosophy / David Hume ; edited, with introduction, by Geoffrey
Sayre-McCord.
    p. cm.
  Includes bibliographical references (p.   ) and index.
  Contents: My own life—Letter from Adam Smith, LL.D., to William
Strahan, Esq.—A treatise of human nature: volume II, Of the passions—
A treatise of human nature: volume III, Of morals—An enquiry concerning
the principles of morals—A dialogue—Essays, moral and political.
  ISBN-13: 978-0-87220-600-7 (cloth)
  ISBN-13: 978-0-87220-599-4 (paper)
  1. Ethics.   I. Sayre-McCord, Geoffrey, 1956-   II. Title.
  B1455.S39 2006
  170—dc22   2006043572

CONTENTS

To my mother, Joan McCord,
who introduced me to Hume and who showed me that
philosophical skepticism can be combined
with genuine commitment and personal optimism.

ACKNOWLEDGMENTS

The University of North Carolina at Chapel Hill provided much needed funding and resources (including access to copies of the relevant editions of Hume's work) for which I am extremely grateful. Just as important has been the careful research and editing assistance provided by Angela Coventry and Nancy Lawrence. Deborah Wilkes' extraordinary patience, wise counsel, and commitment to quality are appreciated beyond words.

HUME'S MORAL PHILOSOPHY: AN INTRODUCTION

Geoffrey Sayre–McCord

David Hume died in 1776, succumbing to what was probably intestinal cancer.[1] He was sixty-five years old. Working and entertaining visitors right to the end, Hume faced death with an equanimity that was a comfort to his friends and a disappointment to those who had hoped that confronting his own mortality would bring Hume back to religion. Although he had been raised a Calvinist, Hume's faith waned when, as a teenager, he read John Locke and Samuel Clarke. Their work convinced him that the boundaries of reasonable belief were set by experience, and was convinced too that religion inevitably required moving beyond those boundaries. Comfortable acknowledging the limits of his own understanding, Hume recognized that there might be, for all he knew, an afterlife. Yet he regarded the alternative, that death would mean he ceases to exist, with the same attitude he brought to the recognition that there had been a time, before he was born, when he had not yet come into existence.

After attending the University of Edinburgh, Hume took up the study of law for a short time, but abandoned that path to make a career as a philosopher and man of letters. He soon exhausted himself in study, however, and suffered a malaise that led him eventually to try his hand at business. Hume quickly discovered business was not to his liking. So he moved to France and eventually settled in La Flèche, home to a Jesuit college where René Descartes had studied. There, living on a modest stipend from this family, Hume continued his study of philosophy. During this period, Hume relentlessly pursued "the experimental method of reasoning" that

---

Thanks are due to Don Garrett and Deborah Wilkes for helpful comments and suggestions.

[1] Hume's brief account of his life, *My Own Life* (1777), is wonderfully fair minded, by all accounts largely accurate, and a nice testimony to the character of its author. Ernest C. Mossner, Hume's biographer, notes that Hume was no saint but rightly goes on to describe him as "humane, charitable, pacific, tolerant, and encouraging of others, morally sincere and intellectually honest" (*The Life of David Hume*, 4).

had been used to such spectacular effect by Isaac Newton in explaining the natural world. Yet Hume's interest, unlike Newton's, was in the study specifically of human nature. According to Hume, developing the "science of man" was both important in its own right and the key to progress in other fields as well. "All the sciences," he argued, "are in some measure dependent on the science of MAN; since they lie under the cognizance of men, and are judg'd of by their powers and faculties."[2]

Hume's studies culminated in the magisterial *A Treatise of Human Nature*, which he had more or less finished writing by the time he was twenty-five. It was published soon after, with Books I and II appearing in 1739 and Book III appearing in 1740. Covering the Understanding (in Book I), the Passions (in Book II), and Morality (in Book III), the *Treatise* manages to be comprehensive and, in section after section, challenging, provocative, and engaging. Hume's thoroughgoing empiricism, and his consequent willingness to reject whatever could not be founded on experience, failed to earn his work the reception he had hoped for.

Hume later described his *Treatise* as having fallen "dead-born from the press, without reaching such distinction, as even to excite a murmur among the zealots."[3] But he was exaggerating. The *Treatise* attracted enough attention among the zealots and others both to enable him to make a bid for the Chair of Ethics and Pneumatical Philosophy at Edinburgh University in 1746, and to ensure that his bid would fail. Some years later, Hume was a candidate for the Chair of Logic at the University of Glasgow and was again unsuccessful, almost surely because of the views set forth in the *Treatise*. In the end, he never held a position in a university. He did, however, serve for a number of years as the librarian to the Edinburgh Faculty of Advocates, which gave him easy access to an extraordinary collection. During that period he wrote his influential six-volume *History of England*.[4]

One suspects that Hume would not have minded a little scandal and the reputation of a renegade. Still, Hume was disappointed that so many clearly misunderstood his views. Characteristically, he took responsibility for the *Treatise*'s failure, saying he had been "carry'd away by the Heat of Youth &

---

[2] *A Treatise of Human Nature*, edited by David Fate Norton and Mary J. Norton (Oxford: Clarendon Press, 2000), 4.

[3] *My Own Life*, 2.

[4] In the course of his life Hume found employment, very briefly, as a tutor (to an insane marquis), as secretary to a general, as a private secretary to an ambassador to France, and as the undersecretary of state. These positions moved him from Vienna to Turin, Paris, and London. Despite his notable popularity in France, Hume eventually settled permanently in Edinburgh.

Invention to publish too precipitately."[5] Without significantly changing the main principles and theses of his view, Hume worked hard to re-present them—most notably in the *Enquiry Concerning Human Understanding* (which overlaps with Book I of the *Treatise*) and the *Enquiry Concerning the Principles of Morals* (which overlaps with Book III of the *Treatise*)—to make them more easily understood and, he hoped, more likely to be appreciated.

The extent to which the *Treatise* was misunderstood is some indication of just how new and unorthodox Hume's views were. Yet the *Treatise* has from the beginning been given vastly different interpretations, each finding more than a little support in the text. A number of very different philosophical schools (logical positivism, naturalism, skepticism, to mention a few) have each claimed to be Hume's rightful heir. Novelty and a lack of orthodoxy do not fully explain this. Some of the explanation is found in the striking richness of Hume's work, and some in the fact that Hume did not always work to show how all the positions and arguments he offers might fit comfortably together. In any case, there is no doubt that the *Treatise* is a work of genius and that Hume clearly stands as one of the world's great philosophers.

In seeking to establish a science of man, Hume was set on identifying fundamental principles that would both explain and be supported by our experiences. He realized that whatever the fundamental principles may be, they cannot themselves be explained precisely because they are fundamental. "But if this impossibility of explaining ultimate principles shou'd be esteem'd a defect in the science of man, I will venture to affirm, that 'tis a defect common to it with all the sciences, and all the arts . . . whether they be such as are cultivated in the schools of the philosophers, or practic'd in the shops of the meanest artizans. None of them can go beyond experience, or establish any principles which are not founded on that authority."[6] In pursuing this science, then, Hume was simultaneously and self-consciously setting out to discover the limits of our understanding. Throughout his life, and despite the glorious ambitions of his projects, Hume manifested an admirable willingness to mark the limits of his own arguments.

Hume's awareness of the boundaries of human understanding, and his concern to note when theories and hypotheses have overreached, quickly earned him a reputation as a skeptic and atheist.[7] Not surprisingly, there is

---

[5] In a letter to Gilbert Elliot of Minto in March or April of 1751. *The Letters of David Hume*, edited by J. Y. T. Greig (Oxford: Clarendon Press, 1932), I:158.

[6] *A Treatise of Human Nature*, ed. Norton and Norton, 5–6.

[7] Hume was unmistakably opposed to established religions. Whether he was an atheist or an agnostic is perhaps more difficult to say. In any case, there is no doubt that Hume thought that a positive belief in God, or in an afterlife, was unreasonable.

more than a little truth in this reputation, and understandably it continues to shape how Hume's central works are read.

Hume's skeptical portfolio is unmistakably thick. In Book I of the *Treatise*, for example, Hume argues (i) that we do not have even an idea of necessary connection, let alone any knowledge of such connections, (ii) that the idea we do have of cause and effect reflects more the nature of our own minds than the structure of the world, and (iii) that any attempt to offer a justification for inductive reasoning, which plays such a central role in our understanding of the world, will fail. He argues as well that we have no idea of substance, of a soul, or even of ourselves, other than the ideas we have of the qualities that these things are supposed to possess (which, of course, is different from actually having an idea of them).

Yet Hume is not merely a skeptic. He consistently offers detailed theories, positive proposals, and ingenious supporting arguments that are clearly part of an effort to extend and deepen our knowledge of human nature. No reading of Hume that treats him solely as a skeptic will do him justice.

MORAL THEORY AND THE SCIENCE OF HUMAN NATURE

Hume's positive aims are nowhere more evident than in his discussion of morality (and of the passions on which morality depends). He develops a systematic account of morality that takes as its starting point a catalog of the virtues and the vices, and proceeds to "discover the circumstances on both sides, which are common to these qualities; to observe that particular in which the estimable qualities agree on the one hand, and the blameable on the other; and thence to reach the foundation of ethics, and find those universal principles, from which all censure or approbation is ultimately derived" (E. 190). Hume sets out in this way to explain moral thought and practice, and to make sense of how and why we think in the moral terms that we do.

Hume contrasts his experimental method with an alternative that starts not with cases, observation, and experience, but with some general abstract principle that is then extended "into a variety of inferences and conclusions" (E. 190). The architectonic of such an approach, he grants, is appealing, yet he thinks that this approach is a regular cause of error, one that tempts people all too quickly to forsake the evidence they actually have in pursuit of a perfect form they have no reason to think exists.[8] Newton, Hume empha-

---

[8] "I found," Hume wrote to Dr. George Cheyne in March 1734, "that the moral Philosophy transmitted to us by Antiquity, labor'd under the same Inconvenience that

sizes, taught us the folly of this approach when it comes to understanding the natural world. "Men are now cured of passion for hypotheses and systems in natural philosophy, and will hearken to no arguments but those which are derived from experience. It is full time they should attempt a like reformation in all moral disquisitions; and reject every system of ethics, however subtle or ingenious, which is not founded on fact and observation" (E. 191).

Hume attempts that reformation. Moral theory, no less than natural science and human psychology, needs to be approached using the 'experimental method of reasoning' and needs, in the process, to make sense of and explain our capacity to think in moral terms. Yet Hume's method of cataloging, systematizing, and explaining the moral distinctions we draw seems to be a recipe for discovering only what we *think* is moral, not what *is* moral. As a result, many have thought that Hume's emphasis on observation, experience, and explanation, as opposed to justification, means that the results of his enquiry will be irrelevant to what ought to be, and therefore irrelevant to moral theory.

Hume is of course well aware that there is a difference between how things are and how they should be—that there is a difference between, as he puts it, 'is' and 'ought.' Indeed, he is famous for having stressed the point when he complained of systems where

> the author proceeds for some time in the ordinary way of reasoning, and establishes the being of a God, or makes observations concerning human affairs; when of a sudden . . . instead of the usual copulations of propositions, *is*, and *is not*, I meet with no proposition that is not connected with an *ought*, or an *ought not*. This change is imperceptible; but is, however, of the last consequence. For as this *ought*, or *ought not*, expresses some new relation or affirmation, 'tis necessary that it shou'd be observ'd and explain'd; and at the same time that a reason shou'd be given, for what seems altogether inconceivable, how this new relation can be a deduction from others, which are entirely different from it. (T. 77)

Of all people, Hume would reject inferring an 'ought' from an 'is.'

So how might the experimental method of reasoning shed light on morality, according to Hume? In applying this method to morality, Hume

---

has been found in their natural Philosophy, of being entirely Hypothetical, & depending more upon Invention than Experience. Every one consulted his Fancy in erecting Schemes of Virtue & of Happiness, without regarding human Nature, upon which every moral Conclusion must depend. This therefore I resolved to make my principal Study, & the Source from which I wou'd derive every Truth in Criticism as well as Morality." *The Letters of David Hume*, 16.

has two aims. First, he wants to explain *what* specifically we are thinking of people when we think that they have a virtue or a vice or think that what they have done is just or unjust. Second, he hopes to explain *why* we think in the terms we do. The first project, which consists in identifying the content of our moral thought, involves articulating the criteria for virtue and vice, justice and injustice, while the second involves explaining why we came to have thoughts with that content. Both projects are explanatory projects; both are built on the recognition that it is a contingent, and empirical, matter that we think in moral terms at all and that we think specifically in the moral terms we do. To carry out the two projects successfully is to makes sense of how things are, not how they should be. Yet, to determine what it takes for something to count genuinely as a virtue (assuming there is a fact of the matter) is to discover, in an important sense, how things should be (because it is to discover the nature of virtue). Although there is a big difference between something being a virtue and someone thinking that it is a virtue, there is no difference between being a virtue and actually satisfying the relevant criteria.

To say that, however, is compatible with thinking that the term 'virtue' fails to express any idea at all (as Hume thinks of *immaterial substance*)—in which case there are no criteria to satisfy. And it is compatible as well with holding that the criteria that something would have to satisfy to count as a virtue are not actually satisfied by anything—in which case nothing would genuinely count as virtuous, no matter what people think. Many have argued that Hume's arguments, properly understood, commit him to holding one of these two views about our moral thought. So, for instance, various emotivists, prescriptivists, and other noncognitivists appeal to Humean considerations in support of their views, as do others who reject noncognitivism but embrace instead an error theory, according to which moral thought supposes there to be features of the world that we actually have no reason to think exist.

Hume, however, sees himself as rejecting both of those views. According to Hume, "Those who have denied the reality of moral distinctions, may be ranked among the disingenuous disputants" (E. 187).[9] He has no

---

[9] Whether he is right about his own view is itself a matter of dispute. Many have thought that Hume shows, despite his protests to the contrary, that moral terms express no genuine ideas and are, as a result, meaningless. These are the noncognitivists mentioned above. Others have thought that Hume's arguments leave intact the idea that moral distinctions are real but show that those distinctions correspond to nothing in the world. These are the error theorists. In any case, it is relatively common for people to argue that Hume's arguments establish something more, or at least different, than Hume himself maintains.

doubt that moral distinctions are real and account for the difference between those who are "entitled to the affection and regard of everyone"
and those who are not. Nevertheless, Hume thinks that there are serious
questions to be answered concerning both the ground of the distinctions
and how we might learn of them. He does not shy away from that challenge.

MORALITY, REASON, AND MOTIVATION

One might hold that moral distinctions are grounded in reason alone and
are, therefore, discoverable independent of experience. In fact, there is a
long tradition that would place morality on the side of reason and see it as
staunchly opposed to the influences of passion and appetite. Despite the
tradition, Hume maintains that the view simply cannot be sustained and
he offers three main arguments for this conclusion.

First, Hume notes that morality is distinctively practical and, of its nature, not a matter of indifference. This feature of morality, Hume maintains, cannot be accounted for by appeal to reason alone. " '[T]is
impossible," he argues, "that the distinction betwixt moral good and evil,
can be made by reason; since that distinction has an influence upon our
actions, of which reason alone is incapable" (T. 72).

What exactly the influence of the distinction between moral good and
evil is supposed to be is unclear. What is clear is that Hume thinks that
reason (and its distinctions) have an impact on action only contingently
and not in a way directly tied to virtue and vice. Some have interpreted
Hume as assuming here that in making a moral judgment—a judgment
that draws a moral distinction—one must necessarily be motivated to act,
at least to some degree. Judgments based on distinctions of reason seem at
most only contingently to motivate action. If that is right, there would be
a clear contrast between moral distinctions and those that might be established by reason. Yet Hume himself, in several places, seems to acknowledge that a person might well make a moral judgment and be left totally
unmoved. For instance, he considers seriously a sensible knave who grants
"[t]hat *honesty is the best policy*, may be a good general rule; but is liable to
many exceptions: And he . . . conducts himself with most wisdom, who
observes the general rule, and takes advantage of all the exceptions" (E.
267). Hume also notes that " 'Tis one thing to know virtue, and another to
conform the will to it" (T. 74).

Alternatively, Hume might have had in mind that moral distinctions
necessarily have an influence on action not because the making of the

judgments concerning those distinctions always influences action, but because the distinctions themselves mark a difference among people as to how they will be influenced, with the virtuous necessarily being motivated to act virtuously, the vicious not. No similar connection between the distinctions of reason and motivation exists.

Or perhaps Hume had in mind some other way in which morality is practical that would disqualify it as grounded on reason. However the details are to be worked out, Hume obviously thought that paying proper attention to the influencing motives of the will would reveal that a wholly dispassionate nature would be a wholly inactive one. So reason operating alone, without the collusion of passion, would never engage humanity in the way it so manifestly, and importantly, does.

In any case, Hume offers a second argument for thinking that moral distinctions are not grounded on reason. It starts with the assumption that reason's role and office is to discover relations among ideas and to discover truth and falsity in matters of fact. Reason then approves or condemns by discovering something to be true or false. Yet the objects of moral evaluation—volitions and actions and characters—are none of them true or false. "'Tis impossible, therefore, they can be pronounc'd . . . either contrary or conformable to reason" (T. 69). Nor can good sense be made of morally evaluating the volition, actions, and characters on the grounds that either their causes or their effects happen to be true or false. Hume acknowledges that someone who "sees any lewd behaviour of mine with my neighbour's wife, may be so simple as to imagine she is certainly my own" (T. 71). So one might think that the action is, in some sense, analogous to a lie. But the immorality of the action, Hume points out, surely does not rest with the falseness of that person's belief. After all, if it did, then closing the curtains would eliminate the immorality (T. 71n). Other proposals for tracing the distinction between virtue and vice to the truth or falsity of things associated with the motive, action, or character being evaluated fare no better. The difference between virtue and vice is not the difference between truth and falsehood, nor can it be explained by such a difference.

All the same, it is worth noting that once the distinction is in place and there is a difference between virtue and vice, there is no bar to reason, with the help of experience, discovering that distinction and declaring moral opinions true or false. That moral distinctions are not distinctions between the true and the false, and so are not founded on reason alone, does not mean that claims concerning virtue and vice cannot be conformable or contrary to reasons. They are unlike motives, actions and characters, after all, in that they apparently can be true or false. It is just that the distinc-

tions on which the truth of such claims depend cannot themselves be a difference in truth and falsehood.

The third argument Hume offers for thinking that moral distinctions
are not grounded on reason requires canvassing the various relations that
might be discovered by reason and showing that they all consistently fail
to line up with the contours of moral distinctions. No relation, nor any set
of relations, discoverable by reason, is always and only present in cases of
morality (or cases of immorality). Hume considers, for instance, the moral
crime of patricide and points out that the very relations (of parent to child
and killer to victim) might show up between a sapling and a tree without
there being any immorality at all. For any other moral offense, he argues,
there will always be available cases where the relation(s) in question are
present but the offense is not, especially because it appears that all the relations discoverable by reason are relations that might hold among non-
moral beings and even inanimate objects. One might try either to find
some new relation that can be borne only by moral agents, or one might
argue that moral distinctions depend not on the relations but rather in
some way on the rational capacity to recognize right and wrong, virtue
and vice. In response to the first possibility, Hume acknowledges that
finding such a relation would be sufficient and merely records his failure
at finding any plausible candidate. In response to the second possibility, he
points out that it simply presupposes the very distinctions we are trying to
explain; some other account still must be offered to explain the distinction
these agents are supposed to be able to draw.

MORAL SENTIMENTS AND THE DISTINCTION BETWEEN VIRTUE AND VICE

With all three of these arguments in place, Hume believes he has shown
that moral distinctions cannot possibly be founded on reason alone. The
only alternative, he holds, is that such distinctions are in some way
grounded in experience. Happily, this alternative provides resources for
explaining how it is that moral distinctions might regularly have the impact on action that reason alone seems not to have. For if the experiences
that matter to the drawing of moral distinctions are the sorts of experience
that regularly and understandably influence behavior, then the explanation for the distinctions in question might also explain how it is that they
serve to guide behavior.

As it happens, Hume argues, if we turn our attention to the question

"What feeling, or impression, or experience provides the distinction between virtue and vice?" we will quickly discover "the impression arising from virtue, to be agreeable, and that proceeding from vice to be uneasy" (T. 78). These agreeable and uneasy feelings, on which the distinction between vice and virtue depends, understandably both prompt action and engage the heart. Once we discover the sort of experience that underwrites moral distinctions, we discover, Hume thinks, how it is that such distinctions can of their nature matter to action. Just which feelings they are, and why they underwrite the distinction between vice and virtue, are questions Hume takes very seriously.

One might think that if the relevant feelings manage to motivate they must somehow be tied to self-love. This, anyway, would be the implication of Hume's arguments if one accepted the idea, defended by Thomas Hobbes and others, that our only motive is self-love. But Hume argues against this view of motivation, maintaining not only that there are others motives, but that a realistic appreciation of the motive of self-love will reveal that it depends on having concerns that do not have ourselves as objects.[10] In any case, he argues against self-love as the source of moral distinctions on the grounds that "[a]varice, ambition, vanity, and all passions vulgarly . . . comprised under the denomination of *self-love*, are here excluded from our theory concerning the origin of morals, not because they are too weak, but because they have not a proper direction, for that purpose" (E. 259).

In order to have the proper "direction," the feeling or sentiment in question must work to explain two important features of moral judgment. First, we expect people to concur in their moral judgments and to treat differences of evaluation as disagreements to be resolved.[11] Second, we see those judgments as appropriately made not only of those with whom one interacts but also of those in distant lands and ages. Only a sentiment that is commonly shared, more or less unified in its deliverances, and far reaching in its scope will work. Our capacity for sympathy, our humanity,

---

[10] See the *Enquiry*, Appendix II: "Of Self-Love," where Hume responds in detail to the proposal that we are all motivated solely by a concern for our own interest.

[11] Hume of course knew that people did not actually always agree on moral questions. His point is that, when people disagree, they regard those with whom they disagree as having made a mistake—and they expect that if sources of error were set aside the differences in opinion would disappear. In this respect, questions of morality differ importantly from matters of simple preference and taste where differences are not normally regarded as reflecting defects.

xxIntroduction

he points out, meets these requirements and no other sentiment does.[12] Hume maintains, "One man's ambition is not another's ambition; nor will the same event or object satisfy both: But the humanity of one man is the humanity of every one; and the same object touches this passion in all human creatures" (E. 260), and this is true "however remote the person: But every man, so far removed as neither to cross nor serve my avarice and ambition, is regarded as wholly indifferent by those passions" (E. 261).

Keeping in mind that Hume's ultimate aim is to "reach the foundation of ethics" by collecting together all the virtues and vices and then working "to discover the circumstances on both sides, which are common to these qualities; to observe that particular in which the estimable qualities agree on the one hand, and the blamable on the other," it is worth noting how nicely Hume's appeal to sympathy fits with what he discovers.[13]

WHAT IS USEFUL OR AGREEABLE
TO SELF OR OTHERS

According to Hume, "whatever mental quality in ourselves or others gives us a satisfaction, by the survey or reflection, is of course virtuous; as every thing of this nature that gives uneasiness is vicious."[14] Virtue thus turns

---

[12] See the *Enquiry*, p. 259.

[13] Hume, the *Enquiry*, p. 189; see also pp. 190 and 288. Hume "proposed simply to collect on the one hand, a list of those mental qualities which are the object of love or esteem, and form a part of personal merit, and on the other hand, a catalogue of those qualities, which are the object of censure or reproach, and which detract from the character of the person, possessed of them" (E. 288); "we shall," he says in another place, "analyze that complication of mental qualities, which form what, in common life, we call PERSONAL MERIT: We shall consider every attribute of the mind, which renders a man an object either of esteem and affection, or of hatred and contempt; every habit or sentiment or faculty, which, if ascribed to any person, implies either praise or blame, and may enter into any panegyric or satire of his character and manners" (E. 190).

[14] See the *Treatise*, p. 151; the same view is advanced on T. 27, T. 78, and T. 97, as well as on E. 252n. He writes, in another place: "The hypothesis which we embrace is plain. It maintains that morality is determined by sentiment. It defines virtue to be *whatever mental action or quality gives to a spectator the pleasing sentiment of approbation*; and vice the contrary. We then proceed to examine a plain matter of fact" (E. 270). Hume claims, "It is the nature, and, indeed the definition of virtue, that it is *a quality of the mind agreeable to or approved of by every one, who considers or contemplates it*" (E. 252n). See T. 78: "An action, or sentiment, or character is virtuous or vicious; why? because its view causes a pleasure or uneasiness of a particular kind. . . . To have the sense of virtue, is nothing but to *feel* a satisfaction of a particular kind from the contemplation of a character. . . . The case is the same as in our judgments concerning all

out to be *"whatever mental action or quality gives to a spectator the pleasing sentiment of approbation*; and vice the contrary" (E. 270).

Moreover, everything we count as a virtue (because we approve of it in the relevant way) falls into one of four categories: either it is useful to others or to the possessor, or it is immediately agreeable to others, or to the possessor. Many traits, he notes, fall into more than one of these categories. *"Honesty, fidelity, truth*, are praised for their immediate tendency to promote the interests of society; but after those virtues are once established upon this foundation, they are also considered as advantageous to the person himself, and as the source of that trust and confidence, which can alone give a man any consideration in life" (E. 235). What is crucial is that they must fall into at least one of these four categories in order to count as virtues.

How is it that these qualities give rise to the relevant sort of approbation? Why do we get "the pleasing sentiment of approbation" from what is useful or agreeable either to the possessor or those with whom the possessor interacts? The answer is found in our capacity for sympathy—in our ability, on thinking about the pleasures or pains of others, to feel a pleasure or pain ourselves, without regard to our own interests. In considering anyone who has agreeable or useful traits, Hume argues, the "idea, which we form of their effect on his acquaintance, has an agreeable influence on our imagination, and gives us the sentiment of approbation. This principle enters into all the judgments, which we form concerning manners and characters" (E. 256).[15]

If we ask what all the virtues have in common, one answer is: they give rise, on reflection, to approbation, while all vices give rise to disapprobation. Another answer is: they are all useful or agreeable to the possessor or others, while the vices are the inverse. Combining the first answer with the second, Hume writes, "Every quality of the mind is denominated virtuous, which gives pleasure by the mere survey; as every quality, which produces pain, is call'd vicious. This pleasure and this pain may arise from

---

kinds of beauty, and tastes, and sensations"; T. 97: "every thing which gives uneasiness in human actions, upon the general survey, is call'd Vice, and whatever produces satisfaction, in the same manner, is denominated Virtue." And, though he has not yet committed himself, Hume describes as the most probable hypothesis an account according to which the distinction between virtue and vice is traceable to the fact that certain characters "by the very view and contemplation, produce a pain, and others in like manner excite a pleasure" (T. 27).

[15] Although in the *Enquiry* Hume does not invoke explicitly the mechanism of sympathy that is prominent in the *Treatise*, he is here and elsewhere in the *Enquiry* clearly relying on its effect.

four different sources. For we reap a pleasure from the view of a character, which is naturally fitted to be useful to others, or to the person himself, or which is agreeable to others, or to the person himself" (T. 162–3).

If we ask why the traits that are useful or agreeable give rise to this plea-sure and so to approbation "by the mere survey," the answer is: because we are sympathetic beings, capable of being moved by the weal and woe of others. If the welfare of others had been a matter of indifference to us, we never would have developed the capacity to distinguish virtue and vice, and we would have no idea of either; just as, if we never had the visual ex-perience of colors, we never would have developed the capacity to distin-guish between red and blue, and we would have no idea of either.

MORAL APPROBATION AND DISAPPROBATION

It is worth noting what is often missed: that although sympathy prompts pleasure or pain directly on contemplating the pleasures and pains of oth-ers, the distinctively moral feelings are not the pleasures or pains we feel directly as a result of sympathy.[16] Rather the moral feelings are the 'indi-rect passions' of approbation and disapprobation, the having of which de-pend on, but are distinct from, sympathetic pleasures and pains. These indirect passions simultaneously direct one's attention back to the quali-ties of the object that, thanks to sympathy, generated the original pleasure or pain.[17]

The direct pleasures are caused immediately by the idea of the pleasure the person or others might have. The indirect pleasures of moral approba-tion, in contrast, are pleasant feelings *about the person* whose character is causing her or someone else pleasure (the idea of which causes us pleasure because of her character). The fact that approbation is an indirect, rather than a direct, passion gives Hume the resources to explain how it is that we approve of people *because* of their character traits, *in light of* the effect those traits have on someone or another. At the same time—though Hume does not make use of this fact—the complex structure of indirect passions makes it possible to identify, within a broadly Humean account of psychol-ogy, the considerations that lead us to approve of the people, characters,

---

[16] A few people have noticed this. See Páll Árdal's *Passion and Value in Hume's* Trea-tise (Edinburgh: Edinburgh University Press, 1966) and James Baillie's *Hume on Morality* (London: Routledge, 2000).

[17] "The pain or pleasure which arises from the general survey or view of any action or quality of the *mind*, constitutes its vice or virtue," Hume holds, and that pleasure or pain then "gives rise to our approbation or blame, which is nothing but a fainter and more imperceptible love or hatred" (T. 179).

and actions that we do. For instance, in the case of our moral approval of someone as virtuous, the considerations that support that approval will be that she has a certain character and that her character has certain effects on her or others. These are, in a perfectly recognizable sense, the reasons we would have, and would offer, for approving of her. We would not approve in the way we do if our understanding of her character and its effects left us cold, but our reasons for approving of her are found in the considerations that lead us to approve, not in the fact that we do approve. Locating within Hume's account of approval the structure needed to see people as approving or disapproving for reasons is important to working out how he could make sense of moral deliberation and discussion, even though he does not try. Making sense of moral deliberation and discussion is essential to developing a fully satisfying account of morality.

Although Hume's account is already complex, it cannot be right as it stands, which Hume recognizes. Not everything that gives rise to an agreeable feeling of approbation is actually a virtue, nor do actual virtues always give rise to approbation. Our sympathetic feelings can be ill informed, biased, or otherwise influenced in ways that mean the distinction between virtue and vice does not line up reliably with the distinction between those who happen to secure our approbation and those who do not. As a result, there is a difference between appearing to be a virtue (which is a matter of securing moral approbation) and actually being one. The feelings we happen to have are not a reliable guide to the difference.

Indeed, the feelings of approbation and disapprobation prompted by sympathy vary predictably in ways that our moral judgments do not, and they are sensitive to influences that we commonly regard as irrelevant.[18] For example, our sympathetic responses, even as they abstract from our own interests, are influenced "by our acquaintance or connexion with the persons, or even by an eloquent recital of the case" (E. 230). Yet our judgments do not vary accordingly. We hold that two people with the same character are equally virtuous regardless of their connection to us, even as we are more engaged by one than the other: "Our servant, if diligent and faithful, may excite stronger sentiments of love and kindness than Marcus Brutus, as represented in history; but we say not, upon that account, that the former character is more laudable than the latter" (T. 157). And: "A statesman or patriot, who serves our own country, in our own time, has always a more passionate regard paid to him, than one whose beneficial influence operated on distant ages or remote nations . . ." even though

---

[18] This is not a problem solely for accounts that appeal to sympathy, but is one for any theory of moral judgment that identifies the judgments with some sentiment or other as all sentiments vary in ways that our judgments do not. See T. 156–7.

"[w]e may own the merit to be equally great, though our sentiments are not raised to an equal height, in both cases" (E. 228).

Moreover, our sympathetic responses are more or less engaged by the actual effects of someone's character, though we judge those who have the same character equally virtuous (or vicious). "[T]he tendencies of actions and characters," Hume argues, "not their real accidental consequences, are alone regarded in our moral determinations or general judgements; though in our real feeling or sentiment, we cannot help paying greater regard to one whose station, joined to virtue, renders him really useful to society, than to one, who exerts the social virtues only in good intentions and benevolent affections" (E. 229n).[19]

Taken together, these considerations show that moral judgments are not properly thought of as mere expressions of our sympathetic (or, indeed, any sentimental or emotional) response. Moral judgments exhibit both a stability and an independence from individual perspectives that our sympathetic responses do not.

That said, Hume is committed to holding (i) that the distinctions we draw in making moral judgments exists at all only because certain character traits give rise to approbation under particular circumstances and (ii) that we can learn the distinction only because we have the capacity to have the relevant feelings.

THE STANDARD OF MORALITY

What is needed is an account of moral judgment that makes sense of moral judgments as genuine judgments (as opposed to expressions of sentiment) that underwrite a difference between appearance and reality—between something seeming to be a virtue and it actually being one—while at the same time taking account of how moral distinctions depend upon our capacity to feel approbation and disapprobation.

An appropriate model is our capacity to distinguish the colors of objects. Not everything that gives rise to a perceptual experience of seeing blue is in fact blue, nor does everything that is blue actually give rise to such an experience. Moreover, one can judge that something is blue in

---

[19] Hume makes the same point in the *Treatise*: When "a good disposition is attended with good fortune, . . . it gives a stronger pleasure to the spectator, and is attended with a more lively sympathy. We are more affected by it; and yet we do not say that it is more virtuous, or that we esteem it more" (T. 159). And: "Where a person is possess'd of a character, that in its natural tendency is beneficial to society, we esteem him virtuous, . . . even tho' particular accidents prevent its operation, and incapacitate him from being serviceable to his friends and country" (T. 158).

contexts where one has no color experience at all (as when, for instance, you think that your bedspread is blue although, because the lights are out, you do not see it as blue). Nonetheless, it is only because certain things give rise to such perceptual experiences that we have the color distinctions we do, and it is only because we have the capacity to have those perceptual experiences that we can learn color distinctions.

An equally good model is our capacity to distinguish shapes. Here too Hume maintains that the distinctions among the shapes, and our ability to learn such distinctions, depend on our capacity to have certain experiences. Just as an object counts as genuinely blue (or circular) if, but only if, it has the power to produce a specific sort of *perceptual* experience under particular circumstances, so too, Hume holds, a character trait counts as genuinely a virtue if, but only if, it has the power to produce a specific sort of *affective* experience, under particular circumstances.

In the case of colors and shapes, the particular circumstances that work to set the standard involve a perceiver with the appropriate perceptual capacities, in good order, exercising them in the appropriate light (in the case of colors), or from the right perspective (in the case of shapes), and from not too far away. That these are the relevant conditions can, to a significant degree, be read off of the sorts of criticisms that can be leveled against particular perceptions: they are made by someone with defective vision, our under poor light, or from too far away. However, it would be a mistake to think that these are the relevant conditions because they allow people to judge correctly. There is, Hume thinks, no independent criteria we could use to evaluate the conditions as being conducive to accuracy. Rather, the role of the conditions in question is to help constitute criteria we can then use to mark the difference between which objects do have the colors or shapes in question and which do not. Settling on these conditions, as setting the standard, works to make the judgments possible in the first place.

It is easy to misunderstand this view. There is no claim here that the objects that prompt the various perceptual experiences have no qualities, or that the qualities these objects have are whatever we might decide. Instead, the point is that what counts as the correct way to describe the qualities of these things depends on the concepts that we are deploying. These concepts are human creations that, if Hume is right, are properly understood as applying correctly to what would give rise to the appropriate experiences under certain particular circumstances.

To say that these concepts are human creations is not to say that they are arbitrary. They are not. But they are contingent features of our cognitive repertoire, and understanding the concepts, and the standards we rely on in deploying them, requires understanding the conditions that give point and purpose to the concepts. The reasons we have for privileging how things look under specific circumstances to people with specific perceptual capacities have to do with why we need concepts of color and shape in the first place. The various circumstances and capacities come to set the standard for the concept because relying on them solves problems of communication, prediction, and explanation that we otherwise would not be able to address as well. We could, for instance, have a concept of color that privileged very special lighting conditions or relied on how objects appeared to those with peculiar visual equipment. We could. But why? Such concepts would not be useful to us, especially if we are unable to figure out how things would look under the special lighting conditions to those with the peculiar visual equipment.

With these models in mind, the challenge is to identify correctly the circumstances under which the feelings of approbation and disapprobation set the standard for virtue and vice. Hume holds that, in making moral judgments, we commonly do, and in any case should, adjust the deliverances of sympathy according to a "steady rule of right." This steady rule works both to explain the relative stability (and intersubjectivity) of moral judgment and to articulate what he describes as "a just sentiment of morals" ("Taste," 346). The standard for our moral judgments, he maintains, is set not by how we individually feel at any given time, but instead by how we all would feel were we to take up a particular general point of view.[20]

One succeeds in taking up that point of view, according to Hume, by (i) considering the type of character in question with an informed eye to its usual effects on whoever would standardly be affected by those with such a character, and then (ii) responding sympathetically to that character, so considered. In cases where, having taken up that point of view, a person whose sympathetic capacities are in good order would respond with approbation, the character trait is a virtue. If, on this general survey, it would garner disapprobation from a person so situated, it is a vice.

That this is the standard of virtue and vice explains both how it is that our capacity to think morally depends not merely on reason but on sentiment, even as it accounts also for the fact that in making moral judgments we are not merely expressing our sentiments but are making claims that mark a real difference among the people we judge.

It matters to Hume that this account of the standard of moral judgment

---

[20] Hume's appeals to "points of view," not just in ethics but elsewhere, suggest that he treats a point of view primarily as a way of thinking of something, and not as the occupying of a particular position in the viewing of something. See, for instance, Book I, Part III, Section XIV and Book I, Part IV, Section III of the *Treatise* (pp. 114 and 145–6, respectively, in the Norton and Norton edition) and "Of the Standard of Taste," p. 354.

does not just fit well as an explanation of our moral judgments but simultaneously offers a standard that, on reflection, we can judge to be worth embracing. We have good reason, he thinks, to regulate our thought, talk, and action by what we would approve of if we were to take the general point of view. Far from being an arbitrary standard of right, it is, he maintains, essential to avoiding the perennial conflicts that would come from our failing to put in place a common, mutually accessible, standard of the sort set by the general point of view.

Of course, on Hume's view, to say we have this good reason is, in effect, to claim that we would, from the general point of view, approve of adopting our reactions from that point of view as setting the standard. Whether this is true is not a trivial question. It could be that, when we consider a point of view in the appropriate way, we would actually not approve of it. Hume would see that as grounds for thinking either that he had identified the wrong standard in the first place or that we had reason to change our existing standard. In either case, we would have grounds for disregarding the general point of view. Fortunately, Hume thinks, things do not turn out that way. A clear-eyed and informed appreciation of the alternatives, and the problems they would leave unsolved, would lead us all (Hume thinks) to respond with approval from a sympathy with all who benefit (including ourselves) from having the standard in place.[21]

THE SPECIFIC VIRTUES

To know that the various virtues fall into one of four categories—being useful or being agreeable, to the person who has them or to others—and to know too that the traits that count as virtues are those that would give rise to approval from the general point of view, does not tell one very much about the particular duties. In both the *Treatise* and the *Enquiry* Hume spends a good deal of time exploring specific virtues: principally justice, fidelity to promises, chastity, modesty, generosity, and humanity; but prudence, temperance, frugality, industry, assiduity, and enterprise, receive attention too. Hume's interest is in explaining the conditions under which each of these would emerge as virtues, and characterizing

---

21 I set out, in more detail, Hume's account of the general point of view and the roles it plays in his moral theory in "On Why Hume's 'General Point of View' Isn't Ideal—and Shouldn't Be," *Social Philosophy & Policy* 11, no. 1 (1994): 202–28. See also Rachel Cohon's "The Common Point of View in Hume's Ethics," *Philosophy and Phenomenological Research* 57, no. 4 (1997): 827–50 and Christine Korsgaard's "The General Point of View: Love and Moral Approval in Hume's Ethics," *Hume Studies* 25, no. 1–2 (1999): 3–41.

the features that make each of them useful or agreeable in the ways that earn them approbation from the general point of view.

In the *Treatise* Hume divides the virtues into two categories: the natural and the artificial. This distinction plays out against his view that moral evaluations of virtue and vice are primarily of character traits, not actions. According to Hume, "If any *action* be either virtuous or vicious, 'tis only as a sign of some quality or character. It must depend upon durable principles of the mind, which extend over the whole conduct, and enter into the personal character. Actions themselves, not proceeding from any constant principle, have no influence on love or hatred, pride or humility; and consequently are never consider'd in morality" (T. 151). The durable principles of the mind manifest themselves in the motives that people have in doing what they do. So, in treating an action or a person as virtuous or vicious one must turn one's attention to the motives behind the conduct. In fact, according to Hume, "*no action can be virtuous, or morally good, unless there be in human nature some motive to produce it distinct from the sense of its morality*" (T. 83).

The natural virtues are those that depend on people's motives independent of the various conventions within which they might find themselves acting. Being a benevolent person is being moved to help others in need. Although this motive will find expression in different ways in different contexts, depending on how it seems one might be of help, the motive itself is a part of the normal human frame, needing convention neither for its existence nor for its direction. Its evident usefulness to others, assuming we do not live in a world in which the road to hell is paved with good intentions, is sufficient to secure it approval from the general point of view.

In contrast, Hume maintains, in the absence of conventions establishing mine and thine, there is no sense to be made of the motive of justice and— even if sense of the motive could be made—no particular direction for it. Were there no such convention "no one wou'd ever have dream'd, that there was such a virtue as justice, or have been induc'd to conform his actions to it" (T. 96). Moreover, and more dramatically, Hume holds that were one to have and act on a recognizable motive of justice (say, thanks to the prior existence of the necessary conventions), there would be no virtue in acting on it if the relevant conventions are no longer in place. According to Hume, not only do the motives in question require the conventions, but so too does the approval from the general point of view. The same holds when it comes to fidelity to promises. Whereas Hume agrees that fidelity is most certainly a virtue, the possibility of recognizing some course of action as keeping one's promise, and so the possibility of having the required motive, presupposes the existence of certain conventions. And should the motive be present, though the relevant conventions have changed or disappeared, he again thinks the conditions required for the motive to secure approval from the general point of view would no longer be in place.

The artificial virtues thus depend on conventions along two dimensions. First, the possibility of acting on the motives, the having of which is required for these virtues, is possible only when certain conventions (of property or promising) are in place. Second, once those motives are available, their ability to secure approval from the general point of view, and so their standing as virtuous, depends upon the conventions being in place.

In the course of arguing that there is no natural motive to justice, Hume turns to a discussion of whether a person, lacking other motives to do the just thing, might nonetheless act from the motive of duty or a "regard to the virtue of the action" (T. 82). It highlights an intriguing puzzle. Hume grants that acting on this motive may well be a virtue—it might, that is, garner approval from the general point of view. But we need an answer to the question: What is a person thinking when she is thinking of some action, that it is her duty? It is no answer to say that she is thinking, in effect, that someone taking up the general point of view would approve of her acting from a sense of duty. That assumes we already have an account of what that sense is a sense of, which is the question we were originally trying to answer.

Perhaps the person is motivated by a benevolent concern for the welfare of those her just action would benefit. That is a perfectly intelligible and virtuous motive, Hume grants. Yet it is clearly distinct from the motive of duty, since in some cases one has a duty of justice to do what one recognizes will not answer to benevolence.

Another proposal might be that the person is motivated by a recognition that it is in her own interest to abide by the rules in place. This too is an intelligible motive and it is one that falls within the virtue of prudence. Still, acting on this motive, when one does one's duty, is clearly not the same as doing one's duty *from a sense of duty*.

One might suggest, then, that being motivated by a sense of duty is just a matter of being motivated by the thought that some conventional rule requires some action. Although such a motive requires the existence of the conventions in question, and so is not a natural motive, it is nonetheless a candidate for being the motive of duty. There are two problems with this suggestion. One is that acting in a certain way because the rules require it is different than acting in that way because one sees it as a duty, so the motive on offer still does not seem to be the right one. The other problem, which is connected to the first, is that being motivated simply to abide by rules, without regard to whether the rules are good, seems more of a rule-fetishism than a virtue and is very likely the sort of trait that would secure disapproval from the general point of view.

Hume never actually offers an explicit answer to this problem. However, anyone tempted by the thought that acting from a sense of duty is virtuous has reason to wrestle with it. What content can be given to the thought that something is one's duty such that being motivated by that thought is, itself, virtuous? My proposal, on Hume's behalf, would be that the relevant motive is not the rule-fetishistic motive mentioned above but is rather the complex motive constituted by recognizing that compliance with the rules in questions would secure approval from the general point of view. One who has this motive is not disposed merely to comply with rules simply because they are in place, but she is disposed to take the fact that an action conforms to the rules as grounds for acting, on the condition that acting on those grounds would survive scrutiny from the general point of view.

MORALITY AND UTILITY

Whatever account one accepts, it is important at this point to step back from the distinction between the artificial and the natural virtues to highlight the specific way in which Hume thinks morality is related to utility. Hume clearly takes considerations of utility to be at the heart of morality. "It appears to be a matter of fact," he observes,

> that the circumstances of *utility*, in all subjects, is a source of praise and approbation: That it is constantly appealed to in all moral decisions concerning the merit and demerit of actions: That it is the *sole* source of that high regard paid to justice, fidelity, honour, allegiance, and chastity: That it is inseparable from all the other social virtues, humanity, generosity, charity, affability, leniency, mercy, and moderation: And, in a word, that it is a foundation of the chief part of morals, which has a reference to mankind and our fellow-creatures. (E. 231)

Hume's appeals to utility are so extensive, and so central to the thrust of his whole account of morality, that it is natural to suppose that he embraces some version of utilitarianism. At the same time, it is clear that Hume's theory differs markedly from the version of utilitarianism advanced by Bentham (who reported learning from Hume "[t]hat the foundations of all *virtue* are laid in *utility*").[22] Specifically, although Bentham

---

[22] Jeremy Bentham, *A Fragment on Government*, in *A Comment on the Commentaries and A Fragment on the Government*, edited by J. H. Burns and H. L. A. Hart (London: University of London Athlone Press, 1977), Chapter 1, sec. 36, note 1, p. 440. In the following note, Bentham describes feeling, when he read Book III of the *Treatise*, "as if the scales had fallen from my eyes."

and many other utilitarians focus on actions as the primary objects of evaluation, Hume clearly thinks we properly focus on durable traits of mind or character and evaluate actions only as they reflect such traits. If he is a utilitarian, he is clearly what is called a motive or virtue utilitarian. Furthermore, although many utilitarians see the value of the primary objects of evaluation as turning on their actual contribution to welfare, Hume emphasizes that "[v]irtue in rags is still virtue; and the love which it procures attends a man into a dungeon or desert, where the virtue can no longer be exerted in action, and is lost to all the world" (T. 158). No version of utilitarianism that evaluates people or their motives or characters by the actual or expected impact they have will fit what Hume takes to be the facts of moral evaluation. Nonetheless there is both room and reason for a version of utilitarianism that concentrates instead on *types* of people, motives, or character. On this sort of view, a particular person's character might count as a virtue because it is the *kind* of character that makes a salutary contribution to utility even though, in this instance, it makes no such contribution.

If Hume is a utilitarian, he almost surely should be viewed as one who holds that a person counts as having a virtue not because of the contribution his character actually makes to utility but because he has the kind of character that makes such a contribution. Yet even this formulation fails to fit Hume's actual view comfortably, not if one gives much weight to the idea that the utility at issue is a measure of interpersonal value that might underwrite elaborate cost-benefit analyses. Hume seems never to have embraced Francis Hutcheson's concern for "the greatest happiness for the greatest numbers," and he steered clear of invoking anything like the "moral arithmetic" Hutcheson had introduced.[23] He also resisted the temptation to think that various virtues might usefully be compared to one another in an attempt to determine their relative value. Hume's theory neither requires nor supports the idea that such comparisons make sense.

More significantly, reading Hume as a utilitarian hides from view the degree to which he saw the particular virtues, as well as our practice of thinking in moral terms, as more or less specific solutions to problems we otherwise would face. An appreciation of their value comes, Hume thought, not from seeing how they measure up to some overarching scale of value nor from determining their over-all contribution to welfare, but from recognizing how they work to alleviate practical problems or to advance the projects

---

[23] Hutcheson offered the famous phrase and a moral calculus in "An Inquiry Concerning the Original of Our Ideas of Virtue or Moral Good," selections reprinted in *British Moralists*, edited by L. A. Selby-Bigge (New York: Dover Publications, 1965), on 107 and 110–13, respectively.

of particular individuals.[24] Hume was, in fact, perfectly prepared to acknowledge that genuine virtues, say of a statesman or a soldier, may not
benefit humanity over all. It is enough that they are useful or agreeable to
that person's countrymen.

Hume's theory seems well captured by saying that a durable feature of
mind or character is a virtue if (i) it would secure approval from the general point of view, and (ii) it will do this if it is *well suited* for the achieving
of certain ends or the solving of certain problems, because (iii) on taking
up the general point of view, sympathy will engage us with the advantages
enjoyed by those whose ends would be advance or problems solved. No
part of this view carries a commitment to an overarching measure of interpersonal value that is distinctive of utilitarianism.

Of course, if taking up the general point of view had one surveying the
impact of the sort of character in question on all of humanity, Hume's
view would match utilitarianism in its deliverances. However, Hume
clearly sees taking up the general point of view as a matter of focusing on
a trait's impact on, what Hume calls, the "narrow circle." Just how wide
the narrow circle seems, on Hume's view, to vary with the character trait
in question. Thus, in evaluating someone as a parent, the relevant circle is
largely limited to those in the family, whereas when it comes to evaluating
someone as a statesman the focus (from the general point of view) is properly on the nation as a whole (but not on other nations). Different sorts of
problems—those faced by parents and those faced by statesmen—may
call for different, and perhaps incompatible, solutions. A character trait
might be well suited for the solving of certain problems in the appropriate
way, even if it is never actually used to solve those problems, and even if
people know that it will never be so used. This is the case of virtue in rags.
Finally, a trait might be well suited to the achieving of the relevant ends
even if using it to secure those ends will frustrate others (as sometimes
justice frustrates benevolence [see E. 281–2]).

The fact that character traits count as virtues because they are well
suited to solving problems that we are concerned to avoid explains in a satisfying way why morality, as Hume understands it, is genuinely practical.
This advantage amplifies once one appreciates that the very same account
Hume offers of the virtues applies as well to moral thought, talk, and action. No less than the particular virtues, Hume holds, our capacity to
think and talk together about moral matters and then regulate our behavior accordingly, plays an essential role in making it possible for us to live
together harmoniously.

---

[24] I try to work out the details of this interpretation of Hume in "Hume and the
Bauhaus Theory of Ethics," *Midwest Studies in Philosophy* 20 (1996): 280–98.

That moral thought and talk is a human creation that answers to problems we would otherwise face invites a serious concern. "Most of the inventions of men are subject to change. They depend," Hume notes, "upon humour and caprice. They have a vogue for a time, and then sink into oblivion" (T. 183). One might worry that Hume's view that the artificial virtues of justice—fidelity to promises—is based on convention, and that, in fact, the very practice of judging things in moral terms is based on convention, puts morality on a similarly shaky foundation. In reply, Hume argues that although the conventions central to morality are "inventions of men," they are founded on an interest that is "the greatest imaginable, and extends to all times and places. It cannot possibly be serv'd by any other invention. It is obvious, and discovers itself on the very first formation of society" (T. 183). As a result, he argues, the conventions that constitute morality are "steadfast and immutable; at least, as immutable as human nature" (T. 183).

NOTE ON THE TEXTS

The aim in putting this collection together has been to provide a careful, though not a critical, edition of Hume's work on ethics and political philosophy. Every effort has been made to ensure that the text reflects Hume's final judgment concerning how the texts should be, so a number of revisions made by Hume are included. What is not included, which would be in a critical edition, is an apparatus of variant readings that tracks changes in the texts over various editions. Those interested in following such changes should consult the masterful critical edition of the *Enquiry Concerning the Principles of Morals* edited by Tom L. Beauchamp (Oxford: Oxford University Press, 1998) and the forthcoming critical edition of the *Treatise of Human Nature* edited by David Fate Norton and Mary J. Norton, prepared for the Clarendon edition of *The Philosophical, Political and Literary Works of David Hume* (Oxford: Clarendon Press, 2006). They set the standard for accuracy and for judicious editorial judgment, and they contain an elaborate and nicely refined critical apparatus, along with informative annotations and helpful glossaries. Consequently, they supersede the editions of the *Enquiries* and the *Treatise* edited by L. A. Selby-Bigge (revised by P. H. Nidditch; 1975 for the *Enquiries*, 1978 for the *Treatise*) that have long served as the standard editions. Eugene F. Miller's elegant critical edition of the *Essays: Moral, Political, and Literary*, is, far and away, the best edition of Hume's essays (rev. ed., Indianapolis: LibertyClassics, 1987).

This edition of the *Treatise* is based on that published in 1739–40, while the *Enquiry* and the *Essays* (except for "On Suicide") are based on the 1777 posthumous edition of *Essays and Treatises on Several Subjects* that Hume prepared at the end of his life. "My Own Life" and "A Letter from Adam Smith, LL.D. to William Strahan, Esq." are taken from *The Life of David Hume, Esq., written by himself*, published by Strahan in 1777. Hume withdrew "On Suicide" from publication in 1756, for fear of repercussions from the Church, but arranged to have it published upon his death. Following Miller, this edition relies on a prepublication copy that Hume amended rather than the first published edition, which appeared in 1777 (without attribution). There is at least some reason to think the version used here better reflects Hume's intentions. The prepublication copy is housed in the National Library of Scotland and is being used with the much appreciated permission of The Trustees of the National Library of Scotland.

The resulting text has, in each case, been compared with, and sometimes corrected in light of, the editions cited above. In general, the temptation to regularize Hume's spelling and punctuation has been resisted and the changes made have been governed by a concern to limit alterations to ones that Hume himself indicated or authorized.

All translations of Greek and Latin (which are set off by square brackets in the text) are taken from the Loeb Classical Library (published by Harvard University Press) except for: Hugo Grotius, *The Rights of War and Peace*, translated by John Morrice (Indianapolis: Liberty Fund, 2005); and Justinian, *Justinian's Institutes*, translated by Peter Birks and Grant McLeod (London: Duckworth, 1987); and Flavius Vegetius Renatus, *De re militari*, translated by Lieutenant John Clarke (London: W. Griffin, 1767). The French translation of St. Evremond's *Letters*, volume 1, is from the edition by Rene Ternois (Paris: Didier, 1967–8).

In order to facilitate a system of textual reference that will work across editions, paragraphs in this collection are numbered consecutively within each section and essay.

SELECT BIBLIOGRAPHY

HUME'S WRITINGS

A Treatise of Human Nature (1739–40)

An Abstract of . . . *A Treatise of Human Nature* (1740)

Essays, Moral and Political (1741–2, 1748)

An Enquiry Concerning Human Understanding; first published as *Philosophical Essays Concerning Human Understanding* (1748)

An Enquiry Concerning the Principles of Morals (1751)

Political Discourses (1752)

The History of England (1754–62)

Four Dissertations: "The Natural History of Religion," "Of the Passions" ("A Dissertation on the Passions"), "Of Tragedy," and "Of the Standard of Taste" (1757)

My Own Life (1777)

Dialogues Concerning Natural Religion (1779)

Essays on Suicide and the Immortality of the Soul (1783)

USEFUL SECONDARY SOURCES
Books

Árdal, Páll. *Passion and Value in Hume's Treatise*. Edinburgh: Edinburgh University Press, 1966.

Baier, Annette C. *A Progress of Sentiments: Reflections on Hume's Treatise*. Cambridge: Harvard University Press, 1991.

Baillie, James. *Hume on Morality*. London: Routledge, 2000.

Box, M. A. *The Suasive Art of David Hume*. Princeton: Princeton University Press, 1990.

Bricke, John. *Mind and Morality: An Examination of Hume's Moral Psychology*. New York: Oxford University Press, 1996.

Cohon, Rachel. *Hume: Moral and Political Philosophy*. Aldershot: Ashgate, 2001.

Darwall, Stephen. *The British Moralists and the Internal 'Ought.'* Cambridge: Cambridge University Press, 1995.

Fogelin, Robert J. *Hume's Skepticism in the* Treatise of Human Nature. London: Routledge, 1985.

Forbes, Duncan. *Hume's Philosophical Politics.* Cambridge: Cambridge University Press, 1975.

Garrett, Don. *Cognition and Commitment in Hume's Philosophy.* New York: Oxford University Press, 1997.

Glathe, A. B. *Hume's Theory of the Passions and of Morals: A Study of Books II and III of the* Treatise. Berkeley: University of California Press, 1950.

Haakonssen, Knud. *The Science of a Legislator: The Natural Jurisprudence of David Hume and Adam Smith.* Cambridge: Cambridge University Press, 1981.

Harrison, Jonathan. *Hume's Moral Epistemology.* Oxford: Clarendon Press, 1976.

————. *Hume's Theory of Justice.* Oxford: Clarendon Press, 1981.

Jones, Peter. *Hume's Sentiments: Their Ciceronian and French Context.* Edinburgh: Edinburgh University Press, 1982.

Kydd, Rachel M. *Reason and Conduct in Hume's Treatise.* Oxford: Clarendon Press, 1946.

Livingston, Donald W. *Hume's Philosophy of Common Life.* Chicago: University of Chicago Press, 1984.

Mackie, J. L. *Hume's Moral Theory.* London: Routledge, 1980.

Mercer, Philip. *Sympathy and Ethics: A Study of the Relationship between Sympathy and Morality, with Special Reference to Hume's* Treatise. Oxford: Clarendon Press, 1972.

Miller, David. *Philosophy and Ideology in Hume's Political Thought.* Oxford: Clarendon Press, 1981.

Mossner, Ernest C. *The Life of David Hume,* 2nd ed. Oxford: Clarendon Press, 1980.

Norton, David Fate. *David Hume: Common Sense Moralist, Sceptical Metaphysician,* rev. ed. Princeton: Princeton University Press, 1984.

Norton, David Fate, ed. *The Cambridge Companion to Hume.* Cambridge: Cambridge University Press, 1993.

Raphael, D. D. *The Moral Sense.* London: Oxford University Press, 1947.

Russell, Paul. *Freedom and Moral Sentiment: Hume's Way of Naturalizing Responsibility.* New York: Oxford University Press, 1995.

Schneewind, J. B. *The Invention of Autonomy.* Cambridge: Cambridge University Press, 1998.

Smith, Norman Kemp. *The Philosophy of David Hume*. London: Macmillan, 1941.

Snare, Francis. *Morals, Motivation, and Convention: Hume's Influential Doctrines*. Cambridge: Cambridge University Press, 1991.

Stewart, John B. *Opinion and Reform in Hume's Political Philosophy*. Princeton: Princeton University Press, 1992.

Stroud, Barry. *Hume*. London: Routledge, 1977.

Whelan, Frederick. *Order and Artifice in Hume's Political Philosophy*. Princeton: Princeton University Press, 1981.

Articles

Árdal, Páll. "Another Look at Hume's Account of Moral Evaluation." *Journal of the History of Philosophy* 15 (October 1977): 405–21.

———. "Convention and Value." In *David Hume: Bicentenary Papers*, edited by G. P. Morice, 51–68. Austin: University of Texas Press, 1977.

Baier, Annette. "Artificial Virtues and the Equally Sensible Non-Knaves: A Response to Gauthier." *Hume Studies* 18, no. 2 (1992): 429–39.

———. "Hume's Account of Social Artifice: Its Origin and Originality." *Ethics* 98 (July 1988): 757–78.

———. "Hume's Analysis of Pride." *Journal of Philosophy* 75 (1978): 27–40.

———. "Master Passions." In *Explaining Emotions*, edited by Amélie Oksenberg Rorty, 403–23. Berkeley: University of California Press, 1980.

Baron, Marcia. "Hume's Noble Lie: An Account of His Artificial Virtues." *Canadian Journal of Philosophy* 12 (1982): 539–55.

Blackburn, Simon. "Hume on the Mezzanine Level." *Hume Studies* 19, no. 2 (1993): 273–88.

Bricke, John. "Hume, Motivation and Morality." *Hume Studies* 14, no. 1 (1988): 1–24.

Brown, Charlotte. "Is Hume an Internalist?" *Journal of the History of Philosophy* 26, no. 1 (1988): 69–87.

Cohon, Rachel. "The Common Point of View in Hume's Ethics." *Philosophy and Phenomenological Research* 57, no. 4 (1997): 827–50.

———. "Hume's Difficulty with the Virtue of Honesty." *Hume Studies* 23, no. 1 (1997): 91–112.

———. "Is Hume a Noncognitivist in the Motivation Argument?" *Philosophical Studies* 85 (1997): 251–66.

Darwall, Stephen. "Hume and the Invention of Utilitarianism." In *Hume and Hume's Connections*, edited by M. A. Stewart and John P. Wright, 58–82. Edinburgh: Edinburgh University Press, 1994.

—————. "Motive and Obligation in Hume's Ethics." *Noûs* 27, no. 4 (1993): 415–48.

Davidson, Donald. "Hume's Cognitive Theory of Pride." *Journal of Philosophy* 73 (1967): 744–57.

Dees, Richard. "Hume on the Characters of Virtue." *Journal of the History of Philosophy* 35, no. 1 (1997): 45–64.

Falk, W. D. "Hume on Is and Ought." *Canadian Journal of Philosophy* 6 (1976): 359–78.

—————. "Hume on Practical Reason." *Philosophical Studies* 27 (1975): 1–8.

Flew, Antony. "On the Interpretation of Hume." *Philosophy* 38 (1963): 178–81.

Foot, Philippa. "Hume on Moral Judgement." In *David Hume: A Symposium*, by Stuart Hampshire et al., edited by D. F. Pears, 74–80. London: Macmillan, 1963.

Forbes, Duncan. "Hume's Science of Politics." In *David Hume: Bicentenary Papers*, edited by G. P. Morice, 39–50. Austin: University of Texas Press, 1977.

Gauthier, David. "Artificial Virtues and the Sensible Knave." *Hume Studies* 18, no. 2 (1992): 401–27.

—————. "David Hume, Contractarian." *Philosophical Review* 88 (1979): 3–38.

—————. "Three against Justice: The Foole, the Sensible Knave, and the Lydian Shepherd." *Midwest Studies in Philosophy* 7 (1982): 11–29.

Glossop, Ronald J. "Is Hume a 'Classical Utilitarian'?" *Hume Studies* 2, no. 1 (1976): 1–16.

Haakonssen, Knud. "Hume's Obligations." *Hume Studies* 4, no. 1 (1978): 7–17.

Hampton, Jean. "Does Hume Have an Instrumental Conception of Practical Reason?" *Hume Studies* 21, no. 1 (1995): 57–74.

Hearn, Thomas K. "General Rules and the Moral Sentiments in Hume's *Treatise*." *Review of Metaphysics* 30 (1976): 57–72.

Hudson, W. D. "Hume on Is and Ought." *The Philosophical Quaterly* 14 (1964): 246–52.

Hunter, Geoffrey. "Hume on Is and Ought." *Philosophy* 37 (1962): 148–52.

Jenkins, John J. "Hume's Account of Sympathy—Some Difficulties." In *Philosophers of the Scottish Enlightenment*, edited by V. Hope, 91–104. Edinburgh: Edinburgh University Press, 1984.

Jensen, Henning. "Hume on Moral Agreement." *Mind* 86 (1977): 497–513.

Kivy, Peter. "Hume's Standard of Taste: Breaking the Circle." *British Journal of Aesthetics* 7 (1967): 57–66.

Korsgaard, Christine. "The General Point of View: Love and Moral Approval in Hume's Ethics." *Hume Studies* 25, no. 1–2 (1999): 3–41.

Loeb, Louis. "Hume's Moral Sentiments and the Structure of the *Treatise*." *Journal of the History of Philosophy* 15 (1977): 395–403.

MacIntyre, Alasdair C. "Hume on 'Is' and 'Ought.'" *Philosophical Review* 68 (1959): 451–68.

Magri, Tito. "Natural Obligations and Normative Motivation in Hume's *Treatise*." *Hume Studies* 22, no. 2 (1996): 231–53.

McCracken, D. J. "David Hume and the Sentiment of Humanity." *Actes du XI Congress International de Philosophie* 8 (1953): 100–103.

McIntyre, Jane. "Character: A Humean Account." *History of Philosophy Quarterly* 7 (1990): 193–206.

Millgram, Elijah. "Was Hume a Humean?" *Hume Studies* 21, no. 1 (1995): 75–93.

Norton, David Fate. "Hume, Human Nature, and the Foundations of Morality." In *The Cambridge Companion to Hume*, edited by David Fate Norton, 148–82. Cambridge: Cambridge University Press, 1993.

———. "Hume's Moral Ontology." *Hume Studies* (special volume) (1985): 189–214.

Nuyen, A. T. "David Hume on Reason, Passions and Morals." *Hume Studies* 10, no. 1 (1984): 26–45.

Persson, Ingmar. "Hume—Not a 'Humean' about Motivation." *History of Philosophy Quarterly* 14, no. 2 (1997): 189–206.

Postema, Gerald. "Hume's Reply to the Sensible Knave." *History of Philosophy Quarterly* 5 (1988): 23–40.

Radcliffe, Elizabeth. "How Does the Humean Sense of Duty Motivate?" *Journal of the History of Philosophy* 34 (July 1996): 47–70.

———. "Kantian Tunes on a Humean Instrument: Why Hume Is Not Really a Skeptic about Practical Reasoning." *Canadian Journal of Philosophy* 27 (June 1997): 247–69.

Sayre-McCord, Geoffrey. "Hume and the Bauhaus Theory of Ethics." *Midwest Studies in Philosophy* 20 (1996): 280–98.

————. "On Why Hume's 'General Point of View' Isn't Ideal—and Shouldn't Be." *Social Philosophy & Policy* 11, no. 1 (1994): 202–28.

Shaver, Robert. "Hume and the Duties of Humanity." *Journal of the History of Philosophy* 30 (1992): 545–56.

Stroud, Barry. "'Gilding or Staining' the World with 'Sentiments' and 'Phantasms.'" *Hume Studies* 19, no. 2 (1993): 253–72.

Sturgeon, Nicholas. "Moral Skepticism and Moral Naturalism in Hume's *Treatise*." *Hume Studies* 21, no. 1 (2001): 3–83.

Swain, Corliss. "Passionate Objectivity." *Noûs* 26, no. 4 (1992): 465–90.

Taylor, Jacqueline. "Justice and the Foundations of Social Morality in Hume's *Treatise*." *Hume Studies* 24, no. 1 (1998): 5–30.

Wiggins, David. "A Sensible Subjectivism?" In *Needs, Values, Truth*, 3rd ed., 185–210. Oxford: Clarendon Press, 1998.

MY OWN LIFE

It is difficult for a man to speak long of himself without vanity; therefore, 1
I shall be short. It may be thought an instance of vanity that I pretend at
all to write my life; but this Narrative shall contain little more than the
History of my Writings; as, indeed, almost all my life has been spent in literary pursuits and occupations. The first success of most of my writings
was not such as to be an object of vanity.

I was born the 26th of April 1711, old style, at Edinburgh. I was of a 2
good family, both by father and mother: my father's family is a branch of
the Earl of Home's, or Hume's; and my ancestors had been proprietors of
the estate, which my brother possesses, for several generations. My
mother was daughter of Sir David Falconer, President of the College of
Justice: the title of Lord Halkerton came by succession to her brother.

My family, however, was not rich, and being myself a younger brother, 3
my patrimony, according to the mode of my country, was of course very
slender. My father, who passed for a man of parts, died when I was an infant, leaving me, with an elder brother and a sister, under the care of our
mother, a woman of singular merit, who, though young and handsome,
devoted herself entirely to the rearing and educating of her children. I
passed through the ordinary course of education with success, and was
seized very early with a passion for literature, which has been the ruling
passion of my life, and the great source of my enjoyments. My studious
disposition, my sobriety, and my industry, gave my family a notion that
the law was a proper profession for me; but I found an unsurmountable
aversion to every thing but the pursuits of philosophy and general learning; and while they fancied I was poring upon Voet and Vinnius, Cicero
and Virgil were the authors which I was secretly devouring.

My very slender fortune, however, being unsuitable to this plan of 4
life, and my health being a little broken by my ardent application, I was
tempted, or rather forced, to make a very feeble trial for entering into a
more active scene of life. In 1734, I went to Bristol, with some recom-
mendations to eminent merchants, but in a few months found that scene
totally unsuitable to me. I went over to France, with a view of prosecut-
ing my studies in a country retreat; and I there laid that plan of life,
which I have steadily and successfully pursued. I resolved to make a very
rigid frugality supply my deficiency of fortune, to maintain unimpaired

my independency, and to regard every object as contemptible, except
the improvement of my talents in literature.

5   During my retreat in France, first at Reims, but chiefly at La Fleche, in
Anjou, I composed my *Treatise of Human Nature*. After passing three
years very agreeably in that country, I came over to London in 1737. In
the end of 1738, I published my Treatise, and immediately went down to
my mother and my brother, who lived at his country-house, and was employing himself very judiciously and successfully in the improvement of
his fortune.

6   Never literary attempt was more unfortunate than my Treatise of
Human Nature. It fell *dead-born from the press*, without reaching such distinction, as even to excite a murmur among the zealots. But being naturally of a cheerful and sanguine temper, I very soon recovered the blow,
and prosecuted with great ardour my studies in the country. In 1742, I
printed at Edinburgh the first part of my Essays: the work was favourably
received, and soon made me entirely forget my former disappointment. I
continued with my mother and brother in the country, and in that time recovered the knowledge of the Greek language, which I had too much neglected in my early youth.

7   In 1745, I received a letter from the Marquis of Annandale, inviting me
to come and live with him in England; I found also, that the friends and
family of that young nobleman were desirous of putting him under my care
and direction, for the state of his mind and health required it.—I lived
with him a twelvemonth. My appointments during that time made a
considerable accession to my small fortune. I then received an invitation
from General St. Clair to attend him as a secretary to his expedition, which
was at first meant against Canada, but ended in an incursion on the coast of
France. Next year, to wit, 1747, I received an invitation from the General to
attend him in the same station in his military embassy to the courts of Vienna and Turin. I then wore the uniform of an officer, and was introduced
at these courts as aide-de-camp to the general, along with Sir Harry Ersk-
ine and Captain Grant, now General Grant. These two years were almost
the only interruptions which my studies have received during the course of
my life: I passed them agreeably and in good company; and my appointments, with my frugality, had made me reach a fortune, which I called independent, though most of my friends were inclined to smile when I said
so; in short, I was now master of near a thousand pounds.

8   I had always entertained a notion, that my want of success in publishing
the Treatise of Human Nature, had proceeded more from the manner than
the matter, and that I had been guilty of a very usual indiscretion, in going
to the press too early. I, therefore, cast the first part of that work anew in
the Enquiry concerning Human Understanding, which was published

while I was at Turin. But this piece was at first little more successful than the Treatise of Human Nature. On my return from Italy, I had the mortification to find all England in a ferment, on account of Dr. Middleton's Free Enquiry, while my performance was entirely overlooked and neglected. A new edition, which had been published at London of my Essays, moral and political, met not with a much better reception.

Such is the force of natural temper, that these disappointments made little or no impression on me. I went down in 1749, and lived two years with my brother at his country-house, for my mother was now dead. I there composed the second part of my Essays, which I called Political Discourses, and also my Enquiry concerning the Principles of Morals, which is another part of my treatise that I cast anew. Meanwhile, my bookseller, A. Millar, informed me, that my former publications (all but the unfortunate Treatise) were beginning to be the subject of conversation; that the sale of them was gradually increasing, and that new editions were demanded. Answers by Reverends, and Right Reverends, came out two or three in a year; and I found, by Dr. Warburton's railing, that the books were beginning to be esteemed in good company. However, I had fixed a resolution, which I inflexibly maintained, never to reply to any body; and not being very irascible in my temper, I have easily kept myself clear of all literary squabbles. These symptoms of a rising reputation gave me encouragement, as I was ever more disposed to see the favourable than unfavourable side of things; a turn of mind which it is more happy to possess, than to be born to an estate of ten thousand a year.

In 1751, I removed from the country to the town, the true scene for a man of letters. In 1752, were published at Edinburgh, where I then lived, my Political Discourses, the only work of mine that was successful on the first publication. It was well received abroad and at home. In the same year was published at London, my Enquiry concerning the Principles of Morals; which, in my own opinion (who ought not to judge on that subject), is of all my writings, historical, philosophical, or literary, incomparably the best. It came unnoticed and unobserved into the world.

In 1752, the Faculty of Advocates chose me their Librarian, an office from which I received little or no emolument, but which gave me the command of a large library. I then formed the plan of writing the History of England; but being frightened with the notion of continuing a narrative through a period of 1700 years, I commenced with the accession of the House of Stuart, an epoch when, I thought, the misrepresentations of faction began chiefly to take place. I was, I own, sanguine in my expectations of the success of this work. I thought that I was the only historian, that had at once neglected present power, interest, and authority, and the cry of popular prejudices; and as the subject was suited to every capacity, I expected proportional applause. But miserable was my disappointment: I was assailed by one cry of reproach, disapprobation, and even detestation; English, Scotch, and Irish, Whig and Tory, churchman and sectary, free-thinker and religionist, patriot and courtier, united in their rage against the man, who had presumed to shed a generous tear for the fate of Charles I. and the Earl of Strafford; and after the first ebullitions of their fury were over, what was still more mortifying, the book seemed to sink into oblivion. Mr. Millar told me, that in a twelvemonth he sold only forty-five copies of it. I scarcely, indeed, heard of one man in the three kingdoms, considerable for rank or letters, that could endure the book. I must only except the primate of England, Dr. Herring, and the primate of Ireland, Dr. Stone, which seem two odd exceptions. These dignified prelates separately sent me messages not to be discouraged.

12   I was, however, I confess, discouraged; and had not the war been at that time breaking out between France and England, I had certainly retired to some provincial town of the former kingdom, have changed my name, and never more have returned to my native country. But as this scheme was not now practicable, and the subsequent volume was considerably advanced, I resolved to pick up courage and to persevere.

13   In this interval[1] I published at London my Natural History of Religion, along with some other small pieces: its public entry was rather obscure, except only that Dr. Hurd wrote a pamphlet against it, with all the illiberal petulance, arrogance, and scurrility which distinguish the Warburtonian school. This pamphlet gave me some consolation for the otherwise indifferent reception of my performance.

14   In 1756, two years after the fall of the first volume, was published the second volume of my History, containing the period from the death of Charles I. till the Revolution. This performance happened to give less displeasure to the Whigs, and was better received. It not only rose itself, but helped to buoy up its unfortunate brother.

15   But though I had been taught by experience, that the Whig party were in possession of bestowing all places, both in the state and in literature, I was so little inclined to yield to their senseless clamour, that in about a hundred alterations, which farther study, reading, or reflection engaged me to make in the reigns of the first two Stuarts, I have made all of them invariably to the Tory side. It is ridiculous to consider the English constitution before that period as a regular plan of liberty.

16   In 1759, I published my History of the House of Tudor. The clamour against this performance was almost equal to that against the History of

---

[1] In 1757.

the two first Stuarts. The reign of Elizabeth was particularly obnoxious. But I was now callous against the impressions of public folly, and continued very peaceably and contentedly in my retreat at Edinburgh, to finish, in two volumes, the more early part of the English History, which I gave to the public in 1761, with tolerable, and but tolerable success.

But, notwithstanding this variety of winds and seasons, to which my writings had been exposed, they had still been making such advances, that the copy-money given me by the booksellers, much exceeded any thing formerly known in England; I was become not only independent, but opulent. I retired to my native country of Scotland, determined never more to set my foot out of it; and retaining the satisfaction of never having preferred a request to one great man, or even making advances of friendship to any of them. As I was now turned of fifty, I thought of passing all the rest of my life in this philosophical manner, when I received, in 1763, an invitation from the Earl of Hertford, with whom I was not in the least acquainted, to attend him on his embassy to Paris, with a near prospect of being appointed secretary to the embassy; and, in the meanwhile, of performing the functions of that office. This offer, however inviting, I at first declined, both because I was reluctant to begin connexions with the great, and because I was afraid that the civilities and gay company of Paris, would prove disagreeable to a person of my age and humour: but on his lordship's repeating the invitation, I accepted of it. I have every reason, both of pleasure and interest, to think myself happy in my connexions with that nobleman, as well as afterwards with his brother, General Conway. 17

Those who have not seen the strange effects of modes, will never imagine the reception I met with at Paris, from men and women of all ranks and stations. The more I resiled from their excessive civilities, the more I was loaded with them. There is, however, a real satisfaction in living at Paris, from the great number of sensible, knowing, and polite company with which that city abounds above all places in the universe. I thought once of settling there for life. 18

I was appointed secretary to the embassy; and in summer 1765, Lord Hertford left me, being appointed Lord Lieutenant of Ireland. I was *chargé d'affaires* till the arrival of the Duke of Richmond, towards the end of the year. In the beginning of 1766, I left Paris, and next summer went to Edinburgh, with the same view as formerly, of burying myself in a philosophical retreat. I returned to that place, not richer, but with much more money, and a much larger income, by means of Lord Hertford's friendship, than I left it; and I was desirous of trying what superfluity could produce, as I had formerly made an experiment of a competency. But in 1767, I received from Mr. Conway an invitation to be Under-secretary; 19 and this invitation, both the character of the person, and my connexions with Lord Hertford, prevented me from declining. I returned to Edinburgh in 1769, very opulent (for I possessed a revenue of 1000 *l.* a year), healthy, and though somewhat stricken in years, with the prospect of enjoying long my ease, and of seeing the increase of my reputation.

20   In spring 1775, I was struck with a disorder in my bowels, which at first gave me no alarm, but has since, as I apprehend it, become mortal and incurable. I now reckon upon a speedy dissolution. I have suffered very little pain from my disorder; and what is more strange, have, notwithstanding the great decline of my person, never suffered a moment's abatement of my spirits; insomuch, that were I to name the period of my life, which I should most choose to pass over again, I might be tempted to point to this later period. I possess the same ardour as ever in study, and the same gaiety in company. I consider, besides, that a man of sixty-five, by dying, cuts off only a few years of infirmities; and though I see many symptoms of my literary reputation's breaking out at last with additional lustre, I knew that I could have but few years to enjoy it. It is difficult to be more detached from life than I am at present.

21   To conclude historically with my own character. I am, or rather was (for that is the style I must now use in speaking of myself, which emboldens me the more to speak my sentiments); I was, I say, a man of mild dispositions, of command of temper, of an open, social, and cheerful humour, capable of attachment, but little susceptible of enmity, and of great moderation in all my passions. Even my love of literary fame, my ruling passion, never soured my temper, notwithstanding my frequent disappointments. My company was not unacceptable to the young and careless, as well as to the studious and literary; and as I took a particular pleasure in the company of modest women, I had no reason to be displeased with the reception I met with from them. In a word, though most men any wise eminent, have found reason to complain of calumny, I never was touched, or even attacked by her baleful tooth: and though I wantonly exposed myself to the rage of both civil and religious factions, they seemed to be disarmed in my behalf of their wonted fury. My friends never had occasion to vindicate any one circumstance of my character and conduct: not but that the zealots, we may well suppose, would have been glad to invent and propagate any story to my disadvantage, but they could never find any which they thought would wear the face of probability. I cannot say there is no vanity in making this funeral oration of myself, but I hope it is not a misplaced one; and this is a matter of fact which is easily cleared and ascertained.

April 18, 1776.

Letter from Adam Smith, LL.D. to William Strahan, Esq.

Kirkaldy, Fifeshire, Nov. 9, 1776.

Dear Sir,

It is with a real, though a very melancholy pleasure, that I sit down to give you some account of the behaviour of our late excellent friend, Mr. Hume, during his last illness. 1

Though, in his own judgment, his disease was mortal and incurable, yet he allowed himself to be prevailed upon, by the entreaty of his friends, to try what might be the effects of a long journey. A few days before he set out, he wrote that account of his own life, which, together with his other papers, he has left to your care. My account, therefore, shall begin where his ends. 2

He set out for London towards the end of April, and at Morpeth met with Mr. John Home and myself, who had both come down from London on purpose to see him, expecting to have found him at Edinburgh. Mr. Home returned with him, and attended him during the whole of his stay in England, with that care and attention which might be expected from a temper so perfectly friendly and affectionate. As I had written to my mother that she might expect me in Scotland, I was under the necessity of continuing my journey. His disease seemed to yield to exercise and change of air, and when he arrived in London, he was apparently in much better health than when he left Edinburgh. He was advised to go to Bath to drink the waters, which appeared for some time to have so good an effect upon him, that even he himself began to entertain, what he was not apt to do, a better opinion of his own health. His symptoms, however, soon returned with their usual violence, and from that moment he gave up all thoughts of recovery, but submitted with the utmost cheerfulness, and the most perfect complacency and resignation. Upon his return to Edinburgh, though he found himself much weaker, yet his cheerfulness never abated, and he continued to divert himself, as usual, with correcting his own works for a new edition, with reading books of amusement, with the conversation of his friends; and sometimes in the evening with a party at his 3 favourite game of whist. His cheerfulness was so great, and his conversation and amusements ran so much in their usual strain, that notwithstanding all bad symptoms, many people could not believe he was dying. "I shall tell your friend Colonel Edmondstone," said Doctor Dundas to him one day, "that I left you much better, and in a fair way of recovery." "Doctor," said he, "as I believe you would not chuse to tell any thing but the truth, you had better tell him I am dying as fast as my enemies, if I have any, could wish, and as easily and cheerfully as my best friends could desire." Colonel Edmonstoune soon afterwards came to see him, and take leave of him; and on his way home, he could not forbear writing him a letter bidding him once more an eternal adieu, and applying to him, as to a dying man, the beautiful French verses in which the Abbé Chaulieu, in expectation of his own death, laments his approaching separation from his friend, the Marquis de la Fare. Mr. Hume's magnanimity and firmness were such, that his most affectionate friends knew, that they hazarded nothing in talking and writing to him as to a dying man, and that so far from being hurt by this frankness, he was rather pleased and flattered by it. I happened to come into his room while he was reading this letter, which he had just received, and which he immediately showed me. I told him, that though I was sensible how very much he was weakened, and that appearances were in many respects very bad, yet his cheerfulness was still so great, the spirit of life seemed still to be so very strong in him, that I could not help entertaining some faint hopes. He answered, "Your hopes are groundless. An habitual diarrhœa of more than a year's standing, would be a very bad disease at any age: at my age it is a mortal one. When I lie down in the evening, I feel myself weaker than when I rose in the morning; and when I rise in the morning, weaker than when I lay down in the evening. I am sensible, besides, that some of my vital parts are affected, so that I must soon die." "Well," said I, "if it must be so, you have at least the satisfaction of leaving all your friends, your brother's family in particular, in great prosperity." He said that he felt that satisfaction so sensibly, that when he was reading a few days before, Lucian's Dialogues of the Dead, among all the excuses which are alleged to Charon for not entering readily into his boat, he could not find one that fitted him; he had no house to finish, he had no daughter to provide for, he had no enemies upon whom he wished to revenge himself. "I could not well imagine," said he, "what excuse I could make to Charon in order to obtain a little delay. I have done every thing of consequence which I ever meant to do, and I could at no time expect to leave my relations and friends in a better situation than that in which I am now likely to leave them; I, therefore, have all reason to die contented." He then diverted himself with inventing several jocular excuses, which he supposed he might make to Charon, and with imagining the very surly answers which it might suit the character of Charon to return to them. "Upon further consideration," said he, "I thought I might say to him, Good Charon, I have been correcting my works for a new edition. Allow me a little time, that I may see how the Public receives the alterations." But Charon would answer, "When you have seen the effect of these, you will be for making other alterations. There will be no end of such excuses; so, honest friend, please step into the boat." But I might still urge, "Have a little patience, good Charon, I have been endeavouring to open the eyes of the Public. If I live a few years longer, I may have the satisfaction of seeing the downfall of some of the prevailing systems of superstition." But Charon would then lose all temper and decency. "You loitering rogue, that will not happen these many hundred years. Do you fancy I will grant you a lease for so long a term? Get into the boat this instant, you lazy loitering rogue."

But though Mr. Hume always talked of his approaching dissolution 4 with great cheerfulness, he never affected to make any parade of his great magnanimity. He never mentioned the subject but when the conversation naturally led to it, and never dwelt longer upon it than the course of the conversation happened to require: it was a subject indeed which occurred pretty frequently, in consequence of the inquiries which his friends, who came to see him, naturally made concerning the state of his health. The conversation which I mentioned above, and which passed on Thursday the 8th of August, was the last, except one, that I ever had with him. He had now become so very weak, that the company of his most intimate friends fatigued him; for his cheerfulness was still so great, his complaisance and social disposition were still so entire, that when any friend was with him, he could not help talking more, and with greater exertion, than suited the weakness of his body. At his own desire, therefore, I agreed to leave Edinburgh, where I was staying partly upon his account, and returned to my mother's house here, at Kirkaldy, upon condition that he would send for me whenever he wished to see me; the physician who saw him most frequently, Doctor Black, undertaking, in the mean time, to write me occasionally an account of the state of his health.

On the 22nd of August, the Doctor wrote me the following letter: 5

"Since my last, Mr. Hume has passed his time pretty easily, but is 6 much weaker. He sits up, goes down stairs once a day, and amuses himself with reading, but seldom sees anybody. He finds that even the conversation of his most intimate friends fatigues and oppresses him; and it is happy that he does not need it, for he is quite free from anxiety, impatience, or low spirits, and passes his time very well with the assistance of amusing books."

7   I received the day after a letter from Mr. Hume himself, of which the following is an extract.

8   Edinburgh, 23rd August, 1776.
    "MY DEAREST FRIEND,
        "I am obliged to make use of my nephew's hand in writing to you, as I do not rise to-day. . . .
        "I go very fast to decline, and last night had a small fever, which I hoped might put a quicker period to this tedious illness, but unluckily it has, in a great measure, gone off. I cannot submit to your coming over here on my account, as it is possible for me to see you so small a part of the day, but Doctor Black can better inform you concerning the degree of strength which may from time to time remain with me. Adieu, &c."

    Three days after I received the following letter from Doctor Black.

9   Edinburgh, Monday, 26th August, 1776.
    "DEAR SIR,
        "Yesterday about four o'clock afternoon, Mr. Hume expired. The near approach of his death became evident in the night between Thursday and Friday, when his disease became excessive, and soon weakened him so much, that he could no longer rise out of his bed. He continued to the last perfectly sensible, and free from much pain or feelings of distress. He never dropped the smallest expression of impatience; but when he had occasion to speak to the people about him, always did it with affection and tenderness. I thought it improper to write to bring you over, especially as I heard that he had dictated a letter to you desiring you not to come. When he became very weak, it cost him an effort to speak, and he died in such a happy composure of mind, that nothing could exceed it."

10   Thus died our most excellent, and never to be forgotten friend; concerning whose philosophical opinions men will, no doubt, judge variously, every one approving, or condemning them, according as they happen to coincide or disagree with his own; but concerning whose character and conduct there can scarce be a difference of opinion. His temper, indeed, seemed to be more happily balanced, if I may be allowed such an expression, than that perhaps of any other man I have ever known. Even in the lowest state of his fortune, his great and necessary frugality never hindered him from exercising, upon proper occasions, acts both of charity and generosity. It was a frugality founded, not upon avarice, but upon the love of independency. The extreme gentleness of his nature never weak-

ened either the firmness of his mind or the steadiness of his resolutions. His constant pleasantry was the genuine effusion of good-nature and good-humour, tempered with delicacy and modesty, and without even the slightest tincture of malignity, so frequently the disagreeable source of what is called wit in other men. It never was the meaning of his raillery to mortify; and therefore, far from offending, it seldom failed to please and delight, even those who were the objects of it. To his friends, who were frequently the objects of it, there was not perhaps any one of all his great and amiable qualities, which contributed more to endear his conversation. And that gaiety of temper, so agreeable in society, but which is so often accompanied with frivolous and superficial qualities, was in him certainly attended with the most severe application, the most extensive learning, the greatest depth of thought, and a capacity in every respect the most comprehensive. Upon the whole, I have always considered him, both in his lifetime and since his death, as approaching as nearly to the idea of a perfectly wise and virtuous man, as perhaps the nature of human frailty will permit.

> I am ever, dear Sir,
> Most affectionately your's,
> ADAM SMITH.

A
TREATISE

OF

Human Nature:

BEING

An ATTEMPT to introduce the
experimental Method of Reasoning

INTO

MORAL SUBJECTS.

*Rara temporum felicitas, ubi sentire, quæ velis; & quæ
sentias, dicere licet.*
TACIT.*

Book II.

OF THE

PASSIONS.

---

* ["The rare good fortune of an age in which we may feel what we wish and may say
what we feel" (Tacitus, *Histories*, I, 1; trans. by Clifford H. Moore).]

A TREATISE OF HUMAN NATURE

BOOK II: OF THE PASSIONS

Part I:
Of Pride and Humility.

Section I. Division of the subject.

As all the perceptions of the mind may be divided into *impressions* and   1
ideas, so the impressions admit of another division into *original* and *secondary*. This division of the impressions is the same with that which[1] I
formerly made use of when I distinguish'd them into impressions of *sensation* and *reflection*. Original impressions or impressions of sensation are
such as without any antecedent perception arise in the soul, from the constitution of the body, from the animal spirits, or from the application of
objects to the external organs. Secondary, or reflective impressions are
such as proceed from some of these original ones, either immediately or
by the interposition of its idea. Of the first kind are all the impressions of
the senses, and all bodily pains and pleasures: Of the second are the passions, and other emotions resembling them.

'Tis certain, that the mind, in its perceptions, must begin somewhere;   2
and that since the impressions precede their correspondent ideas, there
must be some impressions, which without any introduction make their appearance in the soul. As these depend upon natural and physical causes,
the examination of them wou'd lead me too far from my present subject,
into the sciences of anatomy and natural philosophy. For this reason I shall
here confine myself to those other impressions, which I have call'd secondary and reflective, as arising either from the original impressions, or
from their ideas. Bodily pains and pleasures are the source of many passions, both when felt and consider'd by the mind; but arise originally in
the soul, or in the body, which-ever you please to call it, without any preceding thought or perception. A fit of the gout produces a long train of
passions, as grief, hope, fear; but is not deriv'd immediately from any affection or idea.

The reflective impressions may be divided into two kinds, *viz.* the   3
calm and the *violent*. Of the first kind is the sense of beauty and deformity in action, composition, and external objects. Of the second are the

---

[1] Book I. Part I. Sect. 2.

13

passions of love and hatred, grief and joy, pride and humility. This division is far from being exact. The raptures of poetry and music frequently rise to the greatest height; while those other impressions, properly call'd *passions*, may decay into so soft an emotion, as to become, in a manner, imperceptible. But as in general the passions are more violent than the emotions arising from beauty and deformity, these impressions have been commonly distinguish'd from each other. The subject of the human mind being so copious and various, I shall here take advantage of this vulgar and specious division, that I may proceed with the greater order; and having said all I thought necessary concerning our ideas, shall now explain those violent emotions or passions, their nature, origin, causes, and effects.

4   When we take a survey of the passions, there occurs a division of them into *direct* and *indirect*. By direct passions I understand such as arise immediately from good or evil, from pain or pleasure. By indirect, such as proceed from the same principles, but by the conjunction of other qualities. This distinction I cannot at present justify or explain any farther. I can only observe in general, that under the indirect passions I comprehend pride, humility, ambition, vanity, love, hatred, envy, pity, malice, generosity, with their dependants. And under the direct passions, desire, aversion, grief, joy, hope, fear, despair and security. I shall begin with the former.

Section II. Of pride and humility; their objects and causes.

1   The passions of PRIDE and HUMILITY being simple and uniform impressions, 'tis impossible we can ever, by a multitude of words, give a just definition of them, or indeed of any of the passions. The utmost we can pretend to is a description of them, by an enumeration of such circumstances, as attend them: But as these words, *pride* and *humility*, are of general use, and the impressions they represent the most common of any, every one, of himself, will be able to form a just idea of them, without any danger of mistake. For which reason, not to lose time upon preliminaries, I shall immediately enter upon the examination of these passions.

2   'Tis evident, that pride and humility, tho' directly contrary, have yet the same OBJECT. This object is self, or that succession of related ideas and impressions, of which we have an intimate memory and consciousness. Here the view always fixes when we are actuated by either of these passions. According as our idea of ourself is more or less advantageous, we feel either of those opposite affections, and are elated by pride, or dejected with humility. Whatever other objects may be comprehended by the mind, they are always consider'd with a view to ourselves; otherwise they

wou'd never be able either to excite these passions, or produce the smallest encrease or diminution of them. When self enters not into the consideration, there is no room either for pride or humility.

But tho' that connected succession of perceptions, which we call *self*, be 3 always the object of these two passions, 'tis impossible it can be their CAUSE, or be sufficient alone to excite them. For as these passions are directly contrary, and have the same object in common; were their object also their cause; it cou'd never produce any degree of the one passion, but at the same time it must excite an equal degree of the other; which opposition and contrariety must destroy both. 'Tis impossible a man can at the same time be both proud and humble; and where he has different reasons for these passions, as frequently happens, the passions either take place alternately; or if they encounter, the one annihilates the other, as far as its strength goes, and the remainder only of that, which is superior, continues to operate upon the mind. But in the present case neither of the passions cou'd ever become superior; because supposing it to be the view only of ourself, which excited them, that being perfectly indifferent to either, must produce both in the very same proportion; or in other words, can produce neither. To excite any passion, and at the same time raise an equal share of its antagonist, is immediately to undo what was done, and must leave the mind at last perfectly calm and indifferent.

We must, therefore, make a distinction betwixt the cause and the object 4 of these passions; betwixt that idea, which excites them, and that to which they direct their view when excited. Pride and humility, being once rais'd, immediately turn our attention to ourself, and regard that as their ultimate and final object; but there is something farther requisite in order to raise them: Something, which is peculiar to one of the passions, and produces not both in the very same degree. The first idea, that is presented to the mind, is that of the cause or productive principle. This excites the passion, connected with it; and that passion, when excited, turns our view to another idea, which is that of self. Here then is a passion plac'd betwixt two ideas, of which the one produces it, and the other is produc'd by it. The first idea, therefore, represents the *cause*, the second the *object* of the passion.

To begin with the causes of pride and humility; we may observe, that 5 their most obvious and remarkable property is the vast variety of *subjects*, on which they may be plac'd. Every valuable quality of the mind, whether of the imagination, judgment, memory or disposition; wit, good-sense, learning, courage, justice, integrity; all these are the causes of pride; and their opposites of humility. Nor are these passions confin'd to the mind, but extend their view to the body likewise. A man may be proud of his beauty, strength, agility, good mien, address in dancing, riding, fencing, and of his dexterity in any manual business or manufacture. But this is not all. The passions looking farther, comprehend whatever objects are in the least ally'd or related to us. Our country, family, children, relations, riches, houses, gardens, horses, dogs, cloaths; any of these may become a cause either of pride or of humility.

6   From the consideration of these causes, it appears necessary we shou'd make a new distinction in the causes of the passion, betwixt that *quality*, which operates, and the *subject*, on which it is plac'd. A man, for instance, is vain of a beautiful house, which belongs to him, or which he has himself built and contriv'd. Here the object of the passion is himself, and the cause is the beautiful house: Which cause again is sub-divided into two parts, *viz.* the quality, which operates upon the passion, and the subject, in which the quality inheres. The quality is the beauty, and the subject is the house, consider'd as his property or contrivance. Both these parts are essential, nor is the distinction vain and chimerical. Beauty, consider'd merely as such, unless plac'd upon something related to us, never produces any pride or vanity; and the strongest relation alone, without beauty, or something else in its place, has as little influence on that passion. Since, therefore, these two particulars are easily separated, and there is a necessity for their conjunction, in order to produce the passion, we ought to consider them as component parts of the cause; and infix in our minds an exact idea of this distinction.

Section III. Whence these objects and causes are deriv'd.

1   Being so far advanc'd as to observe a difference betwixt the *object* of the passions and their *cause*, and to distinguish in the cause the *quality*, which operates on the passions, from the *subject*, in which it inheres; we now proceed to examine what determines each of them to be what it is, and assigns such a particular object, and quality, and subject to these affections. By this means we shall fully understand the origin of pride and humility.

2   'Tis evident in the first place, that these passions are determin'd to have self for their *object*, not only by a natural but also by an original property. No one can doubt but this property is *natural* from the constancy and steadiness of its operations. 'Tis always self, which is the object of pride and humility; and whenever the passions look beyond, 'tis still with a view to ourselves, nor can any person or object otherwise have any influence upon us.

3   That this proceeds from an *original* quality or primary impulse, will likewise appear evident, if we consider that 'tis the distinguishing characteristic of these passions. Unless nature had given some original qualities to the mind, it cou'd never have any secondary ones; because in that case it wou'd have no foundation for action, nor cou'd ever begin to exert itself.

Now these qualities, which we must consider as original, are such as are most inseparable from the soul, and can be resolv'd into no other: And such is the quality, which determines the object of pride and humility.

We may, perhaps, make it a greater question, whether the *causes*, that produce the passion, be as *natural* as the object, to which it is directed, and whether all that vast variety proceeds from caprice or from the constitution of the mind. This doubt we shall soon remove, if we cast our eye upon human nature, and consider that in all nations and ages, the same objects still give rise to pride and humility; and that upon the view even of a stranger, we can know pretty nearly, what will either encrease or diminish his passions of this kind. If there be any variation in this particular, it proceeds from nothing but a difference in the tempers and complexions of men; and is besides very inconsiderable. Can we imagine it possible, that while human nature remains the same, men will ever become entirely indifferent to their power, riches, beauty or personal merit, and that their pride and vanity will not be affected by these advantages? 4

But tho' the causes of pride and humility be plainly *natural*, we shall find upon examination, that they are not *original*, and that 'tis utterly impossible they shou'd each of them be adapted to these passions by a particular provision, and primary constitution of nature. Beside their prodigious number, many of them are the effects of art, and arise partly from the industry, partly from the caprice, and partly from the good fortune of men. Industry produces houses, furniture, cloaths. Caprice determines their particular kinds and qualities. And good fortune frequently contributes to all this, by discovering the effects that result from the different mixtures and combinations of bodies. 'Tis absurd, therefore, to imagine, that each of these was foreseen and provided for by nature, and that every new production of art, which causes pride or humility; instead of adapting itself to the passion by partaking of some general quality, that naturally operates on the mind; is itself the object of an original principle, which till then lay conceal'd in the soul, and is only by accident at last brought to light. Thus the first mechanic, that invented a fine scritoire, produc'd pride in him, who became possest of it, by principles different from those, which made him proud of handsome chairs and tables. As this appears evidently ridiculous, we must conclude, that each cause of pride and humility is not adapted to the passions by a distinct original quality; but that there are some one or more circumstances common to all of them, on which their efficacy depends. 5

Besides, we find in the course of nature, that tho' the effects be many, the principles, from which they arise, are commonly but few and simple, and that 'tis the sign of an unskilful naturalist to have recourse to a different quality, in order to explain every different operation. How much more 6

must this be true with regard to the human mind, which being so confin'd
a subject may justly be thought incapable of containing such a monstrous
heap of principles, as wou'd be necessary to excite the passions of pride
and humility, were each distinct cause adapted to the passion by a distinct
set of principles?

7   Here, therefore, moral philosophy is in the same condition as natural,
with regard to astronomy before the time of *Copernicus*. The antients, tho'
sensible of that maxim, *that nature does nothing in vain*, contriv'd such intricate systems of the heavens, as seem'd inconsistent with true philosophy, and gave place at last to something more simple and natural. To
invent without scruple a new principle to every new phænomenon, instead of adapting it to the old; to overload our hypothesis with a variety of
this kind, are certain proofs that none of these principles is the just one,
and that we only desire, by a number of falsehoods, to cover our ignorance
of the truth.

Section IV. Of the relations of impressions and ideas.

1   Thus we have establish'd two truths without any obstacle or difficulty,
*that 'tis from natural principles this variety of causes excites pride and humil-
ity*, and *that 'tis not by a different principle each different cause is adapted to
its passion*. We shall now proceed to enquire how we may reduce these
principles to a lesser number, and find among the causes something common, on which their influence depends.

2   In order to this we must reflect on certain properties of human nature,
which tho' they have a mighty influence on every operation both of the
understanding and passions, are not commonly much insisted on by
philosophers. The *first* of these is the association of ideas, which I have so
often observ'd and explain'd. 'Tis impossible for the mind to fix itself
steadily upon one idea for any considerable time; nor can it by its utmost
efforts ever arrive at such a constancy. But however changeable our
thoughts may be, they are not entirely without rule and method in their
changes. The rule, by which they proceed, is to pass from one object to
what is resembling, contiguous to, or produc'd by it. When one idea is
present to the imagination, any other, united by these relations, naturally
follows it, and enters with more facility by means of that introduction.

3   The *second* property I shall observe in the human mind is a like association of impressions. All resembling impressions are connected together,
and no sooner one arises than the rest immediately follow. Grief and disappointment give rise to anger, anger to envy, envy to malice, and malice
to grief again, till the whole circle be compleated. In like manner our temper, when elevated with joy, naturally throws itself into love, generosity,
pity, courage, pride, and the other resembling affections. 'Tis difficult for

the mind, when actuated by any passion, to confine itself to that passion alone, without any change or variation. Human nature is too inconstant to admit of any such regularity. Changeableness is essential to it. And to what can it so naturally change as to affections or emotions, which are suitable to the temper, and agree with that set of passions, which then prevail? 'Tis evident, then, there is an attraction or association among impressions, as well as among ideas; tho' with this remarkable difference, that ideas are associated by resemblance, contiguity, and causation, and impressions only by resemblance.

In the *third* place, 'tis observable of these two kinds of association, that   4
they very much assist and forward each other, and that the transition is more easily made where they both concur in the same object. Thus a man, who, by any injury from another, is very much discompos'd and ruffled in his temper, is apt to find a hundred subjects of discontent, impatience, fear, and other uneasy passions; especially if he can discover these subjects in or near the person, who was the cause of his first passion. Those principles, which forward the transition of ideas, here concur with those, which operate on the passions; and both uniting in one action, bestow on the mind a double impulse. The new passion, therefore, must arise with so much greater violence, and the transition to it must be render'd so much more easy and natural.

Upon this occasion I may cite the authority of an elegant writer, who   5
expresses himself in the following manner: "As the fancy delights in every thing that is great, strange, or beautiful, and is still more pleas'd the more it finds of these perfections in the *same* object, so it is capable of receiving a new satisfaction by the assistance of another sense. Thus any continu'd sound, as the music of birds, or a fall of waters, awakens every moment the mind of the beholder, and makes him more attentive to the several beauties of the place, that lie before him. Thus if there arises a fragrancy of smells or perfumes, they heighten the pleasure of the imagination, and make even the colours and verdure of the landschape appear more agreeable; for the ideas of both senses recommend each other, and are pleasanter together than when they enter the mind separately: As the different colours of a picture, when they are well disposed, set off one another, and receive an additional beauty from the advantage of the situation." In this phænomenon we may remark the association both of impressions and ideas, as well as the mutual assistance they lend each other.

Section V. Of the influence of these relations on pride and humility.

These principles being establish'd on unquestionable experience, I begin   1
to consider how we shall apply them, by revolving over all the causes of pride and humility, whether these causes be regarded, as the qualities, that

operate, or as the subjects, on which the qualities are plac'd. In examining these *qualities* I immediately find many of them to concur in producing the sensation of pain and pleasure, independent of those affections, which I here endeavour to explain. Thus the beauty of our person, of itself, and by its very appearance, gives pleasure, as well as pride; and its deformity, pain as well as humility. A magnificent feast delights us, and a sordid one displeases. What I discover to be true in some instances, I *suppose* to be so in all; and take it for granted at present, without any farther proof, that every cause of pride, by its peculiar qualities, produces a separate pleasure, and of humility a separate uneasiness.

2   Again, in considering the *subjects*, to which these qualities adhere, I make a new *supposition*, which also appears probable from many obvious instances, *viz.* that these subjects are either parts of ourselves, or something nearly related to us. Thus the good and bad qualities of our actions and manners constitute virtue and vice, and determine our personal character, than which nothing operates more strongly on these passions. In like manner, 'tis the beauty or deformity of our person, houses, equipage, or furniture, by which we are render'd either vain or humble. The same qualities, when transfer'd to subjects, which bear us no relation, influence not in the smallest degree either of these affections.

3   Having thus in a manner suppos'd two properties of the causes of these affections, *viz.* that the *qualities* produce a separate pain or pleasure, and that the *subjects*, on which the qualities are plac'd, are related to self; I proceed to examine the passions themselves, in order to find something in them, correspondent to the suppos'd properties of their causes. *First*, I find, that the peculiar object of pride and humility is determin'd by an original and natural instinct, and that 'tis absolutely impossible, from the primary constitution of the mind, that these passions shou'd ever look beyond self, or that individual person, of whose actions and sentiments each of us is intimately conscious. Here at last the view always rests, when we are actuated by either of these passions; nor can we, in that situation of mind, ever lose sight of this object. For this I pretend not to give any reason; but consider such a peculiar direction of the thought as an original quality.

4   The *second* quality, which I discover in these passions, and which I likewise consider as an original quality, is their sensations, or the peculiar emotions they excite in the soul, and which constitute their very being and essence. Thus pride is a pleasant sensation, and humility a painful; and upon the removal of the pleasure and pain, there is in reality no pride nor humility. Of this our very feeling convinces us; and beyond our feeling, 'tis here in vain to reason or dispute.

5   If I compare, therefore, these two *establish'd* properties of the passions, *viz.* their object, which is self, and their sensation, which is either pleasant

or painful, to the two *suppos'd* properties of the causes, *viz.* their relation to self, and their tendency to produce a pain or pleasure, independent of the passion; I immediately find, that taking these suppositions to be just, the true system breaks in upon me with an irresistible evidence. That cause, which excites the passion, is related to the object, which nature has attributed to the passion; the sensation, which the cause separately produces, is related to the sensation of the passion: From this double relation of ideas and impressions, the passion is deriv'd. The one idea is easily converted into its correlative; and the one impression into that, which resembles and corresponds to it: With how much greater facility must this transition be made, where these movements mutually assist each other, and the mind receives a double impulse from the relations both of its impressions and ideas?

That we may comprehend this the better, we must suppose, that nature 6 has given to the organs of the human mind, a certain disposition fitted to produce a peculiar impression or emotion, which we call *pride*: To this emotion she has assign'd a certain idea, *viz.* that of *self*, which it never fails to produce. This contrivance of nature is easily conceiv'd. We have many instances of such a situation of affairs. The nerves of the nose and palate are so dispos'd, as in certain circumstances to convey such peculiar sensations to the mind: The sensations of lust and hunger always produce in us the idea of those peculiar objects, which are suitable to each appetite. These two circumstances are united in pride. The organs are so dispos'd as to produce the passion; and the passion, after its production, naturally produces a certain idea. All this needs no proof. 'Tis evident we never shou'd be possest of that passion, were there not a disposition of mind proper for it; and 'tis as evident, that the passion always turns our view to ourselves, and makes us think of our own qualities and circumstances.

This being fully comprehended, it may now be ask'd, *Whether nature* 7 *produces the passion immediately, of herself; or whether she must be assisted by the co-operation of other causes?* For 'tis observable, that in this particular her conduct is different in the different passions and sensations. The palate must be excited by an external object, in order to produce any relish: But hunger arises internally, without the concurrence of any external object. But however the case may stand with other passions and impressions, 'tis certain, that pride requires the assistance of some foreign object, and that the organs, which produce it, exert not themselves like the heart and arteries, by an original internal movement. For *first*, daily experience convinces us, that pride requires certain causes to excite it, and languishes when unsupported by some excellency in the character, in bodily accomplishments, in cloaths, equipage or fortune. *Secondly*, 'tis evident pride wou'd be perpetual, if it arose immediately from nature; since the object is always the same, and there is no disposition of body peculiar to pride, as there is to thirst and hunger. *Thirdly*, Humility is in the very same situation with pride; and therefore, either must, upon this supposition, be perpetual likewise, or must destroy the contrary passion from the very first moment; so that none of them cou'd ever make its appearance. Upon the whole, we may rest satisfy'd with the foregoing conclusion, that pride must have a cause, as well as an object, and that the one has no influence without the other.

8   The difficulty, then, is only to discover this cause, and find what it is that gives the first motion to pride, and sets those organs in action, which are naturally fitted to produce that emotion. Upon my consulting experience, in order to resolve this difficulty, I immediately find a hundred different causes, that produce pride; and upon examining these causes, I suppose, what at first I perceive to be probable, that all of them concur in two circumstances; which are, that of themselves they produce an impression, ally'd to the passion, and are plac'd on a subject, ally'd to the object of the passion. When I consider after this the nature of *relation*, and its effects both on the passions and ideas, I can no longer doubt, upon these suppositions, that 'tis the very principle, which gives rise to pride, and bestows motion on those organs, which being naturally dispos'd to produce that affection, require only a first impulse or beginning to their action. Any thing, that gives a pleasant sensation, and is related to self, excites the passion of pride, which is also agreeable, and has self for its object.

9   What I have said of pride is equally true of humility. The sensation of humility is uneasy, as that of pride is agreeable; for which reason the separate sensation, arising from the causes, must be revers'd, while the relation to self continues the same. Tho' pride and humility are directly contrary in their effects, and in their sensations, they have notwithstanding the same object; so that 'tis requisite only to change the relation of impressions, without making any change upon that of ideas. Accordingly we find, that a beautiful house, belonging to ourselves, produces pride; and that the same house, still belonging to ourselves, produces humility, when by any accident its beauty is chang'd into deformity, and thereby the sensation of pleasure, which corresponded to pride, is transform'd into pain, which is related to humility. The double relation between the ideas and impressions subsists in both cases, and produces an easy transition from the one emotion to the other.

10   In a word, nature has bestow'd a kind of attraction on certain impressions and ideas, by which one of them, upon its appearance, naturally introduces its correlative. If these two attractions or associations of impressions and ideas concur on the same object, they mutually assist each other, and the transition of the affections and of the imagination is made with the greatest ease and facility. When an idea produces an

impression, related to an impression, which is connected with an idea, related to the first idea, these two impressions must be in a manner inseparable, nor will the one in any case be unattended with the other. 'Tis after this manner, that the particular causes of pride and humility are determin'd. The quality, which operates on the passion, produces separately an impression resembling it; the subject, to which the quality adheres, is related to self, the object of the passion: No wonder the whole cause, consisting of a quality and of a subject, does so unavoidably give rise to the passion.

To illustrate this hypothesis, we may compare it to that, by which I have   11
already explain'd the belief attending the judgments, which we form from causation. I have observ'd, that in all judgments of this kind, there is always a present impression, and a related idea; and that the present impression gives a vivacity to the fancy, and the relation conveys this vivacity, by an easy transition, to the related idea. Without the present impression, the attention is not fix'd, nor the spirits excited. Without the relation, this attention rests on its first object, and has no farther consequence. There is evidently a great analogy betwixt that hypothesis, and our present one of an impression and idea, that transfuse themselves into another impression and idea by means of their double relation: Which analogy must be allow'd to be no despicable proof of both hypotheses.

Section VI. Limitations of this system.

But before we proceed farther in this subject, and examine particularly all   1
the causes of pride and humility, 'twill be proper to make some limitations to the general system, *that all agreeable objects, related to ourselves, by an association of ideas and of impressions, produce pride, and disagreeable ones, humility*: And these limitations are deriv'd from the very nature of the subject.

I. Suppose an agreeable object to acquire a relation to self, the first pas-   2
sion, that appears on this occasion, is joy; and this passion discovers itself upon a slighter relation than pride and vain-glory. We may feel joy upon being present at a feast, where our senses are regal'd with delicacies of every kind: But 'tis only the master of the feast, who, beside the same joy, has the additional passion of self-applause and vanity. 'Tis true, men sometimes boast of a great entertainment, at which they have only been present; and by so small a relation convert their pleasure into pride: But, however, this must in general be own'd, that joy arises from a more inconsiderable relation than vanity, and that many things, which are too foreign to produce pride, are yet able to give us a delight and pleasure. The reason of the difference may be explain'd thus. A relation is requisite to joy, in order to

approach the object to us, and make it give us any satisfaction. But beside this, which is common to both passions, 'tis requisite to pride, in order to produce a transition from one passion to another, and convert the satisfaction into vanity. As it has a double task to perform, it must be endow'd with double force and energy. To which we may add, that where agreeable objects bear not a very close relation to ourselves, they commonly do to some other person; and this latter relation not only excels, but even diminishes, and sometimes destroys the former, as we shall see afterwards.[1]

3   Here then is the first limitation, we must make to our general position, *that every thing related to us, which produces pleasure or pain, produces likewise pride or humility*. There is not only a relation requir'd, but a close one, and a closer than is requir'd to joy.

4   II. The second limitation is, that the agreeable or disagreeable object be not only closely related, but also peculiar to ourselves, or at least common to us with a few persons. 'Tis a quality observable in human nature, and which we shall endeavour to explain afterwards, that every thing, which is often presented, and to which we have been long accustom'd, loses its value in our eyes, and is in a little time despis'd and neglected. We likewise judge of objects more from comparison than from their real and intrinsic merit; and where we cannot by some contrast enhance their value, we are apt to overlook even what is essentially good in them. These qualities of the mind have an effect upon joy as well as pride; and 'tis remarkable, that goods, which are common to all mankind, and have become familiar to us by custom, give us little satisfaction; tho' perhaps of a more excellent kind, than those on which, for their singularity, we set a much higher value. But tho' this circumstance operates on both these passions, it has a much greater influence on vanity. We are rejoic'd for many goods, which, on account of their frequency, give us no pride. Health, when it returns after a long absence, affords us a very sensible satisfaction; but is seldom regarded as a subject of vanity, because 'tis shar'd with such vast numbers.

5   The reason, why pride is so much more delicate in this particular than joy, I take to be, as follows. In order to excite pride, there are always two objects we must contemplate, *viz.* the *cause* or that object which produces pleasure; and self, which is the real object of the passion. But joy has only one object necessary to its production, *viz.* that which gives pleasure; and tho' it be requisite, that this bear some relation to self, yet that is only requisite in order to render it agreeable; nor is self, properly speaking, the object of this passion. Since, therefore, pride has in a manner two objects, to which it directs our view; it follows, that where neither of them have any

---

[1] Part II. Sect. 4.

singularity, the passion must be more weaken'd upon that account, than a passion, which has only one object. Upon comparing ourselves with others, as we are every moment apt to do, we find we are not in the least distinguish'd; and upon comparing the object we possess, we discover still the same unlucky circumstance. By two comparisons so disadvantageous the passion must be entirely destroy'd.

III. The third limitation is, that the pleasant or painful object be very discernible and obvious, and that not only to ourselves but to others also. This circumstance, like the two foregoing, has an effect upon joy, as well as pride. We fancy ourselves more happy, as well as more virtuous or beautiful, when we appear so to others; but are still more ostentatious of our virtues than of our pleasures. This proceeds from causes, which I shall endeavour to explain afterwards. 6

IV. The fourth limitation is deriv'd from the inconstancy of the cause of these passions, and from the short duration of its connexion with ourselves. What is casual and inconstant gives but little joy, and less pride. We are not much satisfy'd with the thing itself; and are still less apt to feel any new degrees of self-satisfaction upon its account. We foresee and anticipate its change by the imagination; which makes us little satisfy'd with the thing: We compare it to ourselves, whose existence is more durable; by which means its inconstancy appears still greater. It seems ridiculous to infer an excellency in ourselves from an object, which is of so much shorter duration, and attends us during so small a part of our existence. 'Twill be easy to comprehend the reason, why this cause operates not with the same force in joy as in pride; since the idea of self is not so essential to the former passion as to the latter. 7

V. I may add as a fifth limitation, or rather enlargement of this system, that *general rules* have a great influence upon pride and humility, as well as on all the other passions. Hence we form a notion of different ranks of men, suitable to the power or riches they are possest of; and this notion we change not upon account of any peculiarities of the health or temper of the persons, which may deprive them of all enjoyment in their possessions. This may be accounted for from the same principles, that explain'd the influence of general rules on the understanding. Custom readily carries us beyond the just bounds in our passions, as well as in our reasonings. 8

It may not be amiss to observe on this occasion, that the influence of general rules and maxims on the passions very much contributes to facilitate the effects of all the principles, which we shall explain in the progress of this treatise. For 'tis evident, that if a person full-grown, and of the same nature with ourselves, were on a sudden transported into our world, he wou'd be very much embarrass'd with every object, and wou'd not 9 readily find what degree of love or hatred, pride or humility, or any other passion he ought to attribute to it. The passions are often vary'd by very inconsiderable principles; and these do not always play with a perfect regularity, especially on the first trial. But as custom and practice have brought to light all these principles, and have settled the just value of every thing; this must certainly contribute to the easy production of the passions, and guide us, by means of general establish'd maxims, in the proportions we ought to observe in preferring one object to another. This remark may, perhaps, serve to obviate difficulties, that may arise concerning some causes, which I shall hereafter ascribe to particular passions, and which may be esteem'd too refin'd to operate so universally and certainly, as they are found to do.

10   I shall close this subject with a reflection deriv'd from these five limitations. This reflection is, that the persons, who are proudest, and who in the eye of the world have most reason for their pride, are not always the happiest; nor the most humble always the most miserable, as may at first sight be imagin'd from this system. An evil may be real, tho' its cause has no relation to us: It may be real, without being peculiar: It may be real without shewing itself to others: It may be real, without being constant: And it may be real, without falling under the general rules. Such evils as these will not fail to render us miserable, tho' they have little tendency to diminish pride: And perhaps the most real and the most solid evils of life will be found of this nature.

Section VII. Of vice and virtue

1   Taking these limitations along with us, let us proceed to examine the causes of pride and humility; and see, whether in every case we can discover the double relations, by which they operate on the passions. If we find that all these causes are related to self, and produce a pleasure or uneasiness separate from the passion, there will remain no farther scruple with regard to the present system. We shall principally endeavour to prove the latter point; the former being in a manner self-evident.

2   To begin with VICE and VIRTUE, which are the most obvious causes of these passions; 'twou'd be entirely foreign to my present purpose to enter upon the controversy, which of late years has so much excited the curiosity of the publick, *whether these moral distinctions be founded on natural and original principles, or arise from interest and education.* The examination of this I reserve for the following book; and in the mean time shall endeavour to show, that my system maintains its ground upon either of these hypotheses; which will be a strong proof of its solidity.

3   For granting that morality had no foundation in nature, it must still be allow'd, that vice and virtue, either from self-interest or the prejudices of

education, produce in us a real pain and pleasure; and this we may observe to be strenuously asserted by the defenders of that hypothesis. Every passion, habit, or turn of character (say they) which has a tendency to our advantage or prejudice, gives a delight or uneasiness; and 'tis from thence the approbation or disapprobation arises. We easily gain from the liberality of others, but are always in danger of losing by their avarice: Courage defends us, but cowardice lays us open to every attack: Justice is the support of society, but injustice, unless check'd, wou'd quickly prove its ruin: Humility exalts; but pride mortifies us. For these reasons the former qualities are esteem'd virtues, and the latter regarded as vices. Now since 'tis granted there is a delight or uneasiness still attending merit or demerit of every kind, this is all that is requisite for my purpose.

But I go farther, and observe, that this moral hypothesis and my present   4
system not only agree together, but also that, allowing the former to be just, 'tis an absolute and invincible proof of the latter. For if all morality be founded on the pain or pleasure, which arises from the prospect of any loss or advantage, that may result from our own characters, or from those of others, all the effects of morality must be deriv'd from the same pain or pleasure, and among the rest, the passions of pride and humility. The very essence of virtue, according to this hypothesis, is to produce pleasure, and that of vice to give pain. The virtue and vice must be part of our character in order to excite pride or humility. What farther proof can we desire for the double relation of impressions and ideas?

The same unquestionable argument may be deriv'd from the opinion of   5
those, who maintain that morality is something real, essential, and founded on nature. The most probable hypothesis, which has been advanc'd to explain the distinction betwixt vice and virtue, and the origin of moral rights and obligations, is, that from a primary constitution of nature certain characters and passions, by the very view and contemplation, produce a pain, and others in like manner excite a pleasure. The uneasiness and satisfaction are not only inseparable from vice and virtue, but constitute their very nature and essence. To approve of a character is to feel an original delight upon its appearance. To disapprove of it is to be sensible of an uneasiness. The pain and pleasure, therefore, being the primary causes of vice and virtue, must also be the causes of all their effects, and consequently of pride and humility, which are the unavoidable attendants of that distinction.

But supposing this hypothesis of moral philosophy shou'd be allow'd to   6
be false, 'tis still evident, that pain and pleasure, if not the causes of vice and virtue, are at least inseparable from them. A generous and noble character affords a satisfaction even in the survey; and when presented to us, tho' only in a poem or fable, never fails to charm and delight us. On the other hand cruelty and treachery displease from their very nature; nor is it

possible ever to reconcile us to these qualities, either in ourselves or others. Thus one hypothesis of morality is an undeniable proof of the foregoing system, and the other at worst agrees with it.

7   But pride and humility arise not from these qualities alone of the mind, which, according to the vulgar systems of ethicks, have been comprehended as parts of moral duty, but from any other that has a connexion with pleasure and uneasiness. Nothing flatters our vanity more than the talent of pleasing by our wit, good humour, or any other accomplishment; and nothing gives us a more sensible mortification than a disappointment in any attempt of that nature. No one has ever been able to tell what *wit* is, and to shew why such a system of thought must be receiv'd under that denomination, and such another rejected. 'Tis only by taste we can decide concerning it, nor are we possest of any other standard, upon which we can form a judgment of this kind. Now what is this *taste*, from which true and false wit in a manner receive their being, and without which no thought can have a title to either of these denominations? 'Tis plainly nothing but a sensation of pleasure from true wit, and of uneasiness from false, without our being able to tell the reasons of that pleasure or uneasiness. The power of bestowing these opposite sensations is, therefore, the very essence of true and false wit; and consequently the cause of that pride or humility, which arises from them.

8   There may, perhaps, be some, who being accustom'd to the style of the schools and pulpit, and having never consider'd human nature in any other light, than that in which *they* place it, may here be surpriz'd to hear me talk of virtue as exciting pride, which they look upon as a vice; and of vice as producing humility, which they have been taught to consider as a virtue. But not to dispute about words, I observe, that by *pride* I understand that agreeable impression, which arises in the mind, when the view either of our virtue, beauty, riches or power makes us satisfy'd with ourselves: And that by *humility* I mean the opposite impression. 'Tis evident the former impression is not always vicious, nor the latter virtuous. The most rigid morality allows us to receive a pleasure from reflecting on a generous action; and 'tis by none esteem'd a virtue to feel any fruitless remorses upon the thoughts of past villainy and baseness. Let us, therefore, examine these impressions, consider'd in themselves; and enquire into their causes, whether plac'd on the mind or body, without troubling ourselves at present with that merit or blame, which may attend them.

Section XI. Of the love of fame

1   But beside these original causes of pride and humility, there is a secondary one in the opinions of others, which has an equal influence on the affections. Our reputation, our character, our name are considerations of vast

weight and importance; and even the other causes of pride; virtue, beauty and riches; have little influence, when not seconded by the opinions and sentiments of others. In order to account for this phænomenon 'twill be necessary to take some compass, and first explain the nature of *sympathy*.

No quality of human nature is more remarkable, both in itself and in its consequences, than that propensity we have to sympathize with others, and to receive by communication their inclinations and sentiments, however different from, or even contrary to our own. This is not only conspicuous in children, who implicitly embrace every opinion propos'd to them; but also in men of the greatest judgment and understanding, who find it very difficult to follow their own reason or inclination, in opposition to that of their friends and daily companions. To this principle we ought to ascribe the great uniformity we may observe in the humours and turn of thinking of those of the same nation; and 'tis much more probable, that this resemblance arises from sympathy, than from any influence of the soil and climate, which, tho' they continue invariably the same, are not able to preserve the character of a nation the same for a century together. A goodnatur'd man finds himself in an instant of the same humour with his company; and even the proudest and most surly take a tincture from their countrymen and acquaintance. A chearful countenance infuses a sensible complacency and serenity into my mind; as an angry or sorrowful one throws a sudden damp upon me. Hatred, resentment, esteem, love, courage, mirth and melancholy; all these passions I feel more from communication than from my own natural temper and disposition. So remarkable a phænomenon merits our attention, and must be trac'd up to its first principles. 2

When any affection is infus'd by sympathy, it is at first known only by its effects, and by those external signs in the countenance and conversation, which convey an idea of it. This idea is presently converted into an impression, and acquires such a degree of force and vivacity, as to become the very passion itself, and produce an equal emotion, as any original affection. However instantaneous this change of the idea into an impression may be, it proceeds from certain views and reflections, which will not escape the strict scrutiny of a philosopher, tho' they may the person himself, who makes them. 3

'Tis evident, that the idea, or rather impression of ourselves is always intimately present with us, and that our consciousness gives us so lively a conception of our own person, that 'tis not possible to imagine, that any thing can in this particular go beyond it. Whatever object, therefore, is related to ourselves must be conceiv'd with a like vivacity of conception, according to the foregoing principles; and tho' this relation shou'd not be so strong as that of causation, it must still have a considerable influence. 4

Resemblance and contiguity are relations not to be neglected; especially when by an inference from cause and effect, and by the observation of external signs, we are inform'd of the real existence of the object, which is resembling or contiguous.

5   Now 'tis obvious, that nature has preserv'd a great resemblance among all human creatures, and that we never remark any passion or principle in others, of which, in some degree or other, we may not find a parallel in ourselves. The case is the same with the fabric of the mind, as with that of the body. However the parts may differ in shape or size, their structure and composition are in general the same. There is a very remarkable resemblance, which preserves itself amidst all their variety; and this resemblance must very much contribute to make us enter into the sentiments of others, and embrace them with facility and pleasure. Accordingly we find, that where, beside the general resemblance of our natures, there is any peculiar similarity in our manners, or character, or country, or language, it facilitates the sympathy. The stronger the relation is betwixt ourselves and any object, the more easily does the imagination make the transition, and convey to the related idea the vivacity of conception, with which we always form the idea of our own person.

6   Nor is resemblance the only relation, which has this effect, but receives new force from other relations, that may accompany it. The sentiments of others have little influence, when far remov'd from us, and require the relation of contiguity, to make them communicate themselves entirely. The relations of blood, being a species of causation, may sometimes contribute to the same effect; as also acquaintance, which operates in the same manner with education and custom; as we shall see more fully afterwards.[1] All these relations, when united together, convey the impression or consciousness of our own person to the idea of the sentiments or passions of others, and makes us conceive them in the strongest and most lively manner.

7   It has been remark'd in the beginning of this treatise, that all ideas are borrow'd from impressions, and that these two kinds of perceptions differ only in the degrees of force and vivacity, with which they strike upon the soul. The component parts of ideas and impressions are precisely alike. The manner and order of their appearance may be the same. The different degrees of their force and vivacity are, therefore, the only particulars, that distinguish them: And as this difference may be remov'd, in some measure, by a relation betwixt the impressions and ideas, 'tis no wonder an idea of a sentiment or passion, may by this means be so inliven'd as to become the very sentiment or passion. The lively idea of any object always

---

[1] Part II. Sect. 4.

approaches its impression; and 'tis certain we may feel sickness and pain from the mere force of imagination, and make a malady real by often thinking of it. But this is most remarkable in the opinions and affections; and 'tis there principally that a lively idea is converted into an impression. Our affections depend more upon ourselves, and the internal operations of the mind, than any other impressions; for which reason they arise more naturally from the imagination, and from every lively idea we form of them. This is the nature and cause of sympathy; and 'tis after this manner we enter so deep into the opinions and affections of others, whenever we discover them.

What is principally remarkable in this whole affair is the strong confir-   8
mation these phænomena give to the foregoing system concerning the understanding, and consequently to the present one concerning the passions; since these are analogous to each other. 'Tis indeed evident, that when we sympathize with the passions and sentiments of others, these movements appear at first in *our* mind as mere ideas, and are conceiv'd to belong to another person, as we conceive any other matter of fact. 'Tis also evident, that the ideas of the affections of others are converted into the very impressions they represent, and that the passions arise in conformity to the images we form of them. All this is an object of the plainest experience, and depends not on any hypothesis of philosophy. That science can only be admitted to explain the phænomena; tho' at the same time it must be confest, they are so clear of themselves, that there is but little occasion to employ it. For besides the relation of cause and effect, by which we are convinc'd of the reality of the passion, with which we sympathize; besides this, I say, we must be assisted by the relations of resemblance and contiguity, in order to feel the sympathy in its full perfection. And since these relations can entirely convert an idea into an impression, and convey the vivacity of the latter into the former, so perfectly as to lose nothing of it in the transition, we may easily conceive how the relation of cause and effect alone, may serve to strengthen and inliven an idea. In sympathy there is an evident conversion of an idea into an impression. This conversion arises from the relation of objects to ourself. Ourself is always intimately present to us. Let us compare all these circumstances, and we shall find, that sympathy is exactly correspondent to the operations of our understanding; and even contains something more surprising and extraordinary.

'Tis now time to turn our view from the general consideration of sym-   9
pathy, to its influence on pride and humility, when these passions arise from praise and blame, from reputation and infamy. We may observe, that no person is ever prais'd by another for any quality, which wou'd not, if real, produce, of itself, a pride in the person possest of it. The elogiums

either turn upon his power, or riches, or family, or virtue; all of which are subjects of vanity, that we have already explain'd and accounted for. 'Tis certain, then, that if a person consider'd himself in the same light, in which he appears to his admirer, he wou'd first receive a separate pleasure, and afterwards a pride or self-satisfaction, according to the hypothesis above-explain'd. Now nothing is more natural than for us to embrace the opinions of others in this particular; both from *sympathy*, which renders all their sentiments intimately present to us; and from *reasoning*, which makes us regard their judgment, as a kind of argument for what they affirm. These two principles of authority and sympathy influence almost all our opinions; but must have a peculiar influence, when we judge of our own worth and character. Such judgments are always attended with passion;[2] and nothing tends more to disturb our understanding, and precipitate us into any opinions, however unreasonable, than their connexion with passion; which diffuses itself over the imagination, and gives an additional force to every related idea. To which we may add, that being conscious of great partiality in our own favour, we are peculiarly pleas'd with any thing, that confirms the good opinion we have of ourselves, and are easily shock'd with whatever opposes it.

10   All this appears very probable in theory; but in order to bestow a full certainty on this reasoning, we must examine the phænomena of the passions, and see if they agree with it.

11   Among these phænomena we may esteem it a very favourable one to our present purpose, that tho' fame in general be agreeable, yet we receive a much greater satisfaction from the approbation of those, whom we ourselves esteem and approve of, than of those, whom we hate and despise. In like manner we are principally mortify'd with the contempt of persons, upon whose judgment we set some value, and are, in a great measure, indifferent about the opinions of the rest of mankind. But if the mind receiv'd from any original instinct a desire of fame, and aversion to infamy, fame and infamy wou'd influence us without distinction; and every opinion, according as it were favourable or unfavourable, wou'd equally excite that desire or aversion. The judgment of a fool is the judgment of another person, as well as that of a wise man, and is only inferior in its influence on our own judgment.

12   We are not only better pleas'd with the approbation of a wise man than with that of a fool, but receive an additional satisfaction from the former, when 'tis obtain'd after a long and intimate acquaintance. This is accounted for after the same manner.

---

[2] Book I. Part III. Sect. 10.

The praises of others never give us much pleasure, unless they concur 13
with our own opinion, and extol us for those qualities, in which we chiefly
excel. A mere soldier little values the character of eloquence: A gownman
of courage: A bishop of humour: Or a merchant of learning. Whatever esteem a man may have for any quality, abstractedly consider'd; when he is
conscious he is not possest of it; the opinions of the whole world will give
him little pleasure in that particular, and that because they never will be
able to draw his own opinion after them.

Nothing is more usual than for men of good families, but narrow cir- 14
cumstances, to leave their friends and country, and rather seek their liveli-
hood by mean and mechanical employments among strangers, than
among those, who are acquainted with their birth and education. We shall
be unknown, say they, where we go. No body will suspect from what family we are sprung. We shall be remov'd from all our friends and acquaintance, and our poverty and meanness will by that means sit more easy
upon us. In examining these sentiments, I find they afford many very convincing arguments for my present purpose.

First, We may infer from them, that the uneasiness of being contemn'd 15
depends on sympathy, and that sympathy depends on the relation of objects to ourselves; since we are most uneasy under the contempt of persons, who are both related to us by blood, and contiguous in place. Hence
we seek to diminish this sympathy and uneasiness by separating these relations, and placing ourselves in a contiguity to strangers, and at a distance
from relations.

Secondly, We may conclude, that relations are requisite to sympathy, 16
not absolutely consider'd as relations, but by their influence in converting
our ideas of the sentiments of others into the very sentiments, by means
of the association betwixt the idea of their persons, and that of our own.
For here the relations of kindred and contiguity both subsist; but not
being united in the same persons, they contribute in a less degree to the
sympathy.

Thirdly, This very circumstance of the diminution of sympathy by the 17
separation of relations is worthy of our attention. Suppose I am plac'd in a
poor condition among strangers, and consequently am but lightly treated;
I yet find myself easier in that situation, than when I was every day expos'd
to the contempt of my kindred and countrymen. Here I feel a double contempt; from my relations, but they are absent; from those about me, but
they are strangers. This double contempt is likewise strengthen'd by the
two relations of kindred and contiguity. But as the persons are not the
same, who are connected with me by those two relations, this difference of
ideas separates the impressions arising from the contempt, and keeps them
from running into each other. The contempt of my neighbours has a cer-

tain influence; as has also that of my kindred: But these influences are distinct, and never unite; as when the contempt proceeds from persons who
are at once both my neighbours and kindred. This phænomenon is analogous to the system of pride and humility above-explain'd, which may seem
so extraordinary to vulgar apprehensions.

18   *Fourthly*, A person in these circumstances naturally conceals his birth
from those among whom he lives, and is very uneasy, if any one suspects
him to be of a family, much superior to his present fortune and way of living. Every thing in this world is judg'd of by comparison. What is an immense fortune for a private gentleman is beggary for a prince. A peasant
wou'd think himself happy in what cannot afford necessaries for a gentleman. When a man has either been accustom'd to a more splendid way of
living, or thinks himself entitled to it by his birth and quality, every thing
below is disagreeable and even shameful; and 'tis with the greatest industry he conceals his pretensions to a better fortune. Here he himself knows
his misfortunes; but as those, with whom he lives, are ignorant of them, he
has the disagreeable reflection and comparison suggested only by his own
thoughts, and never receives it by a sympathy with others; which must
contribute very much to his ease and satisfaction.

19   If there be any objections to this hypothesis, *that the pleasure, which we
receive from praise, arises from a communication of sentiments*, we shall find,
upon examination, that these objections, when taken in a proper light, will
serve to confirm it. Popular fame may be agreeable even to a man, who despises the vulgar; but 'tis because their multitude gives them additional
weight and authority. Plagiaries are delighted with praises, which they are
conscious they do not deserve; but this is a kind of castle-building, where
the imagination amuses itself with its own fictions, and strives to render
them firm and stable by a sympathy with the sentiments of others. Proud
men are most shock'd with contempt, tho' they do not most readily assent
to it; but 'tis because of the opposition betwixt the passion, which is natural to them, and that receiv'd by sympathy. A violent lover in like manner
is very much displeas'd when you blame and condemn his love; tho' 'tis
evident your opposition can have no influence, but by the hold it takes of
himself, and by his sympathy with you. If he despises you, or perceives
you are in jest, whatever you say has no effect upon him.

Part II:
Of Love and Hatred.

Section I. Of the objects and causes of love and hatred.

'Tis altogether impossible to give any definition of the passions of LOVE   1
and HATRED; and that because they produce merely a simple impression,
without any mixture or composition. 'Twou'd be as unnecessary to attempt any description of them, drawn from their nature, origin, causes
and objects; and that both because these are the subjects of our present
enquiry, and because these passions of themselves are sufficiently known
from our common feeling and experience. This we have already observ'd
concerning pride and humility, and here repeat it concerning love and hatred; and indeed there is so great a resemblance betwixt these two sets of
passions, that we shall be oblig'd to begin with a kind of abridgment of our
reasonings concerning the former, in order to explain the latter.

As the immediate *object* of pride and humility is self or that identical   2
person, of whose thoughts, actions, and sensations we are intimately conscious; so the *object* of love and hatred is some other person, of whose
thoughts, actions, and sensations we are not conscious. This is sufficiently
evident from experience. Our love and hatred are always directed to some
sensible being external to us; and when we talk of *self-love*, 'tis not in a
proper sense, nor has the sensation it produces any thing in common with
that tender emotion, which is excited by a friend or mistress. 'Tis the
same case with hatred. We may be mortify'd by our own faults and follies;
but never feel any anger or hatred, except from the injuries of others.

But tho' the object of love and hatred be always some other person, 'tis   3
plain that the object is not, properly speaking, the *cause* of these passions,
or alone sufficient to excite them. For since love and hatred are directly
contrary in their sensation, and have the same object in common, if that
object were also their cause, it wou'd produce these opposite passions in
an equal degree; and as they must, from the very first moment, destroy
each other, none of them wou'd ever be able to make its appearance. There
must, therefore, be some cause different from the object.

If we consider the causes of love and hatred, we shall find they are very   4
much diversify'd, and have not many things in common. The virtue,
knowledge, wit, good sense, good humour of any person, produce love and
esteem; as the opposite qualities, hatred and contempt. The same passions
arise from bodily accomplishments, such as beauty, force, swiftness, dexterity; and from their contraries; as likewise from the external advantages
and disadvantages of family, possessions, cloaths, nation and climate.
There is not one of these objects, but what by its different qualities may
produce love and esteem, or hatred and contempt.

5   From the view of these causes we may derive a new distinction betwixt the *quality* that operates, and the *subject* on which it is plac'd. A prince, that is possess'd of a stately palace, commands the esteem of the people upon that account; and that *first*, by the beauty of the palace, and *secondly*, by the relation of property, which connects it with him. The removal of either of these destroys the passion; which evidently proves that the cause is a compounded one.

6   'Twou'd be tedious to trace the passions of love and hatred, thro' all the observations which we have form'd concerning pride and humility, and which are equally applicable to both sets of passions. 'Twill be sufficient to *remark* in general, that the object of love and hatred is evidently some thinking person; and that the sensation of the former passion is always agreeable, and of the latter uneasy. We may also *suppose* with some shew of probability, *that the cause of both these passions is always related to a thinking being*, and *that the cause of the former produces a separate pleasure, and of the latter a separate uneasiness.*

7   One of these suppositions, *viz.* that the cause of love and hatred must be related to a person or thinking being, in order to produce these passions, is not only probable, but too evident to be contested. Virtue and vice, when consider'd in the abstract; beauty and deformity, when plac'd on inanimate objects; poverty and riches, when belonging to a third person, excite no degree of love or hatred, esteem or contempt towards those, who have no relation to them. A person looking out at a window, sees me in the street, and beyond me a beautiful palace, with which I have no concern: I believe none will pretend, that this person will pay me the same respect, as if I were owner of the palace.

8   'Tis not so evident at first sight, that a relation of impressions is requisite to these passions, and that because in the transition the one impression is so much confounded with the other, that they become in a manner undistinguishable. But as in pride and humility, we have easily been able to make the separation, and to prove, that every cause of these passions produces a separate pain or pleasure, I might here observe the same method with the same success, in examining particularly the several causes of love and hatred. But as I hasten to a full and decisive proof of these systems, I delay this examination for a moment: And in the mean time shall endeavour to convert to my present purpose all my reasonings concerning pride and humility, by an argument that is founded on unquestionable experience.

9   There are few persons, that are satisfy'd with their own character, or genius, or fortune, who are not desirous of shewing themselves to the world, and of acquiring the love and approbation of mankind. Now 'tis evident, that the very same qualities and circumstances, which are the

causes of pride or self-esteem, are also the causes of vanity or the desire of reputation; and that we always put to view those particulars with which in ourselves we are best satisfy'd. But if love and esteem were not produc'd by the same qualities as pride, according as these qualities are related to ourselves or others, this method of proceeding wou'd be very absurd, nor cou'd men expect a correspondence in the sentiments of every other person, with those themselves have entertain'd. 'Tis true, few can form exact systems of the passions, or make reflections on their general nature and resemblances. But without such a progress in philosophy, we are not subject to many mistakes in this particular, but are sufficiently guided by common experience, as well as by a kind of *presentation*; which tells us what will operate on others, by what we feel immediately in ourselves. Since then the same qualities that produce pride or humility, cause love or hatred; all the arguments that have been employ'd to prove, that the causes of the former passions excite a pain or pleasure independent of the passion, will be applicable with equal evidence to the causes of the latter.

Section II. Experiments to confirm this system.

Upon duly weighing these arguments, no one will make any scruple to assent to that conclusion I draw from them, concerning the transition along related impressions and ideas, especially as 'tis a principle, in itself, so easy and natural. But that we may place this system beyond doubt both with regard to love and hatred, pride and humility, 'twill be proper to make some new experiments upon all these passions, as well as to recal a few of these observations, which I have formerly touch'd upon.   1

In order to make these experiments, let us suppose I am in company with a person, whom I formerly regarded without any sentiments either of friendship or enmity. Here I have the natural and ultimate object of all these four passions plac'd before me. Myself am the proper object of pride or humility; the other person of love or hatred.   2

Regard now with attention the nature of these passions, and their situation with respect to each other. 'Tis evident here are four affections, plac'd, as it were, in a square or regular connexion with, and distance from each other. The passions of pride and humility, as well as those of love and hatred, are connected together by the identity of their object, which to the first set of passions is self, to the second some other person. These two lines of communication or connexion form two opposite sides of the square. Again, pride and love are agreeable passions; hatred and humility uneasy. This similitude of sensation betwixt pride and love, and that betwixt humility and hatred, form a new connexion, and may be consider'd as the other two sides of the square. Upon the whole, pride is connected   3 with humility, love with hatred, by their objects or ideas: Pride with love, humility with hatred, by their sensations or impressions.

4   I say then, that nothing can produce any of these passions without bearing it a double relation, *viz.* of ideas to the object of the passion, and of sensation to the passion itself. This we must prove by our experiments.

5   *First Experiment.* To proceed with the greater order in these experiments, let us first suppose, that being plac'd in the situation abovemention'd, *viz.* in company with some other person, there is an object presented, that has no relation either of impressions or ideas to any of these passions. Thus suppose we regard together an ordinary stone, or other common object, belonging to neither of us, and causing of itself no emotion, or independent pain and pleasure: 'Tis evident such an object will produce none of these four passions. Let us try it upon each of them successively. Let us apply it to love, to hatred, to humility, to pride; none of them ever arises in the smallest degree imaginable. Let us change the object as oft as we please; provided still we choose one, that has neither of these two relations. Let us repeat the experiment in all the dispositions, of which the mind is susceptible. No object, in the vast variety of nature, will, in any disposition, produce any passion without these relations.

6   *Second Experiment.* Since an object, that wants both these relations can never produce any passion, let us bestow on it only one of these relations; and see what will follow. Thus suppose, I regard a stone or any common object, that belongs either to me or my companion, and by that means acquires a relation of ideas to the object of the passions: 'Tis plain, that to consider the matter *a priori*, no emotion of any kind can reasonably be expected. For besides, that a relation of ideas operates secretly and calmly on the mind, it bestows an equal impulse towards the opposite passions of pride and humility, love and hatred, according as the object belongs to ourselves or others; which opposition of the passions must destroy both, and leave the mind perfectly free from any affection or emotion. This reasoning *a priori* is confirm'd by experience. No trivial or vulgar object, that causes not a pain or pleasure, independent of the passion, will ever, by its property or other relations, either to ourselves or others, be able to produce the affections of pride or humility, love or hatred.

7   *Third Experiment.* 'Tis evident, therefore, that a relation of ideas is not able alone to give rise to these affections. Let us now remove this relation, and in its stead place a relation of impressions, by presenting an object, which is agreeable or disagreeable, but has no relation either to ourself or companion; and let us observe the consequences. To consider the matter first *a priori*, as in the preceding experiment; we may conclude, that the object will have a small, but an uncertain connexion with these passions. For besides, that this relation is not a cold and imperceptible one, it has

not the inconvenience of the relation of ideas, nor directs us with equal force to two contrary passions, which by their opposition destroy each other. But if we consider, on the other hand, that this transition from the sensation to the affection is not forwarded by any principle, that produces a transition of ideas; but, on the contrary, that tho' the one impression be easily transfus'd into the other, yet the change of objects is suppos'd contrary to all the principles, that cause a transition of that kind; we may from thence infer, that nothing will ever be a steady or durable cause of any passion, that is connected with the passion merely by a relation of impressions. What our reason wou'd conclude from analogy, after ballancing these arguments, wou'd be, that an object, which produces pleasure or uneasiness, but has no manner of connexion either with ourselves or others, may give such a turn to the disposition, as that it may naturally fall into pride or love, humility or hatred, and search for other objects, upon which, by a double relation, it can found these affections; but that an object, which has only one of these relations, tho' the most advantageous one, can never give rise to any constant and establish'd passion.

Most fortunately all this reasoning is found to be exactly conformable 8 to experience, and the phænomena of the passions. Suppose I were travelling with a companion thro' a country, to which we are both utter strangers; 'tis evident, that if the prospects be beautiful, the roads agreeable, and the inns commodious, this may put me into good humour both with myself and fellow-traveller. But as we suppose, that this country has no relation either to myself or friend, it can never be the immediate cause of pride or love; and therefore if I found not the passion on some other object, that bears either of us a closer relation, my emotions are rather to be consider'd as the overflowings of an elevate or humane disposition, than as an establish'd passion. The case is the same where the object produces uneasiness.

Fourth Experiment. Having found, that neither an object without any re- 9 lation of ideas or impressions, nor an object, that has only one relation, can ever cause pride or humility, love or hatred; reason alone may convince us, without any farther experiment, that whatever has a double relation must necessarily excite these passions; since 'tis evident they must have some cause. But to leave as little room for doubt as possible, let us renew our experiments, and see whether the event in this case answers our expectation. I choose an object, such as virtue, that causes a separate satisfaction: On this object I bestow a relation to self; and find, that from this disposition of affairs, there immediately arises a passion. But what passion? That very one of pride, to which this object bears a double relation. Its idea is related to that of self, the object of the passion: The sensation it causes resembles the sensation of the passion. That I may be sure I am not mistaken in this experiment, I remove first one relation; then another; and find, that each removal destroys the passion, and leaves the object perfectly indifferent. But I am not content with this. I make a still farther trial; and instead of removing the relation, I only change it for one of a different kind. I suppose the virtue to belong to my companion, not to myself; and observe what follows from this alteration. I immediately perceive the affections to wheel about, and leaving pride, where there is only one relation, *viz.* of impressions, fall to the side of love, where they are attracted by a double relation of impressions and ideas. By repeating the same experiment, in changing anew the relation of ideas, I bring the affections back to pride; and by a new repetition I again place them at love or kindness. Being fully convinc'd of the influence of this relation, I try the effects of the other; and by changing virtue for vice, convert the pleasant impression, which arises from the former, into the disagreeable one, which proceeds from the latter. The effect still answers expectation. Vice, when plac'd on another, excites, by means of its double relations, the passion of hatred, instead of love, which for the same reason arises from virtue. To continue the experiment, I change anew the relation of ideas, and suppose the vice to belong to myself. What follows? What is usual. A subsequent change of the passion from hatred to humility. This humility I convert into pride by a new change of the impression; and find after all that I have compleated the round, and have by these changes brought back the passion to that very situation, in which I first found it.

10   But to make the matter still more certain, I alter the object; and instead of vice and virtue, make the trial upon beauty and deformity, riches and poverty, power and servitude. Each of these objects runs the circle of the passions in the same manner, by a change of their relations: And in whatever order we proceed, whether thro' pride, love, hatred, humility, or thro' humility, hatred, love, pride, the experiment is not in the least diversify'd. Esteem and contempt, indeed, arise on some occasions instead of love and hatred; but these are at the bottom the same passions, only diversify'd by some causes, which we shall explain afterwards.

11   *Fifth Experiment*. To give greater authority to these experiments, let us change the situation of affairs as much as possible, and place the passions and objects in all the different positions, of which they are susceptible. Let us suppose, beside the relations above-mention'd, that the person, along with whom I make all these experiments, is closely connected with me either by blood or friendship. He is, we shall suppose, my son or brother, or is united to me by a long and familiar acquaintance. Let us next suppose, that the cause of the passion acquires a double relation of impressions and ideas to this person; and let us see what the effects are of all these complicated attractions and relations.

Before we consider what they are in fact, let us determine what they 12 ought to be, conformable to my hypothesis. 'Tis plain, that, according as the impression is either pleasant or uneasy, the passion of love or hatred must arise towards the person, who is thus connected to the cause of the impression by these double relations, which I have all along requir'd. The virtue of a brother must make me love him; as his vice or infamy must excite the contrary passion. But to judge only from the situation of affairs, I shou'd not expect, that the affections wou'd rest there, and never transfuse themselves into any other impression. As there is here a person, who by means of a double relation is the object of my passion, the very same reasoning leads me to think the passion will be carry'd farther. The person has a relation of ideas to myself, according to the supposition; the passion, of which he is the object, by being either agreeable or uneasy, has a relation of impressions to pride or humility. 'Tis evident, then, that one of these passions must arise from the love or hatred.

This is the reasoning I form in conformity to my hypothesis; and am 13 pleas'd to find upon trial that every thing answers exactly to my expectation. The virtue or vice of a son or brother not only excites love or hatred, but by a new transition, from similar causes, gives rise to pride or humility. Nothing causes greater vanity than any shining quality in our relations; as nothing mortifies us more than their vice or infamy. This exact conformity of experience to our reasoning is a convincing proof of the solidity of that hypothesis, upon which we reason.

Sixth Experiment. This evidence will be still augmented, if we reverse 14 the experiment, and preserving still the same relations, begin only with a different passion. Suppose, that instead of the virtue or vice of a son or brother, which causes first love or hatred, and afterwards pride or humility, we place these good or bad qualities on ourselves, without any immediate connexion with the person, who is related to us: Experience shews us, that by this change of situation the whole chain is broke, and that the mind is not convey'd from one passion to another, as in the preceding instance. We never love or hate a son or brother for the virtue or vice we discern in ourselves; tho' 'tis evident the same qualities in him give us a very sensible pride or humility. The transition from pride or humility to love or hatred is not so natural as from love or hatred to pride or humility. This may at first sight be esteem'd contrary to my hypothesis; since the relations of impressions and ideas are in both cases precisely the same. Pride and humility are impressions related to love and hatred. Myself am related to the person. It shou'd, therefore, be expected, that like causes must produce like effects, and a perfect transition arise from the double relation, as in all other cases. This difficulty we may easily solve by the following reflections.

15   'Tis evident, that as we are at all times intimately conscious of ourselves, our sentiments and passions, their ideas must strike upon us with
greater vivacity than the ideas of the sentiments and passions of any other
person. But every thing, that strikes upon us with vivacity, and appears in
a full and strong light, forces itself, in a manner, into our consideration,
and becomes present to the mind on the smallest hint and most trivial relation. For the same reason, when it is once present, it engages the attention, and keeps it from wandering to other objects, however strong may be
their relation to our first object. The imagination passes easily from obscure to lively ideas, but with difficulty from lively to obscure. In the one
case the relation is aided by another principle: In the other case, 'tis oppos'd by it.

16   Now I have observ'd, that those two faculties of the mind, the imagination and passions, assist each other in their operation, when their propensities are similar, and when they act upon the same object. The mind has
always a propensity to pass from a passion to any other related to it; and
this propensity is forwarded when the object of the one passion is related
to that of the other. The two impulses concur with each other, and render
the whole transition more smooth and easy. But if it shou'd happen, that
while the relation of ideas, strictly speaking, continues the same, its influence, in causing a transition of the imagination, shou'd no longer take
place, 'tis evident its influence on the passions must also cease, as being
dependent entirely on that transition. This is the reason why pride or humility is not transfus'd into love or hatred with the same ease, that the latter passions are chang'd into the former. If a person be my brother I am
his likewise: But tho' the relations be reciprocal, they have very different
effects on the imagination. The passage is smooth and open from the consideration of any person related to us to that of ourself, of whom we are
every moment conscious. But when the affections are once directed to
ourself, the fancy passes not with the same facility from that object to any
other person, how closely so ever connected with us. This easy or difficult
transition of the imagination operates upon the passions, and facilitates or
retards their transition; which is a clear proof, that these two faculties of
the passions and imagination are connected together, and that the relations of ideas have an influence upon the affections. Besides innumerable
experiments that prove this, we here find, that even when the relation remains; if by any particular circumstance its usual effect upon the fancy in
producing an association or transition of ideas, is prevented; its usual effect upon the passions, in conveying us from one to another, is in like
manner prevented.

17   Some may, perhaps, find a contradiction betwixt this phænomenon and
that of sympathy, where the mind passes easily from the idea of ourselves

to that of any other object related to us. But this difficulty will vanish, if
we consider that in sympathy our own person is not the object of any passion, nor is there any thing, that fixes our attention on ourselves; as in the
present case, where we are suppos'd to be actuated with pride or humility.
Ourself, independent of the perception of every other object, is in reality
nothing: For which reason we must turn our view to external objects; and
'tis natural for us to consider with most attention such as lie contiguous to
us, or resemble us. But when self is the object of a passion, 'tis not natural
to quit the consideration of it, till the passion be exhausted; in which case
the double relations of impressions and ideas can no longer operate.

Seventh Experiment. To put this whole reasoning to a farther trial, let us   18
make a new experiment; and as we have already seen the effects of related
passions and ideas, let us here suppose an identity of passions along with
a relation of ideas; and let us consider the effects of this new situation.
'Tis evident a transition of the passions from the one object to the other is
here in all reason to be expected; since the relation of ideas is suppos'd
still to continue, and an identity of impressions must produce a stronger
connexion, than the most perfect resemblance, that can be imagin'd. If a
double relation, therefore, of impressions and ideas is able to produce a
transition from one to the other, much more an identity of impressions
with a relation of ideas. Accordingly we find, that when we either love or
hate any person, the passions seldom continue within their first bounds;
but extend themselves towards all the contiguous objects, and comprehend the friends and relations of him we love or hate. Nothing is more
natural than to bear a kindness to one brother on account of our friendship for another, without any farther examination of his character. A quarrel with one person gives us a hatred for the whole family, tho' entirely
innocent of that, which displeases us. Instances of this kind are every
where to be met with.

There is only one difficulty in this experiment, which it will be neces-   19
sary to account for, before we proceed any farther. 'Tis evident, that tho' all
passions pass easily from one object to another related to it, yet this transition is made with greater facility, where the more considerable object is
first presented, and the lesser follows it, than where this order is revers'd,
and the lesser takes the precedence. Thus 'tis more natural for us to love the
son upon account of the father, than the father upon account of the son;
the servant for the master, than the master for the servant; the subject for
the prince, than the prince for the subject. In like manner we more readily
contract a hatred against a whole family, where our first quarrel is with the
head of it, than where we are displeas'd with a son, or servant, or some inferior member. In short, our passions, like other objects, descend with
greater facility than they ascend.

20   That we may comprehend, wherein consists the difficulty of explaining this phænomenon, we must consider, that the very same reason, which determines the imagination to pass from remote to contiguous objects, with more facility than from contiguous to remote, causes it likewise to change with more ease, the less for the greater, than the greater for the less. Whatever has the greatest influence is most taken notice of; and whatever is most taken notice of, presents itself most readily to the imagination. We are more apt to over-look in any subject, what is trivial, than what appears of considerable moment; but especially if the latter takes the precedence, and first engages our attention. Thus if any accident makes us consider the *Satellites* of *Jupiter*, our fancy is naturally determin'd to form the idea of that planet; but if we first reflect on the principal planet, 'tis more natural for us to overlook its attendants. The mention of the provinces of any empire conveys our thought to the seat of the empire; but the fancy returns not with the same facility to the consideration of the provinces. The idea of the servant makes us think of the master; that of the subject carries our view to the prince. But the same relation has not an equal influence in conveying us back again. And on this is founded that reproach of *Cornelia* to her sons, that they ought to be asham'd she shou'd be more known by the title of the daughter of *Scipio,* than by that of the mother of the *Gracchi.* This was, in other words, exhorting them to render themselves as illustrious and famous as their grandfather, otherwise the imagination of the people, passing from her who was intermediate, and plac'd in an equal relation to both, wou'd always leave them, and denominate her by what was more considerable and of greater moment. On the same principle is founded that common custom of making wives bear the name of their husbands, rather than husbands that of their wives; as also the ceremony of giving the precedency to those, whom we honour and respect. We might find many other instances to confirm this principle, were it not already sufficiently evident.

21   Now since the fancy finds the same facility in passing from the lesser to the greater, as from remote to contiguous, why does not this easy transition of ideas assist the transition of passions in the former case, as well as in the latter? The virtues of a friend or brother produce first love, and then pride; because in that case the imagination passes from remote to contiguous, according to its propensity. Our own virtues produce not first pride, and then love to a friend or brother; because the passage in that case wou'd be from contiguous to remote, contrary to its propensity. But the love or hatred of an inferior causes not readily any passion to the superior, tho' that be the natural propensity of the imagination: While the love or hatred of a superior, causes a passion to the inferior, contrary to its propensity. In short, the same facility of transition operates not in the same manner

upon superior and inferior as upon contiguous and remote. These two phænomena appear contradictory, and require some attention to be reconcil'd.

As the transition of ideas is here made contrary to the natural propensity of the imagination, that faculty must be over-power'd by some stronger principle of another kind; and as there is nothing ever present to the mind but impressions and ideas, this principle must necessarily lie in the impressions. Now it has been observ'd, that impressions or passions are connected only by their resemblance, and that where any two passions place the mind in the same or in similar dispositions, it very naturally passes from the one to the other: As on the contrary, a repugnance in the dispositions produces a difficulty in the transition of the passions. But 'tis observable, that this repugnance may arise from a difference of degree as well as of kind; nor do we experience a greater difficulty in passing suddenly from a small degree of love to a small degree of hatred, than from a small to a great degree of either of these affections. A man, when calm or only moderately agitated, is so different, in every respect, from himself, when disturb'd with a violent passion, that no two persons can be more unlike; nor is it easy to pass from the one extreme to the other, without a considerable interval betwixt them. 22

The difficulty is not less, if it be not rather greater, in passing from the strong passion to the weak, than in passing from the weak to the strong, provided the one passion upon its appearance destroys the other, and they do not both of them exist at once. But the case is entirely alter'd, when the passions unite together, and actuate the mind at the same time. A weak passion, when added to a strong, makes not so considerable a change in the disposition, as a strong when added to a weak; for which reason there is a closer connexion betwixt the great degree and the small, than betwixt the small degree and the great. 23

The degree of any passion depends upon the nature of its object; and an affection directed to a person, who is considerable in our eyes, fills and possesses the mind much more than one, which has for its object a person we esteem of less consequence. Here then the contradiction betwixt the propensities of the imagination and passion displays itself. When we turn our thought to a great and a small object, the imagination finds more facility in passing from the small to the great, than from the great to the small; but the affections find a greater difficulty: And as the affections are a more powerful principle than the imagination, no wonder they prevail over it, and draw the mind to their side. In spite of the difficulty in passing from the idea of great to that of little, a passion directed to the former, produces always a similar passion towards the latter; when the great and little are related together. The idea of the servant conveys our thought most readily 24 to the master; but the hatred or love of the master produces with greater facility anger or good-will to the servant. The strongest passion in this case takes the precedence; and the addition of the weaker making no considerable change on the disposition, the passage is by that means render'd more easy and natural betwixt them.

25   As in the foregoing experiment we found, that a relation of ideas, which, by any particular circumstance, ceases to produce its usual effect of facilitating the transition of ideas, ceases likewise to operate on the passions; so in the present experiment we find the same property of the impressions. Two different degrees of the same passion are surely related together; but if the smaller be first present, it has little or no tendency to introduce the greater; and that because the addition of the great to the little, produces a more sensible alteration on the temper, than the addition of the little to the great. These phænomena, when duly weigh'd, will be found convincing proofs of this hypothesis.

26   And these proofs will be confirm'd, if we consider the manner in which the mind here reconciles the contradiction, I have observ'd betwixt the passions and the imagination. The fancy passes with more facility from the less to the greater, than from the greater to the less: But on the contrary a violent passion produces more easily a feeble, than that does a violent. In this opposition the passion in the end prevails over the imagination; but 'tis commonly by complying with it, and by seeking another quality, which may counter-ballance that principle, from whence the opposition arises. When we love the father or master of a family, we little think of his children or servants. But when these are present with us, or when it lies any ways in our power to serve them, the nearness and contiguity in this case encreases their magnitude, or at least removes that opposition, which the fancy makes to the transition of the affections. If the imagination finds a difficulty in passing from greater to less, it finds an equal facility in passing from remote to contiguous, which brings the matter to an equality, and leaves the way open from the one passion to the other.

27   *Eighth Experiment.* I have observ'd that the transition from love or hatred to pride or humility, is more easy than from pride or humility to love or hatred; and that the difficulty, which the imagination finds in passing from contiguous to remote, is the cause why we scarce have any instance of the latter transition of the affections. I must, however, make one exception, *viz.* when the very cause of the pride and humility is plac'd in some other person. For in that case the imagination is necessitated to consider the person, nor can it possibly confine its view to ourselves. Thus nothing more readily produces kindness and affection to any person, than his approbation of our conduct and character: As on the other hand, nothing inspires us with a stronger hatred, than his blame or contempt. Here 'tis

evident, that the original passion is pride or humility, whose object is self; and that this passion is transfus'd into love or hatred, whose object is some other person, notwithstanding the rule I have already establish'd, *that the imagination passes with difficulty from contiguous to remote.* But the transition in this case is not made merely on account of the relation betwixt ourselves and the person; but because that very person is the real cause of our first passion, and of consequence is intimately connected with it. 'Tis his approbation that produces pride; and disapprobation, humility. No wonder, then, the imagination returns back again attended with the related passions of love and hatred. This is not a contradiction, but an exception to the rule; and an exception that arises from the same reason with the rule itself.

Such an exception as this is, therefore, rather a confirmation of the   28
rule. And indeed, if we consider all the eight experiments I have explain'd, we shall find that the same principle appears in all of them, and that 'tis by means of a transition arising from a double relation of impressions and ideas, pride and humility, love and hatred are produc'd. An object without a relation,[1] or with but one,[2] never produces either of these passions; and 'tis found[3] that the passion always varies in conformity to the relation. Nay we may observe, that where the relation, by any particular circumstance, has not its usual effect of producing a transition either of ideas or of impressions,[4] it ceases to operate upon the passions, and gives rise neither to pride nor love, humility nor hatred. This rule we find still to hold good, even under the appearance of its contrary;[5] and as relation is frequently experienc'd to have no effect; which upon examination is found to proceed from some particular circumstance, that prevents the transition; so even in instances, where that circumstance, tho' present, prevents not the transition, 'tis found to arise from some other circumstance, which counter-ballances it. Thus not only the variations resolve themselves into the general principle, but even the variations of these variations.

Section III. Difficulties solv'd.

After so many and such undeniable proofs drawn from daily experience   1
and observation, it may seem superfluous to enter into a particular examination of all the causes of love and hatred. I shall, therefore, employ the

---

[1] First Experiment.
[2] Second and Third Experiments.
[3] Fourth Experiment.
[4] Sixth Experiment.
[5] Seventh and Eighth Experiments.

sequel of this part, *First*, In removing some difficulties, concerning particular causes of these passions. *Secondly*, In examining the compound affections, which arise from the mixture of love and hatred with other emotions.

2   Nothing is more evident, than that any person acquires our kindness, or is expos'd to our ill-will, in proportion to the pleasure or uneasiness we receive from him, and that the passions keep pace exactly with the sensations in all their changes and variations. Whoever can find the means either by his services, his beauty, or his flattery, to render himself useful or agreeable to us, is sure of our affections: As on the other hand, whoever harms or displeases us never fails to excite our anger or hatred. When our own nation is at war with any other, we detest them under the character of cruel, perfidious, unjust and violent: But always esteem ourselves and allies equitable, moderate, and merciful. If the general of our enemies be successful, 'tis with difficulty we allow him the figure and character of a man. He is a sorcerer: He has a communication with dæmons; as is reported of *Oliver Cromwell*, and the *Duke of Luxembourg*: He is bloody-minded, and takes a pleasure in death and destruction. But if the success be on our side, our commander has all the opposite good qualities, and is a pattern of virtue, as well as of courage and conduct. His treachery we call policy: His cruelty is an evil inseparable from war. In short, every one of his faults we either endeavour to extenuate, or dignify it with the name of that virtue, which approaches it. 'Tis evident the same method of thinking runs thro' common life.

3   There are some, who add another condition, and require not only that the pain and pleasure arise from the person, but likewise that it arise knowingly, and with a particular design and intention. A man, who wounds and harms us by accident, becomes not our enemy upon that account, nor do we think ourselves bound by any ties of gratitude to one, who does us any service after the same manner. By the intention we judge of the actions, and according as that is good or bad, they become causes of love or hatred.

4   But here we must make a distinction. If that quality in another, which pleases or displeases, be constant and inherent in his person and character, it will cause love or hatred independent of the intention: But otherwise a knowledge and design is requisite, in order to give rise to these passions. One that is disagreeable by his deformity or folly is the object of our aversion, tho' nothing be more certain, than that he has not the least intention of displeasing us by these qualities. But if the uneasiness proceed not from a quality, but an action, which is produc'd and annihilated in a moment, 'tis necessary, in order to produce some relation, and connect this action sufficiently with the person, that it be deriv'd from a particular fore-thought

and design. 'Tis not enough, that the action arise from the person, and have him for its immediate cause and author. This relation alone is too feeble and inconstant to be a foundation for these passions. It reaches not the sensible and thinking part, and neither proceeds from any thing *durable* in him, nor leaves any thing behind it; but passes in a moment, and is as if it had never been. On the other hand, an intention shews certain qualities, which remaining after the action is perform'd, connect it with the person, and facilitate the transition of ideas from one to the other. We can never think of him without reflecting on these qualities; unless repentance and a change of life have produc'd an alteration in that respect: In which case the passion is likewise alter'd. This therefore is one reason, why an intention is requisite to excite either love or hatred.

But we must farther consider, that an intention, besides its strengthening the relation of ideas, is often necessary to produce a relation of impressions, and give rise to pleasure and uneasiness. For 'tis observable, that the principal part of an injury is the contempt and hatred, which it shews in the person, that injures us; and without that, the mere harm gives us a less sensible uneasiness. In like manner, a good office is agreeable, chiefly because it flatters our vanity, and is a proof of the kindness and esteem of the person, who performs it. The removal of the intention, removes the mortification in the one case, and vanity in the other; and must of course cause a remarkable diminution in the passions of love and hatred. 5

I grant, that these effects of the removal of design, in diminishing the relations of impressions and ideas, are not entire, nor able to remove every degree of these relations. But then I ask, if the removal of design be able entirely to remove the passion of love and hatred? Experience, I am sure, informs us of the contrary, nor is there any thing more certain, than that men often fall into a violent anger for injuries, which they themselves must own to be entirely involuntary and accidental. This emotion, indeed, cannot be of long continuance; but still is sufficient to shew, that there is a natural connexion betwixt uneasiness and anger, and that the relation of impressions will operate upon a very small relation of ideas. But when the violence of the impression is once a little abated, the defect of the relation begins to be better felt; and as the character of a person is no wise interested in such injuries as are casual and involuntary, it seldom happens that on their account, we entertain a lasting enmity. 6

To illustrate this doctrine by a parallel instance, we may observe, that not only the uneasiness, which proceeds from another by accident, has but little force to excite our passion, but also that which arises from an acknowledg'd necessity and duty. One that has a real design of harming us, proceeding not from hatred and ill-will, but from justice and equity, 7 draws not upon him our anger, if we be in any degree reasonable; notwith-standing he is both the cause, and the knowing cause of our sufferings. Let us examine a little this phænomenon.

8   'Tis evident in the first place, that this circumstance is not decisive; and tho' it may be able to diminish the passions, 'tis seldom it can entirely re-move them. How few criminals are there, who have no ill-will to the per-son, that accuses them, or to the judge, that condemns them, even tho' they be conscious of their own deserts? In like manner our antagonist in a law-suit, and our competitor for any office, are commonly regarded as our enemies; tho' we must acknowledge, if we wou'd but reflect a moment, that their motive is entirely as justifiable as our own.

9   Besides we may consider, that when we receive harm from any person, we are apt to imagine him criminal, and 'tis with extreme difficulty we allow of his justice and innocence. This is a clear proof, that, independent of the opinion of iniquity, any harm or uneasiness has a natural tendency to excite our hatred, and that afterwards we seek for reasons upon which we may justify and establish the passion. Here the idea of injury produces not the passion, but arises from it.

10   Nor is it any wonder that passion shou'd produce the opinion of injury; since otherwise it must suffer a considerable diminution, which all the passions avoid as much as possible. The removal of injury may remove the anger, without proving that the anger arises only from the injury. The harm and the justice are two contrary objects, of which the one has a ten-dency to produce hatred, and the other love; and 'tis according to their different degrees, and our particular turn of thinking, that either of the objects prevails, and excites its proper passion.

Part III:
Of the Will and Direct Passions.

Section I. Of liberty and necessity.

We come now to explain the *direct* passions, or the impressions, which 1
arise immediately from good or evil, from pain or pleasure. Of this kind
are, *desire* and *aversion*, *grief* and *joy*, *hope* and *fear*.

Of all the immediate effects of pain and pleasure, there is none more re- 2
markable than the WILL, and tho', properly speaking, it be not comprehended among the passions, yet as the full understanding of its nature and
properties, is necessary to the explanation of them, we shall here make it
the subject of our enquiry. I desire it may be observ'd, that by the *will*, I
mean nothing but the *internal impression we feel and are conscious of, when
we knowingly give rise to any new motion of our body, or new perception of our
mind*. This impression, like the preceding ones of pride and humility, love
and hatred, 'tis impossible to define, and needless to describe any farther;
for which reason we shall cut off all those definitions and distinctions,
with which philosophers are wont to perplex rather than clear up this
question; and entering at first upon the subject, shall examine that long
disputed question concerning *liberty and necessity*; which occurs so naturally in treating of the will.

'Tis universally acknowledg'd, that the operations of external bodies 3
are necessary, and that in the communication of their motion, in their attraction, and mutual cohesion, there are not the least traces of indifference or liberty. Every object is determin'd by an absolute fate to a certain
degree and direction of its motion, and can no more depart from that precise line, in which it moves, than it can convert itself into an angel, or
spirit, or any superior substance. The actions, therefore, of matter are to
be regarded as instances of necessary actions; and whatever is in this respect on the same footing with matter, must be acknowledg'd to be necessary. That we may know whether this be the case with the actions of the
mind, we shall begin with examining matter, and considering on what the
idea of a necessity in its operations is founded, and why we conclude one
body or action to be the infallible cause of another.

It has been observ'd already, that in no single instance the ultimate 4
connexion of any objects is discoverable, either by our senses or reason,
and that we can never penetrate so far into the essence and construction
of bodies, as to perceive the principle, on which their mutual influence
depends. 'Tis their constant union alone, with which we are acquainted;
and 'tis from the constant union the necessity arises. If objects had not
an uniform and regular conjunction with each other, we shou'd never
arrive at any idea of cause and effect; and even after all, the necessity,

which enters into that idea, is nothing but a determination of the mind to pass from one object to its usual attendant, and infer the existence of one from that of the other. Here then are two particulars, which we are to consider as essential to necessity, *viz.* the constant *union* and the *inference* of the mind; and wherever we discover these we must acknowledge a necessity. As the actions of matter have no necessity, but what is deriv'd from these circumstances, and it is not by any insight into the essence of bodies we discover their connexion, the absence of this insight, while the union and inference remain, will never, in any case, remove the necessity. 'Tis the observation of the union, which produces the inference; for which reason it might be thought sufficient, if we prove a constant union in the actions of the mind, in order to establish the inference, along with the necessity of these actions. But that I may bestow a greater force on my reasoning, I shall examine these particulars apart, and shall first prove from experience, that our actions have a constant union with our motives, tempers, and circumstances, before I consider the inferences we draw from it.

5   To this end a very slight and general view of the common course of human affairs will be sufficient. There is no light, in which we can take them, that does not confirm this principle. Whether we consider mankind according to the difference of sexes, ages, governments, conditions, or methods of education; the same uniformity and regular operation of natural principles are discernible. Like causes still produce like effects; in the same manner as in the mutual action of the elements and powers of nature.

6   There are different trees, which regularly produce fruit, whose relish is different from each other; and this regularity will be admitted as an instance of necessity and causes in external bodies. But are the products of *Guienne* and of *Champagne* more regularly different than the sentiments, actions, and passions of the two sexes, of which the one are distinguish'd by their force and maturity, the other by their delicacy and softness?

7   Are the changes of our body from infancy to old age more regular and certain than those of our mind and conduct? And wou'd a man be more ridiculous, who wou'd expect that an infant of four years old will raise a weight of three hundred pounds, than one, who from a person of the same age, wou'd look for a philosophical reasoning, or a prudent and well-concerted action?

8   We must certainly allow, that the cohesion of the parts of matter arises from natural and necessary principles, whatever difficulty we may find in explaining them: And for a like reason we must allow, that human society is founded on like principles; and our reason in the latter case is better than even that in the former; because we not only observe, that men *always* seek society, but can also explain the principles, on which

this universal propensity is founded. For is it more certain, that two flat pieces of marble will unite together, than that two young savages of different sexes will copulate? Do the children arise from this copulation more uniformly, than does the parents care for their safety and preservation? And after they have arriv'd at years of discretion by the care of their parents, are the inconveniences attending their separation more certain than their foresight of these inconveniences, and their care of avoiding them by a close union and confederacy?

The skin, pores, muscles, and nerves of a day-labourer are different 9 from those of a man of quality: So are his sentiments, actions and manners. The different stations of life influence the whole fabric, external and internal; and these different stations arise necessarily, because uniformly, from the necessary and uniform principles of human nature. Men cannot live without society, and cannot be associated without government. Government makes a distinction of property, and establishes the different ranks of men. This produces industry, traffic, manufactures, law-suits, war, leagues, alliances, voyages, travels, cities, fleets, ports, and all those other actions and objects, which cause such a diversity, and at the same time maintain such an uniformity in human life.

Shou'd a traveller, returning from a far country, tell us, that he had seen 10 a climate in the fiftieth degree of northern latitude, where all the fruits ripen and come to perfection in the winter, and decay in the summer, after the same manner as in *England* they are produc'd and decay in the contrary seasons, he wou'd find few so credulous as to believe him. I am apt to think a traveller wou'd meet with as little credit, who shou'd inform us of people exactly of the same character with those in *Plato's Republic* on the one hand, or those in *Hobbes's Leviathan* on the other. There is a general course of nature in human actions, as well as in the operations of the sun and the climate. There are also characters peculiar to different nations and particular persons, as well as common to mankind. The knowledge of these characters is founded on the observation of an uniformity in the actions, that flow from them; and this uniformity forms the very essence of necessity.

I can imagine only one way of eluding this argument, which is by deny- 11 ing that uniformity of human actions, on which it is founded. As long as actions have a constant union and connexion with the situation and temper of the agent, however we may in words refuse to acknowledge the necessity, we really allow the thing. Now some may, perhaps, find a pretext to deny this regular union and connexion. For what is more capricious than human actions? What more inconstant than the desires of man? And what creature departs more widely, not only from right reason, but from his own character and disposition? An hour, a moment is sufficient to make him change from one extreme to another, and overturn what cost the greatest pain and labour to establish. Necessity is regular and certain. Human conduct is irregular and uncertain. The one, therefore, proceeds not from the other.

12   To this I reply, that in judging of the actions of men we must proceed upon the same maxims, as when we reason concerning external objects. When any phænomena are constantly and invariably conjoin'd together, they acquire such a connexion in the imagination, that it passes from one to the other, without any doubt or hesitation. But below this there are many inferior degrees of evidence and probability, nor does one single contrariety of experiment entirely destroy all our reasoning. The mind ballances the contrary experiments, and deducting the inferior from the superior, proceeds with that degree of assurance or evidence, which remains. Even when these contrary experiments are entirely equal, we remove not the notion of causes and necessity; but supposing that the usual contrariety proceeds from the operation of contrary and conceal'd causes, we conclude, that the chance or indifference lies only in our judgment on account of our imperfect knowledge, not in the things themselves, which are in every case equally necessary, tho' to appearance not equally constant or certain. No union can be more constant and certain, than that of some actions with some motives and characters; and if in other cases the union is uncertain, 'tis no more than what happens in the operations of body, nor can we conclude any thing from the one irregularity, which will not follow equally from the other.

13   'Tis commonly allow'd that mad-men have no liberty. But were we to judge by their actions, these have less regularity and constancy than the actions of wise-men, and consequently are farther remov'd from necessity. Our way of thinking in this particular is, therefore, absolutely inconsistent; but is a natural consequence of these confus'd ideas and undefin'd terms, which we so commonly make use of in our reasonings, especially on the present subject.

14   We must now shew, that as the *union* betwixt motives and actions has the same constancy, as that in any natural operations, so its influence on the understanding is also the same, in *determining* us to infer the existence of one from that of another. If this shall appear, there is no known circumstance, that enters into the connexion and production of the actions of matter, that is not to be found in all the operations of the mind; and consequently we cannot, without a manifest absurdity, attribute necessity to the one, and refuse it to the other.

15   There is no philosopher, whose judgment is so riveted to this fantastical system of liberty, as not to acknowledge the force of *moral evidence*, and both in speculation and practice proceed upon it, as upon a reasonable

foundation. Now moral evidence is nothing but a conclusion concerning the actions of men, deriv'd from the consideration of their motives, temper and situation. Thus when we see certain characters or figures describ'd upon paper, we infer that the person, who produc'd them, wou'd affirm such facts, the death of *Cæsar*, the success of *Augustus*, the cruelty of *Nero*; and remembring many other concurrent testimonies we conclude, that those facts were once really existent, and that so many men, without any interest, wou'd never conspire to deceive us; especially since they must, in the attempt, expose themselves to the derision of all their contemporaries, when these facts were asserted to be recent and universally known. The same kind of reasoning runs thro' politics, war, commerce, œconomy, and indeed mixes itself so entirely in human life, that 'tis impossible to act or subsist a moment without having recourse to it. A prince, who imposes a tax upon his subjects, expects their compliance. A general, who conducts an army, makes account of a certain degree of courage. A merchant looks for fidelity and skill in his factor or supercargo. A man, who gives orders for his dinner, doubts not of the obedience of his servants. In short, as nothing more nearly interests us than our own actions and those of others, the greatest part of our reasonings is employ'd in judgments concerning them. Now I assert, that whoever reasons after this manner, does *ipso facto* believe the actions of the will to arise from necessity, and that he knows not what he means, when he denies it.

All those objects, of which we call the one *cause* and the other *effect*, 16 consider'd in themselves, are as distinct and separate from each other, as any two things in nature, nor can we ever, by the most accurate survey of them, infer the existence of the one from that of the other. 'Tis only from experience and the observation of their constant union, that we are able to form this inference; and even after all, the inference is nothing but the effects of custom on the imagination. We must not here be content with saying, that the idea of cause and effect arises from objects constantly united; but must affirm, that 'tis the very same with the idea of these objects, and that the *necessary connexion* is not discover'd by a conclusion of the understanding, but is merely a perception of the mind. Wherever, therefore, we observe the same union, and wherever the union operates in the same manner upon the belief and opinion, we have the idea of causes and necessity, tho' perhaps we may avoid those expressions. Motion in one body in all past instances, that have fallen under our observation, is follow'd upon impulse by motion in another. 'Tis impossible for the mind to penetrate farther. From this constant union it *forms* the idea of cause and effect, and by its influence *feels* the necessity. As there is the same constancy, and the same influence in what we call moral evidence, I ask no more. What remains can only be a dispute of words.

17   And indeed, when we consider how aptly *natural* and *moral* evidence
cement together, and form only one chain of argument betwixt them, we
shall make no scruple to allow, that they are of the same nature, and deriv'd from the same principles. A prisoner, who has neither money nor interest, discovers the impossibility of his escape, as well from the obstinacy
of the gaoler, as from the walls and bars with which he is surrounded; and
in all attempts for his freedom chuses rather to work upon the stone and
iron of the one, than upon the inflexible nature of the other. The same
prisoner, when conducted to the scaffold, foresees his death as certainly
from the constancy and fidelity of his guards as from the operation of the
axe or wheel. His mind runs along a certain train of ideas: The refusal of
the soldiers to consent to his escape, the action of the executioner; the
separation of the head and body; bleeding, convulsive motions, and death.
Here is a connected chain of natural causes and voluntary actions; but the
mind feels no difference betwixt them in passing from one link to another;
nor is less certain of the future event than if it were connected with the
present impressions of the memory and senses by a train of causes ce-
mented together by what we are pleas'd to call a *physical necessity*. The
same experienc'd union has the same effect on the mind, whether the
united objects be motives, volitions and actions; or figure and motion. We
may change the names of things; but their nature and their operation on
the understanding never change.

18   I dare be positive no one will ever endeavour to refute these reasonings
otherwise than by altering my definitions, and assigning a different meaning to the terms of *cause*, and *effect*, and *necessity*, and *liberty*, and *chance*.
According to my definitions, necessity makes an essential part of causation; and consequently liberty, by removing necessity, removes also
causes, and is the very same thing with chance. As chance is commonly
thought to imply a contradiction, and is at least directly contrary to experience, there are always the same arguments against liberty or free-will. If
any one alters the definitions, I cannot pretend to argue with him, till I
know the meaning he assigns to these terms.

Section II. The same subject continu'd.

1   I believe we may assign the three following reasons for the prevalence of
the doctrine of liberty, however absurd it may be in one sense, and unintelligible in any other. *First*, After we have perform'd any action; tho' we
confess we were influenc'd by particular views and motives; 'tis difficult
for us to perswade ourselves we were govern'd by necessity, and that 'twas
utterly impossible for us to have acted otherwise; the idea of necessity
seeming to imply something of force, and violence, and constraint, of
which we are not sensible. Few are capable of distinguishing betwixt the

liberty of *spontaneity*, as it is call'd in the schools, and the liberty of *indifference*; betwixt that which is oppos'd to violence, and that which means a negation of necessity and causes. The first is even the most common sense of the word; and as 'tis only that species of liberty, which it concerns us to preserve, our thoughts have been principally turn'd towards it, and have almost universally confounded it with the other.

Secondly, There is a *false sensation or experience* even of the liberty of indifference; which is regarded as an argument for its real existence. The necessity of any action, whether of matter or of the mind, is not properly a quality in the agent, but in any thinking or intelligent being, who may consider the action, and consists in the determination of his thought to infer its existence from some preceding objects: As liberty or chance, on the other hand, is nothing but the want of that determination, and a certain looseness, which we feel in passing or not passing from the idea of one to that of the other. Now we may observe, that tho' in reflecting on human actions we seldom feel such a looseness or indifference, yet it very commonly happens, that in performing the actions themselves we are sensible of something like it: And as all related or resembling objects are readily taken for each other, this has been employ'd as a demonstrative or even an intuitive proof of human liberty. We feel that our actions are subject to our will on most occasions, and imagine we feel that the will itself is subject to nothing; because when by a denial of it we are provok'd to try, we feel that it moves easily every way, and produces an image of itself even on that side, on which it did not settle. This image or faint motion, we perswade ourselves, cou'd have been compleated into the thing itself; because, shou'd that be deny'd, we find, upon a second trial, that it can. But these efforts are all in vain; and whatever capricious and irregular actions we may perform; as the desire of showing our liberty is the sole motive of our actions; we can never free ourselves from the bonds of necessity. We may imagine we feel a liberty within ourselves; but a spectator can commonly infer our actions from our motives and character; and even where he cannot, he concludes in general, that he might, were he perfectly acquainted with every circumstance of our situation and temper, and the most secret springs of our complexion and disposition. Now this is the very essence of necessity, according to the foregoing doctrine.

A *third* reason why the doctrine of liberty has generally been better receiv'd in the world, than its antagonist, proceeds from *religion*, which has been very unnecessarily interested in this question. There is no method of reasoning more common, and yet none more blameable, than in philosophical debates to endeavour to refute any hypothesis by a pretext of its dangerous consequences to religion and morality. When any opinion leads us into absurdities, 'tis certainly false; but 'tis not certain an opinion is false, because 'tis of dangerous consequence. Such topics, therefore, ought entirely to be foreborn, as serving nothing to the discovery of truth, but only to make the person of an antagonist odious. This I observe in general, without pretending to draw any advantage from it. I submit myself frankly to an examination of this kind, and dare venture to affirm, that the doctrine of necessity, according to my explication of it, is not only innocent, but even advantageous to religion and morality.

4   I define necessity two ways, conformable to the two definitions of *cause*, of which it makes an essential part. I place it either in the constant union and conjunction of like objects, or in the inference of the mind from the one to the other. Now necessity, in both these senses, has universally, tho' tacitly, in the schools, in the pulpit, and in common life, been allow'd to belong to the will of man, and no one has ever pretended to deny, that we can draw inferences concerning human actions, and that those inferences are founded on the experienc'd union of like actions with like motives and circumstances. The only particular in which any one can differ from me, is either, that perhaps he will refuse to call this necessity. But as long as the meaning is understood, I hope the word can do no harm. Or that he will maintain there is something else in the operations of matter. Now whether it be so or not is of no consequence to religion, whatever it may be to natural philosophy. I may be mistaken in asserting, that we have no idea of any other connexion in the actions of body, and shall be glad to be farther instructed on that head: But sure I am, I ascribe nothing to the actions of the mind, but what must readily be allow'd of. Let no one, therefore, put an invidious construction on my words, by saying simply, that I assert the necessity of human actions, and place them on the same footing with the operations of senseless matter. I do not ascribe to the will that unintelligible necessity, which is suppos'd to lie in matter. But I ascribe to matter, that intelligible quality, call it necessity or not, which the most rigorous orthodoxy does or must allow to belong to the will. I change, therefore, nothing in the receiv'd systems, with regard to the will, but only with regard to material objects.

5   Nay I shall go farther, and assert, that this kind of necessity is so essential to religion and morality, that without it there must ensue an absolute subversion of both, and that every other supposition is entirely destructive to all laws both *divine* and *human*. 'Tis indeed certain, that as all human laws are founded on rewards and punishments, 'tis suppos'd as a fundamental principle, that these motives have an influence on the mind, and both produce the good and prevent the evil actions. We may give to this influence what name we please; but as 'tis usually conjoin'd with the action, common sense requires it shou'd be esteem'd a cause, and be looked upon as an instance of that necessity, which I wou'd establish.

This reasoning is equally solid, when apply'd to *divine* laws, so far as the   6
deity is consider'd as a legislator, and is suppos'd to inflict punishment
and bestow rewards with a design to produce obedience. But I also maintain, that even where he acts not in his magisterial capacity, but is regarded
as the avenger of crimes merely on account of their odiousness and deformity, not only 'tis impossible, without the necessary connexion of cause
and effect in human actions, that punishments cou'd be inflicted compatible with justice and moral equity; but also that it cou'd ever enter into the
thoughts of any reasonable being to inflict them. The constant and universal object of hatred or anger is a person or creature endow'd with thought
and consciousness; and when any criminal or injurious actions excite that
passion, 'tis only by their relation to the person or connexion with him.
But according to the doctrine of liberty or chance, this connexion is reduc'd to nothing, nor are men more accountable for those actions, which
are design'd and premeditated, than for such as are the most casual and
accidental. Actions are by their very nature temporary and perishing; and
where they proceed not from some cause in the characters and disposition
of the person, who perform'd them, they infix not themselves upon him,
and can neither redound to his honour, if good, nor infamy, if evil. The action itself may be blameable; it may be contrary to all the rules of morality
and religion: But the person is not responsible for it; and as it proceeded
from nothing in him, that is durable or constant, and leaves nothing of
that nature behind it, 'tis impossible he can, upon its account, become the
object of punishment or vengeance. According to the hypothesis of liberty, therefore, a man is as pure and untainted, after having committed the
most horrid crimes, as at the first moment of his birth, nor is his character
any way concern'd in his actions; since they are not deriv'd from it, and
the wickedness of the one can never be us'd as a proof of the depravity of
the other. 'Tis only upon the principles of necessity, that a person acquires any merit or demerit from his actions, however the common opinion may incline to the contrary.

But so inconsistent are men with themselves, that tho' they often as-   7
sert, that necessity utterly destroys all merit and demerit either towards
mankind or superior powers, yet they continue still to reason upon these
very principles of necessity in all their judgments concerning this matter.
Men are not blam'd for such evil actions as they perform ignorantly and
casually, whatever may be their consequences. Why? But because the
causes of these actions are only momentary, and terminate in them alone.
Men are less blam'd for such evil actions, as they perform hastily and un-
premeditatedly, than for such as proceed from thought and deliberation.
For what reason? But because a hasty temper, tho' a constant cause in the
mind, operates only by intervals, and infects not the whole character.

Again, repentance wipes off every crime, especially if attended with an evident reformation of life and manners. How is this to be accounted for? But by asserting that actions render a person criminal, merely as they are proofs of criminal passions or principles in the mind; and when by any alteration of these principles they cease to be just proofs, they likewise cease to be criminal. But according to the doctrine of *liberty* or *chance* they never were just proofs, and consequently never were criminal.

8   Here then I turn to my adversary, and desire him to free his own system from these odious consequences before he charge them upon others. Or if he rather chuses, that this question shou'd be decided by fair arguments before philosophers, than by declamations before the people, let him return to what I have advanc'd to prove that liberty and chance are synonimous; and concerning the nature of moral evidence and the regularity of human actions. Upon a review of these reasonings, I cannot doubt of an entire victory; and therefore having prov'd, that all actions of the will have particular causes, I proceed to explain what these causes are, and how they operate.

Section III. Of the influencing motives of the will.

1   Nothing is more usual in philosophy, and even in common life, than to talk of the combat of passion and reason, to give the preference to reason, and assert that men are only so far virtuous as they conform themselves to its dictates. Every rational creature, 'tis said, is oblig'd to regulate his actions by reason; and if any other motive or principle challenge the direction of his conduct, he ought to oppose it, 'till it be entirely subdu'd, or at least brought to a conformity with that superior principle. On this method of thinking the greatest part of moral philosophy, antient and modern, seems to be founded; nor is there an ampler field, as well for metaphysical arguments, as popular declamations, than this suppos'd pre-eminence of reason above passion. The eternity, invariableness, and divine origin of the former have been display'd to the best advantage: The blindness, inconstancy, and deceitfulness of the latter have been as strongly insisted on. In order to shew the fallacy of all this philosophy, I shall endeavour to prove *first*, that reason alone can never be a motive to any action of the will; and *secondly*, that it can never oppose passion in the direction of the will.

2   The understanding exerts itself after two different ways, as it judges from demonstration or probability; as it regards the abstract relations of our ideas, or those relations of objects, of which experience only gives us information. I believe it scarce will be asserted, that the first species of reasoning alone is ever the cause of any action. As its proper province is the world of ideas, and as the will always places us in that of realities, demonstration and volition seem, upon that account, to be totally remov'd, from

each other. Mathematics, indeed, are useful in all mechanical operations, and arithmetic in almost every art and profession: But 'tis not of themselves they have any influence. Mechanics are the art of regulating the motions of bodies *to some design'd end or purpose*; and the reason why we employ arithmetic in fixing the proportions of numbers, is only that we may discover the proportions of their influence and operation. A merchant is desirous of knowing the sum total of his accounts with any person: Why? But that he may learn what sum will have the same *effects* in paying his debt, and going to market, as all the particular articles taken together. Abstract or demonstrative reasoning, therefore, never influences any of our actions, but only as it directs our judgment concerning causes and effects; which leads us to the second operation of the understanding.

'Tis obvious, that when we have the prospect of pain or pleasure from   3
any object, we feel a consequent emotion of aversion or propensity, and are carry'd to avoid or embrace what will give us this uneasiness or satisfaction. 'Tis also obvious, that this emotion rests not here, but making us cast our view on every side, comprehends whatever objects are connected with its original one by the relation of cause and effect. Here then reasoning takes place to discover this relation; and according as our reasoning varies, our actions receive a subsequent variation. But 'tis evident, in this case, that the impulse arises not from reason, but is only directed by it. 'Tis from the prospect of pain or pleasure that the aversion or propensity arises towards any object: And these emotions extend themselves to the causes and effects of that object, as they are pointed out to us by reason and experience. It can never in the least concern us to know, that such objects are causes, and such others effects, if both the causes and effects be indifferent to us. Where the objects themselves do not affect us, their connexion can never give them any influence; and 'tis plain, that as reason is nothing but the discovery of this connexion, it cannot be by its means that the objects are able to affect us.

Since reason alone can never produce any action, or give rise to voli-   4
tion, I infer, that the same faculty is as incapable of preventing volition, or of disputing the preference with any passion or emotion. This consequence is necessary. 'Tis impossible reason cou'd have the latter effect of preventing volition, but by giving an impulse in a contrary direction to our passion; and that impulse, had it operated alone, wou'd have been able to produce volition. Nothing can oppose or retard the impulse of passion, but a contrary impulse; and if this contrary impulse ever arises from reason, that latter faculty must have an original influence on the will, and must be able to cause, as well as hinder any act of volition. But if reason has no original influence, 'tis impossible it can withstand any principle, which has such an efficacy, or ever keep the mind in suspense a moment.

Thus it appears, that the principle, which opposes our passion, cannot be the same with reason, and is only call'd so in an improper sense. We speak not strictly and philosophically when we talk of the combat of passion and of reason. Reason is, and ought only to be the slave of the passions, and can never pretend to any other office than to serve and obey them. As this opinion may appear somewhat extraordinary, it may not be improper to confirm it by some other considerations.

5   A passion is an original existence, or, if you will, modification of existence, and contains not any representative quality, which renders it a copy of any other existence or modification. When I am angry, I am actually possest with the passion, and in that emotion have no more a reference to any other object, than when I am thirsty, or sick, or more than five foot high. 'Tis impossible, therefore, that this passion can be oppos'd by, or be contradictory to truth and reason; since this contradiction consists in the disagreement of ideas, consider'd as copies, with those objects, which they represent.

6   What may at first occur on this head, is, that as nothing can be contrary to truth or reason, except what has a reference to it, and as the judgments of our understanding only have this reference, it must follow, that passions can be contrary to reason only so far as they are *accompany'd* with some judgment or opinion. According to this principle, which is so obvious and natural, 'tis only in two senses that any affection can be call'd unreasonable. First, When a passion, such as hope or fear, grief or joy, despair or security, is founded on the supposition of the existence of objects, which really do not exist. Secondly, When in exerting any passion in action, we chuse means insufficient for the design'd end, and deceive ourselves in our judgment of causes and effects. Where a passion is neither founded on false suppositions, nor chuses means insufficient for the end, the understanding can neither justify nor condemn it. 'Tis not contrary to reason to prefer the destruction of the whole world to the scratching of my finger. 'Tis not contrary to reason for me to chuse my total ruin, to prevent the least uneasiness of an *Indian* or person wholly unknown to me. 'Tis as little contrary to reason to prefer even my own acknowledg'd lesser good to my greater, and have a more ardent affection for the former than the latter. A trivial good may, from certain circumstances, produce a desire superior to what arises from the greatest and most valuable enjoyment; nor is there any thing more extraordinary in this, than in mechanics to see one pound weight raise up a hundred by the advantage of its situation. In short, a passion must be accompany'd with some false judgment, in order to its being unreasonable; and even then 'tis not the passion, properly speaking, which is unreasonable, but the judgment.

7   The consequences are evident. Since a passion can never, in any sense,

be call'd unreasonable, but when founded on a false supposition, or when it chuses means insufficient for the design'd end, 'tis impossible, that reason and passion can ever oppose each other, or dispute for the government of the will and actions. The moment we perceive the falsehood of any supposition, or the insufficiency of any means our passions yield to our reason without any opposition. I may desire any fruit as of an excellent relish; but whenever you convince me of my mistake, my longing ceases. I may will the performance of certain actions as means of obtaining any desir'd good; but as my willing of these actions is only secondary, and founded on the supposition, that they are causes of the propos'd effect; as soon as I discover the falshood of that supposition, they must become indifferent to me.

'Tis natural for one, that does not examine objects with a strict philosophic eye, to imagine, that those actions of the mind are entirely the same, which produce not a different sensation, and are not immediately distinguishable to the feeling and perception. Reason, for instance, exerts itself without producing any sensible emotion; and except in the more sublime disquisitions of philosophy, or in the frivolous subtilties of the schools, scarce ever conveys any pleasure or uneasiness. Hence it proceeds, that every action of the mind, which operates with the same calmness and tranquillity, is confounded with reason by all those, who judge of things from the first view and appearance. Now 'tis certain, there are certain calm desires and tendencies, which, tho' they be real passions, produce little emotion in the mind, and are more known by their effects than by the immediate feeling or sensation. These desires are of two kinds; either certain instincts originally implanted in our natures, such as benevolence and resentment, the love of life, and kindness to children; or the general appetite to good, and aversion to evil, consider'd merely as such. When any of these passions are calm, and cause no disorder in the soul, they are very readily taken for the determinations of reason, and are suppos'd to proceed from the same faculty, with that, which judges of truth and falshood. Their nature and principles have been suppos'd the same, because their sensations are not evidently different.   8

Beside these calm passions, which often determine the will, there are certain violent emotions of the same kind, which have likewise a great influence on that faculty. When I receive any injury from another, I often feel a violent passion of resentment, which makes me desire his evil and punishment, independent of all considerations of pleasure and advantage to myself. When I am immediately threaten'd with any grievous ill, my fears, apprehensions, and aversions rise to a great height, and produce a sensible emotion.   9

The common error of metaphysicians has lain in ascribing the direction   10 of the will entirely to one of these principles, and supposing the other to have no influence. Men often act knowingly against their interest: For which reason the view of the greatest possible good does not always influence them. Men often counter-act a violent passion in prosecution of their interests and designs: 'Tis not therefore the present uneasiness alone, which determines them. In general we may observe, that both these principles operate on the will; and where they are contrary, that either of them prevails, according to the *general* character or *present* disposition of the person. What we call strength of mind, implies the prevalence of the calm passions above the violent; tho' we may easily observe, there is no man so constantly possess'd of this virtue, as never on any occasion to yield to the sollicitations of passion and desire. From these variations of temper proceeds the great difficulty of deciding concerning the actions and resolutions of men, where there is any contrariety of motives and passions.

A

TREATISE

OF

Human Nature:

BEING

An ATTEMPT to introduce the
experimental Method of Reasoning

INTO

MORAL SUBJECTS.

—*Duræ semper virtutis amator,*
Quære quid est virtus, et posce exemplar honesti
LUCAN.*

WITH AN

APPENDIX

Wherein some Passages of the foregoing
Volumes are illustrated and explain'd.

Book III.

OF

MORALS.

---

* ["A lover of austere virtue, you should at least ask now what Virtue is and demand to see Goodness in her visible shape" (Lucan, *Civil Wars*, IX, 562–3; trans. by J. D. Duff).]

Advertisement

I think it proper to inform the public, that tho' this be a third volume of the Treatise of Human Nature, *yet 'tis in some measure independent of the other two, and requires not that the reader shou'd enter into all the abstract reasonings contain'd in them. I am hopeful it may be understood by ordinary readers, with as little attention as is usually given to any books of reasoning. It must only be observ'd, that I continue to make use of the terms,* impressions *and* ideas, *in the same sense as formerly; and that by* impressions *I mean our stronger perceptions, such as our sensations, affections and sentiments; and by* ideas *the fainter perceptions, or the copies of these in the memory and imagination.*

BOOK III: OF MORALS

Part I:
Of Virtue and Vice in General.

Section I. Moral distinctions not deriv'd from reason.

There is an inconvenience which attends all abstruse reasoning, that it 1
may silence, without convincing an antagonist, and requires the same
intense study to make us sensible of its force, that was at first requisite
for its invention. When we leave our closet, and engage in the common
affairs of life, its conclusions seem to vanish, like the phantoms of the
night on the appearance of the morning; and 'tis difficult for us to retain
even that conviction, which we had attain'd with difficulty. This is still
more conspicuous in a long chain of reasoning, where we must preserve
to the end the evidence of the first propositions, and where we often lose
sight of all the most receiv'd maxims, either of philosophy or common
life. I am not, however, without hopes, that the present system of philosophy will acquire new force as it advances; and that our reasonings concerning *morals* will corroborate whatever has been said concerning the
understanding and the *passions*. Morality is a subject that interests us
above all others: We fancy the peace of society to be at stake in every decision concerning it; and 'tis evident, that this concern must make our
speculations appear more real and solid, than where the subject is, in a
great measure, indifferent to us. What affects us, we conclude can never
be a chimera; and as our passion is engag'd on the one side or the other,
we naturally think that the question lies within human comprehension;
which, in other cases of this nature, we are apt to entertain some doubt
of. Without this advantage I never shou'd have ventur'd upon a third
volume of such abstruse philosophy, in an age, wherein the greatest part
of men seem agreed to convert reading into an amusement, and to reject
every thing that requires any considerable degree of attention to be
comprehended.

It has been observ'd, that nothing is ever present to the mind but its 2
perceptions; and that all the actions of seeing, hearing, judging, loving,
hating, and thinking, fall under this denomination. The mind can never
exert itself in any action, which we may not comprehend under the term
of *perception*; and consequently that term is no less applicable to those
judgments, by which we distinguish moral good and evil, than to every
other operation of the mind. To approve of one character, to condemn another, are only so many different perceptions.

Now as perceptions resolve themselves into two kinds, viz. *impressions* 3 and *ideas*, this distinction gives rise to a question, with which we shall open up our present enquiry concerning morals, *Whether 'tis by means of our* ideas *or* impressions *we distinguish betwixt vice and virtue, and pronounce an action blameable or praise-worthy?* This will immediately cut off all loose discourses and declamations, and reduce us to something precise and exact on the present subject.

4   Those who affirm that virtue is nothing but a conformity to reason; that there are eternal fitnesses and unfitnesses of things, which are the same to every rational being that considers them; that the immutable measures of right and wrong impose an obligation, not only on human creatures, but also on the Deity himself: All these systems concur in the opinion, that morality, like truth, is discern'd merely by ideas, and by their juxta-position and comparison. In order, therefore, to judge of these systems, we need only consider, whether it be possible, from reason alone, to distinguish betwixt moral good and evil, or whether there must concur some other principles to enable us to make that distinction.

5   If morality had naturally no influence on human passions and actions, 'twere in vain to take such pains to inculcate it; and nothing wou'd be more fruitless than that multitude of rules and precepts, with which all moralists abound. Philosophy is commonly divided into *speculative* and *practical*; and as morality is always comprehended under the latter division, 'tis suppos'd to influence our passions and actions, and to go beyond the calm and indolent judgments of the understanding. And this is confirm'd by common experience, which informs us, that men are often govern'd by their duties, and are deter'd from some actions by the opinion of injustice, and impell'd to others by that of obligation.

6   Since morals, therefore, have an influence on the actions and affections, it follows, that they cannot be deriv'd from reason; and that because reason alone, as we have already prov'd, can never have any such influence. Morals excite passions, and produce or prevent actions. Reason of itself is utterly impotent in this particular. The rules of morality, therefore, are not conclusions of our reason.

7   No one, I believe, will deny the justness of this inference; nor is there any other means of evading it, than by denying that principle, on which it is founded. As long as it is allow'd, that reason has no influence on our passions and actions, 'tis in vain to pretend, that morality is discover'd only by a deduction of reason. An active principle can never be founded on an inactive; and if reason be inactive in itself, it must remain so in all its shapes and appearances, whether it exerts itself in natural or moral subjects, whether it considers the powers of external bodies, or the actions of rational beings.

It would be tedious to repeat all the arguments, by which I have prov'd,[1] that reason is perfectly inert, and can never either prevent or produce any action or affection. 'Twill be easy to recollect what has been said upon that subject. I shall only recal on this occasion one of these arguments, which I shall endeavour to render still more conclusive, and more applicable to the present subject.

Reason is the discovery of truth or falshood. Truth or falshood consists in an agreement or disagreement either to the *real* relations of ideas, or to *real* existence and matter of fact. Whatever, therefore, is not susceptible of this agreement or disagreement, is incapable of being true or false, and can never be an object of our reason. Now 'tis evident our passions, volitions, and actions, are not susceptible of any such agreement or disagreement; being original facts and realities, compleat in themselves, and implying no reference to other passions, volitions, and actions. 'Tis impossible, therefore, they can be pronounc'd either true or false, and be either contrary or conformable to reason.

This argument is of double advantage to our present purpose. For it proves *directly*, that actions do not derive their merit from a conformity to reason, nor their blame from a contrariety to it; and it proves the same truth more *indirectly*, by shewing us, that as reason can never immediately prevent or produce any action by contradicting or approving of it, it cannot be the source of the distinction betwixt moral good and evil, which are found to have that influence. Actions may be laudable or blameable; but they cannot be reasonable or unreasonable: Laudable or blameable, therefore, are not the same with reasonable or unreasonable. The merit and demerit of actions frequently contradict, and sometimes controul our natural propensities. But reason has no such influence. Moral distinctions, therefore, are not the offspring of reason. Reason is wholly inactive, and can never be the source of so active a principle as conscience, or a sense of morals.

But perhaps it may be said, that tho' no will or action can be immediately contradictory to reason, yet we may find such a contradiction in some of the attendants of the action, that is, in its causes or effects. The action may cause a judgment, or may be *obliquely* caus'd by one, when the judgment concurs with a passion; and by an abusive way of speaking, which philosophy will scarce allow of, the same contrariety may, upon that account, be ascrib'd to the action. How far this truth or falshood may be the source of morals, 'twill now be proper to consider.

---

[1] Book II. Part III. Sect. 3.

12   It has been observ'd, that reason, in a strict and philosophical sense, can
have an influence on our conduct only after two ways: Either when it excites a passion by informing us of the existence of something which is a
proper object of it; or when it discovers the connexion of causes and effects, so as to afford us means of exerting any passion. These are the only
kinds of judgment, which can accompany our actions, or can be said to
produce them in any manner; and it must be allow'd, that these judgments
may often be false and erroneous. A person may be affected with passion,
by supposing a pain or pleasure to lie in an object, which has no tendency
to produce either of these sensations, or which produces the contrary to
what is imagin'd. A person may also take false measures for the attaining
his end, and may retard, by his foolish conduct, instead of forwarding the
execution of any project. These false judgments may be thought to affect
the passions and actions, which are connected with them, and may be said
to render them unreasonable, in a figurative and improper way of speaking. But tho' this be acknowledg'd, 'tis easy to observe, that these errors
are so far from being the source of all immorality, that they are commonly
very innocent, and draw no manner of guilt upon the person who is so unfortunate as to fall into them. They extend not beyond a mistake of *fact*,
which moralists have not generally suppos'd criminal, as being perfectly
involuntary. I am more to be lamented than blam'd, if I am mistaken with
regard to the influence of objects in producing pain or pleasure, or if I
know not the proper means of satisfying my desires. No one can ever regard such errors as a defect in my moral character. A fruit, for instance,
that is really disagreeable, appears to me at a distance, and thro' mistake, I
fancy it to be pleasant and delicious. Here is one error. I choose certain
means of reaching this fruit, which are not proper for my end. Here is a
second error; nor is there any third one, which can ever possibly enter into
our reasonings concerning actions. I ask, therefore, if a man, in this situation, and guilty of these two errors, is to be regarded as vicious and criminal, however unavoidable they might have been? Or if it be possible to
imagine, that such errors are the sources of all immorality?

13   And here it may be proper to observe, that if moral distinctions be deriv'd from the truth or falsehood of those judgments, they must take place
wherever we form the judgments; nor will there be any difference,
whether the question be concerning an apple or a kingdom, or whether
the error be avoidable or unavoidable. For as the very essence of morality
is suppos'd to consist in an agreement or disagreement to reason, the
other circumstances are entirely arbitrary, and can never either bestow on
any action the character of virtuous or vicious, or deprive it of that character. To which we may add, that this agreement or disagreement, not admitting of degrees, all virtues and vices wou'd of course be equal.

Shou'd it be pretended, that tho' a mistake of *fact* be not criminal, yet a   14
mistake of *right* often is; and that this may be the source of immorality: I
wou'd answer, that 'tis impossible such a mistake can ever be the original
source of immorality, since it supposes a real right and wrong; that is, a
real distinction in morals, independent of these judgments. A mistake,
therefore, of right may become a species of immorality; but 'tis only a secondary one, and is founded on some other, antecedent to it.

As to those judgments which are the *effects* of our actions, and which,   15
when false, give occasion to pronounce the actions contrary to truth and
reason; we may observe, that our actions never cause any judgment, either
true or false, in ourselves, and that 'tis only on others they have such an influence. 'Tis certain, that an action, on many occasions, may give rise to
false conclusions in others; and that a person, who thro' a window sees any
lewd behaviour of mine with my neighbour's wife, may be so simple as to
imagine she is certainly my own. In this respect my action resembles somewhat a lye or falshood; only with this difference, which is material, that I
perform not the action with any intention of giving rise to a false judgment
in another, but merely to satisfy my lust and passion. It causes, however, a
mistake and false judgment by accident; and the falsehood of its effects may
be ascrib'd, by some odd figurative way of speaking, to the action itself. But
still I can see no pretext of reason for asserting, that the tendency to cause
such an error is the first spring or original source of all immorality.[2]

---

[2] One might think it were entirely superfluous to prove this, if a late author, who has
had the good fortune to obtain some reputation, had not seriously affirmed, that such a
falshood is the foundation of all guilt and moral deformity. That we may discover the
fallacy of his hypothesis, we need only consider, that a false conclusion is drawn from
an action, only by means of an obscurity of natural principles, which makes a cause be
secretly interrupted in its operation, by contrary causes, and renders the connexion betwixt two objects uncertain and variable. Now, as a like uncertainty and variety of
causes take place, even in natural objects, and produce a like error in our judgment, if
that tendency to produce error were the very essence of vice and immorality, it shou'd
follow, that even inanimate objects might be vicious and immoral.

'Tis in vain to urge, that inanimate objects act without liberty and choice. For as liberty and choice are not necessary to make an action produce in us an erroneous conclusion, they can be, in no respect, essential to morality; and I do not readily perceive,
upon this system, how they can ever come to be regarded by it. If the tendency to cause
error be the origin of immorality, that tendency and immorality wou'd in every case be
inseparable.

Add to this, that if I had used the precaution of shutting the windows, while I indulg'd
myself in those liberties with my neighbour's wife, I should have been guilty of no immorality; and that because my action, being perfectly conceal'd, wou'd have had no tendency to produce any false conclusion.

For the same reason, a thief, who steals in by a ladder at a window, and takes all

16   Thus upon the whole, 'tis impossible, that the distinction betwixt
moral good and evil, can be made by reason; since that distinction has an
influence upon our actions, of which reason alone is incapable. Reason
and judgment may, indeed, be the mediate cause of an action, by prompt-
ing, or by directing a passion: But it is not pretended that a judgment of
this kind, either in its truth or falshood, is attended with virtue or vice.
And as to the judgments, which are caus'd by our actions, they can still
less bestow those moral qualities on the actions, which are their causes.

17   But to be more particular, and to shew, that those eternal immutable fitnesses and unfitnesses of things cannot be defended by sound philosophy,
we may weigh the following considerations.

18   If the thought and understanding were alone capable of fixing the
boundaries of right and wrong, the character of virtuous and vicious either must lie in some relations of objects, or must be a matter of fact,

---

imaginable care to cause no disturbance, is in no respect criminal. For either he will not
be perceiv'd, or if he be, 'tis impossible he can produce any error, nor will any one, from
these circumstances, take him to be other than what he really is.

'Tis well known, that those who are squint-sighted, do very readily cause mistakes in
others, and that we imagine they salute or are talking to one person, while they address
themselves to another. Are they therefore, upon that account, immoral?

Besides, we may easily observe, that in all those arguments there is an evident reasoning in a circle. A person who takes possession of *another*'s goods, and uses them as
his *own*, in a manner declares them to be his own; and this falshood is the source of the
immorality of injustice. But is property, or right, or obligation, intelligible, without an
antecedent morality?

A man that is ungrateful to his benefactor, in a manner affirms, that he never received any favours from him. But in what manner? Is it because 'tis his duty to be
grateful? But this supposes, that there is some antecedent rule of duty and morals. Is it
because human nature is generally grateful, and makes us conclude, that a man who
does any harm never received any favour from the person he harm'd? But human nature is not so generally grateful, as to justify such a conclusion. Or if it were, is an exception to a general rule in every case criminal, for no other reason than because it is an
exception?

But what may suffice entirely to destroy this whimsical system is, that it leaves us
under the same difficulty to give a reason why truth is virtuous and falshood vicious, as
to account for the merit or turpitude of any other action. I shall allow, if you please, that
all immorality is derived from this supposed falshood in action, provided you can give
me any plausible reason, why such a falshood is immoral. If you consider rightly of the
matter, you will find yourself in the same difficulty as at the beginning.

This last argument is very conclusive; because, if there be not an evident merit or
turpitude annex'd to this species of truth or falshood, it can never have any influence
upon our actions. For, who ever thought of forbearing any action, because others might
possibly draw false conclusions from it? Or, who ever perform'd any, that he might give
rise to true conclusions?

which is discover'd by our reasoning. This consequence is evident. As the operations of human understanding divide themselves into two kinds, the comparing of ideas, and the inferring of matter of fact; were virtue discover'd by the understanding; it must be an object of one of these operations; nor is there any third operation of the understanding, which can discover it. There has been an opinion very industriously propagated by certain philosophers, that morality is susceptible of demonstration; and tho' no one has ever been able to advance a single step in those demonstrations; yet 'tis taken for granted that this science may be brought to an equal certainty with geometry or algebra. Upon this supposition, vice and virtue must consist in some relations; since 'tis allow'd on all hands, that no matter of fact is capable of being demonstrated. Let us, therefore, begin with examining this hypothesis, and endeavour, if possible, to fix those moral qualities, which have been so long the objects of our fruitless researches. Point out distinctly the relations, which constitute morality or obligation, that we may know wherein they consist, and after what manner we must judge of them.

If you assert, that vice and virtue consist in relations susceptible of certainty and demonstration, you must confine yourself to those *four* relations which alone admit of that degree of evidence; and in that case you run into absurdities, from which you will never be able to extricate yourself. For as you make the very essence of morality to lie in the relations, and as there is no one of these relations but what is applicable, not only to an irrational but also to an inanimate object; it follows, that even such objects must be susceptible of merit or demerit. *Resemblance, contrariety, degrees in quality,* and *proportions in quantity and number;* all these relations belong as properly to matter as to our actions, passions, and volitions. 'Tis unquestionable, therefore, that morality lies not in any of these relations, nor the sense of it in their discovery.[3]

19

---

[3] As a proof, how confus'd our way of thinking on this subject commonly is, we may observe, that those who assert, that morality is demonstrable, do not say, that morality lies in the relations, and that the relations are distinguishable by reason. They only say, that reason can discover such an action, in such relations, to be virtuous, and such another vicious. It seems they thought it sufficient, if they cou'd bring the word, Relation, into the proposition, without troubling themselves whether it was to the purpose or not. But here, I think, is plain argument. Demonstrative reason discovers only relations. But that reason, according to this hypothesis, discovers also vice and virtue. These moral qualities, therefore, must be relations. When we blame any action, in any situation, the whole complicated object, of action and situation, must form certain relations, wherein the essence of vice consists. This hypothesis is not otherwise intelligible. For what does reason discover, when it pronounces any action vicious? Does it discover a relation or a matter of fact? These questions are decisive, and must not be eluded.

20   Shou'd it be asserted, that the sense of morality consists in the discovery of some relation, distinct from these, and that our enumeration was not compleat, when we comprehended all demonstrable relations under four general heads: To this I know not what to reply, till some one be so good as to point out to me this new relation. 'Tis impossible to refute a system, which has never yet been explain'd. In such a manner of fighting in the dark, a man loses his blows in the air, and often places them where the enemy is not present.

21   I must, therefore, on this occasion, rest contented with requiring the two following conditions of any one that wou'd undertake to clear up this system. *First*, As moral good and evil belong only to the actions of the mind, and are deriv'd from our situation with regard to external objects, the relations, from which these moral distinctions arise, must lie only betwixt internal actions, and external objects, and must not be applicable either to internal actions, compar'd among themselves, or to external objects, when plac'd in opposition to other external objects. For as morality is suppos'd to attend certain relations, if these relations cou'd belong to internal actions consider'd singly, it wou'd follow, that we might be guilty of crimes in ourselves, and independent of our situation, with respect to the universe: And in like manner, if these moral relations cou'd be apply'd to external objects, it wou'd follow, that even inanimate beings wou'd be susceptible of moral beauty and deformity. Now it seems difficult to imagine, that any relation can be discover'd betwixt our passions, volitions and actions, compar'd to external objects, which relation might not belong either to these passions and volitions, or to these external objects, compar'd among *themselves*.

22   But it will be still more difficult to fulfil the *second* condition, requisite to justify this system. According to the principles of those who maintain an abstract rational difference betwixt moral good and evil, and a natural fitness and unfitness of things, 'tis not only suppos'd, that these relations, being eternal and immutable, are the same, when consider'd by every rational creature, but their *effects* are also suppos'd to be necessarily the same; and 'tis concluded they have no less, or rather a greater, influence in directing the will of the deity, than in governing the rational and virtuous of our own species. These two particulars are evidently distinct. 'Tis one thing to know virtue, and another to conform the will to it. In order, therefore, to prove that the measures of right and wrong are eternal laws, *obligatory* on every rational mind, 'tis not sufficient to shew the relations upon which they are founded: We must also point out the connexion betwixt the relation and the will; and must prove that this connexion is so necessary, that in every well-dispos'd mind, it must take place and have its influence; tho' the difference betwixt these minds be in other respects

immense and infinite. Now besides what I have already prov'd, that even in human nature no relation can ever alone produce any action; besides this, I say, it has been shewn, in treating of the understanding, that there is no connexion of cause and effect, such as this is suppos'd to be, which is discoverable otherwise than by experience, and of which we can pretend to have any security by the simple consideration of the objects. All beings in the universe, consider'd in themselves, appear entirely loose and independent of each other. 'Tis only by experience we learn their influence and connexion; and this influence we ought never to extend beyond experience.

Thus it will be impossible to fulfil the *first* condition required to the system of eternal rational measures of right and wrong; because it is impossible to shew those relations, upon which such a distinction may be founded: And 'tis as impossible to fulfil the *second* condition; because we cannot prove *a priori*, that these relations, if they really existed and were perceiv'd, wou'd be universally forcible and obligatory. 23

But to make these general reflections more clear and convincing, we may illustrate them by some particular instances, wherein this character of moral good or evil is the most universally acknowledg'd. Of all crimes that human creatures are capable of committing, the most horrid and unnatural is ingratitude, especially when it is committed against parents, and appears in the more flagrant instances of wounds and death. This is acknowledg'd by all mankind, philosophers as well as the people; the question only arises among philosophers, whether the guilt or moral deformity of this action be discover'd by demonstrative reasoning, or be felt by an internal sense, and by means of some sentiment, which the reflecting on such an action naturally occasions. This question will soon be decided against the former opinion, if we can shew the same relations in other objects, without the notion of any guilt or iniquity attending them. Reason or science is nothing but the comparing of ideas, and the discovery of their relations; and if the same relations have different characters, it must evidently follow, that those characters are not discover'd merely by reason. To put the affair, therefore, to this trial, let us chuse any inanimate object, such as an oak or elm; and let us suppose, that by the dropping of its seed, it produces a sapling below it, which springing up by degrees, at last overtops and destroys the parent tree: I ask, if in this instance there be wanting any relation, which is discoverable in parricide or ingratitude? Is not the one tree the cause of the other's existence; and the latter the cause of the destruction of the former, in the same manner as when a child murders his parent? 'Tis not sufficient to reply, that a choice or will is wanting. For in the case of parricide, a will does not give rise to any *different* relations, but is only the cause from which the action is deriv'd; and consequently 24 produces the *same* relations, that in the oak or elm arise from some other principles. 'Tis a will or choice, that determines a man to kill his parent; and they are the laws of matter and motion, that determine a sapling to destroy the oak, from which it sprung. Here then the same relations have different causes; but still the relations are the same: And as their discovery is not in both cases attended with a notion of immorality, it follows, that that notion does not arise from such a discovery.

25   But to chuse an instance, still more resembling; I wou'd fain ask any one, why incest in the human species is criminal, and why the very same action, and the same relations in animals have not the smallest moral turpitude and deformity? If it be answer'd, that this action is innocent in animals, because they have not reason sufficient to discover its turpitude; but that man, being endow'd with that faculty, which *ought* to restrain him to his duty, the same action instantly becomes criminal to him; shou'd this be said, I wou'd reply, that this is evidently arguing in a circle. For before reason can perceive this turpitude, the turpitude must exist; and consequently is independent of the decisions of our reason, and is their object more properly than their effect. According to this system, then, every animal, that has sense, and appetite, and will; that is, every animal must be susceptible of all the same virtues and vices, for which we ascribe praise and blame to human creatures. All the difference is, that our superior reason may serve to discover the vice or virtue, and by that means may augment the blame or praise: But still this discovery supposes a separate being in these moral distinctions, and a being, which depends only on the will and appetite, and which, both in thought and reality, may be distinguish'd from the reason. Animals are susceptible of the same relations, with respect to each other, as the human species, and therefore wou'd also be susceptible of the same morality, if the essence of morality consisted in these relations. Their want of a sufficient degree of reason may hinder them from perceiving the duties and obligations of morality, but can never hinder these duties from existing; since they must antecedently exist, in order to their being perceiv'd. Reason must find them, and can never produce them. This argument deserves to be weigh'd, as being, in my opinion, entirely decisive.

26   Nor does this reasoning only prove, that morality consists not in any relations, that are the objects of science; but if examin'd, will prove with equal certainty, that it consists not in any *matter of fact*, which can be discover'd by the understanding. This is the *second* part of our argument; and if it can be made evident, we may conclude, that morality is not an object of reason. But can there be any difficulty in proving, that vice and virtue are not matters of fact, whose existence we can infer by reason? Take any action allow'd to be vicious: Wilful murder, for instance. Examine it in all

lights, and see if you can find that matter of fact, or real existence, which you call *vice*. In which-ever way you take it, you find only certain passions, motives, volitions, and thoughts. There is no other matter of fact in the case. The vice entirely escapes you, as long as you consider the object. You never can find it, till you turn your reflection into your own breast, and find a sentiment of disapprobation, which arises in you, towards this action. Here is a matter of fact; but 'tis the object of feeling, not of reason. It lies in yourself, not in the object. So that when you pronounce any action or character to be vicious, you mean nothing, but that from the constitution of your nature you have a feeling or sentiment of blame from the contemplation of it. Vice and virtue, therefore, may be compar'd to sounds, colours, heat and cold, which, according to modern philosophy, are not qualities in objects, but perceptions in the mind: And this discovery in morals, like that other in physics, is to be regarded as a considerable advancement of the speculative sciences; tho', like that too, it has little or no influence on practice. Nothing can be more real, or concern us more, than our own sentiments of pleasure and uneasiness; and if these be favourable to virtue, and unfavourable to vice, no more can be requisite to the regulation of our conduct and behaviour.

I cannot forbear adding to these reasonings an observation, which may,   27
perhaps, be found of some importance. In every system of morality, which I have hitherto met with, I have always remark'd, that the author proceeds for some time in the ordinary way of reasoning, and establishes the being of a God, or makes observations concerning human affairs; when of a sudden I am surpriz'd to find, that instead of the usual copulations of propositions, *is*, and *is not*, I meet with no proposition that is not connected with an *ought*, or an *ought not*. This change is imperceptible; but is, however, of the last consequence. For as this *ought*, or *ought not*, expresses some new relation or affirmation, 'tis necessary that it shou'd be observ'd and explain'd; and at the same time that a reason shou'd be given, for what seems altogether inconceivable, how this new relation can be a deduction from others, which are entirely different from it. But as authors do not commonly use this precaution, I shall presume to recommend it to the readers; and am persuaded, that this small attention wou'd subvert all the vulgar systems of morality, and let us see, that the distinction of vice and virtue is not founded merely on the relations of objects, nor is perceiv'd by reason.

Section II. Moral distinctions deriv'd from a moral sense.

Thus the course of the argument leads us to conclude, that since vice and   1
virtue are not discoverable merely by reason, or the comparison of ideas, it must be by means of some impression or sentiment they occasion, that we

are able to mark the difference betwixt them. Our decisions concerning moral rectitude and depravity are evidently perceptions; and as all perceptions are either impressions or ideas, the exclusion of the one is a convincing argument for the other. Morality, therefore, is more properly felt than judg'd of; tho' this feeling or sentiment is commonly so soft and gentle, that we are apt to confound it with an idea, according to our common custom of taking all things for the same, which have any near resemblance to each other.

2   The next question is, of what nature are these impressions, and after what manner do they operate upon us? Here we cannot remain long in suspense, but must pronounce the impression arising from virtue, to be agreeable, and that proceeding from vice to be uneasy. Every moment's experience must convince us of this. There is no spectacle so fair and beautiful as a noble and generous action; nor any which gives us more abhorrence than one that is cruel and treacherous. No enjoyment equals the satisfaction we receive from the company of those we love and esteem; as the greatest of all punishments is to be oblig'd to pass our lives with those we hate or contemn. A very play or romance may afford us instances of this pleasure, which virtue conveys to us; and pain, which arises from vice.

3   Now since the distinguishing impressions, by which moral good or evil is known, are nothing but *particular* pains or pleasures; it follows, that in all enquiries concerning these moral distinctions, it will be sufficient to shew the principles, which make us feel a satisfaction or uneasiness from the survey of any character, in order to satisfy us why the character is laudable or blameable. An action, or sentiment, or character is virtuous or vicious; why? because its view causes a pleasure or uneasiness of a particular kind. In giving a reason, therefore, for the pleasure or uneasiness, we sufficiently explain the vice or virtue. To have the sense of virtue, is nothing but to *feel* a satisfaction of a particular kind from the contemplation of a character. The very *feeling* constitutes our praise or admiration. We go no farther; nor do we enquire into the cause of the satisfaction. We do not infer a character to be virtuous, because it pleases: But in feeling that it pleases after such a particular manner, we in effect feel that it is virtuous. The case is the same as in our judgments concerning all kinds of beauty, and tastes, and sensations. Our approbation is imply'd in the immediate pleasure they convey to us.

4   I have objected to the system, which establishes eternal rational measures of right and wrong, that 'tis impossible to shew, in the actions of reasonable creatures, any relations, which are not found in external objects; and therefore, if morality always attended these relations, 'twere possible for inanimate matter to become virtuous or vicious. Now it may, in like

manner, be objected to the present system, that if virtue and vice be determin'd by pleasure and pain, these qualities must, in every case, arise
from the sensations; and consequently any object, whether animate or
inanimate, rational or irrational, might become morally good or evil, provided it can excite a satisfaction or uneasiness. But tho' this objection
seems to be the very same, it has by no means the same force, in the one
case as in the other. For, *first*, 'tis evident, that under the term *pleasure*, we
comprehend sensations, which are very different from each other, and
which have only such a distant resemblance, as is requisite to make them
be express'd by the same abstract term. A good composition of music and
a bottle of good wine equally produce pleasure; and, what is more, their
goodness is determin'd merely by the pleasure. But shall we say upon that
account, that the wine is harmonious, or the music of a good flavour? In
like manner an inanimate object, and the character or sentiments of any
person may, both of them, give satisfaction; but as the satisfaction is
different, this keeps our sentiments concerning them from being confounded, and makes us ascribe virtue to the one, and not to the other. Nor
is every sentiment of pleasure or pain, which arises from characters and
actions, of that *peculiar* kind, which makes us praise or condemn. The
good qualities of an enemy are hurtful to us; but may still command our
esteem and respect. 'Tis only when a character is consider'd in general,
without reference to our particular interest, that it causes such a feeling or
sentiment, as denominates it morally good or evil. 'Tis true, those sentiments, from interest and morals, are apt to be confounded, and naturally
run into one another. It seldom happens, that we do not think an enemy
vicious, and can distinguish betwixt his opposition to our interest and real
villainy or baseness. But this hinders not, but that the sentiments are, in
themselves, distinct; and a man of temper and judgment may preserve
himself from these illusions. In like manner, tho' 'tis certain a musical
voice is nothing but one that naturally gives a *particular* kind of pleasure;
yet 'tis difficult for a man to be sensible, that the voice of an enemy is
agreeable, or to allow it to be musical. But a person of a fine ear, who has
the command of himself, can separate these feelings, and give praise to
what deserves it.

Secondly, We may call to remembrance the preceding system of the   5
passions, in order to remark a still more considerable difference among
our pains and pleasures. Pride and humility, love and hatred are excited,
when there is any thing presented to us, that both bears a relation to the
object of the passion, and produces a separate sensation related to the sensation of the passion. Now virtue and vice are attended with these circumstances. They must necessarily be plac'd either in ourselves or others, and
excite either pleasure or uneasiness; and therefore must give rise to one of

these four passions; which clearly distinguishes them from the pleasure and pain arising from inanimate objects, that often bear no relation to us: And this is, perhaps, the most considerable effect that virtue and vice have upon the human mind.

6   It may now be ask'd *in general,* concerning this pain or pleasure, that distinguishes moral good and evil, *From what principles is it deriv'd, and whence does it arise in the human mind?* To this I reply, *first,* that 'tis absurd to imagine, that in every particular instance, these sentiments are produc'd by an *original* quality and *primary* constitution. For as the number of our duties is, in a manner, infinite, 'tis impossible that our original instincts shou'd extend to each of them, and from our very first infancy impress on the human mind all that multitude of precepts, which are contain'd in the compleatest system of ethics. Such a method of proceeding is not conformable to the usual maxims, by which nature is conducted, where a few principles produce all that variety we observe in the universe, and every thing is carry'd on in the easiest and most simple manner. 'Tis necessary, therefore, to abridge these primary impulses, and find some more general principles, upon which all our notions of morals are founded.

7   But in the *second* place, shou'd it be ask'd, whether we ought to search for these principles in *nature,* or whether we must look for them in some other origin? I wou'd reply, that our answer to this question depends upon the definition of the word, Nature, than which there is none more ambiguous and equivocal. If *nature* be oppos'd to miracles, not only the distinction betwixt vice and virtue is natural, but also every event, which has ever happen'd in the world, *excepting those miracles, on which our religion is founded.* In saying, then, that the sentiments of vice and virtue are natural in this sense, we make no very extraordinary discovery.

8   But *nature* may also be opposed to rare and unusual; and in this sense of the word, which is the common one, there may often arise disputes concerning what is natural or unnatural; and one may in general affirm, that we are not possess'd of any very precise standard, by which these disputes can be decided. Frequent and rare depend upon the number of examples we have observ'd; and as this number may gradually encrease or diminish, 'twill be impossible to fix any exact boundaries betwixt them. We may only affirm on this head, that if ever there was any thing, which cou'd be call'd natural in this sense, the sentiments of morality certainly may; since there never was any nation of the world, nor any single person in any nation, who was utterly depriv'd of them, and who never, in any instance, showed the least approbation or dislike of manners. These sentiments are so rooted in our constitution and temper, that without entirely confounding the human mind by disease or madness, 'tis impossible to extirpate and destroy them.

But *nature* may also be opposed to artifice, as well as to what is rare and   9
unusual; and in this sense it may be disputed, whether the notions of
virtue be natural or not. We readily forget, that the designs, and projects,
and views of men are principles as necessary in their operation as heat and
cold, moist and dry: But taking them to be free and entirely our own, 'tis
usual for us to set them in opposition to the other principles of nature.
Shou'd it, therefore, be demanded, whether the sense of virtue be natural
or artificial, I am of opinion, that 'tis impossible for me at present to give
any precise answer to this question. Perhaps it will appear afterwards, that
our sense of some virtues is artificial, and that of others natural. The discussion of this question will be more proper, when we enter upon an exact
detail of each particular vice and virtue.[1]

Mean while it may not be amiss to observe from these definitions of *nat-*   10
ural and *unnatural,* that nothing can be more unphilosophical than those
systems, which assert, that virtue is the same with what is natural, and vice
with what is unnatural. For in the first sense of the word, Nature, as opposed to miracles, both vice and virtue are equally natural; and in the second sense, as oppos'd to what is unusual, perhaps virtue will be found to be
the most unnatural. At least it must be own'd, that heroic virtue, being as
unusual, is as little natural as the most brutal barbarity. As to the third sense
of the word, 'tis certain, that both vice and virtue are equally artificial, and
out of nature. For however it may be disputed, whether the notion of a merit
or demerit in certain actions be natural or artificial, 'tis evident, that the actions themselves are artificial, and are perform'd with a certain design and
intention; otherwise they cou'd never be rank'd under any of these denominations. 'Tis impossible, therefore, that the character of natural and unnatural can ever, in any sense, mark the boundaries of vice and virtue.

Thus we are still brought back to our first position, that virtue is distin-   11
guished by the pleasure, and vice by the pain, that any action, sentiment
or character, gives us by the mere view and contemplation. This decision
is very commodious; because it reduces us to this simple question, *Why*
any action or sentiment, upon the general view or survey, gives a certain satis-
faction or uneasiness, in order to shew the origin of its moral rectitude or
depravity, without looking for any incomprehensible relations and qualities, which never did exist in nature, nor even in our imagination, by any
clear and distinct conception. I flatter myself I have executed a great part
of my present design by a state of the question, which appears to me so
free from ambiguity and obscurity.

---

[1] In the following discourse *natural* is also opposed sometimes to *civil*, sometimes to
moral. The opposition will always discover the sense, in which it is taken.

82   *A Treatise of Human Nature*

Part II:
Of Justice and Injustice.

Section I. Justice, whether a natural or artificial virtue?

1   I have already hinted, that our sense of every kind of virtue is not natural; but that there are some virtues, that produce pleasure and approbation by means of an artifice or contrivance, which arises from the circumstances and necessities of mankind. Of this kind I assert *justice* to be; and shall endeavour to defend this opinion by a short, and, I hope, convincing argument, before I examine the nature of the artifice, from which the sense of that virtue is deriv'd.

2   'Tis evident, that when we praise any actions, we regard only the motives that produc'd them, and consider the actions as signs or indications of certain principles in the mind and temper. The external performance has no merit. We must look within to find the moral quality. This we cannot do directly; and therefore fix our attention on actions, as on external signs. But these actions are still consider'd as signs; and the ultimate object of our praise and approbation is the motive, that produc'd them.

3   After the same manner, when we require any action, or blame a person for not performing it, we always suppose, that one in that situation shou'd be influenc'd by the proper motive of that action, and we esteem it vicious in him to be regardless of it. If we find, upon enquiry, that the virtuous motive was still powerful over his breast, tho' check'd in its operation by some circumstances unknown to us, we retract our blame, and have the same esteem for him, as if he had actually perform'd the action, which we require of him.

4   It appears, therefore, that all virtuous actions derive their merit only from virtuous motives, and are consider'd merely as signs of those motives. From this principle I conclude, that the first virtuous motive, which bestows a merit on any action, can never be a regard to the virtue of that action, but must be some other natural motive or principle. To suppose, that the mere regard to the virtue of the action, may be the first motive, which produc'd the action, and render'd it virtuous, is to reason in a circle. Before we can have such a regard, the action must be really virtuous; and this virtue must be deriv'd from some virtuous motive: And consequently the virtuous motive must be different from the regard to the virtue of the action. A virtuous motive is requisite to render an action virtuous. An action must be virtuous, before we can have a regard to its virtue. Some virtuous motive, therefore, must be antecedent to that regard.

5   Nor is this merely a metaphysical subtility; but enters into all our reasonings in common life, tho' perhaps we may not be able to place it in

such distinct philosophical terms. We blame a father for neglecting his child. Why? because it shews a want of natural affection, which is the duty of every parent. Were not natural affection a duty, the care of children cou'd not be a duty; and 'twere impossible we cou'd have the duty in our eye in the attention we give to our offspring. In this case, therefore, all men suppose a motive to the action distinct from a sense of duty.

Here is a man, that does many benevolent actions; relieves the dis- 6
tress'd, comforts the afflicted, and extends his bounty even to the greatest strangers. No character can be more amiable and virtuous. We regard these actions as proofs of the greatest humanity. This humanity bestows a merit on the actions. A regard to this merit is, therefore, a secondary consideration, and deriv'd from the antecedent principle of humanity, which is meritorious and laudable.

In short, it may be establish'd as an undoubted maxim, *that no action* 7
can be virtuous, or morally good, unless there be in human nature some motive to produce it, distinct from the sense of its morality.

But may not the sense of morality or duty produce an action, without 8
any other motive? I answer, It may: But this is no objection to the present doctrine. When any virtuous motive or principle is common in human nature, a person, who feels his heart devoid of that principle, may hate himself upon that account, and may perform the action without the motive, from a certain sense of duty, in order to acquire by practice, that virtuous principle, or at least, to disguise to himself, as much as possible, his want of it. A man that really feels no gratitude in his temper, is still pleas'd to perform grateful actions, and thinks he has, by that means, fulfill'd his duty. Actions are at first only consider'd as signs of motives: But 'tis usual, in this case, as in all others, to fix our attention on the signs, and neglect, in some measure, the thing signify'd. But tho', on some occasions, a person may perform an action merely out of regard to its moral obligation, yet still this supposes in human nature some distinct principles, which are capable of producing the action, and whose moral beauty renders the action meritorious.

Now to apply all this to the present case; I suppose a person to have lent 9
me a sum of money, on condition that it be restor'd in a few days; and also suppose, that after the expiration of the term agreed on, he demands the sum: I ask, *What reason or motive have I to restore the money?* It will, perhaps, be said, that my regard to justice, and abhorrence of villainy and knavery, are sufficient reasons for me, if I have the least grain of honesty, or sense of duty and obligation. And this answer, no doubt, is just and satisfactory to man in his civiliz'd state, and when train'd up according to a certain discipline and education. But in his rude and more *natural* condition, if you are pleas'd to call such a condition natural, this answer wou'd be rejected as perfectly unintelligible and sophistical. For one in that situation

wou'd immediately ask you, *Wherein consists this honesty and justice, which you find in restoring a loan, and abstaining from the property of others?* It does not surely lie in the external action. It must, therefore, be plac'd in the motive, from which the external action is deriv'd. This motive can never be a regard to the honesty of the action. For 'tis a plain fallacy to say, that a virtuous motive is requisite to render an action honest, and at the same time that a regard to the honesty is the motive of the action. We can never have a regard to the virtue of an action, unless the action be antecedently virtuous. No action can be virtuous, but so far as it proceeds from a virtuous motive. A virtuous motive, therefore, must precede the regard to the virtue; and 'tis impossible, that the virtuous motive and the regard to the virtue can be the same.

10   'Tis requisite, then, to find some motive to acts of justice and honesty, distinct from our regard to the honesty; and in this lies the great difficulty. For shou'd we say, that a concern for our private interest or reputation is the legitimate motive to all honest actions; it wou'd follow, that wherever that concern ceases, honesty can no longer have place. But 'tis certain, that self-love, when it acts at its liberty, instead of engaging us to honest actions, is the source of all injustice and violence; nor can a man ever correct those vices, without correcting and restraining the *natural* movements of that appetite.

11   But shou'd it be affirm'd, that the reason or motive of such actions is the *regard to publick interest*, to which nothing is more contrary than examples of injustice and dishonesty; shou'd this be said, I wou'd propose the three following considerations, as worthy of our attention. *First,* public interest is not naturally attach'd to the observation of the rules of justice; but is only connected with it, after an artificial convention for the establishment of these rules, as shall be shewn more at large hereafter. *Secondly,* if we suppose, that the loan was secret, and that it is necessary for the interest of the person, that the money be restor'd in the same manner (as when the lender wou'd conceal his riches), in that case the example ceases, and the public is no longer interested in the actions of the borrower; tho' I suppose there is no moralist, who will affirm, that the duty and obligation ceases. *Thirdly,* experience sufficiently proves, that men, in the ordinary conduct of life, look not so far as the public interest, when they pay their creditors, perform their promises, and abstain from theft, and robbery, and injustice of every kind. That is a motive too remote and too sublime to affect the generality of mankind, and operate with any force in actions so contrary to private interest as are frequently those of justice and common honesty.

12   In general, it may be affirm'd, that there is no such passion in human minds, as the love of mankind, merely as such, independent of personal

qualities, of services, or of relation to ourself. 'Tis true, there is no human, and indeed no sensible, creature, whose happiness or misery does not, in some measure, affect us, when brought near to us, and represented in lively colours: But this proceeds merely from sympathy, and is no proof of such an universal affection to mankind, since this concern extends itself beyond our own species. An affection betwixt the sexes is a passion evidently implanted in human nature; and this passion not only appears in its peculiar symptoms, but also in inflaming every other principle of affection, and raising a stronger love from beauty, wit, kindness, than what wou'd otherwise flow from them. Were there an universal love among all human creatures, it wou'd appear after the same manner. Any degree of a good quality wou'd cause a stronger affection than the same degree of a bad quality wou'd cause hatred; contrary to what we find by experience. Men's tempers are different, and some have a propensity to the tender, and others to the rougher, affections: But in the main, we may affirm, that man in general, or human nature, is nothing but the object both of love and hatred, and requires some other cause, which by a double relation of impressions and ideas, may excite these passions. In vain wou'd we endeavour to elude this hypothesis. There are no phænomena that point out any such kind affection to men, independent of their merit, and every other circumstance. We love company in general; but 'tis as we love any other amusement. An *Englishman* in *Italy* is a friend: A *European* in *China*; and perhaps a man wou'd be belov'd as such, were we to meet him in the moon. But this proceeds only from the relation to ourselves; which in these cases gathers force by being confin'd to a few persons.

If public benevolence, therefore, or a regard to the interests of man-   13
kind, cannot be the original motive to justice, much less can *private benev-olence*, or *a regard to the interests of the party concern'd*, be this motive. For what if he be my enemy, and has given me just cause to hate him? What if he be a vicious man, and deserves the hatred of all mankind? What if he be a miser, and can make no use of what I wou'd deprive him of? What if he be a profligate debauchee, and wou'd rather receive harm than benefit from large possessions? What if I be in necessity, and have urgent motives to acquire something to my family? In all these cases, the original motive to justice wou'd fail; and consequently the justice itself, and along with it all property, right, and obligation.

A rich man lies under a moral obligation to communicate to those in ne-   14
cessity a share of his superfluities. Were private benevolence the original motive to justice, a man wou'd not be oblig'd to leave others in the possession of more than he is oblig'd to give them. At least the difference wou'd be very inconsiderable. Men generally fix their affections more on what they are possess'd of, than on what they never enjoy'd: For this reason, it

wou'd be greater cruelty to dispossess a man of any thing, than not to give it him. But who will assert, that this is the only foundation of justice?

15   Besides, we must consider, that the chief reason why men attach themselves so much to their possessions is, that they consider them as their property, and as secur'd to them inviolably by the laws of society. But this is a secondary consideration, and dependent on the preceding notions of justice and property.

16   A man's property is suppos'd to be fenc'd against every mortal, in every possible case. But private benevolence towards the proprietor is, and ought to be, weaker in some persons, than in others: And in many, or indeed in most persons, must absolutely fail. Private benevolence, therefore, is not the original motive of justice.

17   From all this it follows, that we have naturally no real or universal motive for observing the laws of equity, but the very equity and merit of that observance; and as no action can be equitable or meritorious, where it cannot arise from some separate motive, there is here an evident sophistry and reasoning in a circle. Unless, therefore, we will allow, that nature has establish'd a sophistry, and render'd it necessary and unavoidable, we must allow, that the sense of justice and injustice is not deriv'd from nature, but arises artificially, tho' necessarily from education, and human conventions.

18   I shall add, as a corollary to this reasoning, that since no action can be laudable or blameable, without some motives or impelling passions, distinct from the sense of morals, these distinct passions must have a great influence on that sense. 'Tis according to their general force in human nature, that we blame or praise. In judging of the beauty of animal bodies, we always carry in our eye the economy of a certain species; and where the limbs and features observe that proportion, which is common to the species, we pronounce them handsome and beautiful. In like manner we always consider the *natural* and *usual* force of the passions, when we determine concerning vice and virtue; and if the passions depart very much from the common measures on either side, they are always disapprov'd as vicious. A man naturally loves his children better than his nephews, his nephews better than his cousins, his cousins better than strangers, where every thing else is equal. Hence arise our common measures of duty, in preferring the one to the other. Our sense of duty always follows the common and natural course of our passions.

19   To avoid giving offence, I must here observe, that when I deny justice to be a natural virtue, I make use of the word *natural*, only as oppos'd to *artificial*. In another sense of the word; as no principle of the human mind is more natural than a sense of virtue; so no virtue is more natural than justice. Mankind is an inventive species; and where an invention is obvious and absolutely necessary, it may as properly be said to be natural as any

thing that proceeds immediately from original principles, without the intervention of thought or reflection. Tho' the rules of justice be *artificial*, they are not *arbitrary*. Nor is the expression improper to call them *Laws of Nature*; if by natural we understand what is common to any species, or even if we confine it to mean what is inseparable from the species.

Section II. Of the origin of justice and property.

We now proceed to examine two questions, viz. *concerning the manner, in which the rules of justice are establish'd by the artifice of men*; and *concerning the reasons, which determine us to attribute to the observance or neglect of these rules a moral beauty and deformity*. These questions will appear afterwards to be distinct. We shall begin with the former.

Of all the animals, with which this globe is peopled, there is none towards whom nature seems, at first sight, to have exercis'd more cruelty than towards man, in the numberless wants and necessities, with which she has loaded him, and in the slender means, which she affords to the relieving these necessities. In other creatures these two particulars generally compensate each other. If we consider the lion as a voracious and carnivorous animal, we shall easily discover him to be very necessitous; but if we turn our eye to his make and temper, his agility, his courage, his arms, and his force, we shall find, that his advantages hold proportion with his wants. The sheep and ox are depriv'd of all these advantages; but their appetites are moderate, and their food is of easy purchase. In man alone, this unnatural conjunction of infirmity, and of necessity, may be observ'd in its greatest perfection. Not only the food, which is requir'd for his sustenance, flies his search and approach, or at least requires his labour to be produc'd, but he must be possess'd of cloaths and lodging to defend him against the injuries of the weather; tho' to consider him only in himself, he is provided neither with arms, nor force, nor other natural abilities, which are in any degree answerable to so many necessities.

'Tis by society alone he is able to supply his defects, and raise himself up to an equality with his fellow-creatures, and even acquire a superiority above them. By society all his infirmities are compensated; and tho' in that situation his wants multiply every moment upon him, yet his abilities are still more augmented, and leave him in every respect more satisfy'd and happy, than 'tis possible for him, in his savage and solitary condition, ever to become. When every individual person labours apart, and only for himself, his force is too small to execute any considerable work; his labour being employ'd in supplying all his different necessities, he never attains a perfection in any particular art; and as his force and success are not at all times equal, the least failure in either of these particulars must be attended with inevitable ruin and misery. Society provides a remedy for these *three* inconveniencies. By the conjunction of forces, our power is augmented: By the partition of employments, our ability encreases: And by mutual succour we are less expos'd to fortune and accidents. 'Tis by this additional *force*, *ability*, and *security*, that society becomes advantageous.

4   But in order to form society, 'tis requisite not only that it be advantageous, but also that men be sensible of these advantages; and 'tis impossible, in their wild uncultivated state, that by study and reflection alone, they shou'd ever be able to attain this knowledge. Most fortunately, therefore, there is conjoin'd to those necessities, whose remedies are remote and obscure, another necessity, which having a present and more obvious remedy, may justly be regarded as the first and original principle of human society. This necessity is no other than that natural appetite betwixt the sexes, which unites them together, and preserves their union, till a new tye takes place in their concern for their common offspring. This new concern becomes also a principle of union betwixt the parents and offspring, and forms a more numerous society; where the parents govern by the advantage of their superior strength and wisdom, and at the same time are restrain'd in the exercise of their authority by that natural affection, which they bear their children. In a little time, custom and habit operating on the tender minds of the children, makes them sensible of the advantages, which they may reap from society, as well as fashions them by degrees for it, by rubbing off those rough corners and untoward affections, which prevent their coalition.

5   For it must be confest, that however the circumstances of human nature may render a union necessary, and however those passions of lust and natural affection may seem to render it unavoidable; yet there are other particulars in our *natural temper*, and in our *outward circumstances*, which are very incommodious, and are even contrary to the requisite conjunction. Among the former, we may justly esteem our *selfishness* to be the most considerable. I am sensible, that, generally speaking, the representations of this quality have been carry'd much too far; and that the descriptions, which certain philosophers delight so much to form of mankind in this particular, are as wide of nature as any accounts of monsters, which we meet with in fables and romances. So far from thinking, that men have no affection for any thing beyond themselves, I am of opinion, that tho' it be rare to meet with one, who loves any single person better than himself; yet 'tis as rare to meet with one, in whom all the kind affections, taken together, do not over-balance all the selfish. Consult common experience: Do you not see, that tho' the whole expence of the family be generally under the direction of the master of it, yet there are few that do not bestow the largest part of their fortunes on the pleasures of their wives, and the education of their children, reserving the smallest portion for their own

proper use and entertainment. This is what we may observe concerning such as have those endearing ties; and may presume, that the case wou'd be the same with others, were they plac'd in a like situation.

But tho' this generosity must be acknowledg'd to the honour of human   6
nature, we may at the same time remark, that so noble an affection, instead of fitting men for large societies, is almost as contrary to them, as the most narrow selfishness. For while each person loves himself better than any other single person, and in his love to others bears the greatest affection to his relations and acquaintance, this must necessarily produce an opposition of passions, and a consequent opposition of actions; which cannot but be dangerous to the new-establish'd union.

'Tis however worth while to remark, that this contrariety of passions   7
wou'd be attended with but small danger, did it not concur with a peculiarity in our *outward circumstances*, which affords it an opportunity of exerting itself. There are three different species of goods, which we are possess'd of; the internal satisfaction of our mind, the external advantages of our body, and the enjoyment of such possessions as we have acquir'd by our industry and good fortune. We are perfectly secure in the enjoyment of the first. The second may be ravish'd from us, but can be of no advantage to him who deprives us of them. The last only are both expos'd to the violence of others, and may be transferr'd without suffering any loss or alteration; while at the same time, there is not a sufficient quantity of them to supply every one's desires and necessities. As the improvement, therefore, of these goods is the chief advantage of society, so the *instability* of their possession, along with their *scarcity*, is the chief impediment.

In vain shou'd we expect to find, in *uncultivated nature*, a remedy to this   8
inconvenience; or hope for any inartificial principle of the human mind, which might controul those partial affections, and make us overcome the temptations arising from our circumstances. The idea of justice can never serve to this purpose, or be taken for a natural principle, capable of inspiring men with an equitable conduct towards each other. That virtue, as it is now understood, wou'd never have been dream'd of among rude and savage men. For the notion of injury or injustice implies an immorality or vice committed against some other person: And as every immorality is deriv'd from some defect or unsoundness of the passions, and as this defect must be judg'd of, in a great measure, from the ordinary course of nature in the constitution of the mind; 'twill be easy to know, whether we be guilty of any immorality, with regard to others, by considering the natural and usual force of those several affections, which are directed towards them. Now it appears, that in the original frame of our mind, our strongest attention is confin'd to ourselves; our next is extended to our relations and acquaintance; and 'tis only the weakest which reaches to

strangers and indifferent persons. This partiality, then, and unequal affection, must not only have an influence on our behaviour and conduct in society, but even on our ideas of vice and virtue; so as to make us regard any remarkable transgression of such a degree of partiality, either by too great an enlargement, or contraction of the affections, as vicious and immoral. This we may observe in our common judgments concerning actions, where we blame a person, who either centers all his affections in his family, or is so regardless of them, as, in any opposition of interest, to give the preference to a stranger, or mere chance acquaintance. From all which it follows, that our natural uncultivated ideas of morality, instead of providing a remedy for the partiality of our affections, do rather conform themselves to that partiality, and give it an additional force and influence.

9   The remedy, then, is not deriv'd from nature, but from *artifice*; or more properly speaking, nature provides a remedy in the judgment and understanding, for what is irregular and incommodious in the affections. For when men, from their early education in society, have become sensible of the infinite advantages that result from it, and have besides acquir'd a new affection to company and conversation; and when they have observ'd, that the principal disturbance in society arises from those goods, which we call external, and from their looseness and easy transition from one person to another; they must seek for a remedy, by putting these goods, as far as possible, on the same footing with the fix'd and constant advantages of the mind and body. This can be done after no other manner, than by a convention enter'd into by all the members of the society to bestow stability on the possession of those external goods, and leave every one in the peaceable enjoyment of what he may acquire by his fortune and industry. By this means, every one knows what he may safely possess; and the passions are restrain'd in their partial and contradictory motions. Nor is such a restraint contrary to these passions; for if so, it cou'd never be enter'd into, nor maintain'd; but it is only contrary to their heedless and impetuous movement. Instead of departing from our own interest, or from that of our nearest friends, by abstaining from the possessions of others, we cannot better consult both these interests, than by such a convention; because it is by that means we maintain society, which is so necessary to their well-being and subsistence, as well as to our own.

10   This convention is not of the nature of a *promise*: For even promises themselves, as we shall see afterwards, arise from human conventions. It is only a general sense of common interest; which sense all the members of the society express to one another, and which induces them to regulate their conduct by certain rules. I observe, that it will be for my interest to leave another in the possession of his goods, *provided* he will act in the

same manner with regard to me. He is sensible of a like interest in the regulation of his conduct. When this common sense of interest is mutually express'd, and is known to both, it produces a suitable resolution and behaviour. And this may properly enough be call'd a convention or agreement betwixt us, tho' without the interposition of a promise; since the actions of each of us have a reference to those of the other, and are perform'd upon the supposition, that something is to be perform'd on the other part. Two men, who pull the oars of a boat, do it by an agreement or convention, tho' they have never given promises to each other. Nor is the rule concerning the stability of possession the less deriv'd from human conventions, that it arises gradually, and acquires force by a slow progression, and by our repeated experience of the inconveniences of transgressing it. On the contrary, this experience assures us still more, that the sense of interest has become common to all our fellows, and gives us a confidence of the future regularity of their conduct: And 'tis only on the expectation of this, that our moderation and abstinence are founded. In like manner are languages gradually establish'd by human conventions without any promise. In like manner do gold and silver become the common measures of exchange, and are esteem'd sufficient payment for what is of a hundred times their value.

After this convention, concerning abstinence from the possessions of others, is enter'd into, and every one has acquir'd a stability in his possessions, there immediately arise the ideas of justice and injustice; as also those of *property*, *right*, and *obligation*. The latter are altogether unintelligible without first understanding the former. Our property is nothing but those goods, whose constant possession is establish'd by the laws of society; that is, by the laws of justice. Those, therefore, who make use of the words *property*, or *right*, or *obligation*, before they have explain'd the origin of justice, or even make use of them in that explication, are guilty of a very gross fallacy, and can never reason upon any solid foundation. A man's property is some object related to him. This relation is not natural, but moral, and founded on justice. 'Tis very preposterous, therefore, to imagine, that we can have any idea of property, without fully comprehending the nature of justice, and shewing its origin in the artifice and contrivance of men. The origin of justice explains that of property. The same artifice gives rise to both. As our first and most natural sentiment of morals is founded on the nature of our passions, and gives the preference to ourselves and friends, above strangers; 'tis impossible there can be naturally any such thing as a fix'd right or property, while the opposite passions of men impel them in contrary directions, and are not restrain'd by any convention or agreement.

12   No one can doubt, that the convention for the distinction of property, and for the stability of possession, is of all circumstances the most necessary to the establishment of human society, and that after the agreement for the fixing and observing of this rule, there remains little or nothing to be done towards settling a perfect harmony and concord. All the other passions, beside this of interest, are either easily restrain'd, or are not of such pernicious consequence, when indulg'd. *Vanity* is rather to be esteem'd a social passion, and a bond of union among men. *Pity* and *love* are to be consider'd in the same light. And as to *envy* and *revenge,* tho' pernicious, they operate only by intervals, and are directed against particular persons, whom we consider as our superiors or enemies. This avidity alone, of acquiring goods and possessions for ourselves and our nearest friends, is insatiable, perpetual, universal, and directly destructive of society. There scarce is any one, who is not actuated by it; and there is no one, who has not reason to fear from it, when it acts without any restraint, and gives way to its first and most natural movements. So that upon the whole, we are to esteem the difficulties in the establishment of society, to be greater or less, according to those we encounter in regulating and restraining this passion.

13   'Tis certain, that no affection of the human mind has both a sufficient force, and a proper direction to counter-balance the love of gain, and render men fit members of society, by making them abstain from the possessions of others. Benevolence to strangers is too weak for this purpose; and as to the other passions, they rather inflame this avidity, when we observe, that the larger our possessions are, the more ability we have of gratifying all our appetites. There is no passion, therefore, capable of controlling the interested affection, but the very affection itself, by an alteration of its direction. Now this alteration must necessarily take place upon the least reflection; since 'tis evident, that the passion is much better satisfy'd by its restraint, than by its liberty, and that by preserving society, we make much greater advances in the acquiring possessions, than by running into the solitary and forlorn condition, which must follow upon violence and an universal licence. The question, therefore, concerning the wickedness or goodness of human nature, enters not in the least into that other question concerning the origin of society; nor is there any thing to be consider'd but the degrees of men's sagacity or folly. For whether the passion of self-interest be esteem'd vicious or virtuous, 'tis all a case; since itself alone restrains it: So that if it be virtuous, men become social by their virtue; if vicious, their vice has the same effect.

14   Now as 'tis by establishing the rule for the stability of possession, that this passion restrains itself; if that rule be very abstruse, and of difficult invention; society must be esteem'd, in a manner, accidental, and the

effect of many ages. But if it be found, that nothing can be more simple and obvious than that rule; that every parent, in order to preserve peace among his children, must establish it; and that these first rudiments of justice must every day be improv'd, as the society enlarges: If all this appear evident, as it certainly must, we may conclude, that 'tis utterly impossible for men to remain any considerable time in that savage condition, which precedes society; but that his very first state and situation may justly be esteem'd social. This, however, hinders not, but that philosophers may, if they please, extend their reasoning to the suppos'd *state of nature*; provided they allow it to be a mere philosophical fiction, which never had, and never cou'd have any reality. Human nature being compos'd of two principal parts, which are requisite in all its actions, the affections and understanding; 'tis certain that the blind motions of the former, without the direction of the latter, incapacitate men for society: And it may be allow'd us to consider separately the effects, that result from the separate operations of these two component parts of the mind. The same liberty may be permitted to moral, which is allow'd to natural philosophers; and 'tis very usual with the latter to consider any motion as compounded and consisting of two parts separate from each other, tho' at the same time they acknowledge it to be in itself uncompounded and inseparable.

This *state of nature*, therefore, is to be regarded as a mere fiction, not   15
unlike that of the *golden age*, which poets have invented; only with this difference, that the former is describ'd as full of war, violence and injustice; whereas the latter is painted out to us, as the most charming and most peaceable condition, that can possibly be imagin'd. The seasons, in that first age of nature, were so temperate, if we may believe the poets, that there was no necessity for men to provide themselves with cloaths and houses as a security against the violence of heat and cold. The rivers flow'd with wine and milk: The oaks yielded honey; and nature spontaneously produc'd her greatest delicacies. Nor were these the chief advantages of that happy age. The storms and tempests were not alone remov'd from nature; but those more furious tempests were unknown to human breasts, which now cause such uproar, and engender such confusion. Avarice, ambition, cruelty, selfishness, were never heard of: Cordial affection, compassion, sympathy, were the only movements, with which the human mind was yet acquainted. Even the distinction of *mine* and *thine* was banish'd from that happy race of mortals, and carry'd with them the very notions of property and obligation, justice and injustice.

This, no doubt, is to be regarded as an idle fiction; but yet deserves our   16
attention, because nothing can more evidently shew the origin of those virtues, which are the subjects of our present enquiry. I have already

observ'd, that justice takes its rise from human conventions; and that these are intended as a remedy to some inconveniences, which proceed from the concurrence of certain *qualities* of the human mind with the *situation* of external objects. The qualities of the mind are *selfishness* and *limited generosity*: And the situation of external objects is their *easy change*, join'd to their *scarcity* in comparison of the wants and desires of men. But however philosophers may have been bewilder'd in those speculations, poets have been guided more infallibly, by a certain taste or common instinct, which in most kinds of reasoning goes farther than any of that art and philosophy, with which we have been yet acquainted. They easily perceiv'd, if every man had a tender regard for another, or if nature supplied abundantly all our wants and desires, that the jealousy of interest, which justice supposes, cou'd no longer have place; nor wou'd there be any occasion for those distinctions and limits of property and possession, which at present are in use among mankind. Encrease to a sufficient degree the benevolence of men, or the bounty of nature, and you render justice useless, by supplying its place with much nobler virtues, and more valuable blessings. The selfishness of men is animated by the few possessions we have, in proportion to our wants; and 'tis to restrain this selfishness, that men have been oblig'd to separate themselves from the community, and to distinguish betwixt their own goods and those of others.

17   Nor need we have recourse to the fictions of poets to learn this; but beside the reason of the thing, may discover the same truth by common experience and observation. 'Tis easy to remark, that a cordial affection renders all things common among friends; and that married people in particular mutually lose their property, and are unacquainted with the *mine* and *thine*, which are so necessary, and yet cause such disturbance in human society. The same effect arises from any alteration in the circumstances of mankind; as when there is such a plenty of any thing as satisfies all the desires of men: In which case the distinction of property is entirely lost, and every thing remains in common. This we may observe with regard to air and water, tho' the most valuable of all external objects; and may easily conclude, that if men were supplied with every thing in the same abundance, or if *every one* had the same affection and tender regard for *every one* as for himself; justice and injustice wou'd be equally unknown among mankind.

18   Here then is a proposition, which, I think, may be regarded as certain, *that 'tis only from the selfishness and confin'd generosity of men, along with the scanty provision nature has made for his wants, that justice derives its origin.* If we look backward we shall find, that this proposition bestows an additional force on some of those observations, which we have already made on this subject.

First, we may conclude from it, that a regard to public interest, or a   19
strong extensive benevolence, is not our first and original motive for the
observation of the rules of justice; since 'tis allow'd, that if men were endow'd with such a benevolence, these rules wou'd never have been
dreamt of.

Secondly, we may conclude from the same principle, that the sense of   20
justice is not founded on reason, or on the discovery of certain connexions
and relations of ideas, which are eternal, immutable, and universally obligatory. For since it is confest, that such an alteration as that above-
mention'd, in the temper and circumstances of mankind, wou'd entirely
alter our duties and obligations, 'tis necessary upon the common system,
that the sense of virtue is deriv'd from reason, to shew the change which this
must produce in the relations and ideas. But 'tis evident, that the only
cause, why the extensive generosity of man, and the perfect abundance of
every thing, wou'd destroy the very idea of justice, is because they render
it useless; and that, on the other hand, his confin'd benevolence, and his
necessitous condition, give rise to that virtue, only by making it requisite
to the publick interest, and to that of every individual. 'Twas therefore a
concern for our own, and the public interest, which made us establish the
laws of justice; and nothing can be more certain, than that it is not any relation of ideas, which gives us this concern, but our impressions and sentiments, without which every thing in nature is perfectly indifferent to us,
and can never in the least affect us. The sense of justice, therefore, is not
founded on our ideas, but on our impressions.

Thirdly, we may farther confirm the foregoing proposition, *that those*   21
impressions, which give rise to this sense of justice, are not natural to the mind
of man, but arise from artifice and human conventions. For since any considerable alteration of temper and circumstances destroys equally justice and
injustice; and since such an alteration has an effect only by changing our
own and the publick interest; it follows that the first establishment of the
rules of justice depends on these different interests. But if men pursu'd
the publick interest naturally, and with a hearty affection, they wou'd
never have dream'd of restraining each other by these rules; and if they
pursu'd their own interest, without any precaution, they wou'd run headlong into every kind of injustice and violence. These rules, therefore, are
artificial, and seek their end in an oblique and indirect manner; nor is the
interest, which gives rise to them, of a kind that cou'd be pursu'd by the
natural and inartificial passions of men.

To make this more evident, consider, that tho' the rules of justice are   22
establish'd merely by interest, their connexion with interest is somewhat
singular, and is different from what may be observ'd on other occasions. A
single act of justice is frequently contrary to *public interest*; and were it to

stand alone, without being follow'd by other acts, may, in itself, be very prejudicial to society. When a man of merit, of a beneficent disposition, restores a great fortune to a miser, or a seditious bigot, he has acted justly and laudably, but the public is a real sufferer. Nor is every single act of justice, consider'd apart, more conducive to private interest, than to public; and 'tis easily conceiv'd how a man may impoverish himself by a signal instance of integrity, and have reason to wish, that with regard to that single act, the laws of justice were for a moment suspended in the universe. But however single acts of justice may be contrary, either to public or private interest, 'tis certain, that the whole plan or scheme is highly conducive, or indeed absolutely requisite, both to the support of society, and the well-being of every individual. 'Tis impossible to separate the good from the ill. Property must be stable, and must be fix'd by general rules. Tho' in one instance the public be a sufferer, this momentary ill is amply compensated by the steady prosecution of the rule, and by the peace and order, which it establishes in society. And even every individual person must find himself a gainer, on ballancing the account; since, without justice, society must immediately dissolve, and every one must fall into that savage and solitary condition, which is infinitely worse than the worst situation that can possibly be suppos'd in society. When therefore men have had experience enough to observe, that whatever may be the consequence of any single act of justice, perform'd by a single person, yet the whole system of actions, concurr'd in by the whole society, is infinitely advantageous to the whole, and to every part; it is not long before justice and property take place. Every member of society is sensible of this interest: Every one expresses this sense to his fellows, along with the resolution he has taken of squaring his actions by it, on condition that others will do the same. No more is requisite to induce any one of them to perform an act of justice, who has the first opportunity. This becomes an example to others. And thus justice establishes itself by a kind of convention or agreement; that is, by a sense of interest, suppos'd to be common to all, and where every single act is perform'd in expectation that others are to perform the like. Without such a convention, no one wou'd ever have dream'd, that there was such a virtue as justice, or have been induc'd to conform his actions to it. Taking any single act, my justice may be pernicious in every respect; and 'tis only upon the supposition, that others are to imitate my example, that I can be induc'd to embrace that virtue; since nothing but this combination can render justice advantageous, or afford me any motives to conform myself to its rules.

23   We come now to the *second* question we propos'd, *viz. Why we annex the idea of virtue to justice, and of vice to injustice.* This question will not detain us long after the principles, which we have already establish'd. All we can

say of it at present will be dispatch'd in a few words: And for farther satisfaction, the reader must wait till we come to the *third* part of this book.
The *natural* obligation to justice, *viz.* interest, has been fully explain'd;
but as to the *moral* obligation, or the sentiment of right and wrong, 'twill
first be requisite to examine the natural virtues, before we can give a full
and satisfactory account of it.

After men have found by experience, that their selfishness and confin'd   24
generosity, acting at their liberty, totally incapacitate them for society; and
at the same time have observ'd, that society is necessary to the satisfaction
of those very passions, they are naturally induc'd to lay themselves under
the restraint of such rules, as may render their commerce more safe and
commodious. To the imposition then, and observance of these rules, both
in general, and in every particular instance, they are at first mov'd only by
a regard to interest; and this motive, on the first formation of society, is
sufficiently strong and forcible. But when society has become numerous,
and has encreas'd to a tribe or nation, this interest is more remote; nor do
men so readily perceive, that disorder and confusion follow upon every
breach of these rules, as in a more narrow and contracted society. But tho'
in our own actions we may frequently lose sight of that interest, which we
have in maintaining order, and may follow a lesser and more present interest, we never fail to observe the prejudice we receive, either mediately or
immediately, from the injustice of others; as not being in that case either
blinded by passion, or byass'd by any contrary temptation. Nay when the
injustice is so distant from us as no way to affect our interest, it still displeases us; because we consider it as prejudicial to human society, and
pernicious to every one that approaches the person guilty of it. We partake
of their uneasiness by *sympathy*; and as every thing, which gives uneasiness in human actions, upon the general survey, is call'd Vice, and whatever produces satisfaction, in the same manner, is denominated Virtue;
this is the reason why the sense of moral good and evil follows upon justice and injustice. And tho' this sense, in the present case, be deriv'd only
from contemplating the actions of others, yet we fail not to extend it even
to our own actions. The *general rule* reaches beyond those instances, from
which it arose; while at the same time we naturally *sympathize* with others
in the sentiments they entertain of us. *Thus self-interest is the original motive to the* establishment *of justice: But a* sympathy *with public interest is the
source of the* moral approbation, *which attends that virtue.* This latter principle of sympathy is too weak to controul our passions; but has sufficient
force to influence our taste, and give us the sentiments of approbation or
blame.

Tho' this progress of the sentiments be *natural*, and even necessary, 'tis   25
certain, that it is here forwarded by the artifice of politicians, who, in order

to govern men more easily, and preserve peace in human society, have endeavour'd to produce an esteem for justice, and an abhorrence of injustice.
This, no doubt, must have its effect; but nothing can be more evident,
than that the matter has been carry'd too far by certain writers on morals,
who seem to have employ'd their utmost efforts to extirpate all sense of
virtue from among mankind. Any artifice of politicians may assist nature
in the producing of those sentiments, which she suggests to us, and may
even on some occasions, produce alone an approbation or esteem for any
particular action; but 'tis impossible it shou'd be the sole cause of the distinction we make betwixt vice and virtue. For if nature did not aid us in
this particular, 'twou'd be in vain for politicians to talk of *honourable* or
dishonourable, *praise-worthy* or *blameable*. These words wou'd be perfectly
unintelligible, and wou'd no more have any idea annex'd to them, than if
they were of a tongue perfectly unknown to us. The utmost politicians can
perform, is, to extend the natural sentiments beyond their original
bounds; but still nature must furnish the materials, and give us some notion of moral distinctions.

26   As publick praise and blame encrease our esteem for justice; so private
education and instruction contribute to the same effect. For as parents
easily observe, that a man is the more useful, both to himself and others,
the greater degree of probity and honour he is endow'd with; and that
those principles have greater force, when custom and education assist interest and reflection: For these reasons they are induc'd to inculcate on
their children, from their earliest infancy, the principles of probity, and
teach them to regard the observance of those rules, by which society is
maintain'd, as worthy and honourable, and their violation as base and infamous. By this means the sentiments of honour may take root in their
tender minds, and acquire such firmness and solidity, that they may fall
little short of those principles, which are the most essential to our natures,
and the most deeply radicated in our internal constitution.

27   What farther contributes to encrease their solidity, is the interest of our
reputation, after the opinion, *that a merit or demerit attends justice or injustice*, is once firmly establish'd among mankind. There is nothing which
touches us more nearly than our reputation, and nothing on which our
reputation more depends than our conduct, with relation to the property
of others. For this reason, every one, who has any regard to his character,
or who intends to live on good terms with mankind, must fix an inviolable
law to himself, never, by any temptation, to be induc'd to violate those
principles, which are essential to a man of probity and honour.

28   I shall make only one observation before I leave this subject, *viz.* that,
tho' I assert, that in the *state of nature*, or that imaginary state, which preceded society, there be neither justice nor injustice, yet I assert not, that it

was allowable, in such a state, to violate the property of others. I only maintain, that there was no such thing as property; and consequently cou'd be no such thing as justice or injustice. I shall have occasion to make a similar reflection with regard to *promises*, when I come to treat of them; and I hope this reflection, when duly weigh'd, will suffice to remove all odium from the foregoing opinions, with regard to justice and injustice.

Section III. Of the rules, which determine property.

Tho' the establishment of the rule, concerning the stability of possession, be not only useful, but even absolutely necessary to human society, it can never serve to any purpose, while it remains in such general terms. Some method must be shewn, by which we may distinguish what particular goods are to be assign'd to each particular person, while the rest of mankind are excluded from their possession and enjoyment. Our next business, then, must be to discover the reasons which modify this general rule, and fit it to the common use and practice of the world. 1

'Tis obvious, that those reasons are not deriv'd from any utility or advantage, which either the *particular* person or the public may reap from his enjoyment of any *particular* goods, beyond what wou'd result from the possession of them by any other person. 'Twere better, no doubt, that every one were possess'd of what is most suitable to him, and proper for his use: But besides, that this relation of fitness may be common to several at once, 'tis liable to so many controversies, and men are so partial and passionate in judging of these controversies, that such a loose and uncertain rule wou'd be absolutely incompatible with the peace of human society. The convention concerning the stability of possession is enter'd into, in order to cut off all occasions of discord and contention; and this end wou'd never be attain'd, were we allow'd to apply this rule differently in every particular case, according to every particular utility, which might be discover'd in such an application. Justice, in her decisions, never regards the fitness or unfitness of objects to particular persons, but conducts herself by more extensive views. Whether a man be generous, or a miser, he is equally well receiv'd by her, and obtains with the same facility a decision in his favour, even for what is entirely useless to him. 2

It follows, therefore, that the general rule, *that possession must be stable*, is not apply'd by particular judgments, but by other general rules, which must extend to the whole society, and be inflexible either by spite or favour. To illustrate this, I propose the following instance. I first consider men in their savage and solitary condition; and suppose, that being sensible of the misery of that state, and foreseeing the advantages that wou'd result from society, they seek each other's company, and make an offer of mutual protection and assistance. I also suppose, that they are endow'd with such 3 sagacity as immediately to perceive that the chief impediment to this project of society and partnership lies in the avidity and selfishness of their natural temper; to remedy which, they enter into a convention for the stability of possession, and for mutual restraint and forbearance. I am sensible that this method of proceeding is not altogether natural; but besides that I here only suppose those reflections to be form'd at once, which in fact arise insensibly and by degrees; besides this, I say, 'tis very possible, that several persons, being by different accidents separated from the societies, to which they formerly belong'd, may be oblig'd to form a new society among themselves; in which case they are entirely in the situation above-mention'd.

4   'Tis evident, then, that their first difficulty, in this situation, after the general convention for the establishment of society, and for the constancy of possession, is, how to separate their possessions, and assign to each his particular portion, which he must for the future inalterably enjoy. This difficulty will not detain them long; but it must immediately occur, as the most natural expedient, that every one continue to enjoy what he is at present master of, and that property or constant possession be conjoin'd to the immediate possession. Such is the effect of custom, that it not only reconciles us to any thing we have long enjoy'd, but even gives us an affection for it, and makes us prefer it to other objects, which may be more valuable, but are less known to us. What has long lain under our eye, and has often been employ'd to our advantage, *that* we are always the most unwilling to part with; but can easily live without possessions, which we never have enjoy'd, and are not accustom'd to. 'Tis evident, therefore, that men wou'd easily acquiesce in this expedient, *that every one continue to enjoy what he is at present possess'd of*; and this is the reason, why they wou'd so naturally agree in preferring it.[1]

5   But we may observe, that tho' the rule of the assignment of property to

---

[1] No questions in philosophy are more difficult, than when a number of causes present themselves for the same phænomenon, to determine which is the principal and predominant. There seldom is any very precise argument to fix our choice, and men must be contented to be guided by a kind of taste or fancy, arising from analogy, and a comparison of similar instances. Thus, in the present case, there are, no doubt, motives of public interest for most of the rules, which determine property; but still I suspect, that these rules are principally fix'd by the imagination, or the more frivolous properties of our thought and conception. I shall continue to explain these causes, leaving it to the reader's choice, whether he will prefer those deriv'd from publick utility, or those deriv'd from the imagination. We shall begin with the right of the present possessor.

'Tis a quality, which I have already observ'd [in Book I. Part IV. Sect. 5] in human nature, that when two objects appear in a close relation to each other, the mind is apt to ascribe to them any additional relation, in order to compleat the union; and this inclination is so strong, as often to make us run into errors (such as that of the conjunction of thought and matter) if we find that they can serve to that purpose. Many of our

the present possessor be natural, and by that means useful, yet its utility extends not beyond the first formation of society; nor wou'd any thing be more pernicious, than the constant observance of it; by which restitution wou'd be excluded, and every injustice wou'd be authoriz'd and rewarded. We must, therefore, seek for some other circumstance, that may give rise to property after society is once establish'd; and of this kind I find four most considerable, *viz.* Occupation, Prescription, Accession, and Succession. We shall briefly examine each of these, beginning with *Occupation*.

The possession of all external goods is changeable and uncertain; which   6 is one of the most considerable impediments to the establishment of society, and is the reason why, by universal agreement, express or tacit, men restrain themselves by what we now call the rules of justice and equity. The misery of the condition, which precedes this restraint, is the cause why we submit to that remedy as quickly as possible; and this affords an easy reason, why we annex the idea of property to the first possession, or to *occupation*. Men are unwilling to leave property in suspence, even for the shortest time, or open the least door to violence and disorder. To which we may add, that the first possession always engages the attention

---

impressions are incapable of place or local position; and yet those very impressions we suppose to have a local conjunction with the impressions of sight and touch, merely because they are conjoin'd by causation, and are already united in the imagination. Since, therefore, we can feign a new relation, and even an absurd one, in order to compleat any union, 'twill easily be imagin'd, that if there be any relations, which depend on the mind, 'twill readily conjoin them to any preceding relation, and unite, by a new bond, such objects as have already an union in the fancy. Thus for instance, we never fail, in our arrangement of bodies, to place those which are *resembling* in *contiguity* to each other, or at least in *correspondent* points of view; because we feel a satisfaction in joining the relation of contiguity to that of resemblance, or the resemblance of situation to that of qualities. And this is easily accounted for from the known properties of human nature. When the mind is determin'd to join certain objects, but undetermin'd in its choice of the particular objects, it naturally turns its eye to such as are related together. They are already united in the mind: They present themselves at the same time to the conception; and instead of requiring any new reason for their conjunction, it wou'd require a very powerful reason to make us over-look this natural affinity. This we shall have occasion to explain more fully afterwards, when we come to treat of *beauty*. In the mean time, we may content ourselves with observing, that the same love of order and uniformity, which arranges the books in a library, and the chairs in a parlour, contributes to the formation of society, and to the well-being of mankind, by modifying the general rule concerning the stability of possession. As property forms a relation betwixt a person and an object, 'tis natural to found it on some preceding relation; and as property is nothing but a constant possession, secur'd by the laws of society, 'tis natural to add it to the present possession, which is a relation that resembles it. For this also has its influence. If it be natural to conjoin all sorts of relations, 'tis more so, to conjoin such relations as are resembling, and are related together.

most; and did we neglect it, there wou'd be no colour of reason for assigning property to any succeeding possession.[2]

7   There remains nothing, but to determine exactly, what is meant by possession; and this is not so easy as may at first sight be imagin'd. We are said to be in possession of any thing, not only when we immediately touch it, but also when we are so situated with respect to it, as to have it in our power to use it; and may move, alter, or destroy it, according to our present pleasure or advantage. This relation, then, is a species of cause and effect; and as property is nothing but a stable possession, deriv'd from the rules of justice, or the conventions of men, 'tis to be consider'd as the same species of relation. But here we may observe, that as the power of using any object becomes more or less certain, according as the interruptions we may meet with are more or less probable; and as this probability may encrease by insensible degrees, 'tis in many cases impossible to determine when possession begins or ends; nor is there any certain standard, by which we can decide such controversies. A wild boar, that falls into our snares, is deem'd to be in our possession, if it be impossible for him to escape. But what do we mean by impossible? How do we separate this impossibility from an improbability? And how distinguish that exactly from a probability? Mark the precise limits of the one and the other, and shew the standard, by which we may decide all disputes that may arise, and, as we find by experience, frequently do arise upon this subject.[3]

---

[2] Some philosophers account for the right of occupation, by saying, that every one has a property in his own labour; and when he joins that labour to any thing, it gives him the property of the whole: But, 1. There are several kinds of occupation, where we cannot be said to join our labour to the object we acquire: As when we possess a meadow by grazing our cattle upon it. 2. This accounts for the matter by means of *accession;* which is taking a needless circuit. 3. We cannot be said to join our labour to any thing but in a figurative sense. Properly speaking, we only make an alteration on it by our labour. This forms a relation betwixt us and the object; and thence arises the property, according to the preceding principles.

[3] If we seek a solution of these difficulties in reason and public interest, we never shall find satisfaction; and if we look for it in the imagination, 'tis evident, that the qualities, which operate upon that faculty, run so insensibly and gradually into each other, that 'tis impossible to give them any precise bounds or termination. The difficulties on this head must encrease, when we consider, that our judgment alters very sensibly, according to the subject, and that the same power and proximity will be deem'd possession in one case, which is not esteem'd such in another. A person, who has hunted a hare to the last degree of weariness, wou'd look upon it as an injustice for another to rush in before him, and seize his prey. But the same person, advancing to pluck an apple that hangs within his reach, has no reason to complain, if another, more alert, passes him, and takes possession. What is the reason of this difference, but that immobility, not being natural to the hare, but the effect of industry, forms in that case a strong relation with the hunter, which is wanting in the other?

But such disputes may not only arise concerning the real existence of   8
property and possession, but also concerning their extent; and these
disputes are often susceptible of no decision, or can be decided by no
other faculty than the imagination. A person who lands on the shore of

---

Here then it appears, that a certain and infallible power of enjoyment, without touch
or some other sensible relation, often produces not property: And I farther observe,
that a sensible relation, without any present power, is sometimes sufficient to give a title
to any object. The sight of a thing is seldom a considerable relation, and is only regarded as such, when the object is hidden, or very obscure; in which case we find, that
the view alone conveys a property; according to that maxim, *that even a whole continent
belongs to the nation, which first discover'd it.* 'Tis however remarkable, that both in the
case of discovery and that of possession, the first discoverer and possessor must join to
the relation an intention of rendering himself proprietor, otherwise the relation will not
have its effect; and that because the connexion in our fancy betwixt the property and
the relation is not so great, but that it requires to be help'd by such an intention.

From all these circumstances, 'tis easy to see how perplex'd many questions may become concerning the acquisition of property by occupation; and the least effort of
thought may present us with instances, which are not susceptible of any reasonable decision. If we prefer examples, which are real, to such as are feign'd, we may consider
the following one, which is to be met with in almost every writer, that has treated of the
laws of nature.

Two *Grecian* colonies, leaving their native country, in search of new seats, were inform'd that a city near them was deserted by its inhabitants. To know the truth of this
report, they dispatch'd at once two messengers, one from each colony; who finding on
their approach, that the information was true, begun a race together with an intention
to take possession of the city, each of them for his countrymen. One of these messengers, finding that he was not an equal match for the other, launch'd his spear at the
gates of the city, and was so fortunate as to fix it there before the arrival of his companion. This produc'd a dispute betwixt the two colonies, which of them was the proprietor of the empty city; and this dispute still subsists among philosophers. For my part
I find the dispute impossible to be decided, and that because the whole question hangs
upon the fancy, which in this case is not possess'd of any precise or determinate standard, upon which it can give sentence.

To make this evident, let us consider, that if these two persons had been simply members of the colonies, and not messengers or deputies, their actions wou'd not have been
of any consequence; since in that case their relation to the colonies wou'd have been but
feeble and imperfect. Add to this, that nothing determin'd them to run to the gates
rather than the walls, or any other part of the city, but that the gates, being the most obvious and remarkable part, satisfy the fancy best in taking them for the whole; as we find
by the poets, who frequently draw their images and metaphors from them. Besides we
may consider, that the touch or contact of the one messenger is not properly possession,
no more than the piercing the gates with the spear; but only forms a relation; and there
is a relation, in the other case, equally obvious, tho' not, perhaps, of equal force. Which
of these relations, then, conveys a right and property, or whether any of them be sufficient for that effect, I leave to the decision of such as are wiser than myself.

a small island, that is desart and uncultivated, is deem'd its possessor from the very first moment, and acquires the property of the whole; because the object is there bounded and circumscrib'd in the fancy, and at the same time is proportion'd to the new possessor. The same person landing on a desart island, as large as *Great Britain*, extends his property no farther than his immediate possession; tho' a numerous colony are esteem'd the proprietors of the whole from the instant of their debarkment.

9   But it often happens, that the title of first possession becomes obscure thro' time; and that 'tis impossible to determine many controversies, which may arise concerning it. In that case long possession or *prescription* naturally takes place, and gives a person a sufficient property in any thing he enjoys. The nature of human society admits not of any great accuracy; nor can we always remount to the first origin of things, in order to determine their present condition. Any considerable space of time sets objects at such a distance, that they seem, in a manner, to lose their reality, and have as little influence on the mind, as if they never had been in being. A man's title, that is clear and certain at present, will seem obscure and doubtful fifty years hence, even tho' the facts on which it is founded, shou'd be prov'd with the greatest evidence and certainty. The same facts have not the same influence after so long an interval of time. And this may be receiv'd as a convincing argument for our preceding doctrine with regard to property and justice. Possession during a long tract of time conveys a title to any object. But as 'tis certain, that, however every thing be produc'd in time, there is nothing real, that is produc'd by time; it follows, that property being produc'd by time, is not any thing real in the objects, but is the offspring of the sentiments, on which alone time is found to have any influence.[4]

10   We acquire the property of objects by *accession*, when they are connected in an intimate manner with objects that are already our property, and at the same time are inferior to them. Thus the fruits of our garden, the offspring of our cattle, and the work of our slaves, are all of them esteem'd our property, even before possession. Where objects are connected together in the imagination, they are apt to be put on the same footing, and are commonly suppos'd to be endow'd with the same

---

[4] Present possession is plainly a relation betwixt a person and an object; but is not sufficient to counter-balance the relation of first possession, unless the former be long and uninterrupted: In which case the relation is encreas'd on the side of the present possession, by the extent of time, and diminish'd on that of first possession, by the distance. This change in the relation produces a consequent change in the property.

qualities. We readily pass from one to the other, and make no difference in our judgments concerning them; especially if the latter be inferior to the former.[5]

The right of *succession* is a very natural one, from the presum'd consent   11

---

[5] This source of property can never be explain'd but from the imagination; and one may affirm, that the causes are here unmix'd. We shall proceed to explain them more particularly, and illustrate them by examples from common life and experience.

It has been observ'd above, that the mind has a natural propensity to join relations, especially resembling ones, and finds a kind of fitness and uniformity in such an union. From this propensity are deriv'd these laws of nature, *that upon the first formation of society, property always follows the present possession*; and afterwards, *that it arises from first or from long possession.* Now we may easily observe, that relation is not confin'd merely to one degree; but that from an object, that is related to us, we acquire a relation to every other object, which is related to it, and so on, till the thought loses the chain by too long a progress. However the relation may weaken by each remove, 'tis not immediately destroy'd; but frequently connects two objects by means of an immediate one, which is related to both. And this principle is of such force as to give rise to the right of *accession*, and causes us to acquire the property not only of such objects as we are immediately possess'd of, but also of such as are closely connected with them.

Suppose a *German*, a *Frenchman*, and a *Spaniard* to come into a room, where there are plac'd upon the table three bottles of wine, *Rhenish*, *Burgundy*, and *Port*; and suppose they shou'd fall a quarrelling about the division of them; a person, who was chosen for umpire, wou'd naturally, to shew his impartiality, give every one the product of his own country: And this from a principle, which, in some measure, is the source of those laws of nature, that ascribe property to occupation, prescription and accession.

In all these cases, and particularly that of accession, there is first a *natural* union betwixt the idea of the person and that of the object, and afterwards a new and *moral* union produc'd by that right or property, which we ascribe to the person. But here there occurs a difficulty, which merits our attention, and may afford us an opportunity of putting to tryal that singular method of reasoning, which has been employ'd on the present subject. I have already observ'd, that the imagination passes with greater facility from little to great, than from great to little, and that the transition of ideas is always easier and smoother in the former case than in the latter. Now as the right of accession arises from the easy transition of ideas, by which related objects are connected together, it shou'd naturally be imagin'd, that the right of accession must encrease in strength, in proportion as the transition of ideas is perform'd with greater facility. It may, therefore, be thought, that when we have acquir'd the property of any small object, we shall readily consider any great object related to it as an accession, and as belonging to the proprietor of the small one; since the transition is in that case very easy from the small object to the great one, and shou'd connect them together in the closest manner. But in fact the case is always found to be otherwise. The empire of *Great Britain* seems to draw along with it the dominion of the *Orkneys*, the *Hebrides*, the isle of *Man*, and the isle of *Wight;* but the authority over those lesser islands does not naturally imply any title to *Great Britain*. In short, a small object naturally follows a great one as its accession; but a great one is never suppos'd to belong to the proprietor of a small one related

of the parent or near relation, and from the general interest of mankind, which requires, that men's possessions shou'd pass to those, who are dearest to them, in order to render them more industrious and frugal. Perhaps these causes are seconded by the influence of *relation*, or the as-

---

to it, merely on account of that property and relation. Yet in this latter case the transition of ideas is smoother from the proprietor to the small object, which is his property, and from the small object to the great one, than in the former case from the proprietor to the great object, and from the great one to the small. It may therefore be thought, that these phænomena are objections to the foregoing hypothesis, *that the ascribing of property to accession is nothing but an effect of the relations of ideas, and of the smooth transition of the imagination.*

'Twill be easy to solve this objection, if we consider the agility and unsteadiness of the imagination, with the different views, in which it is continually placing its objects. When we attribute to a person a property in two objects, we do not always pass from the person to one object, and from that to the other related to it. The objects being here to be consider'd as the property of the person, we are apt to join them together, and place them in the same light. Suppose, therefore, a great and a small object to be related together; if a person be strongly related to the great object, he will likewise be strongly related to both the objects, consider'd together, because he is related to the most considerable part. On the contrary, if he be only related to the small object, he will not be strongly related to both, consider'd together, since his relation lies only with the most trivial part, which is not apt to strike us in any great degree, when we consider the whole. And this is the reason, why small objects become accessions to great ones, and not great to small.

'Tis the general opinion of philosophers and civilians, that the sea is incapable of becoming the property of any nation; and that because 'tis impossible to take possession of it, or form any such distinct relation with it, as may be the foundation of property. Where this reason ceases, property immediately takes place. Thus the most strenuous advocates for the liberty of the seas universally allow, that friths and bays naturally belong as an accession to the proprietors of the surrounding continent. These have properly no more bond or union with the land, than the *pacific* ocean wou'd have; but having an union in the fancy, and being at the same time *inferior*, they are of course regarded as an accession.

The property of rivers, by the laws of most nations, and by the natural turn of our thought, is attributed to the proprietors of their banks, excepting such vast rivers as the *Rhine* or the *Danube*, which seem too large to the imagination to follow as an accession the property of the neighbouring fields. Yet even these rivers are consider'd as the property of that nation, thro' whose dominions they run; the idea of a nation being of a suitable bulk to correspond with them, and bear them such a relation in the fancy.

The accessions, which are made to lands bordering upon rivers, follow the land, say the civilians, provided it be made by what they call *alluvion*, that is, insensibly and imperceptibly; which are circumstances that mightily assist the imagination in the conjunction. Where there is any considerable portion torn at once from one bank, and join'd to another, it becomes not his property, whose land it falls on, till it unite with the land, and till the trees or plants have spread their roots into both. Before that, the imagination does not sufficiently join them.

sociation of ideas, by which we are naturally directed to consider the son after the parent's decease, and ascribe to him a title to his father's possessions. Those goods must become the property of some body: But *of whom* is the question. Here 'tis evident the person's children naturally

---

There are other cases, which somewhat resemble this of accession, but which, at the bottom, are considerably different, and merit our attention. Of this kind is the conjunction of the properties of different persons, after such a manner as not to admit of *separation*. The question is, to whom the united mass must belong.

Where this conjunction is of such a nature as to admit of *division*, but not of *separation*, the decision is natural and easy. The whole mass must be suppos'd to be common betwixt the proprietors of the several parts, and afterwards must be divided according to the proportions of these parts. But here I cannot forbear taking notice of a remarkable subtilty of the *Roman* law, in distinguishing betwixt *confusion* and *commixtion*. Confusion is a union of two bodies, such as different liquors, where the parts become entirely undistinguishable. Commixtion is the blending of two bodies, such as two bushels of corn, where the parts remain separate in an obvious and visible manner. As in the latter case the imagination discovers not so entire an union as in the former, but is able to trace and preserve a distinct idea of the property of each; this is the reason, why the *civil* law, tho' it establish'd an entire community in the case of *confusion*, and after that a proportional division, yet in the case of *commixtion*, supposes each of the proprietors to maintain a distinct right; however necessity may at last force them to submit to the same division.

Quod si frumentum Titii frumento tuo mistum fuerit: siquidem ex voluntate vestra, commune est: quia singula corpora, id est, singula grana, quæ cujusque propria fuerunt, ex consensu vestro communicata sunt. Quod si casu id mistum fuerit, vel Titius id miscuerit sine tua voluntate, non videtur id commune esse; quia singula corpora in sua substantia durant. Sed nec magis istis casibus commune sit frumentum quam grex intelligitur esse communis, si pecora Titii tuis pecoribus mista fuerint. Sed si ab alterutro vestrûm totum id frumentum retineatur, in rem quidem actio pro modo frumenti cujusque competit. Arbitrio autem judicis, continetur, ut ipse æstimet quale cujusque frumentum fuerit. Inst. Lib. II. Tit. 1, Sec. 28. ["But suppose that corn owned by Titius is mixed with yours. If you both wanted the mixing done, you own the mass in common, because every particle you each owned, i.e. every grain of corn, is by your agreement made common to you both. But if the mixture happens accidentally or is done by Titius agaist your will, the whole is not held in common, because the individual particles retain their own identity. The corn is not made common property here any more than flocks become common if the animals get mixed up. If one of you keeps the whole lot, a real action lies for the quantity of the other's individual contribution. The judge has the power to allow for the quality of each contribution in assessing his award" (Justinian, *Justinian's Institutes*, 2.1, 28; trans. by Peter Birks and Grant McLeod).]

Where the properties of two persons are united after such a manner as neither to admit of *division* nor *separation*, as when one builds a house on another's ground, in that case, the whole must belong to one of the proprietors: And here I assert, that it naturally is conceiv'd to belong to the proprietor of the most considerable part. For however the compound object may have a relation to two different persons, and carry our view

present themselves to the mind; and being already connected to those possessions by means of their deceas'd parent, we are apt to connect them still farther by the relation of property. Of this there are many parallel instances.[6]

---

at once to both of them, yet as the most considerable part principally engages our attention, and by the strict union draws the inferior along it; for this reason, the whole bears a relation to the proprietor of that part, and is regarded as his property. The only difficulty is, what we shall be pleas'd to call the most considerable part, and most attractive to the imagination.

This quality depends on several different circumstances, which have little connexion with each other. One part of a compound object may become more considerable than another, either because it is more constant and durable; because it is of greater value; because it is more obvious and remarkable; because it is of greater extent; or because its existence is more separate and independent. 'Twill be easy to conceive, that, as these circumstances may be conjoin'd and oppos'd in all the different ways, and according to all the different degrees, which can be imagin'd, there will result many cases, where the reasons on both sides are so equally ballanc'd, that 'tis impossible for us to give any satisfactory decision. Here then is the proper business of municipal laws, to fix what the principles of human nature have left undetermin'd.

The superficies yields to the soil, says the civil law: The writing to the paper: The canvas to the picture. These decisions do not well agree together, and are a proof of the contrariety of those principles, from which they are deriv'd.

But of all the questions of this kind the most curious is that, which for so many ages divided the disciples of *Proculus* and *Sabinus*. Suppose a person shou'd make a cup from the metal of another, or a ship from his wood, and suppose the proprietor of the metal or wood shou'd demand his goods, the question is, whether he acquires a title to the cup or ship. *Sabinus* maintain'd the affirmative, and asserted that the substance or matter is the foundation of all the qualities; that it is incorruptible and immortal, and therefore superior to the form, which is casual and dependent. On the other hand, *Proculus* observ'd, that the form is the most obvious and remarkable part, and that from it bodies are denominated of this or that particular species. To which he might have added, that the matter or substance is in most bodies so fluctuating and uncertain, that 'tis utterly impossible to trace it in all its changes. For my part, I know not from what principles such a controversy can be certainly determin'd. I shall therefore content myself with observing, that the decision of *Trebonian* seems to me pretty ingenious; that the cup belongs to the proprietor of the metal, because it can be brought back to its first form: But that the ship belongs to the author of its form for a contrary reason. But however ingenious this reason may seem, it plainly depends upon the fancy, which by the possibility of such a reduction, finds a closer connexion and relation betwixt a cup and the proprietor of its metal, than betwixt a ship and the proprietor of its wood, where the substance is more fix'd and unalterable.

[6] In examining the different titles to authority in government, we shall meet with many reasons to convince us, that the right of succession depends, in a great measure, on the imagination. Mean while I shall rest contented with observing one example, which belongs to the present subject. Suppose that a person die without children, and

Section IV. Of the transference of property by consent.

However useful, or even necessary, the stability of possession may be to   1
human society, 'tis attended with very considerable inconveniences. The relation of fitness or suitableness ought never to enter into consideration, in
distributing the properties of mankind; but we must govern ourselves by
rules, which are more general in their application, and more free from doubt
and uncertainty. Of this kind is *present* possession upon the first establishment of society; and afterwards *occupation, prescription, accession,* and *succession.* As these depend very much on chance, they must frequently prove
contradictory both to men's wants and desires; and persons and possessions
must often be very ill adjusted. This is a grand inconvenience, which calls
for a remedy. To apply one directly, and allow every man to seize by violence
what he judges to be fit for him, wou'd destroy society; and therefore the
rules of justice seek some medium betwixt a rigid stability, and this changeable and uncertain adjustment. But there is no medium better than that obvious one, that possession and property shou'd always be stable, except
when the proprietor agrees to bestow them on some other person. This rule
can have no ill consequence, in occasioning wars and dissentions; since the
proprietor's consent, who alone is concern'd, is taken along in the alien-
ation: And it may serve to many good purposes in adjusting property to persons. Different parts of the earth produce different commodities; and not
only so, but different men both are by nature fitted for different employments, and attain to greater perfection in any one, when they confine themselves to it alone. All this requires a mutual exchange and commerce; for
which reason the translation of property by consent is founded on a law of
nature, as well as its stability without such a consent.

So far is determin'd by a plain utility and interest. But perhaps 'tis   2
from more trivial reasons, that *delivery*, or a sensible transference of the
object is commonly requir'd by civil laws, and also by the laws of nature,
according to most authors, as a requisite circumstance in the translation
of property. The property of an object, when taken for something real,

---

that a dispute arises among his relations concerning his inheritance; 'tis evident, that if
his riches be deriv'd partly from his father, partly from his mother, the most natural
way of determining such a dispute, is, to divide his possessions, and assign each part to
the family, from whence it is deriv'd. Now as the person is suppos'd to have been once
the full and entire proprietor of those goods; I ask, what is it makes us find a certain equity and natural reason in this partition, except it be the imagination? His affection to
these families does not depend upon his possessions; for which reason his consent can
never be presum'd precisely for such a partition. And as to the public interest, it seems
not to be in the least concern'd on the one side or the other.

without any reference to morality, or the sentiments of the mind, is a quality perfectly insensible, and even inconceivable; nor can we form any distinct notion, either of its stability or translation. This imperfection of our ideas is less sensibly felt with regard to its stability, as it engages less our attention, and is easily past over by the mind, without any scrupulous examination. But as the translation of property from one person to another is a more remarkable event, the defect of our ideas becomes more sensible on that occasion, and obliges us to turn ourselves on every side in search of some remedy. Now as nothing more enlivens any idea than a present impression, and a relation betwixt that impression and the idea; 'tis natural for us to seek some false light from this quarter. In order to aid the imagination in conceiving the transference of property, we take the sensible object, and actually transfer its possession to the person, on whom we wou'd bestow the property. The suppos'd resemblance of the actions, and the presence of this sensible delivery, deceive the mind, and make it fancy, that it conceives the mysterious transition of the property. And that this explication of the matter is just, appears hence, that men have invented a *symbolical* delivery, to satisfy the fancy, where the real one is impracticable. Thus the giving the keys of a granary is understood to be the delivery of the corn contain'd in it: The giving of stone and earth represents the delivery of a mannor. This is a kind of superstitious practice in civil laws, and in the laws of nature, resembling the *Roman Catholic* superstitions in religion. As the *Roman Catholics* represent the inconceivable mysteries of the *Christian* religion, and render them more present to the mind, by a taper, or habit, or grimace, which is suppos'd to resemble them; so lawyers and moralists have run into like inventions for the same reason, and have endeavour'd by those means to satisfy themselves concerning the transference of property by consent.

Section V. Of the obligation of promises.

1   That the rule of morality, which enjoins the performance of promises, is not *natural*, will sufficiently appear from these two propositions, which I proceed to prove, viz. *that a promise wou'd not be intelligible, before human conventions had establish'd it*; and *that even if it were intelligible, it wou'd not be attended with any moral obligation.*

2   I say, *first*, that a promise is not intelligible naturally, nor antecedent to human conventions; and that a man, unacquainted with society, cou'd never enter into any engagements with another, even tho' they cou'd perceive each other's thoughts by intuition. If promises be natural and intelligible, there must be some act of the mind attending these words, *I promise*; and on this act of the mind must the obligation depend. Let us, therefore, run over all the faculties of the soul, and see which of them is exerted in our promises.

The act of the mind, exprest by a promise, is not a *resolution* to perform   3
any thing: For that alone never imposes any obligation. Nor is it a *desire* of
such a performance: For we may bind ourselves without such a desire, or
even with an aversion, declar'd and avow'd. Neither is it the *willing* of that
action, which we promise to perform: For a promise always regards some
future time, and the will has an influence only on present actions. It follows, therefore, that since the act of the mind, which enters into a promise, and produces its obligation, is neither the resolving, desiring, nor
willing any particular performance, it must necessarily be the *willing* of
that *obligation*, which arises from the promise. Nor is this only a conclusion of philosophy; but is entirely conformable to our common ways of
thinking and of expressing ourselves, when we say that we are bound by
our own consent, and that the obligation arises from our mere will and
pleasure. The only question, then, is, whether there be not a manifest absurdity in supposing this act of the mind, and such an absurdity as no man
cou'd fall into, whose ideas are not confounded by prejudice and the fallacious use of language.

All morality depends upon our sentiments; and when any action, or   4
quality of the mind, pleases us *after a certain manner*, we say it is virtuous;
and when the neglect, or non-performance of it, displeases us *after a like
manner*, we say that we lie under an obligation to perform it. A change of
the obligation supposes a change of the sentiment; and a creation of a new
obligation supposes some new sentiment to arise. But 'tis certain we can
naturally no more change our own sentiments, than the motions of the
heavens; nor by a single act of our will, that is, by a promise, render any
action agreeable or disagreeable, moral or immoral; which, without that
act, wou'd have produc'd contrary impressions, or have been endow'd
with different qualities. It wou'd be absurd, therefore, to will any new
obligation, that is, any new sentiment of pain or pleasure; nor is it possible,
that men cou'd naturally fall into so gross an absurdity. A promise, therefore, is *naturally* something altogether unintelligible, nor is there any act
of the mind belonging to it.[1]

---

[1] Were morality discoverable by reason, and not by sentiment, 'twou'd be still more
evident, that promises cou'd make no alteration upon it. Morality is suppos'd to consist
in relation. Every new imposition of morality, therefore, must arise from some new relation of objects; and consequently the will cou'd not produce *immediately* any change
in morals, but cou'd have that effect only by producing a change upon the objects. But
as the moral obligation of a promise is the pure effect of the will, without the least
change in any part of the universe; it follows, that promises have no *natural* obligation.

Shou'd it be said, that this act of the will being in effect a new object, produces new relations and new duties; I wou'd answer, that this is a pure sophism, which may be detected

5   But, *secondly*, if there was any act of the mind belonging to it, it cou'd not *naturally* produce any obligation. This appears evidently from the foregoing reasoning. A promise creates a new obligation. A new obligation supposes new sentiments to arise. The will never creates new sentiments. There cou'd not naturally, therefore, arise any obligation from a promise, even supposing the mind cou'd fall into the absurdity of willing that obligation.

6   The same truth may be prov'd still more evidently by that reasoning, which prov'd justice in general to be an artificial virtue. No action can be requir'd of us as our duty, unless there be implanted in human nature some actuating passion or motive, capable of producing the action. This motive cannot be the sense of duty. A sense of duty supposes an antecedent obligation: And where an action is not requir'd by any natural passion, it cannot be requir'd by any natural obligation; since it may be omitted without proving any defect or imperfection in the mind and temper, and consequently without any vice. Now 'tis evident we have no motive leading us to the performance of promises, distinct from a sense of duty. If we thought, that promises had no moral obligation, we never shou'd feel any inclination to observe them. This is not the case with the natural virtues. Tho' there was no obligation to relieve the miserable, our humanity wou'd lead us to it; and when we omit that duty, the immorality of the omission arises from its being a proof, that we want the natural sentiments of humanity. A father knows it to be his duty to take care of his children: But he has also a natural inclination to it. And if no human creature had that inclination, no one cou'd lie under any such obligation. But as there is naturally no inclination to observe promises, distinct from a sense of their obligation; it follows, that fidelity is no natural virtue, and that promises have no force, antecedent to human conventions.

7   If any one dissent from this, he must give a regular proof of these two propositions, viz. *that there is a peculiar act of the mind, annext to promises*;

---

by a very moderate share of accuracy and exactness. To will a new obligation, is to will a new relation of objects; and therefore, if this new relation of objects were form'd by the volition itself, we shou'd in effect will the volition; which is plainly absurd and impossible. The will has here no object to which it cou'd tend; but must return upon itself *in infinitum*. The new obligation depends upon new relations. The new relations depend upon a new volition. The new volition has for its object a new obligation, and consequently new relations, and consequently a new volition; which volition again has in view a new obligation, relation and volition, without any termination. 'Tis impossible, therefore, we cou'd ever will a new obligation; and consequently 'tis impossible the will cou'd ever accompany a promise, or produce a new obligation of morality.

and *that consequent to this act of the mind, there arises an inclination to per-form, distinct from a sense of duty*. I presume, that it is impossible to prove either of these two points; and therefore I venture to conclude, that prom-ises are human inventions, founded on the necessities and interests of so-ciety.

In order to discover these necessities and interests, we must consider   8 the same qualities of human nature, which we have already found to give rise to the preceding laws of society. Men being naturally selfish, or en-dow'd only with a confin'd generosity, they are not easily induc'd to per-form any action for the interest of strangers, except with a view to some reciprocal advantage, which they had no hope of obtaining but by such a performance. Now as it frequently happens, that these mutual perfor-mances cannot be finish'd at the same instant, 'tis necessary, that one party be contented to remain in uncertainty, and depend upon the grati-tude of the other for a return of kindness. But so much corruption is there among men, that, generally speaking, this becomes but a slender security; and as the benefactor is here suppos'd to bestow his favours with a view to self-interest, this both takes off from the obligation, and sets an example of selfishness, which is the true mother of ingratitude. Were we, therefore, to follow the natural course of our passions and inclinations, we shou'd perform but few actions for the advantage of others, from disinterested views; because we are naturally very limited in our kindness and affection: And we shou'd perform as few of that kind, out of a regard to interest, be-cause we cannot depend upon their gratitude. Here then is the mutual commerce of good offices in a manner lost among mankind, and every one reduc'd to his own skill and industry for his well-being and subsistence. The invention of the law of nature, concerning the *stability* of possession, has already render'd men tolerable to each other; that of the *transference* of property and possession by consent has begun to render them mutually advantageous: But still these laws, however strictly observ'd, are not suffi-cient to render them so serviceable to each other, as by nature they are fit-ted to become. Tho' possession be *stable*, men may often reap but small advantage from it, while they are possess'd of a greater quantity of any species of goods than they have occasion for, and at the same time suffer by the want of others. The *transference* of property, which is the proper remedy for this inconvenience, cannot remedy it entirely; because it can only take place with regard to such objects as are *present* and *individual*, but not to such as are *absent* or *general*. One cannot transfer the property of a particular house, twenty leagues distant; because the consent cannot be attended with delivery, which is a requisite circumstance. Neither can one transfer the property of ten bushels of corn, or five hogsheads of wine, by the mere expression and consent; because these are only general terms, and have no direct relation to any particular heap of corn, or barrels of wine. Besides, the commerce of mankind is not confin'd to the barter of commodities, but may extend to services and actions, which we may exchange to our mutual interest and advantage. Your corn is ripe to-day; mine will be so to-morrow. 'Tis profitable for us both, that I shou'd labour with you to-day, and that you shou'd aid me to-morrow. I have no kindness for you, and know you have as little for me. I will not, therefore, take any pains upon your account; and shou'd I labour with you upon my own account, in expectation of a return, I know I shou'd be disappointed, and that I shou'd in vain depend upon your gratitude. Here then I leave you to labour alone: You treat me in the same manner. The seasons change; and both of us lose our harvests for want of mutual confidence and security.

9   All this is the effect of the natural and inherent principles and passions of human nature; and as these passions and principles are inalterable, it may be thought, that our conduct, which depends on them, must be so too, and that 'twou'd be in vain, either for moralists or politicians, to tamper with us, or attempt to change the usual course of our actions, with a view to public interest. And indeed, did the success of their designs depend upon their success in correcting the selfishness and ingratitude of men, they wou'd never make any progress, unless aided by omnipotence, which is alone able to new-mould the human mind, and change its character in such fundamental articles. All they can pretend to, is, to give a new direction to those natural passions, and teach us that we can better satisfy our appetites in an oblique and artificial manner, than by their headlong and impetuous motion. Hence I learn to do a service to another, without bearing him any real kindness; because I foresee, that he will return my service, in expectation of another of the same kind, and in order to maintain the same correspondence of good offices with me or with others. And accordingly, after I have serv'd him, and he is in possession of the advantage arising from my action, he is induc'd to perform his part, as foreseeing the consequences of his refusal.

10   But tho' this self-interested commerce of men begins to take place, and to predominate in society, it does not entirely abolish the more generous and noble intercourse of friendship and good offices. I may still do services to such persons as I love, and am more particularly acquainted with, without any prospect of advantage; and they may make me a return in the same manner, without any view but that of recompensing my past services. In order, therefore, to distinguish those two different sorts of commerce, the interested and the disinterested, there is a *certain form of words* invented for the former, by which we bind ourselves to the performance of any action. This form of words constitutes what we call a *promise*, which is

the sanction of the interested commerce of mankind. When a man says *he promises any thing*, he in effect expresses a *resolution* of performing it; and along with that, by making use of this *form of words*, subjects himself to the penalty of never being trusted again in case of failure. A resolution is the natural act of the mind, which promises express: But were there no more than a resolution in the case, promises wou'd only declare our former motives, and wou'd not create any new motive or obligation. They are the conventions of men, which create a new motive, when experience has taught us, that human affairs wou'd be conducted much more for mutual advantage, were there certain *symbols* or *signs* instituted, by which we might give each other security of our conduct in any particular incident. After these signs are instituted, whoever uses them is immediately bound by his interest to execute his engagements, and must never expect to be trusted any more, if he refuse to perform what he promis'd.

Nor is that knowledge, which is requisite to make mankind sensible of this interest in the *institution* and *observance* of promises, to be esteem'd superior to the capacity of human nature, however savage and uncultivated. There needs but a very little practice of the world, to make us perceive all these consequences and advantages. The shortest experience of society discovers them to every mortal; and when each individual perceives the same sense of interest in all his fellows, he immediately performs his part of any contract, as being assur'd, that they will not be wanting in theirs. All of them, by concert, enter into a scheme of actions, calculated for common benefit, and agree to be true to their word; nor is there any thing requisite to form this concert or convention, but that every one have a sense of interest in the faithful fulfilling of engagements, and express that sense to other members of the society. This immediately causes that interest to operate upon them; and interest is the *first* obligation to the performance of promises. 11

Afterwards a sentiment of morals concurs with interest, and becomes a new obligation upon mankind. This sentiment of morality, in the performance of promises, arises from the same principles as that in the abstinence from the property of others. *Public interest, education*, and *the artifices of politicians*, have the same effect in both cases. The difficulties, that occur to us, in supposing a moral obligation to attend promises, we either surmount or elude. For instance; the expression of a resolution is not commonly suppos'd to be obligatory; and we cannot readily conceive how the making use of a certain form of words shou'd be able to cause any material difference. Here, therefore, we *feign* a new act of the mind, which we call the *willing* an obligation; and on this we suppose the morality to depend. But we have prov'd already, that there is no such act of the mind, and consequently that promises impose no natural obligation. 12

13   To confirm this, we may subjoin some other reflections concerning that
will, which is suppos'd to enter into a promise, and to cause its obligation.
'Tis evident, that the will alone is never suppos'd to cause the obligation,
but must be express'd by words or signs, in order to impose a tye upon any
man. The expression being once brought in as subservient to the will,
soon becomes the principal part of the promise; nor will a man be less
bound by his word, tho' he secretly give a different direction to his intention, and with-hold himself both from a resolution, and from willing an
obligation. But tho' the expression makes on most occasions the whole of
the promise, yet it does not always so; and one, who shou'd make use of
any expression, of which he knows not the meaning, and which he uses
without any intention of binding himself, wou'd not certainly be bound by
it. Nay, tho' he knows its meaning, yet if he uses it in jest only, and with
such signs as shew evidently he has no serious intention of binding himself, he wou'd not lie under any obligation of performance; but 'tis necessary that the words be a perfect expression of the will, without any
contrary signs. Nay, even this we must not carry so far as to imagine, that
one, whom, by our quickness of understanding, we conjecture, from certain signs, to have an intention of deceiving us, is not bound by his expression or verbal promise, if we accept of it; but must limit this
conclusion to those cases, where the signs are of a different kind from
those of deceit. All these contradictions are easily accounted for, if the
obligation of promises be merely a human invention for the convenience
of society; but will never be explain'd, if it be something *real* and *natural*,
arising from any action of the mind or body.

14   I shall farther observe, that since every new promise imposes a new
obligation of morality on the person who promises, and since this new
obligation arises from his will; 'tis one of the most mysterious and incomprehensible operations that can possibly be imagin'd, and may even be
compar'd to *transubstantiation*, or *holy orders*,[2] where a certain form of
words, along with a certain intention, changes entirely the nature of an external object, and even of a human creature. But tho' these mysteries be so
far alike, 'tis very remarkable that they differ widely in other particulars,
and that this difference may be regarded as a strong proof of the difference of their origins. As the obligation of promises is an invention for the
interest of society, 'tis warp'd into as many different forms as that interest
requires, and even runs into direct contradictions, rather than lose sight of

---

[2] I mean so far as holy orders are suppos'd to produce the *indelible character*. In
other respects they are only a legal qualification.

its object. But as those other monstrous doctrines are mere priestly inventions, and have no public interest in view, they are less disturb'd in their
progress by new obstacles; and it must be own'd, that, after the first absurdity, they follow more directly the current of reason and good sense.
Theologians clearly perceiv'd, that the external form of words, being mere
sound, require an intention to make them have any efficacy; and that this
intention being once consider'd as a requisite circumstance, its absence
must equally prevent the effect, whether avow'd or conceal'd, whether
sincere or deceitful. Accordingly they have commonly determin'd, that
the intention of the priest makes the sacrament, and that when he secretly
withdraws his intention, he is highly criminal in himself; but still destroys
the baptism, or communion, or holy orders. The terrible consequences of
this doctrine were not able to hinder its taking place; as the inconvenience
of a similar doctrine, with regard to promises, have prevented that doctrine from establishing itself. Men are always more concern'd about the
present life than the future; and are apt to think the smallest evil, which
regards the former, more important than the greatest, which regards the
latter.

We may draw the same conclusion, concerning the origin of promises,   15
from the *force*, which is suppos'd to invalidate all contracts, and to free us
from their obligation. Such a principle is a proof, that promises have no
natural obligation, and are mere artificial contrivances for the convenience
and advantage of society. If we consider aright of the matter, force is not
essentially different from any other motive of hope or fear, which may induce us to engage our word, and lay ourselves under any obligation. A
man, dangerously wounded, who promises a competent sum to a surgeon
to cure him, wou'd certainly be bound to performance; tho' the case be
not so much different from that of one who promises a sum to a robber, as
to produce so great a difference in our sentiments of morality, if these sentiments were not built entirely on public interest and convenience.

Section VI. Some farther reflections concerning justice and injustice.

We have now run over the three fundamental laws of nature, *that of the*   1
stability of possession, of its transference by consent, and of the performance of
promises. 'Tis on the strict observance of those three laws, that the peace
and security of human society entirely depend; nor is there any possibility
of establishing a good correspondence among men, where these are neglected. Society is absolutely necessary for the well-being of men; and
these are as necessary to the support of society. Whatever restraint they
may impose on the passions of men, they are the real offspring of those
passions, and are only a more artful and more refin'd way of satisfying

them. Nothing is more vigilant and inventive than our passions; and nothing is more obvious, than the convention for the observance of these rules. Nature has, therefore, trusted this affair entirely to the conduct of men, and has not plac'd in the mind any peculiar original principles, to determine us to a set of actions, into which the other principles of our frame and constitution were sufficient to lead us. And to convince us the more fully of this truth, we may here stop a moment, and from a review of the preceding reasonings, may draw some new arguments, to prove that those laws, however necessary, are entirely artificial, and of human invention; and consequently that justice is an artificial, and not a natural virtue.

2   I. The first argument I shall make use of is deriv'd from the vulgar definition of justice. Justice is commonly defin'd to be *a constant and perpetual will of giving every one his due*. In this definition 'tis suppos'd, that there are such things as right and property, independent of justice, and antecedent to it; and that they wou'd have subsisted, tho' men had never dreamt of practicing such a virtue. I have already observ'd, in a cursory manner, the fallacy of this opinion, and shall here continue to open up a little more distinctly my sentiments on that subject.

3   I shall begin with observing, that this quality, which we call *property*, is like many of the imaginary qualities of the *peripatetic* philosophy, and vanishes upon a more accurate inspection into the subject, when consider'd apart from our moral sentiments. 'Tis evident property does not consist in any of the sensible qualities of the object. For these may continue invariably the same, while the property changes. Property, therefore, must consist in some relation of the object. But 'tis not in its relation with regard to other external and inanimate objects. For these may also continue invariably the same, while the property changes. This quality, therefore, consists in the relations of objects to intelligent and rational beings. But 'tis not the external and corporeal relation, which forms the essence of property. For that relation may be the same betwixt inanimate objects, or with regard to brute creatures; tho' in those cases it forms no property. 'Tis, therefore, in some internal relation, that the property consists; that is, in some influence, which the external relations of the object have on the mind and actions. Thus the external relation, which we call *occupation* or first possession, is not of itself imagin'd to be the property of the object, but only to cause its property. Now 'tis evident, this external relation causes nothing in external objects, and has only an influence on the mind, by giving us a sense of duty in abstaining from that object, and in restoring it to the first possessor. These actions are properly what we call *justice;* and consequently 'tis on that virtue that the nature of property depends, and not the virtue on the property.

If any one, therefore, wou'd assert, that justice is a natural virtue, and   4
injustice a natural vice, he must assert that abstracting from the notions of
property, and *right*, and *obligation*, a certain conduct and train of actions,
in certain external relations of objects, has naturally a moral beauty or deformity, and causes an original pleasure or uneasiness. Thus the restoring
a man's goods to him is consider'd as virtuous, not because nature has annex'd a certain sentiment of pleasure to such a conduct, with regard to the
property of others, but because she has annex'd that sentiment to such a
conduct, with regard to those external objects, of which others have had
the first or long possession, or which they have receiv'd by the consent of
those, who have had first or long possession. If nature has given us no
such sentiment, there is not, naturally, nor antecedent to human conventions, any such thing as property. Now, tho' it seems sufficiently evident,
in this dry and accurate consideration of the present subject, that nature
has annex'd no pleasure or sentiment of approbation to such a conduct;
yet that I may leave as little room for doubt as possible, I shall subjoin a
few more arguments to confirm my opinion.

First, If nature had given us a pleasure of this kind, it wou'd have been   5
as evident and discernible as on every other occasion; nor shou'd we have
found any difficulty to perceive, that the consideration of such actions, in
such a situation, gives a certain pleasure and sentiment of approbation.
We shou'd not have been oblig'd to have recourse to notions of property in
the definition of justice, and at the same time make use of the notions of
justice in the definition of property. This deceitful method of reasoning is
a plain proof, that there are contain'd in the subject some obscurities and
difficulties, which we are not able to surmount, and which we desire to
evade by this artifice.

Secondly, Those rules, by which property, right, and obligation are de-   6
termin'd, have in them no marks of a natural origin, but many of artifice
and contrivance. They are too numerous to have proceeded from nature:
They are changeable by human laws: And have all of them a direct and evident tendency to public good, and the support of society. This last circumstance is remarkable upon two accounts. *First*, because, tho' the cause
of the establishment of these laws had been a *regard* for the public good, as
much as the public good is their natural tendency, they wou'd still have
been artificial, as being purposely contriv'd and directed to a certain end.
Secondly, because, if men had been endow'd with such a strong regard for
public good, they wou'd never have restrain'd themselves by these rules;
so that the laws of justice arise from natural principles in a manner still
more oblique and artificial. 'Tis self-love which is their real origin; and as
the self-love of one person is naturally contrary to that of another, these

several interested passions are oblig'd to adjust themselves after such a manner as to concur in some system of conduct and behaviour. This system, therefore, comprehending the interest of each individual, is of course advantageous to the public; tho' it be not intended for that purpose by the inventors.

7   II. In the second place we may observe, that all kinds of vice and virtue run insensibly into each other, and may approach by such imperceptible degrees as will make it very difficult, if not absolutely impossible, to determine when the one ends, and the other begins; and from this observation we may derive a new argument for the foregoing principle. For whatever may be the case, with regard to all kinds of vice and virtue, 'tis certain, that rights, and obligations, and property, admit of no such insensible gradation, but that a man either has a full and perfect property, or none at all; and is either entirely oblig'd to perform any action, or lies under no manner of obligation. However civil laws may talk of a perfect *dominion*, and of an imperfect, 'tis easy to observe, that this arises from a fiction, which has no foundation in reason, and can never enter into our notions of natural justice and equity. A man that hires a horse, tho' but for a day, has as full a right to make use of it for that time, as he whom we call its proprietor has to make use of it any other day; and 'tis evident, that however the use may be bounded in time or degree, the right itself is not susceptible of any such gradation, but is absolute and entire, so far as it extends. Accordingly we may observe, that this right both arises and perishes in an instant; and that a man entirely acquires the property of any object by occupation, or the consent of the proprietor; and loses it by his own consent; without any of that insensible gradation, which is remarkable in other qualities and relations. Since, therefore, this is the case with regard to property, and rights, and obligations, I ask, how it stands with regard to justice and injustice? After whatever manner you answer this question, you run into inextricable difficulties. If you reply, that justice and injustice admit of degree, and run insensibly into each other, you expressly contradict the foregoing position, that obligation and property are not susceptible of such a gradation. These depend entirely upon justice and injustice, and follow them in all their variations. Where the justice is entire, the property is also entire: Where the justice is imperfect, the property must also be imperfect. And *vice versa*, if the property admit of no such variations, they must also be incompatible with justice. If you assent, therefore, to this last proposition, and assert, that justice and injustice are not susceptible of degrees, you in effect assert, that they are not *naturally* either vicious or virtuous; since vice and virtue, moral good and evil, and indeed all *natural* qualities, run insensibly into each other, and are, on many occasions, undistinguishable.

And here it may be worth while to observe, that tho' abstract reasoning,   8
and the general maxims of philosophy and law establish this position, *that*
property, and right, and obligation admit not of degrees, yet in our common
and negligent way of thinking, we find great difficulty to entertain that
opinion, and do even *secretly* embrace the contrary principle. An object
must either be in the possession of one person or another. An action must
either be perform'd or not. The necessity there is of choosing one side in
these dilemmas, and the impossibility there often is of finding any just
medium, oblige us, when we reflect on the matter, to acknowledge, that all
property and obligations are entire. But on the other hand, when we consider the origin of property and obligation, and find that they depend on
public utility, and sometimes on the propensities of the imagination,
which are seldom entire on any side; we are naturally inclin'd to imagine,
that these moral relations admit of an insensible gradation. Hence it is,
that in references, where the consent of the parties leave the referees entire masters of the subject, they commonly discover so much equity and
justice on both sides, as induces them to strike a medium, and divide the
difference betwixt the parties. Civil judges, who have not this liberty, but
are oblig'd to give a decisive sentence on some one side, are often at a loss
how to determine, and are necessitated to proceed on the most frivolous
reasons in the world. Half rights and obligations, which seem so natural in
common life, are perfect absurdities in their tribunal; for which reason
they are often oblig'd to take half arguments for whole ones, in order to
terminate the affair one way or other.

III. The third argument of this kind I shall make use of may be ex-   9
plain'd thus. If we consider the ordinary course of human actions, we shall
find, that the mind restrains not itself by any general and universal rules;
but acts on most occasions as it is determin'd by its present motives and
inclination. As each action is a particular individual event, it must proceed
from particular principles, and from our immediate situation within ourselves, and with respect to the rest of the universe. If on some occasions
we extend our motives beyond those very circumstances, which gave rise
to them, and form something like *general rules* for our conduct, 'tis easy to
observe, that these rules are not perfectly inflexible, but allow of many exceptions. Since, therefore, this is the ordinary course of human actions,
we may conclude, that the laws of justice, being universal and perfectly inflexible, can never be deriv'd from nature, nor be the immediate offspring
of any natural motive or inclination. No action can be either morally good
or evil, unless there be some natural passion or motive to impel us to it,
or deter us from it; and 'tis evident, that the morality must be susceptible
of all the same variations, which are natural to the passion. Here are two
persons, who dispute for an estate; of whom one is rich, a fool, and a

batchelor; the other poor, a man of sense, and has a numerous family: The first is my enemy; the second my friend. Whether I be actuated in this affair by a view to public or private interest, by friendship or enmity, I must be induc'd to do my utmost to procure the estate to the latter. Nor wou'd any consideration of the right and property of the persons be able to restrain me, were I actuated only by natural motives, without any combination or convention with others. For as all property depends on morality; and as all morality depends on the ordinary course of our passions and actions; and as these again are only directed by particular motives; 'tis evident, such a partial conduct must be suitable to the strictest morality, and cou'd never be a violation of property. Were men, therefore, to take the liberty of acting with regard to the laws of society, as they do in every other affair, they wou'd conduct themselves, on most occasions, by particular judgments, and wou'd take into consideration the characters and circumstances of the persons, as well as the general nature of the question. But 'tis easy to observe, that this wou'd produce an infinite confusion in human society, and that the avidity and partiality of men wou'd quickly bring disorder into the world, if not restrain'd by some general and inflexible principles. 'Twas, therefore, with a view to this inconvenience, that men have establish'd those principles, and have agreed to restrain themselves by general rules, which are unchangeable by spite and favour, and by particular views of private or public interest. These rules, then, are artificially invented for a certain purpose, and are contrary to the common principles of human nature, which accommodate themselves to circumstances, and have no stated invariable method of operation.

10   Nor do I perceive how I can easily be mistaken in this matter. I see evidently, that when any man imposes on himself general inflexible rules in his conduct with others, he considers certain objects as their property, which he supposes to be sacred and inviolable. But no proposition can be more evident, than that property is perfectly unintelligible without first supposing justice and injustice; and that these moral qualities are as unintelligible, unless we have motives, independent of the morality, to impel us to just actions, and deter us from unjust ones. Let those motives, therefore, be what they will, they must accommodate themselves to circumstances, and must admit of all the variations, which human affairs, in their incessant revolutions, are susceptible of. They are consequently a very improper foundation for such rigid inflexible rules as the laws of nature; and 'tis evident these laws can only be deriv'd from human conventions, when men have perceiv'd the disorders that result from following their natural and variable principles.

11   Upon the whole, then, we are to consider this distinction betwixt justice and injustice, as having two different foundations, *viz.* that of *self-interest*, when men observe, that 'tis impossible to live in society without

restraining themselves by certain rules; and that of *morality*, when this interest is once observ'd to be common to all mankind, and men receive a pleasure from the view of such actions as tend to the peace of society, and an uneasiness from such as are contrary to it. 'Tis the voluntary convention and artifice of men, which makes the first interest take place; and therefore those laws of justice are so far to be consider'd as *artificial*. After that interest is once establish'd and acknowledg'd, the sense of morality in the observance of these rules follows *naturally*, and of itself; tho' 'tis certain, that it is also augmented by a new *artifice*, and that the public instructions of politicians, and the private education of parents, contribute to the giving us a sense of honour and duty in the strict regulation of our actions with regard to the properties of others.

Section VII. Of the origin of government.

Nothing is more certain, than that men are, in a great measure, govern'd   1
by interest, and that even when they extend their concern beyond themselves, 'tis not to any great distance; nor is it usual for them, in common life, to look farther than their nearest friends and acquaintance. 'Tis no less certain, that 'tis impossible for men to consult their interest in so effectual a manner, as by an universal and inflexible observance of the rules of justice, by which alone they can preserve society, and keep themselves from falling into that wretched and savage condition, which is commonly represented as the *state of nature*. And as this interest, which all men have in the upholding of society, and the observation of the rules of justice, is great, so is it palpable and evident, even to the most rude and uncultivated of the human race; and 'tis almost impossible for any one, who has had experience of society, to be mistaken in this particular. Since, therefore, men are so sincerely attach'd to their interest, and their interest is so much concern'd in the observance of justice, and this interest is so certain and avow'd; it may be ask'd, how any disorder can ever arise in society, and what principle there is in human nature so *powerful* as to overcome so strong a passion, or so *violent* as to obscure so clear a knowledge?

It has been observ'd, in treating of the passions, that men are mightily   2
govern'd by the imagination, and proportion their affections more to the light, under which any object appears to them, than to its real and intrinsic value. What strikes upon them with a strong and lively idea commonly prevails above what lies in a more obscure light; and it must be a great superiority of value that is able to compensate this advantage. Now as every thing, that is contiguous to us, either in space or time, strikes upon us with such an idea, it has a proportional effect on the will and passions, and commonly operates with more force than any object, that lies in a more distant and obscure light. Tho' we may be fully convinc'd, that the latter object excels the former, we are not able to regulate our actions by this

judgment; but yield to the sollicitations of our passions, which always plead in favour of whatever is near and contiguous.

3   This is the reason why men so often act in contradiction to their known interest; and in particular why they prefer any trivial advantage, that is present, to the maintenance of order in society, which so much depends on the observance of justice. The consequences of every breach of equity seem to lie very remote, and are not able to counter-ballance any immediate advantage, that may be reap'd from it. They are, however, never the less real for being remote; and as all men are, in some degree, subject to the same weakness, it necessarily happens, that the violations of equity must become very frequent in society, and the commerce of men, by that means, be render'd very dangerous and uncertain. You have the same propension, that I have, in favour of what is contiguous above what is remote. You are, therefore, naturally carry'd to commit acts of injustice as well as me. Your example both pushes me forward in this way by imitation, and also affords me a new reason for any breach of equity, by shewing me, that I shou'd be the cully of my integrity, if I alone shou'd impose on myself a severe restraint amidst the licentiousness of others.

4   This quality, therefore, of human nature, not only is very dangerous to society, but also seems, on a cursory view, to be incapable of any remedy. The remedy can only come from the consent of men; and if men be incapable of themselves to prefer remote to contiguous, they will never consent to any thing, which wou'd oblige them to such a choice, and contradict, in so sensible a manner, their natural principles and propensities. Whoever chuses the means, chuses also the end; and if it be impossible for us to prefer what is remote, 'tis equally impossible for us to submit to any necessity, which wou'd oblige us to such a method of acting.

5   But here 'tis observable, that this infirmity of human nature becomes a remedy to itself, and that the provision we make against our negligence about remote objects, proceeds merely from our natural inclination to that negligence. When we consider any objects at a distance, all their minute distinctions vanish, and we always give the preference to whatever is in itself preferable, without considering its situation and circumstances. This gives rise to what in an improper sense we call *reason*, which is a principle, that is often contradictory to those propensities that display themselves upon the approach of the object. In reflecting on any action, which I am to perform a twelve-month hence, I always resolve to prefer the greater good, whether at that time it will be more contiguous or remote; nor does any difference in that particular make a difference in my present intentions and resolutions. My distance from the final determination makes all those minute differences vanish, nor am I affected by any thing, but the general and more discernible qualities of good and evil. But on my nearer

approach, those circumstances, which I at first over-look'd, begin to appear, and have an influence on my conduct and affections. A new inclination to the present good springs up, and makes it difficult for me to adhere inflexibly to my first purpose and resolution. This natural infirmity I may very much regret, and I may endeavour, by all possible means, to free myself from it. I may have recourse to study and reflection within myself; to the advice of friends; to frequent meditation, and repeated resolution: And having experienc'd how ineffectual all these are, I may embrace with pleasure any other expedient, by which I may impose a restraint upon myself, and guard against this weakness.

The only difficulty, therefore, is to find out this expedient, by which 6 men cure their natural weakness, and lay themselves under the necessity of observing the laws of justice and equity, notwithstanding their violent propension to prefer contiguous to remote. 'Tis evident such a remedy can never be effectual without correcting this propensity; and as 'tis impossible to change or correct any thing material in our nature, the utmost we can do is to change our circumstances and situation, and render the observance of the laws of justice our nearest interest, and their violation our most remote. But this being impracticable with respect to all mankind, it can only take place with respect to a few, whom we thus immediately interest in the execution of justice. These are the persons, whom we call civil magistrates, kings and their ministers, our governors and rulers, who being indifferent persons to the greatest part of the state, have no interest, or but a remote one, in any act of injustice; and being satisfy'd with their present condition, and with their part in society, have an immediate interest in every execution of justice, which is so necessary to the upholding of society. Here then is the origin of civil government and allegiance. Men are not able radically to cure, either in themselves or others, that narrowness of soul, which makes them prefer the present to the remote. They cannot change their natures. All they can do is to change their situation, and render the observance of justice the immediate interest of some particular persons, and its violation their more remote. These persons, then, are not only induc'd to observe those rules in their own conduct, but also to constrain others to a like regularity, and enforce the dictates of equity thro' the whole society. And if it be necessary, they may also interest others more immediately in the execution of justice, and create a number of officers, civil and military, to assist them in their government.

But this execution of justice, tho' the principal, is not the only advan- 7 tage of government. As violent passion hinders men from seeing distinctly the interest they have in an equitable behaviour towards others; so it hinders them from seeing that equity itself, and gives them a remarkable partiality in their own favour. This inconvenience is corrected in the same manner as that above-mention'd. The same persons, who execute the laws of justice, will also decide all controversies concerning them; and being indifferent to the greatest part of the society, will decide them more equitably than every one wou'd in his own case.

8   By means of these two advantages, in the *execution* and *decision* of justice, men acquire a security against each other's weakness and passion, as well as against their own, and under the shelter of their governors, begin to taste at ease the sweets of society and mutual assistance. But government extends farther its beneficial influence; and not contented to protect men in those conventions they make for their mutual interest, it often obliges them to make such conventions, and forces them to seek their own advantage, by a concurrence in some common end or purpose. There is no quality in human nature, which causes more fatal errors in our conduct, than that which leads us to prefer whatever is present to the distant and remote, and makes us desire objects more according to their situation than their intrinsic value. Two neighbours may agree to drain a meadow, which they possess in common; because 'tis easy for them to know each other's mind; and each must perceive, that the immediate consequence of his failing in his part, is the abandoning the whole project. But 'tis very difficult, and indeed impossible, that a thousand persons shou'd agree in any such action; it being difficult for them to concert so complicated a design, and still more difficult for them to execute it; while each seeks a pretext to free himself of the trouble and expence, and wou'd lay the whole burden on others. Political society easily remedies both these inconveniences. Magistrates find an immediate interest in the interest of any considerable part of their subjects. They need consult no body but themselves to form any scheme for the promoting of that interest. And as the failure of any one piece in the execution is connected, tho' not immediately, with the failure of the whole, they prevent that failure, because they find no interest in it, either immediate or remote. Thus bridges are built; harbors open'd; ramparts rais'd; canals form'd; fleets equip'd; and armies disciplin'd; every where, by the care of government, which, tho' compos'd of men subject to all human infirmities, becomes, by one of the finest and most subtile inventions imaginable, a composition, that is, in some measure, exempted from all these infirmities.

Section VIII. Of the source of allegiance.

1   Tho' government be an invention very advantageous, and even in some circumstances absolutely necessary to mankind; it is not necessary in all circumstances, nor is it impossible for men to preserve society for some time, without having recourse to such an invention. Men, 'tis true, are always much inclin'd to prefer present interest to distant and remote; nor is

it easy for them to resist the temptation of any advantage, that they may immediately enjoy, in apprehension of an evil, that lies at a distance from them: But still this weakness is less conspicuous, where the possessions, and the pleasures of life are few, and of little value, as they always are in the infancy of society. An *Indian* is but little tempted to dispossess another of his hut, or to steal his bow, as being already provided of the same advantages; and as to any superior fortune, which may attend one above another in hunting and fishing, 'tis only casual and temporary, and will have but small tendency to disturb society. And so far am I from thinking with some philosophers, that men are utterly incapable of society without government, that I assert the first rudiments of government to arise from quarrels, not among men of the same society, but among those of different societies. A less degree of riches will suffice to this latter effect, than is requisite for the former. Men fear nothing from public war and violence but the resistance they meet with, which, because they share it in common, seems less terrible; and because it comes from strangers, seems less pernicious in its consequences, than when they are expos'd singly against one whose commerce is advantageous to them, and without whose society 'tis impossible they can subsist. Now foreign war to a society without government necessarily produces civil war. Throw any considerable goods among men, they instantly fall a quarreling, while each strives to get possession of what pleases him, without regard to the consequences. In a foreign war the most considerable of all goods, life and limbs, are at stake; and as every one shuns dangerous posts, seizes the best arms, seeks excuse for the slightest wounds, the rules of society, which may be well enough observ'd, while men were calm, can now no longer take place, when they are in such commotion.

This we find verified in the *American* tribes, where men live in concord and amity among themselves without any establish'd government; and never pay submission to any of their fellows, except in time of war, when their captain enjoys a shadow of authority, which he loses after their return from the field, and the establishment of peace with the neighbouring tribes. This authority, however, instructs them in the advantages of government, and teaches them to have recourse to it, when either by the pillage of war, by commerce, or by any fortuitous inventions, their riches and possessions have become so considerable as to make them forget, on every emergence, the interest they have in the preservation of peace and justice. Hence we may give a plausible reason, among others, why all governments are at first monarchical, without any mixture and variety; and why republics arise only from the abuses of monarchy and despotic power. Camps are the true mothers of cities; and as war cannot be administered, by reason of the suddenness of every exigency, without some authority in a single person, the same kind of authority naturally takes place in that civil government, which succeeds the military. And this reason I take to be more natural, than the common one deriv'd from patriarchal government, or the authority of a father, which is said first to take place in one family, and to accustom the members of it to the government of a single person. The state of society without government is one of the most natural states of men, and may subsist with the conjunction of many families, and long after the first generation. Nothing but an encrease of riches and possessions cou'd oblige men to quit it; and so barbarous and uninstructed are all societies on their first formation, that many years must elapse before these cou'd encrease to such a degree, as to disturb men in the enjoyment of peace and concord.

3   But tho' it be possible for men to maintain a small uncultivated society without government, 'tis impossible they shou'd maintain a society of any kind without justice, and the observance of those three fundamental laws concerning the stability of possession, its translation by consent, and the performance of promises. These are, therefore, antecedent to government, and are suppos'd to impose an obligation, before the duty of allegiance to civil magistrates has once been thought of. Nay, I shall go farther, and assert, that government, *upon its first establishment*, wou'd naturally be suppos'd to derive its obligation from those laws of nature, and, in particular, from that concerning the performance of promises. When men have once perceiv'd the necessity of government to maintain peace, and execute justice, they wou'd naturally assemble together, wou'd chuse magistrates, determine their power, and *promise* them obedience. As a promise is suppos'd to be a bond or security already in use, and attended with a moral obligation, 'tis to be consider'd as the original sanction of government, and as the source of the first obligation to obedience. This reasoning appears so natural, that it has become the foundation of our fashionable system of politics, and is in a manner the creed of a party amongst us, who value themselves, with reason, on the soundness of their philosophy, and their liberty of thought. *All men*, say they, *are born free and equal: Government and superiority can only be establish'd by consent: The consent of men, in establishing government, imposes on them a new obligation, unknown to the laws of nature. Men, therefore, are bound to obey their magistrates, only because they promise it; and if they had not given their word, either expressly or tacitly, to preserve allegiance, it wou'd never have become a part of their moral duty.* This conclusion, however, when carry'd so far as to comprehend government in all its ages and situations, is entirely erroneous; and I maintain, that tho' the duty of allegiance be at first grafted on the obligation of promises, and be for some time supported by that obligation, yet as soon as the advantages of government are fully known and acknowledg'd, it immediately takes root of itself, and has an original

obligation and authority, independent of all contracts. This is a principle of moment, which we must examine with care and attention, before we proceed any farther.

'Tis reasonable for those philosophers, who assert justice to be a natural virtue, and antecedent to human conventions, to resolve all civil allegiance into the obligation of a promise, and assert that 'tis our own consent alone, which binds us to any submission to magistracy. For as all government is plainly an invention of men, and the origin of most governments is known in history, 'tis necessary to mount higher, in order to find the source of our political duties, if we wou'd assert them to have any *natural* obligation of morality. These philosophers, therefore, quickly observe, that society is as antient as the human species, and those three fundamental laws of nature as antient as society: So that taking advantage of the antiquity, and obscure origin of these laws, they first deny them to be artificial and voluntary inventions of men, and then seek to ingraft on them those other duties, which are more plainly artificial. But being once undeceiv'd in this particular, and having found that *natural*, as well as civil justice, derives its origin from human conventions, we shall quickly perceive, how fruitless it is to resolve the one into the other, and seek, in the laws of nature, a stronger foundation for our political duties than interest, and human conventions; while these laws themselves are built on the very same foundation. On which ever side we turn this subject, we shall find, that these two kinds of duty are exactly on the same footing, and have the same source both of their *first invention* and *moral obligation*. They are contriv'd to remedy like inconveniences, and acquire their moral sanction in the same manner, from their remedying those inconveniences. These are two points, which we shall endeavour to prove as distinctly as possible. 4

We have already shewn, that men *invented* the three fundamental laws of nature, when they observ'd the necessity of society to their mutual subsistence, and found, that 'twas impossible to maintain any correspondence together, without some restraint on their natural appetites. The same self-love, therefore, which renders men so incommodious to each other, taking a new and more convenient direction, produces the rules of justice, and is the *first* motive of their observance. But when men have observ'd, that tho' the rules of justice be sufficient to maintain any society, yet 'tis impossible for them, of themselves, to observe those rules in large and polish'd societies; they establish government, as a new invention to attain their ends, and preserve the old, or procure new advantages, by a more strict execution of justice. So far, therefore, our *civil* duties are connected with our *natural*, that the former are invented chiefly for the sake of the latter; and that the principal object of government is to constrain men to observe the laws of nature. In this respect, however, that law of nature, concerning the performance of promises, is only compriz'd along with the rest; and its 5 exact observance is to be consider'd as an effect of the institution of government, and not the obedience to government as an effect of the obligation of a promise. Tho' the object of our civil duties be the enforcing of our natural, yet the *first*[1] motive of the invention, as well as performance of both, is nothing but self-interest: And since there is a separate interest in the obedience to government, from that in the performance of promises, we must also allow of a separate obligation. To obey the civil magistrate is requisite to preserve order and concord in society. To perform promises is requisite to beget mutual trust and confidence in the common offices of life. The ends, as well as the means, are perfectly distinct; nor is the one subordinate to the other.

6   To make this more evident, let us consider, that men will often bind themselves by promises to the performance of what it wou'd have been their interest to perform, independent of these promises; as when they wou'd give others a fuller security, by super-adding a new obligation of interest to that which they formerly lay under. The interest in the performance of promises, besides its moral obligation, is general, avow'd, and of the last consequence in life. Other interests may be more particular and doubtful; and we are apt to entertain a greater suspicion, that men may indulge their humour, or passion, in acting contrary to them. Here, therefore, promises come naturally in play, and are often requir'd for fuller satisfaction and security. But supposing those other interests to be as general and avow'd as the interest in the performance of a promise, they will be regarded as on the same footing, and men will begin to repose the same confidence in them. Now this is exactly the case with regard to our civil duties, or obedience to the magistrate; without which no government cou'd subsist, nor any peace or order be maintain'd in large societies, where there are so many possessions on the one hand, and so many wants, real or imaginary, on the other. Our civil duties, therefore, must soon detach themselves from our promises, and acquire a separate force and influence. The interest in both is of the very same kind: 'Tis general, avow'd, and prevails in all times and places. There is, then, no pretext of reason for founding the one upon the other; while each of them has a foundation peculiar to itself. We might as well resolve the obligation to abstain from the possessions of others, into the obligation of a promise, as that of allegiance. The interests are not more distinct in the one case than the other. A regard to property is not more necessary to natural society, than obedience is to civil society or government; nor is the former society more necessary to the being of mankind, than the latter to their well-being and happiness. In short, if the performance of promises be advantageous,

---

[1] First in time, not in dignity or force.

so is obedience to government: If the former interest be general, so is the latter: If the one interest be obvious and avow'd, so is the other. And as these two rules are founded on like obligations of interest, each of them must have a peculiar authority, independent of the other.

But 'tis not only the *natural* obligations of interest, which are distinct in promises and allegiance; but also the *moral* obligations of honour and conscience: Nor does the merit or demerit of the one depend in the least upon that of the other. And indeed, if we consider the close connexion there is betwixt the natural and moral obligations, we shall find this conclusion to be entirely unavoidable. Our interest is always engag'd on the side of obedience to magistracy; and there is nothing but a great present advantage, that can lead us to rebellion, by making us over-look the remote interest, which we have in the preserving of peace and order in society. But tho' a present interest may thus blind us with regard to our own actions, it takes not place with regard to those of others; nor hinders them from appearing in their true colours, as highly prejudicial to our own interest, or at least to that of the public, which we partake of by *sympathy*. This naturally gives us an uneasiness, in considering such seditious and disloyal actions, and makes us attach to them the idea of vice and moral deformity. 'Tis the same principle, which causes us to disapprove of all kinds of private injustice, and in particular of the breach of promises. We blame all treachery and breach of faith; because we consider, that the freedom and extent of human commerce depend entirely on a fidelity with regard to promises. We blame all disloyalty to magistrates; because we perceive, that the execution of justice, in the stability of possession, its translation by consent, and the performance of promises, is impossible, without submission to government. As there are here two interests entirely distinct from each other, they must give rise to two moral obligations, equally separate and independant. Tho' there was no such thing as a promise in the world, government wou'd still be necessary in all large and civiliz'd societies; and if promises had only their own proper obligation, without the separate sanction of government, they wou'd have but little efficacy in such societies. This separates the boundaries of our public and private duties, and shews that the latter are more dependent on the former, than the former on the latter. *Education*, and *the artifice of politicians*, concur in bestowing a farther morality on loyalty, and branding all rebellion with a greater degree of guilt and infamy. Nor is it a wonder, that politicians shou'd be very industrious in inculcating such notions, where their interest is so particularly concern'd.

Lest those arguments shou'd not appear entirely conclusive (as I think they are) I shall have recourse to authority, and shall prove, from the universal consent of mankind, that the obligation of submission to government is not deriv'd from any promise of the subjects. Nor need any one wonder, that tho' I have all along endeavour'd to establish my system on pure reason, and have scarce ever cited the judgment even of philosophers or historians on any article, I shou'd now appeal to popular authority, and oppose the sentiments of the rabble to any philosophical reasoning. For it must be observ'd, that the opinions of men, in this case, carry with them a peculiar authority, and are, in a great measure, infallible. The distinction of moral good and evil is founded on the pleasure or pain, which results from the view of any sentiment, or character; and as that pleasure or pain cannot be unknown to the person who feels it, it follows,[2] that there is just so much vice or virtue in any character, as every one places in it, and that 'tis impossible in this particular we can ever be mistaken. And tho' our judgments concerning the *origin* of any vice or virtue, be not so certain as those concerning their *degrees*; yet, since the question in this case regards not any philosophical origin of an obligation, but a plain matter of fact, 'tis not easily conceiv'd how we can fall into an error. A man, who acknowledges himself to be bound to another, for a certain sum, must certainly know whether it be by his own bond, or that of his father; whether it be of his mere good-will, or for money lent him; and under what conditions, and for what purposes he has bound himself. In like manner, it being certain, that there is a moral obligation to submit to government, because every one thinks so; it must be as certain, that this obligation arises not from a promise; since no one, whose judgment has not been led astray by too strict adherence to a system of philosophy, has ever yet dreamt of ascribing it to that origin. Neither magistrates nor subjects have form'd this idea of our civil duties.

9   We find, that magistrates are so far from deriving their authority, and the obligation to obedience in their subjects, from the foundation of a promise or original contract, that they conceal, as far as possible, from their people, especially from the vulgar, that they have their origin from thence. Were this the sanction of government, our rulers wou'd never receive it tacitly, which is the utmost that can be pretended; since what is given tacitly and insensibly can never have such influence on mankind, as what is perform'd expressly and openly. A tacit promise is, where the will is signify'd by other more diffuse signs than those of speech; but a will there must certainly be in the case, and that can never escape the person's

---

[2] This proposition must hold strictly true, with regard to every quality, that is determin'd merely by sentiment. In what sense we can talk either of a *right* or a *wrong* taste in morals, eloquence, or beauty, shall be consider'd afterwards. In the mean time, it may be observ'd, that there is such an uniformity in the *general* sentiments of mankind, as to render such questions of but small importance.

notice, who exerted it, however silent or tacit. But were you to ask the far greatest part of the nation, whether they had ever consented to the authority of their rulers, or promis'd to obey them, they wou'd be inclin'd to think very strangely of you; and wou'd certainly reply, that the affair depended not on their consent, but that they were born to such an obedience. In consequence of this opinion, we frequently see them imagine such persons to be their natural rulers, as are at that time depriv'd of all power and authority, and whom no man, however foolish, wou'd voluntarily chuse; and this merely because they are in that line, which rul'd before, and in that degree of it, which us'd to succeed; tho' perhaps in so distant a period, that scarce any man alive cou'd ever have given any promise of obedience. Has a government, then, no authority over such as these, because they never consented to it, and wou'd esteem the very attempt of such a free choice a piece of arrogance and impiety? We find by experience, that it punishes them very freely for what it calls treason and rebellion, which, it seems, according to this system, reduces itself to common injustice. If you say, that by dwelling in its dominions, they in effect consented to the establish'd government; I answer, that this can only be, where they think the affair depends on their choice, which few or none, beside those philosophers, have ever yet imagin'd. It never was pleaded as an excuse for a rebel, that the first act he perform'd, after he came to years of discretion, was to levy war against the sovereign of the state; and that while he was a child he cou'd not bind himself by his own consent, and having become a man, show'd plainly, by the first act he perform'd, that he had no design to impose on himself any obligation to obedience. We find, on the contrary, that civil laws punish this crime at the same age as any other, which is criminal, of itself, without our consent; that is, when the person is come to the full use of reason: Whereas to this crime they ought in justice to allow some intermediate time, in which a tacit consent at least might be suppos'd. To which we may add, that a man living under an absolute government, wou'd owe it no allegiance; since, by its very nature, it depends not on consent. But as that is as *natural* and *common* a government as any, it must certainly occasion some obligation; and 'tis plain from experience, that men, who are subjected to it, do always think so. This is a clear proof, that we do not commonly esteem our allegiance to be deriv'd from our consent or promise; and a farther proof is, that when our promise is upon any account expressly engag'd, we always distinguish exactly betwixt the two obligations, and believe the one to add more force to the other, than in a repetition of the same promise. Where no promise is given, a man looks not on his faith as broken in private matters, upon account of rebellion; but keeps those two duties of honour and allegiance perfectly distinct and separate. As the uniting of them was thought by these philosophers a very subtile invention, this is a convincing proof, that 'tis not a true one; since no man can either give a promise, or be restrain'd by its sanction and obligation unknown to himself.

Section IX. Of the measures of allegiance.

1   Those political writers, who have had recourse to a promise, or original contract, as the source of our allegiance to government, intended to establish a principle, which is perfectly just and reasonable; tho' the reasoning, upon which they endeavour'd to establish it, was fallacious and sophistical. They wou'd prove, that our submission to government admits of exceptions, and that an egregious tyranny in the rulers is sufficient to free the subjects from all ties of allegiance. Since men enter into society, say they, and submit themselves to government, by their free and voluntary consent, they must have in view certain advantages, which they propose to reap from it, and for which they are contented to resign their native liberty. There is, therefore, something mutual engag'd on the part of the magistrate, *viz.* protection and security; and 'tis only by the hopes he affords of these advantages, that he can ever perswade men to submit to him. But when instead of protection and security, they meet with tyranny and oppression, they are freed from their promises, (as happens in all conditional contracts) and return to that state of liberty, which preceded the institution of government. Men wou'd never be so foolish as to enter into such engagements as shou'd turn entirely to the advantage of others, without any view of bettering their own condition. Whoever proposes to draw any profit from our submission, must engage himself, either expressly or tacitly, to make us reap some advantage from his authority; nor ought he to expect, that without the performance of his part we will ever continue in obedience.

2   I repeat it: This conclusion is just, tho' the principles be erroneous; and I flatter myself, that I can establish the same conclusion on more reasonable principles. I shall not take such a compass, in establishing our political duties, as to assert, that men perceive the advantages of government; that they institute government with a view to those advantages; that this institution requires a promise of obedience; which imposes a moral obligation to a certain degree, but being conditional, ceases to be binding whenever the other contracting party performs not his part of the engagement. I perceive, that a promise itself arises entirely from human conventions, and is invented with a view to a certain interest. I seek, therefore, some such interest more immediately connected with government, and which may be at once the original motive to its institution, and the source of our obedience to it. This interest I find to consist in the security and

protection, which we enjoy in political society, and which we can never attain, when perfectly free and independent. As interest, therefore, is the immediate sanction of government, the one can have no longer being than the other; and whenever the civil magistrate carries his oppression so far as to render his authority perfectly intolerable, we are no longer bound to submit to it. The cause ceases; the effect must cease also.

So far the conclusion is immediate and direct, concerning the *natural*   3 obligation which we have to allegiance. As to the *moral* obligation, we may observe, that the maxim wou'd here be false, that *when the cause ceases the effect must cease also.* For there is a principle of human nature, which we have frequently taken notice of, that men are mightily addicted to *general rules*, and that we often carry our maxims beyond those reasons, which first induc'd us to establish them. Where cases are similar in many circumstances, we are apt to put them on the same footing, without considering, that they differ in the most material circumstances, and that the resemblance is more apparent than real. It may, therefore, be thought, that in the case of allegiance our moral obligation of duty will not cease, even tho' the natural obligation of interest, which is its cause, has ceas'd; and that men may be bound by *conscience* to submit to a tyrannical government against their own and the public interest. And indeed, to the force of this argument I so far submit, as to acknowledge, that general rules commonly extend beyond the principles, on which they are founded; and that we seldom make any exception to them, unless that exception have the qualities of a general rule, and be founded on very numerous and common instances. Now this I assert to be entirely the present case. When men submit to the authority of others, 'tis to procure themselves some security against the wickedness and injustice of men, who are perpetually carry'd, by their unruly passions, and by their present and immediate interest, to the violation of all the laws of society. But as this imperfection is inherent in human nature, we know that it must attend men in all their states and conditions; and that those, whom we chuse for rulers, do not immediately become of a superior nature to the rest of mankind, upon account of their superior power and authority. What we expect from them depends not on a change of their nature but of their situation, when they acquire a more immediate interest in the preservation of order and the execution of justice. But besides that this interest is only more immediate in the execution of justice among their subjects, not in disputes betwixt themselves and their subjects; besides this, I say, we may often expect, from the irregularity of human nature, that they will neglect even this immediate interest, and be transported by their passions into all the excesses of cruelty and ambition. Our general knowledge of human nature, our observation of the past history of mankind, our experience of present times; all these causes must induce us to open the door to exceptions, and must make us conclude, that we may resist the more violent effects of supreme power, without any crime or injustice.

4   Accordingly we may observe, that this is both the general practice and principle of mankind, and that no nation, that cou'd find any remedy, ever yet suffer'd the cruel ravages of a tyrant, or were blam'd for their resistance. Those who took up arms against *Dionysius* or *Nero*, or *Philip the second*, have the favour of every reader in the perusal of their history; and nothing but the most violent perversion of common sense can ever lead us to condemn them. 'Tis certain, therefore, that in all our notions of morals we never entertain such an absurdity as that of passive obedience, but make allowances for resistance in the more flagrant instances of tyranny and oppression. The general opinion of mankind has some authority in all cases; but in this of morals 'tis perfectly infallible. Nor is it less infallible, because men cannot distinctly explain the principles, on which it is founded. Few persons can carry on this train of reasoning: "Government is a mere human invention for the interest of society. Where the tyranny of the governor removes this interest, it also removes the natural obligation to obedience. The moral obligation is founded on the natural, and therefore must cease where *that* ceases; especially where the subject is such as makes us foresee very many occasions wherein the natural obligation may cease, and causes us to form a kind of general rule for the regulation of our conduct in such occurrences." But tho' this train of reasoning be too subtile for the vulgar, 'tis certain, that all men have an implicit notion of it, and are sensible, that they owe obedience to government merely on account of the public interest; and at the same time, that human nature is so subject to frailties and passions, as may easily pervert this institution, and change their governors into tyrants and public enemies. If the sense of interest were not our original motive to obedience, I wou'd fain ask, what other principle is there in human nature capable of subduing the natural ambition of men, and forcing them to such a submission? Imitation and custom are not sufficient. For the question still recurs, what motive first produces those instances of submission, which we imitate, and that train of actions, which produces the custom? There evidently is no other principle than interest; and if interest first produces obedience to government, the obligation to obedience must cease, whenever the interest ceases, in any great degree, and in a considerable number of instances.

Section X. Of the objects of allegiance.

1   But tho', on some occasions, it may be justifiable, both in sound politics and morality, to resist supreme power, 'tis certain, that in the ordinary

course of human affairs nothing can be more pernicious and criminal; and that besides the convulsions, which always attend revolutions, such a practice tends directly to the subversion of all government, and the causing an universal anarchy and confusion among mankind. As numerous and civiliz'd societies cannot subsist without government, so government is entirely useless without an exact obedience. We ought always to weigh the advantages, which we reap from authority, against the disadvantages; and by this means we shall become more scrupulous of putting in practice the doctrine of resistance. The common rule requires submission; and 'tis only in cases of grievous tyranny and oppression, that the exception can take place.

Since then such a blind submission is commonly due to magistracy, the next question is, *To whom it is due, and whom we are to regard as our lawful magistrates?* In order to answer this question, let us recollect what we have already establish'd concerning the origin of government and political society. When men have once experienc'd the impossibility of preserving any steady order in society, while every one is his own master, and violates or observes the laws of society, according to his present interest or pleasure, they naturally run into the invention of government, and put it out of their own power, as far as possible, to transgress the rules of justice. Government, therefore, arises from the voluntary convention of men; and 'tis evident, that the same convention, which establishes government, will also determine the persons who are to govern, and will remove all doubt and ambiguity in this particular. And the voluntary consent of men must here have the greater efficacy, that the authority of the magistrate does *at first* stand upon the foundation of a promise of the subjects, by which they bind themselves to obedience; as in every other contract or engagement. The same promise, then, which binds them to obedience, ties them down to a particular person, and makes him the object of their allegiance. 2

But when government has been establish'd on this footing for some considerable time, and the separate interest, which we have in submission, has produc'd a separate sentiment of morality, the case is entirely alter'd, and a promise is no longer able to determine the particular magistrate; since it is no longer consider'd as the foundation of government. We naturally suppose ourselves born to submission; and imagine, that such particular persons have a right to command, as we on our part are bound to obey. These notions of right and obligation are deriv'd from nothing but the *advantage* reapt from government, which gives us a repugnance to practise resistance ourselves, and makes us displeas'd with any instance of it in others. But here 'tis remarkable, that in this new state of affairs, the original sanction of government, which is *interest*, is not admitted to determine the persons, whom we are to obey, as the original sanction did at 3 first, when affairs were on the footing of a *promise*. A *promise* fixes and determines the persons, without any uncertainty: But 'tis evident, that if men were to regulate their conduct in this particular, by the view of a peculiar *interest*, either public or private, they wou'd involve themselves in endless confusion, and wou'd render all government, in a great measure, ineffectual. The private interest of every one is different; and, tho' the public interest in itself be always one and the same, yet it becomes the source of as great dissensions, by reason of the different opinions of particular persons concerning it. The same interest, therefore, which causes us to submit to magistracy, makes us renounce itself in the choice of our magistrates, and binds us down to a certain form of government, and to particular persons, without allowing us to aspire to the utmost perfection in either. The case is here the same as in that law of nature concerning the stability of possession. 'Tis highly advantageous, and even absolutely necessary to society, that possession shou'd be stable; and this leads us to the establishment of such a rule: But we find, that were we to follow the same advantage, in assigning particular possessions to particular persons, we shou'd disappoint our end, and perpetuate the confusion, which that rule is intended to prevent. We must, therefore, proceed by general rules, and regulate ourselves by general interests, in modifying the law of nature concerning the stability of possession. Nor need we fear, that our attachment to this law will diminish upon account of the seeming frivolousness of those interests, by which it is determin'd. The impulse of the mind is deriv'd from a very strong interest; and those other more minute interests serve only to direct the motion, without adding any thing to it, or diminishing from it. 'Tis the same case with government. Nothing is more advantageous to society than such an invention; and this interest is sufficient to make us embrace it with ardour and alacrity; tho' we are oblig'd afterwards to regulate and direct our devotion to government by several considerations, which are not of the same importance, and to chuse our magistrates without having in view any particular advantage from the choice.

4   The *first* of those principles I shall take notice of, as a foundation of the right of magistracy, is that which gives authority to almost all the establish'd governments of the world: I mean, *long possession* in any one form of government, or succession of princes. 'Tis certain, that if we remount to the first origin of every nation, we shall find, that there scarce is any race of kings, or form of a commonwealth, that is not primarily founded on usurpation and rebellion, and whose title is not at first worse than doubtful and uncertain. Time alone gives solidity to their right; and operating gradually on the minds of men, reconciles them to any authority, and

makes it seem just and reasonable. Nothing causes any sentiment to have a greater influence upon us than custom, or turns our imagination more strongly to any object. When we have been long accustom'd to obey any set of men, that general instinct or tendency, which we have to suppose a moral obligation attending loyalty, takes easily this direction, and chuses that set of men for its objects. 'Tis interest which gives the general instinct; but 'tis custom which gives the particular direction.

And here 'tis observable, that the same length of time has a different influence on our sentiments of morality, according to its different influence on the mind. We naturally judge of every thing by comparison; and since in considering the fate of kingdoms and republics, we embrace a long extent of time, a small duration has not in this case a like influence on our sentiments, as when we consider any other object. One thinks he acquires a right to a horse, or a suit of cloaths, in a very short time; but a century is scarce sufficient to establish any new government, or remove all scruples in the minds of the subjects concerning it. Add to this, that a shorter period of time will suffice to give a prince a title to any additional power he may usurp, than will serve to fix his right, where the whole is an usurpation. The kings of *France* have not been possess'd of absolute power for above two reigns; and yet nothing will appear more extravagant to *Frenchmen* than to talk of their liberties. If we consider what has been said concerning *accession*, we shall easily account for this phænomenon.

When there is no form of government establish'd by *long* possession, the *present* possession is sufficient to supply its place, and may be regarded as the *second* source of all public authority. Right to authority is nothing but the constant possession of authority, maintain'd by the laws of society and the interests of mankind; and nothing can be more natural than to join this constant possession to the present one, according to the principles above-mention'd. If the same principles did not take place with regard to the property of private persons, 'twas because these principles were counter-ballanc'd by very strong considerations of interest; when we observ'd, that all restitution wou'd by that means be prevented, and every violence be authoriz'd and protected. And tho' the same motives may seem to have force, with regard to public authority, yet they are oppos'd by a contrary interest; which consists in the preservation of peace, and the avoiding of all changes, which, however they may be easily produc'd in private affairs, are unavoidably attended with bloodshed and confusion, where the public is interested.

Any one, who finding the impossibility of accounting for the right of the present possessor, by any receiv'd system of ethics, shou'd resolve to deny absolutely that right, and assert, that it is not authoriz'd by morality, wou'd be justly thought to maintain a very extravagant paradox, and to shock the common sense and judgment of mankind. No maxim is more conformable, both to prudence and morals, than to submit quietly to the government, which we find establish'd in the country where we happen to live, without enquiring too curiously into its origin and first establishment. Few governments will bear being examin'd so rigorously. How many kingdoms are there at present in the world, and how many more do we find in history, whose governors have no better foundation for their authority than that of present possession? To confine ourselves to the *Roman* and *Grecian* empire; is it not evident, that the long succession of emperors, from the dissolution of the *Roman* liberty, to the final extinction of that empire by the *Turks*, cou'd not so much as pretend to any other title to the empire? The election of the senate was a mere form, which always follow'd the choice of the legions; and these were almost always divided in the different provinces, and nothing but the sword was able to terminate the difference. 'Twas by the sword, therefore, that every emperor acquir'd, as well as defended his right; and we must either say, that all the known world, for so many ages, had no government, and ow'd no allegiance to any one, or must allow, that the right of the stronger, in public affairs, is to be receiv'd as legitimate, and authoriz'd by morality, when not oppos'd by any other title.

8   The right of *conquest* may be consider'd as a *third* source of the title of sovereigns. This right resembles very much that of present possession; but has rather a superior force, being seconded by the notions of glory and honour, which we ascribe to *conquerors*, instead of the sentiments of hatred and detestation, which attend *usurpers*. Men naturally favour those they love; and therefore are more apt to ascribe a right to successful violence, betwixt one sovereign and another, than to the successful rebellion of a subject against his sovereign.[1]

9   When neither long possession, nor present possession, nor conquest take place, as when the first sovereign, who founded any monarchy, dies; in that case, the right of *succession* naturally prevails in their stead, and men are commonly induc'd to place the son of their late monarch on the throne, and suppose him to inherit his father's authority. The presum'd consent of the father, the imitation of the succession to private families,

---

[1] It is not here asserted, that *present possession* or *conquest* are sufficient to give a title against *long possession* and *positive laws:* But only that they have some force, and will be able to cast the ballance where the titles are otherwise equal, and will even be sufficient *sometimes* to sanctify the weaker title. What degree of force they have is difficult to determine. I believe all moderate men will allow, that they have great force in all disputes concerning the rights of princes.

the interest, which the state has in choosing the person, who is most powerful, and has the most numerous followers; all these reasons lead men to
prefer the son of their late monarch to any other person.[2]

These reasons have some weight; but I am persuaded, that to one, who   10
considers impartially of the matter, 'twill appear, that some principles of
the imagination concur with those views of justice and interest. The royal
authority seems to be connected with the young prince even in his father's
life-time, by the natural transition of the thought; and still more after his
death: So that nothing is more natural than to compleat this union by a
new relation, and by putting him actually in possession of what seems so
naturally to belong to him.

To confirm this we may weigh the following phænomena, which are   11
pretty curious in their kind. In elective monarchies the right of succession
has no place by the laws and settled custom; and yet its influence is so natural, that 'tis impossible entirely to exclude it from the imagination, and
render the subjects indifferent to the son of their deceas'd monarch.
Hence in some governments of this kind, the choice commonly falls on
one or other of the royal family; and in some governments they are all excluded. Those contrary phænomena proceed from the same principle.
Where the royal family is excluded, 'tis from a refinement in politics,
which makes people sensible of their propensity to chuse a sovereign in
that family, and gives them a jealousy of their liberty, lest their new monarch, aided by this propensity, shou'd establish his family, and destroy the
freedom of elections for the future.

The history of *Artaxerxes*, and the younger *Cyrus*, may furnish us with   12
some reflections to the same purpose. *Cyrus* pretended a right to the
throne above his elder brother, because he was born after his father's accession. I do not pretend, that this reason was valid. I wou'd only infer
from it, that he wou'd never have made use of such a pretext, were it not
for the qualities of the imagination above-mention'd, by which we are naturally inclin'd to unite by a new relation whatever objects we find already
united. *Artaxerxes* had an advantage above his brother, as being the eldest
son, and the first in succession: But *Cyrus* was more closely related to the
royal authority, as being begot after his father was invested with it.

Shou'd it here be pretended, that the view of convenience may be the   13
source of all the right of succession, and that men gladly take advantage of
any rule, by which they can fix the successor of their late sovereign, and

---

[2] To prevent mistakes I must observe, that this case of succession is not the same
with that of hereditary monarchies, where custom has fix'd the right of succession.
These depend upon the principle of long possession above explain'd.

prevent that anarchy and confusion, which attends all new elections: To this I wou'd answer, that perhaps that this motive may contribute somewhat to the effect; but, that without another principle, 'tis impossible such a motive shou'd take place. The interest of a nation requires, that the succession to the crown shou'd be fix'd one way or other; but 'tis the same thing to its interest in what way it be fix'd: So that if the relation of blood had not an effect independent of public interest, it wou'd never have been regarded, without a positive law; and 'twou'd have been impossible, that so many positive laws of different nations cou'd ever have concurr'd precisely in the same views and intentions.

14   This leads us to consider the *fifth* source of authority, viz. *positive laws*; when the legislature establishes a certain form of government and succession of princes. At first sight it may be thought, that this must resolve into some of the preceding titles of authority. The legislative power, whence the positive law is deriv'd, must either be establish'd by original contract, long possession, present possession, conquest, or succession; and consequently the positive law must derive its force from some of those principles. But here 'tis remarkable, that tho' a positive law can only derive its force from these principles, yet it acquires not all the force of the principle from whence it is deriv'd, but loses considerably in the transition; as it is natural to imagine. For instance; a government is establish'd for many centuries on a certain system of laws, forms, and methods of succession. The legislative power, establish'd by this long succession, changes all on a sudden the whole system of government, and introduces a new constitution in its stead. I believe few of the subjects will think themselves bound to comply with this alteration, unless it have an evident tendency to the public good: But will think themselves still at liberty to return to the antient government. Hence the notion of *fundamental laws*; which are suppos'd to be inalterable by the will of the sovereign: And of this nature the *Salic* law is understood to be in *France*. How far these fundamental laws extend is not determin'd in any government; nor is it possible it ever shou'd. There is such an insensible gradation from the most material laws to the most trivial, and from the most antient laws to the most modern, that 'twill be impossible to set bounds to the legislative power, and determine how far it may innovate in the principles of government. That is the work more of imagination and passion than of reason.

15   Whoever considers the history of the several nations of the world; their revolutions, conquests, encrease, and diminution; the manner in which their particular governments are establish'd, and the successive right transmitted from one person to another, will soon learn to treat very lightly all disputes concerning the rights of princes, and will be convinc'd, that a strict adherence to any general rules, and the rigid loyalty to particular persons and families, on which some people set so high a value, are

virtues that hold less of reason, than of bigotry and superstition. In this particular, the study of history confirms the reasonings of true philosophy; which, shewing us the original qualities of human nature, teaches us to regard the controversies in politics as incapable of any decision in most cases, and as entirely subordinate to the interests of peace and liberty. Where the public good does not evidently demand a change; 'tis certain, that the concurrence of all those titles, *original contract, long possession, present possession, succession,* and *positive laws,* forms the strongest title to sovereignty, and is justly regarded as sacred and inviolable. But when these titles are mingled and oppos'd in different degrees, they often occasion perplexity; and are less capable of solution from the arguments of lawyers and philosophers, than from the swords of the soldiery. Who shall tell me, for instance, whether *Germanicus,* or *Drusus,* ought to have succeeded *Tiberius,* had he died while they were both alive, without naming any of them for his successor? Ought the right of adoption to be receiv'd as equivalent to that of blood in a nation, where it had the same effect in private families, and had already, in two instances, taken place in the public? Ought *Germanicus* to be esteem'd the eldest son, because he was born before *Drusus;* or the younger, because he was adopted after the birth of his brother? Ought the right of the elder to be regarded in a nation, where the eldest brother had no advantage in the succession to private families? Ought the *Roman* empire at that time to be esteem'd hereditary, because of two examples; or ought it, even so early, to be regarded as belonging to the stronger, or the present possessor, as being founded on so recent an usurpation? Upon whatever principles we may pretend to answer these and such like questions, I am afraid we shall never be able to satisfy an impartial enquirer, who adopts no party in political controversies, and will be satisfy'd with nothing but sound reason and philosophy.

But here an *English* reader will be apt to enquire concerning that famous *revolution,* which has had such a happy influence on our constitution, and has been attended with such mighty consequences. We have already remark'd, that in the case of enormous tyranny and oppression, 'tis lawful to take arms even against supreme power; and that as government is a mere human invention for mutual advantage and security, it no longer imposes any obligation, either natural or moral, when once it ceases to have that tendency. But tho' this *general* principle be authoriz'd by common sense, and the practice of all ages, 'tis certainly impossible for the laws, or even for philosophy, to establish any *particular* rules, by which we may know when resistance is lawful; and decide all controversies, which may arise on that subject. This may not only happen with regard to supreme power; but 'tis possible, even in some constitutions, where the legislative authority is not lodg'd in one person, that there may be a magistrate so eminent and powerful, as to oblige the laws to keep silence in this

16

particular. Nor wou'd this silence be an effect only of their *respect*, but also of their *prudence*; since 'tis certain, that in the vast variety of circumstances, which occur in all governments, a particular exercise of power, in so great a magistrate, may at one time be beneficial to the public, which at another time wou'd be pernicious and tyrannical. But notwithstanding this silence of the laws in limited monarchies, 'tis certain, that the people still retain the right of resistance; since 'tis impossible, even in the most despotic governments, to deprive them of it. The same necessity of self-preservation, and the same motive of public good, give them the same liberty in the one case as in the other. And we may farther observe, that in such mix'd governments, the cases, wherein resistance is lawful, must occur much oftener, and greater indulgence be given to the subjects to defend themselves by force of arms, than in arbitrary governments. Not only where the chief magistrate enters into measures, in themselves, extremely pernicious to the public, but even when he wou'd encroach on the other parts of the constitution, and extend his power beyond the legal bounds, it is allowable to resist and dethrone him; tho' such resistance and violence may, in the general tenor of the laws, be deem'd unlawful and rebellious. For besides that nothing is more essential to public interest, than the preservation of public liberty; 'tis evident, that if such a mix'd government be once suppos'd to be establish'd, every part or member of the constitution must have a right of self-defence, and of maintaining its antient bounds against the encroachment of every other authority. As matter wou'd have been created in vain, were it depriv'd of a power of resistance, without which no part of it cou'd preserve a distinct existence, and the whole might be crowded up into a single point: So 'tis a gross absurdity to suppose, in any government, a right without a remedy, or allow, that the supreme power is shar'd with the people, without allowing, that 'tis lawful for them to defend their share against every invader. Those, therefore, who wou'd seem to respect our free government, and yet deny the right of resistance, have renounc'd all pretensions to common sense, and do not merit a serious answer.

17   It does not belong to my present purpose to shew, that these general principles are applicable to the late *revolution*; and that all the rights and privileges, which ought to be sacred to a free nation, were at that time threaten'd with the utmost danger. I am better pleas'd to leave this controverted subject, if it really admits of controversy; and to indulge myself in some philosophical reflections, which naturally arise from that important event.

18   *First*, We may observe, that shou'd the *lords* and *commons* in our constitution, without any reason from public interest, either depose the king in being, or after his death exclude the prince, who, by laws and settled custom, ought to succeed, no one wou'd esteem their proceedings legal, or

think themselves bound to comply with them. But shou'd the king, by his unjust practices, or his attempts for a tyrannical and despotic power, justly forfeit his legal authority, it then not only becomes morally lawful and suitable to the nature of political society to dethrone him; but what is more, we are apt likewise to think, that the remaining members of the constitution acquire a right of excluding his next heir, and of choosing whom they please for his successor. This is founded on a very singular quality of our thought and imagination. When a king forfeits his authority, his heir ought naturally to remain in the same situation, as if the king were remov'd by death; unless by mixing himself in the tyranny, he forfeit it for himself. But tho' this may seem reasonable, we easily comply with the contrary opinion. The deposition of a king, in such a government as ours, is certainly an act beyond all common authority, and an illegal assuming a power for public good, which, in the ordinary course of government, can belong to no member of the constitution. When the public good is so great and so evident as to justify the action, the commendable use of this licence causes us naturally to attribute to the *parliament* a right of using farther licences; and the antient bounds of the laws being once transgress'd with approbation, we are not apt to be so strict in confining ourselves precisely within their limits. The mind naturally runs on with any train of action, which it has begun; nor do we commonly make any scruple concerning our duty, after the first action of any kind, which we perform. Thus at the *revolution*, none who thought the deposition of the father justifiable, esteem'd themselves to be confin'd to his infant son; tho' had that unhappy monarch died innocent at that time, and had his son, by any accident, been convey'd beyond seas, there is no doubt but a regency wou'd have been appointed till he shou'd come to age, and cou'd be restor'd to his dominions. As the slightest properties of the imagination have an effect on the judgments of the people, it shews the wisdom of the laws and of the parliament to take advantage of such properties, and to chuse the magistrates either in or out of a line, according as the vulgar will most naturally attribute authority and right to them.

Secondly, Tho' the accession of the *Prince* of *Orange* to the throne 19 might at first give occasion to many disputes, and his title be contested, it ought not now to appear doubtful, but must have acquir'd a sufficient authority from those three princes, who have succeeded him upon the same title. Nothing is more usual, tho' nothing may, at first sight, appear more unreasonable, than this way of thinking. Princes often *seem* to acquire a right from their successors, as well as from their ancestors; and a king, who during his life-time might justly be deem'd an usurper, will be regarded by posterity as a lawful prince, because he has had the good fortune to settle his family on the throne, and entirely change the antient form of government. *Julius Caesar* is regarded as the first *Roman* emperor;

while *Sylla* and *Marius*, whose titles were really the same as his, are treated as tyrants and usurpers. Time and custom give authority to all forms of government, and all successions of princes; and that power, which at first was founded only on injustice and violence, becomes in time legal and obligatory. Nor does the mind rest there; but returning back upon its footsteps, transfers to their predecessors and ancestors that right, which it naturally ascribes to the posterity, as being related together, and united in the imagination. The present king of *France* makes *Hugh Capet* a more lawful prince than *Cromwell*; as the establish'd liberty of the *Dutch* is no inconsiderable apology for their obstinate resistance to *Philip* the Second.

Section XI. Of the laws of nations.

1   When civil government has been establish'd over the greatest part of mankind, and different societies have been form'd contiguous to each other, there arises a new set of duties among the neighbouring states, suitable to the nature of that commerce, which they carry on with each other. Political writers tell us, that in every kind of intercourse, a body politic is to be consider'd as one person; and indeed this assertion is so far just, that different nations, as well as private persons, require mutual assistance; at the same time that their selfishness and ambition are perpetual sources of war and discord. But tho' nations in this particular resemble individuals, yet as they are very different in other respects, no wonder they regulate themselves by different maxims, and give rise to a new set of rules, which we call the *laws of nations*. Under this head we may comprize the sacredness of the persons of ambassadors, the declaration of war, the abstaining from poison'd arms, with other duties of that kind, which are evidently calculated for the commerce, that is peculiar to different societies.

2   But tho' these rules be super-added to the laws of nature, the former do not entirely abolish the latter; and one may safely affirm, that the three fundamental rules of justice, the stability of possession, its transference by consent, and the performance of promises, are duties of princes, as well as of subjects. The same interest produces the same effect in both cases. Where possession has no stability, there must be perpetual war. Where property is not transferr'd by consent, there can be no commerce. Where promises are not observ'd, there can be no leagues nor alliances. The advantages, therefore, of peace, commerce, and mutual succour, make us extend to different kingdoms the same notions of justice, which take place among individuals.

3   There is a maxim very current in the world, which few politicians are willing to avow, but which has been authoriz'd by the practice of all ages, *that there is a system of morals calculated for princes, much more free than that*

which ought to govern private persons. 'Tis evident this is not to be understood of the lesser *extent* of public duties and obligations; nor will any one
be so extravagant as to assert, that the most solemn treaties ought to have
no force among princes. For as princes do actually form treaties among
themselves, they must propose some advantage from the execution of
them; and the prospect of such advantage for the future must engage them
to perform their part, and must establish that law of nature. The meaning,
therefore, of this political maxim is, that tho' the morality of princes has
the same *extent,* yet it has not the same *force* as that of private persons, and
may lawfully be transgress'd from a more trivial motive. However shock-
ing such a proposition may appear to certain philosophers, 'twill be easy
to defend it upon those principles, by which we have accounted for the
origin of justice and equity.

When men have found by experience, that 'tis impossible to subsist   4
without society, and that 'tis impossible to maintain society, while they
give free course to their appetites; so urgent an interest quickly restrains
their actions, and imposes an obligation to observe those rules which we
call the *laws of justice.* This obligation of interest rests not here; but by the
necessary course of the passions and sentiments, gives rise to the moral
obligation of duty; while we approve of such actions as tend to the peace
of society, and disapprove of such as tend to its disturbance. The same
natural obligation of interest takes place among independent kingdoms,
and gives rise to the same *morality*; so that no one of ever so corrupt
morals will approve of a prince who voluntarily, and of his own accord,
breaks his word, or violates any treaty. But here we may observe, that tho'
the intercourse of different states be advantageous, and even sometimes
necessary, yet it is not so necessary nor advantageous as that among individuals, without which 'tis utterly impossible for human nature ever to
subsist. Since, therefore, the *natural* obligation to justice, among different
states, is not so strong as among individuals, the *moral* obligation, which
arises from it, must partake of its weakness; and we must necessarily give
a greater indulgence to a prince or minister, who deceives another; than to
a private gentleman, who breaks his word of honour.

Shou'd it be ask'd, *What proportion these two species of morality bear to*   5
each other? I wou'd answer, that this is a question, to which we can never
give any precise answer; nor is it possible to reduce to numbers the proportion, which we ought to fix betwixt them. One may safely affirm, that
this proportion finds itself, without any art or study of men; as we may observe on many other occasions. The practice of the world goes farther in
teaching us the degrees of our duty, than the most subtile philosophy,
which was ever yet invented. And this may serve as a convincing proof,
that all men have an implicit notion of the foundation of those moral rules

concerning natural and civil justice, and are sensible, that they arise merely from human conventions, and from the interest, which we have in the preservation of peace and order. For otherwise the diminution of the interest wou'd never produce a relaxation of the morality, and reconcile us more easily to any transgression of justice among princes and republics, than in the private commerce of one subject with another.

Section XII. Of chastity and modesty.

1   If any difficulty attend this system concerning the laws of nature and nations, 'twill be with regard to the universal approbation or blame, which follows their observance or transgression, and which some may not think sufficiently explain'd from the general interests of society. To remove, as far as possible, all scruples of this kind, I shall here consider another set of duties, *viz.* the *modesty* and *chastity* which belong to the fair sex: And I doubt not but these virtues will be found to be still more conspicuous instances of the operation of those principles, which I have insisted on.

2   There are some philosophers, who attack the female virtues with great vehemence, and fancy they have gone very far in detecting popular errors, when they can show, that there is no foundation in nature for all that exterior modesty, which we require in the expressions, and dress, and behaviour of the fair sex. I believe I may spare myself the trouble of insisting on so obvious a subject, and may proceed, without farther preparation, to examine after what manner such notions arise from education, from the voluntary conventions of men, and from the interest of society.

3   Whoever considers the length and feebleness of human infancy, with the concern which both sexes naturally have for their offspring, will easily perceive, that there must be an union of male and female for the education of the young, and that this union must be of considerable duration. But in order to induce the men to impose on themselves this restraint, and undergo chearfully all the fatigues and expences, to which it subjects them, they must believe, that the children are their own, and that their natural instinct is not directed to a wrong object, when they give a loose to love and tenderness. Now if we examine the structure of the human body, we shall find, that this security is very difficult to be attain'd on our part; and that since, in the copulation of the sexes, the principle of generation goes from the man to the woman, an error may easily take place on the side of the former, tho' it be utterly impossible with regard to the latter. From this trivial and anatomical observation is deriv'd that vast difference betwixt the education and duties of the two sexes.

4   Were a philosopher to examine the matter *a priori*, he wou'd reason after the following manner. Men are induc'd to labour for the maintenance and education of their children, by the persuasion that they are

really their own; and therefore 'tis reasonable, and even necessary, to give them some security in this particular. This security cannot consist entirely in the imposing of severe punishments on any transgressions of conjugal fidelity on the part of the wife; since these public punishments cannot be inflicted without legal proof, which 'tis difficult to meet with in this subject. What restraint, therefore, shall we impose on women, in order to counter-balance so strong a temptation as they have to infidelity? There seems to be no restraint possible, but in the punishment of bad fame or reputation; a punishment, which has a mighty influence on the human mind, and at the same time is inflicted by the world upon surmizes, and conjectures, and proofs, that wou'd never be receiv'd in any court of judicature. In order, therefore, to impose a due restraint on the female sex, we must attach a peculiar degree of shame to their infidelity, above what arises merely from its injustice, and must bestow proportionable praises on their chastity.

But tho' this be a very strong motive to fidelity, our philosopher wou'd　5 quickly discover, that it wou'd not alone be sufficient to that purpose. All human creatures, especially of the female sex, are apt to over-look remote motives in favour of any present temptation: The temptation is here the strongest imaginable: Its approaches are insensible and seducing: And a woman easily finds, or flatters herself she shall find, certain means of securing her reputation, and preventing all the pernicious consequences of her pleasures. 'Tis necessary, therefore, that, beside the infamy attending such licences, there shou'd be some preceding backwardness or dread, which may prevent their first approaches, and may give the female sex a repugnance to all expressions, and postures, and liberties, that have an immediate relation to that enjoyment.

Such wou'd be the reasonings of our speculative philosopher: But I am　6 persuaded, that if he had not a perfect knowledge of human nature, he wou'd be apt to regard them as mere chimerical speculations, and wou'd consider the infamy attending infidelity, and backwardness to all its approaches, as principles that were rather to be wish'd than hop'd for in the world. For what means, wou'd he say, of persuading mankind, that the transgressions of conjugal duty are more infamous than any other kind of injustice, when 'tis evident they are more excusable, upon account of the greatness of the temptation? And what possibility of giving a backwardness to the approaches of a pleasure, to which nature has inspir'd so strong a propensity; and a propensity that 'tis absolutely necessary in the end to comply with, for the support of the species?

But speculative reasonings, which cost so much pains to philosophers,　7 are often form'd by the world naturally, and without reflection: As difficulties, which seem unsurmountable in theory, are easily got over in practice. Those, who have an interest in the fidelity of women, naturally disapprove of their infidelity, and all the approaches to it. Those, who have no interest, are carried along with the stream, and are also apt to be affected with sympathy for the general interests of society. Education takes possession of the ductile minds of the fair sex in their infancy. And when a general rule of this kind is once establish'd, men are apt to extend it beyond those principles, from which it first arose. Thus batchelors, however debauch'd, cannot chuse but be shock'd with any instance of lewdness or impudence in women. And tho' all these maxims have a plain reference to generation, yet women past child-bearing have no more privilege in this respect, than those who are in the flower of their youth and beauty. Men have undoubtedly an implicit notion, that all those ideas of modesty and decency have a regard to generation; since they impose not the same laws, *with the same force*, on the male sex, where that reason takes not place. The exception is there obvious and extensive, and founded on a remarkable difference, which produces a clear separation and disjunction of ideas. But as the case is not the same with regard to the different ages of women, for this reason, tho' men know, that these notions are founded on the public interest, yet the general rule carries us beyond the original principle, and makes us extend the notions of modesty over the whole sex, from their earliest infancy to their extremest old-age and infirmity.

8   Courage, which is the point of honour among men, derives its merit, in a great measure, from artifice, as well as the chastity of women; tho' it has also some foundation in nature, as we shall see afterwards.

9   As to the obligations which the male sex lie under, with regard to chastity, we may observe, that according to the general notions of the world, they bear nearly the same proportion to the obligations of women, as the obligations of the law of nations do to those of the law of nature. 'Tis contrary to the interest of civil society, that men shou'd have an *entire* liberty of indulging their appetites in venereal enjoyment: But as this interest is weaker than in the case of the female sex, the moral obligation, arising from it, must be proportionably weaker. And to prove this we need only appeal to the practice and sentiments of all nations and ages.

Part III:
Of the Other Virtues and Vices.

Section I. Of the origin of the natural virtues and vices.

We come now to the examination of such virtues and vices as are entirely   1
natural, and have no dependence on the artifice and contrivance of men.
The examination of these will conclude this system of morals.

The chief spring or actuating principle of the human mind is pleasure   2
or pain; and when these sensations are remov'd, both from our thought
and feeling, we are, in a great measure, incapable of passion or action, of
desire or volition. The most immediate effects of pleasure and pain are the
propense and averse motions of the mind; which are diversify'd into volition, into desire and aversion, grief and joy, hope and fear, according as
the pleasure or pain changes its situation, and becomes probable or improbable, certain or uncertain, or is consider'd as out of our power for the
present moment. But when along with this, the objects, that cause pleasure or pain, acquire a relation to ourselves or others; they still continue to
excite desire and aversion, grief and joy: But cause, at the same time, the
indirect passions of pride or humility, love or hatred, which in this case
have a double relation of impressions and ideas to the pain or pleasure.

We have already observ'd, that moral distinctions depend entirely on cer-   3
tain peculiar sentiments of pain and pleasure, and that whatever mental
quality in ourselves or others gives us a satisfaction, by the survey or reflection, is of course virtuous; as every thing of this nature, that gives uneasiness, is vicious. Now since every quality in ourselves or others, which gives
pleasure, always causes pride or love; as every one, that produces uneasiness,
excites humility or hatred: It follows, that these two particulars are to be
consider'd as equivalent, with regard to our mental qualities, *virtue* and the
power of producing love or pride, *vice* and the power of producing humility
or hatred. In every case, therefore, we must judge of the one by the other;
and may pronounce any *quality* of the mind virtuous, which causes love or
pride; and any one vicious, which causes hatred or humility.

If any *action* be either virtuous or vicious, 'tis only as a sign of some   4
quality or character. It must depend upon durable principles of the mind,
which extend over the whole conduct, and enter into the personal character. Actions themselves, not proceeding from any constant principle, have
no influence on love or hatred, pride or humility; and consequently are
never consider'd in morality.

This reflection is self-evident, and deserves to be attended to, as being   5
of the utmost importance in the present subject. We are never to consider
any single action in our enquiries concerning the origin of morals; but
only the quality or character from which the action proceeded. These

alone are *durable* enough to affect our sentiments concerning the person. Actions are, indeed, better indications of a character than words, or even wishes and sentiments; but 'tis only so far as they are such indications, that they are attended with love or hatred, praise or blame.

6   To discover the true origin of morals, and of that love or hatred, which arises from mental qualities, we must take the matter pretty deep, and compare some principles, which have been already examin'd and explain'd.

7   We may begin with considering anew the nature and force of *sympathy*. The minds of all men are similar in their feelings and operations; nor can any one be actuated by any affection, of which all others are not, in some degree, susceptible. As in strings equally wound up, the motion of one communicates itself to the rest; so all the affections readily pass from one person to another, and beget correspondent movements in every human creature. When I see the *effects* of passion in the voice and gesture of any person, my mind immediately passes from these effects to their causes, and forms such a lively idea of the passion, as is presently converted into the passion itself. In like manner, when I perceive the *causes* of any emotion, my mind is convey'd to the effects, and is actuated with a like emotion. Were I present at any of the more terrible operations of surgery, 'tis certain, that even before it begun, the preparation of the instruments, the laying of the bandages in order, the heating of the irons, with all the signs of anxiety and concern in the patient and assistants, wou'd have a great effect upon my mind, and excite the strongest sentiments of pity and terror. No passion of another discovers itself immediately to the mind. We are only sensible of its causes or effects. From *these* we infer the passion: And consequently *these* give rise to our sympathy.

8   Our sense of beauty depends very much on this principle; and where any object has a tendency to produce pleasure in its possessor, it is always regarded as beautiful; as every object, that has a tendency to produce pain, is disagreeable and deform'd. Thus the conveniency of a house, the fertility of a field, the strength of a horse, the capacity, security, and swift-sailing of a vessel, form the principal beauty of these several objects. Here the object, which is denominated beautiful, pleases only by its tendency to produce a certain effect. That effect is the pleasure or advantage of some other person. Now the pleasure of a stranger, for whom we have no friendship, pleases us only by sympathy. To this principle, therefore, is owing the beauty, which we find in every thing that is useful. How considerable a part this is of beauty will easily appear upon reflection. Wherever an object has a tendency to produce pleasure in the possessor, or in other words, is the proper *cause* of pleasure, it is sure to please the spectator, by

a delicate sympathy with the possessor. Most of the works of art are es-teem'd beautiful, in proportion to their fitness for the use of man, and even many of the productions of nature derive their beauty from that source. Handsome and beautiful, on most occasions, is not an absolute but a relative quality, and pleases us by nothing but its tendency to produce an end that is agreeable.[1]

The same principle produces, in many instances, our sentiments of   9 morals, as well as those of beauty. No virtue is more esteem'd than justice, and no vice more detested than injustice; nor are there any qualities, which go farther to the fixing the character, either as amiable or odious. Now justice is a moral virtue, merely because it has that tendency to the good of mankind; and, indeed, is nothing but an artificial invention to that purpose. The same may be said of allegiance, of the laws of nations, of modesty, and of good-manners. All these are mere human contrivances for the interest of society. The inventors of them had chiefly in view their own interest. But we carry our approbation of them into the most distant countries and ages, and much beyond our own interest. And since there is a very strong sentiment of morals, which have always attended them, we must allow, that the reflecting on the tendency of characters and mental qualities, is sufficient to give us the sentiments of approbation and blame. Now as the means to an end can only be agreeable, where the end is agree-able; and as the good of society, where our own interest is not concern'd, or that of our friends, pleases only by sympathy: It follows, that sympathy is the source of the esteem, which we pay to all the artificial virtues.

Thus it appears, *that* sympathy is a very powerful principle in human   10 nature, *that* it has a great influence on our taste of beauty, and *that* it pro-duces our sentiment of morals in all the artificial virtues. From thence we may presume, that it also gives rise to many of the other virtues; and that qualities acquire our approbation, because of their tendency to the good of mankind. This presumption must become a certainty, when we find that most of those qualities, which we *naturally* approve of, have actually that tendency, and render a man a proper member of society: While the

---

[1] Decentior equus cujus astricta sunt ilia; sed idem velocior. Pulcher aspectu sit ath-leta, cujus lacertos exercitatio expressit; idem certamini paratior. Nunquam vero *species* ab *utilitate* dividitur. Sed hoc quidem discernere, modici judicii est.—*Quinct.* lib. 8. ["A horse whose flanks are compact looks better, but is also faster. An athlete whose muscles have been developed by exercise may be good to look at; he is also more ready for the fray. True beauty is never separated from usefulness. But it only takes a modest power of judgement to see this." (Quintilian, *The Orator's Education*, VIII, III, 10–11; trans. by Donald A. Russell).]

qualities, which we *naturally* disapprove of, have a contrary tendency, and render any intercourse with the person dangerous or disagreeable. For having found, that such tendencies have force enough to produce the strongest sentiment of morals, we can never reasonably, in these cases, look for any other cause of approbation or blame; it being an inviolable maxim in philosophy, that where any particular cause is sufficient for an effect, we ought to rest satisfy'd with it, and ought not to multiply causes without necessity. We have happily attain'd experiments in the artificial virtues, where the tendency of qualities to the good of society, is the *sole* cause of our approbation, without any suspicion of the concurrence of another principle. From thence we learn the force of that principle. And where that principle may take place, and the quality approv'd of is really beneficial to society, a true philosopher will never require any other principle to account for the strongest approbation and esteem.

11   That many of the natural virtues have this tendency to the good of society, no one can doubt of. Meekness, beneficence, charity, generosity, clemency, moderation, equity, bear the greatest figure among the moral qualities, and are commonly denominated the *social* virtues, to mark their tendency to the good of society. This goes so far, that some philosophers have represented all moral distinctions as the effect of artifice and education, when skilful politicians endeavour'd to restrain the turbulent passions of men, and make them operate to the public good, by the notions of honour and shame. This system, however, is not consistent with experience. For, *first*, there are other virtues and vices beside those which have this tendency to the public advantage and loss. *Secondly*, had not men a natural sentiment of approbation and blame, it cou'd never be excited by politicians; nor wou'd the words *laudable* and *praise-worthy*, *blameable* and *odious*, be any more intelligible, than if they were a language perfectly unknown to us, as we have already observ'd. But tho' this system be erroneous, it may teach us, that moral distinctions arise, in a great measure, from the tendency of qualities and characters to the interests of society, and that 'tis our concern for that interest, which makes us approve or disapprove of them. Now we have no such extensive concern for society but from sympathy; and consequently 'tis that principle, which takes us so far out of ourselves, as to give us the same pleasure or uneasiness in characters which are useful or pernicious to society, as if they had a tendency to our own advantage or loss.

12   The only difference betwixt the natural virtues and justice lies in this, that the good, which results from the former, arises from every single act, and is the object of some natural passion: Whereas a single act of justice, consider'd in itself, may often be contrary to the public good; and 'tis only the concurrence of mankind, in a general scheme or system of action,

which is advantageous. When I relieve persons in distress, my natural humanity is my motive; and so far as my succour extends, so far have I promoted the happiness of my fellow-creatures. But if we examine all the questions, that come before any tribunal of justice, we shall find, that, considering each case apart, it wou'd as often be an instance of humanity to decide contrary to the laws of justice as conformable to them. Judges take from a poor man to give to a rich; they bestow on the dissolute the labour of the industrious; and put into the hands of the vicious the means of harming both themselves and others. The whole scheme, however, of law and justice is advantageous to the society and to every individual; and 'twas with a view to this advantage, that men, by their voluntary conventions, establish'd it. After it is once establish'd by these conventions, it is *naturally* attended with a strong sentiment of morals; which can proceed from nothing but our sympathy with the interests of society. We need no other explication of that esteem, which attends such of the natural virtues, as have a tendency to the public good.

I must farther add, that there are several circumstances, which render   13
this hypothesis much more probable with regard to the natural than the artificial virtues. 'Tis certain, that the imagination is more affected by what is particular, than by what is general; and that the sentiments are always mov'd with difficulty, where their objects are, in any degree, loose and undetermin'd: Now every particular act of justice is not beneficial to society, but the whole scheme or system: And it may not, perhaps, be any individual person, for whom we are concern'd, who receives benefit from justice, but the whole society alike. On the contrary, every particular act of generosity, or relief of the industrious and indigent, is beneficial; and is beneficial to a particular person, who is not undeserving of it. 'Tis more natural, therefore, to think, that the tendencies of the latter virtue will affect our sentiments, and command our approbation, than those of the former; and therefore, since we find, that the approbation of the former arises from their tendencies, we may ascribe, with better reason, the same cause to the approbation of the latter. In any number of similar effects, if a cause can be discover'd for one, we ought to extend that cause to all the other effects, which can be accounted for by it: But much more, if these other effects be attended with peculiar circumstances, which facilitate the operation of that cause.

Before I proceed farther, I must observe two remarkable circumstances   14
in this affair, which may seem objections to the present system. The first may be thus explain'd. When any quality, or character, has a tendency to the good of mankind, we are pleas'd with it, and approve of it; because it presents the lively idea of pleasure; which idea affects us by sympathy, and is itself a kind of pleasure. But as this sympathy is very variable, it may be

thought, that our sentiments of morals must admit of all the same variations. We sympathize more with persons contiguous to us, than with persons remote from us: With our acquaintance, than with strangers: With our countrymen, than with foreigners. But notwithstanding this variation of our sympathy, we give the same approbation to the same moral qualities in *China* as in *England*. They appear equally virtuous, and recommend themselves equally to the esteem of a judicious spectator. The sympathy varies without a variation in our esteem. Our esteem, therefore, proceeds not from sympathy.

15   To this I answer: The approbation of moral qualities most certainly is not deriv'd from reason, or any comparison of ideas; but proceeds entirely from a moral taste, and from certain sentiments of pleasure or disgust, which arise upon the contemplation and view of particular qualities or characters. Now 'tis evident, that those sentiments, whence-ever they are deriv'd, must vary according to the distance or contiguity of the objects; nor can I feel the same lively pleasure from the virtues of a person, who liv'd in *Greece* two thousand years ago, that I feel from the virtues of a familiar friend and acquaintance. Yet I do not say, that I esteem the one more than the other: And therefore, if the variation of the sentiment, without a variation of the esteem, be an objection, it must have equal force against every other system, as against that of sympathy. But to consider the case a-right, it has no force at all; and 'tis the easiest matter in the world to account for it. Our situation, with regard both to persons and things, is in continual fluctuation; and a man, that lies at a distance from us, may, in a little time, become a familiar acquaintance. Besides, every particular man has a peculiar position with regard to others; and 'tis impossible we cou'd ever converse together on any reasonable terms, were each of us to consider characters and persons, only as they appear from his peculiar point of view. In order, therefore, to prevent those continual *contradictions*, and arrive at a more *stable* judgment of things, we fix on some *steady* and *general* points of view; and always, in our thoughts, place ourselves in them, whatever may be our present situation. In like manner, external beauty is determin'd merely by pleasure; and 'tis evident, a beautiful countenance cannot give so much pleasure, when seen at the distance of twenty paces, as when it is brought nearer us. We say not, however, that it appears to us less beautiful: Because we know what effect it will have in such a position, and by that reflection we correct its momentary appearance.

16   In general, all sentiments of blame or praise are variable, according to our situation of nearness or remoteness, with regard to the person blam'd or prais'd, and according to the present disposition of our mind. But these variations we regard not in our general decisions, but still apply the terms

expressive of our liking or dislike, in the same manner, as if we remain'd in one point of view. Experience soon teaches us this method of correcting our sentiments, or at least, of correcting our language, where the sentiments are more stubborn and inalterable. Our servant, if diligent and faithful, may excite stronger sentiments of love and kindness than *Marcus Brutus*, as represented in history; but we say not upon that account, that the former character is more laudable than the latter. We know, that were we to approach equally near to that renown'd patriot, he wou'd command a much higher degree of affection and admiration. Such corrections are common with regard to all the senses; and indeed 'twere impossible we cou'd ever make use of language, or communicate our sentiments to one another, did we not correct the momentary appearances of things, and overlook our present situation.

'Tis therefore from the influence of characters and qualities, upon those who have an intercourse with any person, that we blame or praise him. We consider not whether the persons, affected by the qualities, be our acquaintance or strangers, countrymen or foreigners. Nay, we overlook our own interest in those general judgments; and blame not a man for opposing us in any of our pretensions, when his own interest is particularly concern'd. We make allowance for a certain degree of selfishness in men; because we know it to be inseparable from human nature, and inherent in our frame and constitution. By this reflection we correct those sentiments of blame, which so naturally arise upon any opposition.   17

But however the general principle of our blame or praise may be corrected by those other principles, 'tis certain they are not altogether efficacious, nor do our passions often correspond entirely to the present theory. 'Tis seldom men heartily love what lies at a distance from them, and what no way redounds to their particular benefit; as 'tis no less rare to meet with persons, who can pardon another any opposition he makes to their interest, however justifiable that opposition may be by the general rules of morality. Here we are contented with saying, that reason requires such an impartial conduct, but that 'tis seldom we can bring ourselves to it, and that our passions do not readily follow the determination of our judgment. This language will be easily understood, if we consider what we formerly said concerning that *reason*, which is able to oppose our passion; and which we have found to be nothing but a general calm determination of the passions, founded on some distant view or reflection. When we form our judgments of persons, merely from the tendency of their characters to our own benefit, or to that of our friends, we find so many contradictions to our sentiments in society and conversation, and such an uncertainty from the incessant changes of our situation, that we seek some other standard of merit and demerit, which may not admit of so great variation.   18

Being thus loosen'd from our first station, we cannot afterwards fix ourselves so commodiously by any means as by a sympathy with those, who have any commerce with the person we consider. This is far from being as lively as when our own interest is concern'd, or that of our particular friends; nor has it such an influence on our love and hatred: But being equally conformable to our calm and general principles, 'tis said to have an equal authority over our reason, and to command our judgment and opinion. We blame equally a bad action, which we read of in history, with one perform'd in our neighbourhood t'other day: The meaning of which is, that we know from reflection, that the former action wou'd excite as strong sentiments of disapprobation as the latter, were it plac'd in the same position.

19   I now proceed to the *second* remarkable circumstance, which I propos'd to take notice of. Where a person is possess'd of a character, that in its natural tendency is beneficial to society, we esteem him virtuous, and are delighted with the view of his character, even tho' particular accidents prevent its operation, and incapacitate him from being serviceable to his friends and country. Virtue in rags is still virtue; and the love, which it procures, attends a man into a dungeon or desart, where the virtue can no longer be exerted in action, and is lost to all the world. Now this may be esteem'd an objection to the present system. Sympathy interests us in the good of mankind; and if sympathy were the source of our esteem for virtue, that sentiment of approbation cou'd only take place, where the virtue actually attain'd its end, and was beneficial to mankind. Where it fails of its end, 'tis only an imperfect means; and therefore can never acquire any merit from that end. The goodness of an end can bestow a merit on such means alone as are compleat, and actually produce the end.

20   To this we may reply, that where any object, in all its parts, is fitted to attain any agreeable end, it naturally gives us pleasure, and is esteem'd beautiful, even tho' some external circumstances be wanting to render it altogether effectual. 'Tis sufficient if every thing be compleat in the object itself. A house, that is contriv'd with great judgment for all the commodities of life, pleases us upon that account; tho' perhaps we are sensible, that no-one will ever dwell in it. A fertile soil, and a happy climate, delight us by a reflection on the happiness which they wou'd afford the inhabitants, tho' at present the country be desart and uninhabited. A man, whose limbs and shape promise strength and activity, is esteem'd handsome, tho' condemn'd to perpetual imprisonment. The imagination has a set of passions belonging to it, upon which our sentiments of beauty much depend. These passions are mov'd by degrees of liveliness and strength, which are inferior to *belief,* and independent of the real existence of their objects. Where a character is, in every respect, fitted to be beneficial to society, the imagination passes easily from the cause to the effect, without considering

that there are still some circumstances wanting to render the cause a compleat one. *General rules* create a species of probability, which sometimes influences the judgment, and always the imagination.

'Tis true, when the cause is compleat, and a good disposition is attended with good fortune, which renders it really beneficial to society, it gives a stronger pleasure to the spectator, and is attended with a more lively sympathy. We are more affected by it; and yet we do not say that it is more virtuous, or that we esteem it more. We know, that an alteration of fortune may render the benevolent disposition entirely impotent; and therefore we separate, as much as possible, the fortune from the disposition. The case is the same, as when we correct the different sentiments of virtue, which proceed from its different distances from ourselves. The passions do not always follow our corrections; but these corrections serve sufficiently to regulate our abstract notions, and are alone regarded, when we pronounce in general concerning the degrees of vice and virtue.

'Tis observ'd by critics, that all words or sentences which are difficult to the pronunciation, are disagreeable to the ear. There is no difference, whether a man hear them pronounc'd, or read them silently to himself. When I run over a book with my eye, I imagine I hear it all; and also, by the force of imagination, enter into the uneasiness, which the delivery of it wou'd give the speaker. The uneasiness is not real; but as such a composition of words has a natural tendency to produce it, this is sufficient to affect the mind with a painful sentiment, and render the style harsh and disagreeable. 'Tis a similar case, where any real quality is, by accidental circumstances, render'd impotent, and is depriv'd of its natural influence on society.

Upon these principles we may easily remove any contradiction, which may appear to be betwixt the *extensive sympathy*, on which our sentiments of virtue depend, and that *limited generosity* which I have frequently observ'd to be natural to men, and which justice and property suppose, according to the precedent reasoning. My sympathy with another may give me the sentiment of pain and disapprobation, when any object is presented, that has a tendency to give him uneasiness; tho' I may not be willing to sacrifice any thing of my own interest, or cross any of my passions, for his satisfaction. A house may displease me by being ill-contriv'd for the convenience of the owner; and yet I may refuse to give a shilling towards the rebuilding of it. Sentiments must touch the heart, to make them controul our passions: But they need not extend beyond the imagination, to make them influence our taste. When a building seems clumsy and tottering to the eye, it is ugly and disagreeable; tho' we be fully assur'd of the solidity of the workmanship. 'Tis a kind of fear, which causes this sentiment of disapprobation; but the passion is not the same with that which we feel, when oblig'd to stand under a wall, that we really think tottering

21

22

23

and insecure. The *seeming tendencies* of objects affect the mind: And the emotions they excite are of a like species with those, which proceed from the *real consequences* of objects, but their feeling is different. Nay, these emotions are so different in their feeling, that they may often be contrary, without destroying each other; as when the fortifications of a city belonging to an enemy are esteem'd beautiful upon account of their strength, tho' we cou'd wish that they were entirely destroy'd. The imagination adheres to the *general* views of things, and distinguishes betwixt the feelings they produce, and those which arise from our particular and momentary situation.

24   If we examine the panegyrics that are commonly made of great men, we shall find, that most of the qualities, which are attributed to them, may be divided into two kinds, *viz.* such as make them perform their part in society; and such as render them serviceable to themselves, and enable them to promote their own interest. Their *prudence, temperance, frugality, industry, assiduity, enterprize, dexterity,* are celebrated, as well as their *generosity* and *humanity.* If we ever give an indulgence to any quality, that disables a man from making a figure in life, 'tis to that of *indolence,* which is not suppos'd to deprive one of his parts and capacity, but only suspends their exercise; and that without any inconvenience to the person himself, since 'tis, in some measure, from his own choice. Yet indolence is always allow'd to be a fault, and a very great one, if extreme: Nor do a man's friends ever acknowledge him to be subject to it, but in order to save his character in more material articles. He cou'd make a figure, say they, if he pleas'd to give application: His understanding is sound, his conception quick, and his memory tenacious; but he hates business, and is indifferent about his fortune. And this a man sometimes may make even a subject of vanity; tho' with the air of confessing a fault: Because he may think, that this incapacity for business implies much more noble qualities; such as a philosophical spirit, a fine taste, a delicate wit, or a relish for pleasure and society. But take any other case: Suppose a quality, that without being an indication of any other good qualities, incapacitates a man *always* for business, and is destructive to his interest; such as a blundering understanding, and a wrong judgment of every thing in life; inconstancy and irresolution; or a want of address in the management of men and business: These are all allow'd to be imperfections in a character; and many men wou'd rather acknowledge the greatest crimes, than have it suspected, that they are, in any degree, subject to them.

25   'Tis very happy, in our philosophical researches, when we find the same phænomenon diversify'd by a variety of circumstances; and by discovering what is common among them, can the better assure ourselves of the truth of any hypothesis we may make use of to explain that phænomenon.

Were nothing esteem'd virtue but what were beneficial to society, I am persuaded, that the foregoing explication of the moral sense ought still to be receiv'd, and that upon sufficient evidence: But this evidence must grow upon us, when we find other kinds of virtue, which will not admit of any explication except from that hypothesis. Here is a man, who is not remarkably defective in his social qualities; but what principally recommends him is his dexterity in business, by which he has extricated himself from the greatest difficulties, and conducted the most delicate affairs with a singular address and prudence. I find an esteem for him immediately to arise in me: His company is a satisfaction to me; and before I have any farther acquaintance with him, I wou'd rather do him a service than another, whose character is in every other respect equal, but is deficient in that particular. In this case, the qualities that please me are all consider'd as useful to the person, and as having a tendency to promote his interest and satisfaction. They are only regarded as means to an end, and please me in proportion to their fitness for that end. The end, therefore, must be agreeable to me. But what makes the end agreeable? The person is a stranger: I am no way interested in him, nor lie under any obligation to him: His happiness concerns not me, farther than the happiness of every human, and indeed of every sensible creature: That is, it affects me only by sympathy. From that principle, whenever I discover his happiness and good, whether in its causes or effects, I enter so deeply into it, that it gives me a sensible emotion. The appearance of qualities, that have a *tendency* to promote it, have an agreeable effect upon my imagination, and command my love and esteem.

This theory may serve to explain, why the same qualities, in all cases, 26 produce both pride and love, humility and hatred; and the same man is always virtuous or vicious, accomplish'd or despicable to others, who is so to himself. A person, in whom we discover any passion or habit, which originally is only incommodious to himself, becomes always disagreeable to us merely on its account; as on the other hand, one whose character is only dangerous and disagreeable to others, can never be satisfy'd with himself, as long as he is sensible of that disadvantage. Nor is this observable only with regard to characters and manners, but may be remark'd even in the most minute circumstances. A violent cough in another gives us uneasiness; tho' in itself it does not in the least affect us. A man will be mortify'd, if you tell him he has a stinking breath; tho' 'tis evidently no annoyance to himself. Our fancy easily changes its situation; and either surveying ourselves as we appear to others, or considering others as they feel themselves, makes us enter, by that means, into sentiments, which no way belong to us, and in which nothing but sympathy is able to interest us. And this sympathy we sometimes carry so far, as even to be displeas'd with a quality commodious to us, merely because it displeases others, and renders us disagreeable in their eyes; tho' perhaps we never can have any interest in rendering ourselves agreeable to them.

27   There have been many systems of morality advanc'd by philosophers in all ages; but if they are strictly examin'd, they may be reduc'd to two, which alone merit our attention. Moral good and evil are certainly distinguish'd by our *sentiments*, not by *reason*: But these sentiments may arise either from the mere species or appearance of characters and passions, or from reflections on their tendency to the happiness of mankind, and of particular persons. My opinion is, that both these causes are intermix'd in our judgments of morals; after the same manner as they are in our decisions concerning most kinds of external beauty: Tho' I am also of opinion, that reflections on the tendencies of actions have by far the greatest influence, and determine all the great lines of our duty. There are, however, instances, in cases of less moment, wherein this immediate taste or sentiment produces our approbation. Wit, and a certain easy and disengag'd behaviour, are qualities *immediately agreeable* to others, and command their love and esteem. Some of these qualities produce satisfaction in others by particular *original* principles of human nature, which cannot be accounted for: Others may be resolv'd into principles, which are more general. This will best appear upon a particular enquiry.

28   As some qualities acquire their merit from their being *immediately agreeable* to others, without any tendency to public interest; so some are denominated virtuous from their being *immediately agreeable* to the person himself, who possesses them. Each of the passions and operations of the mind has a particular feeling, which must be either agreeable or disagreeable. The first is virtuous, the second vicious. This particular feeling constitutes the very nature of the passion; and therefore needs not be accounted for.

29   But however directly the distinction of vice and virtue may seem to flow from the immediate pleasure or uneasiness, which particular qualities cause to ourselves or others; 'tis easy to observe, that it has also a considerable dependence on the principle of *sympathy* so often insisted on. We approve of a person, who is possess'd of qualities *immediately agreeable* to those, with whom he has any commerce; tho' perhaps we ourselves never reap'd any pleasure from them. We also approve of one, who is possess'd of qualities, that are *immediately agreeable* to himself; tho' they be of no service to any mortal. To account for this we must have recourse to the foregoing principles.

30   Thus, to take a general review of the present hypothesis: Every quality of the mind is denominated virtuous, which gives pleasure by the mere survey; as every quality, which produces pain, is call'd vicious. This pleasure and this pain may arise from four different sources. For we reap a

pleasure from the view of a character, which is naturally fitted to be useful to others, or to the person himself, or which is agreeable to others, or to the person himself. One may, perhaps, be surpriz'd, that amidst all these interests and pleasures, we shou'd forget our own, which touch us so nearly on every other occasion. But we shall easily satisfy ourselves on this head, when we consider, that every particular person's pleasure and interest being different, 'tis impossible men cou'd ever agree in their sentiments and judgments, unless they chose some common point of view, from which they might survey their object, and which might cause it to appear the same to all of them. Now in judging of characters, the only interest or pleasure, which appears the same to every spectator, is that of the person himself, whose character is examin'd; or that of persons, who have a connexion with him. And tho' such interests and pleasures touch us more faintly than our own, yet being more constant and universal, they counter-ballance the latter even in practice, and are alone admitted in speculation as the standard of virtue and morality. They alone produce that particular feeling or sentiment, on which moral distinctions depend.

As to the good or ill desert of virtue or vice, 'tis an evident consequence   31
of the sentiments of pleasure or uneasiness. These sentiments produce love or hatred; and love or hatred, by the original constitution of human passion, is attended with benevolence or anger; that is, with a desire of making happy the person we love, and miserable the person we hate. We have treated of this more fully on another occasion.

Section II. Of greatness of mind.

It may now be proper to illustrate this general system of morals, by apply-   1
ing it to particular instances of virtue and vice, and shewing how their merit or demerit arises from the four sources here explain'd. We shall begin with examining the passions of *pride* and *humility*, and shall consider the vice or virtue that lies in their excesses or just proportion. An excessive pride or over-weaning conceit of ourselves is always esteem'd vicious, and is universally hated; as modesty, or a just sense of our weakness, is esteem'd virtuous, and procures the good-will of every-one. Of the four sources of moral distinctions, this is to be ascrib'd to the *third*; viz. the immediate agreeableness and disagreeableness of a quality to others, without any reflections on the tendency of that quality.

In order to prove this, we must have recourse to two principles, which   2
are very conspicuous in human nature. The *first* of these is the *sympathy*, and communication of sentiments and passions above-mention'd. So close and intimate is the correspondence of human souls, that no sooner any person approaches me, than he diffuses on me all his opinions, and draws along my judgment in a greater or lesser degree. And tho', on many occasions, my sympathy with him goes not so far as entirely to change my

sentiments, and way of thinking; yet it seldom is so weak as not to disturb the easy course of my thought, and give an authority to that opinion, which is recommended to me by his assent and approbation. Nor is it any way material upon what subject he and I employ our thoughts. Whether we judge of an indifferent person, or of my own character, my sympathy gives equal force to his decision: And even his sentiments of his own merit make me consider him in the same light, in which he regards himself.

3 This principle of sympathy is of so powerful and insinuating a nature, that it enters into most of our sentiments and passions, and often takes place under the appearance of its contrary. For 'tis remarkable, that when a person opposes me in any sentiment, which I am strongly bent upon, and rouzes up my passion by contradiction, I have always a degree of sympathy with him, nor does my commotion proceed from any other origin. We may here observe an evident conflict or rencounter of opposite principles and passions. On the one side there is that passion or sentiment, which is natural to me; and 'tis observable, that the stronger this passion is, the greater is the commotion. There must also be some passion or sentiment on the other side; and this passion can proceed from nothing but sympathy. The sentiments of others can never affect us, but by becoming, in some measure, our own; in which case they operate upon us, by opposing and encreasing our passions, in the very same manner, as if they had been originally deriv'd from our own temper and disposition. While they remain conceal'd in the minds of others, they can never have any influence upon us: And even when they are known, if they went no farther than the imagination, or conception; that faculty is so accustom'd to objects of every different kind, that a mere idea, tho' contrary to our sentiments and inclinations, wou'd never alone be able to affect us.

4 The *second* principle I shall take notice of is that of *comparison*, or the variation of our judgments concerning objects, according to the proportion they bear to those with which we compare them. We judge more of objects by comparison, than by their intrinsic worth and value; and regard every thing as mean, when set in opposition to what is superior of the same kind. But no comparison is more obvious than that with ourselves; and hence it is that on all occasions it takes place, and mixes with most of our passions. This kind of comparison is directly contrary to sympathy in its operation, as we have observ'd in treating of *compassion* and *malice*.[1] *In all kinds of comparison an object makes us always receive from another, to which it is compar'd, a sensation contrary to what arises from itself in its direct and immediate survey. The direct survey of another's pleasure naturally gives*

---

[1] Book II. Part II. Sect.8.

us pleasure, and therefore produces pain when compar'd with our own. His pain, consider'd in itself, is painful; but augments the idea of our own happiness, and gives us pleasure.

Since then those principles of sympathy, and a comparison with our-   5
selves, are directly contrary, it may be worth while to consider, what general rules can be form'd, beside the particular temper of the person, for the prevalence of the one or the other. Suppose I am now in safety at land, and wou'd willingly reap some pleasure from this consideration: I must think on the miserable condition of those who are at sea in a storm, and must endeavour to render this idea as strong and lively as possible, in order to make me more sensible of my own happiness. But whatever pains I may take, the comparison will never have an equal efficacy, as if I were really on the shore,[2] and saw a ship at a distance, tost by a tempest, and in danger every moment of perishing on a rock or sand-bank. But suppose this idea to become still more lively. Suppose the ship to be driven so near me, that I can perceive distinctly the horror, painted on the countenance of the seamen and passengers, hear their lamentable cries, see the dearest friends give their last adieu, or embrace with a resolution to perish in each other's arms: No man has so savage a heart as to reap any pleasure from such a spectacle, or withstand the motions of the tenderest compassion and sympathy. 'Tis evident, therefore, there is a medium in this case; and that if the idea be too faint, it has no influence by comparison; and on the other hand, if it be too strong, it operates on us entirely by sympathy, which is the contrary to comparison. Sympathy being the conversion of an idea into an impression, demands a greater force and vivacity in the idea than is requisite to comparison.

All this is easily apply'd to the present subject. We sink very much in   6
our own eyes, when in the presence of a great man, or one of a superior genius; and this humility makes a considerable ingredient in that *respect*, which we pay our superiors, according to our foregoing reasonings on that passion.[3] Sometimes even envy and hatred arise from the comparison; but

---

[2] Suave mari magno turbantibus æquora ventis
   E terra magnum alterius spectare laborem;
   Non quia vexari quenquam est jucunda voluptas,
   Sed quibus ipse malis careas quia cernere suav' est.
                              Lucret.

["Pleasant it is, when over a great sea the winds trouble the waters, to gaze from shore upon another's great tribulation: not because any man's troubles are a delectable joy, but because to perceive what ills you are free from yourself is pleasant" (Lucretius, *Of the Nature of Things*, Book II; trans. by W. H. D. Rouse).]

[3] Book II. Part II. Sect. 10.

in the greatest part of men, it rests at respect and esteem. As sympathy has such a powerful influence on the human mind, it causes pride to have, in some measure, the same effect as merit; and, by making us enter into those elevated sentiments, which the proud man entertains of himself, presents that comparison, which is so mortifying and disagreeable. Our judgment does not entirely accompany him in the flattering conceit, in which he pleases himself; but still is so shaken as to receive the idea it presents, and to give it an influence above the loose conceptions of the imagination. A man, who, in an idle humour, wou'd form a notion of a person of a merit very much superior to his own, wou'd not be mortified by that fiction: But when a man, whom we are really persuaded to be of inferior merit, is presented to us; if we observe in him any extraordinary degree of pride and self-conceit; the firm persuasion he has of his own merit, takes hold of the imagination, and diminishes us in our own eyes, in the same manner, as if he were really possess'd of all the good qualities which he so liberally attributes to himself. Our idea is here precisely in that medium, which is requisite to make it operate on us by comparison. Were it accompany'd with belief, and did the person appear to have the same merit, which he assumes to himself, it wou'd have a contrary effect, and wou'd operate on us by sympathy. The influence of that principle wou'd then be superior to that of comparison, contrary to what happens where the person's merit seems below his pretensions.

7   The necessary consequence of these principles is, that pride, or an over-weaning conceit of ourselves, must be vicious; since it causes uneasiness in all men, and presents them every moment with a disagreeable comparison. 'Tis a trite observation in philosophy, and even in common life and conversation, that 'tis our own pride, which makes us so much displeas'd with the pride of other people; and that vanity becomes insupportable to us merely because we are vain. The gay naturally associate themselves with the gay, and the amorous with the amorous: But the proud never can endure the proud, and rather seek the company of those who are of an opposite disposition. As we are, all of us, proud in some degree, pride is universally blam'd and condemn'd by all mankind; as having a natural tendency to cause uneasiness in others by means of comparison. And this effect must follow the more naturally, that those, who have an ill-grounded conceit of themselves, are for ever making those comparisons, nor have they any other method of supporting their vanity. A man of sense and merit is pleas'd with himself, independent of all foreign considerations: But a fool must always find some person, that is more foolish, in order to keep himself in good humour with his own parts and understanding.

But tho' an over-weaning conceit of our own merit be vicious and dis- 8
agreeable, nothing can be more laudable, than to have a value for ourselves, where we really have qualities that are valuable. The utility and
advantage of any quality to ourselves is a source of virtue, as well as its
agreeableness to others; and 'tis certain, that nothing is more useful to us
in the conduct of life, than a due degree of pride, which makes us sensible
of our own merit, and gives us a confidence and assurance in all our projects and enterprizes. Whatever capacity any one may be endow'd with, 'tis
entirely useless to him, if he be not acquainted with it, and form not designs suitable to it. 'Tis requisite on all occasions to know our own force;
and were it allowable to err on either side, 'twou'd be more advantageous
to over-rate our merit, than to form ideas of it, below its just standard.
Fortune commonly favours the bold and enterprizing; and nothing inspires us with more boldness than a good opinion of ourselves.

Add to this, that tho' pride, or self-applause, be sometimes disagreeable 9
to others, 'tis always agreeable to ourselves; as on the other hand, modesty,
tho' it give pleasure to every one, who observes it, produces often uneasiness in the person endow'd with it. Now it has been observ'd, that our own
sensations determine the vice and virtue of any quality, as well as those
sensations, which it may excite in others.

Thus self-satisfaction and vanity may not only be allowable, but requi- 10
site in a character. 'Tis, however, certain that good-breeding and decency
require that we shou'd avoid all signs and expressions, which tend directly
to show that passion. We have, all of us, a wonderful partiality for ourselves, and were we always to give vent to our sentiments in this particular, we shou'd mutually cause the greatest indignation in each other, not
only by the immediate presence of so disagreeable a subject of comparison, but also by the contrariety of our judgments. In like manner, therefore, as we establish the *laws of nature*, in order to secure property in
society, and prevent the opposition of self-interest; we establish the *rules
of good-breeding*, in order to prevent the opposition of men's pride, and
render conversation agreeable and inoffensive. Nothing is more disagreeable than a man's over-weaning conceit of himself: Every one almost has a
strong propensity to this vice. No one can well distinguish in *himself* betwixt the vice and virtue, or be certain, that his esteem of his own merit is
well-founded: For these reasons, all direct expressions of this passion are
condemn'd; nor do we make any exception to this rule in favour of men of
sense and merit. They are not allow'd to do themselves justice openly, in
words, no more than other people; and even if they show a reserve and secret doubt in doing themselves justice in their own thoughts, they will be
more applauded. That impertinent, and almost universal propensity of

men, to over-value themselves, has given us such a *prejudice* against self-applause, that we are apt to condemn it, by a *general rule*, wherever we meet with it; and 'tis with some difficulty we give a privilege to men of sense, even in their most secret thoughts. At least, it must be own'd, that some disguise in this particular is absolutely requisite; and that if we harbour pride in our breasts, we must carry a fair outside, and have the appearance of modesty and mutual deference in all our conduct and behaviour. We must, on every occasion, be ready to prefer others to ourselves; to treat them with a kind of deference, even tho' they be our equals; to seem always the lowest and least in the company, where we are not very much distinguish'd above them: And if we observe these rules in our conduct, men will have more indulgence for our secret sentiments, when we discover them in an oblique manner.

11   I believe no one, who has any practice of the world, and can penetrate into the inward sentiments of men, will assert, that the humility, which good-breeding and decency require of us, goes beyond the outside, or that a thorough sincerity in this particular is esteem'd a real part of our duty. On the contrary, we may observe, that a genuine and hearty pride, or self-esteem, if well conceal'd and well founded, is essential to the character of a man of honour, and that there is no quality of the mind, which is more indispensibly requisite to procure the esteem and approbation of mankind. There are certain deferences and mutual submissions, which custom requires of the different ranks of men towards each other; and whoever exceeds in this particular, if thro' interest, is accus'd of meanness, if thro' ignorance, of simplicity. 'Tis necessary, therefore, to know our rank and station in the world, whether it be fix'd by our birth, fortune, employments, talents or reputation. 'Tis necessary to feel the sentiment and passion of pride in conformity to it, and to regulate our actions accordingly. And shou'd it be said, that prudence may suffice to regulate our actions in this particular, without any real pride, I wou'd observe, that here the object of prudence is to conform our actions to the general usage and custom; and that 'tis impossible those tacit airs of superiority shou'd ever have been establish'd and authoriz'd by custom, unless men were generally proud, and unless that passion were generally approv'd, when well-grounded.

12   If we pass from common life and conversation to history, this reasoning acquires new force, when we observe, that all those great actions and sentiments, which have become the admiration of mankind, are founded on nothing but pride and self-esteem. *Go*, says *Alexander* the Great to his soldiers, when they refus'd to follow him to the *Indies*, *go tell your countrymen, that you left Alexander compleating the conquest of the world.* This passage was always particularly admir'd by the prince of *Condé*, as we

learn from *St. Evremond.* "Alexander," said that prince, "abandon'd by his soldiers, among barbarians, not yet fully subdu'd, felt in himself such a dignity and right of empire, that he cou'd not believe it possible any one cou'd refuse to obey him. Whether in *Europe* or in *Asia,* among *Greeks* or *Persians,* all was indifferent to him: Wherever he found men, he fancied he had found subjects."

In general we may observe, that whatever we call *heroic virtue,* and ad- 13
mire under the character of greatness and elevation of mind, is either nothing but a steady and well-establish'd pride and self-esteem, or partakes largely of that passion. Courage, intrepidity, ambition, love of glory, magnanimity, and all the other shining virtues of that kind, have plainly a strong mixture of self-esteem in them, and derive a great part of their merit from that origin. Accordingly we find, that many religious declaimers decry those virtues as purely pagan and natural, and represent to us the excellency of the *Christian* religion, which places humility in the rank of virtues, and corrects the judgment of the world, and even of philosophers, who so generally admire all the efforts of pride and ambition. Whether this virtue of humility has been rightly understood, I shall not pretend to determine. I am content with the concession, that the world naturally esteems a well-regulated pride, which secretly animates our conduct, without breaking out into such indecent expressions of vanity, as may offend the vanity of others.

The merit of pride or self-esteem is deriv'd from two circumstances, 14
viz. its utility and its agreeableness to ourselves; by which it capacitates us for business, and, at the same time, gives us an immediate satisfaction. When it goes beyond its just bounds, it loses the first advantage, and even becomes prejudicial; which is the reason why we condemn an extravagant pride and ambition, however regulated by the decorums of good-breeding and politeness. But as such a passion is still agreeable, and conveys an elevated and sublime sensation to the person, who is actuated by it, the sympathy with that satisfaction diminishes considerably the blame, which naturally attends its dangerous influence on his conduct and behaviour. Accordingly we may observe, that an excessive courage and magnanimity, especially when it displays itself under the frowns of fortune, contributes, in a great measure, to the character of a hero, and will render a person the admiration of posterity; at the same time, that it ruins his affairs, and leads him into dangers and difficulties, with which otherwise he wou'd never have been acquainted.

Heroism, or military glory, is much admir'd by the generality of man- 15
kind. They consider it as the most sublime kind of merit. Men of cool reflection are not so sanguine in their praises of it. The infinite confusions and disorder, which it has caus'd in the world, diminish much of its merit

in their eyes. When they wou'd oppose the popular notions on this head, they always paint out the evils, which this suppos'd virtue has produc'd in human society; the subversion of empires, the devastation of provinces, the sack of cities. As long as these are present to us, we are more inclin'd to hate than admire the ambition of heroes. But when we fix our view on the person himself, who is the author of all this mischief, there is something so dazling in his character, the mere contemplation of it so elevates the mind, that we cannot refuse it our admiration. The pain, which we receive from its tendency to the prejudice of society, is over-power'd by a stronger and more immediate sympathy.

16   Thus our explication of the merit or demerit, which attends the degrees of pride or self-esteem, may serve as a strong argument for the preceding hypothesis, by showing the effects of those principles above-explain'd in all the variations of our judgments concerning that passion. Nor will this reasoning be advantageous to us only by shewing, that the distinction of vice and virtue arises from the *four* principles of the *advantage* and of the *pleasure* of the *person himself*, and of *others*: But may also afford us a strong proof of some under-parts of that hypothesis.

17   No one, who duly considers of this matter, will make any scruple of allowing, that any piece of ill-breeding, or any expression of pride and haughtiness, is displeasing to us, merely because it shocks our own pride, and leads us by sympathy into a comparison, which causes the disagreeable passion of humility. Now as an insolence of this kind is blam'd even in a person who has always been civil to ourselves in particular; nay, in one, whose name is only known to us in history; it follows, that our disapprobation proceeds from a sympathy with others, and from the reflection, that such a character is highly displeasing and odious to every one, who converses or has any intercourse with the person possest of it. We sympathize with those people in their uneasiness; and as their uneasiness proceeds in part from a sympathy with the person who insults them, we may here observe a double rebound of the sympathy; which is a principle very similar to what we have observ'd on another occasion.[4]

Section III. Of goodness and benevolence.

1   Having thus explain'd the origin of that praise and approbation, which attends every thing we call *great* in human affections; we now proceed to give an account of their *goodness*, and shew whence its merit is deriv'd.

2   When experience has once given us a competent knowledge of human affairs, and has taught us the proportion they bear to human passion, we

---

[4] Book II. Part II. Sect. 5.

perceive, that the generosity of men is very limited, and that it seldom extends beyond their friends and family, or, at most, beyond their native country. Being thus acquainted with the nature of man, we expect not any impossibilities from him; but confine our view to that narrow circle, in which any person moves, in order to form a judgment of his moral character. When the natural tendency of his passions leads him to be serviceable and useful within his sphere, we approve of his character, and love his person, by a sympathy with the sentiments of those, who have a more particular connexion with him. We are quickly oblig'd to forget our own interest in our judgments of this kind, by reason of the perpetual contradictions, we meet with in society and conversation, from persons that are not plac'd in the same situation, and have not the same interest with ourselves. The only point of view, in which our sentiments concur with those of others, is, when we consider the tendency of any passion to the advantage or harm of those, who have any immediate connexion or intercourse with the person possess'd of it. And tho' this advantage or harm be often very remote from ourselves, yet sometimes 'tis very near us, and interests us strongly by sympathy. This concern we readily extend to other cases, that are resembling; and when these are very remote, our sympathy is proportionably weaker, and our praise or blame fainter and more doubtful. The case is here the same as in our judgments concerning external bodies. All objects seem to diminish by their distance: But tho' the appearance of objects to our senses be the original standard, by which we judge of them, yet we do not say that they actually diminish by the distance; but correcting the appearance by reflection, arrive at a more constant and establish'd judgment concerning them. In like manner, tho' sympathy be much fainter than our concern for ourselves, and a sympathy with persons remote from us much fainter than that with persons near and contiguous; yet we neglect all these differences in our calm judgments concerning the characters of men. Besides, that we ourselves often change our situation in this particular, we every day meet with persons, who are in a different situation from ourselves, and who cou'd never converse with us on any reasonable terms, were we to remain constantly in that situation and point of view, which is peculiar to us. The intercourse of sentiments, therefore, in society and conversation, makes us form some general inalterable standard, by which we may approve or disapprove of characters and manners. And tho' the *heart* does not always take part with those general notions, or regulate its love and hatred by them, yet are they sufficient for discourse, and serve all our purposes in company, in the pulpit, on the theatre, and in the schools.

From these principles we may easily account for that merit, which is 3 commonly ascrib'd to *generosity, humanity, compassion, gratitude, friendship, fidelity, zeal, disinterestedness, liberality,* and all those other qualities, which form the character of good and benevolent. A propensity to the tender passions makes a man agreeable and useful in all the parts of life; and gives a just direction to all his other qualities, which otherwise may become prejudicial to society. Courage and ambition, when not regulated by benevolence, are fit only to make a tyrant and public robber. 'Tis the same case with judgment and capacity, and all the qualities of that kind. They are indifferent in themselves to the interests of society, and have a tendency to the good or ill of mankind, according as they are directed by these other passions.

4   As love is *immediately agreeable* to the person, who is actuated by it, and hatred *immediately disagreeable*; this may also be a considerable reason, why we praise all the passions that partake of the former, and blame all those that have any considerable share of the latter. 'Tis certain we are infinitely touch'd with a tender sentiment, as well as with a great one. The tears naturally start in our eyes at the conception of it; nor can we forbear giving a loose to the same tenderness towards the person who exerts it. All this seems to me a proof, that our approbation has, in those cases, an origin different from the prospect of utility and advantage, either to ourselves or others. To which we may add, that men naturally, without reflection, approve of that character, which is most like their own. The man of a mild disposition and tender affections, in forming a notion of the most perfect virtue, mixes in it more of benevolence and humanity, than the man of courage and enterprize, who naturally looks upon a certain elevation of mind as the most accomplish'd character. This must evidently proceed from an *immediate* sympathy, which men have with characters similar to their own. They enter with more warmth into such sentiments, and feel more sensibly the pleasure, which arises from them.

5   'Tis remarkable, that nothing touches a man of humanity more than any instance of extraordinary delicacy in love or friendship, where a person is attentive to the smallest concerns of his friend, and is willing to sacrifice to them the most considerable interest of his own. Such delicacies have little influence on society; because they make us regard the greatest trifles: But they are the more engaging, the more minute the concern is, and are a proof of the highest merit in any one, who is capable of them. The passions are so contagious, that they pass with the greatest facility from one person to another, and produce correspondent movements in all human breasts. Where friendship appears in very signal instances, my heart catches the same passion, and is warm'd by those warm sentiments, that display themselves before me. Such agreeable movements must give me an affection to every one that excites them. This is the case with every

thing that is agreeable in any person. The transition from pleasure to love is easy: But the transition must here be still more easy; since the agreeable sentiment, which is excited by sympathy, is love itself; and there is nothing requir'd but to change the object.

Hence the peculiar merit of benevolence in all its shapes and appearances. Hence even its weaknesses are virtuous and amiable; and a person, whose grief upon the loss of a friend were excessive, wou'd be esteem'd upon that account. His tenderness bestows a merit, as it does a pleasure, on his melancholy. 6

We are not, however, to imagine, that all the angry passions are vicious, tho' they are disagreeable. There is a certain indulgence due to human nature in this respect. Anger and hatred are passions inherent in our very frame and constitution. The want of them, on some occasions, may even be a proof of weakness and imbecility. And where they appear only in a low degree, we not only excuse them because they are natural; but even bestow our applauses on them, because they are inferior to what appears in the greatest part of mankind. 7

Where these angry passions rise up to cruelty, they form the most detested of all vices. All the pity and concern which we have for the miserable sufferers by this vice, turns against the person guilty of it, and produces a stronger hatred than we are sensible of on any other occasion. 8

Even when the vice of inhumanity rises not to this extreme degree, our sentiments concerning it are very much influenc'd by reflections on the harm that results from it. And we may observe in general, that if we can find any quality in a person, which renders him incommodious to those, who live and converse with him, we always allow it to be a fault or blemish, without any farther examination. On the other hand, when we enumerate the good qualities of any person, we always mention those parts of his character, which render him a safe companion, an easy friend, a gentle master, an agreeable husband, or an indulgent father. We consider him with all his relations in society; and love or hate him, according as he affects those, who have any immediate intercourse with him. And 'tis a most certain rule, that if there be no relation of life, in which I cou'd not wish to stand to a particular person, his character must so far be allow'd to be perfect. If he be as little wanting to himself as to others, his character is entirely perfect. This is the ultimate test of merit and virtue. 9

Section IV. Of natural abilities.

No distinction is more usual in all systems of ethics, than that betwixt *natural abilities* and *moral virtues*; where the former are plac'd on the same footing with bodily endowments, and are suppos'd to have no merit 1 or moral worth annex'd to them. Whoever considers the matter accurately, will find, that a dispute upon this head wou'd be merely a dispute of words, and that tho' these qualities are not altogether of the same kind, yet they agree in the most material circumstances. They are both of them equally mental qualities: And both of them equally produce pleasure; and have of course an equal tendency to procure the love and esteem of mankind. There are few, who are not as jealous of their character, with regard to sense and knowledge, as to honour and courage; and much more than with regard to temperance and sobriety. Men are even afraid of passing for good-natur'd; lest *that* shou'd be taken for want of understanding: And often boast of more debauches than they have been really engag'd in, to give themselves airs of fire and spirit. In short, the figure a man makes in the world, the reception he meets with in company, the esteem paid him by his acquaintance; all these advantages depend almost as much upon his good sense and judgment, as upon any other part of his character. Let a man have the best intentions in the world, and be the farthest from all injustice and violence, he will never be able to make himself be much regarded, without a moderate share, at least, of parts and understanding. Since then natural abilities, tho', perhaps, inferior, yet are on the same footing, both as to their causes and effects, with those qualities which we call moral virtues, why shou'd we make any distinction betwixt them?

2   Tho' we refuse to natural abilities the title of virtues, we must allow, that they procure the love and esteem of mankind; that they give a new lustre to the other virtues; and that a man possess'd of them is much more intitled to our good-will and services, than one entirely void of them. It may, indeed, be pretended, that the sentiment of approbation, which those qualities produce, besides its being *inferior*, is also somewhat *different* from that, which attends the other virtues. But this, in my opinion, is not a sufficient reason for excluding them from the catalogue of virtues. Each of the virtues, even benevolence, justice, gratitude, integrity, excites a different sentiment or feeling in the spectator. The characters of *Cæsar* and *Cato*, as drawn by *Sallust*, are both of them virtuous, in the strictest sense of the word; but in a different way: Nor are the sentiments entirely the same, which arise from them. The one produces love; the other esteem: The one is amiable; the other awful: We cou'd wish to meet with the one character in a friend; the other character we wou'd be ambitious of in ourselves. In like manner, the approbation, which attends natural abilities, may be somewhat different to the feeling from that, which arises from the other virtues, without making them entirely of a different species. And indeed we may observe, that the natural abilities, no more than the other virtues, produce not, all of them, the

same kind of approbation. Good sense and genius beget esteem: Wit and humour excite love.[1]

Those, who represent the distinction betwixt natural abilities and moral virtues as very material, may say, that the former are entirely involuntary, and have therefore no merit attending them, as having no dependance on liberty and free-will. But to this I answer, *first,* that many of those qualities, which all moralists, especially the antients, comprehend under the title of moral virtues, are equally involuntary and necessary, with the qualities of the judgment and imagination. Of this nature are constancy, fortitude, magnanimity; and, in short, all the qualities which form the *great* man. I might say the same, in some degree, of the others; it being almost impossible for the mind to change its character in any considerable article, or cure itself of a passionate or splenetic temper, when they are natural to it. The greater degree there is of these blameable qualities, the more vicious they become, and yet they are the less voluntary. *Secondly,* I wou'd have any one give me a reason, why virtue and vice may not be involuntary, as well as beauty and deformity. These moral distinctions arise from the natural distinctions of pain and pleasure; and when we receive those feelings from the general consideration of any quality or character, we denominate it vicious or virtuous. Now I believe no one will assert, that a quality can never produce pleasure or pain to the person who considers it, unless it be perfectly voluntary in the person who possesses it. *Thirdly,* As to free-will, we have shewn that it has no place with regard to the actions, no more than the qualities of men. It is not a just consequence, that what is voluntary is free. Our actions are more voluntary than our judgments; but we have not more liberty in the one than in the other.

But tho' this distinction betwixt voluntary and involuntary be not sufficient to justify the distinction betwixt natural abilities and moral virtues, yet the former distinction will afford us a plausible reason, why moralists have invented the latter. Men have observ'd, that tho' natural abilities and moral qualities be in the main on the same footing, there is, however, this difference betwixt them, that the former are almost invariable by any art or industry; while the latter, or at least, the actions, that proceed from them, may be chang'd by the motives of reward and punishment, praise

3

4

---

[1] Love and esteem are at the bottom the same passions, and arise from like causes. The qualities, that produce both, are agreeable, and give pleasure. But where this pleasure is severe and serious; or where its object is great, and makes a strong impression; or where it produces any degree of humility and awe: In all these cases, the passion, which arises from the pleasure, is more properly denominated esteem than love. Benevolence attends both: But is connected with love in a more eminent degree.

and blame. Hence legislators, and divines, and moralists, have principally apply'd themselves to the regulating these voluntary actions, and have endeavour'd to produce additional motives for being virtuous in that particular. They knew, that to punish a man for folly, or exhort him to be prudent and sagacious, wou'd have but little effect; tho' the same punishments and exhortations, with regard to justice and injustice, might have a considerable influence. But as men, in common life and conversation, do not carry those ends in view, but naturally praise or blame whatever pleases or displeases them, they do not seem much to regard this distinction, but consider prudence under the character of virtue as well as benevolence, and penetration as well as justice. Nay, we find, that all moralists, whose judgment is not perverted by a strict adherence to a system, enter into the same way of thinking; and that the antient moralists in particular made no scruple of placing prudence at the head of the cardinal virtues. There is a sentiment of esteem and approbation, which may be excited, in some degree, by any faculty of the mind, in its perfect state and condition; and to account for this sentiment is the business of *philosophers*. It belongs to *grammarians* to examine what qualities are entitled to the denomination of *virtue*; nor will they find, upon trial, that this is so easy a task, as at first sight they may be apt to imagine.

5   The principal reason why natural abilities are esteem'd, is because of their tendency to be useful to the person, who is possess'd of them. 'Tis impossible to execute any design with success, where it is not conducted with prudence and discretion; nor will the goodness of our intentions alone suffice to procure us a happy issue to our enterprizes. Men are superior to beasts principally by the superiority of their reason; and they are the degrees of the same faculty, which set such an infinite difference betwixt one man and another. All the advantages of art are owing to human reason; and where fortune is not very capricious, the most considerable part of these advantages must fall to the share of the prudent and sagacious.

6   When it is ask'd, whether a quick or a slow apprehension be most valuable? whether one, that at first view penetrates into a subject, but can perform nothing upon study; or a contrary character, which must work out every thing by dint of application? whether a clear head, or a copious invention? whether a profound genius, or a sure judgment? in short, what character, or peculiar understanding, is more excellent than another? 'Tis evident we can answer none of these questions, without considering which of those qualities capacitates a man best for the world, and carries him farthest in any of his undertakings.

7   There are many other qualities of the mind, whose merit is deriv'd from the same origin. *Industry, perseverance, patience, activity, vigilance,*

application, constancy, with other virtues of that kind, which 'twill be easy to recollect, are esteem'd valuable upon no other account, than their advantage in the conduct of life. 'Tis the same case with *temperance, frugality, œconomy, resolution*: As on the other hand, *prodigality, luxury, irresolution, uncertainty*, are vicious, merely because they draw ruin upon us, and incapacitate us for business and action.

As wisdom and good-sense are valued, because they are *useful* to the person possess'd of them; so *wit* and *eloquence* are valued because they are *immediately agreeable* to others. On the other hand, *good humour* is lov'd and esteem'd, because it is *immediately agreeable* to the person himself. 'Tis evident, that the conversation of a man of wit is very satisfactory; as a chearful good-humour'd companion diffuses a joy over the whole company, from a sympathy with his gaiety. These qualities, therefore, being agreeable, they naturally beget love and esteem, and answer to all the characters of virtue. 8

'Tis difficult to tell, on many occasions, what it is that renders one man's conversation so agreeable and entertaining, and another's so insipid and distasteful. As conversation is a transcript of the mind as well as books, the same qualities, which render the one valuable, must give us an esteem for the other. This we shall consider afterwards. In the mean time it may be affirm'd in general, that all the merit a man may derive from his conversation (which, no doubt, may be very considerable) arises from nothing but the pleasure it conveys to those who are present. 9

In this view, *cleanliness* is also to be regarded as a virtue; since it naturally renders us agreeable to others, and is a very considerable source of love and affection. No one will deny, that a negligence in this particular is a fault; and as faults are nothing but smaller vices, and this fault can have no other origin than the uneasy sensation, which it excites in others, we may in this instance, seemingly so trivial, clearly discover the origin of the moral distinction of vice and virtue in other instances. 10

Besides all those qualities, which render a person lovely or valuable, there is also a certain *je-ne-sçai-quoi* of agreeable and handsome, that concurs to the same effect. In this case, as well as in that of wit and eloquence, we must have recourse to a certain sense, which acts without reflection, and regards not the tendencies of qualities and characters. Some moralists account for all the sentiments of virtue by this sense. Their hypothesis is very plausible. Nothing but a particular enquiry can give the preference to any other hypothesis. When we find, that almost all the virtues have such particular tendencies; and also find, that these tendencies are sufficient alone to give a strong sentiment of approbation: We cannot doubt, after this, that qualities are approv'd of, in proportion to the advantage, which results from them. 11

12   The *decorum* or *indecorum* of a quality, with regard to the age, or character, or station, contributes also to its praise or blame. This decorum depends, in a great measure, upon experience. 'Tis usual to see men lose
their levity, as they advance in years. Such a degree of gravity, therefore,
and such years, are connected together in our thoughts. When we observe
them separated in any person's character, this imposes a kind of violence
on our imagination, and is disagreeable.

13   That faculty of the soul, which, of all others, is of the least consequence
to the character, and has the least virtue or vice in its several degrees, at
the same time, that it admits of a great variety of degrees, is the *memory*.
Unless it rise up to that stupendous height as to surprize us, or sink so low
as, in some measure, to affect the judgment, we commonly take no notice
of its variations, nor ever mention them to the praise or dispraise of any
person. 'Tis so far from being a virtue to have a good memory, that men
generally affect to complain of a bad one; and, endeavouring to persuade
the world, that what they say is entirely of their own invention, sacrifice it
to the praise of genius and judgment. Yet to consider the matter abstractedly, 'twou'd be difficult to give a reason, why the faculty of recalling past
ideas with truth and clearness, shou'd not have as much merit in it, as the
faculty of placing our present ideas in such an order, as to form true
propositions and opinions. The reason of the difference certainly must be,
that the memory is exerted without any sensation of pleasure or pain, and
in all its middling degrees serves almost equally well in business and affairs. But the least variations in the judgment are sensibly felt in their consequences; while at the same time that faculty is never exerted in any
eminent degree, without an extraordinary delight and satisfaction. The
sympathy with this utility and pleasure bestows a merit on the understanding; and the absence of it makes us consider the memory as a faculty
very indifferent to blame or praise.

14   Before I leave this subject of *natural abilities*, I must observe, that, perhaps, one source of the esteem and affection, which attends them, is deriv'd from the *importance* and *weight*, which they bestow on the person
possess'd of them. He becomes of greater consequence in life. His resolutions and actions affect a greater number of his fellow-creatures. Both his
friendship and enmity are of moment. And 'tis easy to observe that whoever is elevated, after this manner, above the rest of mankind, must excite
in us the sentiments of esteem and approbation. Whatever is important
engages our attention, fixes our thought, and is contemplated with satisfaction. The histories of kingdoms are more interesting than domestic
stories: The histories of great empires more than those of small cities and
principalities: And the histories of wars and revolutions more than those
of peace and order. We sympathize with the persons that suffer, in all the

various sentiments which belong to their fortunes. The mind is occupied by the multitude of the objects, and by the strong passions, that display themselves. And this occupation or agitation of the mind is commonly agreeable and amusing. The same theory accounts for the esteem and regard we pay to men of extraordinary parts and abilities. The good and ill of multitudes are connected with their actions. Whatever they undertake is important, and challenges our attention. Nothing is to be over-look'd and despis'd, that regards them. And where any person can excite these sentiments, he soon acquires our esteem; unless other circumstances of his character render him odious and disagreeable.

Section V. Some farther reflections concerning the natural virtues.

It has been observ'd, in treating of the passions, that pride and humility, love and hatred, are excited by any advantages or disadvantages of the *mind*, *body*, or *fortune*; and that these advantages or disadvantages have that effect by producing a separate impression of pain or pleasure. The pain or pleasure, which arises from the general survey or view of any action or quality of the *mind*, constitutes its vice or virtue, and gives rise to our approbation or blame, which is nothing but a fainter and more imperceptible love or hatred. We have assign'd four different sources of this pain and pleasure; and in order to justify more fully that hypothesis, it may here be proper to observe, that the advantages or disadvantages of the *body* and of *fortune*, produce a pain or pleasure from the very same principles. The tendency of any object to be *useful* to the person possess'd of it, or to others; to convey *pleasure* to him or to others; all these circumstances convey an immediate pleasure to the person, who considers the object, and command his love and approbation. 1

To begin with the advantages of the *body*; we may observe a phænomenon, which might appear somewhat trivial and ludicrous, if any thing cou'd be trivial, which fortified a conclusion of such importance, or ludicrous, which was employ'd in a philosophical reasoning. 'Tis a general remark, that those we call good *women's men*, who have either signaliz'd themselves by their amorous exploits, or whose make of body promises any extraordinary vigour of that kind, are well receiv'd by the fair sex, and naturally engage the affections even of those, whose virtue prevents any design of ever giving employment to those talents. Here 'tis evident, that the ability of such a person to give enjoyment, is the real source of that love and esteem he meets with among the females; at the same time that the women, who love and esteem him, have no prospect of receiving that enjoyment themselves, and can only be affected by means of their sympathy with one, that has a commerce of love with him. This instance is singular, and merits our attention. 2

3   Another source of the pleasure we receive from considering bodily advantages, is their utility to the person himself, who is possess'd of them.
'Tis certain, that a considerable part of the beauty of men, as well as of
other animals, consists in such a conformation of members, as we find by
experience to be attended with strength and agility, and to capacitate the
creature for any action or exercise. Broad shoulders, a lank belly, firm
joints, taper legs; all these are beautiful in our species, because they are
signs of force and vigour, which being advantages we naturally sympathize
with, they convey to the beholder a share of that satisfaction they produce
in the possessor.

4   So far as to the *utility*, which may attend any quality of the body. As to
the immediate *pleasure*, 'tis certain, that an air of health, as well as of
strength and agility, makes a considerable part of beauty; and that a sickly
air in another is always disagreeable, upon account of that idea of pain and
uneasiness, which it conveys to us. On the other hand, we are pleas'd with
the regularity of our own features, tho' it be neither useful to ourselves
nor others; and 'tis necessary for us, in some measure, to set ourselves at a
distance, to make it convey to us any satisfaction. We commonly consider
ourselves as we appear in the eyes of others, and sympathize with the advantageous sentiments they entertain with regard to us.

5   How far the advantages of *fortune* produce esteem and approbation
from the same principles, we may satisfy ourselves by reflecting on our
precedent reasoning on that subject. We have observ'd, that our approbation of those, who are possess'd of the advantages of fortune, may be ascrib'd to three different causes. *First*, To that immediate pleasure, which
a rich man gives us, by the view of the beautiful cloaths, equipage, gardens, or houses, which he possesses. *Secondly*, To the advantage, which
we hope to reap from him by his generosity and liberality. *Thirdly*, To the
pleasure and advantage, which he himself reaps from his possessions, and
which produce an agreeable sympathy in us. Whether we ascribe our esteem of the rich and great to one or all of these causes, we may clearly see
the traces of those principles, which give rise to the sense of vice and
virtue. I believe most people, at first sight, will be inclin'd to ascribe our
esteem of the rich to self-interest, and the prospect of advantage. But as
'tis certain, that our esteem or deference extends beyond any prospect of
advantage to ourselves, 'tis evident, that that sentiment must proceed
from a sympathy with those, who are dependent on the person we esteem
and respect, and who have an immediate connexion with him. We consider him as a person capable of contributing to the happiness or enjoyment of his fellow-creatures, whose sentiments, with regard to him, we
naturally embrace. And this consideration will serve to justify my hypothesis in preferring the *third* principle to the other two, and ascribing

our esteem of the rich to a sympathy with the pleasure and advantage, which they themselves receive from their possessions. For as even the other two principles cannot operate to a due extent, or account for all the phænomena, without having recourse to a sympathy of one kind or other; 'tis much more natural to chuse that sympathy, which is immediate and direct, than that which is remote and indirect. To which we may add, that where the riches or power are very great, and render the person considerable and important in the world, the esteem attending them, may, in part, be ascrib'd to another source, distinct from these three, *viz.* their interesting the mind by a prospect of the multitude, and importance of their consequences: Tho', in order to account for the operation of this principle, we must also have recourse to *sympathy*; as we have observ'd in the preceding section.

It may not be amiss, on this occasion, to remark the flexibility of our   6
sentiments, and the several changes they so readily receive from the objects, with which they are conjoin'd. All the sentiments of approbation, which attend any particular species of objects, have a great resemblance to each other, tho' deriv'd from different sources; and, on the other hand, those sentiments, when directed to different objects, are different to the feeling, tho' deriv'd from the same source. Thus the beauty of all visible objects causes a pleasure pretty much the same, tho' it be sometimes deriv'd from the mere *species* and appearance of the objects; sometimes from sympathy, and an idea of their utility. In like manner, whenever we survey the actions and characters of men, without any particular interest in them, the pleasure, or pain, which arises from the survey (with some minute differences) is, in the main, of the same kind, tho' perhaps there be a great diversity in the causes, from which it is deriv'd. On the other hand, a convenient house, and a virtuous character, cause not the same feeling of approbation; even tho' the source of our approbation be the same, and flow from sympathy and an idea of their utility. There is something very inexplicable in this variation of our feelings; but 'tis what we have experience of with regard to all our passions and sentiments.

Section VI. Conclusion of this book.

Thus upon the whole I am hopeful, that nothing is wanting to an accurate   1
proof of this system of ethics. We are certain, that sympathy is a very powerful principle in human nature. We are also certain, that it has a great influence on our sense of beauty, when we regard external objects, as well as when we judge of morals. We find, that it has force sufficient to give us the strongest sentiments of approbation, when it operates alone, without the concurrence of any other principle; as in the cases of justice, allegiance, chastity, and good-manners. We may observe, that all the circumstances

requisite for its operation are found in most of the virtues; which have, for the most part, a tendency to the good of society, or to that of the person possess'd of them. If we compare all these circumstances, we shall not doubt, that sympathy is the chief source of moral distinctions; especially when we reflect, that no objection can be rais'd against this hypothesis in one case, which will not extend to all cases. Justice is certainly approv'd of for no other reason, than because it has a tendency to the public good: And the public good is indifferent to us, except so far as sympathy interests us in it. We may presume the like with regard to all the other virtues, which have a like tendency to the public good. They must derive all their merit from our sympathy with those, who reap any advantage from them: As the virtues, which have a tendency to the good of the person possess'd of them, derive their merit from our sympathy with him.

2   Most people will readily allow, that the useful qualities of the mind are virtuous, because of their utility. This way of thinking is so natural, and occurs on so many occasions, that few will make any scruple of admitting it. Now this being once admitted, the force of sympathy must necessarily be acknowledg'd. Virtue is consider'd as means to an end. Means to an end are only valued so far as the end is valued. But the happiness of strangers affects us by sympathy alone. To that principle, therefore, we are to ascribe the sentiment of approbation, which arises from the survey of all those virtues, that are useful to society, or to the person possess'd of them. These form the most considerable part of morality.

3   Were it proper in such a subject to bribe the reader's assent, or employ any thing but solid argument, we are here abundantly supply'd with topics to engage the affections. All lovers of virtue (and such we all are in speculation, however we may degenerate in practice) must certainly be pleas'd to see moral distinctions deriv'd from so noble a source, which gives us a just notion both of the *generosity* and *capacity* of our nature. It requires but very little knowledge of human affairs to perceive, that a sense of morals is a principle inherent in the soul, and one of the most powerful that enters into the composition. But this sense must certainly acquire new force, when reflecting on itself, it approves of those principles, from whence it is deriv'd, and finds nothing but what is great and good in its rise and origin. Those who resolve the sense of morals into original instincts of the human mind, may defend the cause of virtue with sufficient authority; but want the advantage, which those possess, who account for that sense by an extensive sympathy with mankind. According to the latter system, not only virtue must be approv'd of, but also the sense of virtue: And not only that sense, but also the principles, from whence it is deriv'd. So that nothing is presented on any side, but what is laudable and good.

This observation may be extended to justice, and the other virtues of   4
that kind. Tho' justice be artificial, the sense of its morality is natural. 'Tis
the combination of men, in a system of conduct, which renders any act of
justice beneficial to society. But when once it has that tendency, we *naturally* approve of it; and if we did not so, 'tis impossible any combination or
convention cou'd ever produce that sentiment.

Most of the inventions of men are subject to change. They depend   5
upon humour and caprice. They have a vogue for a time, and then sink
into oblivion. It may, perhaps, be apprehended, that if justice were allow'd
to be a human invention, it must be plac'd on the same footing. But the
cases are widely different. The interest, on which justice is founded, is the
greatest imaginable, and extends to all times and places. It cannot possibly
be serv'd by any other invention. It is obvious, and discovers itself on the
very first formation of society. All these causes render the rules of justice
stedfast and immutable; at least, as immutable as human nature. And if
they were founded on original instincts, cou'd they have any greater stability?

The same system may help us to form a just notion of the *happiness*,   6
as well as of the *dignity* of virtue, and may interest every principle of our
nature in the embracing and cherishing that noble quality. Who indeed
does not feel an accession of alacrity in his pursuits of knowledge and
ability of every kind, when he considers, that besides the advantage,
which immediately result from these acquisitions, they also give him a
new lustre in the eyes of mankind, and are universally attended with esteem and approbation? And who can think any advantages of fortune a
sufficient compensation for the least breach of the *social* virtues, when
he considers, that not only his character with regard to others, but also
his peace and inward satisfaction entirely depend upon his strict observance of them; and that a mind will never be able to bear its own survey,
that has been wanting in its part to mankind and society? But I forbear
insisting on this subject. Such reflections require a work a-part, very
different from the genius of the present. The anatomist ought never to
emulate the painter; nor in his accurate dissections and portraitures of
the smaller parts of the human body, pretend to give his figures any
graceful and engaging attitude or expression. There is even something
hideous, or at least minute in the views of things, which he presents; and
'tis necessary the objects shou'd be set more at a distance, and be more
cover'd up from sight, to make them engaging to the eye and imagination. An anatomist, however, is admirably fitted to give advice to a
painter; and 'tis even impracticable to excel in the latter art, without the
assistance of the former. We must have an exact knowledge of the parts,

their situation and connexion, before we can design with any elegance or correctness. And thus the most abstract speculations concerning human nature, however cold and unentertaining, become subservient to *practical morality*; and may render this latter science more correct in its precepts, and more persuasive in its exhortations.

AN ENQUIRY
CONCERNING THE
PRINCIPLES OF MORALS

ADVERTISEMENT

MOST of the principles, and reasonings, contained in this volume, were published in a work in three volumes, called A Treatise of Human Nature: *A work which the Author had projected before he left College, and which he wrote and published not long after. But not finding it successful, he was sensible of his error in going to the press too early, and he cast the whole anew in the following pieces, where some negligences in his former reasoning and more in the expression, are, he hopes, corrected. Yet several writers, who have honoured the Author's Philosophy with answers, have taken care to direct all their batteries against that juvenile work, which the Author never acknowledged, and have affected to triumph in any advantages, which, they imagined, they had obtained over it: A practice very contrary to all rules of candour and fair-dealing, and a strong instance of those polemical artifices, which a bigotted zeal thinks itself authorized to employ. Henceforth, the Author desires, that the following Pieces may alone be regarded as containing his philosophical sentiments and principles.*

AN ENQUIRY CONCERNING THE PRINCIPLES OF MORALS

SECTION I.
OF THE GENERAL PRINCIPLES OF MORALS.

DISPUTES with men, pertinaciously obstinate in their principles, are, of all others, the most irksome; except, perhaps, those with persons, entirely disingenuous, who really do not believe the opinions they defend, but engage in the controversy, from affectation, from a spirit of opposition, or from a desire of showing wit and ingenuity, superior to the rest of mankind. The same blind adherence to their own arguments is to be expected in both; the same contempt of their antagonists; and the same passionate vehemence, in inforcing sophistry and falsehood. And as reasoning is not the source, whence either disputant derives his tenets; it is in vain to expect, that any logic, which speaks not to the affections, will ever engage him to embrace sounder principles.

Those who have denied the reality of moral distinctions, may be ranked among the disingenuous disputants; nor is it conceivable, that any human creature could ever seriously believe, that all characters and actions were alike entitled to the affection and regard of every one. The difference, which nature has placed between one man and another, is so wide, and this difference is still so much farther widened, by education, example, and habit, that, where the opposite extremes come at once under our apprehension, there is no scepticism so scrupulous, and scarce any assurance so determined, as absolutely to deny all distinction between them. Let a man's insensibility be ever so great, he must often be touched with the images of RIGHT and WRONG; and let his prejudices be ever so obstinate, he must observe, that others are susceptible of like impressions. The only way, therefore, of converting an antagonist of this kind, is to leave him to himself. For, finding that no body keeps up the controversy with him, it is probable he will, at last, of himself, from mere weariness, come over to the side of common sense and reason.

There has been a controversy started of late, much better worth examination, concerning the general foundation of MORALS; whether they be derived from REASON, or from SENTIMENT; whether we attain the knowledge of them by a chain of argument and induction, or by an immediate feeling and finer internal sense; whether, like all sound judgment of truth and falsehood, they should be the same to every rational intelligent being; or whether, like the perception of beauty and deformity, they be founded entirely on the particular fabric and constitution of the human species.

4   The ancient philosophers, though they often affirm, that virtue is nothing but conformity to reason, yet, in general, seem to consider morals as deriving their existence from taste and sentiment. On the other hand, our modern enquirers, though they also talk much of the beauty of virtue, and deformity of vice, yet have commonly endeavoured to account for these distinctions by metaphysical reasonings, and by deductions from the most abstract principles of the understanding. Such confusion reigned in these subjects, that an opposition of the greatest consequence could prevail between one system and another, and even in the parts of almost each individual system; and yet no body, till very lately, was ever sensible of it. The elegant Lord SHAFTESBURY, who first gave occasion to remark this distinction, and who, in general, adhered to the principles of the ancients, is not, himself, entirely free from the same confusion.

5   It must be acknowledged, that both sides of the question are susceptible of specious arguments. Moral distinctions, it may be said, are discernible by pure *reason*: Else, whence the many disputes that reign in common life, as well as in philosophy, with regard to this subject: The long chain of proofs often produced on both sides; the examples cited, the authorities appealed to, the analogies employed, the fallacies detected, the inferences drawn, and the several conclusions adjusted to their proper principles. Truth is disputable; not taste: What exists in the nature of things is the standard of our judgment; what each man feels within himself is the standard of sentiment. Propositions in geometry may be proved, systems in physics may be controverted; but the harmony of verse, the tenderness of passion, the brilliancy of wit, must give immediate pleasure. No man reasons concerning another's beauty; but frequently concerning the justice or injustice of his actions. In every criminal trial the first object of the prisoner is to disprove the facts alleged, and deny the actions imputed to him: The second to prove, that, even if these actions were real, they might be justified, as innocent and lawful. It is confessedly by deductions of the understanding, that the first point is ascertained: How can we suppose that a different faculty of the mind is employed in fixing the other?

6   On the other hand, those who would resolve all moral determinations into *sentiment*, may endeavour to show, that it is impossible for reason ever to draw conclusions of this nature. To virtue, say they, it belongs to be *amiable*, and vice *odious*. This forms their very nature or essence. But can reason or argumentation distribute these different epithets to any subjects, and pronounce before-hand, that this must produce love, and that

hatred? Or what other reason can we ever assign for these affections, but the original fabric and formation of the human mind, which is naturally adapted to receive them?

The end of all moral speculations is to teach us our duty; and, by proper representations of the deformity of vice and beauty of virtue, beget correspondent habits, and engage us to avoid the one, and embrace the other. But is this ever to be expected from inferences and conclusions of the understanding, which of themselves have no hold of the affections, nor set in motion the active powers of men? They discover truths: But where the truths which they discover are indifferent, and beget no desire or aversion, they can have no influence on conduct and behaviour. What is honourable, what is fair, what is becoming, what is noble, what is generous, takes possession of the heart, and animates us to embrace and maintain it. What is intelligible, what is evident, what is probable, what is true, procures only the cool assent of the understanding; and gratifying a speculative curiosity, puts an end to our researches. 7

Extinguish all the warm feelings and prepossessions in favour of virtue, and all disgust or aversion to vice: Render men totally indifferent towards these distinctions; and morality is no longer a practical study, nor has any tendency to regulate our lives and actions. 8

These arguments on each side (and many more might be produced) are so plausible, that I am apt to suspect, they may, the one as well as the other, be solid and satisfactory, and that *reason* and *sentiment* concur in almost all moral determinations and conclusions. The final sentence, it is probable, which pronounces characters and actions amiable or odious, praise-worthy or blameable; that which stamps on them the mark of honour or infamy, approbation or censure; that which renders morality an active principle, and constitutes virtue our happiness, and vice our misery: It is probable, I say, that this final sentence depends on some internal sense or feeling, which nature has made universal in the whole species. For what else can have an influence of this nature? But in order to pave the way for such a sentiment, and give a proper discernment of its object, it is often necessary, we find, that much reasoning should precede, that nice distinctions be made, just conclusions drawn, distant comparisons formed, complicated relations examined, and general facts fixed and ascertained. Some species of beauty, especially the natural kinds, on their first appearance, command our affection and approbation; and where they fail of this effect, it is impossible for any reasoning to redress their influence, or adapt them better to our taste and sentiment. But in many orders of beauty, particularly those of the finer arts, it is requisite to employ much reasoning, in order to feel the proper sentiment; and a false relish may frequently be corrected by argument and reflection. There are just 9 grounds to conclude, that moral beauty partakes much of this latter species, and demands the assistance of our intellectual faculties, in order to give it a suitable influence on the human mind.

10   But though this question, concerning the general principles of morals, be curious and important, it is needless for us, at present, to employ farther care in our researches concerning it. For if we can be so happy, in the course of this enquiry, as to discover the true origin of morals, it will then easily appear how far either sentiment or reason enters into all determinations of this nature.[1] In order to attain this purpose, we shall endeavour to follow a very simple method: We shall analyze that complication of mental qualities, which form what, in common life, we call PERSONAL MERIT: We shall consider every attribute of the mind, which renders a man an object either of esteem and affection, or of hatred and contempt; every habit or sentiment or faculty, which, if ascribed to any person, implies either praise or blame, and may enter into any panegyric or satire of his character and manners. The quick sensibility, which, on this head, is so universal among mankind, gives a philosopher sufficient assurance, that he can never be considerably mistaken in framing the catalogue, or incur any danger of misplacing the objects of his contemplation: He needs only to enter into his own breast for a moment, and consider whether or not he should desire to have this or that quality ascribed to him, and whether such or such an imputation would proceed from a friend or an enemy. The very nature of language guides us almost infallibly in forming a judgment of this nature; and as every tongue possesses one set of words which are taken in a good sense, and another in the opposite, the least acquaintance with the idiom suffices, without any reasoning, to direct us in collecting and arranging the estimable or blameable qualities of men. The only object of reasoning is to discover the circumstances on both sides, which are common to these qualities; to observe that particular in which the estimable qualities agree on the one hand, and the blameable on the other; and thence to reach the foundation of ethics, and find those universal principles, from which all censure or approbation is ultimately derived. As this is a question of fact, not of abstract science, we can only expect success, by following the experimental method, and deducing general maxims from a comparison of particular instances. The other scientifical method, where a general abstract principle is first established, and is afterwards branched out into a variety of inferences and conclusions, may be more perfect in itself, but suits less the imperfection of human nature, and is a common source of illusion and mistake in this as well as in other

---

[1] See Appendix I.

subjects. Men are now cured of their passion for hypotheses and systems in natural philosophy, and will hearken to no arguments but those which are derived from experience. It is full time they should attempt a like reformation in all moral disquisitions; and reject every system of ethics, however subtle or ingenious, which is not founded on fact and observation.

We shall begin our enquiry on this head by the consideration of social   11 virtues, benevolence and justice. The explication of them will probably give us an opening by which the others may be accounted for.

SECTION II.
OF BENEVOLENCE.
Part I.

1   IT may be esteemed, perhaps, a superfluous task to prove, that the benevolent or softer affections are ESTIMABLE; and wherever they appear, engage the approbation, and good-will of mankind. The epithets, *sociable, good-natured, humane, merciful, grateful, friendly, generous, beneficent,* or their equivalents, are known in all languages, and universally express the highest merit, which *human nature* is capable of attaining. Where these amiable qualities are attended with birth and power and eminent abilities, and display themselves in the good government or useful instruction of mankind, they seem even to raise the possessors of them above the rank of *human nature,* and make them approach in some measure to the divine. Exalted capacity, undaunted courage, prosperous success; these may only expose a hero or politician to the envy and ill-will of the public: But as soon as the praises are added of humane and beneficent; when instances are displayed of lenity, tenderness, or friendship; envy itself is silent, or joins the general voice of approbation and applause.

2   When PERICLES, the great ATHENIAN statesman and general, was on his death-bed, his surrounding friends, deeming him now insensible, began to indulge their sorrow for their expiring patron, by enumerating his great qualities and successes, his conquests and victories, the unusual length of his administration, and his nine trophies erected over the enemies of the republic. *You forget,* cries the dying hero, who had heard all, *you forget the most eminent of my praises, while you dwell so much on those vulgar advantages, in which fortune had a principal share. You have not observed, that no citizen has ever yet worne mourning on my account.*[1]

3   In men of more ordinary talents and capacity, the social virtues become, if possible, still more essentially requisite; there being nothing eminent, in that case, to compensate for the want of them, or preserve the person from our severest hatred, as well as contempt. A high ambition, an elevated courage, is apt, says CICERO, in less perfect characters, to degenerate into a turbulent ferocity. The more social and softer virtues are there chiefly to be regarded. These are always good and amiable.[2]

4   The principal advantage, which JUVENAL discovers in the extensive capacity of the human species is, that it renders our benevolence also more

---

[1]   PLUT. in PERICLE, 38. [Plutarch, *Lives.*]
[2]   CIC. de Officiis, lib. 1. [Cicero, *De officiis.*]

extensive, and gives us larger opportunities of spreading our kindly influence than what are indulged to the inferior creation.[3] It must, indeed, be confessed, that by doing good only, can a man truly enjoy the advantages of being eminent. His exalted station, of itself, but the more exposes him to danger and tempest. His sole prerogative is to afford shelter to inferiors, who repose themselves under his cover and protection.

But I forget, that it is not my present business to recommend generosity and benevolence, or to paint, in their true colours, all the genuine charms of the social virtues. These, indeed, sufficiently engage every heart, on the first apprehension of them; and it is difficult to abstain from some sally of panegyric, as often as they occur in discourse or reasoning. But our object here being more the speculative, than the practical part of morals, it will suffice to remark, (what will readily, I believe, be allowed) that no qualities are more intitled to the general good-will and approbation of mankind than beneficence and humanity, friendship and gratitude, natural affection and public spirit, or whatever proceeds from a tender sympathy with others, and a generous concern for our kind and species. These, wherever they appear, seem to transfuse themselves, in a manner, into each beholder, and to call forth, in their own behalf, the same favourable and affectionate sentiments, which they exert on all around.

Part II.

We may observe, that, in displaying the praises of any humane, beneficent man, there is one circumstance which never fails to be amply insisted on, namely, the happiness and satisfaction, derived to society from his intercourse and good offices. To his parents, we are apt to say, he endears himself by his pious attachment and duteous care, still more than by the connexions of nature. His children never feel his authority, but when employed for their advantage. With him, the ties of love are consolidated by beneficence and friendship. The ties of friendship approach, in a fond observance of each obliging office, to those of love and inclination. His domestics and dependants have in him a sure resource; and no longer dread the power of fortune, but so far as she exercises it over him. From him the hungry receive food, the naked cloathing, the ignorant and slothful skill and industry. Like the sun, an inferior minister of providence, he cheers, invigorates, and sustains the surrounding world.

If confined to private life, the sphere of his activity is narrower; but his influence is all benign and gentle. If exalted into a higher station, mankind and posterity reap the fruit of his labours.

---

[3] Sat. xv. 139. & seq. [Juvenal, *Satires*.]

8   As these topics of praise never fail to be employed, and with success, where we would inspire esteem for any one; may it not thence be concluded, that the UTILITY, resulting from the social virtues, forms, at least, a *part* of their merit, and is one source of that approbation and regard so universally paid to them?

9   When we recommend even an animal or a plant as *useful* and *beneficial*, we give it an applause and recommendation suited to its nature. As, on the other hand, reflection on the baneful influence of any of these inferior beings always inspires us with the sentiment of aversion. The eye is pleased with the prospect of corn-fields and loaded vineyards; horses grazing, and flocks pasturing: But flies the view of briars and brambles, affording shelter to wolves and serpents.

10   A machine, a piece of furniture, a vestment, a house well contrived for use and conveniency, is so far beautiful, and is contemplated with pleasure and approbation. An experienced eye is here sensible to many excellencies, which escape persons ignorant and uninstructed.

11   Can anything stronger be said in praise of a profession, such as merchandize or manufacture, than to observe the advantages which it procures to society? And is not a monk and inquisitor enraged when we treat his order as useless or pernicious to mankind?

12   The historian exults in displaying the benefit arising from his labours. The writer of romance alleviates or denies the bad consequences ascribed to his manner of composition.

13   In general, what praise is implied in the simple epithet *useful*! What reproach in the contrary!

14   Your Gods, says CICERO,[4] in opposition to the EPICUREANS, cannot justly claim any worship or adoration, with whatever imaginary perfections you may suppose them endowed. They are totally useless and inactive. Even the EGYPTIANS, whom you so much ridicule, never consecrated any animal but on account of its utility.

15   The sceptics assert,[5] though absurdly, that the origin of all religious worship was derived from the utility of inanimate objects, as the sun and moon, to the support and well-being of mankind. This is also the common reason assigned by historians, for the deification of eminent heroes and legislators.[6]

---

[4] De Nat. Deor. lib. i. [Cicero, *De natura deorum*.]

[5] SEXT. EMP. adversus MATH. lib. ix. [Sextus Empiricus, *Against the Mathematicians*.]

[6] DIOD. SIC. passim. [Diodorus Siculus, *Historical Library*.]

To plant a tree, to cultivate a field, to beget children; meritorious acts, 16
according to the religion of ZOROASTER.

In all determinations of morality, this circumstance of public utility is 17
ever principally in view; and wherever disputes arise, either in philosophy
or common life, concerning the bounds of duty, the question cannot, by
any means, be decided with greater certainty, than by ascertaining, on any
side, the true interests of mankind. If any false opinion, embraced from
appearances, has been found to prevail; as soon as farther experience and
sounder reasoning have given us juster notions of human affairs; we retract our first sentiment, and adjust anew the boundaries of moral good
and evil.

Giving alms to common beggars is naturally praised; because it seems 18
to carry relief to the distressed and indigent: But when we observe the encouragement thence arising to idleness and debauchery, we regard that
species of charity rather as a weakness than a virtue.

Tyrannicide, or the assassination of usurpers and oppressive princes, 19
was highly extolled in ancient times; because it both freed mankind from
many of these monsters, and seemed to keep the others in awe, whom the
sword or poniard could not reach. But history and experience having since
convinced us, that this practice encreases the jealousy and cruelty of
princes, a TIMOLEON and a BRUTUS, though treated with indulgence on
account of the prejudices of their times, are now considered as very improper models for imitation.

Liberality in princes is regarded as a mark of beneficence: But when it 20
occurs, that the homely bread of the honest and industrious is often
thereby converted into delicious cates for the idle and the prodigal, we
soon retract our heedless praises. The regrets of a prince, for having lost a
day, were noble and generous: But had he intended to have spent it in acts
of generosity to his greedy courtiers, it was better lost than misemployed
after that manner.

Luxury, or a refinement on the pleasures and conveniencies of life, had 21
long been supposed the source of every corruption in government, and
the immediate cause of faction, sedition, civil wars, and the total loss of
liberty. It was, therefore, universally regarded as a vice, and was an object
of declamation to all satirists, and severe moralists. Those, who prove, or
attempt to prove, that such refinements rather tend to the encrease of industry, civility, and arts, regulate anew our *moral* as well as *political* sentiments, and represent, as laudable or innocent, what had formerly been
regarded as pernicious and blameable.

Upon the whole, then, it seems undeniable, *that* nothing can bestow 22
more merit on any human creature than the sentiment of benevolence in

an eminent degree; and *that* a *part*, at least, of its merit arises from its tendency to promote the interests of our species, and bestow happiness on human society. We carry our view into the salutary consequences of such a character and disposition; and whatever has so benign an influence, and forwards so desirable an end, is beheld with complacency and pleasure. The social virtues are never regarded without their beneficial tendencies, nor viewed as barren and unfruitful. The happiness of mankind, the order of society, the harmony of families, the mutual support of friends, are always considered as the result of their gentle dominion over the breasts of men.

23   How considerable a *part* of their merit we ought to ascribe to their utility, will better appear from future disquisitions;[7] as well as the reason, why this circumstance has such a command over our esteem and approbation.[8]

---

[7] Sect. 3d and 4th

[8] Sect. 5th.

SECTION III.
OF JUSTICE.

Part I.

THAT justice is useful to society, and consequently that *part* of its merit, at   1
least, must arise from that consideration, it would be a superfluous undertaking to prove. That public utility is the *sole* origin of justice, and that reflections on the beneficial consequences of this virtue are the *sole*
foundation of its merit; this proposition, being more curious and important, will better deserve our examination and enquiry.

Let us suppose, that nature has bestowed on the human race such pro-   2
fuse *abundance* of all *external* conveniencies, that, without any uncertainty
in the event, without any care or industry on our part, every individual
finds himself fully provided with whatever his most voracious appetites
can want, or luxurious imagination wish or desire. His natural beauty, we
shall suppose, surpasses all acquired ornaments: The perpetual clemency
of the seasons renders useless all cloaths or covering: The raw herbage affords him the most delicious fare; the clear fountain, the richest beverage.
No laborious occupation required: No tillage: No navigation. Music, poetry, and contemplation form his sole business: Conversation, mirth, and
friendship his sole amusement.

It seems evident, that, in such a happy state, every other social virtue   3
would flourish, and receive tenfold encrease; but the cautious, jealous
virtue of justice would never once have been dreamed of. For what purpose make a partition of goods, where every one has already more than
enough? Why give rise to property, where there cannot possibly be any
injury? Why call this object *mine*, when, upon the seizing of it by another, I need but stretch out my hand to possess myself of what is
equally valuable? Justice, in that case, being totally USELESS, would be
an idle ceremonial, and could never possibly have place in the catalogue
of virtues.

We see, even in the present necessitous condition of mankind, that,   4
wherever any benefit is bestowed by nature in an unlimited abundance, we
leave it always in common among the whole human race, and make no
subdivisions of right and property. Water and air, though the most necessary of all objects, are not challenged as the property of individuals; nor
can any man commit injustice by the most lavish use and enjoyment of
these blessings. In fertile extensive countries, with few inhabitants, land is
regarded on the same footing. And no topic is so much insisted on by
those, who defend the liberty of the seas, as the unexhausted use of them

in navigation. Were the advantages, procured by navigation, as inexhaustible, these reasoners had never had any adversaries to refute; nor had any claims ever been advanced of a separate, exclusive dominion over the ocean.

5   It may happen, in some countries, at some periods, that there be established a property in water, none in land;[1] if the latter be in greater abundance than can be used by the inhabitants, and the former be found, with difficulty, and in very small quantities.

6   Again; suppose, that, though the necessities of human race continue the same as at present, yet the mind is so enlarged, and so replete with friendship and generosity, that every man has the utmost tenderness for every man, and feels no more concern for his own interest than for that of his fellows: It seems evident, that the USE of justice would, in this case, be suspended by such an extensive benevolence, nor would the divisions and barriers of property and obligation have ever been thought of. Why should I bind another, by a deed or promise, to do me any good office, when I know that he is already prompted, by the strongest inclination, to seek my happiness, and would, of himself, perform the desired service; except the hurt, he thereby receives, be greater than the benefit accruing to me? In which case, he knows, that, from my innate humanity and friendship, I should be the first to oppose myself to his imprudent generosity. Why raise land-marks between my neighbour's field and mine, when my heart has made no division between our interests; but shares all his joys and sorrows with the same force and vivacity as if originally my own? Every man, upon this supposition, being a second self to another, would trust all his interests to the discretion of every man; without jealousy, without partition, without distinction. And the whole human race would form only one family; where all would lie in common, and be used freely, without regard to property; but cautiously too, with as entire regard to the necessities of each individual, as if our own interests were most intimately concerned.

7   In the present disposition of the human heart, it would, perhaps, be difficult to find compleat instances of such enlarged affections; but still we may observe, that the case of families approaches towards it; and the stronger the mutual benevolence is among the individuals, the nearer it approaches; till all distinction of property be, in a great measure, lost and confounded among them. Between married persons, the cement of friendship is by the laws supposed so strong as to abolish all division of possessions; and has often, in reality, the force ascribed to it. And it is observable,

---

[1] GENESIS, chap. xiii. and xxi.

that, during the ardour of new enthusiasms, when every principle is inflamed into extravagance, the community of goods has frequently been attempted; and nothing but experience of its inconveniencies, from the
returning or disguised selfishness of men, could make the imprudent fanatics adopt anew the ideas of justice and of separate property. So true is it,
that this virtue derives its existence entirely from its necessary *use* to the intercourse and social state of mankind.

To make this truth more evident, let us reverse the foregoing supposi- 8
tions; and carrying every thing to the opposite extreme, consider what
would be the effect of these new situations. Suppose a society to fall into
such want of all common necessaries, that the utmost frugality and industry cannot preserve the greater number from perishing, and the whole
from extreme misery: It will readily, I believe, be admitted, that the strict
laws of justice are suspended, in such a pressing emergence, and give
place to the stronger motives of necessity and self-preservation. Is it any
crime, after a shipwreck, to seize whatever means or instrument of safety
one can lay hold of, without regard to former limitations of property? Or
if a city besieged were perishing with hunger; can we imagine, that men
will see any means of preservation before them, and lose their lives, from a
scrupulous regard to what, in other situations, would be the rules of equity and justice? The USE and TENDENCY of that virtue is to procure
happiness and security, by preserving order in society: But where the society is ready to perish from extreme necessity, no greater evil can be
dreaded from violence and injustice; and every man may now provide for
himself by all the means, which prudence can dictate, or humanity permit. The public, even in less urgent necessities, opens granaries, without
the consent of proprietors; as justly supposing, that the authority of magistracy may, consistent with equity, extend so far: But were any number of
men to assemble, without the tye of laws or civil jurisdiction; would an
equal partition of bread in a famine, though effected by power and even
violence, be regarded as criminal or injurious?

Suppose likewise, that it should be a virtuous man's fate to fall into the 9
society of ruffians, remote from the protection of laws and government;
what conduct must he embrace in that melancholy situation? He sees such
a desperate rapaciousness prevail; such a disregard to equity, such contempt of order, such stupid blindness to future consequences, as must immediately have the most tragical conclusion, and must terminate in
destruction to the greater number, and in a total dissolution of society to
the rest. He, mean while, can have no other expedient than to arm himself,
to whomever the sword he seizes, or the buckler, may belong: To make
provision of all means of defence and security: And his particular regard
to justice being no longer of USE to his own safety or that of others, he

must consult the dictates of self-preservation alone, without concern for those who no longer merit his care and attention.

10   When any man, even in political society, renders himself, by his crimes, obnoxious to the public, he is punished by the laws in his goods and person; that is, the ordinary rules of justice are, with regard to him, suspended for a moment, and it becomes equitable to inflict on him, for the *benefit* of society, what, otherwise, he could not suffer without wrong or injury.

11   The rage and violence of public war; what is it but a suspension of justice among the warring parties, who perceive, that this virtue is now no longer of any *use* or advantage to them? The laws of war, which then succeed to those of equity and justice, are rules calculated for the *advantage* and *utility* of that particular state, in which men are now placed. And were a civilized nation engaged with barbarians, who observed no rules even of war; the former must also suspend their observance of them, where they no longer serve to any purpose; and must render every action or rencounter as bloody and pernicious as possible to the first aggressors.

12   Thus, the rules of equity or justice depend entirely on the particular state and condition, in which men are placed, and owe their origin and existence to that UTILITY, which results to the public from their strict and regular observance. Reverse, in any considerable circumstance, the condition of men: Produce extreme abundance or extreme necessity: Implant in the human breast perfect moderation and humanity, or perfect rapaciousness and malice: By rendering justice totally *useless*, you thereby totally destroy its essence, and suspend its obligation upon mankind.

13   The common situation of society is a medium amidst all these extremes. We are naturally partial to ourselves, and to our friends; but are capable of learning the advantage resulting from a more equitable conduct. Few enjoyments are given us from the open and liberal hand of nature; but by art, labour, and industry, we can extract them in great abundance. Hence the ideas of property become necessary in all civil society: Hence justice derives its usefulness to the public: And hence alone arises its merit and moral obligation.

14   These conclusions are so natural and obvious, that they have not escaped even the poets, in their descriptions of the felicity, attending the golden age or the reign of SATURN. The seasons, in that first period of nature, were so temperate, if we credit these agreeable fictions, that there was no necessity for men to provide themselves with cloaths and houses, as a security against the violence of heat and cold: The rivers flowed with wine and milk: The oaks yielded honey; and nature spontaneously produced her greatest delicacies. Nor were these the chief advantages of that happy age. Tempests were not alone removed from nature; but those more

furious tempests were unknown to human breasts, which now cause such uproar, and engender such confusion. Avarice, ambition, cruelty, selfishness, were never heard of: Cordial affection, compassion, sympathy, were the only movements with which the mind was yet acquainted. Even the punctilious distinction of *mine* and *thine* was banished from among that happy race of mortals, and carried with it the very notion of property and obligation, justice and injustice.

This *poetical* fiction of the *golden age* is, in some respects, of a piece with the *philosophical* fiction of the *state of nature*; only that the former is represented as the most charming and most peaceable condition, which can possibly be imagined; whereas the latter is painted out as a state of mutual war and violence, attended with the most extreme necessity. On the first origin of mankind, we are told, their ignorance and savage nature were so prevalent, that they could give no mutual trust, but must each depend upon himself, and his own force or cunning for protection and security. No law was heard of: No rule of justice known: No distinction of property regarded: Power was the only measure of right; and a perpetual war of all against all was the result of men's untamed selfishness and barbarity.[2]

15

---

[2] This fiction of a state of nature, as a state of war, was not first started by Mr. HOBBES, as is commonly imagined. PLATO endeavours to refute an hypothesis very like it in the 2d, 3d, and 4th books de republica. CICERO, on the contrary, supposes it certain and universally acknowledged in the following passage. "Quis enim vestrum, judices, ignorat, ita naturam rerum tulisse, ut quodam tempore homines, nondum neque naturali, neque civili jure descripto, fusi per agros, ac dispersi vagarentur tantumque haberent quantum manu ac viribus, per cædem ac vulnera, aut eripere aut retinere potuissent? Qui igitur primi virtute & consilio præstanti extiterunt, ii perspecto genere humanæ docilitatis atque ingenii, dissipatos unum in locum congregarunt, eosque ex feritate illa ad justitiam ac mansuetudinem transduxerunt. Tum res ad communem utilitatem, quas publicas appellamus, tum conventicula hominum, quæ postea civitates nominatæ sunt, tum domicilia conjuncta, quas urbes dicamus, invento & divino & humano jure, mœnibus sepserunt. Atque inter hanc vitam, perpolitam humanitate, & illam immanem, nihil tam interest quam JUS atque VIS. Horum utro uti nolimus, altero est utendum. Vim volumus extingui? Jus valeat necesse est, id est, judicia, quibus omne jus continetur. Judicia displicent, aut nulla, sunt? Vis dominetur necesse est? Hæc vident omnes."—*Pro Sext.* l. 42. ["For which of us, gentleman, does not know the natural course of human history—how there was once a time, before either natural or civil law had been formulated, when men roamed, scattered and dispersed over the country, and had no other possessions than just so much as they had been able either to seize by strength and violence, or keep at the cost of slaughter and wounds? So then those who at first showed themselves to be the most eminent for merit and wisdom, having perceived the essential teachableness of human nature, gathered together into one place those who had been scattered abroad, and brought them from tat state of savagery to one of justice and humanity. Then things serving for common use, which we

16   Whether such a condition of human nature could ever exist, or if it did, could continue so long as to merit the appellation of a *state*, may justly be doubted. Men are necessarily born in a family-society, at least; and are trained up by their parents to some rule of conduct and behaviour. But this must be admitted, that, if such a state of mutual war and violence was ever real, the suspension of all laws of justice, from their absolute inutility, is a necessary and infallible consequence.

17   The more we vary our views of human life, and the newer and more unusual the lights are, in which we survey it, the more shall we be convinced, that the origin here assigned for the virtue of justice is real and satisfactory.

18   Were there a species of creatures, intermingled with men, which, though rational, were possessed of such inferior strength, both of body and mind, that they were incapable of all resistance, and could never, upon the highest provocation, make us feel the effects of their resentment; the necessary consequence, I think, is, that we should be bound, by the laws of humanity, to give gentle usage to these creatures, but should not, properly speaking, lie under any restraint of justice with regard to them, nor could they possess any right or property, exclusive of such arbitrary lords. Our intercourse with them could not be called society, which supposes a degree of equality; but absolute command on the one side, and servile obedience on the other. Whatever we covet, they must instantly resign: Our permission is the only tenure, by which they hold their possessions: Our compassion and kindness the only check, by which they curb our lawless will: And as no inconvenience ever results from the exercise of a power, so firmly established in nature, the restraints of justice and property, being totally *useless*, would never have place in so unequal a confederacy.

19   This is plainly the situation of men, with regard to animals; and how far these may be said to possess reason, I leave it to others to determine. The great superiority of civilized EUROPEANS above barbarous INDIANS, tempted us to imagine ourselves on the same footing with regard to them, and made us throw off all restraints of justice, and even of humanity, in

---

call public, associations of men, which were afterwards called states, then continuous series of dwelling-places which we call cities, they enclosed with walls, after divine and human law had been introduced. Now, between life thus refined and humanized, and that life of savagery, nothing marks the difference so clearly as law and violence. Whichever of the two we are unwilling to use, we must use the other. If we would have violence abolished, law must prevail, that is the administration of justice, on which law wholly depends; if we dislike the administration of justice, or if there is none, force must rule. All are aware of this" (Cicero, *Pro Sestio*, XLII, 91; trans. by R. Gardner).]

our treatment of them. In many nations, the female sex are reduced to like slavery, and are rendered incapable of all property, in opposition to their lordly masters. But though the males, when united, have, in all countries, bodily force sufficient to maintain this severe tyranny; yet such are the insinuation, address, and charms of their fair companions, that women are commonly able to break the confederacy, and share with the other sex in all the rights and privileges of society.

Were the human species so framed by nature as that each individual   20 possessed within himself every faculty, requisite both for his own preservation and for the propagation of his kind: Were all society and intercourse cut off between man and man, by the primary intention of the supreme Creator: It seems evident, that so solitary a being would be as much incapable of justice, as of social discourse and conversation. Where mutual regards and forbearance serve to no manner of purpose, they would never direct the conduct of any reasonable man. The headlong course of the passions would be checked by no reflection on future consequences. And as each man is here supposed to love himself alone, and to depend only on himself and his own activity for safety and happiness, he would, on every occasion, to the utmost of his power, challenge the preference above every other being, to none of which he is bound by any ties, either of nature or of interest.

But suppose the conjunction of the sexes to be established in nature, a   21 family immediately arises; and particular rules being found requisite for its subsistence, these are immediately embraced; though without comprehending the rest of mankind within their prescriptions. Suppose, that several families unite together into one society, which is totally disjoined from all others, the rules, which preserve peace and order, enlarge themselves to the utmost extent of that society; but becoming then entirely useless, lose their force when carried one step farther. But again suppose, that several distinct societies maintain a kind of intercourse for mutual convenience and advantage, the boundaries of justice still grow larger, in proportion to the largeness of men's views, and the force of their mutual connexions. History, experience, reason sufficiently instruct us in this natural progress of human sentiments, and in the gradual enlargement of our regards to justice, in proportion as we become acquainted with the extensive utility of that virtue.

Part II.

If we examine the *particular* laws, by which justice is directed, and prop-   22 erty determined; we shall still be presented with the same conclusion. The good of mankind is the only object of all these laws and regulations. Not only it is requisite, for the peace and interest of society, that men's possessions should be separated; but the rules, which we follow, in making the separation, are such as can best be contrived to serve farther the interests of society.

23   We shall suppose, that a creature, possessed of reason, but unacquainted with human nature, deliberates with himself what RULES of justice or property would best promote public interest, and establish peace and security among mankind: His most obvious thought would be, to assign the largest possessions to the most extensive virtue, and give every one the power of doing good, proportioned to his inclination. In a perfect theocracy, where a being, infinitely intelligent, governs by particular volitions, this rule would certainly have place, and might serve to the wisest purposes: But were mankind to execute such a law; so great is the uncertainty of merit, both from its natural obscurity, and from the self-conceit of each individual, that no determinate rule of conduct would ever result from it; and the total dissolution of society must be the immediate consequence. Fanatics may suppose, *that dominion is founded on grace,* and *that saints alone inherit the earth*; but the civil magistrate very justly puts these sublime theorists on the same footing with common robbers, and teaches them by the severest discipline, that a rule, which, in speculation, may seem the most advantageous to society, may yet be found, in practice, totally pernicious and destructive.

24   That there were *religious* fanatics of this kind in ENGLAND, during the civil wars, we learn from history; though it is probable, that the obvious *tendency* of these principles excited such horror in mankind, as soon obliged the dangerous enthusiasts to renounce, or at least conceal their tenets. Perhaps, the *levellers*, who claimed an equal distribution of property, were a kind of *political* fanatics, which arose from the religious species, and more openly avowed their pretensions; as carrying a more plausible appearance, of being practicable in themselves, as well as useful to human society.

25   It must, indeed, be confessed, that nature is so liberal to mankind, that, were all her presents equally divided among the species, and improved by art and industry, every individual would enjoy all the necessaries, and even most of the comforts of life; nor would ever be liable to any ills, but such as might accidentally arise from the sickly frame and constitution of his body. It must also be confessed, that, wherever we depart from this equality, we rob the poor of more satisfaction than we add to the rich, and that the slight gratification of a frivolous vanity, in one individual, frequently costs more than bread to many families, and even provinces. It may appear withal, that the rule of equality, as it would be highly *useful*, is not altogether *impracticable*; but has taken place, at least in an imperfect degree, in some republics; particularly that of SPARTA;

where it was attended, it is said, with the most beneficial consequences. Not to mention, that the AGRARIAN laws, so frequently claimed in ROME, and carried into execution in many GREEK cities, proceeded, all of them, from a general idea of the utility of this principle.

But historians, and even common sense, may inform us, that, however   26
specious these ideas of *perfect* equality may seem, they are really, at bottom, *impracticable*; and were they not so, would be extremely *pernicious* to human society. Render possessions ever so equal, men's different degrees of art, care, and industry will immediately break that equality. Or if you check these virtues, you reduce society to the most extreme indigence; and instead of preventing want and beggary in a few, render it unavoidable to the whole community. The most rigorous inquisition too is requisite to watch every inequality on its first appearance; and the most severe jurisdiction, to punish and redress it. But besides, that so much authority must soon degenerate into tyranny, and be exerted with great partialities; who can possibly be possessed of it, in such a situation as is here supposed? Perfect equality of possessions, destroying all subordination, weakens extremely the authority of magistracy, and must reduce all power nearly to a level, as well as property.

We may conclude, therefore, that, in order to establish laws for the reg-   27
ulation of property, we must be acquainted with the nature and situation of man; must reject appearances, which may be false, though specious; and must search for those rules, which are, on the whole, most *useful* and *beneficial*. Vulgar sense and slight experience are sufficient for this purpose; where men give not way to too selfish avidity, or too extensive enthusiasm.

Who sees not, for instance, that whatever is produced or improved by a   28
man's art or industry ought, for ever, to be secured to him, in order to give encouragement to such *useful* habits and accomplishments? That the property ought also to descend to children and relations, for the same *useful* purpose? That it may be alienated by consent, in order to beget that commerce and intercourse, which is so *beneficial* to human society? And that all contracts and promises ought carefully to be fulfilled, in order to secure mutual trust and confidence, by which the general *interest* of mankind is so much promoted?

Examine the writers on the laws of nature; and you will always find,   29
that, whatever principles they set out with, they are sure to terminate here at last, and to assign, as the ultimate reason for every rule which they establish, the convenience and necessities of mankind. A concession thus extorted, in opposition to systems, has more authority, than if it had been made in prosecution of them.

What other reason, indeed, could writers ever give, why this must be   30 *mine* and that *yours*; since uninstructed nature, surely, never made any such distinction? The objects, which receive those appellations, are, of themselves, foreign to us; they are totally disjoined and separated from us; and nothing but the general interests of society can form the connexion.

31   Sometimes, the interests of society may require a rule of justice in a particular case; but may not determine any particular rule, among several, which are all equally beneficial. In that case, the slightest *analogies* are laid hold of, in order to prevent that indifference and ambiguity, which would be the source of perpetual dissention. Thus possession alone, and first possession, is supposed to convey property, where no body else has any preceding claim and pretension. Many of the reasonings of lawyers are of this analogical nature, and depend on very slight connexions of the imagination.

32   Does any one scruple, in extraordinary cases, to violate all regard to the private property of individuals, and sacrifice to public interest a distinction, which had been established for the sake of that interest? The safety of the people is the supreme law: All other particular laws are subordinate to it, and dependant on it: And if, in the *common* course of things, they be followed and regarded; it is only because the public safety and interest *commonly* demand so equal and impartial an administration.

33   Sometimes both *utility* and *analogy* fail, and leave the laws of justice in total uncertainty. Thus, it is highly requisite, that prescription or long possession should convey property; but what number of days or months or years should be sufficient for that purpose, it is impossible for reason alone to determine. *Civil laws* here supply the place of the natural *code*, and assign different terms for prescription, according to the different *utilities*, proposed by the legislator. Bills of exchange and promissory notes, by the laws of most countries, prescribe sooner than bonds, and mortgages, and contracts of a more formal nature.

34   In general, we may observe, that all questions of property are subordinate to the authority of civil laws, which extend, restrain, modify, and alter the rules of natural justice, according to the particular *convenience* of each community. The laws have, or ought to have, a constant reference to the constitution of government, the manners, the climate, the religion, the commerce, the situation of each society. A late author of genius, as well as learning, has prosecuted this subject at large, and has established, from these principles, a system of political knowledge, which abounds in ingenious and brilliant thoughts, and is not wanting in solidity.[3]

---

[3] The author of *L'Esprit des Loix*. This illustrious writer, however, sets out with a different theory, and supposes all right to be founded on certain *rapports* or relations; which is a system, that, in my opinion, never will be reconciled with true philosophy. Father MALEBRANCHE, as far as I can learn, was the first that started this abstract theory of

What is a man's property? Any thing, which it is lawful for him, and for him alone, to use. *But what rule have we, by which we can distinguish these objects?* Here we must have recourse to statutes, customs, precedents, analogies, and a hundred other circumstances; some of which are constant and inflexible, some variable and arbitrary. But the ultimate point, in which they all professedly terminate, is, the interest and happiness of human society. Where this enters not into consideration, nothing can appear more whimsical, unnatural, and even superstitious, than all or most of the laws of justice and of property. 35

Those, who ridicule vulgar superstitions, and expose the folly of particular regards to meats, days, places, postures, apparel, have an easy task; while they consider all the qualities and relations of the objects, and discover no adequate cause for that affection or antipathy, veneration or horror, which have so mighty an influence over a considerable part of mankind. A SYRIAN would have starved rather than taste pigeon; an EGYPTIAN would not have approached bacon: But if these species of food be examined by the senses of sight, smell, or taste, or scrutinized by the sciences of chymistry, medicine, or physics; no difference is ever found between them and any other species, nor can that precise circumstance be pitched on, which may afford a just foundation for the religious passion. A 36

---

morals, which was afterwards adopted by CUDWORTH, CLARKE, and others; and as it excludes all sentiment, and pretends to found every thing on reason, it has not wanted followers in this philosophic age. See Section I. Appendix I. With regard to justice, the virtue here treated of, the inference against this theory seems short and conclusive. Property is allowed to be dependent on civil laws; civil laws are allowed to have no other object, but the interest of society: This therefore must be allowed to be the sole foundation of property and justice. Not to mention, that our obligation itself to obey the magistrate and his laws is founded on nothing but the interests of society.

If the ideas of justice, sometimes, do not follow the dispositions of civil law; we shall find, that these cases, instead of objections, are confirmations of the theory delivered above. Where a civil law is so perverse as to cross all the interests of society, it loses all its authority, and men judge by the ideas of natural justice, which are conformable to those interests. Sometimes also civil laws, for useful purposes, require a ceremony or form to any deed; and where that is wanting, their decrees run contrary to the usual tenour of justice; but one who takes advantage of such chicanes, is not commonly regarded as an honest man. Thus, the interests of society require, that contracts be fulfilled; and there is not a more material article either of natural or civil justice: But the omission of a trifling circumstance will often, by law, invalidate a contract, *in foro humano*, but not *in foro conscientiæ*, as divines express themselves. In these cases, the magistrate is supposed only to withdraw his power of enforcing the right, not to have altered the right. Where his intention extends to the right, and is conformable to the interests of society; it never fails to alter the right; a clear proof of the origin of justice and of property, as assigned above.

fowl on Thursday is lawful food; on Friday abominable: Eggs, in this house, and in this diocese, are permitted during Lent; a hundred paces farther, to eat them is a damnable sin. This earth or building, yesterday was profane; to-day, by the muttering of certain words, it has become holy and sacred. Such reflections as these, in the mouth of a philosopher, one may safely say, are too obvious to have any influence; because they must always, to every man, occur at first sight; and where they prevail not, of themselves, they are surely obstructed by education, prejudice, and passion, not by ignorance or mistake.

37   It may appear to a careless view, or rather a too abstracted reflection, that there enters a like superstition into all the sentiments of justice; and that, if a man expose its object, or what we call property, to the same scrutiny of sense and science, he will not, by the most accurate enquiry, find any foundation for the difference made by moral sentiment. I may lawfully nourish myself from this tree; but the fruit of another of the same species, ten paces off, it is criminal for me to touch. Had I worne this apparel an hour ago, I had merited the severest punishment; but a man, by pronouncing a few magical syllables, has now rendered it fit for my use and service. Were this house placed in the neighbouring territory, it had been immoral for me to dwell in it; but being built on this side the river, it is subject to a different municipal law, and, by its becoming mine, I incur no blame or censure. The same species of reasoning, it may be thought, which so successfully exposes superstition, is also applicable to justice; nor is it possible, in the one case more than in the other, to point out, in the object, that precise quality or circumstance, which is the foundation of the sentiment.

38   But there is this material difference between *superstition* and *justice*, that the former is frivolous, useless, and burdensome; the latter is absolutely requisite to the well-being of mankind and existence of society. When we abstract from this circumstance (for it is too apparent ever to be over-looked) it must be confessed, that all regards to right and property, seem entirely without foundation, as much as the grossest and most vulgar superstition. Were the interests of society no wise concerned, it is as unintelligible, why another's articulating certain sounds, implying consent, should change the nature of my actions with regard to a particular object, as why the reciting of a liturgy by a priest, in a certain habit and posture, should dedicate a heap of brick and timber, and render it, thenceforth and for ever, sacred.[4]

---

[4] It is evident, that the will or consent alone never transfers property, nor causes the obligation of a promise (for the same reasoning extends to both) but the will must be expressed by words or signs, in order to impose a tye upon any man. The expression

These reflections are far from weakening the obligations of justice, or 39 diminishing any thing from the most sacred attention to property. On the contrary, such sentiments must acquire new force from the present reasoning. For what stronger foundation can be desired or conceived for any

---

being once brought in as subservient to the will, soon becomes the principal part of the promise; nor will a man be less bound by his word, though he secretly give a different direction to his intention, and withhold the assent of his mind. But though the expression makes, on most occasions, the whole of the promise, yet it does not always so; and one who should make use of any expression, of which he knows not the meaning, and which he uses without any sense of the consequences, would not certainly be bound by it. Nay, though he know its meaning, yet if he uses it in jest only, and with such signs as evidently show, that he has no serious intention of binding himself, he would not lie under any obligation of performance; but it is necessary, that the words be a perfect expression of the will, without any contrary signs. Nay, even this we must not carry so far as to imagine, that one, whom, by our quickness of understanding, we conjecture, from certain signs, to have an intention of deceiving us, is not bound by his expression or verbal promise, if we accept of it; but must limit this conclusion to those cases where the signs are of a different nature from those of deceit. All these contradictions are easily accounted for, if justice arise entirely from its usefulness to society; but will never be explained on any other hypothesis.

It is remarkable, that the moral decisions of the *Jesuits* and other relaxed casuists, were commonly formed in prosecution of some such subtilties of reasoning as are here pointed out, and proceed as much from the habit of scholastic refinement as from any corruption of the heart, if we may follow the authority of Mons. BAYLE. See his Dictionary, article LOYOLA. And why has the indignation of mankind risen so high against these casuists; but because every one perceived, that human society could not subsist were such practices authorized, and that morals must always be handled with a view to public interest, more than philosophical regularity? If the secret direction of the intention, said every man of sense, could invalidate a contract; where is our security? And yet a metaphysical schoolman might think, that, where an intention was supposed to be requisite, if that intention really had not place, no consequence ought to follow, and no obligation be imposed. The casuistical subtilties may not be greater than the subtilties of lawyers, hinted at above; but as the former are *pernicious*, and the latter *innocent* and even *necessary*, this is the reason of the very different reception they meet with from the world.

It is a doctrine of the church of ROME, that the priest, by a secret direction of his intention, can invalidate any sacrament. This position is derived from a strict and regular prosecution of the obvious truth, that empty words alone, without any meaning or intention in the speaker, can never be attended with any effect. If the same conclusion be not admitted in reasonings concerning civil contracts, where the affair is allowed to be of so much less consequence than the eternal salvation of thousands, it proceeds entirely from men's sense of the danger and inconvenience of the doctrine in the former case: And we may thence observe, that however positive, arrogant, and dogmatical any superstition may appear, it never can convey any thorough persuasion of the reality of its objects, or put them, in any degree, on a balance with the common incidents of life, which we learn from daily observation and experimental reasoning.

duty, than to observe, that human society, or even human nature could not subsist, without the establishment of it; and will still arrive at greater degrees of happiness and perfection, the more inviolable the regard is, which is paid to that duty?

40   The dilemma seems obvious: As justice evidently tends to promote public utility and to support civil society, the sentiment of justice is either derived from our reflecting on that tendency, or like hunger, thirst, and other appetites, resentment, love of life, attachment to offspring, and other passions, arises from a simple original instinct in the human breast, which nature has implanted for like salutary purposes. If the latter be the case, it follows, that property, which is the object of justice, is also distinguished by a simple, original instinct, and is not ascertained by any argument or reflection. But who is there that ever heard of such an instinct? Or is this a subject, in which new discoveries can be made? We may as well expect to discover, in the body, new senses, which had before escaped the observation of all mankind.

41   But farther, though it seems a very simple proposition to say, that nature, by an instinctive sentiment, distinguishes property, yet in reality we shall find, that there are required for that purpose ten thousand different instincts, and these employed about objects of the greatest intricacy and nicest discernment. For when a definition of *property* is required, that relation is found to resolve itself into any possession acquired by occupation, by industry, by prescription, by inheritance, by contract, &c. Can we think, that nature, by an original instinct, instructs us in all these methods of acquisition?

42   These words too, inheritance and contract, stand for ideas infinitely complicated; and to define them exactly, a hundred volumes of laws, and a thousand volumes of commentators, have not been found sufficient. Does nature, whose instincts in men are all simple, embrace such complicated and artificial objects, and create a rational creature, without trusting any thing to the operation of his reason?

43   But even though all this were admitted, it would not be satisfactory. Positive laws can certainly transfer property. Is it by another original instinct, that we recognize the authority of kings and senates, and mark all the boundaries of their jurisdiction? Judges too, even though their sentence be erroneous and illegal, must be allowed, for the sake of peace and order, to have decisive authority, and ultimately to determine property. Have we original, innate ideas of praetors, and chancellors and juries? Who sees not, that all these institutions arise merely from the necessities of human society?

44   All birds of the same species, in every age and country, build their nests alike: In this we see the force of instinct. Men, in different times and

places, frame their houses differently: Here we perceive the influence of reason and custom. A like inference may be drawn from comparing the instinct of generation and the institution of property.

How great soever the variety of municipal laws, it must be confessed, 45 that their chief outlines pretty regularly concur; because the purposes, to which they tend, are every where exactly similar. In like manner, all houses have a roof and walls, windows and chimneys; though diversified in their shape, figure, and materials. The purposes of the latter, directed to the conveniencies of human life, discover not more plainly their origin from reason and reflection, than do those of the former, which point all to a like end.

I need not mention the variations, which all the rules of property re- 46 ceive from the finer turns and connexions of the imagination, and from the subtilties and abstractions of law-topics and reasonings. There is no possibility of reconciling this observation to the notion of original instincts.

What alone will beget a doubt concerning the theory, on which I insist, 47 is the influence of education and acquired habits, by which we are so accustomed to blame injustice, that we are not, in every instance, conscious of any immediate reflection on the pernicious consequences of it. The views the most familiar to us are apt, for that very reason, to escape us; and what we have very frequently performed from certain motives, we are apt likewise to continue mechanically, without recalling, on every occasion, the reflections, which first determined us. The convenience, or rather necessity, which leads to justice, is so universal, and every where points so much to the same rules, that the habit takes place in all societies; and it is not without some scrutiny, that we are able to ascertain its true origin. The matter, however, is not so obscure, but that, even in common life, we have, every moment, recourse to the principle of public utility, and ask, *What must become of the world, if such practices prevail? How could society subsist under such disorders?* Were the distinction or separation of possessions entirely useless, can any one conceive, that it ever should have obtained in society?

Thus we seem, upon the whole, to have attained a knowledge of the 48 force of that principle here insisted on, and can determine what degree of esteem or moral approbation may result from reflections on public interest and utility. The necessity of justice to the support of society is the SOLE foundation of that virtue; and since no moral excellence is more highly esteemed, we may conclude, that this circumstance of usefulness has, in general, the strongest energy, and most entire command over our sentiments. It must, therefore, be the source of a considerable part of the merit ascribed to humanity, benevolence, friendship, public spirit, and other social virtues of that stamp; as it is the SOLE source of the moral approbation paid to fidelity, justice, veracity, integrity, and those other estimable and useful qualities and principles. It is entirely agreeable to the rules of philosophy, and even of common reason; where any principle has been found to have a great force and energy in one instance, to ascribe to it a like energy in all similar instances. This indeed is NEWTON's chief rule of philosophizing.[5]

---

[5] Principia, lib. iii. [Isaac Newton, *Mathematical Principles of Natural Philosophy*.]

SECTION IV.
OF POLITICAL SOCIETY.

HAD every man sufficient *sagacity* to perceive, at all times, the strong in-   1
terest, which binds him to the observance of justice and equity, and
strength of mind sufficient to persevere in a steady adherence to a general
and a distant interest, in opposition to the allurements of present pleasure
and advantage; there had never, in that case, been any such thing as government or political society, but each man, following his natural liberty,
had lived in entire peace and harmony with all others. What need of positive law where natural justice is, of itself, a sufficient restraint? Why create
magistrates, where there never arises any disorder or iniquity? Why
abridge our native freedom, when, in every instance, the utmost exertion
of it is found innocent and beneficial? It is evident, that, if government
were totally useless, it never could have place, and that the SOLE foundation of the duty of ALLEGIANCE is the *advantage,* which it procures to
society, by preserving peace and order among mankind.

When a number of political societies are erected, and maintain a great   2
intercourse together, a new set of rules are immediately discovered to be
useful in that particular situation; and accordingly take place under the
title of LAWS of NATIONS. Of this kind are, the sacredness of the person of ambassadors, abstaining from poisoned arms, quarter in war, with
others of that kind, which are plainly calculated for the *advantage* of states
and kingdoms, in their intercourse with each other.

The rules of justice, such as prevail among individuals, are not entirely   3
suspended among political societies. All princes pretend a regard to the
rights of other princes; and some, no doubt, without hypocrisy. Alliances
and treaties are every day made between independent states, which would
only be so much waste of parchment, if they were not found, by experience, to have *some* influence and authority. But here is the difference between kingdoms and individuals. Human nature cannot, by any means,
subsist, without the association of individuals; and that association never
could have place, were no regard paid to the laws of equity and justice.
Disorder, confusion, the war of all against all, are the necessary consequences of such a licentious conduct. But nations can subsist without intercourse. They may even subsist, in some degree, under a general war.
The observance of justice, though useful among them, is not guarded by
so strong a necessity as among individuals; and the *moral obligation* holds
proportion with the *usefulness.* All politicians will allow, and most philosophers, that REASONS of STATE may, in particular emergencies, dis-
pense with the rules of justice, and invalidate any treaty or alliance, where

the strict observance of it would be prejudicial, in a considerable degree, to either of the contracting parties. But nothing less than the most extreme necessity, it is confessed, can justify individuals in a breach of promise, or an invasion of the properties of others.

4   In a confederated commonwealth, such as the ACHÆAN republic of old, or the SWISS Cantons and United Provinces in modern times; as the league has here a peculiar *utility*, the conditions of union have a peculiar sacredness and authority, and a violation of them would be regarded as no less, or even as more criminal, than any private injury or injustice.

5   The long and helpless infancy of man requires the combination of parents for the subsistence of their young; and that combination requires the virtue of CHASTITY or fidelity to the marriage bed. Without such a *utility*, it will readily be owned, that such a virtue would never have been thought of.[1]

6   An infidelity of this nature is much more *pernicious* in *women* than in *men*. Hence the laws of chastity are much stricter over the one sex than over the other.

7   These rules have all a reference to generation; and yet women past child-bearing are no more supposed to be exempted from them than those in the flower of their youth and beauty. *General rules* are often extended beyond the principle, whence they first arise; and this in all matters of taste and sentiment. It is a vulgar story at PARIS, that, during the rage of the MISSISSIPPI, a hump-backed fellow went every day into the RUE DE QUINCEMPOIX, where the stock-jobbers met in great crowds, and was well

---

[1] The only solution, which PLATO gives to all the objections that might be raised against the community of women, established in his imaginary commonwealth, is, Κάλλιστα γὰρ δὴ τοῦτο καὶ λέγεται καὶ λελέξεται, ὅτι τὸ μὲν ὠφέλιμον καλόν, τὸ δὲ βλαβερὸν αἰσχρόν. *Scite enim istud & dicitur & dicetur, Id quod utile sit honestum esse, quod autem inutile sit turpe esse.* De Rep. lib. v. p. 457. ex edit. Serr. ["For the fairest thing that is said or ever will be said is this, that the helpful is fair and the harmful foul" (Plato, *The Republic,* Book V, 457; trans. by Paul Shorey).] And this maxim will admit of no doubt, where public utility is concerned; which is PLATO'S meaning. And indeed to what other purpose do all the ideas of chastity and modesty serve? *Nisi utile est quod facimus, frustra est gloria,* says PHÆDRUS. ["Unless what we do is useful, the glory is vain" (Phaedrus, *Fables,* III, 17, 12; trans. by Ben E. Perry).] Καλὸν τῶν βλαβερῶν οὐδέν, says PLUTARCH, *de vitioso pudore.* "Nihil eorum quæ damnosa sunt, pulchrum est." ["Nothing harmful is admirable" (Plutarch, *Moralia,* III; trans. by Frank C. Babbit).] The same was the opinion of the Stoics. Φασὶν οὖν οἱ Στωικοὶ ἀγαθὸν εἶναι ὠφέλειαν ἢ οὐχ ἕτερον ὠφελείας, ὠφελεῖν μὲν λέγοντες τὴν ἀρετὴν καὶ τὴν σπουδαίαν πρᾶξιν. SEXT. EMP. lib. iii cap. 20. ["The Stoics, then, assert that good is 'utility or not other than utility,' meaning by 'utility' virtue and right action" (Sextus Empiricus, *Outlines of Pyrrhonism,* III, XXII; trans. by R. G. Bury).]

paid for allowing them to make use of his hump as a desk, in order to sign their contracts upon it. Would the fortune, which he raised by this expedient, make him a handsome fellow; though it be confessed, that personal beauty arises very much from ideas of utility? The imagination is influenced by associations of ideas; which, though they arise at first from the judgment, are not easily altered by every particular exception that occurs to us. To which we may add, in the present case of chastity, that the example of the old would be pernicious to the young; and that women, continually foreseeing that a certain time would bring them the liberty of indulgence, would naturally advance that period, and think more lightly of this whole duty, so requisite to society.

Those who live in the same family have such frequent opportunities of licence of this kind, that nothing could preserve purity of manners, were marriage allowed, among the nearest relations, or any intercourse of love between them ratified by law and custom. INCEST, therefore, being *pernicious* in a superior degree, has also a superior turpitude and moral deformity annexed to it.   8

What is the reason, why, by the ATHENIAN laws, one might marry a half-sister by the father, but not by the mother? Plainly this: The manners of the ATHENIANS were so reserved, that a man was never permitted to approach the women's apartment, even in the same family, unless where he visited his own mother. His step-mother and her children were as much shut up from him as the women of any other family, and there was as little danger of any criminal correspondence between them. Uncles and nieces, for a like reason, might marry at ATHENS; but neither these, nor half-brothers and sisters, could contract that alliance at ROME, where the intercourse was more open between the sexes. Public utility is the cause of all these variations.   9

To repeat, to a man's prejudice, any thing that escaped him in private conversation, or to make any such use of his private letters, is highly blamed. The free and social intercourse of minds must be extremely checked, where no such rules of fidelity are established.   10

Even in repeating stories, whence we can foresee no ill consequences to result, the giving of one's author is regarded as a piece of indiscretion, if not of immorality. These stories, in passing from hand to hand, and receiving all the usual variations, frequently come about to the persons concerned, and produce animosities and quarrels among people, whose intentions are the most innocent and inoffensive.   11

To pry into secrets, to open or even read the letters of others, to play the spy upon their words and looks and actions; what habits more inconvenient in society? What habits, of consequence, more blameable?   12

This principle is also the foundation of most of the laws of good   13 manners; a kind of lesser morality, calculated for the ease of company and conversation. Too much or too little ceremony are both blamed, and every thing, which promotes ease, without an indecent familiarity, is useful and laudable.

14   Constancy in friendships, attachments, and familiarities, is commendable, and is requisite to support trust and good correspondence in society. But in places of general, though casual concourse, where the pursuit of health and pleasure brings people promiscuously together, public conveniency has dispensed with this maxim; and custom there promotes an unreserved conversation for the time, by indulging the privilege of dropping afterwards every indifferent acquaintance, without breach of civility or good manners.

15   Even in societies, which are established on principles the most immoral, and the most destructive to the interests of the general society, there are required certain rules, which a species of false honour, as well as private interest, engages the members to observe. Robbers and pirates, it has often been remarked, could not maintain their pernicious confederacy, did they not establish a new distributive justice among themselves, and recall those laws of equity, which they have violated with the rest of mankind.

16   I hate a drinking companion, says the GREEK proverb, who never forgets. The follies of the last debauch should be buried in eternal oblivion, in order to give full scope to the follies of the next.

17   Among nations, where an immoral gallantry, if covered with a thin veil of mystery, is, in some degree, authorized by custom, there immediately arise a set of rules, calculated for the conveniency of that attachment. The famous court or parliament of love in PROVENCE formerly decided all difficult cases of this nature.

18   In societies for play, there are laws required for the conduct of the game; and these laws are different in each game. The foundation, I own, of such societies is frivolous; and the laws are, in a great measure, though not altogether, capricious and arbitrary. So far is there a material difference between them and the rules of justice, fidelity, and loyalty. The general societies of men are absolutely requisite for the subsistence of the species; and the public conveniency, which regulates morals, is inviolably established in the nature of man, and of the world, in which he lives. The comparison, therefore, in these respects, is very imperfect. We may only learn from it the necessity of rules, wherever men have any intercourse with each other.

19   They cannot even pass each other on the road without rules. Waggoners, coachmen, and postilions have principles, by which they give the way; and these are chiefly founded on mutual ease and convenience.

Sometimes also they are arbitrary, at least dependent on a kind of capricious analogy, like many of the reasonings of lawyers.[2]

To carry the matter farther, we may observe, that it is impossible for men so much as to murder each other without statutes, and maxims, and an idea of justice and honour. War has its laws as well as peace; and even that sportive kind of war, carried on among wrestlers, boxers, cudgel-players, gladiators, is regulated by fixed principles. Common interest and utility beget infallibly a standard of right and wrong among the parties concerned.

20

---

[2] That the lighter machine yield to the heavier, and, in machines of the same kind, that the empty yield to the loaded; this rule is founded on convenience. That those who are going to the capital take place of those who are coming from it; this seems to be founded on some idea of the dignity of the great city, and of the preference of the future to the past. From like reasons, among foot-walkers, the right-hand intitles a man to the wall, and prevents jostling, which peaceable people find very disagreeable and inconvenient.

SECTION V.
WHY UTILITY PLEASES.
Part I.

1   IT seems so natural a thought to ascribe to their utility the praise, which we bestow on the social virtues, that one would expect to meet with this principle every where in moral writers, as the chief foundation of their reasoning and enquiry. In common life, we may observe, that the circumstance of utility is always appealed to; nor is it supposed, that a greater eulogy can be given to any man, than to display his usefulness to the public, and enumerate the services, which he has performed to mankind and society. What praise, even of an inanimate form, if the regularity and elegance of its parts destroy not its fitness for any useful purpose! And how satisfactory an apology for any disproportion or seeming deformity, if we can show the necessity of that particular construction for the use intended! A ship appears more beautiful to an artist, or one moderately skilled in navigation, where its prow is wide and swelling beyond its poop, than if it were framed with a precise geometrical regularity, in contradiction to all the laws of mechanics. A building, whose doors and windows were exact squares, would hurt the eye by that very proportion; as ill adapted to the figure of a human creature, for whose service the fabric was intended. What wonder then that a man, whose habits and conduct are hurtful to society, and dangerous or pernicious to every one who has an intercourse with him, should, on that account, be an object of disapprobation, and communicate to every spectator the strongest sentiment of disgust and hatred.[1]

---

[1] We ought not to imagine, because an inanimate object may be useful as well as a man, that therefore it ought also, according to this system, to merit the appellation of *virtuous*. The sentiments, excited by utility, are, in the two cases, very different; and the one is mixed with affection, esteem, approbation, &c., and not the other. In like manner, an inanimate object may have good colour and proportions as well as a human figure. But can we ever be in love with the former? There are a numerous set of passions and sentiments, of which thinking rational beings are, by the original constitution of nature, the only proper objects: And though the very same qualities be transferred to an insensible, inanimate being, they will not excite the same sentiments. The beneficial qualities of herbs and minerals are, indeed, sometimes called their *virtues*; but this is an effect of the caprice of language, which ought not to be regarded in reasoning. For though there be a species of approbation attending even inanimate objects, when beneficial, yet this sentiment is so weak, and so different from that which is directed to beneficent magistrates or statesmen; that they ought not to be ranked under the same class or appellation.

A very small variation of the object, even where the same qualities are preserved, will destroy a sentiment. Thus, the same beauty, transferred to a different sex, excites no amorous passion, where nature is not extremely perverted.

But perhaps the difficulty of accounting for these effects of usefulness, 2 or its contrary, has kept philosophers from admitting them into their systems of ethics, and has induced them rather to employ any other principle, in explaining the origin of moral good and evil. But it is no just reason for rejecting any principle, confirmed by experience, that we cannot give a satisfactory account of its origin, nor are able to resolve it into other more general principles. And if we would employ a little thought on the present subject, we need be at no loss to account for the influence of utility, and to deduce it from principles, the most known and avowed in human nature.

From the apparent usefulness of the social virtues, it has readily been 3 inferred by sceptics, both ancient and modern, that all moral distinctions arise from education, and were, at first, invented, and afterwards encouraged, by the art of politicians, in order to render men tractable, and subdue their natural ferocity and selfishness, which incapacitated them for society. This principle, indeed, of precept and education, must so far be owned to have a powerful influence, that it may frequently encrease or diminish, beyond their natural standard, the sentiments of approbation or dislike; and may even, in particular instances, create, without any natural principle, a new sentiment of this kind; as is evident in all superstitious practices and observances: But that *all* moral affection or dislike arises from this origin, will never surely be allowed by any judicious enquirer. Had nature made no such distinction, founded on the original constitution of the mind, the words, *honourable* and *shameful*, *lovely* and *odious*, *noble* and *despicable*, had never had place in any language; nor could politicians, had they invented these terms, ever have been able to render them intelligible, or make them convey any idea to the audience. So that nothing can be more superficial than this paradox of the sceptics; and it were well, if, in the abstruser studies of logic and metaphysics, we could as easily obviate the cavils of that sect, as in the practical and more intelligible sciences of politics and morals.

The social virtues must, therefore, be allowed to have a natural beauty 4 and amiableness, which, at first, antecedent to all precept or education, recommends them to the esteem of uninstructed mankind, and engages their affections. And as the public utility of these virtues is the chief circumstance, whence they derive their merit, it follows, that the end, which they have a tendency to promote, must be some way agreeable to us, and take hold of some natural affection. It must please, either from considerations of self-interest, or from more generous motives and regards.

It has often been asserted, that, as every man has a strong connexion with 5 society, and perceives the impossibility of his solitary subsistence, he becomes, on that account, favourable to all those habits or principles, which promote order in society, and insure to him the quiet possession of so inestimable a blessing. As much as we value our own happiness and welfare, as much must we applaud the practice of justice and humanity, by which alone the social confederacy can be maintained, and every man reap the fruits of mutual protection and assistance.

6　　This deduction of morals from self-love, or a regard to private interest, is an obvious thought, and has not arisen wholly from the wanton sallies and sportive assaults of the sceptics. To mention no others, POLYBIUS, one of the gravest and most judicious, as well as most moral writers of antiquity, has assigned this selfish origin to all our sentiments of virtue.[2] But though the solid, practical sense of that author, and his aversion to all vain subtilties, render his authority on the present subject very considerable; yet is not this an affair to be decided by authority, and the voice of nature and experience seems plainly to oppose the selfish theory.

7　　We frequently bestow praise on virtuous actions, performed in very distant ages and remote countries; where the utmost subtilty of imagination would not discover any appearance of self-interest, or find any connexion of our present happiness and security with events so widely separated from us.

8　　A generous, a brave, a noble deed, performed by an adversary, commands our approbation; while in its consequences it may be acknowledged prejudicial to our particular interest.

9　　Where private advantage concurs with general affection for virtue, we readily perceive and avow the mixture of these distinct sentiments, which have a very different feeling and influence on the mind. We praise, perhaps, with more alacrity, where the generous, humane action contributes to our particular interest: But the topics of praise, which we insist on, are very wide of this circumstance. And we may attempt to bring over others to our sentiments, without endeavouring to convince them, that they reap any advantage from the actions which we recommend to their approbation and applause.

---

[2] Undutifulness to parents is disapproved of by mankind, προορωμένους τὸ μέλλον, καὶ συλλογιζομένους ὅτι τὸ παραπλήσιον ἑκάστοις αὐτῶν συγκυρήσει. ["looking to the future and reflecting that they may all meet with the same treatment."] Ingratitude for a like reason (though he seems there to mix a more generous regard) συναγανακτοῦντας μὲν τῷ πέλας, ἀναφέροντας δ' ἐπ' αὐτοὺς τὸ παραπλήσιον ἐξ ὧν ὑπογίγνεταί τις ἔννοια παρ' ἑκάστῳ τῆς τοῦ καθήκοντος δυνάμεως καὶ θεωρίας. Lib. vi. cap. 4. ["sharing the resentment of their injured neighbour and imagining themselves in the same situation. From all this there arises in everyone a notion of the meaning and theory of duty" (Polybius, *Histories*, VI, VI, 2; trans. by W. R. Paton).] Perhaps the historian only meant, that our sympathy and humanity was more enlivened, by our considering the similarity of our case with that of the person suffering; which is a just sentiment.

Frame the model of a praise-worthy character, consisting of all the 10 most amiable moral virtues: Give instances, in which these display themselves after an eminent and extraordinary manner: You readily engage the esteem and approbation of all your audience, who never so much as enquire in what age and country the person lived, who possessed these noble qualities: A circumstance, however, of all others, the most material to selflove, or a concern for our own individual happiness.

Once on a time, a statesman, in the shock and contest of parties, pre- 11 vailed so far as to procure, by his eloquence, the banishment of an able adversary; whom he secretly followed, offering him money for his support during his exile, and soothing him with topics of consolation in his misfortunes. *Alas!* cries the banished statesman, *with what regret must I leave my friends in this city, where even enemies are so generous!* Virtue, though in an enemy, here pleased him: And we also give it the just tribute of praise and approbation; nor do we retract these sentiments, when we hear, that the action passed at ATHENS, about two thousand years ago, and that the persons' names were ESCHINES and DEMOSTHENES.

What is that to me? There are few occasions, when this question is not 12 pertinent: And had it that universal, infallible influence supposed, it would turn into ridicule every composition, and almost every conversation, which contain any praise or censure of men and manners.

It is but a weak subterfuge, when pressed by these facts and arguments, 13 to say, that we transport ourselves, by the force of imagination, into distant ages and countries, and consider the advantage, which we should have reaped from these characters, had we been contemporaries, and had any commerce with the persons. It is not conceivable, how a *real* sentiment or passion can ever arise from a known *imaginary* interest; especially when our *real* interest is still kept in view, and is often acknowledged to be entirely distinct from the imaginary, and even sometimes opposite to it.

A man, brought to the brink of a precipice, cannot look down without 14 trembling; and the sentiment of *imaginary* danger actuates him, in opposition to the opinion and belief of *real* safety. But the imagination is here assisted by the presence of a striking object; and yet prevails not, except it be also aided by novelty, and the unusual appearance of the object. Custom soon reconciles us to heights and precipices, and wears off these false and delusive terrors. The reverse is observable in the estimates, which we form of characters and manners; and the more we habituate ourselves to an accurate scrutiny of morals, the more delicate feeling do we acquire of the most minute distinctions between vice and virtue. Such frequent occasion, indeed, have we, in common life, to pronounce all kinds of moral determinations, that no object of this kind can be new or unusual to us; nor could any *false* views or prepossessions maintain their ground against an experience, so common and familiar. Experience being chiefly what forms the associations of ideas, it is impossible, that any association could establish and support itself in direct opposition to that principle.

15   Usefulness is agreeable, and engages our approbation. This is a matter of fact, confirmed by daily observation. But, *useful?* For what? For some body's interest, surely. Whose interest then? Not our own only; For our approbation frequently extends farther. It must, therefore, be the interest of those, who are served by the character or action approved of; and these we may conclude, however remote, are not totally indifferent to us. By opening up this principle, we shall discover one great source of moral distinctions.

Part II.

16   Self-love is a principle in human nature of such extensive energy, and the interest of each individual is, in general, so closely connected with that of the community, that those philosophers were excusable, who fancied, that all our concern for the public might be resolved into a concern for our own happiness and preservation. They saw, every moment, instances of approbation or blame, satisfaction or displeasure towards characters and actions; they denominated the objects of these sentiments, *virtues*, or *vices*; they observed, that the former had a tendency to encrease the happiness, and the latter the misery of mankind; they asked, whether it were possible that we could have any general concern for society, or any disinterested resentment of the welfare or injury of others; they found it simpler to consider all these sentiments as modifications of self-love; and they discovered a pretence, at least, for this unity of principle, in that close union of interest, which is so observable between the public and each individual.

17   But notwithstanding this frequent confusion of interests, it is easy to attain what natural philosophers, after lord Bacon, have affected to call the *experimentum crucis,* or that experiment, which points out the right way in any doubt or ambiguity. We have found instances, in which private interest was separate from public; in which it was even contrary: And yet we observed the moral sentiment to continue, notwithstanding this disjunction of interests. And wherever these distinct interests sensibly concurred, we always found a sensible encrease of the sentiment, and a more warm affection to virtue, and detestation of vice, or what we properly call, *gratitude* and *revenge.* Compelled by these instances, we must renounce the theory, which accounts for every moral sentiment by the principle of self-love. We must adopt a more public affection, and allow, that the interests of society are not, even on their own account, entirely indifferent to

us. Usefulness is only a tendency to a certain end; and it is a contradiction in terms, that any thing pleases as means to an end, where the end itself no wise affects us. If usefulness, therefore, be a source of moral sentiment, and if this usefulness be not always considered with a reference to self; it follows, that every thing, which contributes to the happiness of society recommends itself directly to our approbation and good-will. Here is a principle, which accounts, in great part, for the origin of morality: And what need we seek for abstruse and remote systems, when there occurs one so obvious and natural?[3]

Have we any difficulty to comprehend the force of humanity and benevolence? Or to conceive, that the very aspect of happiness, joy, prosperity, gives pleasure; that of pain, suffering, sorrow, communicates uneasiness? The human countenance, says HORACE,[4] borrows smiles or tears from the human countenance. Reduce a person to solitude, and he loses all enjoyment, except either of the sensual or speculative kind; and that because the movements of his heart are not forwarded by correspondent movements in his fellow-creatures. The signs of sorrow and mourning, though arbitrary, affect us with melancholy; but the natural symptoms, tears and cries and groans, never fail to infuse compassion and uneasiness. And if the effects of misery touch us in so lively a manner; can we be supposed altogether insensible or indifferent towards its causes; when a malicious or treacherous character and behaviour are presented to us? 18

We enter, I shall suppose, into a convenient, warm, well-contrived apartment: We necessarily receive a pleasure from its very survey; because 19

---

[3] It is needless to push our researches so far as to ask, why we have humanity or a fellow-feeling with others. It is sufficient, that this is experienced to be a principle in human nature. We must stop somewhere in our examination of causes; and there are, in every science, some general principles, beyond which we cannot hope to find any principle more general. No man is absolutely indifferent to the happiness and misery of others. The first has a natural tendency to give pleasure; the second, pain. This every one may find in himself. It is not probable, that these principles can be resolved into principles more simple and universal, whatever attempts may have been made to that purpose. But if it were possible, it belongs not to the present subject; and we may here safely consider these principles as original: Happy, if we can render all the consequences sufficiently plain and perspicuous!

[4] "Uti ridentibus arrident, ita flentibus adflent
Humani vultus." HOR. A. P. 101.

["As men's faces smile on those who smile, so they respond to those who weep" (Horace, *Art of Poetry*, 101; trans. by H. Rushton Fairclough).]

it presents us with the pleasing ideas of ease, satisfaction, and enjoyment. The hospitable, good-humoured, humane landlord appears. This circumstance surely must embellish the whole; nor can we easily forbear reflecting, with pleasure, on the satisfaction which results to every one from his intercourse and good-offices.

20   His whole family, by the freedom, ease, confidence, and calm enjoyment, diffused over their countenances, sufficiently express their happiness. I have a pleasing sympathy in the prospect of so much joy, and can never consider the source of it, without the most agreeable emotions.

21   He tells me, that an oppressive and powerful neighbour had attempted to dispossess him of his inheritance, and had long disturbed all his innocent and social pleasures. I feel an immediate indignation arise in me against such violence and injury.

22   But it is no wonder, he adds, that a private wrong should proceed from a man, who had enslaved provinces, depopulated cities, and made the field and scaffold stream with human blood. I am struck with horror at the prospect of so much misery, and am actuated by the strongest antipathy against its author.

23   In general, it is certain, that, wherever we go, whatever we reflect on or converse about, every thing still presents us with the view of human happiness or misery, and excites in our breast a sympathetic movement of pleasure or uneasiness. In our serious occupations, in our careless amusements, this principle still exerts its active energy.

24   A man, who enters the theatre, is immediately struck with the view of so great a multitude, participating of one common amusement; and experiences, from their very aspect, a superior sensibility or disposition of being affected with every sentiment, which he shares with his fellow-creatures.

25   He observes the actors to be animated by the appearance of a full audience, and raised to a degree of enthusiasm, which they cannot command in any solitary or calm moment.

26   Every movement of the theatre, by a skilful poet, is communicated, as it were by magic, to the spectators; who weep, tremble, resent, rejoice, and are inflamed with all the variety of passions, which actuate the several personages of the drama.

27   Where any event crosses our wishes, and interrupts the happiness of the favourite characters, we feel a sensible anxiety and concern. But where their sufferings proceed from the treachery, cruelty, or tyranny of an enemy, our breasts are affected with the liveliest resentment against the author of these calamities.

28   It is here esteemed contrary to the rules of art to represent any thing

cool and indifferent. A distant friend, or a confident, who has no immediate interest in the catastrophe, ought, if possible, to be avoided by the poet; as communicating a like indifference to the audience, and checking the progress of the passions.

Few species of poetry are more entertaining than *pastoral*; and every   29
one is sensible, that the chief source of its pleasure arises from those images of a gentle and tender tranquillity, which it represents in its personages, and of which it communicates a like sentiment to the reader. SANNAZARIUS, who transferred the scene to the sea-shore, though he presented the most magnificent object in nature, is confessed to have erred in his choice. The idea of toil, labour, and danger, suffered by the fishermen, is painful; by an unavoidable sympathy, which attends every conception of human happiness or misery.

When I was twenty, says a FRENCH poet, OVID was my favourite: Now I   30
am forty, I declare for HORACE. We enter, to be sure, more readily into sentiments, which resemble those we feel every day: But no passion, when well represented, can be entirely indifferent to us; because there is none, of which every man has not, within him, at least the seeds and first principles. It is the business of poetry to bring every affection near to us by lively imagery and representation, and make it look like truth and reality: A certain proof, that, wherever that reality is found, our minds are disposed to be strongly affected by it.

Any recent event or piece of news, by which the fate of states,   31
provinces, or many individuals is affected, is extremely interesting even to those whose welfare is not immediately engaged. Such intelligence is propagated with celerity, heard with avidity, and enquired into with attention and concern. The interest of society appears, on this occasion, to be, in some degree, the interest of each individual. The imagination is sure to be affected; though the passions excited may not always be so strong and steady as to have great influence on the conduct and behaviour.

The perusal of a history seems a calm entertainment; but would be no   32
entertainment at all, did not our hearts beat with correspondent movements to those which are described by the historian.

THUCYDIDES and GUICCIARDIN support with difficulty our attention;   33
while the former describes the trivial rencounters of the small cities of GREECE, and the latter the harmless wars of PISA. The few persons interested, and the small interest fill not the imagination, and engage not the affections. The deep distress of the numerous ATHENIAN army before SYRACUSE; the danger, which so nearly threatens VENICE; these excite compassion; these move terror and anxiety.

The indifferent, uninteresting stile of SUETONIUS, equally with the   34 masterly pencil of TACITUS, may convince us of the cruel depravity of NERO or TIBERIUS: But what a difference of sentiment! While the former coldly relates the facts; and the latter sets before our eyes the venerable figures of a SORANUS and a THRASEA, intrepid in their fate, and only moved by the melting sorrows of their friends and kindred. What sympathy then touches every human heart! What indignation against the tyrant, whose causeless fear or unprovoked malice gave rise to such detestable barbarity!

35   If we bring these subjects nearer: If we remove all suspicion of fiction and deceit: What powerful concern is excited, and how much superior, in many instances, to the narrow attachments of self-love and private interest! Popular sedition, party zeal, a devoted obedience to factious leaders; these are some of the most visible, though less laudable effects of this social sympathy in human nature.

36   The frivolousness of the subject too, we may observe, is not able to detach us entirely from what carries an image of human sentiment and affection.

37   When a person stutters, and pronounces with difficulty, we even sympathize with this trivial uneasiness, and suffer for him. And it is a rule in criticism, that every combination of syllables or letters, which gives pain to the organs of speech in the recital, appears also, from a species of sympathy, harsh and disagreeable to the ear. Nay, when we run over a book with our eye, we are sensible of such unharmonious composition; because we still imagine, that a person recites it to us, and suffers from the pronunciation of these jarring sounds. So delicate is our sympathy!

38   Easy and unconstrained postures and motions are always beautiful: An air of health and vigour is agreeable: Cloaths which warm, without burdening the body; which cover, without imprisoning the limbs, are well-fashioned. In every judgment of beauty, the feelings of the person affected enter into consideration, and communicate to the spectator similar touches of pain or pleasure.[5] What wonder, then, if we can pronounce no judgment concerning the character and conduct of men, without considering the tendencies of their actions, and the happiness or misery which

---

[5] "Decentior equus cujus astricta sunt ilia; sed idem velocior. Pulcher aspectu sit athleta, cujus lacertos exercitatio expressit; idem certamini paratior. Nunquam enim *species* ab *utilitate* dividitur. Sed hoc quidem discernere modici judicii est." QUINTIL-IAN *Inst.* lib. viii. cap. 3. ["A horse whose flanks are compact looks better, but is also faster. An athlete whose muscles have been developed by exercise may be good to look at; he is also more ready for the fray. True beauty is never separated from usefulness. But it only takes a modest power of judgement to see this." (Quintilian, *The Orator's Education*, VIII, III, 10–11; trans. by Donald A. Russell.)]

thence arises to society? What association of ideas would ever operate, were that principle here totally inactive.[6]

If any man, from a cold insensibility, or narrow selfishness of temper, is unaffected with the images of human happiness or misery, he must be equally indifferent to the images of vice and virtue: As, on the other hand, it is always found, that a warm concern for the interests of our species is attended with a delicate feeling of all moral distinctions; a strong resentment of injury done to men; a lively approbation of their welfare. In this particular, though great superiority is observable of one man above another; yet none are so entirely indifferent to the interest of their fellow-creatures, as to perceive no distinctions of moral good and evil, in consequence of the different tendencies of actions and principles. How, indeed, can we suppose it possible in any one, who wears a human heart, that, if there be subjected to his censure, one character or system of conduct, which is beneficial, and another, which is pernicious, to his species or community, he will not so much as give a cool preference to the former, or ascribe to it the smallest merit or regard? Let us suppose such a person ever so selfish; let private interest have ingrossed ever so much his attention; yet in instances, where that is not concerned, he must unavoidably feel *some* propensity to the good of mankind, and make it an object of choice, if every thing else be equal. Would any man, who is walking along, tread as willingly on another's gouty toes, whom he has no quarrel with, as on the hard flint and pavement? There is here surely a difference in the case. We surely take into consideration the happiness and misery of others, in weighing the several motives of action, and incline to the former, where no private regards draw us to seek our own promotion or advantage by the injury of our fellow-creatures. And if the principles of humanity are capable, in many instances, of influencing our actions, they must, at all times, have *some* authority over our sentiments, and give us a general

39

---

[6] In proportion to the station which a man possesses, according to the relations in which he is placed; we always expect from him a greater or less degree of good, and when disappointed, blame his inutility; and much more do we blame him, if any ill or prejudice arises from his conduct and behaviour. When the interests of one country interfere with those of another, we estimate the merits of a statesman by the good or ill, which results to his own country from his measures and counsils, without regard to the prejudice which he brings on its enemies and rivals. His fellow-citizens are the objects, which lie nearest the eye, while we determine his character. And as nature has implanted in every one a superior affection to his own country, we never expect any regard to distant nations, where a competition arises. Not to mention, that, while every man consults the good of his own community, we are sensible, that the general interest of mankind is better promoted, than by any loose indeterminate views to the good of a species, whence no beneficial action could ever result, for want of a duly limited object, on which they could exert themselves.

approbation of what is useful to society, and blame of what is dangerous or pernicious. The degrees of these sentiments may be the subject of controversy; but the reality of their existence, one should think, must be admitted, in every theory or system.

40   A creature, absolutely malicious and spiteful, were there any such in nature, must be worse than indifferent to the images of vice and virtue. All his sentiments must be inverted, and directly opposite to those, which prevail in the human species. Whatever contributes to the good of mankind, as it crosses the constant bent of his wishes and desires, must produce uneasiness and disapprobation; and on the contrary, whatever is the source of disorder and misery in society, must, for the same reason, be regarded with pleasure and complacency. TIMON, who, probably from his affected spleen, more than any inveterate malice, was denominated the man-hater, embraced ALCIBIADES, with great fondness. *Go on my boy! cried he, acquire the confidence of the people: You will one day, I foresee, be the cause of great calamities to them:*[7] Could we admit the two principles of the MANICHEANS, it is an infallible consequence, that their sentiments of human actions, as well as of every thing else, must be totally opposite, and that every instance of justice and humanity, from its necessary tendency, must please the one deity and displease the other. All mankind so far resemble the good principle, that, where interest or revenge or envy perverts not our disposition, we are always inclined, from our natural philanthropy, to give the preference to the happiness of society, and consequently to virtue, above its opposite. Absolute, unprovoked, disinterested malice has never, perhaps, place in any human breast; or if it had, must there pervert all the sentiments of morals, as well as the feelings of humanity. If the cruelty of NERO be allowed entirely voluntary, and not rather the effect of constant fear and resentment; it is evident, that TIGELLINUS, preferably to SENECA or BURRHUS, must have possessed his steady and uniform approbation.

41   A statesman or patriot, who serves our own country, in our own time, has always a more passionate regard paid to him, than one whose beneficial influence operated on distant ages or remote nations; where the good, resulting from his generous humanity, being less connected with us, seems more obscure, and affects us with a less lively sympathy. We may own the merit to be equally great, though our sentiments are not raised to an equal height, in both cases. The judgment here corrects the inequalities of our internal emotions and perceptions; in like manner, as it preserves us from error, in the several variations of images, presented to our external senses. The same object, at a double distance, really throws on the

---

[7] PLUTARCH in vita ALC. [Plutarch, *Lives*, "Alcibiades".]

eye a picture of but half the bulk; yet we imagine that it appears of the same size in both situations; because we know, that, on our approach to it, its image would expand on the eye, and that the difference consists not in the object itself, but in our position with regard to it. And, indeed, without such a correction of appearances, both in internal and external sentiment, men could never think or talk steadily on any subject; while their fluctuating situations produce a continual variation on objects, and throw them into such different and contrary lights and positions.[8]

The more we converse with mankind, and the greater social intercourse   42
we maintain, the more shall we be familiarized to these general preferences and distinctions, without which our conversation and discourse could scarcely be rendered intelligible to each other. Every man's interest is peculiar to himself, and the aversions and desires, which result from it, cannot be supposed to affect others in a like degree. General language, therefore, being formed for general use, must be moulded on some more general views, and must affix the epithets of praise or blame, in conformity to sentiments, which arise from the general interests of the community. And if these sentiments, in most men, be not so strong as those, which have a reference to private good; yet still they must make some distinction, even in persons the most depraved and selfish; and must attach the notion of good to a beneficent conduct, and of evil to the contrary. Sympathy, we shall allow, is much fainter than our concern for ourselves, and sympathy with persons remote from us, much fainter than that with persons near and contiguous; but for this very reason, it is necessary for us, in our calm judgments and discourse concerning the characters of men, to neglect all these differences, and render our sentiments more public and social. Besides, that we ourselves often change our situation in this particular, we every day meet with persons, who are in a situation different from us, and

---

[8] For a like reason, the tendencies of actions and characters, not their real accidental consequences, are alone regarded in our moral determinations or general judgments; though in our real feeling or sentiment, we cannot help paying greater regard to one whose station, joined to virtue, renders him really useful to society, than to one, who exerts the social virtues only in good intentions and benevolent affections. Separating the character from the fortune, by an easy and necessary effort of thought, we pronounce these persons alike, and give them the same general praise. The judgment corrects or endeavours to correct the appearance: But is not able entirely to prevail over sentiment.

Why is this peach-tree said to be better than that other; but because it produces more or better fruit? And would not the same praise be given it, though snails or vermin had destroyed the peaches, before they came to full maturity? In morals too, is not *the tree known by the fruit?* And cannot we easily distinguish between nature and accident, in the one case as well as in the other?

who could never converse with us, were we to remain constantly in that position and point of view, which is peculiar to ourselves. The intercourse of sentiments, therefore, in society and conversation, makes us form some general unalterable standard, by which we may approve or disapprove of characters and manners. And though the heart takes not part entirely with those general notions, nor regulates all its love and hatred, by the universal, abstract differences of vice and virtue, without regard to self, or the persons with whom we are more intimately connected; yet have these moral differences a considerable influence, and being sufficient, at least, for discourse, serve all our purposes in company, in the pulpit, on the theatre, and in the schools.[9]

43   Thus, in whatever light we take this subject, the merit, ascribed to the social virtues, appears still uniform, and arises chiefly from that regard, which the natural sentiment of benevolence engages us to pay to the interests of mankind and society. If we consider the principles of the human make, such as they appear to daily experience and observation; we must, *a priori*, conclude it impossible for such a creature as man to be totally indifferent to the well or ill-being of his fellow-creatures, and not readily, of himself, to pronounce, where nothing gives him any particular byass, that what promotes their happiness is good, what tends to their misery is evil, without any farther regard or consideration. Here then are the faint rudiments, at least, or out-lines, of a *general* distinction between actions; and in proportion as the humanity of the person is supposed to encrease, his connexion with those who are injured or benefited, and his lively conception of their misery or happiness; his consequent censure or approbation acquires proportionable vigour. There is no necessity, that a generous action, barely mentioned in an old history or remote gazette, should communicate any strong feelings of applause and admiration. Virtue, placed at such a distance, is like a fixed star, which, though to the eye of reason, it may appear as luminous as the sun in his meridian, is so infinitely removed, as to affect the senses, neither with light nor heat. Bring this virtue nearer, by our acquaintance or connexion with the persons, or even by an eloquent recital of the case; our hearts are immediately caught, our sympathy inlivened, and our cool approbation converted into the warmest

---

[9] It is wisely ordained by nature, that private connexions should commonly prevail over universal views and considerations; otherwise our affections and actions would be dissipated and lost, for want of a proper limited object. Thus a small benefit done to ourselves, or our near friends, excites more lively sentiments of love and approbation than a great benefit done to a distant commonwealth: But still we know here, as in all the senses, to correct these inequalities by reflection, and retain a general standard of vice and virtue, founded chiefly on general usefulness.

sentiments of friendship and regard. These seem necessary and infallible consequences of the general principles of human nature, as discovered in common life and practice.

Again; reverse these views and reasonings: Consider the matter *a poste-* 44 *riori*; and, weighing the consequences, enquire if the merit of social virtue be not, in a great measure, derived from the feelings of humanity, with which it affects the spectators. It appears to be matter of fact, that the circumstance of *utility*, in all subjects, is a source of praise and approbation: That it is constantly appealed to in all moral decisions concerning the merit and demerit of actions: That it is the *sole* source of that high regard paid to justice, fidelity, honour, allegiance, and chastity: That it is inseparable from all the other social virtues, humanity, generosity, charity, affability, lenity, mercy, and moderation: And, in a word, that it is a foundation of the chief part of morals, which has a reference to mankind and our fellow-creatures.

It appears also, that, in our general approbation of characters and man- 45 ners, the useful tendency of the social virtues moves us not by any regards to self-interest, but has an influence much more universal and extensive. It appears, that a tendency to public good, and to the promoting of peace, harmony, and order in society, does always, by affecting the benevolent principles of our frame, engage us on the side of the social virtues. And it appears, as an additional confirmation, that these principles of humanity and sympathy enter so deeply into all our sentiments, and have so powerful an influence, as may enable them to excite the strongest censure and applause. The present theory is the simple result of all these inferences, each of which seems founded on uniform experience and observation.

Were it doubtful, whether there were any such principle in our nature as 46 humanity or a concern for others, yet when we see, in numberless instances, that whatever has a tendency to promote the interests of society, is so highly approved of, we ought thence to learn the force of the benevolent principle; since it is impossible for any thing to please as means to an end, where the end is totally indifferent. On the other hand, were it doubtful, whether there were, implanted in our nature, any general principle of moral blame and approbation, yet when we see, in numberless instances, the influence of humanity, we ought thence to conclude, that it is impossible, but that every thing, which promotes the interest of society, must communicate pleasure, and what is pernicious give uneasiness. But when these different reflections and observations concur in establishing the same conclusion, must they not bestow an undisputed evidence upon it?

It is however hoped, that the progress of this argument will bring a far- 47 ther confirmation of the present theory, by showing the rise of other sentiments of esteem and regard from the same or like principles.

SECTION VI.
OF QUALITIES USEFUL TO OURSELVES.

Part I.

1   IT seems evident, that where a quality or habit is subjected to our examination, if it appear, in any respect, prejudicial to the person possessed of it, or such as incapacitates him for business and action, it is instantly blamed, and ranked among his faults and imperfections. Indolence, negligence, want of order and method, obstinacy, fickleness, rashness, credulity; these qualities were never esteemed by any one indifferent to a character; much less, extolled as accomplishments or virtues. The prejudice, resulting from them, immediately strikes our eye, and gives us the sentiment of pain and disapprobation.

2   No quality, it is allowed, is absolutely either blameable or praiseworthy. It is all according to its degree. A due medium, say the PERIPATETICS, is the characteristic of virtue. But this medium is chiefly determined by utility. A proper celerity, for instance, and dispatch in business, is commendable. When defective, no progress is ever made in the execution of any purpose: When excessive, it engages us in precipitate and ill-concerted measures and enterprises: By such reasonings, we fix the proper and commendable mediocrity in all moral and prudential disquisitions; and never lose view of the advantages, which result from any character or habit.

3   Now as these advantages are enjoyed by the person possessed of the character, it can never be *self-love* which renders the prospect of them agreeable to us, the spectators, and prompts our esteem and approbation. No force of imagination can convert us into another person, and make us fancy, that we, being that person, reap benefit from those valuable qualities, which belong to him. Or if it did, no celerity of imagination could immediately transport us back, into ourselves, and make us love and esteem the person, as different from us. Views and sentiments, so opposite to known truth, and to each other, could never have place, at the same time, in the same person. All suspicion, therefore, of selfish regards, is here totally excluded. It is a quite different principle, which actuates our bosom, and interests us in the felicity of the person whom we contemplate. Where his natural talents and acquired abilities give us the prospect of elevation, advancement, a figure in life, prosperous success, a steady command over fortune, and the execution of great or advantageous undertakings; we are struck with such agreeable images, and feel a complacency and regard immediately arise towards him. The ideas of happiness, joy, triumph, prosperity, are connected with every

circumstance of his character, and diffuse over our minds a pleasing sentiment of sympathy and humanity.[1]

Let us suppose a person originally framed so as to have no manner of concern for his fellow-creatures, but to regard the happiness and misery of all sensible beings with greater indifference than even two contiguous shades of the same colour. Let us suppose, if the prosperity of nations were laid on the one hand, and their ruin on the other, and he were desired to choose; that he would stand, like the schoolman's ass, irresolute and undetermined, between equal motives; or rather, like the same ass between two pieces of wood or marble, without any inclination or propensity to either side. The consequence, I believe, must be allowed just, that such a person, being absolutely unconcerned, either for the public good of a community or the private utility of others, would look on every quality, however pernicious, or however beneficial, to society, or to its possessor, with the same indifference as on the most common and uninteresting object.

4

But if, instead of this fancied monster, we suppose a *man* to form a judgment or determination in the case, there is to him a plain foundation of preference, where every thing else is equal; and however cool his choice may be, if his heart be selfish, or if the persons interested be remote from him; there must still be a choice or distinction between what is useful, and what is pernicious. Now this distinction is the same in all its parts, with the *moral distinction*, whose foundation has been so often, and so much in vain, enquired after. The same endowments of the mind, in every circumstance, are agreeable to the sentiment of morals and to that of humanity; the same temper is susceptible of high degrees of the one sentiment and of the other; and the same alteration in the objects, by their nearer approach or by connexions, enlivens the one and the other. By all the rules of philosophy,

5

---

[1] One may venture to affirm, that there is no human creature, to whom the appearance of happiness (where envy or revenge has no place) does not give pleasure, that of misery, uneasiness. This seems inseparable from our make and constitution. But they are only the more generous minds, that are thence prompted to seek zealously the good of others, and to have a real passion for their welfare. With men of narrow and ungenerous spirits, this sympathy goes not beyond a slight feeling of the imagination, which serves only to excite sentiments of complacency or censure, and makes them apply to the object either honourable or dishonourable appellations. A griping miser, for instance, praises extremely *industry* and *frugality* even in others, and sets them, in his estimation, above all the other virtues. He knows the good that results from them, and feels that species of happiness with a more lively sympathy, than any other you could represent to him; though perhaps he would not part with a shilling to make the fortune of the industrious man, whom he praises so highly.

therefore, we must conclude, that these sentiments are originally the same; since, in each particular, even the most minute, they are governed by the same laws, and are moved by the same objects.

6   Why do philosophers infer, with the greatest certainty, that the moon is kept in its orbit by the same force of gravity, that makes bodies fall near the surface of the earth, but because these effects are, upon computation, found similar and equal? And must not this argument bring as strong conviction, in moral as in natural disquisitions?

7   To prove, by any long detail, that all the qualities, useful to the possessor, are approved of, and the contrary censured, would be superfluous. The least reflection on what is every day experienced in life, will be sufficient. We shall only mention a few instances, in order to remove, if possible, all doubt and hesitation.

8   The quality, the most necessary for the execution of any useful enterprise, is DISCRETION; by which we carry on a safe intercourse with others, give due attention to our own and to their character, weigh each circumstance of the business which we undertake, and employ the surest and safest means for the attainment of any end or purpose. To a CROMWELL, perhaps or a DE RETZ, discretion may appear an alderman-like virtue, as Dr. SWIFT calls it; and being incompatible with those vast designs, to which their courage and ambition prompted them, it might really, in them, be a fault or imperfection. But in the conduct of ordinary life, no virtue is more requisite, not only to obtain success, but to avoid the most fatal miscarriages and disappointments. The greatest parts without it, as observed by an elegant writer, may be fatal to their owner; as POLYPHEMUS, deprived of his eye, was only the more exposed, on account of his enormous strength and stature.

9   The best character, indeed, were it not rather too perfect for human nature, is that which is not swayed by temper of any kind; but alternately employs enterprise and caution, as each is *useful* to the particular purpose intended. Such is the excellence which ST. EVREMOND ascribes to mareschal TURENNE, who displayed every campaign, as he grew older, more temerity in his military enterprises; and being now, from long experience, perfectly acquainted with every incident in war, he advanced with greater firmness and security, in a road so well known to him. Fabius, says MACHIAVEL, was cautious; Scipio enterprising: And both succeeded, because the situation of the ROMAN affairs, during the command of each, was peculiarly adapted to his genius; but both would have failed, had these situations been reversed. He is happy, whose circumstances suit his temper; but he is more excellent, who can suit his temper to any circumstances.

10   What need is there to display the praises of INDUSTRY, and to extol

its advantages, in the acquisition of power and riches, or in raising what we call a *fortune* in the world? The tortoise, according to the fable, by his perseverance, gained the race of the hare, though possessed of much superior swiftness. A man's time, when well husbanded, is like a cultivated field, of which a few acres produce more of what is useful to life, than extensive provinces, even of the richest soil, when over-run with weeds and brambles.

But all prospect of success in life, or even of tolerable subsistence, must   11
fail, where a reasonable FRUGALITY is wanting. The heap, instead of encreasing, diminishes daily, and leaves its possessor so much more unhappy, as, not having been able to confine his expences to a large revenue, he will still less be able to live contentedly on a small one. The souls of men, according to PLATO,[2] inflamed with impure appetites, and losing the body, which alone afforded means of satisfaction, hover about the earth, and haunt the places where their bodies are deposited; possessed with a longing desire to recover the lost organs of sensation. So may we see worthless prodigals, having consumed their fortune in wild debauches, thrusting themselves into every plentiful table, and every party of pleasure, hated even by the vicious, and despised even by fools.

The one extreme of frugality is *avarice*, which, as it both deprives a   12
man of all use of his riches, and checks hospitality and every social enjoyment, is justly censured on a double account. *Prodigality*, the other extreme, is commonly more hurtful to a man himself; and each of these extremes is blamed above the other, according to the temper of the person who censures, and according to his greater or less sensibility to pleasure, either social or sensual.

QUALITIES often derive their merit from complicated sources. *Honesty*,   13
fidelity, *truth*, are praised for their immediate tendency to promote the interests of society; but after those virtues are once established upon this foundation, they are also considered as advantageous to the person himself, and as the source of that trust and confidence, which can alone give a man any consideration in life. One becomes contemptible, no less than odious, when he forgets the duty, which, in this particular, he owes to himself as well as to society.

Perhaps, this consideration is one *chief* source of the high blame, which   14
is thrown on any instance of failure among women in point of *chastity*. The greatest regard, which can be acquired by that sex, is derived from their fidelity; and a woman becomes cheap and vulgar, loses her rank, and is exposed to every insult, who is deficient in this particular. The smallest

---

[2] Phædo. 81. [Plato, *Phaedo*.]

failure is here sufficient to blast her character. A female has so many opportunities of secretly indulging these appetites, that nothing can give us
security but her absolute modesty and reserve; and where a breach is once
made, it can scarcely ever be fully repaired. If a man behave with cowardice on one occasion, a contrary conduct reinstates him in his character.
But by what action can a woman, whose behaviour has once been dissolute, be able to assure us, that she has formed better resolutions, and has
self-command enough to carry them into execution?

15   All men, it is allowed, are equally desirous of happiness; but few are
successful in the pursuit: One considerable cause is the want of
STRENGTH of MIND, which might enable them to resist the temptation of present ease or pleasure, and carry them forward in the search of
more distant profit and enjoyment. Our affections, on a general prospect
of their objects, form certain rules of conduct, and certain measures of
preference of one above another: And these decisions, though really the
result of our calm passions and propensities, (for what else can pronounce
any object eligible or the contrary?) are yet said, by a natural abuse of
terms, to be the determinations of pure *reason* and reflection. But when
some of these objects approach nearer to us, or acquire the advantages of
favourable lights and positions, which catch the heart or imagination; our
general resolutions are frequently confounded, a small enjoyment preferred, and lasting shame and sorrow entailed upon us. And however poets
may employ their wit and eloquence, in celebrating present pleasure, and
rejecting all distant views to fame, health, or fortune; it is obvious, that
this practice is the source of all dissoluteness and disorder, repentance and
misery. A man of a strong and determined temper adheres tenaciously to
his general resolutions, and is neither seduced by the allurements of pleasure, nor terrified by the menaces of pain; but keeps still in view those distant pursuits, by which he, at once, ensures his happiness and his honour.

16   Self-satisfaction, at least in some degree, is an advantage, which equally
attends the FOOL and the WISE MAN: But it is the only one; nor is
there any other circumstance in the conduct of life, where they are upon
an equal footing. Business, books, conversation; for all of these, a fool is
totally incapacitated, and except condemned by his station to the coarsest
drudgery, remains a *useless* burthen upon the earth. Accordingly, it is
found, that men are extremely jealous of their character in this particular;
and many instances are seen of profligacy and treachery, the most avowed
and unreserved; none of bearing patiently the imputation of ignorance
and stupidity. DICAEARCHUS, the MACEDONIAN general, who, as POLYBIUS

---

[3] Lib. xvii. cap. 35. [Polybius, *Histories*.]

tells us,[3] openly erected one altar to impiety, another to injustice, in order to bid defiance to mankind; even he, I am well assured, would have started at the epithet of *fool*, and have meditated revenge for so injurious an appellation. Except the affection of parents, the strongest and most indissoluble bond in nature, no connexion has strength sufficient to support the disgust arising from this character. Love itself, which can subsist under treachery, ingratitude, malice, and infidelity, is immediately extinguished by it, when perceived and acknowledged; nor are deformity and old age more fatal to the dominion of that passion. So dreadful are the ideas of an utter incapacity for any purpose or undertaking, and of continued error and misconduct in life!

When it is asked, whether a quick or a slow apprehension be most valu- 17 able? Whether one, that, at first view, penetrates far into a subject, but can perform nothing upon study; or a contrary character, which must work out every thing by dint of application? Whether a clear head or a copious invention? Whether a profound genius or a sure judgment? In short, what character, or peculiar turn of understanding is more excellent than another? It is evident, that we can answer none of these questions, without considering which of those qualities capacitates a man best for the world, and carries him farthest in any undertaking.

If refined sense and exalted sense be not so *useful* as common sense, 18 their rarity, their novelty, and the nobleness of their objects make some compensation, and render them the admiration of mankind: As gold, though less serviceable than iron, acquires, from its scarcity, a value, which is much superior.

The defects of judgment can be supplied by no art or invention; but 19 those of MEMORY frequently may, both in business and in study, by method and industry, and by diligence in committing every thing to writing; and we scarcely ever hear a short memory given as a reason for a man's failure in any undertaking. But in ancient times, when no man could make a figure without the talent of speaking, and when the audience were too delicate to bear such crude, undigested harangues as our extemporary orators offer to public assemblies; the faculty of memory was then of the utmost consequence, and was accordingly much more valued than at present. Scarce any great genius is mentioned in antiquity, who is not celebrated for this talent; and CICERO enumerates it among the other sublime qualities of CÆSAR himself.[4]

Particular customs and manners alter the usefulness of qualities: They 20

---

[4] "Fuit in illo ingenium, ratio, memoria, literæ, cura, cogitatio, diligentia," &c. PHILIP. 2. ["In him there was genius, calculation, memory, letters, industry, thought, diligence" (Cicero, *Philippics*, II, XLV; trans. by Walter C. A. Ker).]

also alter their merit. Particular situations and accidents have, in some degree, the same influence. He will always be more esteemed, who possesses those talents and accomplishments, which suit his station and profession, than he whom fortune has misplaced in the part which she has assigned him. The private or selfish virtues are, in this respect, more arbitrary than the public and social. In other respects, they are, perhaps, less liable to doubt and controversy.

21   In this kingdom, such continued ostentation, of late years, has prevailed among men in *active* life with regard to *public spirit*, and among those in *speculative* with regard to *benevolence*; and so many false pretensions to each have been, no doubt, detected, that men of the world are apt, without any bad intention, to discover a sullen incredulity on the head of those moral endowments, and even sometimes absolutely to deny their existence and reality. In like manner, I find, that, of old, the perpetual cant of the *Stoics* and *Cynics* concerning *virtue*, their magnificent professions and slender performances, bred a disgust in mankind; and Lucian, who, though licentious with regard to pleasure, is yet, in other respects, a very moral writer, cannot, sometimes, talk of virtue, so much boasted, without betraying symptoms of spleen and irony.[5] But surely this peevish delicacy, whence-ever it arises, can never be carried so far as to make us deny the existence of every species of merit, and all distinction of manners and behaviour. Besides *discretion, caution, enterprise, industry, assiduity, frugality, œconomy, good-sense, prudence, discernment*; besides these endowments, I say, whose very names force an avowal of their merit, there are many others, to which the most determined scepticism cannot, for a moment, refuse the tribute of praise and approbation. *Temperance, sobriety, patience, constancy, perseverance, forethought, considerateness, secrecy, order, insinuation, address, presence of mind, quickness of conception, facility of expression*; these, and a thousand more of the same

---

[5] Ἀρετήν τινα καὶ ἀσώματα καὶ λήρους μεγάλῃ τῇ φωνῇ ξυνειρόντων. Luc. Timon 9. ["dinned to death with their harangues about 'virtue' and 'things incorporeal' and other piffle" (Lucian, *Timon or the Misanthrope*, 9; trans. by A. M. Harmon).] Again, Καὶ συνάγοντες (οἱ φιλόσοφοι) εὐεξαπάτητα μειράκια τήν τε πολυθρύλλητον ἀρετὴν τραγῳδοῦσι. Icaro-men 30. ["[C]ollecting lads who are easy to hoodwink, (the philosophers) rant about their far-famed 'Virtue'" (Lucian, *Icaromenippus or the Sky Man*, 30; trans. by A. M. Harmon).] In another place, Ἢ ποῦ γάρ ἐστιν ἡ πολυθρύλλητος ἀρετή, καὶ φύσις, καὶ εἱμαρμένη, καὶ τύχη, ἀνυπόστατα καὶ κενὰ πραγμάτων ὀνόματα. Deor. Concil. 13. ["Where is that famous Virtue, and Nature, and Destiny, and Chance? They are unsubstantial, empty appelations" (Lucian, *The Parliament of the Gods*, 13; trans. by A. M. Harmon).]

kind, no man will ever deny to be excellencies and perfections. As their merit consists in their tendency to serve the person, possessed of them, without any magnificent claim to public and social desert, we are the less jealous of their pretensions, and readily admit them into the catalogue of laudable qualities. We are not sensible, that, by this concession, we have paved the way for all the other moral excellencies, and cannot consistently hesitate any longer, with regard to disinterested benevolence, patriotism, and humanity.

It seems, indeed, certain, that first appearances are here, as usual, extremely deceitful, and that it is more difficult, in a speculative way, to resolve into self-love the merit, which we ascribe to the selfish virtues above-mentioned, than that even of the social virtues, justice and beneficence. For this latter purpose, we need but say, that whatever conduct promotes the good of the community is loved, praised, and esteemed by the community, on account of that utility and interest, of which every one partakes: And though this affection and regard be, in reality, gratitude, not self-love, yet a distinction, even of this obvious nature, may not readily be made by superficial reasoners; and there is room, at least, to support the cavil and dispute for a moment. But as qualities, which tend only to the utility of their possessor, without any reference to us, or to the community, are yet esteemed and valued; by what theory or system can we account for this sentiment from self-love, or deduce it from that favourite origin? There seems here a necessity for confessing that the happiness and misery of others are not spectacles entirely indifferent to us; but that the view of the former, whether in its causes or effects, like sun-shine or the prospect of well-cultivated plains, (to carry our pretensions no higher) communicates a secret joy and satisfaction; the appearance of the latter, like a lowering cloud or barren landskip, throws a melancholy damp over the imagination. And this concession being once made, the difficulty is over; and a natural unforced interpretation of the phænomena of human life will afterwards, we may hope, prevail among all speculative enquirers.

Part II.

It may not be improper, in this place, to examine the influence of bodily endowments, and of the goods of fortune, over our sentiments of regard and esteem, and to consider whether these phænomena fortify or weaken the present theory. It will naturally be expected, that the beauty of the body, as is supposed by all ancient moralists, will be similar, in some respects, to that of the mind; and that every kind of esteem, which is paid to a man, will have something similar in its origin, whether it arise from his mental endowments, or from the situation of his exterior circumstances.

24   It is evident, that one considerable source of *beauty* in all animals is the advantage, which they reap from the particular structure of their limbs and members, suitably to the particular manner of life, to which they are by nature destined. The just proportions of a horse, described by XENOPHON and VIRGIL, are the same, that are received at this day by our modern jockeys; because the foundation of them is the same, namely, experience of what is detrimental or useful in the animal.

25   Broad shoulders, a lank belly, firm joints, taper legs; all these are beautiful in our species, because signs of force and vigour. Ideas of utility and its contrary, though they do not entirely determine what is handsome or deformed, are evidently the source of a considerable part of approbation or dislike.

26   In ancient times, bodily strength and dexterity, being of greater *use* and importance in war, was also much more esteemed and valued, than at present. Not to insist on HOMER and the poets, we may observe, that historians scruple not to mention *force of body* among the other accomplishments even of EPAMINONDAS, whom they acknowledge to be the greatest hero, statesman, and general of all the GREEKS.[6] A like praise is given to POMPEY, one of the greatest of the ROMANS.[7] This instance is similar to what we observed above, with regard to memory.

27   What derision and contempt, with both sexes, attend *impotence*; while the unhappy object is regarded as one deprived of so capital a pleasure in life, and at the same time, as disabled from communicating it to others. *Barrenness* in women, being also a species of *inutility*, is a reproach, but not in the same degree: Of which the reason is very obvious, according to the present theory.

28   There is no rule in painting or statuary more indispensible than that of balancing the figures, and placing them with the greatest exactness on

---

    [6] DIODORUS SICULUS, lib. xv. [Diodorus Siculus, *Historical Library*.] It may not be improper to give the character of EPAMINONDAS, as drawn by the historian, in order to show the ideas of perfect merit, which prevailed in those ages. In other illustrious men, says he, you will observe, that each possessed some one shining quality, which was the foundation of his fame: In EPAMINONDAS all the *virtues* are found united; force of body, eloquence of expression, vigour of mind, contempt of riches, gentleness of disposition, and, *what is chiefly to be regarded*, courage and conduct in war.

    [7] *Cum alacribus, saltu; cum velocibus, cursu; cum validis recte certabat.* SALLUST apud VEGET. ["[H]e disputed the superiority in leaping with the most active, in running with the most swift, and in exercises of strength with the most robust." (Flavius Vegetius Renatus, *De re militari*, Book I; trans. by Lieutenant John Clarke).]

their proper center of gravity. A figure, which is not justly balanced, is ugly; because it conveys the disagreeable ideas of fall, harm, and pain.[8]

A disposition or turn of mind, which qualifies a man to rise in the world, and advance his fortune, is entitled to esteem and regard, as has already been explained. It may, therefore, naturally be supposed, that the actual possession of riches and authority will have a considerable influence over these sentiments.   29

Let us examine any hypothesis, by which we can account for the regard paid to the rich and powerful: We shall find none satisfactory, but that which derives it from the enjoyment communicated to the spectator by the images of prosperity, happiness, ease, plenty, authority, and the gratification of every appetite. Self-love, for instance, which some affect so much to consider as the source of every sentiment, is plainly insufficient for this purpose. Where no good-will or friendship appears, it is difficult to conceive on what we can found our hope of advantage from the riches of others; though we naturally respect the rich, even before they discover any such favourable disposition towards us.   30

We are affected with the same sentiments, when we lie so much out of the sphere of their activity, that they cannot even be supposed to possess the power of serving us. A prisoner of war, in all civilized nations, is treated with a regard suited to his condition; and riches, it is evident, go far towards fixing the condition of any person. If birth and quality enter for a share, this still affords us an argument to our present purpose. For what is it we call a man of birth, but one who is descended from a long succession of rich and powerful ancestors, and who acquires our esteem by his connexion with persons whom we esteem? His ancestors, therefore, though dead, are respected, in some measure, on account of their riches; and consequently, without any kind of expectation.   31

But not to go so far as prisoners of war or the dead, to find instances of this disinterested regard for riches; we may only observe, with a little attention, those phænomena, which occur in common life and conversation.   32

---

[8] All men are equally liable to pain and disease and sickness; and may again recover health and ease. These circumstances, as they make no distinction between one man and another, are no source of pride or humility, regard or contempt. But comparing our own species to superior ones, it is a very mortifying consideration, that we should all be so liable to diseases and infirmities; and divines accordingly employ this topic, in order to depress self-conceit and vanity. They would have more success, if the common bent of our thoughts were not perpetually turned to compare ourselves with others. The infirmities of old age are mortifying; because a comparison with the young may take place. The king's evil is industriously concealed, because it affects others, and is often transmitted to posterity. The case is nearly the same with such diseases as convey any nauseous or frightful images; the epilepsy, for instance, ulcers, sores, scabs, &c.

A man, who is himself, we shall suppose, of a competent fortune, and of no profession, being introduced to a company of strangers, naturally treats them with different degrees of respect, as he is informed of their different fortunes and conditions; though it is impossible that he can so suddenly propose, and perhaps he would not accept of, any pecuniary advantage from them. A traveller is always admitted into company, and meets with civility, in proportion as his train and equipage speak him a man of great or moderate fortune. In short, the different ranks of men are, in a great measure, regulated by riches; and that with regard to superiors as well as inferiors, strangers as well as acquaintance.

33   What remains, therefore, but to conclude, that, as riches are desired for ourselves only as the means of gratifying our appetites, either at present or in some imaginary future period; they beget esteem in others merely from their having that influence. This indeed is their very nature or essence: They have a direct reference to the commodities, conveniencies, and pleasures of life: The bill of a banker, who is broke, or gold in a desart island, would otherwise be full as valuable. When we approach a man, who is, as we say, at his ease, we are presented with the pleasing ideas of plenty, satisfaction, cleanliness, warmth; a chearful house, elegant furniture, ready service, and whatever is desirable in meat, drink, or apparel. On the contrary, when a poor man appears, the disagreeable images of want, penury, hard labour, dirty furniture, coarse or ragged cloaths, nauseous meat and distasteful liquor, immediately strike our fancy. What else do we mean by saying that one is rich, the other poor? And as regard or contempt is the natural consequence of those different situations in life; it is easily seen what additional light and evidence this throws on our preceding theory, with regard to all moral distinctions.[9]

34   A man, who has cured himself of all ridiculous prepossessions, and is fully, sincerely, and steadily convinced, from experience as well as philosophy, that

---

[9] There is something extraordinary, and seemingly unaccountable in the operation of our passions, when we consider the fortune and situation of others. Very often another's advancement and prosperity produces envy, which has a strong mixture of hatred, and arises chiefly from the comparison of ourselves with the person. At the very same time, or at least in very short intervals, we may feel the passion of respect, which is a species of affection or good-will, with a mixture of humility. On the other hand, the misfortunes of our fellows often cause pity, which has in it a strong mixture of good-will. This sentiment of pity is nearly allied to contempt, which is a species of dislike, with a mixture of pride. I only point out these phænomena, as a subject of speculation to such as are curious with regard to moral enquiries. It is sufficient for the present purpose to observe in general, that power and riches commonly cause respect, poverty and meanness contempt, though particular views and incidents may sometimes raise the passions of envy and of pity.

the difference of fortune makes less difference in happiness than is vulgarly imagined; such a one does not measure out degrees of esteem according to the rent-rolls of his acquaintance. He may, indeed, externally pay a superior deference to the great lord above the vassal; because riches are the most convenient, being the most fixed and determinate, source of distinction: But his internal sentiments are more regulated by the personal characters of men, than by the accidental and capricious favours of fortune.

In most countries of EUROPE, family, that is, hereditary riches, marked with titles and symbols from the sovereign, is the chief source of distinction. In ENGLAND, more regard is paid to present opulence and plenty. Each practice has its advantages and disadvantages. Where birth is respected, unactive, spiritless minds remain in haughty indolence, and dream of nothing but pedigrees and genealogies: The generous and ambitious seek honour and authority and reputation and favour. Where riches are the chief idol, corruption, venality, rapine prevail: Arts, manufactures, commerce, agriculture flourish. The former prejudice, being favourable to military virtue, is more suited to monarchies. The latter, being the chief spur to industry, agrees better with a republican government. And we accordingly find, that each of these forms of government, by varying the *utility* of those customs, has commonly a proportionable effect on the sentiments of mankind.

SECTION VII.
OF QUALITIES IMMEDIATELY AGREEABLE TO OURSELVES.

1   WHOEVER has passed an evening with serious melancholy people, and has observed how suddenly the conversation was animated, and what sprightliness diffused itself over the countenance, discourse, and behaviour of every one, on the accession of a good-humoured, lively companion; such a one will easily allow, that CHEARFULNESS carries great merit with it, and naturally conciliates the good-will of mankind. No quality, indeed, more readily communicates itself to all around; because no one has a greater propensity to display itself, in jovial talk and pleasant entertainment. The flame spreads through the whole circle; and the most sullen and morose are often caught by it. That the melancholy hate the merry, even though HORACE says it, I have some difficulty to allow; because I have always observed, that, where the jollity is moderate and decent, serious people are so much the more delighted, as it dissipates the gloom, with which they are commonly oppressed; and gives them an unusual enjoyment.

2   From this influence of chearfulness, both to communicate itself, and to engage approbation, we may perceive, that there is another set of mental qualities, which, without any utility or any tendency to farther good, either of the community or of the possessor, diffuse a satisfaction on the beholders, and procure friendship and regard. Their immediate sensation, to the person possessed of them, is agreeable: Others enter into the same humour, and catch the sentiment, by a contagion or natural sympathy: And as we cannot forbear loving whatever pleases, a kindly emotion arises towards the person, who communicates so much satisfaction. He is a more animating spectacle: His presence diffuses over us more serene complacency and enjoyment: Our imagination, entering into his feelings and disposition, is affected in a more agreeable manner, than if a melancholy, dejected, sullen, anxious temper were presented to us. Hence the affection and approbation, which attend the former: The aversion and disgust, with which we regard the latter.[1]

---

[1] There is no man, who, on particular occasions, is not affected with all the disagreeable passions, fear, anger, dejection, grief, melancholy, anxiety, &c. But these, so far as they are natural, and universal, make no difference between one man and another, and can never be the object of blame. It is only when the disposition gives a *propensity* to any of these disagreeable passions, that they disfigure the character, and by giving uneasiness, convey the sentiment of disapprobation to the spectator.

Few men wou'd envy the character, which CÆSAR gives of CASSIUS.   3

> He loves no play,
> As thou do'st, ANTHONY: He hears no music:
> Seldom he smiles; and smiles in such a sort,
> As if he mock'd himself, and scorn'd his spirit
> That could be mov'd to smile at any thing.

Not only such men, as CÆSAR adds, are commonly *dangerous*, but also, having little enjoyment within themselves, they can never become agreeable to others, or contribute to social entertainment. In all polite nations and ages, a relish for pleasure, if accompanied with temperance and decency, is esteemed a considerable merit, even in the greatest men; and becomes still more requisite in those of inferior rank and character. It is an agreeable representation, which a FRENCH writer gives of the situation of his own mind in this particular, *Virtue I love,* says he, *without austerity: Pleasure, without effeminacy: And life, without fearing its end.*[2]

Who is not struck with any signal instance of GREATNESS of MIND   4
or Dignity of Character; with elevation of sentiment, disdain of slavery, and with that noble pride and spirit, which arises from conscious virtue? The sublime, says LONGINUS, is often nothing but the echo or image of magnanimity; and where this quality appears in any one, even though a syllable be not uttered, it excites our applause and admiration; as may be observed of the famous silence of AJAX in the ODYSSEY, which expresses more noble disdain and resolute indignation than any language can convey.[3]

Were I ALEXANDER, said PARMENIO, *I would accept of these offers made*   5
by DARIUS. *So would I too,* replied ALEXANDER, *were I* PARMENIO. This saying is admirable, says LONGINUS, from a like principle.[4]

Go! cries the same hero to his soldiers, when they refused to follow   6
him to the INDIES, *go tell your countrymen, that you left* ALEXANDER *compleating the conquest of the world.* "ALEXANDER," said the Prince of CONDÉ, who always admired this passage, "abandoned by his soldiers,

---

[2] "J'aime la vertu, sans rudesse;
J'aime le plaisir, sans molesse;
J'aime la vie, & n'en crains point la fin." St. EVREMOND.
["Virtue, if not sour, I choose;
Pleasure, if not wild and loose;
Life I love, but do not fly
At Death's approach, nor fear to die"
(Seigneur de Saint-Évremond, *Letters*; trans. by Rene Ternois).

[3] Cap. 9. [Longinus, *On the Sublime.*]

[4] Idem.

among Barbarians, not yet fully subdued, felt in himself such a dignity and right of empire, that he could not believe it possible, that any one would refuse to obey him. Whether in EUROPE or in ASIA, among GREEKS or PERSIANS, all was indifferent to him: Wherever he found men, he fancied he should find subjects."

7   The confident of MEDEA in the tragedy recommends caution and sub-mission; and enumerating all the distresses of that unfortunate heroine, asks her, what she has to support her against her numerous and implacable enemies. *Myself,* replies she; *Myself, I say, and it is enough.* BOILEAU justly recommends this passage as an instance of true sublime.[5]

8   When PHOCION, the modest, the gentle PHOCION, was led to execution, he turned to one of his fellow-sufferers, who was lamenting his own hard fate. *Is it not glory enough for you,* says he, *that you die with* PHOCION?[6]

9   Place in opposition the picture, which TACITUS draws of VITELLIUS, fallen from empire, prolonging his ignominy from a wretched love of life, delivered over to the merciless rabble; tossed, buffeted, and kicked about; constrained, by their holding a poinard under his chin, to raise his head, and expose himself to every contumely. What abject infamy! What low hu-miliation! Yet even here, says the historian, he discovered some symptoms of a mind not wholly degenerate. To a tribune, who insulted him, he re-plied, *I am still your emperor.*[7]

10   We never excuse the absolute want of spirit and dignity of character, or a proper sense of what is due to one's self, in society and the common inter-course of life. This vice constitutes what we properly call *meanness*; when a man can submit to the basest slavery, in order to gain his ends; fawn upon those who abuse him; and degrade himself by intimacies and familiarities with undeserving inferiors. A certain degree of generous pride or self-value is so requisite, that the absence of it in the mind displeases, after the same

---

[5] Reflexion 10 sur Longin. [Nicolas Boileau-Despréaux, *Réflxions critiques sur quelques passages de Longin.*]

[6] PLUTARCH in PHOC. [Plutarch, *Lives*, "Phocion."]

[7] TACIT. hist. lib. iii. The author entering upon the narration, says, *Laniata veste, fœdum spectaculum ducebatur, multis increpantibus, nullo inlacrimante:* deformitas exitus misericordiam abstulerat. ["With his arms bound behind his back, his garments torn, he presented a grievous sight as he was led away. Many cried out against him, not one shed a tear; the ugliness of the last scene had banished pity" (Tacitus, *Histories*, III, LXXXIV; trans. by Clifford H. Moore).] To enter thoroughly into this method of think-ing, we must make allowance for the ancient maxims, that no one ought to prolong his life after it became dishonourable; but, as he had always a right to dispose of it, it then became a duty to part with it.

manner as the want of a nose, eye, or any of the most material features of the face or members of the body.[8]

The utility of COURAGE, both to the public and to the person pos-   11 sessed of it, is an obvious foundation of merit: But to any one who duly considers of the matter, it will appear, that this quality has a peculiar lustre, which it derives wholly from itself, and from that noble elevation inseparable from it. Its figure, drawn by painters and by poets, displays, in each feature, a sublimity and daring confidence; which catches the eye, engages the affections, and diffuses, by sympathy, a like sublimity of sentiment over every spectator.

Under what shining colours does DEMOSTHENES[9] represent PHILIP;   12 where the orator apologizes for his own administration, and justifies that pertinacious love of liberty, with which he had inspired the ATHENIANS. "I beheld PHILIP," says he, "he with whom was your contest, resolutely, while in pursuit of empire and dominion, exposing himself to every wound; his eye goared, his neck wrested, his arm, his thigh pierced, whatever part of his body fortune should seize on, that chearfully relinquishing; provided that, with what remained, he might live in honour and renown. And shall it be said, that he, born in PELLA, a place heretofore mean and ignoble, should be inspired with so high an ambition and thirst of fame: While you, ATHENIANS, &c." These praises excite the most lively admiration; but the views presented by the orator, carry us not, we see, beyond the hero himself, nor ever regard the future advantageous consequences of his valour.

The martial temper of the ROMANS, inflamed by continual wars, had   13 raised their esteem of courage so high, that, in their language, it was called *virtue*, by way of excellence and of distinction from all other moral qualities. *The* SUEVI, *in the opinion of* TACITUS,[10] *dressed their hair with a laudable intent: Not for the purpose of loving or being loved: They adorned themselves only for their enemies, and in order to appear more terri-*

---

[8] The absence of virtue may often be a vice; and that of the highest kind; as in the instance of ingratitude, as well as meanness. Where we expect a beauty, the disappointment gives an uneasy sensation, and produces a real deformity. An abjectness of character, likewise, is disgustful and contemptible in another view. Where a man has no sense of value in himself, we are not likely to have any higher esteem of him. And if the same person, who crouches to his superiors, is insolent to his inferiors (as often happens), this contrariety of behaviour, instead of correcting the former vice, aggravates it extremely by the addition of a vice still more odious. See Sect. VIII.

[9] Pro corona. [Demosthenes, *On the Crown*, 67–68.]

[10] De moribus Germ. [Tacitus, *Germania*, 38.]

ble. A sentiment of the historian, which would sound a little oddly in other nations and other ages.

14   The SCYTHIANS, according to HERODOTUS,[11] after scalping their enemies, dressed the skin like leather, and used it as a towel; and whoever had the most of those towels was most esteemed among them. So much had martial bravery, in that nation, as well as in many others, destroyed the sentiments of humanity; a virtue surely much more useful and engaging.

15   It is indeed observable, that, among all uncultivated nations, who have not, as yet, had full experience of the advantages attending beneficence, justice, and the social virtues, courage is the predominant excellence; what is most celebrated by poets, recommended by parents and instructors, and admired by the public in general. The ethics of HOMER are, in this particular, very different from those of FENELON, his elegant imitator; and such as were well suited to an age, when one hero, as remarked by THUCYDIDES,[12] could ask another, without offence, whether he were a robber or not. Such also, very lately, was the system of ethics, which prevailed in many barbarous parts of IRELAND; if we may credit SPENCER, in his judicious account of the state of that kingdom.[13]

16   Of the same class of virtues with courage is that undisturbed philosophical TRANQUILLITY, superior to pain, sorrow, anxiety, and each assault of adverse fortune. Conscious of his own virtue, say the philosophers, the sage elevates himself above every accident of life; and securely placed in the temple of wisdom, looks down on inferior mortals, engaged in pursuit of honours, riches, reputation, and every frivolous enjoyment. These pretensions, no doubt, when stretched to the utmost, are, by far, too magnificent for human nature. They carry, however, a grandeur with them, which seizes the spectator, and strikes him with admiration. And the nearer we can approach in practice, to this sublime tranquillity and indifference (for we must distinguish it from a stupid insensibility) the more secure enjoyment shall we attain within ourselves, and the more greatness of mind shall we discover to the world. The philosophical tranquillity may, indeed, be considered only as a branch of magnanimity.

17   Who admires not SOCRATES; his perpetual serenity and contentment, amidst the greatest poverty and domestic vexations; his resolute contempt

---

[11] Lib. iv. [Herodotus, *The Persian Wars.*]

[12] Lib. i. [Thucydides, *History of the Peloponnesian War.*]

[13] It is a common use, says he, amongst their gentlemen's sons, that, as soon as they are able to use their weapons, they strait gather to themselves three or four stragglers or kern, with whom wandering a while up and down idly the country, taking only meat, he at last falleth into some bad occasion, that shall be offered; which being once made known, he is thenceforth counted a man of worth, in whom there is courage.

of riches, and his magnanimous care of preserving liberty, while he re-fused all assistance from his friends and disciples, and avoided even the dependence of an obligation? EPICTETUS had not so much as a door to his little house or hovel; and therefore, soon lost his iron lamp, the only furni-ture which he had worth taking. But resolving to disappoint all robbers for the future, he supplied its place with an earthen lamp, of which he very peaceably kept possession ever after.

Among the ancients, the heroes in philosophy, as well as those in war and patriotism, have a grandeur and force of sentiment, which astonishes our narrow souls, and is rashly rejected as extravagant and supernatural. They, in their turn, I allow, would have had equal reason to consider as romantic and incredible, the degree of humanity, clemency, order, tran-quillity, and other social virtues, to which, in the administration of gov-ernment, we have attained in modern times, had any one been then able to have made a fair representation of them. Such is the compensation, which nature, or rather education, has made in the distribution of excellencies and virtues, in those different ages.

The merit of BENEVOLENCE, arising from its utility, and its ten-dency to promote the good of mankind, has been already explained, and is, no doubt, the source of a *considerable* part of that esteem, which is so universally paid to it. But it will also be allowed, that the very softness and tenderness of the sentiment, its engaging endearments, its fond expres-sions, its delicate attentions, and all that flow of mutual confidence and re-gard, which enters into a warm attachment of love and friendship: It will be allowed, I say, that these feelings, being delightful in themselves, are necessarily communicated to the spectators, and melt them into the same fondness and delicacy. The tear naturally starts in our eye on the appre-hension of a warm sentiment of this nature: Our breast heaves, our heart is agitated, and every humane tender principle of our frame is set in mo-tion, and gives us the purest and most satisfactory enjoyment.

When poets form descriptions of ELYSIAN fields, where the blessed in-habitants stand in no need of each other's assistance, they yet represent them as maintaining a constant intercourse of love and friendship, and sooth our fancy with the pleasing image of these soft and gentle passions. The idea of tender tranquillity in a pastoral ARCADIA is agreeable from a like principle, as has been observed above.[14]

Who would live amidst perpetual wrangling, and scolding, and mutual reproaches? The roughness and harshness of these emotions disturb and displease us: We suffer by contagion and sympathy; nor can we remain

18

19

20

21

---

[14] Sect. v. Part 2.

indifferent spectators, even though certain, that no pernicious consequences would ever follow from such angry passions.

22   As a certain proof, that the whole merit of benevolence is not derived
from its usefulness, we may observe, that, in a kind way of blame, we say, a
person is *too good*; when he exceeds his part in society, and carries his attention for others beyond the proper bounds. In like manner, we say a man
is *too high-spirited, too intrepid, too indifferent about fortune*: Reproaches,
which really, at bottom, imply more esteem than many panegyrics. Being
accustomed to rate the merit and demerit of characters chiefly by their
useful or pernicious tendencies, we cannot forbear applying the epithet of
blame, when we discover a sentiment, which rises to a degree that is hurtful: But it may happen, at the same time, that its noble elevation, or its engaging tenderness so seizes the heart, as rather to encrease our friendship
and concern for the person.[15]

23   The amours and attachments of Harry the IVth of France, during the
civil wars of the league, frequently hurt his interest and his cause; but all
the young, at least, and amorous, who can sympathize with the tender passions, will allow, that this very weakness (for they will readily call it such)
chiefly endears that hero, and interests them in his fortunes.

24   The excessive bravery and resolute inflexibility of Charles the XIIth
ruined his own country, and infested all his neighbours; but have such
splendour and greatness in their appearance, as strikes us with admiration; and they might, in some degree, be even approved of, if they betrayed not sometimes too evident symptoms of madness and disorder.

25   The Athenians pretended to the first invention of agriculture and of
laws; and always valued themselves extremely on the benefit thereby procured to the whole race of mankind. They also boasted, and with reason,
of their warlike enterprizes; particularly against those innumerable fleets
and armies of Persians, which invaded Greece during the reigns of Darius and Xerxes. But though there be no comparison, in point of utility,
between these peaceful and military honours; yet we find, that the orators,
who have writ such elaborate panegyrics on that famous city, have chiefly
triumphed in displaying the warlike atchievements. Lysias, Thucydides,
Plato, and Isocrates discover, all of them, the same partiality; which,
though condemned by calm reason and reflection, appears so natural in
the mind of man.

26   It is observable, that the great charm of poetry consists in lively pictures of the sublime passions, magnanimity, courage, disdain of fortune;

---

[15] Cheerfulness could scarce admit of blame from its excess, were it not that dissolute mirth, without a proper cause or subject, is a sure symptom and characteristic of
folly, and on that account disgustful.

or those of the tender affections, love and friendship; which warm the
heart, and diffuse over it similar sentiments and emotions. And though all
kinds of passion, even the most disagreeable, such as grief and anger, are
observed, when excited by poetry, to convey a satisfaction, from a mechanism of nature, not easy to be explained: Yet those more elevated or softer
affections have a peculiar influence, and please from more than one cause
or principle. Not to mention, that they alone interest us in the fortune of
the persons represented, or communicate any esteem and affection for
their character.

And can it possibly be doubted, that this talent itself of poets, to move   27
the passions, this PATHETIC and SUBLIME of sentiment, is a very
considerable merit; and being enhanced by its extreme rarity, may exalt
the person possessed of it, above every character of the age in which he
lives? The prudence, address, steadiness, and benign government of Au-
GUSTUS, adorned with all the splendour of his noble birth and imperial
crown, render him but an unequal competitor for fame with VIRGIL, who
lays nothing into the opposite scale but the divine beauties of his poetical
genius.

The very sensibility to these beauties, or a DELICACY of taste, is itself   28
a beauty in any character; as conveying the purest, the most durable, and
most innocent of all enjoyments.

These are some instances of the several species of merit, that are valued   29
for the immediate pleasure, which they communicate to the person possessed of them. No views of utility or of future beneficial consequences
enter into this sentiment of approbation; yet is it of a kind similar to that
other sentiment, which arises from views of a public or private utility. The
same social sympathy, we may observe, or fellow-feeling with human happiness or misery, gives rise to both; and this analogy, in all the parts of the
present theory, may justly be regarded as a confirmation of it.

SECTION VIII.
OF QUALITIES IMMEDIATELY AGREEABLE TO OTHERS.[1]

1   As the mutual shocks, in *society*, and the oppositions of interest and self-love have constrained mankind to establish the laws of *justice*; in order to preserve the advantages of mutual assistance and protection: In like manner, the eternal contrarieties, in *company*, of men's pride and self-conceit, have introduced the rules of GOOD-MANNERS or POLITENESS; in order to facilitate the intercourse of minds, and an undisturbed commerce and conversation. Among well-bred people, a mutual deference is affected: Contempt of others disguised: Authority concealed: Attention given to each in his turn: And an easy stream of conversation maintained, without vehemence, without interruption, without eagerness for victory, and without any airs of superiority. These attentions and regards are immediately *agreeable* to others, abstracted from any consideration of utility or beneficial tendencies: They conciliate affection, promote esteem, and extremely enhance the merit of the person, who regulates his behaviour by them.

2   Many of the forms of breeding are arbitrary and casual: But the thing expressed by them is still the same. A SPANIARD goes out of his own house before his guest, to signify that he leaves him master of all. In other countries, the landlord walks out last, as a common mark of deference and regard.

3   But, in order to render a man perfect *good company*, he must have WIT and INGENUITY as well as good-manners. What wit is, it may not be easy to define; but it is easy surely to determine, that it is a quality immediately *agreeable* to others, and communicating, on its first appearance, a lively joy and satisfaction to every one who has any comprehension of it. The most profound metaphysics, indeed, might be employed, in explaining the various kinds and species of wit; and many classes of it, which are now received on the sole testimony of taste and sentiment, might, perhaps, be resolved into more general principles. But this is sufficient for our present purpose, that it does affect taste and sentiment, and bestowing an immediate enjoyment, is a sure source of approbation and affection.

---

[1] It is the nature, and, indeed the definition of virtue, that it is *a quality of the mind agreeable to or approved of by every one, who considers or contemplates it.* But some qualities produce pleasure, because they are useful to society, or useful or agreeable to the person himself; others produce it more immediately: Which is the case with the class of virtues here considered.

In countries, where men pass most of their time in conversation, and   4
visits, and assemblies, these *companionable* qualities, so to speak, are of
high estimation, and form a chief part of personal merit. In countries,
where men live a more domestic life, and either are employed in business,
or amuse themselves in a narrower circle of acquaintance, the more solid
qualities are chiefly regarded. Thus, I have often observed, that, among
the FRENCH, the first questions, with regard to a stranger, are, *Is he polite?*
Has he wit? In our own country, the chief praise bestowed, is always that of
a *good-natured, sensible fellow*.

In conversation, the lively spirit of dialogue is *agreeable*, even to those   5
who desire not to have any share in the discourse: Hence the teller of long
stories, or the pompous declaimer, is very little approved of. But most
men desire likewise their turn in the conversation, and regard, with a very
evil eye, that *loquacity*, which deprives them of a right they are naturally so
jealous of.

There is a sort of harmless *liars*, frequently to be met with in company,   6
who deal much in the marvellous. Their usual intention is to please and
entertain; but as men are most delighted with what they conceive to be
truth, these people mistake extremely the means of pleasing, and incur
universal blame. Some indulgence, however, to lying or fiction is given in
humorous stories; because it is there really agreeable and entertaining; and
truth is not of any importance.

Eloquence, genius of all kinds, even good sense, and sound reasoning,   7
when it rises to an eminent degree, and is employed upon subjects of any
considerable dignity and nice discernment; all these endowments seem
immediately agreeable, and have a merit distinct from their usefulness.
Rarity, likewise, which so much enhances the price of every thing, must
set an additional value on these noble talents of the human mind.

Modesty may be understood in different senses, even abstracted from   8
chastity, which has been already treated of. It sometimes means that tenderness and nicety of honour, that apprehension of blame, that dread of
intrusion or injury towards others, that PUDOR, which is the proper
guardian of every kind of virtue, and a sure preservative against vice and
corruption. But its most usual meaning is when it is opposed to *impudence*
and *arrogance*, and expresses a diffidence of our own judgment, and a due
attention and regard for others. In young men chiefly, this quality is a sure
sign of good sense; and is also the certain means of augmenting that endowment, by preserving their ears open to instruction, and making them
still grasp after new attainments. But it has a farther charm to every spectator; by flattering every man's vanity, and presenting the appearance of a
docile pupil, who receives, with proper attention and respect, every word
they utter.

9   Men have, in general, a much greater propensity to over-value than
under-value themselves; notwithstanding the opinion of ARISTOTLE.[2] This
makes us more jealous of the excess on the former side, and causes us to
regard, with a peculiar indulgence, all tendency to modesty and self-
diffidence; as esteeming the danger less of falling into any vicious extreme
of that nature. It is thus, in countries, where men's bodies are apt to exceed in corpulency, personal beauty is placed in a much greater degree of
slenderness, than in countries where that is the most usual defect. Being
so often struck with instances of one species of deformity, men think they
can never keep at too great a distance from it, and wish always to have a
leaning to the opposite side. In like manner, were the door opened to self-
praise, and were MONTAIGNE'S maxim observed, that one should say as
frankly, *I have sense, I have learning, I have courage, beauty, or wit*; as it is
sure we often think so; were this the case, I say, every one is sensible, that
such a flood of impertinence would break in upon us, as would render society wholly intolerable. For this reason custom has established it as a rule,
in common societies, that men should not indulge themselves in self-
praise, or even speak much of themselves; and it is only among intimate
friends or people of very manly behaviour, that one is allowed to do himself justice. No body finds fault with MAURICE, Prince of ORANGE, for his
reply to one who asked him, whom he esteemed the first general of the
age, *The marquis of* SPINOLA, said he, *is the second*. Though it is observable,
that the self-praise implied is here better implied, than if it had been directly expressed, without any cover or disguise.

10   He must be a very superficial thinker, who imagines, that all instances
of mutual deference are to be understood in earnest, and that a man would
be more esteemable for being ignorant of his own merits and accomplishments. A small bias towards modesty, even in the internal sentiment, is
favourably regarded, especially in young people; and a strong bias is required, in the outward behaviour: But this excludes not a noble pride and
spirit, which may openly display itself in its full extent, when one lies
under calumny or oppression of any kind. The generous contumacy of
SOCRATES, as CICERO calls it, has been highly celebrated in all ages; and
when joined to the usual modesty of his behaviour, forms a shining character. IPHICRATES, the ATHENIAN, being accused of betraying the interests
of his country, asked his accuser, *Would you*, says he, *have, on a like occasion, been guilty of that crime? By no means*, replied the other. *And can you
then imagine*, cried the hero, *that* IPHICRATES *would be guilty?*[3] In short, a

---

2   Ethic. ad Nicomachum. [Aristotle, *Nicomachean Ethics*.]
3   QUINTIL. lib. v. cap. 12. [Quintilian, *Institutes*.]

generous spirit and self-value, well founded, decently disguised, and courageously supported under distress and calumny, is a great excellency, and seems to derive its merit from the noble elevation of its sentiment, or its immediate agreeableness to its possessor. In ordinary characters, we approve of a bias towards modesty, which is a quality immediately agreeable to others: The vicious excess of the former virtue, namely, insolence or haughtiness, is immediately disagreeable to others: The excess of the latter is so to the possessor. Thus are the boundaries of these duties adjusted.

A desire of fame, reputation, or a character with others, is so far from   11 being blameable, that it seems inseparable from virtue, genius, capacity, and a generous or noble disposition. An attention even to trivial matters, in order to please, is also expected and demanded by society; and no one is surprised, if he find a man in company, to observe a greater elegance of dress and more pleasant flow of conversation, than when he passes his time at home, and with his own family. Wherein, then, consists VANITY, which is so justly regarded as a fault or imperfection? It seems to consist chiefly in such an intemperate display of our advantages, honours, and accomplishments; in such an importunate and open demand of praise and admiration, as is offensive to others, and encroaches too far on *their* secret vanity and ambition. It is besides a sure symptom of the want of true dignity and elevation of mind, which is so great an ornament in any character. For why that impatient desire of applause; as if you were not justly entitled to it, and might not reasonably expect, that it would for ever attend you? Why so anxious to inform us of the great company which you have kept; the obliging things which were said to you; the honours, the distinctions which you met with; as if these were not things of course, and what we could readily, of ourselves, have imagined, without being told of them?

DECENCY, or a proper regard to age, sex, character, and station in the   12 world, may be ranked among the qualities, which are immediately agreeable to others, and which, by that means, acquire praise and approbation. An effeminate behaviour in a man, a rough manner in a woman; these are ugly, because unsuitable to each character, and different from the qualities which we expect in the sexes. It is as if a tragedy abounded in comic beauties, or a comedy in tragic. The disproportions hurt the eye, and convey a disagreeable sentiment to the spectators, the source of blame and disapprobation. This is that *indecorum*, which is explained so much at large by CICERO in his Offices.

Among the other virtues, we may also give CLEANLINESS a place;   13 since it naturally renders us agreeable to others, and is no inconsiderable source of love and affection. No one will deny, that a negligence in this particular is a fault; and as faults are nothing but smaller vices, and this

fault can have no other origin than the uneasy sensation, which it excites
in others; we may, in this instance, seemingly so trivial, clearly discover
the origin of moral distinctions, about which the learned have involved
themselves in such mazes of perplexity and error.

14   But besides all the *agreeable* qualities, the origin of whose beauty, we
can, in some degree explain and account for, there still remains something
mysterious and inexplicable, which conveys an immediate satisfaction to
the spectator, but how, or why, or for what reason, he cannot pretend to
determine. There is a MANNER, a grace, an ease, a genteelness, an I-
know-not-what, which some men possess above others, which is very
different from external beauty and comeliness, and which, however,
catches our affection almost as suddenly and powerfully. And though this
manner be chiefly talked of in the passion between the sexes, where the
concealed magic is easily explained, yet surely much of it prevails in all
our estimation of characters, and forms no inconsiderable part of personal
merit. This class of accomplishments, therefore, must be trusted entirely
to the blind, but sure testimony of taste and sentiment; and must be considered as a part of ethics, left by nature to baffle all the pride of philosophy, and make her sensible of her narrow boundaries and slender
acquisitions.

15   We approve of another, because of his wit, politeness, modesty, decency, or any agreeable quality which he possesses; although he be not of
our acquaintance, nor has ever given us any entertainment, by means of
these accomplishments. The idea, which we form of their effect on his acquaintance, has an agreeable influence on our imagination, and gives us
the sentiment of approbation. This principle enters into all the judgments, which we form concerning manners and characters.

SECTION IX.
CONCLUSION.

Part I.

IT may justly appear surprising, that any man, in so late an age, should   1
find it requisite to prove, by elaborate reasoning, that PERSONAL
MERIT consists altogether in the possession of mental qualities, *useful*
or *agreeable* to the *person himself* or to *others*. It might be expected, that
this principle would have occurred even to the first rude, unpracticed enquirers concerning morals, and been received from its own evidence,
without any argument or disputation. Whatever is valuable in any kind,
so naturally classes itself under the division of *useful* or *agreeable*, the
utile or the *dulce*, that it is not easy to imagine, why we should ever seek
farther, or consider the question as a matter of nice research or enquiry.
And as every thing useful or agreeable must possess these qualities with
regard either to the *person himself* or to *others*, the compleat delineation or
description of merit seems to be performed as naturally as a shadow is
cast by the sun, or an image is reflected upon water. If the ground, on
which the shadow is cast, be not broken and uneven; nor the surface,
from which the image is reflected, disturbed and confused; a just figure is
immediately presented, without any art or attention. And it seems a reasonable presumption, that systems and hypotheses have perverted our
natural understanding; when a theory, so simple and obvious, could so
long have escaped the most elaborate examination.

But however the case may have fared with philosophy; in common life,   2
these principles are still implicitly maintained, nor is any other topic of
praise or blame ever recurred to, when we employ any panegyric or satire,
any applause or censure of human action and behaviour. If we observe
men, in every intercourse of business or pleasure, in every discourse and
conversation; we shall find them no where, except in the schools, at any
loss upon this subject. What so natural, for instance, as the following dialogue? You are very happy, we shall suppose one to say, addressing himself to another, that you have given your daughter to CLEANTHES. He is a
man of honour and humanity. Every one, who has any intercourse with
him, is sure of *fair* and *kind* treatment.[1] I congratulate you too, says another on the promising expectations of this son in-law; whose assiduous
application to the study of the laws, whose quick penetration and early
knowledge both of men and business, prognosticate the greatest honours

---

[1] Qualities useful to others.

and advancement.[2] You surprize me, replies a third, when you talk of CLEANTHES as a man of business and application. I met him lately in a circle of the gayest company, and he was the very life and soul of our conversation: So much wit with good manners; so much gallantry without affectation; so much ingenious knowledge so genteelly delivered, I have never before observed in any one.[3] You would admire him still more, says a fourth, if you knew him more familiarly. That chearfulness, which you might remark in him, is not a sudden flash struck out by company: It runs through the whole tenor of his life, and preserves a perpetual serenity on his countenance, and tranquillity in his soul. He has met with severe trials, misfortunes as well as dangers; and by his greatness of mind, was still superior to all of them.[4] The image, gentlemen, which you have here delineated of CLEANTHES, cry'd I, is that of accomplished merit. Each of you has given a stroke of the pencil to his figure; and you have unawares exceeded all the pictures drawn by GRATIAN or CASTIGLIONE. A philosopher might select this character as a model of perfect virtue.

3   And as every quality, which is useful or agreeable to ourselves or others, is, in common life, allowed to be a part of personal merit; so no other will ever be received, where men judge of things by their natural, unprejudiced reason, without the delusive glosses of superstition and false religion. Celibacy, fasting, penance, mortification, self-denial, humility, silence, solitude, and the whole train of monkish virtues; for what reason are they every where rejected by men of sense, but because they serve to no manner of purpose; neither advance a man's fortune in the world, nor render him a more valuable member of society; neither qualify him for the entertainment of company, nor increase his power of self-enjoyment? We observe, on the contrary, that they cross all these desirable ends; stupify the understanding and harden the heart, obscure the fancy and sour the temper. We justly, therefore, transfer them to the opposite column, and place them in the catalogue of vices; nor has any superstition force sufficient among men of the world, to pervert entirely these natural sentiments. A gloomy, hair-brained enthusiast, after his death, may have a place in the calendar; but will scarcely ever be admitted, when alive, into intimacy and society, except by those who are as delirious and dismal as himself.

4   It seems a happiness in the present theory, that it enters not into that vulgar dispute concerning the *degrees* of benevolence or self-love, which

---

[2] Qualities useful to the person himself.

[3] Qualities immediately agreeable to others.

[4] Qualities immediately agreeable to the person himself.

prevail in human nature; a dispute which is never likely to have any issue, both because men, who have taken part, are not easily convinced, and because the phenomena, which can be produced on either side, are so dispersed, so uncertain, and subject to so many interpretations, that it is scarcely possible accurately to compare them, or draw from them any determinate inference or conclusion. It is sufficient for our present purpose, if it be allowed, what surely, without the greatest absurdity, cannot be disputed, that there is some benevolence, however small, infused into our bosom; some spark of friendship for human kind; some particle of the dove, kneaded into our frame, along with the elements of the wolf and serpent. Let these generous sentiments be supposed ever so weak; let them be insufficient to move even a hand or finger of our body; they must still direct the determinations of our mind, and where every thing else is equal, produce a cool preference of what is useful and serviceable to mankind, above what is pernicious and dangerous. A *moral distinction*, therefore, immediately arises; a general sentiment of blame and approbation; a tendency, however faint, to the objects of the one, and a proportionable aversion to those of the other. Nor will those reasoners, who so earnestly maintain the predominant selfishness of human kind, be any wise scandalized at hearing of the weak sentiments of virtue, implanted in our nature. On the contrary, they are found as ready to maintain the one tenet as the other; and their spirit of satire (for such it appears, rather than of corruption) naturally gives rise to both opinions; which have, indeed, a great and almost indissoluble connexion together.

Avarice, ambition, vanity, and all passions vulgarly, though improperly, 5 comprized under the denomination of *self-love*, are here excluded from our theory concerning the origin of morals, not because they are too weak, but because they have not a proper direction, for that purpose. The notion of morals, implies some sentiment common to all mankind, which recommends the same object to general approbation, and makes every man, or most men, agree in the same opinion or decision concerning it. It also implies some sentiment, so universal and comprehensive as to extend to all mankind, and render the actions and conduct, even of the persons the most remote, an object of applause or censure, according as they agree or disagree with that rule of right which is established. These two requisite circumstances belong alone to the sentiment of humanity here insisted on. The other passions produce, in every breast, many strong sentiments of desire and aversion, affection and hatred; but these neither are felt so much in common, nor are so comprehensive, as to be the foundation of any general system and established theory of blame or approbation.

When a man denominates another his *enemy*, his *rival*, his *antagonist*, 6 his *adversary*, he is understood to speak the language of self-love, and to express sentiments, peculiar to himself, and arising from his particular circumstances and situation. But when he bestows on any man the epithets of *vicious* or *odious* or *depraved*, he then speaks another language, and expresses sentiments, in which, he expects, all his audience are to concur with him. He must here, therefore, depart from his private and particular situation, and must chuse a point of view, common to him with others: He must move some universal principle of the human frame, and touch a string, to which all mankind have an accord and symphony. If he mean, therefore, to express, that this man possesses qualities, whose tendency is pernicious to society, he has chosen this common point of view, and has touched the principle of humanity, in which every man, in some degree, concurs. While the human heart is compounded of the same elements as at present, it will never be wholly indifferent to public good, nor entirely unaffected with the tendency of characters and manners. And though this affection of humanity may not generally be esteemed so strong as vanity or ambition, yet, being common to all men, it can alone be the foundation of morals, or of any general system of blame or praise. One man's ambition is not another's ambition; nor will the same event or object satisfy both: But the humanity of one man is the humanity of every one; and the same object touches this passion in all human creatures.

7   But the sentiments, which arise from humanity, are not only the same in all human creatures, and produce the same approbation or censure; but they also comprehend all human creatures; nor is there any one whose conduct or character is not, by their means, an object, to every one, of censure or approbation. On the contrary, those other passions, commonly denominated selfish, both produce different sentiments in each individual, according to his particular situation; and also contemplate the greater part of mankind with the utmost indifference and unconcern. Whoever has a high regard and esteem for me flatters my vanity; whoever expresses contempt mortifies and displeases me: But as my name is known but to a small part of mankind, there are few, who come within the sphere of this passion, or excite, on its account, either my affection or disgust. But if you represent a tyrannical, insolent, or barbarous behaviour, in any country or in any age of the world; I soon carry my eye to the pernicious tendency of such a conduct, and feel the sentiment of repugnance and displeasure towards it. No character can be so remote as to be, in this light, wholly indifferent to me. What is beneficial to society or to the person himself must still be preferred. And every quality or action, of every human being, must, by this means, be ranked under some class or denomination, expressive of general censure or applause.

8   What more, therefore, can we ask to distinguish the sentiments, dependant on humanity, from those connected with any other passion, or to satisfy

us, why the former are the origin of morals, not the latter? Whatever conduct gains my approbation, by touching my humanity, procures also the applause of all mankind, by affecting the same principle in them: But what serves my avarice or ambition pleases these passions in me alone, and affects not the avarice and ambition of the rest of mankind. There is no circumstance of conduct in any man, provided it have a beneficial tendency, that is not agreeable to my humanity, however remote the person: But every man, so far removed as neither to cross nor serve my avarice and ambition, is regarded as wholly indifferent by those passions. The distinction, therefore, between these species of sentiment being so great and evident, language must soon be moulded upon it, and must invent a peculiar set of terms, in order to express those universal sentiments of censure or approbation, which arise from humanity, or from views of general usefulness and its contrary. VIRTUE and VICE become then known: Morals are recognized: Certain general ideas are framed of human conduct and behaviour: Such measures are expected from men, in such situations: This action is determined to be conformable to our abstract rule; that other, contrary. And by such universal principles are the particular sentiments of self-love frequently controuled and limited.[5]

From instances of popular tumults, seditions, factions, panics, and of all passions, which are shared with a multitude; we may learn the influence of society, in exciting and supporting any emotion; while the most ungovernable disorders are raised, we find, by that means, from the slightest and most frivolous occasions. SOLON was no very cruel, though perhaps, an unjust legislator, who punished neuters in civil wars; and few, I

9

---

[5] It seems certain, both from reason and experience, that a rude, untaught savage regulates chiefly his love and hatred by the ideas of private utility and injury, and has but faint conceptions of a general rule or system of behaviour. The man who stands opposite to him in battle, he hates heartily, not only for the present moment, which is almost unavoidable, but for ever after; nor is he satisfied without the most extreme punishment and vengeance. But we, accustomed to society, and to more enlarged reflections, consider that this man is serving his own country and community; that any man, in the same situation, would do the same; that we ourselves, in like circumstances, observe a like conduct; that, in general, human society is best supported on such maxims: And by these suppositions and views, we correct, in some measure, our ruder and narrower passions. And though much of our friendship and enmity be still regulated by private considerations of benefit and harm, we pay, at least, this homage to general rules, which we are accustomed to respect, that we commonly pervert our adversary's conduct, by imputing malice or injustice to him, in order to give vent to those passions, which arise from self-love and private interest. When the heart is full of rage, it never wants pretences of this nature; though sometimes as frivolous, as those from which HORACE, being almost crushed by the fall of a tree, affects to accuse of parricide the first planter of it.

believe, would, in such cases, incur the penalty, were their affection and discourse allowed sufficient to absolve them. No selfishness, and scarce any philosophy, have there force sufficient to support a total coolness and indifference; and he must be more or less than man, who kindles not in the common blaze. What wonder, then, that moral sentiments are found of such influence in life; though springing from principles, which may appear, at first sight, somewhat small and delicate? But these principles, we must remark, are social and universal: They form, in a manner, the *party* of human-kind against vice or disorder, its common enemy: And as the benevolent concern for others is diffused, in a greater or less degree, over all men, and is the same in all, it occurs more frequently in discourse, is cherished by society and conversation, and the blame and approbation, consequent on it, are thereby rouzed from that lethargy, into which they are probably lulled, in solitary and uncultivated nature. Other passions, though perhaps originally stronger, yet being selfish and private, are often overpowered by its force, and yield the dominion of our breast to those social and public principles.

10   Another spring of our constitution, that brings a great addition of force to moral sentiment, is, the love of fame; which rules, with such uncontrouled authority, in all generous minds, and is often the grand object of all their designs and undertakings. By our continual and earnest pursuit of a character, a name, a reputation in the world, we bring our own deportment and conduct frequently in review, and consider how they appear in the eyes of those, who approach and regard us. This constant habit of surveying ourselves, as it were, in reflection, keeps alive all the sentiments of right and wrong, and begets, in noble natures, a certain reverence for themselves as well as others; which is the surest guardian of every virtue. The animal conveniencies and pleasures sink gradually in their value; while every inward beauty and moral grace is studiously acquired, and the mind is accomplished in every perfection, which can adorn or embellish a rational creature.

11   Here is the most perfect morality with which we are acquainted: Here is displayed the force of many sympathies. Our moral sentiment is itself a feeling chiefly of that nature: And our regard to a character with others seems to arise only from a care of preserving a character with ourselves; and in order to attain this end, we find it necessary to prop our tottering judgment on the correspondent approbation of mankind.

12   But, that we may accommodate matters, and remove, if possible, every difficulty, let us allow all these reasonings to be false. Let us allow, that, when we resolve the pleasure, which arises from views of utility, into the sentiments of humanity and sympathy, we have embraced a wrong hypothesis. Let us confess it necessary to find some other explication of that

applause, which is paid to objects, whether inanimate, animate, or rational, if they have a tendency to promote the welfare and advantage of mankind. However difficult it be to conceive, that an object is approved of on account of its tendency to a certain end, while the end itself is totally indifferent; let us swallow this absurdity, and consider what are the consequences. The preceding delineation or definition of PERSONAL MERIT must still retain its evidence and authority: It must still be allowed, that every quality of the mind, which is *useful* or *agreeable* to the *person himself* or to *others*, communicates a pleasure to the spectator, engages his esteem, and is admitted under the honourable denomination of virtue or merit. Are not justice, fidelity, honour, veracity, allegiance, chastity, esteemed solely on account of their tendency to promote the good of society? Is not that tendency inseparable from humanity, benevolence, lenity, generosity, gratitude, moderation, tenderness, friendship, and all the other social virtues? Can it possibly be doubted, that industry, discretion, frugality, secrecy, order, perseverance, forethought, judgment, and this whole class of virtues and accomplishments, of which many pages would not contain the catalogue; can it be doubted, I say, that the tendency of these qualities to promote the interest and happiness of their possessor, is the sole foundation of their merit? Who can dispute that a mind, which supports a perpetual serenity and chearfulness, a noble dignity and undaunted spirit, a tender affection and good-will to all around; as it has more enjoyment within itself, is also a more animating and rejoicing spectacle, than if dejected with melancholy, tormented with anxiety, irritated with rage, or sunk into the most abject baseness and degeneracy? And as to the qualities, immediately *agreeable to others*, they speak sufficiently for themselves; and he must be unhappy, indeed, either in his own temper, or in his situation and company, who has never perceived the charms of a facetious wit or flowing affability, of a delicate modesty or decent genteelness of address and manner.

I am sensible, that nothing can be more unphilosophical than to be positive or dogmatical on any subject; and that, even if *excessive* scepticism could be maintained, it would not be more destructive to all just reasoning and enquiry. I am convinced, that, where men are the most sure and arrogant, they are commonly the most mistaken, and have there given reins to passion, without that proper deliberation and suspence, which can alone secure them from the grossest absurdities. Yet, I must confess, that this enumeration puts the matter in so strong a light, that I cannot, *at present*, be more assured of any truth, which I learn from reasoning and argument, than that personal merit consists entirely in the usefulness or agreeableness of qualities to the person himself possessed of them, or to others, who have any intercourse with him. But when I reflect, that, though the

13

bulk and figure of the earth have been measured and delineated, though
the motions of the tides have been accounted for, the order and economy
of the heavenly bodies subjected to their proper laws, and INFINITE itself reduced to calculation; yet men still dispute concerning the foundation of their moral duties: When I reflect on this, I say, I fall back into
diffidence and scepticism, and suspect, that an hypothesis, so obvious, had
it been a true one, would, long ere now, have been received by the unani-
mous suffrage and consent of mankind.

Part II.

14   Having explained the moral *approbation* attending merit or virtue, there
remains nothing, but briefly to consider our interested *obligation* to it, and
to enquire, whether every man, who has any regard to his own happiness
and welfare, will not best find his account in the practice of every moral
duty. If this can be clearly ascertained from the foregoing theory, we shall
have the satisfaction to reflect, that we have advanced principles, which
not only, it is hoped, will stand the test of reasoning and enquiry, but may
contribute to the amendment of men's lives, and their improvement in
morality and social virtue. And though the philosophical truth of any
proposition by no means depends on its tendency to promote the interests
of society; yet a man has but a bad grace, who delivers a theory, however
true, which, he must confess, leads to a practice dangerous and pernicious. Why rake into those corners of nature, which spread a nuisance all
around? Why dig up the pestilence from the pit, in which it is buried? The
ingenuity of your researches may be admired; but your systems will be detested: And mankind will agree, if they cannot refute them, to sink them,
at least, in eternal silence and oblivion. Truths, which are *pernicious* to society, if any such there be, will yield to errors, which are salutary and *advantageous*.

15   But what philosophical truths can be more advantageous to society,
than those here delivered, which represent virtue in all her genuine and
most engaging charms, and make us approach her with ease, familiarity,
and affection? The dismal dress falls off, with which many divines, and
some philosophers have covered her; and nothing appears but gentleness,
humanity, beneficence, affability; nay even, at proper intervals, play, frolic,
and gaiety. She talks not of useless austerities and rigours, suffering and
self-denial. She declares, that her sole purpose is, to make her votaries and
all mankind, during every instant of their existence, if possible, cheerful
and happy; nor does she ever willingly part with any pleasure but in hopes
of ample compensation in some other period of their lives. The sole
trouble, which she demands, is that of just calculation, and a steady preference of the greater happiness. And if any austere pretenders approach

her, enemies to joy and pleasure, she either rejects them as hypocrites and deceivers; or if she admit them in her train, they are ranked however, among the least favoured of her votaries.

And, indeed, to drop all figurative expression, what hopes can we ever   16
have of engaging mankind to a practice, which we confess full of austerity and rigour? Or what theory of morals can ever serve any useful purpose, unless it can show, by a particular detail, that all the duties, which it rec-ommends, are also the true interest of each individual? The peculiar ad-vantage of the foregoing system seems to be, that it furnishes proper mediums for that purpose.

That the virtues which are immediately *useful* or *agreeable* to the person   17
possessed of them, are desirable in a view to self-interest, it would surely be superfluous to prove. Moralists, indeed, may spare themselves all the pains, which they often take in recommending these duties. To what pur-pose collect arguments to evince, that temperance is advantageous, and the excesses of pleasure hurtful? When it appears, that these excesses are only denominated such, because they are hurtful; and that, if the unlim-ited use of strong liquors, for instance, no more impaired health or the faculties of mind and body than the use of air or water, it would not be a whit more vicious or blameable.

It seems equally superfluous to prove, that the *companionable* virtues of   18
good manners and wit, decency and genteelness, are more desirable than the contrary qualities. Vanity alone, without any other consideration, is a sufficient motive to make us wish for the possession of these accomplish-ments. No man was ever willingly deficient in this particular. All our fail-ures here proceed from bad education, want of capacity, or a perverse and unpliable disposition. Would you have your company coveted, admired, followed; rather than hated, despised, avoided? Can any one seriously de-liberate in the case? As no enjoyment is sincere, without some reference to company and society; so no society can be agreeable, or even tolerable, where a man feels his presence unwelcome, and discovers all around him symptoms of disgust and aversion.

But why, in the greater society or confederacy of mankind, should not   19
the case be the same as in particular clubs and companies? Why is it more doubtful, that the enlarged virtues of humanity, generosity, beneficence, are desirable with a view to happiness and self-interest, than the limited endowments of ingenuity and politeness? Are we apprehensive, lest those social affections interfere, in a greater and more immediate degree than any other pursuits, with private utility, and cannot be gratified, without some important sacrifice of honour and advantage? If so, we are but ill in-structed in the nature of the human passions, and are more influenced by verbal distinctions than by real differences.

20   Whatever contradiction may vulgarly be supposed between the *selfish*
and *social* sentiments or dispositions, they are really no more opposite
than selfish and ambitious, selfish and revengeful, selfish and vain. It is
requisite, that there be an original propensity of some kind, in order to be
a basis to self-love, by giving a relish to the objects of its pursuit; and none
more fit for this purpose than benevolence or humanity. The goods of fortune are spent in one gratification or another: The miser, who accumulates
his annual income, and lends it out at interest, has really spent it in the
gratification of his avarice. And it would be difficult to show, why a man is
more a loser by a generous action, than by any other method of expence;
since the utmost which he can attain, by the most elaborate selfishness, is
the indulgence of some affection.

21   Now if life, without passion, must be altogether insipid and tiresome;
let a man suppose that he has full power of modelling his own disposition,
and let him deliberate what appetite or desire he would choose for the
foundation of his happiness and enjoyment. Every affection, he would observe, when gratified by success, gives a satisfaction proportioned to its
force and violence: but besides this advantage, common to all, the immediate feeling of benevolence and friendship, humanity and kindness, is
sweet, smooth, tender, and agreeable, independent of all fortune and accidents. These virtues are besides attended with a pleasing consciousness or
remembrance, and keep us in humour with ourselves as well as others;
while we retain the agreeable reflection of having done our part towards
mankind and society. And though all men show a jealousy of our success
in the pursuits of avarice and ambition; yet are we almost sure of their
good-will and good-wishes, so long as we persevere in the paths of virtue,
and employ ourselves in the execution of generous plans and purposes.
What other passion is there where we shall find so many advantages
united; an agreeable sentiment, a pleasing consciousness, a good reputation? But of these truths, we may observe, men are of themselves, pretty
much convinced; nor are they deficient in their duty to society, because
they would not wish to be generous, friendly, and humane; but because
they do not feel themselves such.

22   Treating vice with the greatest candour, and making it all possible concessions, we must acknowledge, that there is not, in any instance, the
smallest pretext for giving it the preference above virtue, with a view to
self-interest; except, perhaps, in the case of justice, where a man, taking
things in a certain light, may often seem to be a loser by his integrity. And
though it is allowed, that, without a regard to property, no society could
subsist; yet, according to the imperfect way in which human affairs are
conducted, a sensible knave, in particular incidents, may think, that an act
of iniquity or infidelity will make a considerable addition to his fortune,

without causing any considerable breach in the social union and confederacy. That *honesty is the best policy*, may be a good general rule; but is liable to many exceptions: And he, it may, perhaps, be thought, conducts himself with most wisdom, who observes the general rule, and takes advantage of all the exceptions.

I must confess, that, if a man think, that this reasoning much requires an answer, it will be a little difficult to find any, which will to him appear satisfactory and convincing. If his heart rebel not against such pernicious maxims, if he feel no reluctance to the thoughts of villany or baseness, he has indeed lost a considerable motive to virtue; and we may expect, that his practice will be answerable to his speculation. But in all ingenuous natures, the antipathy to treachery and roguery is too strong to be counterbalanced by any views of profit or pecuniary advantage. Inward peace of mind, consciousness of integrity, a satisfactory review of our own conduct; these are circumstances very requisite to happiness, and will be cherished and cultivated by every honest man, who feels the importance of them. 23

Such a one has, besides, the frequent satisfaction of seeing knaves, with all their pretended cunning and abilities, betrayed by their own maxims; and while they purpose to cheat with moderation and secrecy, a tempting incident occurs, nature is frail, and they give into the snare; whence they can never extricate themselves, without a total loss of reputation, and the forfeiture of all future trust and confidence with mankind. 24

But were they ever so secret and successful, the honest man, if he has any tincture of philosophy, or even common observation and reflection, will discover that they themselves are, in the end, the greatest dupes, and have sacrificed the invaluable enjoyment of a character, with themselves at least, for the acquisition of worthless toys and gewgaws. How little is requisite to supply the *necessities* of nature? And in a view to *pleasure*, what comparison between the unbought satisfaction of conversation, society, study, even health and the common beauties of nature, but above all the peaceful reflection on one's own conduct: What comparison, I say, between these, and the feverish, empty amusements of luxury and expence? These natural pleasures, indeed, are really without price; both because they are below all price in their attainment, and above it in their enjoyment. 25

APPENDIX I.
CONCERNING MORAL SENTIMENT.

1   IF the foregoing hypothesis be received, it will now be easy for us to determine the question first started,[1] concerning the general principles of
morals; and though we postponed the decision of that question, lest it
should then involve us in intricate speculations, which are unfit for moral
discourses, we may resume it at present, and examine how far either *reason*
or *sentiment* enters into all decisions of praise or censure.

2   One principal foundation of moral praise being supposed to lie in the
usefulness of any quality or action; it is evident, that *reason* must enter for
a considerable share in all decisions of this kind; since nothing but that
faculty can instruct us in the tendency of qualities and actions, and point
out their beneficial consequences to society and to their possessors. In
many cases, this is an affair liable to great controversy: Doubts may arise;
opposite interests may occur; and a preference must be given to one side,
from very nice views, and a small overbalance of utility. This is particularly remarkable in questions with regard to justice; as is, indeed, natural
to suppose, from that species of utility, which attends this virtue.[2] Were
every single instance of justice, like that of benevolence, useful to society;
this would be a more simple state of the case, and seldom liable to great
controversy. But as single instances of justice are often pernicious in their
first and immediate tendency, and as the advantage to society results only
from the observance of the general rule, and from the concurrence and
combination of several persons in the same equitable conduct; the case
here becomes more intricate and involved. The various circumstances of
society; the various consequences of any practice; the various interests
which may be proposed: These, on many occasions, are doubtful, and subject to great discussion and enquiry. The object of municipal laws is to fix
all the questions with regard to justice: The debates of civilians; the reflections of politicians; the precedents of history and public records, are
all directed to the same purpose. And a very accurate *reason* or *judgment* is
often requisite, to give the true determination, amidst such intricate
doubts arising from obscure or opposite utilities.

3   But though reason, when fully assisted and improved, be sufficient to
instruct us in the pernicious or useful tendency of qualities and actions; it
is not alone sufficient to produce any moral blame or approbation. Utility

---

[1] Sect. I.

[2] See Appendix III.

is only a tendency to a certain end; and were the end totally indifferent to us, we should feel the same indifference towards the means. It is requisite a *sentiment* should here display itself, in order to give a preference to the useful above the pernicious tendencies. This sentiment can be no other than a feeling for the happiness of mankind, and a resentment of their misery; since these are the different ends which virtue and vice have a tendency to promote. Here, therefore, *reason* instructs us in the several tendencies of actions, and *humanity* makes a distinction in favour of those, which are useful and beneficial.

This partition between the faculties of understanding and sentiment, in all moral decisions, seems clear from the preceding hypothesis. But I shall suppose that hypothesis false. It will then be requisite to look out for some other theory, that may be satisfactory; and I dare venture to affirm, that none such will ever be found, so long as we suppose reason to be the sole source of morals. To prove this, it will be proper to weigh the five following considerations. 4

I. It is easy for a false hypothesis to maintain some appearance of truth, while it keeps wholly in generals, makes use of undefined terms, and employs comparisons, instead of instances. This is particularly remarkable in that philosophy, which ascribes the discernment of all moral distinctions to reason alone, without the concurrence of sentiment. It is impossible that, in any particular instance, this hypothesis can so much as be rendered intelligible; whatever specious figure it may make in general declamations and discourses. Examine the crime of *ingratitude*, for instance; which has place, wherever we observe good-will, expressed and known, together with good offices performed, on the one side, and a return of ill-will or indifference, with ill-offices or neglect on the other: Anatomize all these circumstances, and examine, by your reason alone, in what consists the demerit or blame: You never will come to any issue or conclusion. 5

Reason judges either of *matter of fact* or of *relations*. Enquire then, *first*, where is that matter of fact, which we here call *crime*; point it out; determine the time of its existence; describe its essence or nature; explain the sense or faculty, to which it discovers itself. It resides in the mind of the person, who is ungrateful. He must, therefore, feel it, and be conscious of it. But nothing is there, except the passion of ill-will or absolute indifference. You cannot say, that these, of themselves, always, and in all circumstances, are crimes. No: They are only crimes, when directed towards persons, who have before expressed and displayed good-will towards us. Consequently, we may infer, that the crime of ingratitude is not any particular individual *fact*; but arises from a complication of circumstances, which, being presented to the spectator, excites the *sentiment* of blame, by the particular structure and fabric of his mind. 6

7　　　This representation, you say, is false. Crime, indeed, consists not in a particular *fact*, of whose reality we are assured by *reason*: But it consists in certain *moral relations*, discovered by reason, in the same manner as we discover, by reason, the truths of geometry or algebra. But what are the relations, I ask, of which you here talk? In the case stated above, I see first good-will and good-offices in one person; then ill-will and ill-offices in the other. Between these, there is the relation of *contrariety*. Does the crime consist in that relation? But suppose a person bore me ill-will or did me ill-offices; and I, in return, were indifferent towards him, or did him good-offices: Here is the same relation of *contrariety*; and yet my conduct is often highly laudable. Twist and turn this matter as much as you will, you can never rest the morality on relation; but must have recourse to the decisions of sentiment.

8　　　When it is affirmed, that two and three are equal to the half of ten; this relation of equality, I understand perfectly. I conceive, that if ten be divided into two parts, of which one has as many units as the other; and if any of these parts be compared to two added to three, it will contain as many units as that compound number. But when you draw thence a comparison to moral relations, I own that I am altogether at a loss to understand you. A moral action, a crime, such as ingratitude, is a complicated object. Does the morality consist in the relation of its parts to each other? How? After what manner? Specify the relation: Be more particular and explicit in your propositions; and you will easily see their falsehood.

9　　　No, say you, the morality consists in the relation of actions to the rule of right; and they are denominated good or ill, according as they agree or disagree with it. What then is this rule of right? In what does it consist? How is it determined? By reason, you say, which examines the moral relations of actions. So that moral relations are determined by the comparison of actions to a rule. And that rule is determined by considering the moral relations of objects. Is not this fine reasoning?

10　　All this is metaphysics, you cry: That is enough: There needs nothing more to give a strong presumption of falsehood. Yes, reply I: Here are metaphysics surely: But they are all on your side, who advance an abstruse hypothesis, which can never be made intelligible, nor quadrate with any particular instance or illustration. The hypothesis which we embrace is plain. It maintains, that morality is determined by sentiment. It defines virtue to be *whatever mental action or quality gives to a spectator the pleasing sentiment of approbation*; and vice the contrary. We then proceed to examine a plain matter of fact, to wit, what actions have this influence: We consider all the circumstances, in which these actions agree: And thence endeavour to extract some general observations with regard to these sentiments. If you call this metaphysics, and find any thing abstruse here, you need only conclude, that your turn of mind is not suited to the moral sciences.

II. When a man, at any time, deliberates concerning his own conduct, 11
(as, whether he had better, in a particular emergence, assist a brother or a
benefactor) he must consider these separate relations, with all the circumstances and situations of the persons, in order to determine the superior
duty and obligation: And in order to determine the proportion of lines in
any triangle, it is necessary to examine the nature of that figure, and the
relations which its several parts bear to each other. But notwithstanding
this appearing similarity in the two cases, there is, at bottom, an extreme
difference between them. A speculative reasoner concerning triangles or
circles considers the several known and given relations of the parts of
these figures; and thence infers some unknown relation, which is dependent on the former. But in moral deliberations, we must be acquainted,
before-hand, with all the objects, and all their relations to each other; and
from a comparison of the whole, fix our choice or approbation. No new
fact to be ascertained: No new relation to be discovered. All the circumstances of the case are supposed to be laid before us, ere we can fix any
sentence of blame or approbation. If any material circumstance be yet unknown or doubtful, we must first employ our enquiry or intellectual faculties to assure us of it; and must suspend for a time all moral decision or
sentiment. While we are ignorant, whether a man were aggressor or not,
how can we determine whether the person, who killed him, be criminal or
innocent? But after every circumstance, every relation is known, the understanding has no farther room to operate, nor any object, on which it
could employ itself. The approbation or blame, which then ensues, cannot
be the work of the judgment, but of the heart; and is not a speculative
proposition or affirmation, but an active feeling or sentiment. In the disquisitions of the understanding, from known circumstances and relations,
we infer some new and unknown. In moral decisions, all the circumstances and relations must be previously known; and the mind, from the
contemplation of the whole, feels some new impression of affection or
disgust, esteem or contempt, approbation or blame.

Hence the great difference between a mistake of *fact* and one of *right*; 12
and hence the reason why the one is commonly criminal and not the other.
When ŒDIPUS killed LAIUS, he was ignorant of the relation, and from circumstances, innocent and involuntary, formed erroneous opinions concerning the action which he committed. But when NERO killed
AGRIPPINA, all the relations between himself and the person, and all the
circumstances of the fact were previously known to him: But the motive of
revenge, or fear, or interest, prevailed in his savage heart over the sentiments of duty and humanity. And when we express that detestation

against him, to which he, himself, in a little time, became insensible; it is not, that we see any relations, of which he was ignorant; but that, from the rectitude of our disposition, we feel sentiments, against which he was hardened, from flattery and a long perseverance in the most enormous crimes. In these sentiments, then, not in a discovery of relations of any kind, do all moral determinations consist. Before we can pretend to form any decision of this kind, every thing must be known and ascertained on the side of the object or action. Nothing remains but to feel, on our part, some sentiment of blame or approbation; whence we pronounce the action criminal or virtuous.

13   III. This doctrine will become still more evident, if we compare moral beauty with natural, to which, in many particulars, it bears so near a resemblance. It is on the proportion, relation, and position of parts, that all natural beauty depends; but it would be absurd thence to infer, that the perception of beauty, like that of truth in geometrical problems, consists wholly in the perception of relations, and was performed entirely by the understanding or intellectual faculties. In all the sciences, our mind, from the known relations, investigates the unknown: But in all decisions of taste or external beauty, all the relations are before-hand obvious to the eye; and we thence proceed to feel a sentiment of complacency or disgust, according to the nature of the object, and disposition of our organs.

14   EUCLID has fully explained all the qualities of the circle; but has not, in any proposition, said a word of its beauty. The reason is evident. The beauty is not a quality of the circle. It lies not in any part of the line, whose parts are equally distant from a common center. It is only the effect, which that figure produces upon the mind, whose peculiar fabric or structure renders it susceptible of such sentiments. In vain would you look for it in the circle, or seek it, either by your senses or by mathematical reasonings, in all the properties of that figure.

15   Attend to PALLADIO and PERRAULT, while they explain all the parts and proportions of a pillar: They talk of the cornice and frieze and base and entablature and shaft and architrave; and give the description and position of each of these members. But should you ask the description and position of its beauty, they would readily reply, that the beauty is not in any of the parts or members of a pillar, but results from the whole, when that complicated figure is presented to an intelligent mind, susceptible to those finer sensations. 'Till such a spectator appear, there is nothing but a figure of such particular dimensions and proportions: From his sentiments alone arise its elegance and beauty.

16   Again; attend to CICERO, while he paints the crimes of a VERRES or a CATILINE; you must acknowledge that the moral turpitude results, in the same manner, from the contemplation of the whole, when presented to a

being, whose organs have such a particular structure and formation. The orator may paint rage, insolence, barbarity on the one side: Meekness, suffering, sorrow, innocence on the other: But if you feel no indignation or compassion arise in you from this complication of circumstances, you would in vain ask him, in what consists the crime or villainy, which he so vehemently exclaims against: At what time or on what subject it first began to exist: And what has a few months afterwards become of it, when every disposition and thought of all the actors is totally altered, or annihilated. No satisfactory answer can be given to any of these questions, upon the abstract hypothesis of morals; and we must at last acknowledge, that the crime or immorality is no particular fact or relation, which can be the object of the understanding: But arises entirely from the sentiment of disapprobation, which, by the structure of human nature, we unavoidably feel on the apprehension of barbarity or treachery.

IV. Inanimate objects may bear to each other all the same relations, which we observe in moral agents; though the former can never be the object of love or hatred, nor are consequently susceptible of merit or iniquity. A young tree, which over-tops and destroys its parent, stands in all the same relations with NERO, when he murdered AGRIPPINA; and if morality consisted merely in relations, would, no doubt, be equally criminal. 17

V. It appears evident, that the ultimate ends of human actions can never, in any case, be accounted for by *reason*, but recommend themselves entirely to the sentiments and affections of mankind, without any dependance on the intellectual faculties. Ask a man, *why he uses exercise*; he will answer, *because he desires to keep his health*. If you then enquire, *why he desires health*, he will readily reply, *because sickness is painful*. If you push your enquiries farther, and desire a reason, *why he hates pain*, it is impossible he can ever give any. This is an ultimate end, and is never referred to any other object. 18

Perhaps, to your second question, *why he desires health*, he may also reply, that *it is necessary for the exercise of his calling*. If you ask, *why he is anxious on that head*, he will answer, *because he desires to get money*. If you demand *Why? It is the instrument of pleasure*, says he. And beyond this it is an absurdity to ask for a reason. It is impossible there can be a progress *in infinitum*; and that one thing can always be a reason, why another is desired. Something must be desirable on its own account, and because of its immediate accord or agreement with human sentiment and affection. 19

Now as virtue is an end, and is desirable on its own account, without fee or reward, merely, for the immediate satisfaction which it conveys; it is requisite that there should be some sentiment, which it touches; some internal taste or feeling, or whatever you please to call it, which distinguishes moral good and evil, and which embraces the one and rejects the other. 20

21   Thus the distinct boundaries and offices of *reason* and of *taste* are easily ascertained. The former conveys the knowledge of truth and falsehood: The latter gives the sentiment of beauty and deformity, vice and virtue. The one discovers objects, as they really stand in nature, without addition or diminution: The other has a productive faculty, and gilding or staining all natural objects with the colours, borrowed from internal sentiment, raises, in a manner, a new creation. Reason, being cool and disengaged, is no motive to action, and directs only the impulse received from appetite or inclination, by showing us the means of attaining happiness or avoiding misery: Taste, as it gives pleasure or pain, and thereby constitutes happiness or misery, becomes a motive to action, and is the first spring or impulse to desire and volition. From circumstances and relations, known or supposed, the former leads us to the discovery of the concealed and unknown: After all circumstances and relations are laid before us, the latter makes us feel from the whole a new sentiment of blame or approbation. The standard of the one, being founded on the nature of things, is eternal and inflexible, even by the will of the Supreme Being: The standard of the other, arising from the internal frame and constitution of animals, is ultimately derived from that Supreme Will, which bestowed on each being its peculiar nature, and arranged the several classes and orders of existence.

APPENDIX II.
OF SELF-LOVE.

THERE is a principle, supposed to prevail among many, which is utterly incompatible with all virtue or moral sentiment; and as it can proceed from nothing but the most depraved disposition, so in its turn it tends still further to encourage that depravity. This principle is, that all *benevolence* is mere hypocrisy, friendship a cheat, public spirit a farce, fidelity a snare to procure trust and confidence; and that, while all of us, at bottom, pursue only our private interest, we wear these fair disguises, in order to put others off their guard, and expose them the more to our wiles and machinations. What heart one must be possessed of who professes such principles, and who feels no internal sentiment that belies so pernicious a theory, it is easy to imagine: And also, what degree of affection and benevolence he can bear to a species, whom he represents under such odious colours, and supposes so little susceptible of gratitude or any return of affection. Or if we should not ascribe these principles wholly to a corrupted heart, we must, at least, account for them from the most careless and precipitate examination. Superficial reasoners, indeed, observing many false pretences among mankind, and feeling, perhaps, no very strong restraint in their own disposition, might draw a general and a hasty conclusion, that all is equally corrupted, and that men, different from all other animals, and indeed from all other species of existence, admit of no degrees of good or bad, but are, in every instance, the same creatures under different disguises and appearances. 1

There is another principle, somewhat resembling the former; which has been much insisted on by philosophers, and has been the foundation of many a system; that, whatever affection one may feel, or imagine he feels for others, no passion is, or can be disinterested; that the most generous friendship, however sincere, is a modification of self-love; and that, even unknown to ourselves, we seek only our own gratification, while we appear the most deeply engaged in schemes for the liberty and happiness of mankind. By a turn of imagination, by a refinement of reflection, by an enthusiasm of passion, we seem to take part in the interests of others, and imagine ourselves divested of all selfish considerations: But, at bottom, the most generous patriot and most niggardly miser, the bravest hero and most abject coward, have, in every action, an equal regard to their own happiness and welfare. 2

Whoever concludes, from the seeming tendency of this opinion, that those, who make profession of it, cannot possibly feel the true sentiments of benevolence, or have any regard for genuine virtue, will often find himself, in practice, very much mistaken. Probity and honour were no 3 strangers to EPICURUS and his sect. ATTICUS and HORACE seem to have enjoyed from nature, and cultivated by reflection, as generous and friendly dispositions as any disciple of the austerer schools. And among the moderns, HOBBES and LOCKE, who maintained the selfish system of morals, lived irreproachable lives; though the former lay not under any restraint of religion, which might supply the defects of his philosophy.

4   An EPICUREAN or a HOBBIST readily allows, that there is such a thing as friendship in the world, without hypocrisy or disguise; though he may attempt, by a philosophical chymistry, to resolve the elements of this passion, if I may so speak, into those of another, and explain every affection to be self-love, twisted and moulded, by a particular turn of imagination, into a variety of appearances. But as the same turn of imagination prevails not in every man, nor gives the same direction to the original passion; this is sufficient, even according to the selfish system, to make the widest difference in human characters, and denominate one man virtuous and humane, another vicious and meanly interested. I esteem the man, whose self-love, by whatever means, is so directed as to give him a concern for others, and render him serviceable to society: As I hate or despise him, who has no regard to any thing beyond his own gratifications and enjoyments. In vain would you suggest, that these characters, though seemingly opposite, are, at bottom, the same, and that a very inconsiderable turn of thought forms the whole difference between them. Each character, notwithstanding these inconsiderable differences, appears to me, in practice, pretty durable and untransmutable. And I find not in this, more than in other subjects, that the natural sentiments, arising from the general appearances of things, are easily destroyed by subtile reflections concerning the minute origin of these appearances. Does not the lively, chearful colour of a countenance inspire me with complacency and pleasure; even though I learn from philosophy, that all difference of complexion arises from the most minute differences of thickness, in the most minute parts of the skin; by means of which a superficies is qualified to reflect one of the original colours of light, and absorb the others?

5   But though the question, concerning the universal or partial selfishness of man be not so material, as is usually imagined, to morality and practice, it is certainly of consequence in the speculative science of human nature, and is a proper object of curiosity and enquiry. It may not, therefore, be unsuitable, in this place, to bestow a few reflections upon it.[1]

6   The most obvious objection to the selfish hypothesis, is, that, as it is

---

[1] Benevolence naturally divides into two kinds, the *general* and the *particular*. The first is, where we have no friendship or connexion or esteem for the person, but feel only a general sympathy with him or a compassion for his pains, and a congratulation with his pleasures. The other species of benevolence is founded on an opinion of

contrary to common feeling and our most unprejudiced notions, there is required the highest stretch of philosophy to establish so extraordinary a paradox. To the most careless observer, there appear to be such dispositions as benevolence and generosity; such affections as love, friendship, compassion, gratitude. These sentiments have their causes, effects, objects, and operations, marked by common language and observation, and plainly distinguished from those of the selfish passions. And as this is the obvious appearance of things, it must be admitted; till some hypothesis be discovered, which, by penetrating deeper into human nature, may prove the former affections to be nothing but modifications of the latter. All attempts of this kind have hitherto proved fruitless, and seem to have proceeded entirely, from that love of *simplicity*, which has been the source of much false reasoning in philosophy. I shall not here enter into any detail on the present subject. Many able philosophers have shown the insufficiency of these systems. And I shall take for granted what, I believe, the smallest reflection will make evident to every impartial enquirer.

But the nature of the subject furnishes the strongest presumption, that 7 no better system will ever, for the future, be invented, in order to account for the origin of the benevolent from the selfish affections, and reduce all the various emotions of the human mind to a perfect simplicity. The case is not the same in this species of philosophy as in physics. Many an hypothesis in nature, contrary to first appearances, has been found, on more accurate scrutiny, solid and satisfactory. Instances of this kind are so frequent, that a judicious, as well as witty philosopher,[2] has ventured to affirm, if there be more than one way, in which any phænomenon may be produced, that there is a general presumption for its arising from the causes, which are the least obvious and familiar. But the presumption always lies on the other side, in all enquiries concerning the origin of our passions, and of the internal operations of the human mind. The simplest and most obvious cause, which can there be assigned for any phænomenon, is probably the true one. When a philosopher, in the explication of his system, is obliged to have recourse to some very intricate and refined reflections, and to suppose them essential to the production of any passion or emotion, we have reason to be extremely on our guard against so

---

virtue, on services done us, or on some particular connexions. Both these sentiments must be allowed real in human nature; but whether they will resolve into some nice considerations of self-love, is a question more curious than important. The former sentiment, to wit, that of general benevolence, or humanity, or sympathy, we shall have occasion frequently to treat of in the course of this enquiry; and I assume it as real, from general experience, without any other proof.

[2] Mons. FONTENELLE. [Bernard le Bovier de Fontenelle, *Conversations on the Plurality of Worlds*.]

fallacious an hypothesis. The affections are not susceptible of any impression from the refinements of reason or imagination; and it is always found, that a vigorous exertion of the latter faculties, necessarily, from the narrow capacity of the human mind, destroys all activity in the former. Our predominant motive or intention is, indeed, frequently concealed from ourselves, when it is mingled and confounded with other motives, which the mind, from vanity or self-conceit, is desirous of supposing more prevalent: But there is no instance, that a concealment of this nature has ever arisen from the abstruseness and intricacy of the motive. A man, that has lost a friend and patron, may flatter himself, that all his grief arises from generous sentiments, without any mixture of narrow or interested considerations: But a man, that grieves for a valuable friend, who needed his patronage and protection; how can we suppose, that his passionate tenderness arises from some metaphysical regards to a self-interest, which has no foundation or reality? We may as well imagine, that minute wheels and springs, like those of a watch, give motion to a loaded waggon, as account for the origin of passion from such abstruse reflections.

8 　　　Animals are found susceptible of kindness, both to their own species and to ours; nor is there, in this case, the least suspicion of disguise or artifice. Shall we account for all *their* sentiments too, from refined deductions of self-interest? Or if we admit a disinterested benevolence in the inferior species, by what rule of analogy can we refuse it in the superior?

9 　　　Love between the sexes begets a complacency and good-will, very distinct from the gratification of an appetite. Tenderness to their offspring, in all sensible beings, is commonly able alone to counter-balance the strongest motives of self-love, and has no manner of dependance on that affection. What interest can a fond mother have in view, who loses her health by assiduous attendance on her sick child, and afterwards languishes and dies of grief, when freed, by its death, from the slavery of that attendance?

10 　　Is gratitude no affection of the human breast, or is that a word merely, without any meaning or reality? Have we no satisfaction in one man's company above another's, and no desire of the welfare of our friend, even though absence or death should prevent us from all participation in it? Or what is it commonly, that gives us any participation in it, even while alive and present, but our affection and regard to him?

11 　　These and a thousand other instances are marks of a general benevolence in human nature, where no *real* interest binds us to the object. And how an *imaginary* interest, known and avowed for such, can be the origin of any passion or emotion, seems difficult to explain. No satisfactory hypothesis of this kind has yet been discovered; nor is there the smallest probability, that the future industry of men will ever be attended with more favourable success.

But farther, if we consider rightly of the matter, we shall find, that the   12
hypothesis, which allows of a disinterested benevolence, distinct from
self-love, has really more *simplicity* in it, and is more conformable to the
analogy of nature, than that which pretends to resolve all friendship and
humanity into this latter principle. There are bodily wants or appetites,
acknowledged by every one, which necessarily precede all sensual enjoyment, and carry us directly to seek possession of the object. Thus, hunger
and thirst have eating and drinking for their end; and from the gratification of these primary appetites arises a pleasure, which may become the
object of another species of desire or inclination, that is secondary and interested. In the same manner, there are mental passions, by which we are
impelled immediately to seek particular objects, such as fame, or power, or
vengeance, without any regard to interest; and when these objects are attained, a pleasing enjoyment ensues, as the consequence of our indulged
affections. Nature must, by the internal frame and constitution of the
mind, give an original propensity to fame, ere we can reap any pleasure
from that acquisition, or pursue it from motives of self-love, and a desire
of happiness. If I have no vanity, I take no delight in praise: If I be void of
ambition, power gives me no enjoyment: If I be not angry, the punishment
of an adversary is totally indifferent to me. In all these cases, there is a passion, which points immediately to the object, and constitutes it our good
or happiness; as there are other secondary passions, which afterwards
arise, and pursue it as a part of our happiness, when once it is constituted
such by our original affections. Were there no appetite of any kind antecedent to self-love, that propensity could scarcely ever exert itself; because we should, in that case, have felt few and slender pains or pleasures,
and have little misery or happiness to avoid or to pursue.

Now where is the difficulty in conceiving, that this may likewise be the   13
case with benevolence and friendship, and that, from the original frame of
our temper, we may feel a desire of another's happiness or good, which, by
means of that affection, becomes our own good, and is afterwards pursued, from the combined motives of benevolence and self-enjoyment?
Who sees not that vengeance, from the force alone of passion, may be so
eagerly pursued, as to make us knowingly neglect every consideration of
ease, interest, or safety; and, like some vindictive animals, infuse our very
souls into the wounds we give an enemy?[3] And what a malignant philosophy must it be, that will not allow, to humanity and friendship, the same

---

[3] Animasque in vulnere ponunt. Virg. ["and lay down their lives in the wound"
(Virgil, *Georgics*, IV; trans. by H. Rushton Fairclough).] "Dum alteri noceat, sui negli-
gens," says Seneca of Anger. De Ira, l. i, 1. ["giving no thought to itself if only it can
hurt another" (Seneca, *Moral Essays*, "On Anger," I; trans. by John W. Basore).]

privileges, which are indisputably granted to the darker passions of enmity and resentment? Such a philosophy is more like a satire than a true
delineation or description of human nature; and may be a good foundation for paradoxical wit and raillery, but is a very bad one for any serious
argument or reasoning.

APPENDIX III.
SOME FARTHER CONSIDERATIONS
WITH REGARD TO JUSTICE.

THE intention of this Appendix is to give some more particular explica- 1
tion of the origin and nature of Justice, and to mark some differences between it and the other virtues.

The social virtues of humanity and benevolence exert their influence 2
immediately, by a direct tendency or instinct, which chiefly keeps in view
the simple object, moving the affections, and comprehends not any
scheme or system, nor the consequences resulting from the concurrence,
imitation, or example of others. A parent flies to the relief of his child;
transported by that natural sympathy, which actuates him, and which affords no leisure to reflect on the sentiments or conduct of the rest of mankind in like circumstances. A generous man chearfully embraces an
opportunity of serving his friend; because he then feels himself under the
dominion of the beneficent affections, nor is he concerned whether any
other person in the universe were ever before actuated by such noble motives, or will ever afterwards prove their influence. In all these cases, the
social passions have in view a single individual object, and pursue the
safety or happiness alone of the person loved and esteemed. With this
they are satisfied: In this, they acquiesce. And as the good, resulting from
their benign influence, is in itself compleat and entire, it also excites the
moral sentiment of approbation, without any reflection on farther consequences, and without any more enlarged views of the concurrence or imitation of the other members of society. On the contrary, were the generous
friend or disinterested patriot to stand alone in the practice of beneficence; this would rather enhance his value in our eyes, and join the praise
of rarity and novelty to his other more exalted merits.

The case is not the same with the social virtues of justice and fidelity. 3
They are highly useful, or indeed absolutely necessary to the well-being of
mankind: But the benefit, resulting from them, is not the consequence of
every individual single act; but arises from the whole scheme or system,
concurred in by the whole, or the greater part of the society. General
peace and order are the attendants of justice or a general abstinence from
the possessions of others: But a particular regard to the particular right of
one individual citizen may frequently, considered in itself, be productive
of pernicious consequences. The result of the individual acts is here, in
many instances, directly opposite to that of the whole system of actions;
and the former may be extremely hurtful, while the latter is, to the highest
degree, advantageous. Riches, inherited from a parent, are, in a bad man's

hand, the instruments of mischief. The right of succession may, in one instance, be hurtful. Its benefit arises only from the observance of the general rule; and it is sufficient, if compensation be thereby made for all the ills and inconveniencies, which flow from particular characters and situations.

4   CYRUS, young and inexperienced, considered only the individual case before him, and reflected on a limited fitness and convenience, when he assigned the long coat to the tall boy, and the short coat to the other of smaller size. His governor instructed him better; while he pointed out more enlarged views and consequences, and informed his pupil of the general, inflexible rules, necessary to support general peace and order in society.

5   The happiness and prosperity of mankind, arising from the social virtue of benevolence and its subdivisions, may be compared to a wall, built by many hands; which still rises by each stone, that is heaped upon it, and receives increase proportional to the diligence and care of each workman. The same happiness, raised by the social virtue of justice and its subdivisions, may be compared to the building of a vault, where each individual stone would, of itself, fall to the ground; nor is the whole fabric supported but by the mutual assistance and combination of its corresponding parts.

6   All the laws of nature, which regulate property, as well as all civil laws, are general, and regard alone some essential circumstances of the case, without taking into consideration the characters, situations, and connexions of the person concerned, or any particular consequences which may result from the determination of these laws, in any particular case which offers. They deprive, without scruple, a beneficent man of all his possessions, if acquired by mistake, without a good title; in order to bestow them on a selfish miser, who has already heaped up immense stores of superfluous riches. Public utility requires, that property should be regulated by general inflexible rules; and though such rules are adopted as best serve the same end of public utility, it is impossible for them to prevent all particular hardships, or make beneficial consequences result from every individual case. It is sufficient, if the whole plan or scheme be necessary to the support of civil society, and if the balance of good, in the main, do thereby preponderate much above that of evil. Even the general laws of the universe, though planned by infinite wisdom, cannot exclude all evil or inconvenience, in every particular operation.

7   It has been asserted by some, that justice arises from HUMAN CONVENTIONS, and proceeds from the voluntary choice, consent, or combination of mankind. If by convention be here meant a *promise* (which is the most usual sense of the word) nothing can be more absurd than this

position. The observance of promises is itself one of the most considerable parts of justice; and we are not surely bound to keep our word, because we have given our word to keep it. But if by convention be meant *a sense of common interest*; which sense each man feels in his own breast, which he remarks in his fellows, and which carries him, in concurrence with others, into a general plan or system of actions, which tends to public utility; it must be owned, that, in this sense, justice arises from human conventions. For if it be allowed (what is, indeed, evident) that the particular consequences of a particular act of justice may be hurtful to the public as well as to individuals; it follows, that every man, in embracing that virtue, must have an eye to the whole plan or system, and must expect the concurrence of his fellows in the same conduct and behaviour. Did all his views terminate in the consequences of each act of his own, his benevolence and humanity, as well as his self-love, might often prescribe to him measures of conduct very different from those, which are agreeable to the strict rules of right and justice.

Thus two men pull the oars of a boat by common convention, for common interest, without any promise or contract: Thus gold and silver are made the measures of exchange; thus speech and words and language are fixed, by human convention and agreement. Whatever is advantageous to two or more persons, if all perform their part; but what loses all advantage, if only one perform, can arise from no other principle. There would otherwise be no motive for any one of them to enter into that scheme of conduct.[1]

8

---

[1] This theory concerning the origin of property, and consequently of justice, is, in the main, the same with that hinted at and adopted by GROTIUS. "Hinc discimus, quæ fuerit causa, ob quam a primæva communione rerum primo mobilium, deinde & immobilium discessum est: nimirum quod cum non contenti homines vesci sponte natis, antra habitare, corpore aut nudo agere, aut corticibus arborum ferarumve pellibus vestito, vitæ genus exquisitius delegissent, industria opus fuit, quam singuli rebus singulis adhiberent: Quo minus autem fructus in commune conferrentur, primum obstitit locorum, in quæ homines discesserunt, distantia, deinde justitiæ & amoris defectus, per quem fiebat, ut nec in labore, nec in consumtione fructuum, quæ debebat, æqualitas servaretur. Simul discimus, quomodo res in proprietatem iverint; non animi actu solo, neque enim scire alii poterant, quid alii suum esse vellent, ut eo abstinerent, & idem velle plures poterant; sed pacto quodam aut expresso, ut per divisionem, aut tacito, ut per occupationem." De jure belli & pacis. Lib. ii. cap. 2, sec. 2, art. 4 & 5. ["From hence we learn, upon what Account Men departed from the antient Community, first of *moveable*, and then of *immoveable* Things: Namely, because Men being no longer contented with what the Earth produced of itself for their Nourishment; being no longer willing to dwell in Caves, to go naked, or covered only with the Barks of Trees, or the Skins of wild Beasts, wanted to live in a more commodious and more agreeable

9   The word, *natural*, is commonly taken in so many senses, and is of so loose a signification, that it seems vain to dispute, whether justice be natural or not. If self-love, if benevolence be natural to man; if reason and forethought be also natural; then may the same epithet be applied to justice, order, fidelity, property, society. Men's inclination, their necessities lead them to combine; their understanding and experience tell them, that this combination is impossible, where each governs himself by no rule, and pays no regard to the possessions of others: And from these passions and reflections conjoined, as soon as we observe like passions and reflections in others, the sentiment of justice, throughout all ages, has infallibly and certainly had place, to some degree or other, in every individual of the human species. In so sagacious an animal, what necessarily arises from the exertion of his intellectual faculties, may justly be esteemed natural.[2]

10   Among all civilized nations, it has been the constant endeavour to remove every thing arbitrary and partial from the decision of property, and to fix the sentence of judges by such general views and considerations, as may be equal to every member of the society. For besides, that nothing could be more dangerous than to accustom the bench, even in the smallest instance, to regard private friendship or enmity; it is certain, that men,

---

Manner; to which End Labour and Industry was necessary, which some employed for one Thing, and others for another. And there was no Possibility then of using Things in common; first, by Reason of the Distance of Places where each was settled; and afterwards because of the Defect of Equity and Love, whereby a just Equality would not have been observed, either in their Labour, or in the Consumption of their Fruits and Revenues.

Thus also we see what was the Original of Property, which was derived not from a mere internal Act of the Mind, since one could not possibly guess what others designed to appropriate to themselves, that he might abstain from it; and besides, several might have had a Mind to the same Thing, at the same Time; but it resulted from a certain Compact and Agreement, either expressly, as by a Division; or else tacitly, as by Seizure. For as soon as living in common was no longer approved of, all Men were supposed, and ought to be supposed to have consented, that each should appropriate to himself, by Right of first Possession, what could not have been divided." (Hugo Grotius, *On the Rights of War and Peace*, Book II, Chapter II, 4; trans. by John Morrice).]

[2] Natural may be opposed, either to what is *unusual*, *miraculous*, or *artificial*. In the two former senses, justice and property are undoubtedly natural. But as they suppose reason, forethought, design, and a social union and confederacy among men, perhaps, that epithet cannot strictly, in the last sense, be applied to them. Had men lived without society, property had never been known, and neither justice nor injustice had ever existed. But society among human creatures, had been impossible, without reason, and forethought. Inferior animals, that unite, are guided by instinct, which supplies the place of reason. But all these disputes are merely verbal.

where they imagine, that there was no other reason for the preference of their adversary but personal favour, are apt to entertain the strongest ill-will against the magistrates and judges. When natural reason, therefore, points out no fixed view of public utility, by which a controversy of property can be decided, positive laws are often framed to supply its place, and direct the procedure of all courts of judicature. Where these too fail, as often happens, precedents are called for; and a former decision, though given itself without any sufficient reason, justly becomes a sufficient reason for a new decision. If direct laws and precedents be wanting, imperfect and indirect ones are brought in aid; and the controverted case is ranged under them, by analogical reasonings and comparisons, and similitudes, and correspondencies, which are often more fanciful than real. In general, it may safely be affirmed, that jurisprudence is, in this respect, different from all the sciences; and that in many of its nicer questions, there cannot properly be said to be truth or falsehood on either side. If one pleader bring the case under any former law or precedent, by a refined analogy or comparison; the opposite pleader is not at a loss to find an opposite analogy or comparison: And the preference given by the judge is often founded more on taste and imagination than on any solid argument. Public utility is the general object of all courts of judicature; and this utility too requires a stable rule in all controversies: But where several rules, nearly equal and indifferent, present themselves, it is a very slight turn of thought, which fixes the decision in favour of either party.[3]

---

[3] That there be a separation or distinction of possessions, and that this separation be steady and constant; this is absolutely required by the interests of society, and hence the origin of justice and property. What possessions are assigned to particular persons; this is, generally speaking, pretty indifferent; and is often determined by very frivolous views and considerations. We shall mention a few particulars.

Were a society formed among several independent members, the most obvious rule, which could be agreed on, would be to annex property to *present* possession, and leave every one a right to what he at present enjoys. The relation of possession, which takes place between the person and the object, naturally draws on the relation of property.

For a like reason, occupation or first possession becomes the foundation of property.

Where a man bestows labour and industry upon any object, which before belonged to no body; as in cutting down and shaping a tree, in cultivating a field, &c., the alterations, which he produces, causes a relation between him and the object, and naturally engages us to annex it to him by the new relation of property. This cause here concurs with the public utility, which consists in the encouragement given to industry and labour.

Perhaps too, private humanity towards the possessor, concurs, in this instance, with the other motives, and engages us to leave with him what he has acquired by his sweat and labour; and what he has flattered himself in the constant enjoyment of. For though

11   We may just observe, before we conclude this subject, that, after the laws of justice are fixed by views of general utility, the injury, the hardship, the harm, which result to any individual from a violation of them, enter very much into consideration, and are a great source of that universal blame, which attends every wrong or iniquity. By the laws of society, this coat, this horse is mine, and *ought* to remain perpetually in my possession: I reckon on the secure enjoyment of it: By depriving me of it, you disappoint my expectations, and doubly displease me, and offend every bystander. It is a public wrong, so far as the rules of equity are violated: It is a private harm, so far as an individual is injured. And though the second consideration could have no place, were not the former previously established: For

---

private humanity can, by no means, be the origin of justice; since the latter virtue so often contradicts the former; yet when the rule of separate and constant possession is once formed by the indispensable necessities of society, private humanity, and an aversion to the doing a hardship to another, may, in a particular instance, give rise to a particular rule of property.

I am much inclined to think, that the right of succession or inheritance much depends on those connexions of the imagination, and that the relation to a former proprietor begetting a relation to the object, is the cause why the property is transferred to a man after the death of his kinsman. It is true; industry is more encouraged by the transference of possession to children or near relations: But this consideration will only have place in a cultivated society; whereas the right of succession is regarded even among the greatest Barbarians.

Acquisition of property by *accession* can be explained no way but by having recourse to the relations and connexions of the imagination.

The property of rivers, by the laws of most nations, and by the natural turn of our thought, is attributed to the proprietors of their banks, excepting such vast rivers as the RHINE or the DANUBE, which seem too large to follow as an accession to the property of the neighbouring fields. Yet even these rivers are considered as the property of that nation, through whose dominions they run; the idea of a nation being of a suitable bulk to correspond with them, and bear them such a relation in the fancy.

The accessions, which are made to land, bordering upon rivers, follow the land, say the civilians, provided it be made by what they call *alluvion*, that is, insensibly and imperceptibly; which are circumstances, that assist the imagination in the conjunction.

Where there is any considerable portion torn at once from one bank and added to another, it becomes not *his* property, whose land it falls on, till it unite with the land, and till the trees and plants have spread their roots into both. Before that, the thought does not sufficiently join them.

In short, we must ever distinguish between the necessity of a separation and constancy in men's possession, and the rules, which assign particular objects to particular persons. The first necessity is obvious, strong, and invincible: The latter may depend on a public utility more light and frivolous, on the sentiment of private humanity and aversion to private hardship, on positive laws, on precedents, analogies, and very fine connexions and turns of the imagination.

otherwise the distinction of *mine* and *thine* would be unknown in society: Yet there is no question, but the regard to general good is much enforced by the respect to particular. What injures the community, without hurting any individual, is often more lightly thought of. But where the greatest public wrong is also conjoined with a considerable private one, no wonder the highest disapprobation attends so iniquitous a behaviour.

APPENDIX IV.
OF SOME VERBAL DISPUTES.

1   NOTHING is more usual than for philosophers to encroach upon the province of grammarians; and to engage in disputes of words, while they imagine, that they are handling controversies of the deepest importance and concern. It was in order to avoid altercations, so frivolous and endless, that I endeavoured to state with the utmost caution the object of our present enquiry; and proposed simply to collect on the one hand, a list of those mental qualities which are the object of love or esteem, and form a part of personal merit, and on the other hand, a catalogue of those qualities, which are the object of censure or reproach, and which detract from the character of the person, possessed of them; subjoining some reflections concerning the origin of these sentiments of praise or blame. On all occasions, where there might arise the least hesitation, I avoided the terms *virtue* and *vice*; because some of those qualities, which I classed among the objects of praise, receive, in the ENGLISH language, the appellation of *talents*, rather than of virtues; as some of the blameable or censurable qualities are often called *defects*, rather than vices. It may now, perhaps, be expected, that, before we conclude this moral enquiry, we should exactly separate the one from the other; should mark the precise boundaries of virtues and talents, vices and defects; and should explain the reason and origin of that distinction. But in order to excuse myself from this undertaking, which would, at last, prove only a grammatical enquiry, I shall subjoin the four following reflections, which shall contain all that I intend to say on the present subject.

2   *First*, I do not find, that in the ENGLISH, or any other modern tongue, the boundaries are exactly fixed between virtues and talents, vices and defects, or that a precise definition can be given of the one as contradistinguished from the other. Were we to say, for instance, that the esteemable qualities alone, which are voluntary, are entitled to the appellation of virtues; we should soon recollect the qualities of courage, equanimity, patience, self-command; with many others, which almost every language classes under this appellation, though they depend little or not at all on our choice. Should we affirm, that the qualities alone, which prompt us to act our part in society, are entitled to that honourable distinction; it must immediately occur, that these are indeed the most valuable qualities, and are commonly denominated the *social* virtues; but that this very epithet supposes, that there are also virtues of another species. Should we lay hold of the distinction between *intellectual* and *moral* endowments, and affirm

the last alone to be the real and genuine virtues, because they alone lead to action; we should find that many of those qualities, usually called intellectual virtues, such as prudence, penetration, discernment, discretion, had also a considerable influence on conduct. The distinction between the *heart* and the *head* may also be adopted: The qualities of the first may be defined such as in their immediate exertion are accompanied with a feeling or sentiment; and these alone may be called the genuine virtues: But industry, frugality, temperance, secrecy, perseverance, and many other laudable powers or habits, generally stiled virtues, are exerted without any immediate sentiment in the person possessed of them; and are only known to him by their effects. It is fortunate, amidst all this seeming perplexity, that the question, being merely verbal, cannot possibly be of any importance. A moral, philosophical discourse needs not enter into all these caprices of language, which are so variable in different dialects, and in different ages of the same dialect. But on the whole, it seems to me, that, though it is always allowed, that there are virtues of many different kinds, yet, when a man is called *virtuous*, or is denominated a man of virtue, we chiefly regard his social qualities, which are, indeed, the most valuable. It is, at the same time, certain, that any remarkable defect in courage, temperance, œconomy, industry, understanding, dignity of mind, would bereave even a very good-natured, honest man of this honourable appellation. Who did ever say, except by way of irony, that such a one was a man of great virtue, but an egregious blockhead?

But, *secondly*, it is no wonder, that languages should not be very precise in marking the boundaries between virtues and talents, vices and defects; since there is so little distinction made in our internal estimation of them. It seems indeed certain, that the *sentiment* of conscious worth, the self-satisfaction proceeding from a review of a man's own conduct and character; it seems certain, I say, that this sentiment, which, though the most common of all others, has no proper name in our language,[1] arises from the endowments of courage and capacity, industry and ingenuity, as well as from any other mental excellencies. Who, on the other hand, is not deeply mortified with reflecting on his own folly and dissoluteness, and feels not a secret sting or compunction, whenever his memory presents

---

[1] The term, pride, is commonly taken in a bad sense; but this sentiment seems indifferent, and may be either good or bad, according as it is well or ill founded, and according to the other circumstances which accompany it. The FRENCH express this sentiment by the term, *amour propre*, but as they also express self-love as well as vanity by the same term, there arises thence a great confusion in ROCHEFOUCAULT, and many of their moral writers.

any past occurrence, where he behaved with stupidity or ill-manners? No time can efface the cruel ideas of a man's own foolish conduct, or of affronts, which cowardice or impudence has brought upon him. They still haunt his solitary hours, damp his most aspiring thoughts, and show him, even to himself, in the most contemptible and most odious colours imaginable.

4   What is there too we are more anxious to conceal from others than such blunders, infirmities, and meannesses, or more dread to have exposed by raillery and satire? And is not the chief object of vanity, our bravery or learning, our wit or breeding, our eloquence or address, our taste or abilities? These we display with care, if not with ostentation; and we commonly show more ambition of excelling in them, than even in the social virtues themselves, which are, in reality, of such superior excellence. Good-nature and honesty, especially the latter, are so indispensably required, that, though the greatest censure attends any violation of these duties, no eminent praise follows such common instances of them, as seem essential to the support of human society. And hence the reason, in my opinion, why, though men often extol so liberally the qualities of their heart, they are shy in commending the endowments of their head: Because the latter virtues, being supposed more rare and extraordinary, are observed to be the more usual objects of pride and self-conceit; and when boasted of, beget a strong suspicion of these sentiments.

5   It is hard to tell, whether you hurt a man's character most by calling him a knave or a coward, and whether a beastly glutton or drunkard be not as odious and contemptible, as a selfish, ungenerous miser. Give me my choice, and I would rather, for my own happiness and self-enjoyment, have a friendly, humane heart, than possess all the other virtues of DEMOSTHENES and PHILIP united: But I would rather pass with the world for one endowed with extensive genius and intrepid courage, and should thence expect stronger instances of general applause and admiration. The figure which a man makes in life, the reception which he meets with in company, the esteem paid him by his acquaintance; all these advantages depend as much upon his good sense and judgment, as upon any other part of his character. Had a man the best intentions in the world, and were the farthest removed from all injustice and violence, he would never be able to make himself be much regarded, without a moderate share, at least, of parts and understanding.

6   What is it then we can here dispute about? If sense and courage, temperance and industry, wisdom and knowledge confessedly form a considerable part of *personal merit*: If a man possessed of these qualities, is both better satisfied with himself, and better entitled to the good-will, esteem, and services of others, than one entirely destitute of them; if, in short, the

sentiments are similar, which arise from these endowments and from the social virtues; is there any reason for being so extremely scrupulous about a *word*, or disputing whether they be entitled to the denomination of virtues? It may, indeed, be pretended, that the sentiment of approbation, which those accomplishments produce, besides its being *inferior*, is also somewhat *different* from that, which attends the virtues of justice and humanity. But this seems not a sufficient reason for ranking them entirely under different classes and appellations. The character of CÆSAR and that of CATO, as drawn by SALLUST, are both of them virtuous, in the strictest and most limited sense of the word; but in a different way: Nor are the sentiments entirely the same, which arise from them. The one produces love; the other, esteem: The one is amiable; the other awful: We should wish to meet the one character in a friend; the other we should be ambitious of in ourselves. In like manner the approbation, which attends temperance or industry or frugality, may be somewhat different from that which is paid to the social virtues, without making them entirely of a different species. And, indeed, we may observe, that these endowments, more than the other virtues, produce not, all of them, the same kind of approbation. Good sense and genius beget esteem and regard: Wit and humour excite love and affection.[2]

Most people, I believe, will naturally, without premeditation, assent to the definition of the elegant and judicious poet.   7

> Virtue (for mere good-nature is a fool)
> Is sense and spirit with humanity.[3]

---

[2] Love and esteem are nearly the same passion, and arise from similar causes. The qualities, which produce both, are such as communicate pleasure. But where this pleasure is severe and serious; or where its object is great, and makes a strong impression, or where it produces any degree of humility and awe: In all these cases, the passion, which arises from the pleasure, is more properly denominated esteem than love. Benevolence attends both: But is connected with love in a more eminent degree. There seems to be still a stronger mixture of pride in contempt than of humility in esteem; and the reason would not be difficult to one, who studied accurately the passions. All these various mixtures and compositions and appearances of sentiment form a very curious subject of speculation, but are wide of our present purpose. Throughout this enquiry, we always consider in general, what qualities are a subject of praise or of censure, without entering into all the minute differences of sentiment, which they excite. It is evident, that whatever is contemned, is also disliked, as well as what is hated; and we here endeavour to take objects, according to their most simple views and appearances. These sciences are but too apt to appear abstract to common readers, even with all the precautions which we can take to clear them from superfluous speculations, and bring them down to every capacity.

[3] The Art of preserving Health. Book 4 [by John Armstrong].

8   What pretensions has a man to our generous assistance or good offices, who has dissipated his wealth in profuse expenses, idle vanities, chimerical projects, dissolute pleasures, or extravagant gaming? These vices (for we scruple not to call them such) bring misery unpitied, and contempt on every one addicted to them.

9   ACHÆUS, a wise and prudent prince, fell into a fatal snare, which cost him his crown and life, after having used every reasonable precaution to guard himself against it. On that account, says the historian, he is a just object of regard and compassion: His betrayers alone of hatred and contempt.[4]

10   The precipitate flight and improvident negligence of POMPEY, at the beginning of the civil wars, appeared such notorious blunders to CICERO, as quite palled his friendship towards that great man. *In the same manner,* says he, *as want of cleanliness, decency, or discretion in a mistress are found to alienate our affections.* For so he expresses himself, where he talks, not in the character of a philosopher, but in that of a statesman and man of the world, to his friend ATTICUS.[5]

11   But the same CICERO, in imitation of all the ancient moralists, when he reasons as a philosopher, enlarges very much his ideas of virtue, and comprehends every laudable quality or endowment of the mind, under that honourable appellation. This leads to the *third* reflection, which we proposed to make, to wit, that the ancient moralists, the best models, made no material distinction among the different species of mental endowments and defects, but treated all alike under the appellation of virtues and vices, and made them indiscriminately the object of their moral reasonings. The *prudence* explained in CICERO's *Offices,*[6] is that sagacity, which leads to the discovery of truth, and preserves us from error and mistake. *Magnanimity, temperance, decency,* are there also at large discoursed of. And as that eloquent moralist followed the common received division of the four cardinal virtues, our social duties form but one head, in the general distribution of his subject.[7]

---

[4] POLYBIUS, lib. viii. cap. 2. [Polybius, *Histories.*]

[5] Lib. ix. epist. 10. [Cicero, *Letters to Atticus.*]

[6] Lib. i. cap. 6. [Cicero, *De officiis.*]

[7] The following passage of CICERO is worth quoting, as being the most clear and express to our purpose, that any thing can be imagined, and, in a dispute, which is chiefly verbal, must, on account of the author, carry an authority, from which there can be no appeal.

"Virtus autem, quæ est per se ipsa laudabilis, et sine qua nihil laudari potest, tamen habet plures partes, quarum alia est alia ad laudationem aptior. Sunt enim aliæ virtutes, quæ videntur in moribus hominum, et quadam comitate ac beneficentia positæ: aliæ, quæ in ingenii aliqua facultate, aut animi magnitudine ac robore. Nam clementia,

We need only peruse the titles of chapters in ARISTOTLE'S Ethics to be   12
convinced, that he ranks courage, temperance, magnificence, magnanimity, modesty, prudence, and a manly openness, among the virtues, as well
as justice and friendship.

To *sustain* and to *abstain*, that is, to be patient and continent, appeared   13
to some of the ancients a summary comprehension of all morals.

EPICTETUS has scarcely ever mentioned the sentiment of humanity and   14
compassion, but in order to put his disciples on their guard against it. The
virtue of the STOICS seems to consist chiefly in a firm temper and a sound
understanding. With them, as with SOLOMON and the eastern moralists,
folly and wisdom are equivalent to vice and virtue.

Men will praise thee, says DAVID,[8] when thou dost well unto thyself. I   15
hate a wise man, says the GREEK poet, who is not wise to himself.[9]

---

justitia, benignitas, fides, fortitudo in periculis communibus, jucunda est auditu in
laudationibus. Omnes enim hæ virtutes non tam ipsis, qui eas in se habent, quam
generi hominum fructuosæ putantur. Sapientia et magnitudo animi, qua omnes res
humanæ tenues et pro nihilo putantur; et in cogitando vis quædam ingenii, et ipsa elo-
quentia admirationis habet non minus, jucunditatis minus. Ipsos enim magis videtur,
quos laudamus, quam illos, apud quos laudamus, ornare ac tueri: sed tamen in lau-
denda jungenda sunt etiam hæc genera virtutum. Ferunt enim aures hominum, cum
illa quæ jucunda et grata, tum etiam illa, quæ mirabilia sunt in virtute, laudari." *De
orat.* lib. ii. cap. 84. ["But virtue, which is praiseworthy in itself and is a necessary element in anything that can be praised, nevertheless contains several divisions, one of
which is more fit to be praised than another. For there are some virtues that are manifested as qualities of people's behaviour and by a sort of kindness and beneficence,
while others consist in intellectual ability or in highmindedness and strength of character; inasmuch, as mercy, justice, kindness, fidelity, courage in common dangers are
acceptable topics in a panegyric, since all these virtues are thought to be beneficial not
so much to their possessors as to the human race in general, whereas wisdom, and
magnanimity that count all human fortunes slight and worthless, and strength and
originality of intellect, and eloquence itself are not less admired it is true but give less
pleasure, because they seem to grace and to safeguard the subjects of panegyrics
themselves rather than the persons before whom they are delivered. But nevertheless
virtues of these kinds also should be introduced in a panegyric, since an audience will
accept the bestowal of praise on the aspects of virtue that call for admiration as well as
on those that give pleasure and gratification" (Cicero, *The Orator*, II, LXXXIV, 343–
344; trans. by H. Rackham).]

I suppose, if CICERO were now alive, it would be found difficult to fetter his moral
sentiments by narrow systems; or persuade him, that no qualities were to be admitted
as *virtues*, or acknowledged to be a part of *personal merit*, but what were recommended
by *The Whole Duty of Man*.

   [8] Psalm 49th

   [9] Μισῶ σοφιστὴν ὅστις οὐχ αὑτῷ σοφός. EURIPIDES. Fr. 111. ["The sage, no sage
for his own ends, I loathe" (Euripides, *Papyri*, 111; trans. by Denys L. Page).]

16   PLUTARCH is no more cramped by systems in his philosophy than in his history. Where he compares the great men of GREECE and ROME, he fairly sets in opposition all their blemishes and accomplishments of whatever kind, and omits nothing considerable, which can either depress or exalt their characters. His moral discourses contain the same free and natural censure of men and manners.

17   The character of HANNIBAL, as drawn by LIVY,[10] is esteemed partial, but allows him many eminent virtues. Never was there a genius, says the historian, more equally fitted for those opposite offices of commanding and obeying; and it were, therefore, difficult to determine whether he rendered himself *dearer* to the general or to the army. To none would HAS-DRUBAL entrust more willingly the conduct of any dangerous enterprize; under none, did the soldiers discover more courage and confidence. Great boldness in facing danger; great prudence in the midst of it. No labour could fatigue his body or subdue his mind. Cold and heat were indifferent to him: Meat and drink he sought as supplies to the necessities of nature, not as gratifications of his voluptuous appetites: Waking or rest he used indiscriminately, by night or by day.—These great VIRTUES were balanced by great VICES: Inhuman cruelty; perfidy more than *punic*; no truth, no faith, no regard to oaths, promises, or religion.

18   The character of ALEXANDER the Sixth, to be found in GUICCIARDIN,[11] is pretty similar, but juster; and is a proof, that even the moderns, where they speak naturally, hold the same language with the ancients. In this pope, says he, there was a singular capacity and judgment: Admirable prudence; a wonderful talent of persuasion; and in all momentous enterprizes, a diligence and dexterity incredible. But these *virtues* were infinitely overbalanced by his *vices*; no faith, no religion, insatiable avarice, exorbitant ambition, and a more than barbarous cruelty.

19   POLYBIUS,[12] reprehending TIMÆUS for his partiality against AGATHO-CLES, whom he himself allows to be the most cruel and impious of all tyrants, says: If he took refuge in SYRACUSE, as asserted by that historian, flying the dirt and smoke and toil of his former profession of a potter; and if proceeding from such slender beginnings, he became master, in a little time, of all SICILY; brought the CARTHAGINIAN state into the utmost danger; and at last died in old age, and in possession of sovereign dignity: Must he not be allowed something prodigious and extraordinary, and to have possessed great talents and capacity for business and action? His

---

[10] Lib. xxi. cap. 4. [Livy, *History.*]

[11] Lib. i. [Francesco Guicciardini, *La storia d'Italia.*]

[12] Lib. xii. [Polybius, *Histories.*]

historian, therefore, ought not to have alone related what tended to his reproach and infamy; but also what might redound to his PRAISE and HONOUR.

In general, we may observe, that the distinction of voluntary or involuntary was little regarded by the ancients in their moral reasonings; where they frequently treated the question as very doubtful, *whether virtue could be taught or not?*[13] They justly considered, that cowardice, meanness, levity, anxiety, impatience, folly, and many other qualities of the mind, might appear ridiculous and deformed, contemptible and odious, though independent of the will. Nor could it be supposed, at all times, in every man's power to attain every kind of mental, more than of exterior beauty. 20

And here there occurs the *fourth* reflection which I purposed to make, in suggesting the reason, why modern philosophers have often followed a course, in their moral enquiries, so different from that of the ancients. In later times, philosophy of all kinds, especially ethics, have been more closely united with theology than ever they were observed to be among the Heathens; and as this latter science admits of no terms of composition, but bends every branch of knowledge to its own purpose, without much regard to the phænomena of nature, or to the unbiassed sentiments of the mind, hence reasoning, and even language, have been warped from their natural course, and distinctions have been endeavoured to be established, where the difference of the objects was, in a manner, imperceptible. Philosophers, or rather divines under that disguise, treating all morals, as on a like footing with civil laws, guarded by the sanctions of reward and punishment, were necessarily led to render this circumstance, of *voluntary* or *involuntary*, the foundation of their whole theory. Every one may employ *terms* in what sense he pleases: But this, in the mean time, must be allowed, that *sentiments* are every day experienced of blame and praise, which have objects beyond the dominion of the will or choice, and of which it behoves us, if not as moralists, as speculative philosophers at least, to give some satisfactory theory and explication. 21

A blemish, a fault, a vice, a crime; these expressions seem to denote different degrees of censure and disapprobation; which are, however, all of them, at the bottom, pretty nearly of the same kind or species. The explication of one will easily lead us into a just conception of the others; and it is of greater consequence to attend to things than to verbal appellations. That we owe a duty to ourselves is confessed even in the most 22

---

[13] Vid. PLATO In MENONE, SENECA *de otio sap.* cap. 31. So also HORACE, *Virtutem doctrina paret, naturane donet.* Epist. lib. i. ep. 18. ["Does wisdom beget virtue, or Nature bring her as a gift?" (Horace, *Epistles*, 18, 100–101; trans. by H. Rushton Fairclough).] ÆSCHINES SOCRATICUS, Dial. I. [Aeschines Socraticus, *Dialogues*.]

vulgar system of morals; and it must be of consequence to examine that duty, in order to see, whether it bears any affinity to that which we owe to society. It is probable, that the approbation, attending the observance of both, is of a similar nature, and arises from similar principles; whatever appellation we may give to either of these excellencies.

A DIALOGUE.

MY friend, PALAMEDES, who is as great a rambler in his principles as in his person, and who has run over, by study and travel, almost every region of the intellectual and material world, surprized me lately with an account of a nation, with whom, he told me, he had passed a considerable part of his life, and whom, he found, in the main, a people extremely civilized and intelligent. 1

There is a country, said he, in the world, called FOURLI, no matter for its longitude or latitude, whose inhabitants have ways of thinking, in many things, particularly in morals, diametrically opposite to ours. When I came among them, I found that I must submit to double pains; first to learn the meaning of the terms in their language, and then to know the import of those terms, and the praise or blame attached to them. After a word had been explained to me, and a character which it expressed had been described, I concluded, that such an epithet must necessarily be the greatest reproach in the world; and was extremely surprized to find one in a public company, apply it to a person, with whom he lived in the strictest intimacy and friendship. *You fancy*, said I, one day, to an acquaintance, *that* CHANGUIS *is your mortal enemy: I love to extinguish quarrels; and I must, therefore, tell you, that I heard him talk of you in the most obliging manner.* But to my great astonishment, when I repeated CHANGUIS'S words, though I had both remembered and understood them perfectly, I found, that they were taken for the most mortal affront, and that I had very innocently rendered the breach between these persons altogether irreparable. 2

As it was my fortune to come among this people on a very advantageous footing, I was immediately introduced to the best company; and being desired by ALCHEIC to live with him, I readily accepted of his invitation; as I found him universally esteemed for his personal merit, and indeed regarded by every one in FOURLI, as a perfect character. 3

One evening he invited me, as an amusement, to bear him company in a serenade, which he intended to give to GULKI, with whom, he told me, he was extremely enamoured; and I soon found that his taste was not singular: For we met many of his rivals, who had come on the same errand. I very naturally concluded, that this mistress of his must be one of the finest women in town; and I already felt a secret inclination to see her, and be acquainted with her. But as the moon began to rise, I was much surprized to find that we were in the midst of the university, where GULKI studied: And I was somewhat ashamed for having attended my friend, on such an errand. 4

I was afterwards told, that ALCHEIC'S choice of GULKI was very much 5 approved of by all the good company in town; and that it was expected, while he gratified his own passion, he would perform to that young man the same good office, which he had himself owed to ELCOUF. It seems ALCHEIC had been very handsome in his youth, had been courted by many lovers; but had bestowed his favours chiefly on the sage ELCOUF; to whom he was supposed to owe, in a great measure, the astonishing progress which he had made in philosophy and virtue.

6   It gave me some surprize that ALCHEIC'S wife (who by-the-by happened also to be his sister) was no wise scandalized at this species of infidelity.

7   Much about the same time I discovered (for it was not attempted to be kept a secret from me or any body) that ALCHEIC was a murderer and a parricide, and had put to death an innocent person, the most nearly connected with him, and whom he was bound to protect and defend by all the ties of nature and humanity. When I asked, with all the caution and deference imaginable, what was his motive for this action; he replied coolly, that he was not then so much at ease in his circumstances as he is at present, and that he had acted, in that particular, by the advice of all his friends.

8   Having heard ALCHEIC'S virtue so extremely celebrated, I pretended to join in the general voice of acclamation, and only asked, by way of curiosity, as a stranger, which of all his noble actions was most highly applauded; and I soon found, that all sentiments were united in giving the preference to the assassination of USBEK. This USBEK had been to the last moment ALCHEIC'S intimate friend, had laid many high obligations upon him, had even saved his life on a certain occasion, and had, by his will, which was found after the murder, made him heir to a considerable part of his fortune. ALCHEIC, it seems, conspired with about twenty or thirty more, most of them also USBEK'S friends; and falling all together on that unhappy man, when he was not aware, they had torne him with a hundred wounds; and given him that reward for all his past favours and obligations. USBEK, said the general voice of the people, had many great and good qualities: His very vices were shining, magnificent, and generous: But this action of ALCHEIC'S sets him far above USBEK in the eyes of all judges of merit; and is one of the noblest that ever perhaps the sun shone upon.

9   Another part of ALCHEIC'S conduct, which I also found highly applauded, was his behaviour towards CALISH, with whom he was joined in a project or undertaking of some importance. CALISH, being a passionate man, gave ALCHEIC, one day, a sound drubbing; which he took very patiently, waited the return of CALISH'S good-humour, kept still a fair correspondence with him; and by that means brought the affair, in which they were joined, to a happy issue, and gained to himself immortal honour by his remarkable temper and moderation.

I have lately received a letter from a correspondent in FOURLI, by which   10
I learn, that, since my departure, ALCHEIC, falling into a bad state of
health, has fairly hanged himself; and has died universally regretted and
applauded in that country. So virtuous and noble a life, says each
FOURLIAN, could not be better crowned than by so noble an end; and
ALCHEIC has proved by this, as well as by all his other actions, what was
his constant principle during his life, and what he boasted of near his last
moments, that a wise man is scarcely inferior to the great god, VITZLI.
This is the name of the supreme deity among the FOURLIANS.

The notions of this people, continued PALAMEDES, are as extraordinary   11
with regard to good-manners and sociableness, as with regard to morals.
My friend ALCHEIC formed once a party for my entertainment, composed
of all the prime wits and philosophers of FOURLI; and each of us brought
his mess along with him to the place where we assembled. I observed one
of them to be worse provided than the rest, and offered him a share of my
mess, which happened to be a roasted pullet: And I could not but remark,
that he and all the rest of the company smiled at my simplicity. I was told,
that ALCHEIC had once so much interest with his club as to prevail with
them to eat in common, and that he had made use of an artifice for that
purpose. He persuaded those, whom he observed to be *worst* provided, to
offer their mess to the company; after which, the others, who had brought
more delicate fare, were ashamed not to make the same offer. This is regarded as so extraordinary an event, that it has since, as I learn, been
recorded in the history of ALCHEIC'S life, composed by one of the greatest
geniuses of FOURLI.

Pray, said I, PALAMEDES, when you were at FOURLI, did you also learn   12
the art of turning your friends into ridicule, by telling them strange stories, and then laughing at them, if they believed you. I assure you, replied
he, had I been disposed to learn such a lesson, there was no place in the
world more proper. My friend, so often mentioned, did nothing, from
morning to night, but sneer, and banter, and rally; and you could scarcely
ever distinguish, whether he were in jest or earnest. But you think then,
that my story is improbable; and that I have used, or rather abused the
privilege of a traveller. To be sure, said I, you were but in jest. Such barbarous and savage manners are not only incompatible with a civilized, intelligent people, such as you said these were; but are scarcely compatible
with human nature. They exceed all we ever read of, among the MINGRE-
LIANS, and TOPINAMBOUES.

Have a care, cried he, have a care! You are not aware that you are speak-   13
ing blasphemy, and are abusing your favourites, the GREEKS, especially
the ATHENIANS, whom I have couched, all along, under these bizarre
names I employed. If you consider aright, there is not one stroke of the

foregoing character, which might not be found in the man of highest merit at ATHENS, without diminishing in the least from the brightness of his character. The amours of the GREEKS, their marriages,[1] and the exposing of their children cannot but strike you immediately. The death of USBEK is an exact counter-part to that of CÆSAR.

14   All to a trifle, said I, interrupting him: You did not mention that USBEK was an usurper.

15   I did not, replied he; lest you should discover the parallel I aimed at. But even adding this circumstance, we should make no scruple, according to our sentiments of morals, to denominate BRUTUS, and CASSIUS, ungrateful traitors and assassins: Though you know, that they are, perhaps, the highest characters of all antiquity; and the ATHENIANS erected statues to them; which they placed near those of HARMODIUS and ARISTOGITON, their own deliverers. And if you think this circumstance, which you mention, so material to absolve these patriots, I shall compensate it by another, not mentioned, which will equally aggravate their crime. A few days before the execution of their fatal purpose, they all swore fealty to CÆSAR; and protesting to hold his person ever sacred, they touched the altar with those hands, which they had already armed for his destruction.[2]

16   I need not remind you of the famous and applauded story of THEMISTOCLES, and of his patience towards EURYBIADES, the SPARTAN, his commanding officer, who, heated by debate, lifted his cane to him in a council of war (the same thing as if he had cudgelled him) *Strike!* cries the ATHENIAN, *strike! but hear me.*

17   You are too good a scholar not to discover the ironical SOCRATES and his ATHENIAN club in my last story; and you will certainly observe, that it is exactly copied from XENOPHON, with a variation only of the names.[3] And I think I have fairly made it appear, that an ATHENIAN man of merit might be such a one as with us would pass for incestuous, a parricide, an assassin, an ungrateful, perjured traitor, and something else too abominable to be named; not to mention his rusticity and ill-manners. And having lived in this manner, his death might be entirely suitable: He might conclude the scene by a desperate act of self-murder, and die with the most absurd blasphemies in his mouth. And notwithstanding all this, he shall have statues, if not altars, erected to his memory; poems and orations

---

[1] The laws of ATHENS allowed a man to marry his sister by the father. SOLON's law forbid pæderasty to slaves, as being an act of too great dignity for such mean persons.

[2] APPIAN. Bell. Civ. lib. ii. SUETONIUS in vita CÆSARIS. [Appian, *Roman History*; Suetonius, *Lives of the Caesars*.]

[3] Mem. Soc. lib. iii. sub fine. [Xenophon, *Memorabilia*.]

shall be composed in his praise; great sects shall be proud of calling themselves by his name; and the most distant posterity shall blindly continue their admiration: Though were such a one to arise among themselves, they would justly regard him with horror and execration.

I might have been aware, replied I, of your artifice. You seem to take 18 pleasure in this topic; and are indeed the only man I ever knew, who was well acquainted with the ancients, and did not extremely admire them. But instead of attacking their philosophy, their eloquence, or poetry, the usual subjects of controversy between us, you now seem to impeach their morals, and accuse them of ignorance in a science, which is the only one, in my opinion, in which they are not surpassed by the moderns. Geometry, physics, astronomy, anatomy, botany, geography, navigation; in these we justly claim the superiority: But what have we to oppose to their moralists? Your representation of things is fallacious. You have no indulgence for the manners and customs of different ages. Would you try a GREEK or ROMAN by the common law of ENGLAND? Hear him defend himself by his own maxims; and then pronounce.

There are no manners so innocent or reasonable, but may be rendered 19 odious or ridiculous, if measured by a standard, unknown to the persons; especially, if you employ a little art or eloquence, in aggravating some circumstances, and extenuating others, as best suits the purpose of your discourse. All these artifices may easily be retorted on you. Could I inform the ATHENIANS, for instance, that there was a nation, in which adultery, both active and passive, so to speak, was in the highest vogue and esteem: In which every man of education chose for his mistress a married woman, the wife, perhaps, of his friend and companion; and valued himself upon these infamous conquests, as much as if he had been several times a conqueror in boxing or wrestling at the *Olympic* games: In which every man also took a pride in his tameness and facility with regard to his own wife, and was glad to make friends or gain interest by allowing her to prostitute her charms; and even, without any such motive, gave her full liberty and indulgence: I ask, what sentiments the ATHENIANS would entertain of such a people; they who never mentioned the crime of adultery but in conjunction with robbery and poisoning? Which would they admire most, the villainy or the meanness of such a conduct?

Should I add, that the same people were as proud of their slavery and 20 dependance as the ATHENIANS of their liberty; and though a man among them were oppressed, disgraced, impoverished, insulted, or imprisoned by the tyrant, he would still regard it as the highest merit to love, serve, and obey him; and even to die for his smallest glory or satisfaction: These noble GREEKS would probably ask me, whether I spoke of a human society, or of some inferior, servile species.

21   It was then I might inform my ATHENIAN audience, that these people, however, wanted not spirit and bravery. If a man, say I, though their intimate friend, should throw out, in a private company, a raillery against them, nearly approaching any of those, with which your generals and demagogues every day regale each other, in the face of the whole city, they never can forgive him; but in order to revenge themselves, they oblige him immediately to run them through the body, or be himself murdered. And if a man, who is an absolute stranger to them, should desire them, at the peril of their own life, to cut the throat of their bosom-companion, they immediately obey, and think themselves highly obliged and honoured by the commission. These are their maxims of honour: This is their favourite morality.

22   But though so ready to draw their sword against their friends and countrymen; no disgrace, no infamy, no pain, no poverty will ever engage these people to turn the point of it against their own breast. A man of rank would row in the gallies, would beg his bread, would languish in prison, would suffer any tortures; and still preserve his wretched life. Rather than escape his enemies by a generous contempt of death, he would infamously receive the same death from his enemies, aggravated by their triumphant insults, and by the most exquisite sufferings.

23   It is very usual too, continue I, among this people to erect jails, where every art of plaguing and tormenting the unhappy prisoners is carefully studied and practised: And in these jails it is usual for a parent voluntarily to shut up several of his children; in order, that another child, whom he owns to have no greater or rather less merit than the rest, may enjoy his whole fortune, and wallow in every kind of voluptuousness and pleasure. Nothing so virtuous in their opinion as this barbarous partiality.

24   But what is more singular in this whimsical nation, say I to the ATHENIANS, is, that a frolic of yours during the SATURNALIA,[4] when the slaves are served by their masters, is seriously continued by them throughout the whole year, and throughout the whole course of their lives; accompanied too with some circumstances, which still farther augment the absurdity and ridicule. Your sport only elevates for a few days those whom fortune has thrown down, and whom she too, in sport, may really elevate for ever above you: But this nation gravely exalts those, whom nature has subjected to them, and whose inferiority and infirmities are absolutely incurable. The women, though without virtue, are their masters and sovereigns: These they reverence, praise, and magnify: To these, they pay

---

[4] The GREEKS kept the feast of SATURN or CHRONUS, as well as the ROMANS. See LUCIAN. Epist. SATURN. [Lucian, *Saturnalia*.]

the highest deference and respect: And in all places and all times, the superiority of the females is readily acknowledged and submitted to by every one, who has the least pretensions to education and politeness. Scarce any crime would be so universally detested as an infraction of this rule.

You need go no further, replied PALAMEDES; I can easily conjecture the 25 people whom you aim at. The strokes, with which you have painted them, are pretty just; and yet you must acknowledge, that scarce any people are to be found, either in ancient or modern times, whose national character is, upon the whole, less liable to exception. But I give you thanks for helping me out with my argument. I had no intention of exalting the moderns at the expence of the ancients. I only meant to represent the uncertainty of all these judgments concerning characters; and to convince you, that fashion, vogue, custom, and law, were the chief foundation of all moral determinations. The ATHENIANS surely, were a civilized, intelligent people, if ever there were one; and yet their man of merit might, in this age, be held in horror and execration. The FRENCH are also, without doubt, a very civilized, intelligent people; and yet their man of merit might, with the ATHENIANS, be an object of the highest contempt and ridicule, and even hatred. And what renders the matter more extraordinary: These two people are supposed to be the most similar in their national character of any in ancient and modern times; and while the ENGLISH flatter themselves that they resemble the ROMANS, their neighbours on the continent draw the parallel between themselves and those polite GREEKS. What wide difference, therefore, in the sentiments of morals, must be found between civilized nations and Barbarians, or between nations whose characters have little in common? How shall we pretend to fix a standard for judgments of this nature?

By tracing matters, replied I, a little higher, and examining the first 26 principles, which each nation establishes, of blame or censure. The RHINE flows north, the RHONE south; yet both spring from the *same* mountain, and are also actuated, in their opposite directions, by the *same* principle of gravity. The different inclinations of the ground, on which they run, cause all the difference of their courses.

In how many circumstances would an ATHENIAN and a FRENCH man of 27 merit certainly resemble each other? Good sense, knowledge, wit, eloquence, humanity, fidelity, truth, justice, courage, temperance, constancy, dignity of mind: These you have all omitted; in order to insist only on the points, in which they may, by accident, differ. Very well: I am willing to comply with you; and shall endeavour to account for these differences from the most universal, established principles of morals.

The GREEK loves, I care not to examine more particularly. I shall only 28 observe, that, however blameable, they arose from a very innocent cause,

the frequency of the gymnastic exercises among that people; and were recommended, though absurdly, as the source of friendship, sympathy, mutual
attachment, and fidelity;[5] qualities esteemed in all nations and all ages.

29   The marriage of half-brothers and sisters seems no great difficulty.
Love between the nearer relations is contrary to reason and public utility;
but the precise point, where we are to stop, can scarcely be determined by
natural reason; and is therefore a very proper subject for municipal law or
custom. If the ATHENIANS went a little too far on the one side, the canon
law has surely pushed matters a great way into the other extreme.[6]

30   Had you asked a parent at ATHENS, why he bereaved his child of that
life, which he had so lately given it. It is because I love it, he would reply;
and regard the poverty which it must inherit from me, as a greater evil
than death, which it is not capable of dreading, feeling, or resenting.[7]

31   How is public liberty, the most valuable of all blessings, to be recovered
from the hands of an usurper or tyrant, if his power shields him from
public rebellion, and our scruples from private vengeance? That his crime
is capital by law, you acknowledge: And must the highest aggravation of
his crime, the putting of himself above law, form his full security? You can
reply nothing, but by showing the great inconveniencies of assassination;
which could any one have proved clearly to the ancients, he had reformed
their sentiments in this particular.

32   Again, to cast your eye on the picture which I have drawn of modern
manners; there is almost as great difficulty, I acknowledge, to justify
FRENCH as GREEK gallantry; except only, that the former is much more
natural and agreeable than the latter. But our neighbours, it seems, have
resolved to sacrifice some of the domestic to the sociable pleasures; and to
prefer ease, freedom, and an open commerce to a strict fidelity and constancy. These ends are both good, and are somewhat difficult to reconcile;
nor need we be surprised, if the customs of nations incline too much,
sometimes to the one side, sometimes to the other.

33   The most inviolable attachment to the laws of our country is every
where acknowledged a capital virtue; and where the people are not so
happy, as to have any legislature but a single person, the strictest loyalty is,
in that case, the truest patriotism.

34   Nothing surely can be more absurd and barbarous than the practice of
duelling; but those, who justify it, say, that it begets civility and good-
manners. And a duellist, you may observe, always values himself upon his

---

[5] PLAT. Symp. p. 182. ex. edit. Ser. [Plato, *Symposium*.]

[6] See Enquiry, Sect. IV.

[7] PLUT. de amore prolis, sub fine. ["On Affection for Offspring" (Plutarch, *Moralia*).]

courage, his sense of honour, his fidelity and friendship; qualities, which are here indeed very oddly directed, but which have been esteemed universally, since the foundation of the world.

Have the gods forbid self-murder? An ATHENIAN allows, that it ought 35 to be forborn. Has the Deity permitted it? A FRENCHMAN allows that death is preferable to pain and infamy.

You see then, continued I, that the principles upon which men reason 36 in morals are always the same; though the conclusions which they draw are often very different. That they all reason aright with regard to this subject, more than with regard to any other, it is not incumbent on any moralist to show. It is sufficient, that the original principles of censure or blame are uniform, and that erroneous conclusions can be corrected by sounder reasoning and larger experience. Though many ages have elapsed since the fall of GREECE and ROME; though many changes have arrived in religion, language, laws, and customs; none of these revolutions has ever produced any considerable innovation in the primary sentiments of morals, more than in those of external beauty. Some minute differences, perhaps, may be observed in both. HORACE[8] celebrates a low forehead, and ANACREON joined eye-brows:[9] But the APOLLO and the VENUS of antiquity are still our models for male and female beauty; in like manner as the character of SCIPIO continues our standard for the glory of heroes, and that of CORNELIA for the honour of matrons.

It appears, that there never was any quality recommended by any one, 37 as a virtue or moral excellence, but on account of its being *useful*, or *agreeable* to a man *himself*, or to *others*. For what other reason can ever be assigned for praise or approbation? Or where would be the sense of extolling a *good* character or action, which, at the same time, is allowed to be *good for nothing?* All the differences, therefore, in morals, may be reduced to this one general foundation, and may be accounted for by the different views, which people take of these circumstances.

Sometimes men differ in their judgment about the usefulness of any 38 habit or action: Sometimes also the peculiar circumstances of things render one moral quality more useful than others, and give it a peculiar preference.

It is not surprising, that, during a period of war and disorder, the mili- 39 tary virtues should be more celebrated than the pacific, and attract more the admiration and attention of mankind. "How usual is it," says TULLY,[10]

---

[8] Epist. lib. i. epis. 7. Also lib. i. ode 3. [Horace, *Epistles*.]

[9] Ode 28. [Anacreon, *Anacreontea*.] PETRONIUS (cap. 126) joins both these circumstances as beauties. [Petronius, *Satyricon*.]

[10] Tusc. Quæst. lib. ii. [Cicero, *Tusculan Disputations*.]

"to find CIMBRIANS, CELTIBERIANS, and other Barbarians, who bear, with inflexible constancy, all the fatigues and dangers of the field; but are immediately dispirited under the pain and hazard of a languishing distemper: While, on the other hand, the GREEKS patiently endure the slow approaches of death, when armed with sickness and disease; but timorously fly his presence, when he attacks them violently with swords and falchions!" So different is even the same virtue of courage among warlike or peaceful nations! And indeed, we may observe, that, as the difference between war and peace is the greatest that arises among nations and public societies, it produces also the greatest variations in moral sentiment, and diversifies the most our ideas of virtue and personal merit.

40   Sometimes too, magnanimity, greatness of mind, disdain of slavery, inflexible rigour and integrity, may better suit the circumstances of one age than those of another, and have a more kindly influence, both on public affairs, and on a man's own safety and advancement. Our idea of merit, therefore, will also vary a little with these variations; and LABEO, perhaps, be censured for the same qualities, which procured CATO the highest approbation.

41   A degree of luxury may be ruinous and pernicious in a native of SWITZERLAND, which only fosters the arts, and encourages industry in a FRENCHMAN or ENGLISHMAN. We are not, therefore, to expect, either the same sentiments, or the same laws in BERNE, which prevail in LONDON or PARIS.

42   Different customs have also some influence as well as different utilities; and by giving an early biass to the mind, may produce a superior propensity, either to the useful or the agreeable qualities; to those which regard self, or those which extend to society. These four sources of moral sentiment still subsist; but particular accidents may, at one time, make any one of them flow with greater abundance than at another.

43   The customs of some nations shut up the women from all social commerce: Those of others make them so essential a part of society and conversation, that, except where business is transacted, the male-sex alone are supposed almost wholly incapable of mutual discourse and entertainment. As this difference is the most material that can happen in private life, it must also produce the greatest variation in our moral sentiments.

44   Of all nations in the world, where polygamy was not allowed, the GREEKS seem to have been the most reserved in their commerce with the fair sex, and to have imposed on them the strictest laws of modesty and decency. We have a strong instance of this in an oration of LYSIAS.[11] A

---

[11] Orat. 33. [Lysias, *Orations.*]

widow injured, ruined, undone, calls a meeting of a few of her nearest friends and relations; and though never before accustomed, says the orator, to speak in the presence of men, the distress of her circumstances constrained her to lay the case before them. The very opening of her mouth in such company required, it seems, an apology.

When DEMOSTHENES prosecuted his tutors, to make them refund his 45 patrimony, it became necessary for him, in the course of the law-suit, to prove that the marriage of APHOBUS'S sister with ONETER was entirely fraudulent, and that, notwithstanding her sham marriage, she had lived with her brother at ATHENS for two years past, ever since her divorce from her former husband. And it is remarkable, that though these were people of the first fortune and distinction in the city, the orator could prove this fact no way, but by calling for her female slaves to be put to the question, and by the evidence of one physician, who had seen her in her brother's house during her illness.[12] So reserved were GREEK manners.

We may be assured, that an extreme purity of manners was the conse- 46 quence of this reserve. Accordingly we find, that, except the fabulous stories of an HELEN and a CLYTEMNESTRA, there scarcely is an instance of any event in the GREEK history, which proceeded from the intrigues of women. On the other hand, in modern times, particularly in a neighbouring nation, the females enter into all transactions and all management of church and state: And no man can expect success, who takes not care to obtain their good graces. HARRY the third, by incurring the displeasure of the fair, endangered his crown, and lost his life, as much as by his indulgence to heresy.

It is needless to dissemble: The consequence of a very free commerce 47 between the sexes, and of their living much together, will often terminate in intrigues and gallantry. We must sacrifice somewhat of the *useful*, if we be very anxious to obtain all the *agreeable* qualities; and cannot pretend to reach alike every kind of advantage. Instances of licence, daily multiplying, will weaken the scandal with the one sex, and teach the other, by degrees, to adopt the famous maxim of LA FONTAINE, with regard to female infidelity, *that if one knows it, it is but a small matter; if one knows it not, it is nothing.*[13]

Some people are inclined to think, that the best way of adjusting all 48 differences, and of keeping the proper medium between the *agreeable* and the *useful* qualities of the sex, is to live with them after the manner of the

---

[12] In ONETEREM. [Demosthenes, *Against Oneter*, I, 33.]

[13] "Quand on le sçait, c'est peu de chose;
Quand on l'ignore, ce n'est rien."

ROMANS and the ENGLISH (for the customs of these two nations seem similar in this respect);[14] that is, without gallantry,[15] and without jealousy. By a parity of reason, the customs of the SPANIARDS and of the ITALIANS of an age ago (for the present are very different) must be the worst of any; because they favour both gallantry and jealousy.

49   Nor will these different customs of nations affect the one sex only: Their idea of personal merit in the males must also be somewhat different with regard, at least, to conversation, address, and humour. The one nation, where the men live much apart, will naturally more approve of prudence; the other of gaiety. With the one simplicity of manners will be in the highest esteem; with the other, politeness. The one will distinguish themselves by good sense and judgment; the other, by taste and delicacy. The eloquence of the former will shine most in the senate; that of the other, on the theatre.

50   These, I say, are the *natural* effects of such customs. For it must be confessed, that chance has a great influence on national manners; and many events happen in society, which are not to be accounted for by general rules. Who could imagine, for instance, that the ROMANS, who lived freely with their women, should be very indifferent about music, and esteem dancing infamous: While the GREEKS, who never almost saw a woman but in their own houses, were continually piping, singing, and dancing?

51   The differences of moral sentiment, which naturally arise from a republican or monarchical government, are also very obvious; as well as those which proceed from general riches or poverty, union or faction, ignorance or learning. I shall conclude this long discourse with observing, that different customs and situations vary not the original ideas of merit (however they may, some consequences) in any very essential point, and prevail chiefly with regard to young men, who can aspire to the agreeable qualities, and may attempt to please. The MANNER, the ORNA-MENTS, the GRACES, which succeed in this shape, are more arbitrary and casual: But the merit of riper years is almost every where the same; and consists chiefly in integrity, humanity, ability, knowledge, and the other more solid and useful qualities of the human mind.

---

[14] During the time of the emperors, the ROMANS seem to have been more given to intrigues and gallantry than the ENGLISH are at present: And the women of condition, in order to retain their lovers, endeavoured to fix a name of reproach on those who were addicted to wenching and low amours. They were called Ancillarioli. See SENECA, de beneficiis. Lib. i. cap, 9. [Seneca, *Moral Essays*, "De beneficiis."] See also MARTIAL. lib. xii. epig. 58. [Martial, *Epigrams*.]

[15] The gallantry here meant is that of amours and attachments, not that of complaisance, which is as much paid to the fair-sex in ENGLAND as in any other country.

What you insist on, replied PALAMEDES, may have some foundation, 52
when you adhere to the maxims of common life and ordinary conduct.
Experience and the practice of the world readily correct any great extravagance on either side. But what say you to *artificial* lives and manners?
How do you reconcile the maxims, on which, in different ages and nations, these are founded?

What do you understand by *artificial* lives and manners? said I. I ex- 53
plain myself, replied he. You know, that religion had, in ancient times, very
little influence on common life, and that, after men had performed their
duty in sacrifices and prayers at the temple, they thought, that the gods
left the rest of their conduct to themselves, and were little pleased or of-
fended with those virtues or vices, which only affected the peace and happiness of human society. In those ages, it was the business of philosophy
alone to regulate men's ordinary behaviour and deportment; and accordingly, we may observe, that this being the sole principle, by which a man
could elevate himself above his fellows, it acquired a mighty ascendant
over many, and produced great singularities of maxims and of conduct. At
present, when philosophy has lost the allurement of novelty, it has no such
extensive influence; but seems to confine itself mostly to speculations in
the closet; in the same manner, as the ancient religion was limited to sacrifices in the temple. Its place is now supplied by the modern religion,
which inspects our whole conduct, and prescribes an universal rule to our
actions, to our words, to our very thoughts and inclinations; a rule so
much the more austere, as it is guarded by infinite, though distant, rewards and punishments; and no infraction of it can ever be concealed or
disguised.

DIOGENES is the most celebrated model of extravagant philosophy. Let 54
us seek a parallel to him in modern times. We shall not disgrace any philosophic name by a comparison with the DOMINICS or LOYOLAS, or any can-
onized monk or friar. Let us compare him to PASCAL, a man of parts and
genius as well as DIOGENES himself; and perhaps too, a man of virtue, had
he allowed his virtuous inclinations to have exerted and displayed themselves.

The foundation of DIOGENES's conduct was an endeavour to render 55
himself an independent being as much as possible, and to confine all his
wants and desires and pleasures within himself and his own mind: The
aim of PASCAL was to keep a perpetual sense of his dependence before his
eyes, and never to forget his numberless wants and infirmities. The ancient supported himself by magnanimity, ostentation, pride, and the idea
of his own superiority above his fellow-creatures. The modern made constant profession of humility and abasement, of the contempt and hatred of
himself; and endeavoured to attain these supposed virtues, as far as they

are attainable. The austerities of the GREEK were in order to inure himself to hardships, and prevent his ever suffering: Those of the FRENCHMAN were embraced merely for their own sake, and in order to suffer as much as possible. The philosopher indulged himself in the most beastly pleasures, even in public: The saint refused himself the most innocent, even in private. The former thought it his duty to love his friends, and to rail at them, and reprove them, and scold them: The latter endeavoured to be absolutely indifferent towards his nearest relations, and to love and speak well of his enemies. The great object of DIOGENES'S wit was every kind of superstition, that is every kind of religion known in his time. The mortality of the soul was his standard principle; and even his sentiments of a divine providence seem to have been licentious. The most ridiculous superstitions directed PASCAL'S faith and practice; and an extreme contempt of this life, in comparison of the future, was the chief foundation of his conduct.

56   In such a remarkable contrast do these two men stand: Yet both of them have met with general admiration in their different ages, and have been proposed as models of imitation. Where then is the universal standard of morals, which you talk of? And what rule shall we establish for the many different, nay contrary sentiments of mankind?

57   An experiment, said I, which succeeds in the air, will not always succeed in a vacuum. When men depart from the maxims of common reason, and affect these *artificial* lives, as you call them, no one can answer for what will please or displease them. They are in a different element from the rest of mankind; and the natural principles of their mind play not with the same regularity, as if left to themselves, free from the illusions of religious superstition or philosophical enthusiasm.

ESSAYS: MORAL, POLITICAL, AND LITERARY

ESSAY I.
OF THE DELICACY OF TASTE AND PASSION.

SOME People are subject to a certain *delicacy* of *passion*, which makes 1
them extremely sensible to all the accidents of life, and gives them a
lively joy upon every prosperous event, as well as a piercing grief, when
they meet with misfortunes and adversity. Favours and good offices easily engage their friendship; while the smallest injury provokes their resentment. Any honour or mark of distinction elevates them above
measure; but they are as sensibly touched with contempt. People of this
character have, no doubt, more lively enjoyments, as well as more pun-
gent sorrows, than men of cool and sedate tempers: But, I believe, when
every thing is balanced, there is no one, who would not rather be of the
latter character, were he entirely master of his own disposition. Good or
ill fortune is very little at our disposal: And when a person, that has this
sensibility of temper, meets with any misfortune, his sorrow or resentment takes entire possession of him, and deprives him of all relish in the
common occurrences of life; the right enjoyment of which forms the
chief part of our happiness. Great pleasures are much less frequent than
great pains; so that a sensible temper must meet with fewer trials in the
former way than in the latter. Not to mention, that men of such lively
passions are apt to be transported beyond all bounds of prudence and
discretion, and to take false steps in the conduct of life, which are often
irretrievable.

There is a *delicacy* of *taste* observable in some men, which very much 2
resembles this *delicacy* of *passion*, and produces the same sensibility to
beauty and deformity of every kind, as that does to prosperity and adversity, obligations and injuries. When you present a poem or a picture to a
man possessed of this talent, the delicacy of his feeling makes him be sensibly touched with every part of it; nor are the masterly strokes perceived
with more exquisite relish and satisfaction, than the negligences or absurdities with disgust and uneasiness. A polite and judicious conversation
affords him the highest entertainment; rudeness or impertinence is as
great a punishment to him. In short, delicacy of taste has the same effect

311

as delicacy of passion: It enlarges the sphere both of our happiness and misery, and makes us sensible to pains as well as pleasures, which escape the rest of mankind.

3   I believe, however, every one will agree with me, that, notwithstanding this resemblance, delicacy of taste is as much to be desired and cultivated as delicacy of passion is to be lamented, and to be remedied, if possible. The good or ill accidents of life are very little at our disposal; but we are pretty much masters what books we shall read, what diversions we shall partake of, and what company we shall keep. Philosophers have endeavoured to render happiness entirely independent of every thing external. That degree of perfection is impossible to be *attained:* But every wise man will endeavour to place his happiness on such objects chiefly as depend upon himself: And *that* is not to be *attained* so much by any other means as by this delicacy of sentiment. When a man is possessed of that talent, he is more happy by what pleases his taste, than by what gratifies his appetites, and receives more enjoyment from a poem or a piece of reasoning than the most expensive luxury can afford.

4   Whatever connexion there may be originally between these two species of delicacy, I am persuaded, that nothing is so proper to cure us of this delicacy of passion, as the cultivating of that higher and more refined taste, which enables us to judge of the characters of men, of compositions of genius, and of the productions of the nobler arts. A greater or less relish for those obvious beauties, which strike the senses, depends entirely upon the greater or less sensibility of the temper: But with regard to the sciences and liberal arts, a fine taste is, in some measure, the same with strong sense, or at least depends so much upon it, that they are inseparable. In order to judge aright of a composition of genius, there are so many views to be taken in, so many circumstances to be compared, and such a knowledge of human nature requisite, that no man, who is not possessed of the soundest judgment, will ever make a tolerable critic in such performances. And this is a new reason for cultivating a relish in the liberal arts. Our judgment will strengthen by this exercise: We shall form juster notions of life: Many things, which please or afflict others, will appear to us too frivolous to engage our attention: And we shall lose by degrees that sensibility and delicacy of passion, which is so incommodious.

5   But perhaps I have gone too far in saying, that a cultivated taste for the polite arts extinguishes the passions, and renders us indifferent to those objects, which are so fondly pursued by the rest of mankind. On farther reflection, I find, that it rather improves our sensibility for all the tender and agreeable passions; at the same time that it renders the mind incapable of the rougher and more boisterous emotions.

Ingenuas didicisse fideliter artes,
Emollit mores, nec sinit esse feros.[1]

For this, I think there may be assigned two very natural reasons. In the 6
first place, nothing is so improving to the temper as the study of the beauties, either of poetry, eloquence, music, or painting. They give a certain elegance of sentiment to which the rest of mankind are strangers. The
emotions which they excite are soft and tender. They draw off the mind
from the hurry of business and interest; cherish reflection; dispose to
tranquillity; and produce an agreeable melancholy, which, of all dispositions of the mind, is the best suited to love and friendship.

In the *second* place, a delicacy of taste is favourable to love and friend- 7
ship, by confining our choice to few people, and making us indifferent to
the company and conversation of the greater part of men. You will seldom
find, that mere men of the world, whatever strong sense they may be endowed with, are very nice in distinguishing characters, or in marking
those insensible differences and gradations, which make one man preferable to another. Any one, that has competent sense, is sufficient for their
entertainment: They talk to him, of their pleasure and affairs, with the
same frankness that they would to another; and finding many, who are fit
to supply his place, they never feel any vacancy or want in his absence. But
to make use of the allusion of a celebrated French[2] author, the judgment
may be compared to a clock or watch, where the most ordinary machine is
sufficient to tell the hours; but the most elaborate alone can point out the
minutes and seconds, and distinguish the smallest differences of time.
One that has well digested his knowledge both of books and men, has little
enjoyment but in the company of a few select companions. He feels too
sensibly, how much all the rest of mankind fall short of the notions which
he has entertained. And, his affections being thus confined within a narrow circle, no wonder he carries them further, than if they were more general and undistinguished. The gaiety and frolic of a bottle companion
improves with him into a solid friendship: And the ardours of a youthful
appetite become an elegant passion.

---

[1] ["A faithful study of the liberal arts humanizes character and permits it not to be
cruel." Ovid, *Epistulae ex Ponto* (*Letters from Pontus*; trans. by A. L. Wheeler).]

[2] *Mons.* FONTENELLE, *Pluralité des Mondes*. Soir. 6. [Bernard le Bovier de
Fontenelle, *Conversations on the Plurality of Worlds*.]

ESSAY II.
OF THE ORIGIN OF GOVERNMENT.

1   MAN, born in a family, is compelled to maintain society, from necessity, from natural inclination, and from habit. The same creature, in his farther progress, is engaged to establish political society, in order to administer justice; without which there can be no peace among them, nor safety, nor mutual intercourse. We are, therefore, to look upon all the vast apparatus of our government, as having ultimately no other object or purpose but the distribution of justice, or, in other words, the support of the twelve judges. Kings and parliaments, fleets and armies, officers of the court and revenue, ambassadors, ministers, and privy-counsellors, are all subordinate in their end to this part of administration. Even the clergy, as their duty leads them to inculcate morality, may justly be thought, so far as regards this world, to have no other useful object of their institution.

2   All men are sensible of the necessity of justice to maintain peace and order; and all men are sensible of the necessity of peace and order for the maintenance of society. Yet, notwithstanding this strong and obvious necessity, such is the frailty or perverseness of our nature! It is impossible to keep men, faithfully and unerringly, in the paths of justice. Some extraordinary circumstances may happen, in which a man finds his interests to be more promoted by fraud or rapine, than hurt by the breach which his injustice makes in the social union. But much more frequently, he is seduced from his great and important, but distant interests, by the allurement of present, though often very frivolous temptations. This great weakness is incurable in human nature.

3   Men must, therefore, endeavour to palliate what they cannot cure. They must institute some persons, under the appellation of magistrates, whose peculiar office it is, to point out the decrees of equity, to punish transgressors, to correct fraud and violence, and to oblige men, however reluctant, to consult their own real and permanent interests. In a word, OBEDIENCE is a new duty which must be invented to support that of JUSTICE; and the tyes of equity must be corroborated by those of allegiance.

4   But still, viewing matters in an abstract light, it may be thought, that nothing is gained by this alliance, and that the factitious duty of obedience, from its very nature, lays as feeble a hold of the human mind, as the primitive and natural duty of justice. Peculiar interests and present temptations may overcome the one as well as the other. They are equally exposed to the same inconvenience. And the man, who is inclined to be a bad neighbour, must be led by the same motives, well or ill understood, to be a bad citizen and subject. Not to mention, that the magistrate himself may often be negligent, or partial, or unjust in his administration.

Experience, however, proves, that there is a great difference between 5
the cases. Order in society, we find, is much better maintaind by means of
government; and our duty to the magistrate is more strictly guarded by
the principles of human nature, than our duty to our fellow-citizens. The
love of dominion is so strong in the breast of man, that many, not only
submit to, but court all the dangers, and fatigues, and cares of government; and men, once raised to that station, though often led astray by private passions, find, in ordinary cases, a visible interest in the impartial
administration of justice. The persons, who first attain this distinction by
the consent, tacit or express, of the people, must be endowed with superior personal qualities of valour, force, integrity, or prudence, which command respect and confidence: and after government is established, a
regard to birth, rank, and station has a mighty influence over men, and en-
forces the decrees of the magistrate. The prince or leader exclaims against
every disorder, which disturbs his society. He summons all his partizans
and all men of probity to aid him in correcting and redressing it: and he is
readily followed by all indifferent persons in the execution of his office.
He soon acquires the power of rewarding these services; and in the
progress of society, he establishes subordinate ministers and often a military force, who find an immediate and a visible interest, in supporting his
authority. Habit soon consolidates what other principles of human nature
had imperfectly founded; and men, once accustomed to obedience, never
think of departing from that path, in which they and their ancestors have
constantly trod, and to which they are confined by so many urgent and
visible motives.

But though this progress of human affairs may appear certain and in- 6
evitable, and though the support which allegiance brings to justice, be
founded on obvious principles of human nature, it cannot be expected
that men should beforehand be able to discover them, or foresee their operation. Government commences more casually and more imperfectly. It
is probable, that the first ascendant of one man over multitudes begun
during a state of war; where the superiority of courage and of genius discovers itself most visibly, where unanimity and concert are most requisite,
and where the pernicious effects of disorder are most sensibly felt. The
long continuance of that state, an incident common among savage tribes,
enured the people to submission; and if the chieftain possessed as much
equity as prudence and valour, he became, even during peace, the arbiter
of all differences, and could gradually, by a mixture of force and consent,
establish his authority. The benefit sensibly felt from his influence, made
it be cherished by the people, at least by the peaceable and well disposed
among them; and if his son enjoyed the same good qualities, government
advanced the sooner to maturity and perfection; but was still in a feeble
state, till the farther progress of improvement procured the magistrate a

revenue, and enabled him to bestow rewards on the several instruments of his administration, and to inflict punishments on the refractory and disobedient. Before that period, each exertion of his influence must have been particular, and founded on the peculiar circumstances of the case. After it, submission was no longer a matter of choice in the bulk of the community, but was rigorously exacted by the authority of the supreme magistrate.

7   In all governments, there is a perpetual intestine struggle, open or secret, between AUTHORITY and LIBERTY; and neither of them can ever absolutely prevail in the contest. A great sacrifice of liberty must necessarily be made in every government; yet even the authority, which confines liberty, can never, and perhaps ought never, in any constitution, to become quite entire and uncontroulable. The sultan is master of the life and fortune of any individual; but will not be permitted to impose new taxes on his subjects: A French monarch can impose taxes at pleasure; but would find it dangerous to attempt the lives and fortunes of individuals. Religion also, in most countries, is commonly found to be a very intractable principle; and other principles or prejudices frequently resist all the authority of the civil magistrate; whose power, being founded on opinion, can never subvert other opinions, equally rooted with that of his title to dominion. The government, which, in common appellation, receives the appellation of free, is that which admits of a partition of power among several members, whose united authority is no less, or is commonly greater than that of any monarch; but who, in the usual course of administration, must act by general and equal laws, that are previously known to all the members and to all their subjects. In this sense, it must be owned, that liberty is the perfection of civil society; but still authority must be acknowledged essential to its very existence: and in those contests, which so often take place between the one and the other, the latter may, on that account, challenge the preference. Unless perhaps one may say (and it may be said with some reason) that a circumstance, which is essential to the existence of civil society, must always support itself, and needs be guarded with less jealousy, than one that contributes only to its perfection, which the indolence of men is so apt to neglect, or their ignorance to overlook.

ESSAY III.
OF THE DIGNITY OR MEANNESS
OF HUMAN NATURE.

THERE are certain sects, which secretly form themselves in the learned   1
world, as well as factions in the political; and though sometimes they
come not to an open rupture, they give a different turn to the ways of
thinking of those who have taken part on either side. The most remarkable
of this kind are the sects, founded on the different sentiments with regard
to the *dignity of human nature;* which is a point that seems to have divided
philosophers and poets, as well as divines, from the beginning of the
world to this day. Some exalt our species to the skies, and represent man as
a kind of human demigod, who derives his origin from heaven, and retains
evident marks of his lineage and descent. Others insist upon the blind
sides of human nature, and can discover nothing, except vanity, in which
man surpasses the other animals, whom he affects so much to despise. If
an author possess the talent of rhetoric and declamation, he commonly
takes part with the former: If his turn lie towards irony and ridicule, he
naturally throws himself into the other extreme.

I am far from thinking, that all those, who have depreciated our species,   2
have been enemies to virtue, and have exposed the frailties of their fellow
creatures with any bad intention. On the contrary, I am sensible that a delicate sense of morals, especially when attended with a splenetic temper, is
apt to give a man a disgust of the world, and to make him consider the
common course of human affairs with too much indignation. I must, however, be of opinion, that the sentiments of those, who are inclined to think
favourably of mankind, are more advantageous to virtue, than the contrary principles, which give us a mean opinion of our nature. When a man
is prepossessed with a high notion of his rank and character in the creation, he will naturally endeavour to act up to it, and will scorn to do a
base or vicious action, which might sink him below that figure which he
makes in his own imagination. Accordingly we find, that all our polite and
fashionable moralists insist upon this topic, and endeavour to represent
vice as unworthy of man, as well as odious in itself.

We find few disputes, that are not founded on some ambiguity in the   3
expression; and I am persuaded, that the present dispute, concerning the
dignity or meanness of human nature, is not more exempt from it than any
other. It may, therefore, be worth while to consider, what is real, and what
is only verbal, in this controversy.

That there is a natural difference between merit and demerit, virtue   4
and vice, wisdom and folly, no reasonable man will deny: Yet is it evident,

that in affixing the term, which denotes either our approbation or blame, we are commonly more influenced by comparison than by any fixed unalterable standard in the nature of things. In like manner, quantity, and extension, and bulk, are by every one acknowledged to be real things: But when we call any animal *great* or *little*, we always form a secret comparison between that animal and others of the same species; and it is that comparison which regulates our judgment concerning its greatness. A dog and a horse may be of the very same size, while the one is admired for the greatness of its bulk, and the other for the smallness. When I am present, therefore, at any dispute, I always consider with myself, whether it be a question of comparison or not that is the subject of the controversy; and if it be, whether the disputants compare the same objects together, or talk of things that are widely different.

5   In forming our notions of human nature, we are apt to make a comparison between men and animals, the only creatures endowed with thought that fall under our senses. Certainly this comparison is favourable to mankind. On the one hand, we see a creature, whose thoughts are not limited by any narrow bounds, either of place or time; who carries his researches into the most distant regions of this globe, and beyond this globe, to the planets and heavenly bodies; looks backward to consider the first origin, at least, the history of human race; casts his eye forward to see the influence of his actions upon posterity, and the judgments which will be formed of his character a thousand years hence; a creature, who traces causes and effects to a great length and intricacy; extracts general principles from particular appearances; improves upon his discoveries; corrects his mistakes; and makes his very errors profitable. On the other hand, we are presented with a creature the very reverse of this; limited in its observations and reasonings to a few sensible objects which surround it; without curiosity, without foresight; blindly conducted by instinct, and attaining, in a short time, its utmost perfection, beyond which it is never able to advance a single step. What a wide difference is there between these creatures! And how exalted a notion must we entertain of the former, in comparison of the latter!

6   There are two means commonly employed to destroy this conclusion: *First*, By making an unfair representation of the case, and insisting only upon the weaknesses of human nature. And *secondly*, By forming a new and secret comparison between man and beings of the most perfect wisdom. Among the other excellencies of man, this is one, that he can form an idea of perfections much beyond what he has experience of in himself; and is not limited in his conception of wisdom and virtue. He can easily exalt his notions and conceive a degree of knowledge, which, when compared to his own, will make the latter appear very contemptible, and will

cause the difference between that and the sagacity of animals, in a manner, to disappear and vanish. Now this being a point, in which all the world is agreed, that human understanding falls infinitely short of perfect wisdom; it is proper we should know when this comparison takes place, that we may not dispute where there is no real difference in our sentiments. Man falls much more short of perfect wisdom, and even of his own ideas of perfect wisdom, than animals do of man; yet the latter difference is so considerable, that nothing but a comparison with the former can make it appear of little moment.

It is also usual to *compare* one man with another; and finding very few 7 whom we can call *wise* or *virtuous*, we are apt to entertain a contemptible notion of our species in general. That we may be sensible of the fallacy of this way of reasoning, we may observe, that the honourable appellations of wise and virtuous, are not annexed to any particular degree of those qualities of *wisdom* and *virtue;* but arise altogether from the comparison we make between one man and another. When we find a man, who arrives at such a pitch of wisdom as is very uncommon, we pronounce him a wise man: So that to say, there are few wise men in the world, is really to say nothing; since it is only by their scarcity, that they merit that appellation. Were the lowest of our species as wise as TULLY, or lord BACON, we should still have reason to say, that there are few wise men. For in that case we should exalt our notions of wisdom, and should not pay a singular honour to any one, who was not singularly distinguished by his talents. In like manner, I have heard it observed by thoughtless people, that there are few women possessed of beauty, in comparison of those who want it; not considering, that we bestow the epithet of *beautiful* only on such as possess a degree of beauty, that is common to them with a few. The same degree of beauty in a woman is called deformity, which is treated as real beauty in one of our sex.

As it is usual, in forming a notion of our species, to *compare* it with the 8 other species above or below it, or to compare the individuals of the species among themselves; so we often compare together the different motives or actuating principles of human nature, in order to regulate our judgment concerning it. And, indeed, this is the only kind of comparison, which is worth our attention, or decides any thing in the present question. Were our selfish and vicious principles so much predominant above our social and virtuous, as is asserted by some philosophers, we ought undoubtedly to entertain a contemptible notion of human nature.

There is much of a dispute of words in all this controversy. When a man 9 denies the sincerity of all public spirit or affection to a country and community, I am at a loss what to think of him. Perhaps he never felt this passion in so clear and distinct a manner as to remove all his doubts concerning its force and reality. But when he proceeds afterwards to reject all private friendship, if no interest or self-love intermix itself; I am then confident that he abuses terms, and confounds the ideas of things; since it is impossible for any one to be so selfish, or rather so stupid, as to make no difference between one man and another, and give no preference to qualities, which engage his approbation and esteem. Is he also, say I, as insensible to anger as he pretends to be to friendship? And does injury and wrong no more affect him than kindness or benefits? Impossible: He does not know himself: He has forgotten the movements of his heart; or rather he makes use of a different language from the rest of his countrymen, and calls not things by their proper names. What say you of natural affection? (I subjoin) Is that also a species of self-love? Yes: All is self-love. *Your* children are loved only because they are yours: *Your* friend for a like reason: And *your* country engages you only so far as it has a connexion with *yourself:* Were the idea of self removed, nothing would affect you: You would be altogether unactive and insensible: Or, if you ever gave yourself any movement, it would only be from vanity, and a desire of fame and reputation to this same self. I am willing, reply I, to receive your interpretation of human actions, provided you admit the facts. That species of self-love, which displays itself in kindness to others, you must allow to have great influence over human actions, and even greater, on many occasions, than that which remains in its original shape and form. For how few are there, who, having a family, children, and relations, do not spend more on the maintenance and education of these than on their own pleasures? This, indeed, you justly observe, may proceed from their self-love, since the prosperity of their family and friends is one, or the chief of their pleasures, as well as their chief honour. Be you also one of these selfish men, and you are sure of every one's good opinion and good will; or not to shock your ears with these expressions, the self-love of every one, and mine among the rest, will then incline us to serve you, and speak well of you.

10   In my opinion, there are two things which have led astray those philosophers, that have insisted so much on the selfishness of man. In the *first* place, they found, that every act of virtue or friendship was attended with a secret pleasure; whence they concluded, that friendship and virtue could not be disinterested. But the fallacy of this is obvious. The virtuous sentiment or passion produces the pleasure, and does not arise from it. I feel a pleasure in doing good to my friend, because I love him; but do not love him for the sake of that pleasure.

11   In the *second* place, it has always been found, that the virtuous are far from being indifferent to praise; and therefore they have been represented as a set of vain-glorious men, who had nothing in view but the applauses of others. But this also is a fallacy. It is very unjust in the world, when they

find any tincture of vanity in a laudable action, to depreciate it upon that account, or ascribe it entirely to that motive. The case is not the same with vanity, as with other passions. Where avarice or revenge enters into any seemingly virtuous action, it is difficult for us to determine how far it enters, and it is natural to suppose it the sole actuating principle. But vanity is so closely allied to virtue, and to love the fame of laudable actions approaches so near the love of laudable actions for their own sake, that these passions are more capable of mixture, than any other kinds of affection; and it is almost impossible to have the latter without some degree of the former. Accordingly, we find, that this passion for glory is always warped and varied according to the particular taste or disposition of the mind on which it falls. NERO had the same vanity in driving a chariot, that TRAJAN had in governing the empire with justice and ability. To love the glory of virtuous deeds is a sure proof of the love of virtue.

ESSAY IV.
OF CIVIL LIBERTY.

1   THOSE who employ their pens on political subjects, free from party-rage, and party-prejudices, cultivate a science, which, of all others, contributes most to public utility, and even to the private satisfaction of those who addict themselves to the study of it. I am apt, however, to entertain a suspicion, that the world is still too young to fix many general truths in politics, which will remain true to the latest posterity. We have not as yet had experience of three thousand years; so that not only the art of reasoning is still imperfect in this science, as in all others, but we even want sufficient materials upon which we can reason. It is not fully known, what degree of refinement, either in virtue or vice, human nature is susceptible of; nor what may be expected of mankind from any great revolution in their education, customs, or principles. MACHIAVEL was certainly a great genius; but having confined his study to the furious and tyrannical governments of ancient times, or to the little disorderly principalities of ITALY, his reasonings especially upon monarchical government, have been found extremely defective; and there scarcely is any maxim in his *prince*, which subsequent experience has not entirely refuted. *A weak prince, says he, is incapable of receiving good counsel; for if he consult with several, he will not be able to choose among their different counsels. If he abandon himself to one, that minister may, perhaps, have capacity, but he will not long be a minister: He will be sure to dispossess his master, and place himself and his family upon the throne.* I mention this, among many instances of the errors of that politician, proceeding, in a great measure, from his having lived in too early an age of the world, to be a good judge of political truth. Almost all the princes of EUROPE are at present governed by their ministers; and have been so for near two centuries; and yet no such event has ever happened, or can possibly happen. SEJANUS might project dethroning the CÆSARS; but FLEURY, though ever so vicious, could not, while in his senses, entertain the least hopes of dispossessing the BOURBONS.

2   Trade was never esteemed an affair of state till the last century; and there scarcely is any ancient writer on politics, who has made mention of it.[1] Even the ITALIANS have kept a profound silence with regard to it,

---

[1]   XENOPHON mentions it; but with a doubt if it be of any advantage to a state. Εἰ δὲ καὶ ἐμπορία ὠφελεῖ τι πόλιν, &c. XEN. HIERO. 9.9. ["If commerce also brings gain to a city" (Xenophon, *Hiero* IX, 9; trans. by E. C. Marchant).] PLATO totally excludes it from his imaginary republic. De legibus, lib. iv. [Plato, *Laws*, Book IV.]

though it has now engaged the chief attention, as well of ministers of state, as of speculative reasoners. The great opulence, grandeur, and military atchievements of the two maritime powers seem first to have instructed mankind in the importance of an extensive commerce.

Having, therefore, intended in this essay to make a full comparison of   3
civil liberty and absolute government, and to show the great advantages of the former above the latter; I began to entertain a suspicion, that no man in this age was sufficiently qualified for such an undertaking; and that whatever any one should advance on that head would, in all probability, be refuted by further experience, and be rejected by posterity. Such mighty revolutions have happened in human affairs, and so many events have arisen contrary to the expectation of the ancients, that they are sufficient to beget the suspicion of still further changes.

It had been observed by the ancients, that all the arts and sciences arose   4
among free nations; and, that the PERSIANS and EGYPTIANS, notwith-standing their ease, opulence, and luxury, made but faint efforts towards a relish in those finer pleasures, which were carried to such perfection by the GREEKS, amidst continual wars, attended with poverty, and the great-est simplicity of life and manners. It had also been observed, that, when the GREEKS lost their liberty, though they increased mightily in riches, by means of the conquests of ALEXANDER; yet the arts, from that moment, declined among them, and have never since been able to raise their head in that climate. Learning was transplanted to ROME, the only free nation at that time in the universe; and having met with so favourable a soil, it made prodigious shoots for above a century; till the decay of liberty produced also the decay of letters, and spread a total barbarism over the world. From these two experiments, of which each was double in its kind, and shewed the fall of learning in absolute governments, as well as its rise in popular ones, LONGINUS thought himself sufficiently justified, in assert-ing, that the arts and sciences could never flourish, but in a free govern-ment: And in this opinion, he has been followed by several eminent writers[2] in our own country, who either confined their view merely to an-cient facts, or entertained too great a partiality in favour of that form of government, established amongst us.

But what would these writers have said, to the instances of modern   5
ROME and of FLORENCE? Of which the former carried to perfection all the finer arts of sculpture, painting, and music, as well as poetry, though it groaned under tyranny, and under the tyranny of priests: While the latter made its chief progress in the arts and sciences, after it began to lose its

---

[2] Mr. ADDISON and LORD SHAFTESBURY

liberty by the usurpation of the family of MEDICI. ARIOSTO, TASSO, GALILEO, more than RAPHAEL, and MICHAEL ANGELO, were not born in republics. And though the LOMBARD school was famous as well as the ROMAN, yet the VENETIANS have had the smallest share in its honours, and seem rather inferior to the other ITALIANS, in their genius for the arts and sciences. RUBENS established his school at ANTWERP, not at AMSTER-DAM: DRESDEN, not HAMBURGH, is the centre of politeness in GERMANY.

6   But the most eminent instance of the flourishing of learning in absolute governments, is that of FRANCE, which scarcely ever enjoyed any established liberty, and yet has carried the arts and sciences as near perfection as any other nation. The ENGLISH are, perhaps, greater philosophers; the ITALIANS better painters and musicians; the ROMANS were greater orators: But the FRENCH are the only people, except the GREEKS, who have been at once philosophers, poets, orators, historians, painters, architects, sculptors, and musicians. With regard to the stage, they have excelled even the GREEKS, who far excelled the ENGLISH. And, in common life, they have, in a great measure, perfected that art, the most useful and agreeable of any, *l'Art de Vivre*, the art of society and conversation.

7   If we consider the state of the sciences and polite arts in our own country, HORACE'S observation, with regard to the ROMANS, may, in a great measure, be applied to the BRITISH.

—Sed in longum tamen ævum
Manserunt, hodieque manent vestigia ruris.[3]

8   The elegance and propriety of style have been very much neglected among us. We have no dictionary of our language, and scarcely a tolerable grammar. The first polite prose we have, was writ by a man who is still alive.[4] As to SPRAT, LOCKE and, even TEMPLE, they knew too little of the rules of art to be esteemed elegant writers. The prose of BACON, HAR-RINGTON, and MILTON, is altogether stiff and pedantic; though their sense be excellent. Men, in this country, have been so much occupied in the great disputes of *Religion*, *Politics*, and *Philosophy*, that they had no relish for the seemingly minute observations of grammar and criticism. And though this turn of thinking must have considerably improved our sense and our talent of reasoning; it must be confessed, that, even in those sciences above-mentioned, we have not any standard-book, which we can transmit to posterity: And the utmost we have to boast of, are a few essays

---

    [3] [". . . yet for many a year lived on, and still live on, traces of our rustic past" (Horace, *Epistles* II, I, 160; trans. by H. Rushton Fairclough).]
    [4] Dr. SWIFT

towards a more just philosophy; which, indeed, promise well, but have not, as yet, reached any degree of perfection.

It has become an established opinion, that commerce can never flourish but in a free government; and this opinion seems to be founded on a longer and larger experience than the foregoing, with regard to the arts and sciences. If we trace commerce in its progress through TYRE, ATHENS, SYRACUSE, CARTHAGE, VENICE, FLORENCE, GENOA, ANTWERP, HOLLAND, ENGLAND, &c. we shall always find it to have fixed its seat in free governments. The three greatest trading towns now in Europe, are LONDON, AMSTERDAM, and HAMBURGH; all free cities, and protestant cities; that is, enjoying a double liberty. It must, however, be observed, that the great jealousy entertained of late, with regard to the commerce of FRANCE, seems to prove, that this maxim is no more certain and infallible than the foregoing, and that the subjects of an absolute prince may become our rivals in commerce, as well as in learning.   9

Durst I deliver my opinion in an affair of so much uncertainty, I would assert, that, notwithstanding the efforts of the FRENCH, there is something hurtful to commerce inherent in the very nature of absolute government, and inseparable from it: Though the reason I should assign for this opinion, is somewhat different from that which is commonly insisted on. Private property seems to me almost as secure in a civilized EUROPEAN monarchy, as in a republic; nor is danger much apprehended in such a government, from the violence of the sovereign; more than we commonly dread harm from thunder, or earthquakes, or any accident the most unusual and extraordinary. Avarice, the spur of industry, is so obstinate a passion, and works its way through so many real dangers and difficulties, that it is not likely to be scared by an imaginary danger, which is so small, that it scarcely admits of calculation. Commerce, therefore, in my opinion, is apt to decay in absolute governments, not because it is there less *secure*, but because it is less *honourable*. A subordination of ranks is absolutely necessary to the support of monarchy. Birth, titles, and place, must be honoured above industry and riches. And while these notions prevail, all the considerable traders will be tempted to throw up their commerce, in order to purchase some of those employments, to which privileges and honours are annexed.   10

Since I am upon this head, of the alterations which time has produced, or may produce in politics, I must observe, that all kinds of government, free and absolute, seem to have undergone, in modern times, a great change for the better, with regard both to foreign and domestic management. The *balance of power* is a secret in politics, fully known only to the present age; and I must add, that the internal POLICE of states has also received great improvements within the last century. We are informed by   11

SALLUST, that CATILINE'S army was much augmented by the accession of
the highwaymen about ROME; though I believe, that all of that profession,
who are at present dispersed over EUROPE, would not amount to a regi-
ment. In CICERO'S pleadings for MILO, I find this argument, among others, made use of to prove, that his client had not assassinated CLODIUS.
Had MILO, said he, intended to have killed CLODIUS, he had not attacked
him in the day-time, and at such a distance from the city: He had way-laid
him at night, near the suburbs, where it might have been pretended, that
he was killed by robbers; and the frequency of the accident would have
favoured the deceit. This is a surprizing proof of the loose police of ROME,
and of the number and force of these robbers; since CLODIUS[5] was at that
time attended by thirty slaves, who were compleatly armed, and sufficiently accustomed to blood and danger in the frequent tumults excited by
that seditious tribune.

12   But though all kinds of government be improved in modern times, yet
monarchical government seems to have made the greatest advances towards perfection. It may now be affirmed of civilized monarchies, what
was formerly said in praise of republics alone, *that they are a government of
Laws, not of Men.* They are found susceptible of order, method, and constancy, to a surprizing degree. Property is there secure; industry encouraged; the arts flourish; and the prince lives secure among his subjects, like
a father among his children. There are perhaps, and have been for two
centuries, near two hundred absolute princes, great and small, in EUROPE;
and allowing twenty years to each reign, we may suppose, that there have
been in the whole two thousand monarchs or tyrants, as the GREEKS
would have called them: Yet of these there has not been one, not even
PHILIP II. of Spain, so bad as TIBERIUS, CALIGULA, NERO, or DOMITIAN,
who were four in twelve amongst the ROMAN emperors. It must, however,
be confessed, that, though monarchical governments have approached
nearer to popular ones, in gentleness and stability; they are still inferior.
Our modern education and customs instil more humanity and moderation
than the ancient; but have not as yet been able to overcome entirely the
disadvantages of that form of government.

13   But here I must beg leave to advance a conjecture, which seems probable, but which posterity alone can fully judge of. I am apt to think, that,
in monarchical governments there is a source of improvement, and in
popular governments a source of degeneracy, which in time will bring
these species of civil polity still nearer an equality. The greatest abuses,

---

[5] *Vide Asc. Ped. in Orat. pro Milone.* [Cicero, *The Speech on Behalf of Milo.*]

which arise in FRANCE, the most perfect model of pure monarchy, proceed not from the number or weight of the taxes, beyond what are to be met with in free countries; but from the expensive, unequal, arbitrary, and intricate method of levying them, by which the industry of the poor, especially of the peasants and farmers, is, in a great measure, discouraged, and agriculture rendered a beggarly and slavish employment. But to whose advantage do these abuses tend? If to that of the nobility, they might be esteemed inherent in that form of government; since the nobility are the true supports of monarchy; and it is natural their interest should be more consulted, in such a constitution, than that of the people. But the nobility are, in reality, the chief losers by this oppression; since it ruins their estates, and beggars their tenants. The only gainers by it are the *Finançiers*, a race of men rather odious to the nobility and the whole kingdom. If a prince or minister, therefore, should arise, endowed with sufficient discernment to know his own and the public interest, and with sufficient force of mind to break through ancient customs, we might expect to see these abuses remedied; in which case, the difference between that absolute government and our free one, would not appear so considerable as at present.

The source of degeneracy, which may be remarked in free governments, consists in the practice of contracting debt, and mortgaging the public revenues, by which taxes may, in time, become altogether intolerable, and all the property of the state be brought into the hands of the public. This practice is of modern date. The ATHENIANS, though governed by a republic, paid near two hundred *per Cent*. for those sums of money, which any emergence made it necessary for them to borrow; as we learn from XENOPHON.[6] Among the moderns, the DUTCH first introduced the practice of borrowing great sums at low interest, and have well nigh ruined themselves by it. Absolute princes have also contracted debt; but as an absolute prince may make a bankruptcy when he pleases, his people

14

---

[6] Κτῆσιν δὲ ἀπ' οὐδενὸς ἂν οὕτω καλὴν κτήσαιντο, ὥσπερ ἀφ' οὗ ἂν προτελέσωσιν εἰς τὴν ἀφορμήν—οἱ δέ γε πλεῖστοι Ἀθηναίων πλείονα λήψονται κατ' ἐνιαυτόν ἢ ὅσα ἂν εἰσενέγκωσιν· οἱ γὰρ μνᾶν προτελέσαντες, ἐγγὺς δυοῖν μναῖν πρόσοδον ἕξουσι—ὃ δοκεῖ τῶν ἀνθρωπίνων ἀσφαλέτατόν τε καὶ πολυχρονιώτατον εἶναι. ΞΕΝ. ΠΟΡΟΙ. III. 9. 10. ["But no investment can yield them so fine a return as the money advanced by them to form the capital fund. . . . But most of the Athenians will get over a hundred per cent. in a year, for those who advance one *mina* will draw an income of nearly two *minae*, guaranteed by the state, which is to all appearances the safest and most durable of human institutions" (Xenophon, *Ways and Means*, III, 9–10; trans. by E. C. Marchant).]

can never be oppressed by his debts. In popular governments, the people, and chiefly those who have the highest offices, being commonly the public creditors, it is difficult for the state to make use of this remedy, which, however it may sometimes be necessary, is always cruel and barbarous. This, therefore seems to be an inconvenience, which nearly threatens all free governments; especially our own, at the present juncture of affairs. And what a strong motive is this, to encrease our frugality of public money; lest for want of it, we be reduced, by the multiplicity of taxes, or what is worse, by our public impotence and inability for defence, to curse our very liberty, and wish ourselves in the same state of servitude with all the nations that surround us?

ESSAY V.
THE SCEPTIC.

I have long entertained a suspicion, with regard to the decisions of   1
philosophers upon all subjects, and found in myself a greater inclination
to dispute, than assent to their conclusions. There is one mistake, to which
they seem liable, almost without exception; they confine too much their
principles, and make no account of that vast variety, which nature has so
much affected in all her operations. When a philosopher has once laid
hold of a favourite principle, which perhaps accounts for many natural effects, he extends the same principle over the whole creation, and reduces
to it every phænomenon, though by the most violent and absurd reasoning. Our own mind being narrow and contracted, we cannot extend our
conception to the variety and extent of nature; but imagine, that she is as
much bounded in her operations, as we are in our speculation.

But if ever this infirmity of philosophers is to be suspected on any oc-   2
casion, it is in their reasonings concerning human life, and the methods of
attaining happiness. In that case, they are led astray, not only by the narrowness of their understandings, but by that also of their passions. Almost
every one has a predominant inclination, to which his other desires and
affections submit, and which governs him, though, perhaps, with some
intervals, through the whole course of his life. It is difficult for him to apprehend, that any thing, which appears totally indifferent to him, can ever
give enjoyment to any person, or can possess charms, which altogether escape his observation. His own pursuits are always, in his account, the most
engaging: The objects of his passion, the most valuable: And the road,
which he pursues, the only one that leads to happiness.

But would these prejudiced reasoners reflect a moment, there are many   3
obvious instances and arguments, sufficient to undeceive them, and make
them enlarge their maxims and principles. Do they not see the vast variety
of inclinations and pursuits among our species; where each man seems
fully satisfied with his own course of life, and would esteem it the greatest
unhappiness to be confined to that of his neighbour? Do they not feel in
themselves, that what pleases at one time, displeases at another, by the
change of inclination; and that it is not in their power, by their utmost efforts, to recall that taste or appetite, which formerly bestowed charms on
what now appears indifferent or disagreeable? What is the meaning therefore of those general preferences of the town or country life, of a life of action or one of pleasure, of retirement or society; when besides the
different inclinations of different men, every one's experience may convince him, that each of these kinds of life is agreeable in its turn, and that

their variety or their judicious mixture chiefly contributes to the rendering all of them agreeable.

4   But shall this business be allowed to go altogether at adventures? And must a man consult only his humour and inclination, in order to determine his course of life, without employing his reason to inform him what road is preferable, and leads most surely to happiness? Is there no difference then between one man's conduct and another?

5   I answer, there is a great difference. One man, following his inclination, in chusing his course of life, may employ much surer means for succeeding than another, who is led by his inclination into the same course of life, and pursues the same object. *Are riches the chief object of your desires?* Acquire skill in your profession; be diligent in the exercise of it; enlarge the circle of your friends and acquaintance; avoid pleasure and expence; and never be generous, but with a view of gaining more than you could save by frugality. *Would you acquire the public esteem?* Guard equally against the extremes of arrogance and fawning. Let it appear that you set a value upon yourself, but without despising others. If you fall into either of the extremes, you either provoke men's pride by your insolence, or teach them to despise you by your timorous submission, and by the mean opinion which you seem to entertain of yourself.

6   These, you say, are the maxims of common prudence, and discretion; what every parent inculcates on his child, and what every man of sense pursues in the course of life, which he has chosen.—What is it then you desire more? Do you come to a philosopher as to a *cunning man*, to learn something by magic or witchcraft, beyond what can be known by common prudence and discretion?—Yes; we come to a philosopher to be instructed, how we shall chuse our ends, more than the means for attaining these ends: We want to know what desire we shall gratify, what passion we shall comply with, what appetite we shall indulge. As to the rest, we trust to common sense, and the general maxims of the world for our instruction.

7   I am sorry then, I have pretended to be a philosopher: For I find your questions very perplexing; and am in danger, if my answer be too rigid and severe, of passing for a pedant and scholastic; if it be too easy and free, of being taken for a preacher of vice and immorality. However, to satisfy you, I shall deliver my opinion upon the matter, and shall only desire you to esteem it of as little consequence as I do myself. By that means you will neither think it worthy of your ridicule nor your anger.

8   If we can depend upon any principle, which we learn from philosophy, this, I think, may be considered as certain and undoubted, that there is nothing, in itself, valuable or despicable, desirable or hateful, beautiful or

deformed; but that these attributes arise from the particular constitution and fabric of human sentiment and affection. What seems the most delicious food to one animal, appears loathsome to another: What affects the feeling of one with delight, produces uneasiness in another. This is confessedly the case with regard to all the bodily senses: But if we examine the matter more accurately, we shall find, that the same observation holds even where the mind concurs with the body, and mingles its sentiment with the exterior appetite.

Desire this passionate lover to give you a character of his mistress: He will tell you, that he is at a loss for words to describe her charms, and will ask you very seriously if ever you were acquainted with a goddess or an angel? If you answer that you never were: He will then say, that it is impossible for you to form a conception of such divine beauties as those which his charmer possesses; so complete a shape; such well-proportioned features; so engaging an air; such sweetness of disposition; such gaiety of humour. You can infer nothing, however, from all this discourse, but that the poor man is in love; and that the general appetite between the sexes, which nature has infused into all animals, is in him determined to a particular object by some qualities, which give him pleasure. The same divine creature, not only to a different animal, but also to a different man, appears a mere mortal being, and is beheld with the utmost indifference. 9

Nature has given all animals a like prejudice in favour of their offspring. As soon as the helpless infant sees the light, though in every other eye it appears a despicable and a miserable creature, it is regarded by its fond parent with the utmost affection, and is preferred to every other object, however perfect and accomplished. The passion alone, arising from the original structure and formation of human nature, bestows a value on the most insignificant object. 10

We may push the same observation further, and may conclude, that, even when the mind operates alone, and feeling the sentiment of blame or approbation, pronounces one object deformed and odious, another beautiful and amiable; I say, that, even in this case, those qualities are not really in the objects, but belong entirely to the sentiment of that mind which blames or praises. I grant, that it will be more difficult to make this proposition evident, and as it were, palpable, to negligent thinkers; because nature is more uniform in the sentiments of the mind than in most feelings of the body, and produces a nearer resemblance in the inward than in the outward part of human kind. There is something approaching to principles in mental taste; and critics can reason and dispute more plausibly than cooks or perfumers. We may observe, however, that this uniformity 11 among human kind, hinders not, but that there is a considerable diversity in the sentiments of beauty and worth, and that education, custom, prejudice, caprice, and humour, frequently vary our taste of this kind. You will never convince a man, who is not accustomed to ITALIAN music, and has not an ear to follow its intricacies, that a SCOTCH tune is not preferable. You have not even any single argument, beyond your own taste, which you can employ in your behalf: And to your antagonist, his particular taste will always appear a more convincing argument to the contrary. If you be wise, each of you will allow, that the other may be in the right; and having many other instances of this diversity of taste, you will both confess, that beauty and worth are merely of a relative nature, and consist in an agreeable sentiment, produced by an object in a particular mind, according to the peculiar structure and constitution of that mind.

12   By this diversity of sentiment, observable in human kind, nature has, perhaps, intended to make us sensible of her authority, and let us see what surprizing changes she could produce on the passions and desires of mankind, merely by the change of their inward fabric, without any alteration on the objects. The vulgar may even be convinced by this argument: But men, accustomed to thinking, may draw a more convincing, at least a more general argument, from the very nature of the subject.

13   In the operation of reasoning, the mind does nothing but run over its objects, as they are supposed to stand in reality, without adding any thing to them, or diminishing any thing from them. If I examine the PTOLO-MAIC and COPERNICAN systems, I endeavour only, by my enquiries, to know the real situation of the planets; that is in other words, I endeavour to give them, in my conception, the same relations, that they bear towards each other in the heavens. To this operation of the mind, therefore, there seems to be always a real, though often an unknown standard, in the nature of things; nor is truth or falsehood variable by the various apprehensions of mankind. Though all human race should for ever conclude, that the sun moves, and the earth remains at rest, the sun stirs not an inch from his place for all these reasonings; and such conclusions are eternally false and erroneous.

14   But the case is not the same with the qualities of *beautiful and deformed, desirable and odious*, as with truth and falsehood. In the former case, the mind is not content with merely surveying its objects, as they stand in themselves: It also feels a sentiment of delight or uneasiness, approbation or blame, consequent to that survey; and this sentiment determines it to affix the epithet *beautiful or deformed, desirable or odious*. Now, it is evident, that this sentiment must depend upon the particular fabric or structure of the mind, which enables such particular forms to operate in such a particular manner, and produces a sympathy or conformity between the mind

and its objects. Vary the structure of the mind or inward organs, the sentiment no longer follows, though the form remains the same. The sentiment
being different from the object, and arising from its operation upon the
organs of the mind, an alteration upon the latter must vary the effect, nor
can the same object, presented to a mind totally different, produce the
same sentiment.

This conclusion every one is apt to draw of himself, without much phi-   15
losophy, where the sentiment is evidently distinguishable from the object.
Who is not sensible, that power, and glory, and vengeance, are not desirable of themselves, but derive all their value from the structure of human
passions, which begets a desire towards such particular pursuits? But with
regard to beauty, either natural or moral, the case is commonly supposed
to be different. The agreeable quality is thought to lie in the object, not in
the sentiment; and that merely because the sentiment is not so turbulent
and violent as to distinguish itself, in an evident manner, from the perception of the object.

But a little reflection suffices to distinguish them. A man may know ex-   16
actly all the circles and ellipses of the COPERNICAN system, and all the irregular spirals of the PTOLOMAIC, without perceiving that the former is
more beautiful than the latter. EUCLID has fully explained every quality of
the circle, but has not, in any proposition, said a word of its beauty. The
reason is evident. Beauty is not a quality of the circle. It lies not in any part
of the line *whose* parts are all equally distant from a common center. It is
only the effect, which that figure produces upon a mind, whose particular
fabric or structure renders it susceptible of such sentiments. In vain
would you look for it in the circle, or seek it, either by your senses, or by
mathematical reasonings, in all the properties of that figure.

The mathematician, who took no other pleasure in reading VIRGIL, but   17
that of examining ENEAS'S voyage by the map, might perfectly understand
the meaning of every Latin word, employed by that divine author; and
consequently, might have a distinct idea of the whole narration. He would
even have a more distinct idea of it, than they could attain who had not
studied so exactly the geography of the poem. He knew, therefore, every
thing in the poem: But he was ignorant of its beauty; because the beauty,
properly speaking, lies not in the poem, but in the sentiment or taste of
the reader. And where a man has no such delicacy of temper, as to make
him feel this sentiment, he must be ignorant of the beauty, though possessed of the science and understanding of an angel.[1]

---

[1] Were I not afraid of appearing too philosophical, I should remind my reader of
that famous doctrine, supposed to be fully proved in modern times, "That tastes and

18   The inference upon the whole is, that it is not from the value or worth of the object, which any person pursues, that we can determine his enjoyment, but merely from the passion with which he pursues it, and the success which he meets with in his pursuit. Objects have absolutely no worth or value in themselves. They derive their worth merely from the passion. If that be strong, and steady, and successful, the person is happy. It cannot reasonably be doubted, but a little miss, dressed in a new gown for a dancing-school ball, receives as compleat enjoyment as the greatest orator, who triumphs in the splendor of his eloquence, while he governs the passions and resolutions of a numerous assembly.

19   All the difference, therefore, between one man and another, with regard to life, consists either in the *passion,* or in the *enjoyment:* And these differences are sufficient to produce the wide extremes of happiness and misery.

20   To be happy, the *passion* must neither be too violent nor too remiss. In the first case, the mind is in a perpetual hurry and tumult; in the second, it sinks into a disagreeable indolence and lethargy.

21   To be happy, the passion must be benign and social; not rough or fierce. The affections of the latter kind are not near so agreeable to the feeling, as those of the former. Who will compare rancour and animosity, envy and revenge, to friendship, benignity, clemency, and gratitude?

22   To be happy, the passion must be chearful and gay, not gloomy and melancholy. A propensity to hope and joy is real riches: One to fear and sorrow, real poverty.

23   Some passions or inclinations, in the *enjoyment* of their object, are not so steady or constant as others, nor convey such durable pleasure and satisfaction. *Philosophical devotion,* for instance, like the enthusiasm of a poet, is the transitory effect of high spirits, great leisure, a fine genius, and a habit of study and contemplation: But notwithstanding all these circumstances, an abstract, invisible object, like that which *natural* religion alone presents to us, cannot long actuate the mind, or be of any moment in life. To render the passion of continuance, we must find some method of affecting the senses and imagination, and must embrace some *historical,* as

colours, and all other sensible qualities, lie not in the bodies, but merely in the senses." The case is the same with beauty and deformity, virtue and vice. This doctrine, however, takes off no more from the reality of the latter qualities, than from that of the former; nor need it give any umbrage either to critics or moralists. Though colours were allowed to lie only in the eye, would dyers or painters ever be less regarded or esteemed? There is a sufficient uniformity in the senses and feelings of mankind, to make all these qualities the objects of art and reasoning, and to have the greatest influence on life and manners. And as it is certain, that the discovery above-mentioned in natural philosophy, makes no alteration on action and conduct; why should a like discovery in moral philosophy make any alteration?

well as *philosophical* account of the divinity. Popular superstitions and observances are even found to be of use in this particular.

Though the tempers of men be very different, yet we may safely pronounce in general, that a life of pleasure cannot support itself so long as one of business, but is much more subject to satiety and disgust. The amusements, which are the most durable, have all a mixture of application and attention in them; such as gaming and hunting. And in general, business and action fill up all the great vacancies in human life.   24

But where the temper is the best disposed for any *enjoyment*, the object is often wanting: And in this respect, the passions, which pursue external objects, contribute not so much to happiness, as those which rest in ourselves; since we are neither so certain of attaining such objects, nor so secure in possessing them. A passion for learning is preferable, with regard to happiness, to one for riches.   25

Some men are possessed of great strength of mind; and even when they pursue *external* objects, are not much affected by a disappointment, but renew their application and industry with the greatest chearfulness. Nothing contributes more to happiness than such a turn of mind.   26

According to this short and imperfect sketch of human life, the happiest disposition of mind is the *virtuous;* or, in other words, that which leads to action and employment, renders us sensible to the social passions, steels the heart against the assaults of fortune, reduces the affections to a just moderation, makes our own thoughts an entertainment to us, and inclines us rather to the pleasures of society and conversation, than to those of the senses. This, in the mean time, must be obvious to the most careless reasoner, that all dispositions of mind are not alike favourable to happiness, and that one passion or humour may be extremely desirable, while another is equally disagreeable. And indeed, all the difference between the conditions of life depends upon the mind; nor is there any one situation of affairs, in itself, preferable to another. Good and ill, both natural and moral, are entirely relative to human sentiment and affection. No man would ever be unhappy, could he alter his feelings. PROTEUS-like, he would elude all attacks, by the continual alterations of his shape and form.   27

But of this resource nature has, in a great measure, deprived us. The fabric and constitution of our mind no more depends on our choice, than that of our body. The generality of men have not even the smallest notion, that any alteration in this respect can ever be desirable. As a stream necessarily follows the several inclinations of the ground, on which it runs; so are the ignorant and thoughtless part of mankind actuated by their natural propensities. Such are effectually excluded from all pretensions to philosophy, and the *medicine of the mind*, so much boasted. But even upon the wise and thoughtful, nature has a prodigious influence; nor is it always in a man's power, by the utmost art and industry, to correct his temper, and   28

attain that virtuous character, to which he aspires. The empire of philosophy extends over a few; and with regard to these too, her authority is very
weak and limited. Men may well be sensible of the value of virtue, and
may desire to attain it; but it is not always certain, that they will be successful in their wishes.

29   Whoever considers, without prejudice, the course of human actions,
will find, that mankind are almost entirely guided by constitution and
temper, and that general maxims have little influence, but so far as they affect our taste or sentiment. If a man have a lively sense of honour and
virtue, with moderate passions, his conduct will always be conformable to
the rules of morality; or if he depart from them, his return will be easy
and expeditious. On the other hand, where one is born of so perverse a
frame of mind, of so callous and insensible a disposition, as to have no relish for virtue and humanity, no sympathy with his fellow-creatures, no desire of esteem and applause; such a one must be allowed entirely incurable,
nor is there any remedy in philosophy. He reaps no satisfaction but from
low and sensual objects, or from the indulgence of malignant passions: He
feels no remorse to controul his vicious inclinations: He has not even that
sense or taste, which is requisite to make him desire a better character: For
my part, I know not how I should address myself to such a one, or by what
arguments I should endeavour to reform him. Should I tell him of the inward satisfaction which results from laudable and humane actions, the
delicate pleasure of disinterested love and friendship, the lasting enjoyments of a good name and an established character, he might still reply,
that these were, perhaps, pleasures to such as were susceptible of them;
but that, for his part, he finds himself of a quite different turn and disposition. I must repeat it; my philosophy affords no remedy in such a case,
nor could I do any thing but lament this person's unhappy condition. But
then I ask, If any other philosophy can afford a remedy; or if it be possible,
by any system, to render all mankind virtuous, however perverse may be
their natural frame of mind? Experience will soon convince us of the contrary; and I will venture to affirm, that, perhaps, the chief benefit, which
results from philosophy, arises in an indirect manner, and proceeds more
from its secret, insensible influence, than from its immediate application.

30   It is certain, that a serious attention to the sciences and liberal arts soft-
ens and humanizes the temper, and cherishes those fine emotions, in
which true virtue and honour consists. It rarely, very rarely happens, that
a man of taste and learning is not, at least, an honest man, whatever frailties may attend him. The bent of his mind to speculative studies must
mortify in him the passions of interest and ambition, and must, at the
same time, give him a greater sensibility of all the decencies and duties of
life. He feels more fully a moral distinction in characters and manners;

nor is his sense of this kind diminished, but, on the contrary, it is much encreased, by speculation.

Besides such insensible changes upon the temper and disposition, it is 31 highly probable, that others may be produced by study and application. The prodigious effects of education may convince us, that the mind is not altogether stubborn and inflexible, but will admit of many alterations from its original make and structure. Let a man propose to himself the model of a character, which he approves: Let him be well acquainted with those particulars, in which his own character deviates from this model: Let him keep a constant watch over himself, and bend his mind, by a continual effort, from the vices, towards the virtues; and I doubt not but, in time, he will find, in his temper, an alteration for the better.

Habit is another powerful means of reforming the mind, and implant- 32 ing in it good dispositions and inclinations. A man, who continues in a course of sobriety and temperance, will hate riot and disorder: If he engage in business or study, indolence will seem a punishment to him: If he constrain himself to practise beneficence and affability, he will soon abhor all instances of pride and violence. Where one is thoroughly convinced that the virtuous course of life is preferable; if he have but resolution enough, for some time, to impose a violence on himself; his reformation needs not be despaired of. The misfortune is, that this conviction and this resolution never can have place, unless a man be, before-hand, tolerably virtuous.

Here then is the chief triumph of art and philosophy: It insensibly re- 33 fines the temper, and it points out to us those dispositions which we should endeavour to attain, by a constant *bent* of mind, and by repeated *habit*. Beyond this I cannot acknowledge it to have great influence; and I must entertain doubts concerning all those exhortations and consolations, which are in such vogue among speculative reasoners.

We have already observed, that no objects are, in themselves, desirable 34 or odious, valuable or despicable; but that objects acquire these qualities from the particular character and constitution of the mind, which surveys them. To diminish therefore, or augment any person's value for an object, to excite or moderate his passions, there are no direct arguments or reasons, which can be employed with any force or influence. The catching of flies, like DOMITIAN, if it give more pleasure, is preferable to the hunting of wild beasts, like WILLIAM RUFUS, or conquering of kingdoms, like ALEXANDER.

But though the value of every object can be determined only by the 35 sentiment or passion of every individual, we may observe, that the passion, in pronouncing its verdict, considers not the object simply, as it is in itself, but surveys it with all the circumstances, which attend it. A man transported with joy, on account of his possessing a diamond, confines not his view to the glistering stone before him: He also considers its rarity, and thence chiefly arises his pleasure and exultation. Here therefore a philosopher may step in, and suggest particular views, and considerations, and circumstances, which otherwise would have escaped us; and, by that means, he may either moderate or excite any particular passion.

36   It may seem unreasonable absolutely to deny the authority of philosophy in this respect: But it must be confessed, that there lies this strong presumption against it, that, if these views be natural and obvious, they would have occurred of themselves, without the assistance of philosophy; if they be not natural, they never can have any influence on the affections. *These* are of a very delicate nature, and cannot be forced or constrained by the utmost art or industry. A consideration, which we seek for on purpose, which we enter into with difficulty, which we cannot retain without care and attention, will never produce those genuine and durable movements of passion, which are the result of nature, and the constitution of the mind. A man may as well pretend to cure himself of love, by viewing his mistress through the *artificial* medium of a microscope or prospect, and beholding there the coarseness of her skin, and monstrous disproportion of her features, as hope to excite or moderate any passion by the *artificial* arguments of a SENECA or an EPICTETUS. The remembrance of the natural aspect and situation of the object, will, in both cases, still recur upon him. The reflections of philosophy are too subtile and distant to take place in common life, or eradicate any affection. The air is too fine to breathe in, where it is above the winds and clouds of the atmosphere.

37   Another defect of those refined reflections, which philosophy suggests to us, is, that commonly they cannot diminish or extinguish our vicious passions, without diminishing or extinguishing such as are virtuous, and rendering the mind totally indifferent and unactive. They are, for the most part, general, and are applicable to all our affections. In vain do we hope to direct their influence only to one side. If by incessant study and meditation we have rendered them intimate and present to us, they will operate throughout, and spread an universal insensibility over the mind. When we destroy the nerves, we extinguish the sense of pleasure, together with that of pain, in the human body.

38   It will be easy, by one glance of the eye, to find one or other of these defects in most of those philosophical reflections, so much celebrated both in ancient and modern times. *Let not the injuries or violence of men,* say the philosophers,[2] *ever discompose you by anger or hatred. Would you be angry at*

---

[2] PLUT. *de ira cohibenda.* ["On the Control of Anger" (Plutarch, *Moralia*).]

the ape for its malice, or the tyger for its ferocity? This reflection leads us into
a bad opinion of human nature, and must extinguish the social affections.
It tends also to prevent all remorse for a man's own crimes; when he considers, that vice is as natural to mankind, as the particular instincts to
brute-creatures.

All ills arise from the order of the universe, which is absolutely perfect. Would　39
you wish to disturb so divine an order for the sake of your own particular inter-
est? What if the ills I suffer arise from malice or oppression? *But the vices*
and imperfections of men are also comprehended in the order of the universe:

> *If plagues and earthquakes break not heav'n's design,*
> *Why then a* BORGIA *or a* CATILINE?

Let this be allowed; and my own vices will also be a part of the same order.

To one who said, that none were happy, who were not above opinion, a　40
SPARTAN replied, *then none are happy but knaves and robbers.*[3]

Man is born to be miserable; and is he surprized at any particular misfor-　41
tune? And can he give way to sorrow and lamentation upon account of any dis-
aster? Yes: He very reasonably laments, that he should be born to be
miserable. Your consolation presents a hundred ills for one, of which you
pretend to ease him.

You should always have before your eyes death, disease, poverty, blindness,　42
exile, calumny, and infamy, as ills which are incident to human nature. If any
one of these ills falls to your lot, you will bear it the better, when you have reck-
oned upon it. I answer, if we confine ourselves to a general and distant reflection on the ills of human life, *that* can have no effect to prepare us for
them. If by close and intense meditation we render them present and intimate to us, *that* is the true secret for poisoning all our pleasures, and rendering us perpetually miserable.

Your sorrow is fruitless, and will not change the course of destiny. Very true:　43
And for that very reason I am sorry.

Cicero's consolation for deafness is somewhat curious. *How many lan-*　44
guages are there, says he, *which you do not understand? The* PUNIC, SPANISH,
GALLIC, ÆGYPTIAN, *&c. With regard to all these, you are as if you were*
deaf, yet you are indifferent about the matter. Is it then so great a misfortune to
be deaf to one language more?[4]

I like better the repartee of ANTIPATER the CYRENIAC, when some　45
women were condoling with him for his blindness: *What!* says he, *Do you*
think there are no pleasures in the dark?

---

[3] PLUT. *Lacon. Apophtheg.* ["Sayings of Spartans" (Plutarch, *Moralia*).]
[4] TUSC. *Quest.* lib. v. [Cicero, *Tusculan Disputations*.]

46   *Nothing can be more destructive,* says FONTENELLE, *to ambition, and the passion for conquest, than the true system of astronomy. What a poor thing is even the whole globe in comparison of the infinite extent of nature?* This consideration is evidently too distant ever to have any effect. Or, if it had any, would it not destroy patriotism as well as ambition? The same gallant author adds with some reason, that the bright eyes of the ladies are the only objects, which lose nothing of their lustre or value from the most extensive views of astronomy, but stand proof against every system. Would philosophers advise us to limit our affection to them?

47   *Exile,* says PLUTARCH to a friend in banishment, *is no evil: Mathematicians tell us, that the whole earth is but a point, compared to the heavens. To change one's country then is little more than to remove from one street to another. Man is not a plant, rooted to a certain spot of earth: All soils and all climates are alike suited to him.*[5] These topics are admirable, could they fall only into the hands of banished persons. But what if they come also to the knowledge of those who are employed in public affairs, and destroy all their attachment to their native country? Or will they operate like the quack's medicine, which is equally good for a diabetes and a dropsy?

48   It is certain, were a superior being thrust into a human body, that the whole of life would to him appear so mean, contemptible, and puerile, that he never could be induced to take part in any thing, and would scarcely give attention to what passes around him. To engage him to such a condescension as to play even the part of a PHILIP with zeal and alacrity, would be much more difficult, than to constrain the same PHILIP, after having been a king and a conqueror during fifty years, to mend old shoes with proper care and attention; the occupation which LUCIAN assigns him in the infernal regions. Now all the same topics of disdain towards human affairs, which could operate on this supposed being, occur also to a philosopher; but being, in some measure, disproportioned to human capacity, and not being fortified by the experience of any thing better, they make not a full impression on him. He sees, but he feels not sufficiently their truth; and is always a sublime philosopher, when he needs not; that is, as long as nothing disturbs him, or rouzes his affections. While others play, he wonders at their keenness and ardour; but he no sooner puts in his own stake, than he is commonly transported with the same passions, that he had so much condemned, while he remained a simple spectator.

49   There are two considerations chiefly, to be met with in books of philosophy, from which any important effect is to be expected, and that because these considerations are drawn from common life, and occur upon the

---

[5] *De exilio.* ["On Exile" (Plutarch, *Moralia*).]

most superficial view of human affairs. When we reflect on the shortness and uncertainty of life, how despicable seem all our pursuits of happiness? And even, if we would extend our concern beyond our own life, how frivolous appear our most enlarged and most generous projects; when we consider the incessant changes and revolutions of human affairs, by which laws and learning, books and governments are hurried away by time, as by a rapid stream, and are lost in the immense ocean of matter? Such a reflection certainly tends to mortify all our passions: But does it not thereby counterwork the artifice of nature, who has happily deceived us into an opinion, that human life is of some importance? And may not such a reflection be employed with success by voluptuous reasoners, in order to lead us, from the paths of action and virtue, into the flowery fields of indolence and pleasure?

We are informed by THUCYDIDES, that, during the famous plague of ATHENS, when death seemed present to every one, a dissolute mirth and gaiety prevailed among the people, who exhorted one another to make the most of life as long as it endured. The same observation is made by BOCCACE with regard to the plague of FLORENCE. A like principle makes soldiers, during war, be more addicted to riot and expence, than any other race of men. Present pleasure is always of importance; and whatever diminishes the importance of all other objects must bestow on it an additional influence and value. 50

The *second* philosophical consideration, which may often have an influence on the affections, is derived from a comparison of our own condition with the condition of others. This comparison we are continually making, even in common life; but the misfortune is, that we are rather apt to compare our situation with that of our superiors, than with that of our inferiors. A philosopher corrects this natural infirmity, by turning his view to the other side, in order to render himself easy in the situation, to which fortune has confined him. There are few people, who are not susceptible of some consolation from this reflection, though, to a very good-natured man, the view of human miseries should rather produce sorrow than comfort, and add, to his lamentations for his own misfortunes, a deep compassion for those of others. Such is the imperfection, even of the best of these philosophical topics of consolation.[6] 51

---

[6] The Sceptic, perhaps, carries the matter too far, when he limits all philosophical topics and reflections to these two. There seem to be others, whose truth is undeniable, and whose natural tendency is to tranquillize and soften all the passions. Philosophy greedily seizes these, studies them, weighs them, commits them to the memory, and familiarizes them to the mind: And their influence on tempers, which are thoughtful, gentle, and moderate, may be considerable. But what is their influence, you will say, if the temper be

52   I shall conclude this subject with observing, that, though virtue be undoubtedly the best choice, when it is attainable; yet such is the disorder
and confusion of human affairs, that no perfect or regular distribution of
happiness and misery is ever, in this life, to be expected. Not only the

---

antecedently disposed after the same manner as that to which they pretend to form it?
They may, at least, fortify that temper, and furnish it with views, by which it may entertain and nourish itself. Here are a few examples of such philosophical reflections.

1. Is it not certain, that every condition has concealed ills? Then why envy any
   body?
2. Every one has known ills; and there is a compensation throughout. Why not be
   contented with the present?
3. Custom deadens the sense both of the good and the ill, and levels everything.
4. Health and humour all. The rest of little consequence, except these be affected.
5. How many other good things have I? Then why be vexed for one ill?
6. How many are happy in the condition of which I complain? How many envy me?
7. Every good must be paid for: Fortune by labour, favour by flattery. Would I keep
   the price, yet have the commodity?
8. Expect not too great happiness in life. Human nature admits it not.
9. Propose not a happiness too complicated. But does that depend on me? Yes: The
   first choice does. Life is like a game: One may choose the game: And passion, by
   degrees, seizes the proper object.
10. Anticipate by your hopes and fancy future consolation, which time infallibly
    brings to every affliction.
11. I desire to be rich. Why? That I may possess many fine objects; houses, gardens,
    equipage, &c. How many fine objects does nature offer to every one without ex-
    pence? If enjoyed, sufficient. If not: See the effect of custom or of temper, which
    would soon take off the relish of the riches.
12. I desire fame. Let this occur: If I act well, I shall have the esteem of all my ac-
    quaintance. And what is all the rest to me?

These reflections are so obvious, that it is a wonder they occur not to every man: So
convincing, that it is a wonder they persuade not every man. But perhaps they do occur
to and persuade most men; when they consider human life, by a general and calm survey: But where any real, affecting incident happens; when passion is awakened, fancy agitated, example draws, and counsel urges; the philosopher is lost in the man, and he
seeks in vain for that persuasion which before seemed so firm and unshaken. What remedy for this inconvenience? Assist yourself by a frequent perusal of the entertaining
moralists: Have recourse to the learning of PLUTARCH, the imagination of LUCIAN, the
eloquence of CICERO, the wit of SENECA, the gaiety of MONTAIGNE, the sublimity of
SHAFTESBURY. Moral precepts, so couched, strike deep, and fortify the mind against the
illusions of passion. But trust not altogether to external aid: By habit and study acquire
that philosophical temper which both gives force to reflection, and by rendering a great
part of your happiness independent, takes off the edge from all disorderly passions, and
tranquillizes the mind. Despise not these helps; but confide not too much in them neither; unless nature has been favourable in the temper, with which she has endowed you.

goods of fortune, and the endowments of the body (both of which are important), not only these advantages, I say, are unequally divided between the virtuous and vicious, but even the mind itself partakes, in some degree, of this disorder, and the most worthy character, by the very constitution of the passions, enjoys not always the highest felicity.

It is observable, that, though every bodily pain proceeds from some disorder in the part or organ, yet the pain is not always proportioned to the disorder; but is greater or less, according to the greater or less sensibility of the part, upon which the noxious humours exert their influence. A *tooth-ach* produces more violent convulsions of pain than a *phthisis* or a *dropsy*. In like manner, with regard to the œconomy of the mind, we may observe, that all vice is indeed pernicious; yet the disturbance or pain is not measured out by nature with exact proportion to the degree of vice, nor is the man of highest virtue, even abstracting from external accidents, always the most happy. A gloomy and melancholy disposition is certainly, *to our sentiments*, a vice or imperfection; but as it may be accompanied with great sense of honour and great integrity, it may be found in very worthy characters; though it is sufficient alone to imbitter life, and render the person affected with it completely miserable. On the other hand, a selfish villain may possess a spring and alacrity of temper, a certain *gaiety of heart*, which is indeed a good quality, but which is rewarded much beyond its merit, and when attended with good fortune, will compensate for the uneasiness and remorse arising from all the other vices. 53

I shall add, as an observation to the same purpose, that, if a man be liable to a vice or imperfection, it may often happen, that a good quality, which he possesses along with it, will render him more miserable, than if he were completely vicious. A person of such imbecility of temper as to be easily broken by affliction, is more unhappy for being endowed with a generous and friendly disposition, which gives him a lively concern for others, and exposes him the more to fortune and accidents. A sense of shame, in an imperfect character, is certainly a virtue; but produces great uneasiness and remorse, from which the abandoned villain is entirely free. A very amorous complexion, with a heart incapable of friendship, is happier than the same excess in love, with a generosity of temper, which transports a man beyond himself, and renders him a total slave to the object of his passion. 54

In a word, human life is more governed by fortune than by reason; is to be regarded more as a dull pastime than as a serious occupation; and is more influenced by particular humour, than by general principles. Shall we engage ourselves in it with passion and anxiety? It is not worthy of so much concern. Shall we be indifferent about what happens? We lose all the pleasure of the game by our phlegm and carelessness. While we are 55 reasoning concerning life, life is gone; and death, though *perhaps* they receive him differently, yet treats alike the fool and the philosopher. To reduce life to exact rule and method, is commonly a painful, oft a fruitless occupation: And is it not also a proof, that we overvalue the prize for which we contend? Even to reason so carefully concerning it, and to fix with accuracy its just idea, would be overvaluing it, were it not that, to some tempers, this occupation is one of the most amusing, in which life could possibly be employed.

ESSAY VI.
OF THE STANDARD OF TASTE.

THE great variety of Taste, as well as of opinion, which prevails in the   1
world, is too obvious not to have fallen under every one's observation.
Men of the most confined knowledge are able to remark a difference of
taste in the narrow circle of their acquaintance, even where the persons
have been educated under the same government, and have early imbibed
the same prejudices. But those, who can enlarge their view to contemplate
distant nations and remote ages, are still more surprized at the great in-
consistence and contrariety. We are apt to call *barbarous* whatever departs
widely from our own taste and apprehension: But soon find the epithet of
reproach retorted on us. And the highest arrogance and self-conceit is at
last startled, on observing an equal assurance on all sides, and scruples,
amidst such a contest of sentiment, to pronounce positively in its own
favour.

As this variety of taste is obvious to the most careless enquirer; so will it   2
be found, on examination, to be still greater in reality than in appearance.
The sentiments of men often differ with regard to beauty and deformity
of all kinds, even while their general discourse is the same. There are certain terms in every language, which import blame, and others praise; and
all men, who use the same tongue, must agree in their application of them.
Every voice is united in applauding elegance, propriety, simplicity, spirit
in writing; and in blaming fustian, affectation, coldness, and a false brilliancy: But when critics come to particulars, this seeming unanimity vanishes; and it is found, that they had affixed a very different meaning to
their expressions. In all matters of opinion and science, the case is opposite: The difference among men is there oftener found to lie in generals
than in particulars; and to be less in reality than in appearance. An explanation of the terms commonly ends the controversy; and the disputants
are surprized to find, that they had been quarrelling, while at bottom they
agreed in their judgment.

Those who found morality on sentiment, more than on reason, are in-   3
clined to comprehend ethics under the former observation, and to maintain, that, in all questions, which regard conduct and manners, the
difference among men is really greater than at first sight it appears. It is
indeed obvious, that writers of all nations and all ages concur in applauding justice, humanity, magnanimity, prudence, veracity; and in blaming
the opposite qualities. Even poets and other authors, whose compositions
are chiefly calculated to please the imagination, are yet found from
HOMER down to FENELON, to inculcate the same moral precepts, and to

bestow their applause and blame on the same virtues and vices. This great unanimity is usually ascribed to the influence of plain reason; which, in all these cases, maintains similar sentiments in all men, and prevents those controversies, to which the abstract sciences are so much exposed. So far as the unanimity is real, this account may be admitted as satisfactory: But we must also allow that some part of the seeming harmony in morals may be accounted for from the very nature of language. The word *virtue*, with its equivalent in every tongue, implies praise; as that of *vice* does blame: And no one, without the most obvious and grossest impropriety, could affix reproach to a term, which in general acceptation is understood in a good sense; or bestow applause, where the idiom requires disapprobation. HOMER'S general precepts, where he delivers any such, will never be controverted; but it is obvious, that, when he draws particular pictures of manners, and represents heroism in ACHILLES and prudence in ULYSSES, he intermixes a much greater degree of ferocity in the former, and of cunning and fraud in the latter, than FENELON would admit of. The sage ULYSSES in the GREEK poet seems to delight in lies and fictions, and often employs them without any necessity or even advantage: But his more scrupulous son, in the FRENCH epic writer, exposes himself to the most imminent perils, rather than depart from the most exact line of truth and veracity.

4   The admirers and followers of the ALCORAN insist on the excellent moral precepts interspersed throughout that wild and absurd performance. But it is to be supposed, that the ARABIC words, which correspond to the ENGLISH, equity, justice, temperance, meekness, charity, were such as, from the constant use of that tongue, must always be taken in a good sense; and it would have argued the greatest ignorance, not of morals, but of language, to have mentioned them with any epithets, besides those of applause and approbation. But would we know, whether the pretended prophet had really attained a just sentiment of morals? Let us attend to his narration; and we shall soon find, that he bestows praise on such instances of treachery, inhumanity, cruelty, revenge, bigotry, as are utterly incompatible with civilized society. No steady rule of right seems there to be attended to; and every action is blamed or praised, so far only as it is beneficial or hurtful to the true believers.

5   The merit of delivering true general precepts in ethics is indeed very small. Whoever recommends any moral virtues, really does no more than is implied in the terms themselves. That people, who invented the word *charity*, and used it in a good sense, inculcated more clearly and much more efficaciously, the precept, *be charitable*, than any pretended legislator or prophet, who should insert such a *maxim* in his writings. Of all expressions, those, which, together with their other meaning, imply a degree ei-

ther of blame or approbation, are the least liable to be perverted or mistaken.

It is natural for us to seek a *Standard of Taste;* a rule, by which the various sentiments of men may be reconciled; at least, a decision, afforded, confirming one sentiment, and condemning another.   6

There is a species of philosophy, which cuts off all hopes of success in such an attempt, and represents the impossibility of ever attaining any standard of taste. The difference, it is said, is very wide between judgment and sentiment. All sentiment is right; because sentiment has a reference to nothing beyond itself, and is always real, wherever a man is conscious of it. But all determinations of the understanding are not right; because they have a reference to something beyond themselves, to wit, real matter of fact; and are not always conformable to that standard. Among a thousand different opinions which different men may entertain of the same subject, there is one, and but one, that is just and true; and the only difficulty is to fix and ascertain it. On the contrary, a thousand different sentiments, excited by the same object, are all right: Because no sentiment represents what is really in the object. It only marks a certain conformity or relation between the object and the organs or faculties of the mind; and if that conformity did not really exist, the sentiment could never possibly have being. Beauty is no quality in things themselves: It exists merely in the mind which contemplates them; and each mind perceives a different beauty. One person may even perceive deformity, where another is sensible of beauty; and every individual ought to acquiesce in his own sentiment, without pretending to regulate those of others. To seek the real beauty, or real deformity, is as fruitless an enquiry, as to pretend to ascertain the real sweet or real bitter. According to the disposition of the organs, the same object may be both sweet and bitter; and the proverb has justly determined it to be fruitless to dispute concerning tastes. It is very natural, and even quite necessary, to extend this axiom to mental, as well as bodily taste; and thus common sense, which is so often at variance with philosophy, especially with the sceptical kind, is found, in one instance at least, to agree in pronouncing the same decision.   7

But though this axiom, by passing into a proverb, seems to have attained the sanction of common sense; there is certainly a species of common sense which opposes it, at least serves to modify and restrain it. Whoever would assert an equality of genius and elegance between OGILBY and MILTON, or BUNYAN and ADDISON, would be thought to defend no less an extravagance, than if he had maintained a mole-hill to be as high as TENERIFFE, or a pond as extensive as the ocean. Though there may be found persons, who give the preference to the former authors; no one pays attention to such a taste; and we pronounce without scruple the sen-   8 timent of these pretended critics to be absurd and ridiculous. The principle of the natural equality of tastes is then totally forgot, and while we admit it on some occasions, where the objects seem near an equality, it appears an extravagant paradox, or rather a palpable absurdity, where objects so disproportioned are compared together.

9   It is evident that none of the rules of composition are fixed by reasonings *a priori*, or can be esteemed abstract conclusions of the understanding, from comparing those habitudes and relations of ideas, which are eternal and immutable. Their foundation is the same with that of all the practical sciences, experience; nor are they any thing but general observations, concerning what has been universally found to please in all countries and in all ages. Many of the beauties of poetry and even of eloquence are founded on falsehood and fiction, on hyperboles, metaphors, and an abuse or perversion of terms from their natural meaning. To check the sallies of the imagination, and to reduce every expression to geometrical truth and exactness, would be the most contrary to the laws of criticism; because it would produce a work, which, by universal experience, has been found the most insipid and disagreeable. But though poetry can never submit to exact truth, it must be confined by rules of art, discovered to the author either by genius or observation. If some negligent or irregular writers have pleased, they have not pleased by their transgressions of rule or order, but in spite of these transgressions: They have possessed other beauties, which were conformable to just criticism; and the force of these beauties has been able to overpower censure, and give the mind a satisfaction superior to the disgust arising from the blemishes. ARIOSTO pleases; but not by his monstrous and improbable fictions, by his bizarre mixture of the serious and comic styles, by the want of coherence in his stories, or by the continual interruptions of his narration. He charms by the force and clearness of his expression, by the readiness and variety of his inventions, and by his natural pictures of the passions, especially those of the gay and amorous kind: And however his faults may diminish our satisfaction, they are not able entirely to destroy it. Did our pleasure really arise from those parts of his poem, which we denominate faults, this would be no objection to criticism in general: It would only be an objection to those particular rules of criticism, which would establish such circumstances to be faults, and would represent them as universally blameable. If they are found to please, they cannot be faults; let the pleasure, which they produce, be ever so unexpected and unaccountable.

10   But though all the general rules of art are founded only on experience and on the observation of the common sentiments of human nature, we must not imagine, that, on every occasion, the feelings of men will be conformable to these rules. Those finer emotions of the mind are of a very

tender and delicate nature, and require the concurrence of many favourable circumstances to make them play with facility and exactness, according to their general and established principles. The least exterior hindrance to such small springs, or the least internal disorder, disturbs their motion, and confounds the operation of the whole machine. When we would make an experiment of this nature, and would try the force of any beauty or deformity, we must choose with care a proper time and place, and bring the fancy to a suitable situation and disposition. A perfect serenity of mind, a recollection of thought, a due attention to the object; if any of these circumstances be wanting, our experiment will be fallacious, and we shall be unable to judge of the catholic and universal beauty. The relation, which nature has placed between the form and the sentiment, will at least be more obscure; and it will require greater accuracy to trace and discern it. We shall be able to ascertain its influence not so much from the operation of each particular beauty, as from the durable admiration, which attends those works, that have survived all the caprices of mode and fashion, all the mistakes of ignorance and envy.

The same HOMER, who pleased at ATHENS and ROME two thousand   11
years ago, is still admired at PARIS and at LONDON. All the changes of climate, government, religion, and language, have not been able to obscure his glory. Authority or prejudice may give a temporary vogue to a bad poet or orator; but his reputation will never be durable or general. When his compositions are examined by posterity or by foreigners, the enchantment is dissipated, and his faults appear in their true colours. On the contrary, a real genius, the longer his works endure, and the more wide they are spread, the more sincere is the admiration which he meets with. Envy and jealousy have too much place in a narrow circle; and even familiar acquaintance with his person may diminish the applause due to his performances: But when these obstructions are removed, the beauties, which are naturally fitted to excite agreeable sentiments, immediately display their energy; and while the world endures, they maintain their authority over the minds of men.

It appears then, that, amidst all the variety and caprice of taste, there   12
are certain general principles of approbation or blame, whose influence a careful eye may trace in all operations of the mind. Some particular forms or qualities, from the original structure of the internal fabric, are calculated to please, and others to displease; and if they fail of their effect in any particular instance, it is from some apparent defect or imperfection in the organ. A man in a fever would not insist on his palate as able to decide concerning flavours; nor would one, affected with the jaundice, pretend to give a verdict with regard to colours. In each creature, there is a sound and a defective state; and the former alone can be supposed to afford us a true

standard of taste and sentiment. If, in the sound state of the organ, there be an entire or a considerable uniformity of sentiment among men, we may thence derive an idea of the perfect beauty; in like manner as the appearance of objects in day-light, to the eye of a man in health, is denominated their true and real colour, even while colour is allowed to be merely a phantasm of the senses.

13   Many and frequent are the defects in the internal organs, which prevent or weaken the influence of those general principles, on which depends our sentiment of beauty or deformity. Though some objects, by the structure of the mind, be naturally calculated to give pleasure, it is not to be expected, that in every individual the pleasure will be equally felt. Particular incidents and situations occur, which either throw a false light on the objects, or hinder the true from conveying to the imagination the proper sentiment and perception.

14   One obvious cause, why many feel not the proper sentiment of beauty, is the want of that *delicacy* of imagination, which is requisite to convey a sensibility of those finer emotions. This delicacy every one pretends to: Every one talks of it; and would reduce every kind of taste or sentiment to its standard. But as our intention in this essay is to mingle some light of the understanding with the feelings of sentiment, it will be proper to give a more accurate definition of delicacy, than has hitherto been attempted. And not to draw our philosophy from too profound a source, we shall have recourse to a noted story in DON QUIXOTE.

15   It is with good reason, says SANCHO to the squire with the great nose, that I pretend to have a judgment in wine: This is a quality hereditary in our family. Two of my kinsmen were once called to give their opinion of a hogshead, which was supposed to be excellent, being old and of a good vintage. One of them tastes it; considers it; and after mature reflection pronounces the wine to be good, were it not for a small taste of leather, which he perceived in it. The other, after using the same precautions, gives also his verdict in favour of the wine; but with the reserve of a taste of iron, which he could easily distinguish. You cannot imagine how much they were both ridiculed for their judgment. But who laughed in the end? On emptying the hogshead, there was found at the bottom, an old key with a leathern thong tied to it.

16   The great resemblance between mental and bodily taste will easily teach us to apply this story. Though it be certain, that beauty and deformity, more than sweet and bitter, are not qualities in objects, but belong entirely to the sentiment, internal or external; it must be allowed, that there are certain qualities in objects, which are fitted by nature to produce those particular feelings. Now as these qualities may be found in a small

degree, or may be mixed and confounded with each other, it often happens, that the taste is not affected with such minute qualities, or is not able to distinguish all the particular flavours, amidst the disorder, in which they are presented. Where the organs are so fine, as to allow nothing to escape them; and at the same time so exact as to perceive every ingredient in the composition: This we call delicacy of taste, whether we employ these terms in the literal or metaphorical sense. Here then the general rules of beauty are of use; being drawn from established models, and from the observation of what pleases or displeases, when presented singly and in a high degree: And if the same qualities, in a continued composition and in a smaller degree, affect not the organs with a sensible delight or uneasiness, we exclude the person from all pretensions to this delicacy. To produce these general rules or avowed patterns of composition is like finding the key with the leathern thong; which justified the verdict of SANCHO'S kinsmen, and confounded those pretended judges who had condemned them. Though the hogshead had never been emptied, the taste of the one was still equally delicate, and that of the other equally dull and languid: But it would have been more difficult to have proved the superiority of the former, to the conviction of every by-stander. In like manner, though the beauties of writing had never been methodized, or reduced to general principles; though no excellent models had ever been acknowledged; the different degrees of taste would still have subsisted, and the judgment of one man been preferable to that of another; but it would not have been so easy to silence the bad critic, who might always insist upon his particular sentiment, and refuse to submit to his antagonist. But when we show him an avowed principle of art; when we illustrate this principle by examples, whose operation, from his own particular taste, he acknowledges to be conformable to the principle; when we prove, that the same principle may be applied to the present case, where he did not perceive or feel its influence: He must conclude, upon the whole, that the fault lies in himself, and that he wants the delicacy, which is requisite to make him sensible of every beauty and every blemish, in any composition or discourse.

It is acknowledged to be the perfection of every sense or faculty, to perceive with exactness its most minute objects, and allow nothing to escape its notice and observation. The smaller the objects are, which become sensible to the eye, the finer is that organ, and the more elaborate its make and composition. A good palate is not tried by strong flavours; but by a mixture of small ingredients, where we are still sensible of each part, notwithstanding its minuteness and its confusion with the rest. In like manner, a quick and acute perception of beauty and deformity must be the perfection of our mental taste; nor can a man be satisfied with himself while he suspects, that any excellence or blemish in a discourse has passed him unobserved. In this case, the perfection of the man, and the perfection of the sense or feeling, are found to be united. A very delicate palate, on many occasions, may be a great inconvenience both to a man himself and to his friends: But a delicate taste of wit or beauty must always be a desirable quality; because it is the source of all the finest and most innocent enjoyments, of which human nature is susceptible. In this decision the sentiments of all mankind are agreed. Wherever you can ascertain a delicacy of taste, it is sure to meet with approbation; and the best way of ascertaining it is to appeal to those models and principles, which have been established by the uniform consent and experience of nations and ages.

18   But though there be naturally a wide difference in point of delicacy between one person and another, nothing tends further to encrease and improve this talent, than *practice* in a particular art, and the frequent survey or contemplation of a particular species of beauty. When objects of any kind are first presented to the eye or imagination, the sentiment, which attends them, is obscure and confused; and the mind is, in a great measure, incapable of pronouncing concerning their merits or defects. The taste cannot perceive the several excellencies of the performance; much less distinguish the particular character of each excellency, and ascertain its quality and degree. If it pronounce the whole in general to be beautiful or deformed, it is the utmost that can be expected; and even this judgment, a person, so unpractised, will be apt to deliver with great hesitation and reserve. But allow him to acquire experience in those objects, his feeling becomes more exact and nice: He not only perceives the beauties and defects of each part, but marks the distinguishing species of each quality, and assigns it suitable praise or blame. A clear and distinct sentiment attends him through the whole survey of the objects; and he discerns that very degree and kind of approbation or displeasure, which each part is naturally fitted to produce. The mist dissipates, which seemed formerly to hang over the object: The organ acquires greater perfection in its operations; and can pronounce, without danger of mistake, concerning the merits of every performance. In a word, the same address and dexterity, which practice gives to the execution of any work, is also acquired by the same means, in the judging of it.

19   So advantageous is practice to the discernment of beauty, that, before we can give judgment on any work of importance, it will even be requisite, that that very individual performance be more than once perused by us, and be surveyed in different lights with attention and deliberation. There is a flutter or hurry of thought which attends the first perusal of any piece, and which confounds the genuine sentiment of beauty. The relation of the parts is not discerned: The true characters of style are little distinguished:

The several perfections and defects seem wrapped up in a species of confusion, and present themselves indistinctly to the imagination. Not to mention, that there is a species of beauty, which, as it is florid and superficial, pleases at first; but being found incompatible with a just expression either of reason or passion, soon palls upon the taste, and is then rejected with disdain, at least rated at a much lower value.

It is impossible to continue in the practice of contemplating any order 20 of beauty, without being frequently obliged to form *comparisons* between the several species and degrees of excellence, and estimating their proportion to each other. A man, who has had no opportunity of comparing the different kinds of beauty, is indeed totally unqualified to pronounce an opinion with regard to any object presented to him. By comparison alone we fix the epithets of praise or blame, and learn how to assign the due degree of each. The coarsest daubing contains a certain lustre of colours and exactness of imitation, which are so far beauties, and would affect the mind of a peasant or Indian with the highest admiration. The most vulgar ballads are not entirely destitute of harmony or nature; and none but a person, familiarized to superior beauties, would pronounce their numbers harsh, or narration uninteresting. A great inferiority of beauty gives pain to a person conversant in the highest excellence of the kind, and is for that reason pronounced a deformity: As the most finished object, with which we are acquainted, is naturally supposed to have reached the pinnacle of perfection, and to be entitled to the highest applause. One accustomed to see, and examine, and weigh the several performances, admired in different ages and nations, can alone rate the merits of a work exhibited to his view, and assign its proper rank among the productions of genius.

But to enable a critic the more fully to execute this undertaking, he 21 must preserve his mind free from all *prejudice*, and allow nothing to enter into his consideration, but the very object which is submitted to his examination. We may observe, that every work of art, in order to produce its due effect on the mind, must be surveyed in a certain point of view, and cannot be fully relished by persons, whose situation, real or imaginary, is not conformable to that which is required by the performance. An orator addresses himself to a particular audience, and must have a regard to their particular genius, interests, opinions, passions, and prejudices; otherwise he hopes in vain to govern their resolutions, and inflame their affections. Should they even have entertained some prepossessions against him, however unreasonable, he must not overlook this disadvantage; but, before he enters upon the subject, must endeavour to conciliate their affection, and acquire their good graces. A critic of a different age or nation, who should peruse this discourse, must have all these circumstances in his eye, and must place himself in the same situation as the audience, in order to form a true judgment of the oration. In like manner, when any work is addressed to the public, though I should have a friendship or enmity with the author, I must depart from this situation; and considering myself as a man in general, forget, if possible, my individual being and my peculiar circumstances. A person influenced by prejudice, complies not with this condition; but obstinately maintains his natural position, without placing himself in that point of view, which the performance supposes. If the work be addressed to persons of a different age or nation, he makes no allowance for their peculiar views and prejudices; but, full of the manners of his own age and country, rashly condemns what seemed admirable in the eyes of those for whom alone the discourse was calculated. If the work be executed for the public, he never sufficiently enlarges his comprehension, or forgets his interest as a friend or enemy, as a rival or commentator. By this means, his sentiments are perverted; nor have the same beauties and blemishes the same influence upon him, as if he had imposed a proper violence on his imagination, and had forgotten himself for a moment. So far his taste evidently departs from the true standard; and of consequence loses all credit and authority.

22   It is well known, that in all questions, submitted to the understanding, prejudice is destructive of sound judgment, and perverts all operations of the intellectual faculties: It is no less contrary to good taste; nor has it less influence to corrupt our sentiment of beauty. It belongs to *good sense* to check its influence in both cases; and in this respect, as well as in many others, reason, if not an essential part of taste, is at least requisite to the operations of this latter faculty. In all the nobler productions of genius, there is a mutual relation and correspondence of parts; nor can either the beauties or blemishes be perceived by him, whose thought is not capacious enough to comprehend all those parts, and compare them with each other, in order to perceive the consistence and uniformity of the whole. Every work of art has also a certain end or purpose, for which it is calculated; and is to be deemed more or less perfect, as it is more or less fitted to attain this end. The object of eloquence is to persuade, of history to instruct, of poetry to please by means of the passions and the imagination. These ends we must carry constantly in our view, when we peruse any performance; and we must be able to judge how far the means employed are adapted to their respective purposes. Besides, every kind of composition, even the most poetical, is nothing but a chain of propositions and reasonings; not always, indeed, the justest and most exact, but still plausible and specious, however disguised by the colouring of the imagination. The persons introduced in tragedy and epic poetry, must be represented as reasoning, and thinking, and concluding, and acting, suitably to their character and circumstances; and without judgment, as well as taste and

invention, a poet can never hope to succeed in so delicate an undertaking. Not to mention, that the same excellence of faculties which contributes to the improvement of reason, the same clearness of conception, the same exactness of distinction, the same vivacity of apprehension, are essential to the operations of true taste, and are its infallible concomitants. It seldom, or never happens, that a man of sense, who has experience in any art, cannot judge of its beauty; and it is no less rare to meet with a man who has a just taste without a sound understanding.

Thus, though the principles of taste be universal, and nearly, if not entirely the same in all men; yet few are qualified to give judgment on any work of art, or establish their own sentiment as the standard of beauty. The organs of internal sensation are seldom so perfect as to allow the general principles their full play, and produce a feeling correspondent to those principles. They either labour under some defect, or are vitiated by some disorder; and by that means, excite a sentiment, which may be pronounced erroneous. When the critic has no delicacy, he judges without any distinction, and is only affected by the grosser and more palpable qualities of the object: The finer touches pass unnoticed and disregarded. Where he is not aided by practice, his verdict is attended with confusion and hesitation. Where no comparison has been employed, the most frivolous beauties, such as rather merit the name of defects, are the object of his admiration. Where he lies under the influence of prejudice, all his natural sentiments are perverted. Where good sense is wanting, he is not qualified to discern the beauties of design and reasoning, which are the highest and most excellent. Under some or other of these imperfections, the generality of men labour; and hence a true judge in the finer arts is observed, even during the most polished ages, to be so rare a character: Strong sense, united to delicate sentiment, improved by practice, perfected by comparison, and cleared of all prejudice, can alone entitle critics to this valuable character; and the joint verdict of such, wherever they are to be found, is the true standard of taste and beauty. 23

But where are such critics to be found? By what marks are they to be known? How distinguish them from pretenders? These questions are embarrassing; and seem to throw us back into the same uncertainty, from which, during the course of this essay, we have endeavoured to extricate ourselves. 24

But if we consider the matter aright, these are questions of fact, not of sentiment. Whether any particular person be endowed with good sense and a delicate imagination, free from prejudice, may often be the subject of dispute, and be liable to great discussion and enquiry: But that such a character is valuable and estimable will be agreed in by all mankind. Where these doubts occur, men can do no more than in other disputable 25 questions, which are submitted to the understanding: They must produce the best arguments, that their invention suggests to them; they must acknowledge a true and decisive standard to exist somewhere, to wit, real existence and matter of fact; and they must have indulgence to such as differ from them in their appeals to this standard. It is sufficient for our present purpose, if we have proved, that the taste of all individuals is not upon an equal footing, and that some men in general, however difficult to be particularly pitched upon, will be acknowledged by universal sentiment to have a preference above others.

26   But in reality the difficulty of finding, even in particulars, the standard of taste, is not so great as it is represented. Though in speculation, we may readily avow a certain criterion in science and deny it in sentiment, the matter is found in practice to be much more hard to ascertain in the former case than in the latter. Theories of abstract philosophy, systems of profound theology, have prevailed during one age: In a successive period, these have been universally exploded: Their absurdity has been detected: Other theories and systems have supplied their place, which again gave place to their successors: And nothing has been experienced more liable to the revolutions of chance and fashion than these pretended decisions of science. The case is not the same with the beauties of eloquence and poetry. Just expressions of passion and nature are sure, after a little time, to gain public applause, which they maintain for ever. ARISTOTLE, and PLATO, and EPICURUS, and DESCARTES, may successively yield to each other: But TERENCE and VIRGIL maintain an universal, undisputed empire over the minds of men. The abstract philosophy of CICERO has lost its credit: The vehemence of his oratory is still the object of our admiration.

27   Though men of delicate taste be rare, they are easily to be distinguished in society, by the soundness of their understanding and the superiority of their faculties above the rest of mankind. The ascendant, which they acquire, gives a prevalence to that lively approbation, with which they receive any productions of genius, and renders it generally predominant. Many men, when left to themselves, have but a faint and dubious perception of beauty, who yet are capable of relishing any fine stroke, which is pointed out to them. Every convert to the admiration of the real poet or orator is the cause of some new conversion. And though prejudices may prevail for a time, they never unite in celebrating any rival to the true genius, but yield at last to the force of nature and just sentiment. Thus, though a civilized nation may easily be mistaken in the choice of their admired philosopher, they never have been found long to err, in their affection for a favourite epic or tragic author.

28   But notwithstanding all our endeavours to fix a standard of taste, and reconcile the discordant apprehensions of men, there still remain two sources of variation, which are not sufficient indeed to confound all the

boundaries of beauty and deformity, but will often serve to produce a difference in the degrees of our approbation or blame. The one is the different humours of particular men; the other, the particular manners and opinions of our age and country. The general principles of taste are uniform in human nature: Where men vary in their judgments, some defect or perversion in the faculties may commonly be remarked; proceeding either from prejudice, from want of practice, or want of delicacy; and there is just reason for approving one taste, and condemning another. But where there is such a diversity in the internal frame or external situation as is entirely blameless on both sides, and leaves no room to give one the preference above the other; in that case a certain degree of diversity in judgment is unavoidable, and we seek in vain for a standard, by which we can reconcile the contrary sentiments.

A young man, whose passions are warm, will be more sensibly touched   29
with amorous and tender images, than a man more advanced in years, who takes pleasure in wise, philosophical reflections concerning the conduct of life and moderation of the passions. At twenty, OVID may be the favourite author; HORACE at forty; and perhaps TACITUS at fifty. Vainly would we, in such cases, endeavour to enter into the sentiments of others, and divest ourselves of those propensities, which are natural to us. We choose our favourite author as we do our friend, from a conformity of humour and disposition. Mirth or passion, sentiment or reflection; whichever of these most predominates in our temper, it gives us a peculiar sympathy with the writer who resembles us.

One person is more pleased with the sublime; another with the tender;   30
a third with raillery. One has a strong sensibility to blemishes, and is extremely studious of correctness: Another has a more lively feeling of beauties, and pardons twenty absurdities and defects for one elevated or pathetic stroke. The ear of this man is entirely turned towards conciseness and energy; that man is delighted with a copious, rich, and harmonious expression. Simplicity is affected by one; ornament by another. Comedy, tragedy, satire, odes, have each its partizans, who prefer that particular species of writing to all others. It is plainly an error in a critic, to confine his approbation to one species or style of writing, and condemn all the rest. But it is almost impossible not to feel a predilection for that which suits our particular turn and disposition. Such preferences are innocent and unavoidable, and can never reasonably be the object of dispute, because there is no standard, by which they can be decided.

For a like reason, we are more pleased, in the course of our reading,   31
with pictures and characters, that resemble objects which are found in our own age or country, than with those which describe a different set of customs. It is not without some effort, that we reconcile ourselves to the simplicity of ancient manners, and behold princesses carrying water from the

spring, and kings and heroes dressing their own victuals. We may allow in general, that the representation of such manners is no fault in the author, nor deformity in the piece; but we are not so sensibly touched with them. For this reason, comedy is not easily transferred from one age or nation to another. A FRENCHMAN or ENGLISHMAN is not pleased with the ANDRIA of TERENCE, or CLITIA of MACHIAVEL; where the fine lady, upon whom all the play turns, never once appears to the spectators, but is always kept behind the scenes, suitably to the reserved humour of the ancient GREEKS and modern ITALIANS. A man of learning and reflection can make allowance for these peculiarities of manners; but a common audience can never divest themselves so far of their usual ideas and sentiments, as to relish pictures which no wise resemble them.

32   But here there occurs a reflection, which may, perhaps, be useful in examining the celebrated controversy concerning ancient and modern learning; where we often find the one side excusing any seeming absurdity in the ancients from the manners of the age, and the other refusing to admit this excuse, or at least, admitting it only as an apology for the author, not for the performance. In my opinion, the proper boundaries in this subject have seldom been fixed between the contending parties. Where any innocent peculiarities of manners are represented, such as those above mentioned, they ought certainly to be admitted; and a man, who is shocked with them, gives an evident proof of false delicacy and refinement. The poet's *monument more durable than brass*, must fall to the ground like common brick or clay, were men to make no allowance for the continual revolutions of manners and customs, and would admit of nothing but what was suitable to the prevailing fashion. Must we throw aside the pictures of our ancestors, because of their ruffs and fardingales? But where the ideas of morality and decency alter from one age to another, and where vicious manners are described, without being marked with the proper characters of blame and disapprobation; this must be allowed to disfigure the poem, and to be a real deformity. I cannot, nor is it proper I should, enter into such sentiments; and however I may excuse the poet, on account of the manners of his age, I never can relish the composition. The want of humanity and of decency, so conspicuous in the characters drawn by several of the ancient poets, even sometimes by HOMER and the GREEK tragedians, diminishes considerably the merit of their noble performances, and gives modern authors an advantage over them. We are not interested in the fortunes and sentiments of such rough heroes: We are displeased to find the limits of vice and virtue so much confounded: And whatever indulgence we may give to the writer on account of his prejudices, we cannot prevail on ourselves to enter into his sentiments, or bear an affection to characters, which we plainly discover to be blameable.

The case is not the same with moral principles, as with speculative   33
opinions of any kind. These are in continual flux and revolution. The son
embraces a different system from the father. Nay, there scarcely is any
man, who can boast of great constancy and uniformity in this particular.
Whatever speculative errors may be found in the polite writings of any age
or country, they detract but little from the value of those compositions.
There needs but a certain turn of thought or imagination to make us enter
into all the opinions, which then prevailed, and relish the sentiments or
conclusions derived from them. But a very violent effort is requisite to
change our judgment of manners, and excite sentiments of approbation or
blame, love or hatred, different from those to which the mind from long
custom has been familiarized. And where a man is confident of the rectitude of that moral standard, by which he judges, he is justly jealous of it,
and will not pervert the sentiments of his heart for a moment, in complaisance to any writer whatsoever.

Of all speculative errors, those, which regard religion, are the most ex-   34
cusable in compositions of genius; nor is it ever permitted to judge of the
civility or wisdom of any people, or even of single persons, by the gross-
ness or refinement of their theological principles. The same good sense,
that directs men in the ordinary occurrences of life, is not hearkened to in
religious matters, which are supposed to be placed altogether above the
cognizance of human reason. On this account, all the absurdities of the
pagan system of theology must be overlooked by every critic, who would
pretend to form a just notion of ancient poetry; and our posterity, in their
turn, must have the same indulgence to their forefathers. No religious
principles can ever be imputed as a fault to any poet, while they remain
merely principles, and take not such strong possession of his heart, as to
lay him under the imputation of *bigotry* or *superstition*. Where that happens, they confound the sentiments of morality, and alter the natural
boundaries of vice and virtue. They are therefore eternal blemishes, according to the principle abovementioned; nor are the prejudices and false
opinions of the age sufficient to justify them.

It is essential to the ROMAN catholic religion to inspire a violent hatred   35
of every other worship, and to represent all pagans, mahometans, and
heretics as the objects of divine wrath and vengeance. Such sentiments,
though they are in reality very blameable, are considered as virtues by the
zealots of that communion, and are represented in their tragedies and epic
poems as a kind of divine heroism. This bigotry has disfigured two very
fine tragedies of the FRENCH theatre, POLIEUCTE and ATHALIA; where an
intemperate zeal for particular modes of worship is set off with all the
pomp imaginable, and forms the predominant character of the heroes.
"What is this," says the sublime JOAD to JOSABET, finding her in discourse

with MATHAN, the priest of BAAL, "Does the daughter of DAVID speak to this traitor? Are you not afraid, lest the earth should open and pour forth flames to devour you both? Or lest these holy walls should fall and crush you together? What is his purpose? Why comes that enemy of God hither to poison the air, which we breathe, with his horrid presence?" Such sentiments are received with great applause on the theatre of PARIS; but at LONDON the spectators would be full as much pleased to hear ACHILLES tell AGAMEMNON, that he was a dog in his forehead, and a deer in his heart, or JUPITER threaten JUNO with a sound drubbing, if she will not be quiet.

36   RELIGIOUS principles are also a blemish in any polite composition, when they rise up to superstition, and intrude themselves into every sentiment, however remote from any connection with religion. It is no excuse for the poet, that the customs of his country had burthened life with so many religious ceremonies and observances, that no part of it was exempt from that yoke. It must for ever be ridiculous in PETRARCH to compare his mistress, LAURA, to JESUS CHRIST. Nor is it less ridiculous in that agreeable libertine, BOCCACE, very seriously to give thanks to GOD ALMIGHTY and the ladies, for their assistance in defending him against his enemies.

ESSAY VII.
OF THE ORIGINAL CONTRACT.

As no party, in the present age, can well support itself, without a philo-   1
sophical or speculative system of principles, annexed to its political or
practical one; we accordingly find, that each of the factions, into which
this nation is divided, has reared up a fabric of the former kind, in order to
protect and cover that scheme of actions, which it pursues. The people
being commonly very rude builders, especially in this speculative way, and
more especially still, when actuated by party-zeal; it is natural to imagine,
that their workmanship must be a little unshapely, and discover evident
marks of that violence and hurry, in which it was raised. The one party, by
tracing up government to the DEITY, endeavour to render it so sacred and
inviolate, that it must be little less than sacrilege, however tyrannical it
may become, to touch or invade it, in the smallest article. The other party,
by founding government altogether on the consent of the PEOPLE, suppose that there is a kind of *original contract*, by which the subjects have
tacitly reserved the power of resisting their sovereign, whenever they find
themselves aggrieved by that authority, with which they have, for certain
purposes, voluntarily entrusted him. These are the speculative principles
of the two parties; and these too are the practical consequences deduced
from them.

I shall venture to affirm, *That both these* systems *of speculative principles*   2
are just; though not in the sense, intended by the parties: And, *That both the*
schemes of practical consequences are prudent; though not in the extremes, to
which each party, in opposition to the other, has commonly endeavoured to
carry them.

That the DEITY is the ultimate author of all government, will never be   3
denied by any, who admit a general providence, and allow, that all events
in the universe are conducted by an uniform plan, and directed to wise
purposes. As it is impossible for the human race to subsist, at least in any
comfortable or secure state, without the protection of government; this
institution must certainly have been intended by that beneficent Being,
who means the good of all his creatures: And as it has universally, in fact,
taken place, in all countries, and all ages; we may conclude, with still
greater certainty, that it was intended by that omniscient Being, who can
never be deceived by any event or operation. But since he gave rise to it,
not by any particular or miraculous interposition, but by his concealed
and universal efficacy; a sovereign cannot, properly speaking, be called
his vice-gerent, in any other sense than every power or force, being derived from him, may be said to act by his commission. Whatever actually

happens is comprehended in the general plan or intention of providence; nor has the greatest and most lawful prince any more reason, upon that account, to plead a peculiar sacredness or inviolable authority, than an inferior magistrate, or even an usurper, or even a robber and a pyrate. The same divine superintendant, who, for wise purposes, invested a TITUS or a TRAJAN with authority, did also, for purposes, no doubt, equally wise, though unknown, bestow power on a BORGIA or an ANGRIA. The same causes, which gave rise to the sovereign power in every state, established likewise every petty jurisdiction in it, and every limited authority. A constable, therefore, no less than a king, acts by a divine commission, and possesses an indefeasible right.

4   When we consider how nearly equal all men are in their bodily force, and even in their mental powers and faculties, till cultivated by education; we must necessarily allow, that nothing but their own consent could, at first, associate them together, and subject them to any authority. The people, if we trace government to its first origin in the woods and desarts, are the source of all power and jurisdiction, and voluntarily, for the sake of peace and order, abandoned their native liberty, and received laws from their equal and companion. The conditions, upon which they were willing to submit, were either expressed, or were so clear and obvious, that it might well be esteemed superfluous to express them. If this, then, be meant by the *original contract*, it cannot be denied, that all government is, at first, founded on a contract, and that the most ancient rude combinations of mankind were formed chiefly by that principle. In vain, are we asked in what records this charter of our liberties is registered. It was not written on parchment, nor yet on leaves or barks of trees. It preceded the use of writing and all the other civilized arts of life. But we trace it plainly in the nature of man, and in the equality, or something approaching equality, which we find in all the individuals of that species. The force, which now prevails, and which is founded on fleets and armies, is plainly political, and derived from authority, the effect of established government. A man's natural force consists only in the vigour of his limbs, and the firmness of his courage; which could never subject multitudes to the command of one. Nothing but their own consent, and their sense of the advantages resulting from peace and order, could have had that influence.

5   Yet even this consent was long very imperfect, and could not be the basis of a regular administration. The chieftain, who had probably acquired his influence during the continuance of war, ruled more by persuasion than command; and till he could employ force to reduce the refractory and disobedient, the society could scarcely be said to have attained a state of civil government. No compact or agreement, it is evident,

was expressly formed for general submission; an idea far beyond the comprehension of savages: Each exertion of authority in the chieftain must have been particular, and called forth by the present exigencies of the case: The sensible utility, resulting from his interposition, made these exertions become daily more frequent; and their frequency gradually produced an habitual, and, if you please to call it so, a voluntary, and therefore precarious, acquiescence in the people.

But philosophers, who have embraced a party (if that be not a contradiction in terms) are not contented with these concessions. They assert, not only that government in its earliest infancy arose from consent or rather the voluntary acquiescence of the people; but also, that, even at present, when it has attained full maturity, it rests on no other foundation. They affirm, that all men are still born equal, and owe allegiance to no prince or government, unless bound by the obligation and sanction of a *promise*. And as no man, without some equivalent, would forego the advantages of his native liberty, and subject himself to the will of another; this promise is always understood to be conditional, and imposes on him no obligation, unless he meet with justice and protection from his sovereign. These advantages the sovereign promises him in return; and if he fail in the execution, he has broken, on his part, the articles of engagement, and has thereby freed his subject from all obligations to allegiance. Such, according to these philosophers, is the foundation of authority in every government; and such the right of resistance, possessed by every subject.

But would these reasoners look abroad into the world, they would meet with nothing that, in the least, corresponds to their ideas, or can warrant so refined and philosophical a system. On the contrary, we find, every where, princes, who claim their subjects as their property, and assert their independent right of sovereignty, from conquest or succession. We find also, every where, subjects, who acknowledge this right in their prince, and suppose themselves born under obligations of obedience to a certain sovereign, as much as under the ties of reverence and duty to certain parents. These connexions are always conceived to be equally independent of our consent, in PERSIA and CHINA; in FRANCE and SPAIN; and even in HOLLAND and ENGLAND, wherever the doctrines above-mentioned have not been carefully inculcated. Obedience or subjection becomes so familiar, that most men never make any enquiry about its origin or cause, more than about the principle of gravity, resistance, or the most universal laws of nature. Or if curiosity ever move them; as soon as they learn, that they themselves and their ancestors have, for several ages, or from time immemorial, been subject to such a form of government or such a family; they immediately acquiesce, and acknowledge their obligation to allegiance.

Were you to preach, in most parts of the world, that political connexions are founded altogether on voluntary consent or a mutual promise, the magistrate would soon imprison you, as seditious, for loosening the ties of obedience; if your friends did not before shut you up as delirious, for advancing such absurdities. It is strange, that an act of the mind, which every individual is supposed to have formed, and after he came to the use of reason too, otherwise it could have no authority; that this act, I say, should be so much unknown to all of them, that, over the face of the whole earth, there scarcely remain any traces or memory of it.

8   But the contract, on which government is founded, is said to be the *original contract;* and consequently may be supposed too old to fall under the knowledge of the present generation. If the agreement, by which savage men first associated and conjoined their force, be here meant, this is acknowledged to be real; but being so ancient, and being obliterated by a thousand changes of government and princes, it cannot now be supposed to retain any authority. If we would say any thing to the purpose, we must assert, that every particular government, which is lawful, and which imposes any duty of allegiance on the subject, was, at first, founded on consent and a voluntary compact. But besides that this supposes the consent of the fathers to bind the children, even to the most remote generations, (which republican writers will never allow) besides this, I say, it is not justified by history or experience, in any age or country of the world.

9   Almost all the governments, which exist at present, or of which there remains any record in story, have been founded originally, either on usurpation or conquest, or both, without any pretence of a fair consent, or voluntary subjection of the people. When an artful and bold man is placed at the head of an army or faction, it is often easy for him, by employing, sometimes violence, sometimes false pretences, to establish his dominion over a people a hundred times more numerous than his partizans. He allows no such open communication, that his enemies can know, with certainty, their number or force. He gives them no leisure to assemble together in a body to oppose him. Even all those, who are the instruments of his usurpation, may wish his fall; but their ignorance of each other's intention keeps them in awe, and is the sole cause of his security. By such arts as these, many governments have been established; and this is all the *original contract*, which they have to boast of.

10   The face of the earth is continually changing, by the encrease of small kingdoms into great empires, by the dissolution of great empires into smaller kingdoms, by the planting of colonies, by the migration of tribes. Is there any thing discoverable in all these events, but force and violence? Where is the mutual agreement or voluntary association so much talked of?

Even the smoothest way, by which a nation may receive a foreign mas-	11
ter, by marriage or a will, is not extremely honourable for the people; but
supposes them to be disposed of, like a dowry or a legacy, according to the
pleasure or interest of their rulers.

But where no force interposes, and election takes place; what is this	12
election so highly vaunted? It is either the combination of a few great
men, who decide for the whole, and will allow of no opposition: Or it is
the fury of a multitude, that follow a seditious ringleader, who is not
known, perhaps, to a dozen among them, and who owes his advancement
merely to his own impudence, or to the momentary caprice of his fellows.

Are these disorderly elections, which are rare too, of such mighty au-	13
thority, as to be the only lawful foundation of all government and allegiance?

In reality, there is not a more terrible event, than a total dissolution of	14
government, which gives liberty to the multitude, and makes the determination or choice of a new establishment depend upon a number, which
nearly approaches to that of the body of the people: For it never comes entirely to the whole body of them. Every wise man, then, wishes to see, at
the head of a powerful and obedient army, a general, who may speedily
seize the prize, and give to the people a master, which they are so unfit to
chuse for themselves. So little correspondent is fact and reality to those
philosophical notions.

Let not the establishment at the *Revolution* deceive us, or make us so	15
much in love with a philosophical origin to government, as to imagine all
others monstrous and irregular. Even that event was far from corresponding to these refined ideas. It was only the succession, and that only in the
regal part of the government, which was then changed: And it was only
the majority of seven hundred, who determined that change for near ten
millions. I doubt not, indeed, but the bulk of those ten millions acquiesced willingly in the determination: But was the matter left, in the least,
to their choice? Was it not justly supposed to be, from that moment, decided, and every man punished, who refused to submit to the new sovereign? How otherwise could the matter have ever been brought to any issue
or conclusion?

The republic of ATHENS was, I believe, the most extensive democracy,	16
that we read of in history: Yet if we make the requisite allowances for the
women, the slaves, and the strangers, we shall find, that that establishment
was not, at first, made, nor any law ever voted, by a tenth part of those who
were bound to pay obedience to it: Not to mention the islands and foreign
dominions, which the ATHENIANS claimed as theirs by right of conquest.
And as it is well known, that popular assemblies in that city were always
full of licence and disorder, notwithstanding the institutions and laws by

which they were checked: How much more disorderly must they prove, where they form not the established constitution, but meet tumultuously on the dissolution of the ancient government, in order to give rise to a new one? How chimerical must it be to talk of a choice in such circumstances?

17   The ACHÆANS enjoyed the freest and most perfect democracy of all antiquity; yet they employed force to oblige some cities to enter into their league, as we learn from POLYBIUS.[1]

18   HARRY the IVth and HARRY the VIIth of ENGLAND, had really no title to the throne but a parliamentary election; yet they never would acknowledge it, lest they should thereby weaken their authority. Strange, if the only real foundation of all authority be consent and promise!

19   It is in vain to say, that all governments are or should be, at first, founded on popular consent, as much as the necessity of human affairs will admit. This favours entirely my pretension. I maintain, that human affairs will never admit of this consent; seldom of the appearance of it. But that conquest or usurpation, that is, in plain terms, force, by dissolving the ancient governments, is the origin of almost all the new ones, which were ever established in the world. And that in the few cases, where consent may seem to have taken place, it was commonly so irregular, so confined, or so much intermixed either with fraud or violence, that it cannot have any great authority.

20   My intention here is not to exclude the consent of the people from being one just foundation of government where it has place. It is surely the best and most sacred of any. I only pretend, that it has very seldom had place in any degree, and never almost in its full extent. And that therefore some other foundation of government must also be admitted.

21   Were all men possessed of so inflexible a regard to justice, that, of themselves, they would totally abstain from the properties of others; they had for ever remained in a state of absolute liberty, without subjection to any magistrate or political society: But this is a state of perfection, of which human nature is justly deemed incapable. Again; were all men possessed of so perfect an understanding, as always to know their own interests, no form of government had ever been submitted to, but what was established on consent, and was fully canvassed by every member of the society: But this state of perfection is likewise much superior to human nature. Reason, history, and experience shew us, that all political societies have had an origin much less accurate and regular; and were one to choose a period of time, when the people's consent was the least regarded in public transactions, it would be precisely on the establishment of a new government. In a settled constitution, their inclinations are often consulted;

[1] Lib. ii. cap. 38. [Polybius, *The Histories.*]

but during the fury of revolutions, conquests, and public convulsions, military force or political craft usually decides the controversy.

When a new government is established, by whatever means, the people are commonly dissatisfied with it, and pay obedience more from fear and necessity, than from any idea of allegiance or of moral obligation. The prince is watchful and jealous, and must carefully guard against every beginning or appearance of insurrection. Time, by degrees, removes all these difficulties, and accustoms the nation to regard, as their lawful or native princes, that family, which, at first, they considered as usurpers or foreign conquerors. In order to found this opinion, they have no recourse to any notion of voluntary consent or promise, which, they know, never was, in this case, either expected or demanded. The original establishment was formed by violence, and submitted to from necessity. The subsequent administration is also supported by power, and acquiesced in by the people, not as a matter of choice, but of obligation. They imagine not, that their consent gives their prince a title: But they willingly consent, because they think, that, from long possession, he has acquired a title, independent of their choice or inclination.

Should it be said, that, by living under the dominion of a prince, which one might leave, every individual has given a *tacit* consent to his authority, and promised him obedience; it may be answered, that such an implied consent can only have place, where a man imagines, that the matter depends on his choice. But where he thinks (as all mankind do who are born under established governments) that by his birth he owes allegiance to a certain prince or certain form of government; it would be absurd to infer a consent or choice, which he expressly, in this case, renounces and disclaims.

Can we seriously say, that a poor peasant or artizan has a free choice to leave his country, when he knows no foreign language or manners, and lives from day to day, by the small wages which he acquires? We may as well assert, that a man, by remaining in a vessel, freely consents to the dominion of the master; though he was carried on board while asleep, and must leap into the ocean, and perish, the moment he leaves her.

What if the prince forbid his subjects to quit his dominions; as in TIBERIUS'S time, it was regarded as a crime in a ROMAN knight that he had attempted to fly to the PARTHIANS, in order to escape the tyranny of that emperor?[2] Or as the ancient MUSCOVITES prohibited all travelling under pain of death? And did a prince observe, that many of his subjects were seized with the frenzy of migrating to foreign countries, he would doubtless, with great reason and justice, restrain them, in order to prevent the

22

23

24

25

---

[2] TACIT. Ann. vi. cap. 14. [Tacitus, *The Annals*.]

depopulation of his own kingdom. Would he forfeit the allegiance of all his subjects, by so wise and reasonable a law? Yet the freedom of their choice is surely, in that case, ravished from them.

26   A company of men, who should leave their native country, in order to people some uninhabited region, might dream of recovering their native freedom; but they would soon find, that their prince still laid claim to them, and called them his subjects, even in their new settlement. And in this he would but act conformably to the common ideas of mankind.

27   The truest *tacit* consent of this kind, that is ever observed, is when a foreigner settles in any country, and is beforehand acquainted with the prince, and government, and laws, to which he must submit: Yet is his allegiance, though more voluntary, much less expected or depended on, than that of a natural born subject. On the contrary, his native prince still asserts a claim to him. And if he punish not the renegade, when he seizes him in war with his new prince's commission; this clemency is not founded on the municipal law, which in all countries condemns the prisoner; but on the consent of princes, who have agreed to this indulgence, in order to prevent reprisals.

28   Did one generation of men go off the stage at once, and another succeed, as is the case with silk-worms and butterflies, the new race, if they had sense enough to choose their government, which surely is never the case with men, might voluntarily, and by general consent, establish their own form of civil polity, without any regard to the laws or precedents, which prevailed among their ancestors. But as human society is in perpetual flux, one man every hour going out of the world, another coming into it, it is necessary, in order to preserve stability in government, that the new brood should conform themselves to the established constitution, and nearly follow the path which their fathers, treading in the footsteps of theirs, had marked out to them. Some innovations must necessarily have place in every human institution, and it is happy where the enlightened genius of the age give these a direction to the side of reason, liberty, and justice: but violent innovations no individual is entitled to make: they are even dangerous to be attempted by the legislature: more ill than good is ever to be expected from them: and if history affords examples to the contrary, they are not to be drawn into precedent, and are only to be regarded as proofs, that the science of politics affords few rules, which will not admit of some exception, and which may not sometimes be controuled by fortune and accident. The violent innovations in the reign of HENRY VIII. proceeded from an imperious monarch, seconded by the appearance of legislative authority: Those in the reign of CHARLES I. were derived from faction and fanaticism; and both of them have proved happy in the issue: But even the former were long the source of many disorders, and still

more dangers; and if the measures of allegiance were to be taken from the latter, a total anarchy must have place in human society, and a final period at once be put to every government.

Suppose, that an usurper, after having banished his lawful prince and   29
royal family, should establish his dominion for ten or a dozen years in any country, and should preserve so exact a discipline in his troops, and so regular a disposition in his garrisons, that no insurrection had ever been raised, or even murmur heard, against his administration: Can it be asserted, that the people, who in their hearts abhor his treason, have tacitly consented to his authority, and promised him allegiance, merely because, from necessity, they live under his dominion? Suppose again their native prince restored, by means of an army, which he levies in foreign countries: They receive him with joy and exultation, and shew plainly with what reluctance they had submitted to any other yoke. I may now ask, upon what foundation the prince's title stands? Not on popular consent surely: For though the people willingly acquiesce in his authority, they never imagine, that their consent made him sovereign. They consent; because they apprehend him to be already, by birth, their lawful sovereign. And as to that tacit consent, which may now be inferred from their living under his dominion, this is no more than what they formerly gave to the tyrant and usurper.

When we assert, that all lawful government arises from the consent of   30
the people, we certainly do them a great deal more honour than they deserve, or even expect and desire from us. After the ROMAN dominions became too unwieldly for the republic to govern them, the people, over the whole known world, were extremely grateful to AUGUSTUS for that authority, which, by violence, he had established over them; and they shewed an equal disposition to submit to the successor, whom he left them, by his last will and testament. It was afterwards their misfortune, that there never was, in one family, any long regular succession; but that their line of princes was continually broken, either by private assassinations or public rebellions. The *prætorian* bands, on the failure of every family, set up one emperor; the legions in the East a second; those in GERMANY, perhaps, a third: And the sword alone could decide the controversy. The condition of the people, in that mighty monarchy, was to be lamented, not because the choice of the emperor was never left to them; for that was impracticable: But because they never fell under any succession of masters, who might regularly follow each other. As to the violence and wars and bloodshed, occasioned by every new settlement; these were not blameable, because they were inevitable.

The house of LANCASTER ruled in this island about sixty years; yet the   31
partizans of the white rose seemed daily to multiply in ENGLAND. The

present establishment has taken place during a still longer period. Have all views of right in another family been utterly extinguished; even though scarce any man now alive had arrived at years of discretion, when it was expelled, or could have consented to its dominion, or have promised it allegiance? A sufficient indication surely of the general sentiment of mankind on this head. For we blame not the partizans of the abdicated family, merely on account of the long time, during which they have preserved their imaginary loyalty. We blame them for adhering to a family, which, we affirm, has been justly expelled, and which, from the moment the new settlement took place, had forfeited all title to authority.

32   But would we have a more regular, at least a more philosophical, refutation of this principle of an original contract or popular consent; perhaps, the following observations may suffice.

33   All *moral* duties may be divided into two kinds. The *first* are those, to which men are impelled by a natural instinct or immediate propensity, which operates on them, independent of all ideas of obligation, and of all views, either to public or private utility. Of this nature are, love of children, gratitude to benefactors, pity to the unfortunate. When we reflect on the advantage, which results to society from such humane instincts, we pay them the just tribute of moral approbation and esteem: But the person, actuated by them, feels their power and influence, antecedent to any such reflection.

34   The *second* kind of moral duties are such as are not supported by any original instinct of nature, but are performed entirely from a sense of obligation, when we consider the necessities of human society, and the impossibility of supporting it, if these duties were neglected. It is thus *justice* or a regard to the property of others, *fidelity* or the observance of promises, become obligatory, and acquire an authority over mankind. For as it is evident, that every man loves himself better than any other person, he is naturally impelled to extend his acquisitions as much as possible; and nothing can restrain him in this propensity, but reflection and experience, by which he learns the pernicious effects of that licence, and the total dissolution of society which must ensue from it. His original inclination, therefore, or instinct, is here checked and restrained by a subsequent judgment or observation.

35   The case is precisely the same with the political or civil duty of *allegiance*, as with the natural duties of justice and fidelity. Our primary instincts lead us, either to indulge ourselves in unlimited freedom, or to seek dominion over others: And it is reflection only, which engages us to sacrifice such strong passions to the interests of peace and public order. A small degree of experience and observation suffices to teach us, that society cannot possibly be maintained without the authority of magistrates,

and that this authority must soon fall into contempt, where exact obedience is not payed to it. The observation of these general and obvious interests is the source of all allegiance, and of that moral obligation, which we attribute to it.

What necessity, therefore, is there to found the duty of *allegiance* or obedience to magistrates on that of *fidelity* or a regard to promises, and to suppose, that it is the consent of each individual, which subjects him to government; when it appears, that both allegiance and fidelity stand precisely on the same foundation, and are both submitted to by mankind, on account of the apparent interests and necessities of human society? We are bound to obey our sovereign, it is said; because we have given a tacit promise to that purpose. But why are we bound to observe our promise? It must here be asserted, that the commerce and intercourse of mankind, which are of such mighty advantage, can have no security where men pay no regard to their engagements. In like manner, may it be said, that men could not live at all in society, at least in a civilized society, without laws and magistrates and judges, to prevent the encroachments of the strong upon the weak, of the violent upon the just and equitable. The obligation to allegiance being of like force and authority with the obligation to fidelity, we gain nothing by resolving the one into the other. The general interests or necessities of society are sufficient to establish both. 36

If the reason be asked of that obedience, which we are bound to pay to government, I readily answer, *because society could not otherwise subsist*: And this answer is clear and intelligible to all mankind. Your answer is, *because we should keep our word*. But besides, that no body, till trained in a philosophical system, can either comprehend or relish this answer: Besides this, I say, you find yourself embarrassed, when it is asked, *why we are bound to keep our word?* Nor can you give any answer, but what would, immediately, without any circuit, have accounted for our obligation to allegiance. 37

But *to whom is allegiance due? And who is our lawful sovereign?* This question is often the most difficult of any, and liable to infinite discussions. When people are so happy, that they can answer, *Our present sovereign, who inherits, in a direct line, from ancestors, that have governed us for many ages*; this answer admits of no reply; even though historians, in tracing up to the remotest antiquity, the origin of that royal family, may find, as commonly happens, that its first authority was derived from usurpation and violence. It is confessed, that private justice, or the abstinence from the properties of others, is a most cardinal virtue: Yet reason tells us, that there is no property in durable objects, such as lands or houses, when carefully examined in passing from hand to hand, but must, in some period, have been founded on fraud and injustice. The necessities of human society, neither 38 in private nor public life, will allow of such an accurate enquiry: And there is no virtue or moral duty, but what may, with facility, be refined away, if we indulge a false philosophy, in sifting and scrutinizing it, by every captious rule of logic, in every light or position, in which it may be placed.

39   The questions with regard to private property have filled infinite volumes of law and philosophy, if in both we add the commentators to the original text; and in the end, we may safely pronounce, that many of the rules, there established, are uncertain, ambiguous, and arbitrary. The like opinion may be formed with regard to the succession and rights of princes and forms of government. Several cases, no doubt, occur, especially in the infancy of any constitution, which admit of no determination from the laws of justice and equity: And our historian RAPIN pretends, that the controversy between EDWARD the Third and PHILIP DE VALOIS was of this nature, and could be decided only by an appeal to heaven, that is, by war and violence.

40   Who shall tell me, whether GERMANICUS or DRUSUS ought to have succeeded to TIBERIUS, had he died, while they were both alive, without naming any of them for his successor? Ought the right of adoption to be received as equivalent to that of blood, in a nation, where it had the same effect in private families, and had already, in two instances, taken place in the public? Ought GERMANICUS to be esteemed the elder son because he was born before DRUSUS; or the younger, because he was adopted after the birth of his brother? Ought the right of the elder to be regarded in a nation, where he had no advantage in the succession of private families? Ought the ROMAN empire at that time to be deemed hereditary, because of two examples; or ought it, even so early, to be regarded as belonging to the stronger or to the present possessor, as being founded on so recent an usurpation?

41   COMMODUS mounted the throne after a pretty long succession of excellent emperors, who had acquired their title, not by birth, or public election, but by the fictitious rite of adoption. That bloody debauchee being murdered by a conspiracy suddenly formed between his wench and her gallant, who happened at that time to be *Prætorian Præfect;* these immediately deliberated about choosing a master to human kind, to speak in the style of those ages; and they cast their eyes on PERTINAX. Before the tyrant's death was known, the *Præfect* went secretly to that senator, who, on the appearance of the soldiers, imagined that his execution had been ordered by COMMODUS. He was immediately saluted emperor by the officer and his attendants; chearfully proclaimed by the populace; unwillingly submitted to by the guards; formally recognized by the senate; and passively received by the provinces and armies of the empire.

The discontent of the *Prætorian* bands broke out in a sudden sedition, 42
which occasioned the murder of that excellent prince: And the world
being now without a master and without government, the guards thought
proper to set the empire formally to sale. JULIAN, the purchaser, was proclaimed by the soldiers, recognized by the senate, and submitted to by the
people; and must also have been submitted to by the provinces, had not
the envy of the legions begotten opposition and resistance. PESCENNIUS
NIGER in SYRIA elected himself emperor, gained the tumultuary consent
of his army, and was attended with the secret good-will of the senate and
people of ROME. ALBINUS in BRITAIN found an equal right to set up his
claim; but SEVERUS, who governed PANNONIA, prevailed in the end above
both of them. That able politician and warrior, finding his own birth and
dignity too much inferior to the imperial crown, professed, at first, an intention only of revenging the death of PERTINAX. He marched as general
into ITALY; defeated JULIAN; and without our being able to fix any precise
commencement even of the soldiers' consent, he was from necessity acknowledged emperor by the senate and people; and fully established in his
violent authority by subduing NIGER and ALBINUS.[3]

Inter hæc Gordianus CÆSAR (says CAPITOLINUS, speaking of another pe- 43
riod) *sublatus a militibus.* Imperator *est appellatus, quia non erat alius in
præsenti.*[4] It is to be remarked, that GORDIAN was a boy of fourteen years
of age.

Frequent instances of a like nature occur in the history of the emperors; 44
in that of ALEXANDER'S successors; and of many other countries: Nor can
any thing be more unhappy than a despotic government of this kind;
where the succession is disjointed and irregular, and must be determined,
on every vacancy, by force or election. In a free government, the matter is
often unavoidable, and is also much less dangerous. The interests of liberty may there frequently lead the people, in their own defence, to alter
the succession of the crown. And the constitution, being compounded of
parts, may still maintain a sufficient stability, by resting on the aristocrati-
cal or democratical members, though the monarchical be altered, from
time to time, in order to accommodate it to the former.

In an absolute government, when there is no legal prince, who has a title 45
to the throne, it may safely be determined to belong to the first occupant.

---

[3] HERODIAN, lib. ii. [Herodian, *History of the Empire*.]

[4] ["In the meantime Gordian Caesar was lifted up by the soldiers and hailed emperor, there being no one else at hand" (Julius Capitolinus, *Maximus and Balbinus* in
Scriptores Historiae Augustae, sec. 14; trans. by David Magie).]

Instances of this kind are but too frequent, especially in the eastern monarchies. When any race of princes expires, the will or destination of the last sovereign will be regarded as a title. Thus the edict of LEWIS the XIVth, who called the bastard princes to the succession in case of the failure of all the legitimate princes, would, in such an event, have some authority.[5] Thus the will of CHARLES the Second disposed of the whole SPANISH monarchy. The cession of the ancient proprietor, especially when joined to conquest, is likewise deemed a good title. The general obligation, which binds us to government, is the interest and necessities of society; and this obligation is very strong. The determination of it to this or that particular prince or form of government is frequently more uncertain and dubious. Present possession has considerable authority in these cases, and greater than in private property; because of the disorders which attend all revolutions and changes of government.

46   We shall only observe, before we conclude, that, though an appeal to general opinion may justly, in the speculative sciences of metaphysics, natural philosophy, or astronomy, be deemed unfair and inconclusive, yet in all questions with regard to morals, as well as criticism, there is really no other standard, by which any controversy can ever be decided. And nothing is a clearer proof, that a theory of this kind is erroneous, than to find, that it leads to paradoxes, repugnant to the common sentiments of mankind, and to the practice and opinion of all nations and all ages. The doctrine, which founds all lawful government on an *original contract*, or consent of the people, is plainly of this kind; nor has the most noted of its partizans, in prosecution of it, scrupled to affirm, *that absolute monarchy is*

---

[5] It is remarkable, that, in the remonstrance of the duke of BOURBON and the legitimate princes, against this destination of LOUIS the XIVth, the doctrine of the *original contract* is insisted on, even in that absolute government. The FRENCH nation, say they, chusing HUGH CAPET and his posterity to rule over them and their posterity, where the former line fails, there is a tacit right reserved to choose a new royal family; and this right is invaded by calling the bastard princes to the throne, without the consent of the nation. But the Comte de BOULAINVILLIERS, who wrote in defence of the bastard princes, ridicules this notion of an original contract, especially when applied to HUGH CAPET; who mounted the throne, says he, by the same arts, which have ever been employed by all conquerors and usurpers. He got his title, indeed, recognized by the states after he had put himself in possession: But is this a choice or contract? The Comte de BOULAINVILLIERS, we may observe, was a noted republican; but being a man of learning, and very conversant in history, he knew that the people were never almost consulted in these revolutions and new establishments, and that time alone bestowed right and authority on what was commonly at first founded on force and violence. See *Etat de la France*, Vol. III.

inconsistent with civil society, and so can be no form of civil government at all;[6] *and* that *the supreme power in a state cannot take from any man, by taxes and impositions, any part of his property, without his own consent or that of his representatives.*[7] What authority any moral reasoning can have, which leads into opinions so wide of the general practice of mankind, in every place but this single kingdom, it is easy to determine.

The only passage I meet with in antiquity, where the obligation of obe-   47
dience to government is ascribed to a promise, is in PLATO'S *Crito:* where
SOCRATES refuses to escape from prison, because he had tacitly promised
to obey the laws. Thus he builds a *tory* consequence of passive obedience,
on a *whig* foundation of the original contract.

New discoveries are not to be expected in these matters. If scarce any   48
man, till very lately, ever imagined that government was founded on compact, it is certain, that it cannot, in general, have any such foundation.

The crime of rebellion among the ancients was commonly expressed by   49
the terms νεωτερίζειν, *novas res moliri.*[8]

---

[6] See LOCKE *On Government*, chap. vii. sec. 90.

[7] Id., chap. xi. sec. 138, 139, 140.

[8] [The Greek and Latin alike mean "to make a change."]

ESSAY VIII.
OF SUICIDE.

1   ONE considerable advantage, that arises from philosophy, consists in the
sovereign antidote, which it affords to superstition and false religion. All
other remedies against that pestilent distemper are vain, or, at least, uncertain. Plain good-sense, and the practice of the world, which alone serve
most purposes of life, are here found ineffectual: History, as well as daily
experience, affords instances of men, endowed with the strongest capacity
for business and affairs, who have all their lives crouched under slavery to
the grossest superstition. Even gaiety and sweetness of temper, which infuse a balm into every other wound, afford no remedy to so virulent a poison; as we may particularly observe of the fair sex, who, tho' commonly
possessed of these rich presents of nature, feel many of their joys blasted
by this importunate intruder. But when sound philosophy has once
gained possession of the mind, superstition is effectually excluded; and
one may safely affirm, that her triumph over this enemy is more compleat
than over most of the vices and imperfections, incident to human nature.
Love or anger, ambition or avarice, have their root in the temper and affections, which the soundest reason is scarce ever able fully to correct. But
superstition, being founded on false opinion, must immediately vanish,
when true philosophy has inspired juster sentiments of superior powers.
The contest is here more equal between the distemper and the medicine:
And nothing can hinder the latter from proving effectual, but its being
false and sophisticated.

2   It will here be superfluous to magnify the merits of philosophy, by displaying the pernicious tendency of that vice, of which it cures the human
mind. The superstitious man, says *Tully*,[1] is miserable in every scene, in
every incident of life. Even sleep itself, which banishes all other cares of
unhappy mortals, affords to him matter of new terror; while he examines
his dreams, and finds in those visions of the night, prognostications of future calamities. I may add, that, tho' death alone can put a full period to
his misery, he dares not fly to this refuge, but still prolongs a miserable existence, from a vain fear, lest he offend his maker, by using the power, with
which that beneficent being has endowed him. The presents of God and
Nature are ravished from us by this cruel enemy; and notwithstanding
that one step would remove us from the regions of pain and sorrow, her

---

[1] *De Divin.* lib. ii. [Cicero, *On Divination*, II, 72.]

menaces still chain us down to a hated being, which she herself chiefly contributes to render miserable.

It is observed of such as have been reduced by the calamities of life to 3 the necessity of employing this fatal remedy, that, if the unseasonable care of their friends deprive them of that species of death, which they proposed to themselves, they seldom venture upon any other, or can summon up so much resolution, a second time, as to execute their purpose. So great is our horror of death, that when it presents itself under any form, besides that to which a man has endeavoured to reconcile his imagination, it acquires new terrors, and overcomes his feeble courage. But when the menaces of superstition are joined to this natural timidity, no wonder it quite deprives men of all power over their lives; since even many pleasures and enjoyments, to which we are carried by a strong propensity, are torn from us by this inhuman tyrant. Let us here endeavour to restore men to their native liberty, by examining all the common arguments against Suicide, and shewing, that That action may be free from every imputation of guilt or blame; according to the sentiments of all the antient philosophers.

If Suicide be criminal, it must be a transgression of our duty, either to 4 God, our neighbour, or ourselves.

To prove, that Suicide is no transgression of our duty to God, the fol- 5 lowing considerations may perhaps suffice. In order to govern the material world, the almighty creator has established general and immutable laws, by which all bodies, from the greatest planet to the smallest particle of matter, are maintained in their proper sphere and function. To govern the animal world, he has endowed all living creatures with bodily and mental powers; with senses, passions, appetites, memory, and judgment; by which they arc impelled or regulated in that course of life, to which they are destined. These two distinct principles of the material and animal world continually encroach upon each other, and mutually retard or forward each other's operation. The powers of men and of all other animals are restrained and directed by the nature and qualities of the surrounding bodies; and the modifications and actions of these bodies are incessantly altered by the operation of all animals. Man is stopped by rivers in his passage over the surface of the earth; and rivers, when properly directed, lend their force to the motion of machines, which serve to the use of man. But tho' the provinces of the material and animal powers are not kept entirely separate, there result from thence no discord or disorder in the creation: On the contrary, from the mixture, union, and contrast of all the various powers of inanimate bodies and living creatures, arises that surprizing harmony and proportion, which affords the surest argument of supreme wisdom.

6   The providence of the deity appears not immediately in any operation, but governs every thing by those general and immutable laws, which have been established from the beginning of time. All events, in one sense, may be pronounced the action of the almighty: They all proceed from those powers, with which he has endowed his creatures. A house, which falls by its own weight, is not brought to ruin by his providence more than one destroyed by the hands of men; nor are the human faculties less his workmanship than the laws of motion and gravitation. When the passions play, when the judgment dictates, when the limbs obey; this is all the operation of God; and upon these animate principles, as well as upon the inanimate, has he established the government of the universe.

7   Every event is alike important in the eyes of that infinite being, who takes in, at one glance, the most distant regions of space and remotest periods of time. There is no one event, however important to us, which he has exempted from the general laws that govern the universe, or which he has peculiarly reserved for his own immediate action and operation. The revolutions of states and empires depend upon the smallest caprice or passion of single men; and the lives of men are shortened or extended by the smallest accident of air or diet, sunshine or tempest. Nature still continues her progress and operation; and if general laws be ever broke by particular volitions of the deity, 'tis after a manner which entirely escapes human observation. As on the one hand, the elements and other inanimate parts of the creation carry on their action without regard to the particular interest and situation of men; so men are entrusted to their own judgment and discretion in the various shocks of matter, and may employ every faculty, with which they are endowed, in order to provide for their ease, happiness, or preservation.

8   What is the meaning, then, of that principle, that a man, who, tired of life, and hunted by pain and misery, bravely overcomes all the natural terrors of death, and makes his escape from this cruel scene; that such a man, I say, has incurred the indignation of his creator, by encroaching on the office of divine providence, and disturbing the order of the universe? Shall we assert, that the Almighty has reserved to himself, in any peculiar manner, the disposal of the lives of men, and has not submitted that event, in common with others, to the general laws, by which the universe is governed? This is plainly false. The lives of men depend upon the same laws as the lives of all other animals; and these are subjected to the general laws of matter and motion. The fall of a tower or the infusion of a poison will destroy a man equally with the meanest creature: An inundation sweeps away every thing, without distinction, that comes within the reach of its fury. Since therefore the lives of men are for ever dependent on the general laws of matter and

motion; is a man's disposing of his life criminal, because, in every case, it is criminal to encroach upon these laws, or disturb their operation? But this seems absurd. All animals are entrusted to their own prudence and skill for their conduct in the world, and have full authority, as far as their power extends, to alter all the operations of nature. Without the exercise of this authority, they could not subsist a moment. Every action, every motion of a man innovates in the order of some parts of matter, and diverts, from their ordinary course, the general laws of motion. Putting together, therefore, these conclusions, we find, *that* human life depends upon the general laws of matter and motion, and *that* 'tis no encroachment on the office of providence to disturb or alter these general laws. Has not every one, of consequence, the free disposal of his own life? And may he not lawfully employ that power with which nature has endowed him?

In order to destroy the evidence of this conclusion, we must shew a reason, why this particular case is excepted. Is it because human life is of so great importance, that it is a presumption for human prudence to dispose of it? But the life of man is of no greater importance to the universe than that of an oyster. And were it of ever so great importance, the order of nature has actually submitted it to human prudence, and reduced us to a necessity, in every incident, of determining concerning it. 9

Were the disposal of human life so much reserved as the peculiar province of the almighty that it were an encroachment on his right for men to dispose of their own lives; it would be equally criminal to act for the preservation of life as for its destruction. If I turn aside a stone, which is falling upon my head, I disturb the course of nature, and I invade the peculiar province of the almighty, by lengthening out my life, beyond the period, which, by the general laws of matter and motion, he had assigned to it. 10

A hair, a fly, an insect is able to destroy this mighty being, whose life is of such importance. Is it an absurdity to suppose, that human prudence may lawfully dispose of what depends on such insignificant causes? 11

It would be no crime in me to divert the *Nile* or *Danube* from its course, were I able to effect such purposes. Where then is the crime of turning a few ounces of blood from their natural chanels! 12

Do you imagine that I repine at providence or curse my creation, because I go out of life, and put a period to a being, which, were it to continue, would render me miserable? Far be such sentiments from me. I am only convinced of a matter of fact, which you yourself acknowledge possible, that human life may be unhappy, and that my existence, if farther prolonged, would become uneligible. But I thank providence, both for the good, which I have already enjoyed, and for the power, with which I am 13 endowed, of escaping the ill that threatens me.[2] To you it belongs to repine at providence, who foolishly imagine that you have no such power, and who must still prolong a hated being, tho' loaded with pain and sickness, with shame and poverty.

14 Do you not teach, that when any ill befalls me, tho' by the malice of my enemies, I ought to be resigned to providence; and that the actions of men are the operations of the almighty as much as the actions of inanimate beings? When I fall upon my own sword, therefore, I receive my death equally from the hands of the deity, as if it had proceeded from a lion, a precipice, or a fever.

15 The submission, which you require to providence, in every calamity, that befalls me, excludes not human skill and industry; if possibly, by their means, I can avoid or escape the calamity. And why may I not employ one remedy as well as another?

16 If my life be not my own, it were criminal for me to put it in danger, as well as to dispose of it: Nor could one man deserve the appellation of *Hero*, whom glory or friendship transports into the greatest dangers, and another merit the reproach of *Wretch* or *Miscreant*, who puts a period to his life, from the same or like motives.

17 There is no being, which possesses any power or faculty, that it receives not from its creator; nor is there any one, which, by ever so irregular an action, can encroach upon the plan of his providence, or disorder the universe. Its operations are his work equally with that chain of events, which it invades; and which ever principle prevails, we may, for that very reason, conclude it to be most favoured by him. Be it animate or inanimate, rational or irrational, 'tis all a case: Its power is still derived from the supreme creator, and is alike comprehended in the order of his providence. When the horror of pain prevails over the love of life: When a voluntary action anticipates the effect of blind causes; it is only in consequence of those powers and principles, which he has implanted in his creatures. Divine providence is still inviolate, and placed far beyond the reach of human injuries.

18 It is impious, says the old *Roman* superstition,[3] to divert rivers from their course, or invade the prerogatives of nature. 'Tis impious, says the *French* superstition, to inoculate for the small-pox, or usurp the business of providence, by voluntarily producing distempers and maladies. 'Tis

---

[2] *Agamus Deo gratias, quod nemo in vita teneri potest.* SEN., *Epist.* xii. ["And let us thank God that no man can be kept in life" (Seneca, *Epistles*, XII; trans. by Richard M. Gummere).]

[3] TACIT. *Ann.* lib. i. [Tacitus, *Annals*.]

impious, says the modern *European* superstition, to put a period to our own life, and thereby rebel against our creator. And why not impious, say I, to build houses, cultivate the ground, and sail upon the ocean? In all these actions, we employ our powers of mind and body to produce some innovation in the course of nature; and in none of them do we any more. They are all of them, therefore, equally innocent or equally criminal.

But you are placed by providence, like a sentinel, in a particular station; 19 *and when you desert it, without being recalled, you are guilty of rebellion against your almighty sovereign, and have incurred his displeasure.* I ask, why do you conclude, that Providence has placed me in this station? For my part, I find, that I owe my birth to a long chain of causes, of which many and even the principal, depended upon voluntary actions of men. *But Providence guided all these causes, and nothing happens in the universe without its consent and co-operation.* If so, then neither does my death, however voluntary, happen without its consent; and whenever pain and sorrow so far overcome my patience as to make me tired of life, I may conclude, that I am recalled from my station, in the clearest and most express terms.

It is providence, surely, that has placed me at present in this chamber: 20 But may I not leave it, when I think proper, without being liable to the imputation of having deserted my post or station? When I shall be dead, the principles, of which I am composed, will still perform their part in the universe, and will be equally useful in the grand fabric, as when they composed this individual creature. The difference to the whole will be no greater than between my being in a chamber and in the open air. The one change is of more importance to me than the other; but not more so to the universe.

It is a kind of blasphemy to imagine, that any created being can disturb 21 the order of the world, or invade the business of providence. It supposes, that that being possesses powers and faculties, which it received not from its creator, and which are not subordinate to his government and authority. A man may disturb society, no doubt; and thereby incur the displeasure of the almighty: But the government of the world is placed far beyond his reach and violence. And how does it appear, that the almighty is displeased with those actions, that disturb society? By the principles which he has implanted in human nature, and which inspire us with a sentiment of remorse, if we ourselves have been guilty of such actions, and with that of blame and disapprobation, if we ever observe them in others. Let us now examine, according to the method proposed, whether Suicide be of this kind of actions, and be a breach of our duty to our *neighbour* and to society.

A man, who retires from life, does no harm to society. He only ceases to 22 do good; which, if it be an injury, is of the lowest kind.

23   All our obligations to do good to society seem to imply something reciprocal. I receive the benefits of society, and therefore ought to promote its interest. But when I withdraw myself altogether from society, can I be bound any longer?

24   But allowing, that our obligations to do good were perpetual, they have certainly some bounds. I am not obliged to do a small good to society, at the expence of a great harm to myself. Why then should I prolong a miserable existence, because of some frivolous advantage, which the public may, perhaps, receive from me? If upon account of age and infirmities, I may lawfully resign any office, and employ my time altogether in fencing against these calamities, and alleviating, as much as possible, the miseries of my future life: Why may I not cut short these miseries at once by an action, which is no more prejudicial to society?

25   But suppose, that it is no longer in my power to promote the interest of the public: Suppose, that I am a burthen to it: Suppose, that my life hinders some person from being much more useful to the public. In such cases my resignation of life must not only be innocent but laudable. And most people, who lie under any temptation to abandon existence, are in some such situation. Those, who have health, or power, or authority, have commonly better reason to be in humour with the world.

26   A man is engaged in a conspiracy for the public interest; is seized upon suspicion; is threatened with the rack; and knows, from his own weakness, that the secret will be extorted from him: Could such a one consult the public interest better than by putting a quick period to a miserable life? This was the case of the famous and brave *Strozzi* of *Florence*.

27   Again, suppose a malefactor justly condemned to a shameful death; can any reason be imagined, why he may not anticipate his punishment, and save himself all the anguish of thinking on its dreadful approaches? He invades the business of providence no more than the magistrate did, who ordered his execution; and his voluntary death is equally advantageous to society, by ridding it of a pernicious member.

28   That Suicide may often be consistent with interest and with our duty to *ourselves*, no one can question, who allows, that age, sickness, or misfortune may render life a burthen, and make it worse even than annihilation. I believe that no man ever threw away life, while it was worth keeping. For such is our natural horror of death, that small motives will never be able to reconcile us to it. And tho' perhaps the situation of a man's health or fortune did not seem to require this remedy, we may at least be assured, that any one, who, without apparent reason, has had recourse to it, was curst with such an incurable depravity or gloominess of temper, as must poison all enjoyment, and render him equally miserable as if he had been loaded with the most grievous misfortunes.

If Suicide be supposed a crime, 'tis only cowardice can impel us to it. If   29
it be no crime, both prudence and courage should engage us to rid ourselves at once of existence, when it becomes a burthen. 'Tis the only way,
that we can then be useful to society, by setting an example, which, if imi-
tated, would preserve to every one his chance for happiness in life, and
would effectually free him from all danger of misery.[4]

---

[4] It would be easy to prove, that Suicide is as lawful under the *christian* dispensation
as it was to the heathens. There is not a single text of scripture, which prohibits it. That
great and infallible rule of faith and practice, which must controul all philosophy and
human reasoning, has left us, in this particular, to our natural liberty. Resignation to
providence is, indeed, recommended in scripture; but that implies only submission to
ills, which are unavoidable, not to such as may be remedied by prudence or courage.
Thou shalt not kill is evidently meant to exclude only the killing of others, over whose
life we have no authority. That this precept like most of the scripture precepts, must be
modified by reason and common sense, is plain from the practice of magistrates, who
punish criminals capitally, notwithstanding the letter of this law. But were this com-
mandment ever so express against Suicide, it could now have no authority. For all the
law of *Moses* is abolished, except so far as it is established by the law of nature; and we
have already endeavoured to prove, that Suicide is not prohibited by that law. In all
cases, *Christians* and *Heathens* are precisely upon the same footing; and if *Cato* and *Brutus*, *Arria* and *Portia* acted heroically, those who now imitate their example ought to receive the same praises from posterity. The power of committing Suicide is regarded by
Pliny as an advantage which men possess even above the deity himself. *Deus non sibi
potest mortem consciscere, si velit, quod homini dedit optimum in tantis vitæ pœnis.* Lib. ii.
Cap. 7. ["(God cannot) even if he wishes, commit suicide, the supreme boon that he has
bestowed on man among all the penalties of life" (Pliny, *Natural History* II, v, 27; trans.
by H. Rackham).]

INDEX

385

275, 279, 281, 282, 290, 309, 311,
312, 329, 330, 334, 335, 341, 342,
378, 383; of others, causes pleasure, 223, 227, 233, 239, 241
Harmodius, 300
Harrington, James, 324
Harry III, 307
Harry IV, 250, 366
Harry VII, 366
Hasdrubal, 294
hatred: and blame, xxii, 179; cause
of, 25, 35, 36; indirect passion of,
xx, xxii, xxviii, 14, 26, 35, 36, 37,
38, 39, 40, 41, 42, 44, 46, 47, 48,
49, 51, 79, 85, 150, 151, 152, 158,
163, 171, 179, 190, 230, 261, 292,
359; object of, xx, 35, 36, 38, 288;
quality and subject of cause of, 16
haughtiness, 170, 255
health, 1, 2, 6, 7, 9, 25, 180, 216, 226,
236, 241, 265, 267, 273, 278, 299,
350, 382
Helen of Troy, 307
Henry VIII, 368
Herodian, 373
Herodotus, 248
heroism, 346, 359, 383
Herring, Doctor, 4
A History of England, 3, 4, 5
Hobbes, Thomas, xix, 53, 201
Holland, 325, 363
Home, Earl of, 1
Home, John, 7
Homer, 240, 248, 345, 346, 349,
358
homosexuality, 303
honesty, x, xvi, 9, 83, 84, 195, 207,
267, 289, 290, 336
honor, xxx, 59, 89, 98, 123, 131, 133,
140, 147, 150, 154, 168, 174, 189,
216, 217, 219, 231, 233, 236, 243,
246, 247, 253, 257, 263, 265, 275,
288, 289, 292, 295, 298, 302, 305,
311, 319, 320, 325, 336, 343, 365,
369
hope, a direct passion, 14

Horace, 223, 225, 244, 261, 276, 295,
305, 324, 357
horror, 165, 204, 207, 224, 301, 303,
377, 380, 382
House of Stuart, 3, 4, 5
humanity: humankind, xxxii, 336;
laws of, 202; sentiment or motive
of, xvii, xix, xx, 112, 155, 172,
198, 227, 228, 230, 231, 233,
248, 259, 260, 261, 262, 263,
266, 269, 271, 279, 283, 293,
298, 326, 358; the same for all,
260; virtue of, xxvii, xxx, 83,
160, 171, 172, 173, 193, 199,
200, 201, 211, 220, 223, 228,
231, 239, 249, 257, 264, 265,
281, 291, 303, 308, 345
human nature, xi, xiii, xxviii, xxxiii,
17, 18, 24, 28, 66, 72, 75, 83, 85,
86, 88, 89, 92, 100, 101, 112, 113,
114, 115, 123, 124, 126, 135, 136,
143, 147, 149, 153, 157, 163, 173,
181, 182, 183, 184, 190, 192, 201,
202, 204, 210, 219, 222, 223, 226,
231, 234, 248, 259, 273, 276, 277,
278, 280, 299, 312, 314, 315, 317,
318, 319, 322, 331, 339, 348, 352,
357, 366, 376, 381; dignity or
meanness of, 317–21
humility, 14, 15, 17, 20, 22, 23, 26,
28, 36, 37, 38, 39, 40, 41, 46, 47,
151, 161, 165, 168, 169, 170, 175,
242, 258, 291, 309; cause of, 14,
15, 17, 18, 19, 23, 26, 27, 28, 46;
definition of, 28; indirect passion
of, 14, 15, 16, 17, 18, 19, 22, 25,
27, 28, 31, 34, 35, 36, 37, 38, 41,
47, 51, 79, 163, 179; object of, 14,
15, 16, 17, 20, 22, 35, 38; and
pride, xxviii, 14, 15, 16, 17, 18,
22, 24, 25, 26, 27, 28, 31, 34, 35,
36, 37, 38, 39, 41, 42, 43, 46, 47,
51, 150, 151, 163, 179, 241; quality and subject of cause of, 19
humor, good, 11, 28, 35, 39, 166, 177
Hurd, Doctor, 4

reason: and morality, xvi–xviii, 67–77, 187–91; slave to the passion, 62

reasoning: *a posteriori*, 231; *a priori*, 38, 75, 148, 230, 348; abstract, 66, 121; abstruse, 67; analogical, 23, 188, 206, 207, 217, 251, 278, 279, 285, 286; demonstrative, 57, 61, 75; mathematical, 61, 272, 333; metaphysical, 60, 82, 188; moral, 292, 295, 375

rebellion, 131, 133, 138, 140, 304, 375, 381

reflection, xxi, xxvii, 4, 13, 26, 34, 77, 87, 88, 92, 98, 99, 125, 149, 151, 156, 157, 158, 170, 177, 189, 194, 203, 208, 210, 211, 230, 234, 236, 250, 262, 266, 267, 275, 276, 277, 281, 292, 295, 312, 313, 333, 339, 341, 342, 350, 357, 358, 370

Reims, 2

relation, double, 21, 22, 23, 26, 27, 38, 39, 40, 41, 43, 47, 85, 150

religion, x, xii, 57, 58, 59, 80, 110, 195, 206, 276, 294, 305, 309, 310, 349, 359, 360; Christian, 110, 169; false, 258, 376; and morality, 57, 58; natural, 334; Roman Catholic, 110; of Zoroaster, 195

repentance, 49, 60, 236

republic: Achaean, 214; Athenian, 327, 365; Roman, 369; Spartan, 204

reputation, as cause of pride and humility, 28–34

resistance, 127, 136, 137, 143, 144, 146, 202, 363, 373; doctrine of, 137; right of, 144, 363

respect, 44, 144, 165, 166, 180, 241, 242, 315

Retz, Cardinal Jean-François-Paul-Gondi de, 234

revenge, 8, 92, 222, 228, 233, 237, 266, 271, 302, 321, 334, 346

revolution, 122, 137, 142, 143, 145, 178, 305, 322, 323, 341, 356, 358, 359, 367, 374, 378

Rhine, 106, 286, 303

Rhone, 303

riches, 16, 17, 25, 28, 29, 32, 36, 40, 84, 109, 127, 128, 181, 235, 240, 241, 242, 243, 248, 249, 282, 308, 323, 325, 330, 334, 335, 342

Richmond, Duke of, 5

Rochefoucault, 289

Romans, 247, 302, 303, 308, 324

Rome, 205, 209, 215, 294, 305, 323, 326, 349, 373

Rubens, Peter Paul, 324

Rue de Quincempoix, 214

Rufus, William, 337

rules: of art, 224, 324, 348; general, xvi, 25, 26, 72, 96, 97, 99, 101, 121, 122, 135, 136, 138, 142, 150, 157, 165, 168, 261, 267, 268, 282, 308, 348, 351; moral, 59, 68, 147, 283, 336; that determine property, 99–108

Sabinus, 108

St. Clair, General, 2

Saint-Evremond, xxxv, 169, 234, 245

Sallust, 174, 240, 291, 326

Sancho, 350, 351

Sannazarius, 225

Sannazarius, Jacobus, 225

satire, xx, 190, 257, 259, 280, 290, 357

satisfaction, on reflection, xx, xxi, 27, 78, 81, 97, 150, 256

Saturn, 200, 302

"The Sceptic," 329–44

scepticism, 187, 238, 263, 264, 329–44

sceptics, 194, 219, 220, 329–44

science: abstract, 190, 346; anatomy, 13; and the arts, 323, 324, 325; astronomy, 18, 301, 340, 374; chemistry, 207; geometry, 73, 188, 270; of man or human nature, xi, xii, xiii–xvi; physics, 77, 188, 207, 277, 301; speculative, 77, 276, 374